Theories
of American
Literature

Donald M. Kartiganer

Malcolm A. Griffith

UNIVERSITY OF WASHINGTON

The Macmillan Company, New York

The Macmillan Company
866 Third Avenue, New York, New York 10022

Collier-Macmillan Canada, Ltd., Toronto, Ontario

Library of Congress catalog card number: 73–150070

First Printing

ACKNOWLEDGMENTS

ERRAND INTO THE WILDERNESS   Perry Miller
   Reprinted by permission of the publishers from Perry Miller, Errand into the Wilderness, Cambridge, Mass.: The Belknap Press of Harvard University Press, Copyright, 1956, by the President and Fellows of Harvard University.

THE BROKEN CIRCUIT   Richard Chase
   From The American Novel and Its Tradition by Richard Chase. Copyright © 1957 by Richard Chase. Reprinted by permission of Doubleday & Company, Inc.

CULTURAL AND LITERARY BACKGROUND: THE TYPE OF AMERICAN EXPERIENCE
A. N. Kaul
   Reprinted by permission of Yale University Press from A. N. Kaul, The American Vision, pp. 1–38. Copyright © 1963 by Yale University.

TWO KINGDOMS OF FORCE   Leo Marx
   Reprinted from The Massachusetts Review. Copyright © 1959 The Massachusetts Review, Inc.

SELF AND ENVIRONMENT   Richard Poirier
   From A World Elsewhere: The Place of Style in American Literature by Richard Poirier. Copyright © 1966 by Richard Poirier. Reprinted by permission of Oxford University Press, Inc.

THE AMERICAN ADAM AND THE FORTUNATE FALL   R. W. B. Lewis
   From R. W. B. Lewis, The American Adam, pp. 28–32, 40–52, 55, 57–62, 111–116. Copyright © The University of Chicago, 1955. Copyright under the International Copyright Union, 1955. All rights reserved. Reprinted by permission of The University of Chicago Press and the author. (Titles of this essay and its parts added by editors.)

THE CONTINUITY OF AMERICAN POETRY   Roy Harvey Pearce
   Selections from Roy Harvey Pearce, The Continuity of American Poetry (copyright © 1961 by Princeton University Press; Princeton Paperback, 1965), pp. 3–6, 41–42,

187, 285–286, 296–306, 376–382, 421–423, 429–433. Reprinted by permission of Princeton University Press. (Titles of this essay and its parts added by editors.)

THE AMERICAN HERO: HIS MASQUERADE   *Daniel G. Hoffman*
 From *Form and Fable in American Fiction* by Daniel Hoffman. Copyright © 1961 by Daniel Hoffman. Reprinted by permission of Oxford University Press, Inc.

FENIMORE COOPER'S LEATHERSTOCKING NOVELS   *D. H. Lawrence*
 From *Studies in Classic American Literature* by D. H. Lawrence. Copyright 1923, renewed 1951 by Frieda Lawrence. Reprinted by permission of The Viking Press, Inc.

THE AMERICAN HERO AND THE EVASION OF LOVE   *Leslie Fiedler*
 Copyright © 1966, 1960 by Leslie Fiedler. From the book *Love and Death in the American Novel*. Reprinted with permission of Stein and Day/Publishers. (Title of this essay added by editors.)

THE WHITE NEGRO: SUPERFICIAL REFLECTIONS ON THE HIPSTER   *Norman Mailer*
 Reprinted by permission of C. P. Putnam's Sons from *Advertisements for Myself* by Norman Mailer. Copyright © 1959 by Norman Mailer.

THE DESIGN OF PURITAN EXPERIENCE   *John F. Lynen*
 Reprinted by permission of Yale University Press from John F. Lynen, *The Design of the Present*, pp. 29–31, 35–46, 51–63, 70–76. Copyright © 1969 by Yale University. (Title of this essay added by editors.)

FROM EDWARDS TO EMERSON   *Perry Miller*
 Reprinted by permission of the publishers from Perry Miller, *Errand into the Wilderness*, Cambridge, Mass.: The Belknap Press of Harvard University Press, Copyright, 1956, by the President and Fellows of Harvard College.

MAN IN THE OPEN AIR   *F. O. Matthiessen*
 From *The American Renaissance*, Oxford University Press, pp. 626–635, 646–656. Copyright 1941 by Oxford University Press, Inc. Reprinted by permission.

THE UNBROKEN TRADITION   *Leslie Fiedler*
 Copyright © 1964 by Leslie A. Fiedler. From the book *Waiting for the End*. Reprinted with permission of Stein and Day/Publishers.

REALISM TO NATURALISM   *Everett Carter*
 From the book *Howells and the Age of Realism* by Everett Carter. Copyright, 1954, by Everett Carter. Reprinted by permission of J. B. Lippincott Company. (Title of this essay added by editors.)

THE MODERN ELEMENT IN MODERN LITERATURE   *Lionel Trilling*
 From *Beyond Culture: Essays on Literature & Learning* by Lionel Trilling. Copyright © 1961 by Lionel Trilling. Reprinted by permission of The Viking Press, Inc.

THE POETRY OF REALITY   *J. Hillis Miller*
 Reprinted by permission of the publishers from J. Hillis Miller, *Poets of Reality*, Cambridge, Mass.: The Belknap Press of Harvard University Press, Copyright, 1965, by the President and Fellows of Harvard College.

FORM AND THE AMERICAN EXPERIENCE   *Ralph Ellison*
 Copyright © 1963, 1964 by Ralph Ellison. Reprinted from *Shadow and Act*, by Ralph Ellison, by permission of Random House, Inc. (Title of this essay added by editors.)

 For poetry cited in this volume grateful acknowledgment is made to the following publishers:
 Harcourt Brace Jovanovich, Inc. E. E. CUMMINGS, From "Memorabilia" (p. 184) by E. E. Cummings, copyright, 1935, by E. E. Cummings, renewed, 1963, by Marion Morehouse Cummings. Reprinted from *Poems 1923–1954* by E. E. Cummings by permission of Harcourt Brace Jovanovich, Inc. T. S. ELIOT, from "The Dry Salvages" (p. 130), "Portrait of a Lady" (p. 11), "The Love Song of J. Alfred Prufrock" (p. 4), "Gerontion" (p. 22), "Burnt Norton" (pp. 117, 121), "The Waste Land" (p. 44), and "Five-Finger Exercises" (p. 93) by T. S. Eliot in *T. S. Eliot, The Collected*

Poems and Plays, 1909–1950. Copyright © 1952 by Harcourt Brace Jovanovich, Inc. Reprinted by permission of the publisher and Faber and Faber Ltd. From "East Coker" (p. 15) in *Four Quartets,* copyright, 1943, by T. S. Eliot. Reprinted by permission of Harcourt Brace Jovanovich, Inc., and Faber and Faber Ltd.

Harvard University Press. EMILY DICKINSON, from "Because I could not stop for Death" (p. 546). Reprinted by permission of the publishers and the Trustees of Amherst College from Thomas H. Johnson, Editor, *The Poems of Emily Dickinson,* Cambridge, Mass.: The Belknap Press of Harvard University Press, Copyright, 1951, 1955, by the President and Fellows of Harvard College.

Holt, Rinehart and Winston, Inc. ROBERT FROST, from "Provide, Provide" (p. 307) from *The Poetry of Robert Frost* edited by Edward Connery Lathem. Copyright © 1969 by Holt, Rinehart and Winston, Inc. Reprinted by permission of Holt, Rinehart and Winston, Inc.

Liveright Publishing Corporation. HART CRANE, from "The Bridge" (p. 38) in *The Collected Poems of Hart Crane* by Hart Crane. Permission of Liveright Publishers. Copyright Renewed (R) 1966 by Liveright Publishing Corporation.

The Macmillan Company. EDWIN ARLINGTON ROBINSON, from "New England" (p. 900). Reprinted with permission of The Macmillan Company from *Collected Poems* by Edwin Arlington Robinson. Copyright 1925 by Edwin Arlington, renewed 1953 by Ruth Nivison and Barbara R. Holt. WILLIAM BUTLER YEATS, from "The Scholars" (p. 139). Reprinted with permission of The Macmillan Company, New York. M. B. Yeats, and Macmillan & Company, London, from *Collected Poems of W. B. Yeats* by William Butler Yeats. Copyright 1919 by The Macmillan Company, renewed 1947 by Bertha Georgie Yeats.

Random House, Inc. Alfred A. Knopf, Inc. W. H. AUDEN, from "Under Which Lyre" (p. 224) from *Collected Shorter Poems 1927–1957* by W. H. Auden. Copyright 1946 by W. H. Auden. Reprinted by permission of Random House, Inc. WALLACE STEVENS, from "Ploughing on Sunday" (p. 20), "Like Decorations in a Nigger Cemetery" (p. 150), "Anecdote of the Jar" (p. 76), "Large Red Man Reading" (pp. 423, 424), "Not Ideas About the Thing But the Thing Itself" (p. 534), "Metaphor as Degeneration" (p. 444), "A Primitive Like an Orb" (p. 440), and "An Ordinary Evening in New Haven" (pp. 471, 472) from *The Collected Poems of Wallace Stevens.* Copyright © 1954 by Wallace Stevens. Reprinted by permission of Alfred A. Knopf, Inc.

Preface

THIS collection of critical essays is designed as a companion text for students of American literature. The distinctive feature of these essays is their attempt to see American literature as some kind of integrated whole, to discover in as deep and imaginative ways as possible the underlying unities of a literature that often appears unusually fragmentary. Whatever the differences in their findings the intention is always to move toward a theory of American literature, to create the synthesis that will at last identify the most decisive lines of an American literary tradition. In making such attempts these critics reflect and respond to a similar quest in our writers, for they too have been in constant search of a unifying tradition. Not that either the writers or the critics ever succeed in their aims; the tradition is never definitely set, the great American book is never written. If we have learned anything of our country's literature, it is that its goal is inseparable from its quest, that the only constant structure is the drive *toward* definition.

Our purpose, then, in putting this collection together, is hardly to produce a single theory to which all the others lead. It is, rather, to illustrate some of the most dynamic ways in which our books have been read and related to one another. We also hope to help the student in his own creative task of reading American literature, not only as a series of unique texts but as a fluid sequence of notes toward a definition of what that literature, for some three hundred years now, has been trying to become.

In most cases the essays are newer rather than older. This is not because more recent essays are necessarily better, but because they frequently assimilate and therefore move beyond the older ones. In other words, we have not attempted to document the history of Americans' thinking about American literature, but instead to bring together the most comprehensive examples of this thinking that we have been able to find.

Part I of this collection focuses on the various and particular tensions that have existed between major American authors and within major American works. Part II deals with some of the significant "character" types who appear in much of our fiction. Part III, something of a departure from the rest of the book, consists of essays each of which attempts to define one of the several chronological segments into which American literature is usually divided. The total emphasis in this last section, however, is not to "survey" major literary modes or to provide a series of thumbnail sketches of authors. Instead it is on discovering the underlying pattern, the complex of related statements that may organize a period.

We have left to students and teachers the ways in which this book can be used, but it is obvious that, depending on the primary texts being read, certain critical essays will be more germane than others. Those in Part III can serve as introductions to the basic periods in American literature—to be studied before, during, or after the student has read the primary material. And those in Parts I and II can prove valuable for class discussions and for papers. Students, for example, may apply the various critical theses to primary works not discussed in detail in the essays themselves, or they may try to show how individual works can insist in their complexity on the need to synthesize several critical approaches. Leo Marx on the conflict of technology and nature, A. N. Kaul on the individual and the community, Leslie Fiedler on the avoidance of heterosexuality—these, like the rest of the essays in this collection, can provide stimulating entrances into the central problems of the texts themselves. Once the student understands those problems, it will be up to him to create his own, more detailed interpretations.

In preparing this book we have assumed that students are quite capable of dealing with individual texts. What we have tried to provide are some of those larger perspectives that allow us to see books not only as individual achievements but also as the significant contexts of other books. It is these perspectives that, in turn, will finally raise the single work to its fullest meaning.

One final note: the student who is interested in more extended studies of particular works than these essays provide (see Index for detailed listings) can do no better than to begin with those books from which many of the following essays come. There he will find the close study of individual poems and novels from which the larger theories have grown. There, also, in the arguments of those books and in their bibliographies, students will find still more paths to follow in their reading.

D. M. K.
M. A. G.

Contents

I American Literature as Dialectic

II   Representative Men

III   From Puritanism to the Present

Epilogue

Index

Introduction

I<small>N</small> the third of his *Letters from an American Farmer* (1782), Hector St. John de Crèvecoeur begins his famous definition of the American, "this new man," by a description of the locale which is to be so much a part of that definition:

He is arrived on a new continent; a modern society offers itself to his contemplation, different from what he had hitherto seen. It is not composed, as in Europe, of great lords who possess everything and of a herd of people who have nothing. Here are no aristocratical families, no courts, no kings, no bishops, no ecclesiastical dominion, no invisible power giving to a few a very visible one, no great manufactures employing thousands, no great refinements of luxury. The rich and the poor are not so far removed from each other as they are in Europe.

The passage is important, not only for what it tells us of how an eighteenth-century French immigrant viewed the new land, but especially for its curious mode of definition, best described as one of exuberant negativism: definition as a richly detailed itemization of all that America lacks. The strategy is not an uncommon one in several of the more notable commentaries on life in America; and, in particular, it has seemed a necessary one in defining the character of our literature and our writers' own sense of what they are doing in their work. For the European mind at least—and it is this mind which, in its collision with the New World, largely creates the foundations of our thought and culture—America has been the arena in which, for good or ill, much that traditionally goes into the social, political, and cultural life of man is missing.

1

The attitude toward this condition, of course, has frequently varied from Crèvecoeur's assurance in the passage above that what is missing is well gotten rid of. In such works as Tocqueville's *Democracy in America* (1835), Cooper's *Notions of the Americans* (1828), Hawthorne's preface to *The Marble Faun* (1860), and James's critical study of Hawthorne (1879), there is a considerable skepticism about a country so empty of what has always seemed necessary to civilized life—and especially a skepticism about the possibilities of literature in a land where there is a marked absence of all those materials which are the traditional basis of *belles lettres:* a complex social structure, a native accumulation of legend and myth, and an already existent literary tradition from which to draw. Yet even in these writers, at least the American ones, the dubiousness barely conceals a pride that in this most recalcitrant locale they have indeed created a literature—however difficult they may find the problem of defining it.

This whole practice of negative description achieves its grand climax in James's *Hawthorne,* where we find neither the boastfulness of Emerson nor the self-pity of Hawthorne in comparable moments, but rather a provocative slyness combining a lengthy string of reservations, deliberately comic in their tedious enumeration, with an astute recognition of the complex American condition:

one might enumerate the items of high civilisation, as it exists in other countries, which are absent from the texture of American life, until it should become a wonder to know what was left. No State, in the European sense of the word, and indeed barely a specific national name. No sovereign, no court, no personal loyalty, no aristocracy, no church, no clergy, no army, no diplomatic service, no country gentlemen, no palaces, no castles, nor manors, nor old country-houses, nor parsonages, nor thatched cottages, nor ivied ruins; no cathedrals, nor abbeys, nor little Norman churches; no great Universities nor public schools—no Oxford, nor Eton, nor Harrow; no literature, no novels, no museums, no pictures, no political society, no sporting class—no Epsom nor Ascot! . . . . The natural remark, in the almost lurid light of such an indictment, would be that if these things are left out, everything is left out. The American knows that a good deal remains; what it is that remains—that is his secret, his joke, as one may say.

What remains is still a palpable reality—a social and cultural structure which, despite James's and the other commentators' reservations, is still an abiding force in our literature. But what these commentaries prepare us for is the unusual manner in which our writers have portrayed that reality in their most representative works. For them it has become merely the first of the two worlds which polarize most American books, the available—and lesser—reality which is continually challenged or abandoned in deference to a larger, yet vaguer, "reality" still to be imagined.

The primary American narrative, obsessed with process, with *transition,* is this complex movement from one context to another. The first context is quite capable of being described in detail (and is somewhat diminished by that very fact); the second is, comparatively speaking, shadowy in its conception, being no more than the dream which threatens the clarity, and undermines the value, of the first. It is, as the critic Richard Poirier has written, "a world elsewhere."

The world challenged, whether it be Hawthorne's several Puritan societies, the land communities of *Moby Dick* and *Huckleberry Finn,* or the somber Chicago of *The Adventures of Augie March,* is a world in which every level of existence has its appropriate behavior, where the conduct of life is a matter of habit, and most of all where the place of each member of society is sharply defined. The first context, in other words, is analogous to that stable "Europe" from which the American is *supposed* to be free simply by being an American. The drama of our fictions—and this includes the work of those whose critical observations are referred to above—is the attempt to assert that freedom, to reveal the poverty of a reality inadequate to the hope of "this new man."

As for the nature of the New World, the definition of what it is that must replace a reality which is always less than desire—this has indeed been the problem, the "joke" as Henry James put it. In the inadequacy of an available world, what world does one imagine?

One consequence of posing the question is the creation of those dim structures, the vague "quests," which preside over and direct, but rarely resolve decisively, our most characteristic works. Another has been the continuing concern with the dynamics of creation itself, the precise means of filling in the huge spaces which remain when the real is abandoned, when, in Crèvecoeur's terms, "He is arrived on a new continent." This "new continent," we discover, is not so much an actual virgin land, a literal vacancy, but rather the condition which the writer *wills,* a peculiarly American conviction that what is given is not good enough. The sense of absence which James, Crèvecoeur, and the others describe is a situation not of the country but of the country's mind—the American writer's sense that he must imagine, in terms uniquely appropriate to it, the shape of a New World.

Because of the interest in form—the preoccupation with creating a peculiarly American art—our literature appears, from the largest perspective, as a sequence of improvisations, complex notes toward the creation of some grand fiction. It is as if with each new work our writers feel they must invent again the complete world of a literary form.

Such a condition of nearly absolute freedom to create has appeared to our authors both as possibility and liability, an utter openness suggesting limitless opportunity for the imagination, or an enormous vacancy in which they create from nothing. For some it has meant an opportunity to play Adam, to assume the role of an original namer of experience, the full positive possibilities of which Emerson was perhaps the first to realize: "Why should not we also enjoy an original relation to the universe? Why should not we have a poetry and philosophy of insight and not of tradition, and a religion by revelation to us, and not the history of theirs?"

Whitman is our first great poet, perhaps has to be, because he establishes in his verse an unaccommodating version of precisely what an "original relation" might look like, an extreme form by which every succeeding poet has been able to measure himself—and thus know better the form he chooses or refuses to choose. "There is scarcely a poem of Whitman's before, say, 1867," R. W. B. Lewis writes in one of the following reprinted essays, "which does not have the air of being the first poem ever written, the first formulation in language of the nature of persons and of things and of the relations between them." Others, such as Cooper and James, have seen more the impoverishment of this freedom. Whitman's pride that a radical invention is possible becomes in Hawthorne a deep guilt that it is necessary.

However our writers have viewed their situation, as privileged or handicapped, the result has been a high degree of self-consciousness: "The American poet," Roy Harvey Pearce observes, "has always felt obliged, for well and for ill, to catch himself in the act of being a poet." Some of this self-awareness reveals itself in the writers' extraliterary comments, in their occasional gestures of self-pity and severe self-criticism, or sometimes in an excessive and strident ambitiousness. Hawthorne, for example, in the essay which introduces his greatest novel, is still bemoaning the book he has *not* written, the story of the life of the customhouse in which he had been employed: "The fault was mine. The page of life that was spread out before me seemed dull and commonplace, only because I had not fathomed its deeper import. A better book than I shall ever write was there. . . ."

Norman Mailer, on the other hand, in his *Advertisements for Myself*, sounds a different note. Also discussing a still unwritten work (does anyone but an American spend so much time talking about books that do not exist?), he writes: "the book will be fired to its fuse by the rumor that once I pointed to the farthest fence and said that within ten years I would try to hit the longest ball ever to go up into the accelerated hurricane air of our American letters."

Aside from the self-conscious, probably strategic, posturing, the fact remains that the American's creative stance comes at considerable risk, the risk indigenous to an art of constant improvisation. As vital as some of our books have been—and that vitality has been at least partly the consequence of their "tentativeness," the risk in which they are composed—they have tended to be terribly uneven in merit. If we have our masterpieces or, probably more accurate, near-masterpieces, we have also had a considerable number of very fascinating, very flawed works—works of obvious genius which still pale in the light of critical scrutiny.

The problem is touched upon by Daniel Hoffman:

it is incontestable that each of our authors has suffered from these very advantages of flexibility and freedom. For who can tell how much of his creative energy had to be expended on the continual invention of adequate forms, perhaps at the expense of works that might have come into being had the chief problem been merely how to write within a given tradition?

What all this amounts to—the "negative" descriptions, the uneasiness with the merely real, the emphasis on quest rather than completion, the excessive concern with the aesthetic problems of portraying an experience that has always seemed in transition—what it amounts to is a national literature which, for all its some three hundred years of history, is essentially modern in its concerns and its shape.

The modern poem, according to Wallace Stevens, is "The poem of the mind in the act of finding/ What will suffice"—essentially a drama of the process of acquiring adequate form. Modern literature, in other words, is nothing so much as the study of what it is possible for literature to be. From its very beginnings American literature has revealed a similar concern. The Puritan—as described in Perry Miller's essay, "Errand into the Wilderness," which opens this book —is the first in our country to endure the shock of learning that his condition is something other than what he has supposed it to be, the first to discover himself in the existential condition of having to create anew the terms of his identity: "Who, they are forever asking themselves, who are we?" And it is the very space between old and new, between the context of European preconceptions and the not quite manageable American facts, which becomes the vague arena for the process of self-realization. Ralph Ellison, in this book's concluding essay, articulates the degree to which that process has been all along the American writer's appropriate subject and style, and thus implies the extent to which our literature has perhaps always been "modern."

II

One of the results of the American writer's preoccupation with form has been the frequency with which "expression," the difficult relationship between mind, imagination, and experience, has become a work's central thematic concern. Our writers have presented two versions of this theme: one focusing on the gap between language and experience, the other on the gap between experience and Man.

In the first of these they explore the differences between what they have assumed to be a unique American experience and the limited language with which they have been forced to describe it. "Experience" here is not the solid structures even an American society requires, but the larger, almost "transcendent" encounter which the American sees as his peculiar destiny. This second experience, being American, is new; the language, being English, is old.

Some of our earlier writers and critics speak with an absolute pride of the inability of language, any language, to embody this experience. Sometimes, as in Crèvecoeur, this takes the form of a familiar anti-intellectualism, the feeling that the American's crude expression is a sign of his actual superiority to the European: "Pray do not laugh in thus seeing an artless countryman tracing himself through the simple modifications of his life . . . I endeavour to follow the thread of my feelings, but I cannot tell you all." In Emerson the emphasis is on the divine law, perfectly intelligible but inexpressible: "These laws refuse to be adequately stated. They will not be written out on paper, or spoken by the tongue . . . . yet we read them hourly in each other's faces. . . ."

While it may be at best a precarious activity for the writer to stress the failure of the language which is his only tool, the habit has continued into the twentieth century. Thus, Faulkner's Addie Bundren remarks memorably, "I would think how words go straight up in a thin line, quick and harmless, and how terribly doing goes along the earth clinging to it"; and T. S. Eliot: words "crack and sometimes break . . . slip, slide, perish/ Decay with imprecision."

A gap of this sort is basic to works as disparate as *Song of Myself* and *Four Quartets, Moby Dick* and *Absalom, Absalom!*. In each of these we have the sense that for all the abundance of words, for all the quite unconcealed *straining* after the meaning of some awesome event or condition, this meaning is never really going to get said, at least not all of it. And in this situation we have exactly the paradox which conditions the American writer's attitude to begin with: a certain pride in the novelty of living an experience too large for expression itself; a certain anguish that one is never to complete one's work.

A second approach sees experience as being considerably *less* than man himself—experience now as that palpable, often mundane, existence that opposes an expansive consciousness. Our writers tend to present their characters as images of generic Man, or, taking Crèvecoeur literally when he refers to the American as "this new man," they have seen their own American heroes and personae as being larger than any context, and larger even than the particular deeds they might perform.

A major tension in *The Scarlet Letter* is that of character and context, the expansiveness of Hester Prynne and the narrow and unyielding Puritan society. Hawthorne is able to suggest both the greatness of her character as well as its victimization by the forces which conspire against it. By these forces Hawthorne means not only seventeenth-century Boston but the entire fabric of a world that by its very nature must gain the subservience of its souls or crush them. The scarlet A is but the visible sign of restrictive experience itself, which tries to comprehend by a single letter, a single law, that being who both creates the conditions which constrain her and makes apparent their inadequacy. The paradox, and peculiar tragedy of the tale, is that Hester's supreme identity can only manifest itself in those stultifying conditions.

If, in *Moby Dick,* Ishmael is the one who tries desperately, through his language and vision, to tell the full significance of the voyage of the *Pequod,* then Ahab is the one whose breadth of self is both the impulse for the voyage and its victim. In his attempt to find a deed commensurate with the sense of his power, he is forced to that terrible constriction of being which is necessary to the continuation of the voyage. If Ahab possesses his "humanities," as one of the *Pequod* owners suggests, he has almost entirely stamped them out by the time, several hundred pages later, he encounters the white whale. He has become, for all his greatness, no more than the pure impulse toward his own destruction, the single stone of his desire. The great irony of the book is that out of the brutal narrowing of Ahab, this man who seems grander even than his grand voyage, comes the very action which allows the consciousness of Ishmael to expand wondrously.

In Whitman's *Song of Myself* we find similar conflicts at work. On the one hand there is the man, the voice and to a certain extent the very content of the poem, who makes it very clear that nothing of what he sees—the accumulation of roles, occupations, historical events—is equal to the private being, is capable of really containing or providing adequate outlet for it: "People I meet . . . The latest news . . . My dinner, dress, associates, looks, business, compliments, dues/ . . . They come to me days and nights and go from me again,/ But they are not the Me myself." On the other hand there is a sense of there being no *language* sufficient to what the poet is trying to say, no language for the vision of "form and union and plan" which the poem is supposed to embody: "I do not know it. . . . it is without name. . . . it is a word unsaid,/ It is not in any dictionary or utterance or symbol."

This kind of dynamic emerges out of the American writer's very special concern with the problems of defining his experience, problems finally of the relationship of language and the real, man and the available actions by which he defines himself. They are the problems, present from the beginning, of trying to create coherent and vital expression of American experience.

III

Our critics have approached American literature in a spirit similar to that in which our writers have composed their works. As the writers have attempted to create a distinctive American form, our critics have tried to discover those elements in the existing literature, the characteristic modes and themes, which might be said to constitute a genuine tradition. If the Puritans (and apparently all Americans since) are forever asking, Who are we? and if our writers are forever wondering, How and what am I supposed to write? then the critic seems forever occupied with the question, Is there an American book—and what does it look like?

Many of our critics, some of whom are represented in this collection, have insisted on asking this kind of question; and their answers, consisting of large attempts at creating a comprehensive synthesis of American literature, have been among our finest critical studies. Whatever the biases, the directions, even the particular authors singled out for close analysis, inevitably in these critics we perceive the need to bring all or most of the disparate parts together, to uncover at least one of the possible patterns that will provide some unity. In a very real sense, such critics are firmly in the "American tradition."

Even as there is a cost to the American writer, perhaps there is a similar cost to these most American of critics. Perhaps at times they have seemed to ignore the trees for the forest, perhaps been too insistent on "Americanness" when an author they are discussing has been intensely conscious of something else—such as Europe. Perhaps in their eagerness to define a national tradition, encompassing as many books as possible, they have failed to be sensitive enough to the sheer individuality of any work of art. And perhaps—at the worst—they have failed to pay sufficient respect to books not sufficiently American.

But here again, as in the art itself, we would insist that such criticism has been extraordinarily vital; and that that vitality has sprung directly from the intensity of the search to define, "once and for all," the nature of our literature.

Prologue

Errand into the Wilderness

PERRY MILLER

It was a happy inspiration that led the staff of the John Carter Brown Library to choose as the title of its New England exhibition of 1952 a phrase from Samuel Danforth's election sermon, delivered on May 11, 1670: *A Brief Recognition of New England's Errand into the Wilderness.* It was of course an inspiration, if not of genius at least of talent, for Danforth to invent his title in the first place. But all the election sermons of this period—that is to say, the major expressions of the second generation, which, delivered on these forensic occasions, were in the fullest sense community expression—have interesting titles; a mere listing tells the story of what was happening to the minds and emotions of the New England people: John Higginson's *The Cause of God and His People in New-England* in 1663, William Stoughton's *New England's True Interest, Not to Lie* in 1668, Thomas Shepard's *Eye-Salve* in 1672, Urian Oakes's *New England Pleaded With* in 1673, and, climactically and most explicitly, Increase Mather's *A Discourse Concerning the Danger of Apostasy* in 1677.

All of these show by their title pages alone—and, as those who have looked into them know, infinitely more by their contents—a deep disquietude. They are troubled utterances, worried, fearful. Something has gone wrong. As in 1662 Wigglesworth already was saying in verse, God has a controversy with New England; He has cause to be angry and to punish it because of its innumerable defections. They say, unanimously, that New England was sent on an errand, and that it has failed.

To our ears these lamentations of the second generation sound strange indeed. We think of the founders as heroic men—of the towering stature of Bradford, Winthrop, and Thomas Hooker—who braved the ocean and the wilderness, who conquered both, and left to their children a goodly heritage. Why then this whimpering?

11

Some historians suggest that the second and third generations suffered a failure of nerve; they weren't the men their fathers had been, and they knew it. Where the founders could range over the vast body of theology and ecclesiastical polity and produce profound works like the treatises of John Cotton or the subtle psychological analyses of Hooker, or even such a gusty though wrongheaded book as Nathaniel Ward's *Simple Cobler,* let alone such lofty and rightheaded pleas as Roger Williams' *Bloudy Tenent,* all these children could do was tell each other that they were on probation and that their chances of making good did not seem very promising.

Since Puritan intellectuals were thoroughly grounded in grammar and rhetoric, we may be certain that Danforth was fully aware of the ambiguity concealed in his word "errand." It already had taken on the double meaning which it still carries with us. Originally, as the word first took form in English, it meant exclusively a short journey on which an inferior is sent to convey a message or to perform a service for his superior. In that sense we today speak of an "errand boy"; or the husband says that while in town on his lunch hour, he must run an errand for his wife. But by the end of the Middle Ages, errand developed another connotation: it came to mean the actual business on which the actor goes, the purpose itself, the conscious intention in his mind. In this signification, the runner of the errand is working for himself, is his own boss; the wife, while the husband is away at the office, runs her own errands. Now in the 1660's the problem was this: which had New England originally been— an errand boy or a doer of errands? In which sense had it failed? Had it been despatched for a further purpose, or was it an end in itself? Or had it fallen short not only in one or the other, but in both of the meanings? If so, it was indeed a tragedy, in the primitive sense of a fall from a mighty designation.

If the children were in grave doubts about which had been the original errand—if, in fact, those of the founders who lived into the later period and who might have set their progeny to rights found themselves wondering and confused—there is little chance of our answering clearly. Of course, there is no problem about Plymouth Colony. That is the charm about Plymouth: its clarity. The Pilgrims, as we have learned to call them, were reluctant voyagers; they had never wanted to leave England, but had been obliged to depart because the authorities made life impossible for Separatists. They could, naturally, have stayed at home had they given up being Separatists, but that idea simply did not occur to them. Yet they did not go to Holland as though on an errand; neither can we extract the notion of a mission out of the reasons which, as Bradford tells us, persuaded them to leave Leyden for "Virginia." The war with Spain was about to be resumed, and the economic threat was ominous; their migration was not so much an errand as a shrewd forecast, a plan to get out while the getting was good, lest, should they stay, they would be "in-trapped or surrounded by their enemies, so as they should neither be able to fight nor flie." True, once the decision was taken, they congratulated themselves that they might become a means for propagating the gospel in remote parts of the world, and thus of serving as steppingstones to others in the performance of this great work; nevertheless, the substance of their decision was that they "thought it better to dislodge betimes to some place of better advantage and less danger, if any such could be found." The great hymn that Bradford, looking back in his old age, chanted about the landfall is one of the greatest passages, if not the very greatest, in all New England's literature; yet it does not resound with the sense of a mission accomplished—instead, it vibrates with the sorrow and exultation of suffering, the sheer endurance, the pain and the anguish, with the somberness of death faced unflinchingly:

May not and ought not the children of these fathers rightly say: Our fathers were Englishmen which came over this great ocean, and were ready to perish in this wilderness; but they cried unto the Lord, and he heard their voyce, and looked on their adversitie. . . .

We are bound, I think, to see in Bradford's account the prototype of the vast majority of subsequent immigrants—of those Oscar Handlin calls "The Uprooted": they came for better advantage and for less danger, and to give their posterity the opportunity of success.

The Great Migration of 1630 is an entirely other story. True, among the reasons John Winthrop drew up in 1629 to persuade himself and his colleagues that they should commit themselves to the enterprise, the economic motive frankly figures. Wise men thought that England was overpopulated and that the poor would have a better chance in the new land. But Massachusetts Bay was not just an organization of immigrants seeking advantage and opportunity. It had a positive sense of mission—either it was sent on an errand or it had its own intention, but in either case the deed was deliberate. It was an act of will, perhaps of willfulness. These Puritans were not driven out of England (thousands of their fellows stayed and fought the Cavaliers)—they went of their own accord.

So, concerning them, we ask the question, why? If we are not altogether clear about precisely how we should phrase the answer, this is not because they themselves were reticent. They spoke as fully as they knew how, and none more magnificently or cogently than John Winthrop in the midst of the passage itself, when he delivered a lay sermon aboard the flagship *Arbella* and called it "A Modell of Christian Charity." It distinguishes the motives of this great enterprise from those of Bradford's forlorn retreat, and especially from those of the masses who later have come in quest of advancement. Hence, for the student of New England and of America, it is a fact demanding incessant brooding that John Winthrop selected as the "doctrine" of his discourse, and so as the basic proposition to which, it then seemed to him, the errand was committed, the thesis that God had disposed mankind in a hierarchy of social classes, so that "in all times some must be rich, some poor, some highe and eminent in power and dignitie; others mean and in subjeccion." It is as though, preternaturally sensing what the promise of America might come to signify for the rank and file, Winthrop took the precaution to drive out of their heads any notion that in the wilderness the poor and the mean were ever so to improve themselves as to mount above the rich or the eminent in dignity. Were there any who had signed up under the mistaken impression that such was the purpose of their errand, Winthrop told them that, although other peoples, lesser breeds, might come for wealth or pelf, this migration was specifically dedicated to an avowed end that had nothing to do with incomes. We have entered into an explicit covenant with God, "we haue professed to enterprise these Accions vpon these and these ends"; we have drawn up indentures with the Almighty, wherefore if we succeed and do not let ourselves get diverted into making money, He will reward us. Whereas if we fail, if we "fall to embrace this present world and prosecute our carnall intencions, seeking greate things for our selves and our posterity, the Lord will surely breake out in wrathe against us be revenged of such a periured people and make us knowe the price of the breache of such a Covenant."

Well, what terms were agreed upon in this covenant? Winthrop could say precisely—"It is by a mutuall consent through a specially overruleing providence, and a more than ordinary approbation of the Churches of Christ to seeke out a place of Cohabitation and Consorteshipp under a due form of Government both civill and ecclesiasticall." If it could be said thus concretely, why should there be any ambiguity? There was no doubt whatsoever about what Winthrop meant by a due form of ecclesiastical government: he meant the pure Biblical polity set forth in full detail by the New Testament, that method which later generations, in the days of increasing confusion, would settle down to calling Congregational, but which for Winthrop was no denominational peculiarity but the very essence of organized Christianity. What a due form of civil government meant, therefore, became crystal clear: a political regime, possessing power, which would consider its main function to be the erecting, protecting, and preserving of this form of polity. This due form would have, at the very beginning of its list of responsibilities, the duty of suppressing heresy, of subduing or somehow getting rid of dissenters—of being, in short, deliberately, vigorously, and consistently intolerant.

Regarded in this light, the Massachusetts Bay Company came on an errand in the second and later sense of the word: it was, so to speak, on its own business. What it set out to do was the sufficient reason for its setting out. About this Winthrop seems to be perfectly certain, as he declares specifically what the due forms will be attempting: the end is to improve our lives to do more service to the Lord, to increase the body of Christ, and to preserve our posterity from the corruptions of this evil world, so that they in turn shall work out their salvation under the purity and power of Biblical ordinances. Because the errand was so definable in advance, certain conclusions about the method of conducting it were equally evident: one, obviously, was that those sworn to the covenant should not be allowed to turn aside in a lust for mere physical rewards; but another was, in Winthrop's simple but splendid words, "we must be knit togeher in this worke as one man, wee must entertaine each other in brotherly affection." we must actually delight in each other, "always having before our eyes our Commission and community in the worke, our community as members of the same body." This was to say, were the great purpose kept steadily in mind, if all gazed only at it and strove only for it, then social solidarity (within a scheme of fixed and unalterable class distinctions) would be an automatic consequence. A society despatched upon an errand that is its own reward would want no other rewards: it could go forth to possess a land without ever becoming possessed by it; social gradations would remain eternally what God had originally appointed; there would be no internal contention among groups or interests, and though there would be hard work for everybody, prosperity would be bestowed not as a consequence of labor but as a sign of approval upon the mission itself. For once in the history of humanity (with all its sins), there would be a society so dedicated to holy cause that success would prove innocent and triumph not raise up sinful pride or arrogant dissension.

Or, at least, this would come about if the people did not deal falsely with God, if they would live up to the articles of their bond. If we do not perform these terms, Winthrop warned, we may expect immediate manifestations of divine wrath; we shall perish out of the land we are crossing the sea to possess. And here in the 1660's and 1670's, all the jeremiads (of which Danforth's is one of the most poignant) are castigations of the people for having defaulted on precisely these articles. They recite the long list of afflictions an angry God had rained upon them, surely enough to prove how abysmally they had deserted the covenant: crop failures, epidemics, grasshoppers, caterpillars, torrid summers, arctic winters, Indian wars, hurricanes, shipwrecks, accidents, and (most grievous of all) unsatisfactory children. The solemn work of the election day, said Stoughton in 1668, is "Foundation-work"—not, that is, to lay a new one, "but to continue, and strengthen, and beautifie, and build upon that which has been laid." It had been laid in the covenant before even a foot was set ashore, and thereon New England should rest. Hence the terms of survival, let alone of prosperity, remained what had first been propounded:

If we should so frustrate and deceive the Lords Expectations, that his Covenant-interest in us, and the Workings of his Salvation be made to cease, then All were lost indeed; Ruine upon Ruine, Destruction upon Destruction would come, until one stone were not left upon another.

Since so much of the literature after 1660—in fact, just about all of it—dwells on this theme of declension and apostasy, would not the story of New England seem to be simply that of the failure of a mission? Winthrop's dread was realized: posterity had not found their salvation amid pure ordinances but had, despite the ordinances, yielded to the seductions of the good land. Hence distresses were being piled upon them, the slaughter of King Philip's War and now the attack of a profligate king upon the sacred charter. By about 1680, it did in truth seem that shortly no stone would be left upon another, that history would record of New England that the founders had been great men, but that their children and grandchildren progressively deteriorated.

This would certainly seem to be the impression conveyed by the assembled clergy and lay leaders who, in 1679, met at Boston in a formal synod, under the leadership of Increase Mather, and there prepared a report on why the land suffered. The result of their deliberation, published under the title *The Necessity of Reformation*, was the first in what has proved to be a distressingly long succession of investigations into the civic health of Americans, and it is probably the most pessimistic. The land was afflicted, it said, because corruption had proceeded apace; assuredly, if the people did not quickly reform, the last blow would fall and nothing but desolation be left. Into what a moral quagmire this dedicated community had sunk, the synod did not leave to imagination; it published a long and detailed inventory of sins, crimes, misdemeanors, and nasty habits, which makes, to say the least, interesting reading.

We hear much talk nowadays about corruption, most of it couched in generalized terms. If we ask our current Jeremiahs to descend to particulars, they tell us that the republic is going on the rocks, or to the dogs, because the wives of politicians aspire to wear mink coats and their husbands take a moderate five per cent cut on certain deals to pay for the garments. The Puritans were devotees of logic, and the verb "methodize" ruled their thinking. When the synod went to work, it had before it a succession of sermons, such as that of Danforth and the other election-day or fast-day orators, as well as such works as Increase Mather's *A Brief History of the Warr With the Indians*, wherein the decimating conflict with Philip was presented as a revenge upon the people for their transgressions. When the synod felt obliged to enumerate the enormities of the land so that the people could recognize just how far short of their errand they had fallen, it did not, in the modern manner, assume that regeneration would be accomplished at the next election by turning the rascals out, but it digested this body of literature; it reduced the contents to method. The result is a staggering compendium of inquity, organized into twelve headings.

First, there was a great and visible decay of godliness. Second, there were several manifestations of pride—contention in the churches, insubordination of inferiors toward superiors, particularly of those inferiors who had, unaccountably, acquired more wealth than their betters, and, astonishingly, a shocking extravagance in attire, especially on the part of these of the meaner sort, who persisted in dressing beyond their means. Third, there were heretics, especially Quakers and Anabaptists. Fourth, a notable increase in swearing and a spreading disposition to sleep at sermons (these two phenomena seemed basically connected). Fifth, the Sabbath was wantonly violated. Sixth, family government had decayed, and fathers no longer kept their sons and daughters from prowling at night. Seventh, instead of people being knit together as one man in mutual love, they were full of contention, so that lawsuits were on the increase and lawyers were thriving. Under the eighth head, the synod described the sins of sex and alcohol, thus producing some of the juiciest prose of the period: militia days had become orgies, taverns were crowded; women threw temptation in the way of befuddled men by wearing false locks and displaying naked necks and arms "or, which is more abominable, naked Breasts"; there were "mixed Dancings," along with light behavior and "Company-keeping" with vain persons, wherefore the bastardy rate was rising. In 1672, there was actually an attempt to supply Boston with a brothel (it was suppressed, but the synod was bearish about the future). Ninth, New Englanders were betraying a marked disposition to tell lies, especially when selling anything. In the tenth place, the business morality of even the most righteous left everything to be desired: the wealthy speculated in land and raised prices excessively; "Day-Labourers and Mechanicks are unreasonable in their demands." In the eleventh place, the people showed no disposition to reform, and in the twelfth, they seemed utterly destitute of civic spirit.

"The things here insisted on," said the synod, "have been oftentimes mentioned and inculcated by those whom the Lord hath set as Watchmen to the house of Israel." Indeed they had been, and thereafter they continued to be even more inculcated. At the end of the century, the synod's report was serving as a kind of handbook for preachers: they would take some verse of Isaiah or Jeremiah, set up the doctrine that God avenges the iniquities of a chosen people, and then run down the twelve heads, merely bringing the list up to date by inserting the new and still more depraved practices an ingenious people kept on devising. I suppose that in the whole literature of the world, including the satirists of imperial Rome, there is hardly such another uninhibited and unrelenting documentation of a people's descent into corruption.

I have elsewhere endeavored to argue[1] that, while the social or economic historian may read this literature for its contents—and so con-

---

[1] See *The New England Mind: From Colony to Province* (1952), Chapter II.

struct from the expanding catalogue of denunciations a record of social progress—the cultural anthropologist will look slightly askance at these jeremiads; he will exercise a methodological caution about taking them at face value. If you read them all through, the total effect, curiously enough, is not at all depressing: you come to the paradoxical realization that they do not bespeak a despairing frame of mind. There is something of a ritualistic incantation about them; whatever they may signify in the realm of theology, in that of psychology they are purgations of soul; they do not discourage but actually encourage the community to persist in its heinous conduct. The exhortation to a reformation which never materializes serves as a token payment upon the obligation, and so liberates the debtors. Changes there had to be: adaptations to environment, expansion of the frontier, mansions constructed, commercial adventures undertaken. These activities were not specifically nominated in the bond Winthrop had framed. They were thrust upon the society by American experience; because they were not only works of necessity but of excitement, they proved irresistible—whether making money, haunting taverns, or committing fornication. Land speculation meant not only wealth but dispersion of the people, and what was to stop the march of settlement? The covenant doctrine preached on the *Arbella* had been formulated in England, where land was not to be had for the taking; its adherents had been utterly oblivious of what the fact of a frontier would do for an imported order, let alone for a European mentality. Hence I suggest that under the guise of this mounting wail of sinfulness, this incessant and never successful cry for repentance, the Puritans launched themselves upon the process of Americanization.

However, there are still more pertinent or more analytical things to be said of this body of expression. If you compare it with the great productions of the founders, you will be struck by the fact that the second and third generations had become oriented toward the social, and only the social, problem; herein they were deeply and profoundly different from their fathers. The finest creations of the founders—the disquisitions of Hooker, Shepard, and Cotton—were written in Europe, or else, if actually penned in the colonies, proceeded from a thoroughly European mentality, upon which the American scene made no impression whatsoever. The most striking example of this imperviousness is the poetry of Anne Bradstreet: she came to Massachusetts at the age of eighteen, already two years married to Simon Bradstreet; there, she says, "I found a new world and new manners, at which my heart rose" in rebellion, but soon convincing herself that it was the way of God, she submitted and joined the church. She bore Simon eight children, and loved him sincerely, as her most charming poem, addressed to him, reveals:

> If ever two were one, then surely we;
> If ever man were loved by wife, then thee.

After the house burned, she wrote a lament about how her pleasant things in ashes lay and how no more the merriment of guests would sound in the hall; but there is nothing in the poem to suggest that the house stood in North Andover or that the things so tragically consumed were doubly precious because they had been transported across the ocean and were utterly irreplaceable in the wilderness. In between rearing children and keeping house she wrote her poetry; her brother-in-law carried the manuscript to London, and there published it in 1650 under the ambitious title, *The Tenth Muse Lately Sprung Up in America*. But the title is the only thing about the volume which shows any sense of America, and that little merely in order to prove that the plantations had something in the way of European wit and learning, that they had not receded into barbarism. Anne's flowers are English flowers, the birds, English birds, and the landscape is Lincolnshire. So also with the productions of immigrant scholarship: such a learned and acute work as Hooker's *Survey of the Summe of Church Discipline*, which is specifically about the regime set up in America, is written entirely within the logical patterns, and out of the religious experience, of Europe; it makes no concession to new and peculiar circumstances.

The titles alone of productions in the next generation show how concentrated have become emotion and attention upon the interest of New England, and none is more revealing than Samuel Danforth's conception of an errand into the wilderness. Instead of being able to compose abstract treatises like those of Hooker upon the soul's preparation, humiliation, or exultation, or such a collection of wisdom and theology as John Cotton's *The Way of Life* or Shepard's *The Sound Believer*, these later saints must, over and over again, dwell upon the specific sins of New England, and the more they denounce, the more they must narrow their focus to the provincial problem. If they write upon anything else, it must be about the halfway covenant and its manifold consequences—a development enacted wholly in this country—or else upon their wars with the Indians. Their range is sadly constricted, but every effort, no matter how brief, is addressed to the persistent question: what is the meaning of this society in the wilderness? If it does not mean what Winthrop said it must mean, what under Heaven is it? Who, they are forever asking themselves, who are we?—and sometimes they are on the verge of saying, who the Devil are we, anyway?

This brings us back to the fundamental ambiguity concealed in the word "errand," that *double entente* of which I am certain Danforth was aware when he published the words that give point to the exhibition. While it was true that in 1630, the covenant philosophy of a special and peculiar bond lifted the migration out of the ordinary realm of nature, provided it with a definite mission which might in the secondary sense be called its errand, there was always present in Puritan thinking the suspicion that God's saints are at best inferiors, dispatched by their

Superior upon particular assignments. Anyone who has run errands for other people, particularly for people of great importance with many things on their minds, such as army commanders, knows how real is the peril that, by the time he returns with the report of a message delivered or a bridge blown up, the Superior may be interested in something else; the situation at headquarters may be entirely changed, and the gallant errand boy, or the husband who desperately remembered to buy the ribbon, may be told that he is too late. This tragic pattern appears again and again in modern warfare: an agent is dropped by parachute and, after immense hardships, comes back to find that, in the shifting tactical or strategic situations, his contribution is no longer of value. If he gets home in time and his service proves useful, he receives a medal; otherwise, no matter what prodigies he has performed, he may not even be thanked. He has been sent, as the devastating phrase has it, upon a fool's errand, than which there can be a no more shattering blow to self-esteem.

The Great Migration of 1630 felt insured against such treatment from on high by the covenant; nevertheless, the God of the covenant always remained an unpredictable Jehovah, a *Deus Absconditus*. When God promises to abide by stated terms, His word, of course, is to be trusted; but then, what is man that he dare accuse Omnipotence of tergiversation? But if any such apprehension was in Winthrop's mind as he spoke on the *Arbella*, or in the minds of other apologists for the enterprise, they kept it far back and allowed it no utterance. They could stifle the thought, not only because Winthrop and his colleagues believed fully in the covenant, but because they could see in the pattern of history that their errand was not a mere scouting expedition: it was an essential maneuver in the drama of Christendom. The Bay Company was not a battered remnant of suffering Separatists thrown up on a rocky shore; it was an organized task force of Christians, executing a flank attack on the corruptions of Christendom. These Puritans did not flee to America; they went in order to work out that complete reformation which was not yet accomplished in England and Europe, but which would quickly be accomplished if only the saints back there had a working model to guide them. It is impossible to say that any who sailed from Southampton really expected to lay his bones in the new world; were it to come about—as all in their heart of hearts anticipated—that the forces of righteousness should prevail against Laud and Wentworth, that England after all should turn toward reformation, where else would the distracted country look for leadership except to those who in New England had perfected the ideal polity and who would know how to administer it? This was the large unspoken assumption in the errand of 1630: if the conscious intention were realized, not only would a federated Jehovah bless the new land, but He would bring back these temporary colonials to govern England.

In this respect, therefore, we may say that the migration was running an errand in the earlier and more primitive sense of the word—performing a job not so much for Jehovah as for history, which was the wisdom of Jehovah expressed through time. Winthrop was aware of this aspect of the mission—fully conscious of it. "For wee must Consider that wee shall be as a Citty upon a Hill, the eies of all people are uppon us." More was at stake than just one little colony. If we deal falsely with God, not only will He descend upon us in wrath, but even more terribly, He will make us "a story and a by-word through the world, wee shall open the mouthes of enemies to speake evill of the wayes of god and all professours for Gods sake." No less than John Milton was New England to justify God's ways to man, though not, like him, in the agony and confusion of defeat but in the confidence of approaching triumph. This errand was being run for the sake of Reformed Christianity; and while the first aim was indeed to realize in America the due form of government, both civil and ecclesiastical, the aim behind that aim was to vindicate the most rigorous ideal of the Reformation, so that ultimately all Europe would imitate New England. If we succeed, Winthrop told his audience, men will say of later plantations, "the lord make it like that of New England." There was an elementary prudence to be observed: Winthrop said that the prayer would arise from subsequent plantations, yet what was England itself but one of God's plantations? In America, he promised, we shall see, or may see, more of God's wisdom, power, and truth "then formerly wee have beene acquainted with." The situation was such that, for the moment, the model had no chance to be exhibited in England; Puritans could talk about it, theorize upon it, but they could not display it, could not prove that it would actually work. But if they had it set up in America—in a bare land, devoid of already established (and corrupt) institutions, empty of bishops and courtiers, where they could start *de novo,* and the eyes of the world were upon it—and if then it performed just as the saints had predicted of it, the Calvinist internationale would know exactly how to go about completing the already begun but temporarily stalled revolution in Europe.[2]

When we look upon the enterprise from this point of view, the psychology of the second and third generations becomes more comprehensible. We realize that the migration was not sent upon its errand in order to found the United States of America, nor even the New England conscience. Actually, it would not perform its errand even when the colonists did erect a due form of government in church and state: what was further required in order for this mission to be a success

---

[2] See the perceptive analysis of Alan Heimert (*The New England Quarterly, XXVI,* September 1953) of the ingredients that ultimately went into the Puritan's metaphor of the "wilderness," all the more striking a concoction because they attached no significance a priori to their wilderness destination. To begin with, it was simply a void.

was that the eyes of the world be kept fixed upon it in rapt attention. If the rest of the world, or at least of Protestantism, looked elsewhere, or turned to another model, or simply got distracted and forgot about New England, if the new land was left with a polity nobody in the great world of Europe wanted—then every success in fulfilling the terms of the covenant would become a diabolical measure of failure. If the due form of government were not everywhere to be saluted, what would New England have upon its hands? How give it a name, this victory nobody could utilize? How provide an identity for something conceived under misapprehensions? How could a universal which turned out to be nothing but a provincial particular be called anything but a blunder or an abortion?

If an actor, playing the leading role in the greatest dramatic spectacle of the century, were to attire himself and put on his make-up, rehearse his lines, take a deep breath, and stride onto the stage, only to find the theater dark and empty, no spotlight working, and himself entirely alone, he would feel as did New England around 1650 or 1660. For in the 1640's, during the Civil Wars, the colonies, so to speak, lost their audience. First of all, there proved to be, deep in the Puritan movement, an irreconcilable split between the Presbyterian and Independent wings, wherefore no one system could be imposed upon England, and so the New England model was unserviceable. Secondly—most horrible to relate—the Independents, who in polity were carrying New England's banner and were supposed, in the schedule of history, to lead England into imitation of the colonial order, betrayed the sacred cause by yielding to the heresy of toleration. They actually welcomed Roger Williams, whom the leaders of the model had kicked out of Massachusetts so that his nonsense about liberty of conscience would not spoil the administrations of charity.

In other words, New England did not lie, did not falter; it made good everything Winthrop demanded—wonderfully good—and then found that its lesson was rejected by those choice spirits for whom the exertion had been made. By casting out Williams, Anne Hutchinson, and the Antinomians, along with an assortment of Gortonists and Anabaptists, into that cesspool then becoming known as Rhode Island, Winthrop, Dudley, and the clerical leaders showed Oliver Cromwell how he should go about governing England. Instead, he developed the utterly absurd theory that so long as a man made a good soldier in the New Model Army, it did not matter whether he was a Calvinist, an Antinomian, an Arminian, an Anabaptist or even—horror of horrors—a Socinian! Year after year, as the circus tours this country, crowds howl with laughter, no matter how many times they have seen the stunt, at the bustle that walks by itself: the clown comes out dressed in a large skirt with a bustle behind; he turns sharply to the left, and the bustle continues blindly and obstinately straight ahead, on the original course. It is funny in a circus, but not in history. There is nothing but tragedy in the realization that one was in the main path of events, and now is side-tracked and disregarded. One is always able, of course, to stand firm on his first resolution, and to condemn the clown of history for taking the wrong turning: yet this is a desolating sort of stoicism, because it always carries with it the recognition that history will never come back to the predicted path, and that with one's own demise, righteousness must die out of the world.

The most humiliating element in the experience was the way the English brethren turned upon the colonials for precisely their greatest achievement. It must have seemed, for those who came with Winthrop in 1630 and who remembered the clarity and brilliance with which he set forth the conditions of their errand, that the world was turned upside down and inside out when, in June 1645, thirteen leading Independent divines—such men as Goodwin, Owen, Nye, Burroughs, formerly friends and allies of Hooker and Davenport, men who might easily have come to New England and helped extirpate heretics—wrote the General Court that the colony's law banishing Anabaptists was an embarrassment to the Independent cause in England. Opponents were declaring, said these worthies, "that persons of our way, principall and spirit cannot beare with Dissentors from them, but Doe correct, fine, imprison and banish them wherever they have power soe to Doe." There were indeed people in England who admired the severities of Massachusetts, but we assure you, said the Independents, these "are utterly your enemyes and Doe seeke your extirpation from the face of the earth: those who now in power are your friends are quite otherwise minded, and doe professe they are much offended with your proceedings." Thus early commenced that chronic weakness in the foreign policy of Americans, an inability to recognize who in truth constitute their best friends abroad.

We have lately accustomed ourselves to the fact that there does exist a mentality which will take advantage of the liberties allowed by society in order to conspire for the ultimate suppression of those same privileges. The government of Charles I and Archbishop Laud had not, where that danger was concerned, been liberal, but it had been conspicuously inefficient; hence, it did not liquidate the Puritans (although it made halfhearted efforts), nor did it herd them into prison camps. Instead, it generously, even lavishly, gave a group of them a charter to Massachusetts Bay, and obligingly left out the standard clause requiring that the document remain in London, that the grantees keep their office within reach of Whitehall. Winthrop's revolutionaries availed themselves of this liberty to get the charter overseas, and thus to set up a regime dedicated to the worship of God in the manner they desired—which meant allowing nobody else to worship any other way, especially adherents of Laud and King Charles. All this was perfectly logical and consistent. But what happened to the thought processes of their fellows in England made no sense whatsoever. Out of the New Model Army came the fantastic notion that a party struggling for power should proclaim that, once it captured the state, it would recognize the right of dissenters to disagree and to have their own worship, to hold their own opinions. Oliver Cromwell was so far gone in this idiocy as to become a dictator, in order to impose toleration by force! Amid this shambles, the errand of New England collapsed. There was nobody left at headquarters to whom reports could be sent.

Many a man has done a brave deed, been hailed as a public hero, had honors and ticker tape heaped upon him—and then had to live, day after day, in the ordinary routine, eating breakfast and brushing his teeth, in what seems protracted anticlimax. A couple may win their way to each other across insuperable obstacles, elope in a blaze of passion and glory—and then have to learn that life is a matter of buying the groceries and getting the laundry done. This sense of the meaning having gone out of life, that all adventures are over, that no great days and no heroism lie ahead, is particularly galling when it falls upon a son whose father once was the public hero or the great lover. He has to put up with the daily routine without ever having known at first hand the thrill of danger of the ecstasy of passion. True, he has his own hardships—clearing rocky pastures, hauling in the cod during a storm, fighting Indians in a swamp—but what are these compared with the magnificence of leading an exodus of saints to found a city on a hill, for the eyes of all the world to behold? He might wage a stout fight against the Indians, and one out of ten of his fellows might perish in the struggle, but the world was no longer interested. He would be reduced to writing accounts of himself and scheming to get a publisher in London, in a desperate effort to tell a heedless world, "Look, I exist!"

His greatest difficulty would be not the stones, storms, and Indians, but the problem of his identity. In something of this sort, I should like to suggest, consists the anxiety and torment that inform productions of the late seventeenth and early eighteenth centuries—and should I say, some thereafter? It appears most clearly in *Magnalia Christi Americana*, the work of that soul most tortured by the problem, Cotton Mather: "I write the Wonders of the Christian Religion, flying from the Depravations of Europe, to the American Strand." Thus he proudly begins, and at once trips over the acknowledgement that the founders had not simply fled from depraved Europe but had intended to redeem it. And so the book is full of lamentations over the declension of the children, who appear, page after page, in contrast to their mighty progenitors, about as profligate a lot as ever squandered a great inheritance.

And yet, the *Magnalia* is not an abject book; neither are the election sermons abject, nor is the inventory of sins offered by the synod of 1679. There is a bewilderment, confusion, chagrin, but there is no surrender. A task has been assigned upon which the populace are in fact intensely engaged. But they are not sure any more for just whom they are working;

they know they are moving, but they do not know where they are going. They seem still to be on an errand, but if they are no longer inferiors sent by the superior forces of the Reformation, to whom they should report, then their errand must be wholly of the second sort, something with a purpose and an intention sufficient unto itself. If so, what is it? If it be not the due form of government, civil and ecclesiastical, that they brought into being, how otherwise can it be described?

The literature of self-condemnation must be read for meanings far below the surface, for meanings of which, we may be so rash as to surmise, the authors were not fully conscious, but by which they were troubled and goaded. They looked in vain to history for an explanation of themselves; more and more it appeared that the meaning was not to be found in theology, even with the help of the covenantal dialectic. Thereupon, these citizens found that they had no other place to search but within themselves—even though, at first sight, that repository appeared to be nothing but a sink of iniquity. Their errand having failed in the first sense of the term, they were left with the second, and required to fill it with meaning by themselves and out of themselves. Having failed to rivet the eyes of the world upon their city on the hill, they were left alone with America.

American Literature as Dialectic

I

A culture is not a flow, nor even a confluence; the form of its existence is struggle, or at least debate—it is nothing if not a dialectic. And in any culture there are likely to be certain artists who contain a large part of the dialectic within themselves, their meaning and power lying in their contradictions; they contain within themselves, it may be said, the very essence of the culture, and the sign of this is that they do not submit to serve the ends of any one ideological group or tendency. It is a significant circumstance of American culture, and one which is susceptible of explanation, that an unusually large proportion of its notable writers of the nineteenth century were such repositories of the dialectic of their times—they contained both the yes and the no of their culture, and by that token they were prophetic of the future.

LIONEL TRILLING
The Liberal Imagination

common practice among many prominent American critics of the last half-century or so has been to discuss American life and literature in terms of tension and polarity, to view our culture as essentially an expression of radical oppositions. The identity of these unreconciled forces has varied with the critics who have tried to name them, but among the different versions have been the tensions of the New World vs. the Old, America vs. Europe, liberal vs. conservative, agrarian vs. technological, the individual vs. the community, the private imagination vs. cultural convention—ultimately man, or Man, vs. all the apparatus, natural and civilized, which make up his splendid if necessarily resistant environment.

A tendency toward dialectical thinking, of course, is not peculiarly American, although it may achieve an unusual range and intensity, not to mention a dogged persistence, in our literature. Dialecticism, in various guises, was basic to the whole Romantic revolution of the nineteenth century—particularly in Germany and, to a lesser extent, England—emerging in large part from the Kantian recognition of the split between mind and world, a split which could be healed only by that dramatic turn into the self which altered the course of European thinking, and shaped our own. Through subjectivism, through imagination and art, man could recognize all those antinomies that blocked a rational approach to knowledge, and yet embrace them in an imaginative structure enabling the human mind to survive in what might very well be an actual chaos. This containment of opposition was less (or more) than a total reconciliation of it; the great romantic poem of unity as an enormous and perpetual struggle to reconcile opposing forces was Goethe's *Faust,* in which the conflicting energies of Faust and Mephistopheles (or God and the devil *within* Faust), the tensions of affirmation and negation, action and passivity, the limitless and the limited, were merged into a single dynamic action of creation itself, encompassing yet by no means submerging its discordant principles. Morse Peckham defines the special quality of this tension in *Beyond the Tragic Vision:* "Faust's problem, it turns out, is not, as we might expect, either to succumb to the devil or to deny his existence; it is to learn to hold in a single vision the two forces symbolized by God and the devil. Like Coleridge, he needs to reconcile them without draining them of their contraries and oppositions."

Thus the European mind was characterized by a capacity to comprehend the meaning of tension, of genuine opposition in a world fallen from order, and at the same time to erect elaborate structures of order, rescuing the necessarily disparate into the dynamically interactive. A harmony of some kind could be imagined despite all.

In America the case seems to have been different; the American writer has demonstrated a willingness, as Richard Chase has argued, to imagine and accept a "world of radical, even irreconcilable contradictions." He has tended toward "romance" rather than the "novel," toward melodrama rather than tragedy, toward an expression of "disconnected and uncontrolled experience." Our literature has resisted synthesis, or it has been so remorseless in the articulation of its polarities as to make synthesis nearly impossible. Remarkably aware of the inconsistencies in our culture, our writers have been unwilling or unable to create more orderly structures than their country could genuinely sustain. In this sense American literature has been perhaps not so much a true dialectic, of question and response leading to reconciliation, as a perpetual argument of persistently antithetical positions.

Why American literature, itself clearly a branch of English literature, should fail to move in similar ways, should be unable to "move through contradictions to forms of harmony, reconciliation, catharsis, and transfiguration," is a question that A. N. Kaul and Leo Marx take up in two of the following essays; Kaul refers to the very special problems, dating from the Puritans, of reconciling the needs of individual and society, Marx to the effects of rapid industrialization in the nineteenth century. Perhaps this failure has something to do with that lack of a developed society, the absence of tradition and convention which so many writers, American and foreign, have pointed to. In *The Eccentric Design,* Marius Bewley observes: "These same divisions existed in Europe also, but there they were ballasted by a denser social medium, a richer sense of the past, a more inhibited sense of material possibilities." Perhaps too it is a part of the consequence of lacking an established *literary* tradition equipped to deal with the problems of a radical dualism. And perhaps it has even been not so much a failure as an anticipation of a much later, existential response, which achieves reconciliation, if at all, only at a cost and complexity which even the great European romantics were not prepared to pay. At any rate, from whatever need, or insight, the American writer has forever been calling attention to the essential dissonances of his American experience, and to the tensions between himself as creator and that which will not be

compelled into form: to the problem of the "maker" who brings himself again and again to the difficulties of creating coherent order.

One of the earliest American critics to deal directly with this question of tensions was Van Wyck Brooks, in his *America's Coming of
Age,* published in 1915. Unlike some of our more recent commentators, Brooks views the existence of these tensions as the core of our
culture's inadequacy, the essential split in our national life and
literature which has prevented maturity. He views the Puritan
colonist of the seventeenth century as a sort of essential American, a
"whole" man who yet contains within him, quite unreconciled even
then, the seeds of division which would soon become isolated into
completely separate bodies of thought, separate writers, separate
cultural responses. Brooks' critical approach here, interestingly
enough, is a foreshadowing of T. S. Eliot's famous notion of a "dissociation of sensibility," first proposed in 1921. Quite indifferent to the
failure of American literature to develop, Eliot tries to account for
the tendency of English literature to decline, by pointing to a
division of "thought" and "feeling" which he believes occurred in
seventeenth-century English poetry. Brooks, using not altogether
different terms, sees the Puritan as being at once committed to both
practical and idealistic, materialistic and transcendent goals; most
important, these "threw almost no light on one another; there was
no middle ground between to mitigate, combine, or harmonize
them."

So it is that from the beginning we find two main currents in the
American mind running side by side but rarely mingling—a current
of overtones and a current of undertones—and both equally unsocial:
on the one hand, the current of Transcendentalism, originating in the
piety of the Puritans, becoming a philosophy in Jonathan Edwards,
passing through Emerson, producing the fastidious refinement and
aloofness of the chief American writers, and, as the coherent ideals and
beliefs of Transcendentalism gradually faded out, resulting in the final
unreality of most contemporary American culture; and on the other
hand the current of catchpenny opportunism, originating in the practical
shifts of Puritan life, becoming a philosophy in Franklin, passing through
the American humorists, and resulting in the atmosphere of contemporary
business life.

Thus the literature of the seventeenth century in America is composed
in equal parts, one may fairly say, of piety and advertisement; and the
revered chronicles of New England had the double effect of proving
how many pilgrim souls had been elected to salvation and of populating
with hopeful immigrants a land where heaven had proved so indulgent.

For three generations the prevailing American character was compact in one type, the man of action who was also the man of God. Not until the eighteenth century did the rift appear and with it the essential distinction between "Highbrow" and "Lowbrow." It appeared in the two philosophers, Jonathan Edwards and Benjamin Franklin, who share the eighteenth century between them. In their amazing purity of type and in the apparent incompatibility of their aims they determined the American character as a racial fact, and after them the Revolution became inevitable.

What Brooks seems to be searching for in 1915 is a harmony of forces, a genuine blending of disparate energies similar to what existed in nineteenth-century Europe: reconciliation in which opposition is not emptied of its power, but reconciliation nonetheless, a "middle ground" in which "bare facts and metaphysics" can throw "light on one another." He is searching for the Goethean synthesis of forces, the formation of the "single narrative," altering yet not diminishing the identity of each component within the synthesis. This is the union which Chase refers to as following the pattern of "tragic art and Christian art," which finally transfigures or redeems its inherent conflict into completed form.

It is a kind of art which at least three of the following critics, in addition to Chase, think does not exist in our most representative and greatest literature. In the essays of Kaul, Marx, and Richard Poirier, for example, we find an emphasis on the presence of two dominant images coexistent in our major books. One is an image of *division,* between the radical individual and an oppressive, sometimes tyrannical society; between a wild or rural landscape and some instrument of advanced technology, such as a locomotive; between the conscious self and an environment of established custom and convention which severely limits consciousness. The other is an image of *reconciliation,* far more tenuous and insubstantial than the first image: the formation, for example, of an ideal community, such as the one embodied in the "marriage" of Ishmael and Queequeg; or a merger of technology and wilderness as imagined in the vision and language of Huck Finn, when he absorbs both river and steamboat into a "unified mode of perception"; or the imagination of Lambert Strether's "world elsewhere" in *The Ambassadors,* created out of, but different from, both the severe New England morality and the European sense of beauty which clash in this novel. What is significant about these images of reconciliation is that they cannot withstand the pressure of those images of division which they only temporarily resolve. In *Moby Dick* ideal community gives way to the monomaniacal Ahab, who tyrannizes, then destroys his Pequod society; Huck and Jim's raft is soon invaded again by representatives of the land society, as it has earlier been shattered by the steamboat; and Strether's comprehensive awareness of beauty and decency harmonized gives way to a "lesser" reality as Chad returns to his advertising position and Madame de Vionnet to her need for another wealthy American.

The images of reconciliation, in other words, are seen by these critics in terms of their very failure to reconcile. The images of division remain—solid and supremely intact—the repository of a brooding sorrow and frustration underlying much American literature. Yet they are juxtaposed to a series of imaginative visions, temporary, perhaps unreal, which cannot mitigate a divided experience, but which become part of the larger drama of maker and matter, namer and unnameable, the contest of consciousness and inflexible world which seems basic to the classic pattern of our literature.

II

Richard Chase's *The American Novel and Its Tradition,* from which his essay "The Broken Circuit" is taken, is the primary argument for the notion of American literature as the expression of a "profound poetry of disorder," a literature which, unlike its English counterpart, tends strongly toward a Manichean vision "less interested in redemption than in the melodrama of the eternal struggle of good and evil, less interested in incarnation and reconciliation than in alienation and disorder." Following his distinctions between novel and romance—in which he declares the essential American prose-fiction form to be, in fact, the romance—Chase proceeds to refine his definition by working with some of the important statements of American writers on the subject of romance. He shows how that genre separates itself, not only from the traditional English novel, but from a distinctly lesser kind of romance, one which, neglecting the demands of Hawthorne, can tell us nothing of "the truth of the human heart." He concludes with a discussion of the theories of Henry James who, despite his own insistence on the need for reconciliation, for connecting at last the circuits of "real and ideal," "the known and the mysterious," which made his own works *novels,* still provided us with the best statements we have on the nature of our characteristic romance.

While they by no means always agree with him, at times take explicit exception to what they consider to be the rigidity of his theories, the books of Kaul, Marx, and Poirier are in a certain sense elaborate glosses on the work of Chase. All begin with an acute awareness of the difficulties of order in our literature, each trying to account for the presence of those difficulties and at the same time trying to point out the ways in which the American writer has tried to come to terms with them. In one sense they believe in the possibility of reconciliation within individual works of literature—in apparent disagreement with Chase. Yet the reconciliations they see are clearly tenuous ones: ideals or imaginative worlds only, by which the real may be measured but hardly altered. In this respect they confirm Chase's central point.

A. N. Kaul's "Cultural and Literary Background" is a concise survey of some of the most influential historical and social pressures of the seventeenth and eighteenth centuries, which produced in the nineteenth century (in literature and in real life) numerous attempts to conceive of an ideal society in which those pressures would be unified. Kaul emphasizes two splits in American life. One is the conflict basic to the first Puritan settlements: the spiritual motivation—the drive to set up a model Christian community—and the economic motivation—the drive to accumulate whatever was to be accumulated in a virgin world. The experiment "was at the same time robustly material and highly spiritual." The second conflict is that of the individual and society, reaching a greater intensity here than in Europe chiefly because of a radical individualism, European-bred, which in America was allowed to blossom, with "no older order, no constituted order at all, to hinder its growth."

These two sets of opposed forces are seen by Kaul as revolving around a vague but highly influential notion of "communitarianism," the theory of an ideal community of persons which underlies some of the intentions of the Plymouth and Massachusetts Bay settlements, and which is present in the fiction of Cooper, Hawthorne, Melville, and Twain. Kaul identifies the essential American quest as the search for such a "community" (as opposed to mere "society"), to which the individual can belong without danger to his own integrity: "A common theme of the American imagination has been the problem of reconciling individual freedom with a mode of social life to which the individual can give his allegiance without danger of impairing his moral, spiritual, or psychological integrity."

Utilizing some of the statements of Bradford, Winthrop, Crèvecoeur, and Henry Adams, Kaul is arguing essentially that American fiction is by no means socially indifferent, or anarchic in its political values—as some critics have reputed it to be—but is actually committed to this notion of *ideal* community. Through the language of fiction, most of it "romantic" and removed from the structures of existing society, our major writers have actually been commenting on that society, and at the same time attempting to suggest the outlines of a better one. What he says of Crèvecoeur's very sympathetic description of Indian tribal community in the last of his *Letters from an American Farmer* Kaul later applies to our nineteenth-century novelists: "his purpose in introducing this example of ideal community life is not to describe an actual people in a factual place but rather to create a set of values by means of which he can evaluate the society of his time." Later in his book, Kaul points to such "communities" as the relationship of Leatherstocking and the Indian Chingachgook, Ishmael and Queequeg, Huck and Jim as examples of his contention that the American hero is not so much escaping from an oppressive society as conducting a search, invariably doomed, for a more ideal one. The chief barriers in that search are, on the one hand, restrictive society such as exists in *The Scarlet Letter*, "utterly lacking in the elementary Christian virtues of love and compassion"; and on the other, a totally unrestrained individual like Ahab, who stands as an ultimate example of a "Calvinistic self-absorption [which] had finally issued into action as the unfettered activity of isolated and self-sufficient individuals."

Like Kaul, Leo Marx is concerned with the American writer's attempt to articulate—and perhaps bridge—an impressive gap, in this case the one that exists between the ideal of the "middle landscape" (not a wild but a partially "cultivated" nature) and the nineteenth century's ideal of technological advancements, imaged in the locomotive, the steamboat, and the dynamo: "considered in their totality [these two ideals] constitute a supreme metaphor of contradiction in our culture." Although brought about in large part by the "unbelievably rapid mechanization of an under-developed society," this contradiction becomes, in the hands of our best writers, a means of articulating still deeper conflicts, sometimes of a psychic nature, becoming finally the characteristic American dialectic of mind and an opposed reality. In *The Education of Henry Adams*, Marx sees the American penchant for dialectic in a kind of ultimate embodiment, as the Virgin and the Dynamo become the giant images of "past and present, unity and diversity, love and power."

In his book *The Machine and the Garden,* which impressively extends and illustrates the argument of the essay we reprint, Marx makes it clear that our most vital expressions of reconciliation, for example, in Thoreau, Melville, and Twain, have been imaginative rather than literal ones. The moments of achieved harmony, in other words, have occurred not in actual or fictionalized scenes and events (as Kaul argues) but only in the transcendent and absorbing imaginations of the narrator of *Walden,* of Ishmael, and occasionally in the supple language of Huck Finn. In *Walden,* Marx notes, "Thoreau is clear, as Emerson seldom was, about the location of meaning and value. He is saying that it does not reside in the natural facts or in social institutions or in anything 'out there,' but in consciousness."

A full recognition of reconciliation as an achievement of mind rather than fact is the purpose of Richard Poirier's *A World Elsewhere,* from which the essay "Self and Environment" is excerpted. Poirier is concerned here with style, with the actual language of our authors and their most articulate heroes, as they struggle "to create a world in which consciousness might be free." It is "a style filled with an agitated desire to make a world in which tensions and polarities are fully developed and then resolved." And yet it is the "struggle of consciousness" which Poirier emphasizes. The opponent of this consciousness is nothing more, and nothing less, than what he calls the "provided environment," which is to say the entirety of the "given" American experience: the facts of its space, its social structures, as well as the huge apparatus of convention, both in behavior and language, which constitutes the limitations of mind. The American fictional hero, who is often seen struggling to free himself from an environment less pure, less ideal than the one of his own moral and psychic needs, is thus the resonant echo of the American writer who, particularly as he was described in Emerson's "American Scholar," must free himself from the modes and language of European literary convention. And these come together in the languages of *Walden,* of Huck Finn, of all those Jamesian characters who articulate nothing so much as the gap between reality and a sensitive consciousness miraculously larger than the very tools with which it must perforce articulate itself.

The pathos of our literature, a pathos which Kaul and Marx also imply, becomes the result of these attempts to "externalize the inner consciousness," to "insert it" in an environment that simply will not conform to it, even as it will not conform to those larger-than-life wishes of our most characteristic heroes.

An interesting qualification to Poirier's theory can be found in a passage in Alfred Kazin's *Contemporaries,* on the contemporary American writer's refusal to deal with the world as is. Although he is talking about the same phenomenon in our literature, his evaluation of it differs sharply from Poirier's:

Life in America changes so quickly, and people are so quick to change into each other, that the everlasting thinness and abstractness of American writing, which comes from our lack of "society," of a solid core of leaders, manners, traditions, is likely to be intensified by our new writers, who have a society but don't believe in it enough to describe it—to deal with it not merely as it is but as something that *is.* One of the things we now long for in contemporary literature is escape from the tyranny of symbolic "meaning." We want to return to life not as a figure in the carpet but as life in its beautiful and inexpressible materiality—life as the gift that it actually is rather than the "material" that we try to remake.

That such a return to reality can be executed, however, without a greater modification of mind than the American writer or his hero can afford, is the brunt of Poirier's argument. The deliberateness with which our best-known characters attempt to preserve their "integrity," analogous to the attempt to retain an inviolate and expansive consciousness, is of course a major force in the preservation of that insistent dialectic we have been describing.

R. W. B. Lewis' *The American Adam* is something of a classic of modern American criticism, one of the few works with which other critics, skeptical or enthusiastic, must come to terms. The earliest of the essays included here, it stands as an impressive rebuttal to much of what the others maintain. Although it recognizes tensions in our literature similar to those already described, *The American Adam* is finally about the transformation of those tensions "into conscious and coherent narrative." Lewis sees two major oppositions in nineteenth-century America: what he calls the Party of Hope, epitomized in Emerson, Thoreau, and Whitman, and the Party of Memory, found largely in the orthodox Calvinism of the day. These he finds ultimately reconciled in a Party of Irony—Hawthorne, Melville, and James, who accept the notion of an American Adam, but who insist that he must "fall," must be initiated into the full complexity of experience (including his own capacity for evil), if he is to attain significant value. In *The Marble Faun* and *Billy Budd,* to a greater extent even than in what are generally considered their greatest works, Hawthorne and Melville give form to what Lewis calls "the whole of their experience of America": "These novels were perhaps as close as American culture ever came to the full and conscious realization of the myth it had so long secreted." It is clear from Lewis' book that while he would agree with Chase that our literature has had its "poetry of disorder," he believes that genuine reconciliation was achieved by our greatest authors, and in a manner not essentially different from that of the great European authors. What Lewis calls "the authentic American narrative" is finally the single complex stream of its dissonant yet contained parts.

Part of Lewis' reservations about the poetry of Whitman is, in fact, that it is insensitive to dialectic, that it remains unaware of opposing forces which mightily threaten the Whitmanian notion of man as a God-like creator, naming the parts of his world without a single voice to contradict his right or his capacity to do so. The recognition of dialectic, however, of an alternative force that threatens to nullify a primary one, becomes necessary *in order* for the American Adam to fulfill the limits of the largest narrative available to him; and this is a narrative that ultimately restores essential harmony to what proves to be only an apparent dissonance.

At first glance the selections printed from Roy Harvey Pearce's *The Continuity of American Poetry* will appear to resemble (in his notion of the "shape" if not the content of our literature) the ultimate position of Lewis: that American poetry reveals a single, consistent "narrative," which Pearce defines as "antinomian." The antinomian or Adamic impulse is the strain of the "simple, separate person," the heart of a poetry which, more than anything else, calls attention to itself as the product of an individual mind—standing in a kind of opposition to group and culture. This impulse is part of the radical shift in sensibility, emerging out of certain qualities inherent in Puritanism, resulting in the poet's altered version of what constitutes his role as poet. Instead of "coming upon" reality, as the product of a powerful and controlling God external to himself, the poet begins to see himself as, in certain important ways, the creator and maker of the real. The poem ultimately becomes the thing "which manifests above all man's power to make and to order."

But this single current of national poetic impulse calls forth in the twentieth century a "counter current," what Pearce calls the "mythic" as opposed to the Adamic mode. This mythic mode, epitomized in the poetry and criticism of T. E. Eliot, is the attempt to see man once again "as the creature, not the creator of his world," and to urge, in opposition to Whitman and the Adamic poem, that man "submit [him]self to history." Eliot proposes that the poet return to a mode of verse which recognizes the past, tradition, which submerges the self to a "mythic" awareness of that which is infinitely larger than self; finally that the poet must seek in verse some echo, not of the private order of the independent imagination, but of that permanent order belonging to the history of poetry and of the world.

Unlike Lewis, who begins with a sense of dialectic which finally refines itself into a single narrative, Pearce begins with the single narrative and then follows it through its division into a dialogue in the twentieth century. In response to the "challenge" of the mythic countercurrent, the Adamic mode produces its own ultimate poet, Wallace Stevens, whose poetry is preoccupied with its own status as created object, and whose "implicit Adamic protagonist" is concerned solely "with what *he* can make, his own creations": "if there is a transcendent reality, he can conceive of it only in his own image and know it only as his own creation." Between Adamic and mythic, Stevens and Eliot, there can be, according to Pearce, no reconciliation, although both modes are themselves involved in an identical quest to reconcile individual man to his community. One emphasizes the freedom a man must have, the other the freedom he cannot afford.

III

The concern with tension is a concern with literary form, with the characteristic shapes our literature has taken. And as varied as these shapes have been, the following essayists agree that underlying our classic American books, especially the fiction, has been some kind of radical opposition, whether ultimately reconciled or not.

It is clear that this radical opposition has continued into the twentieth century and that it continues also to dominate our literature, whatever the modifications that may have occurred in complexity, attitude, and tone. In *Of Mice and Men*, for example, Steinbeck dramatizes with an almost formulaic clarity the conflict between the ideal and the actual community. Through the mere fact that they "travel together" and through their dream of owning their own farm, George and Lennie set themselves apart from the other farm laborers. The friendship and the dreaming, of course, are indissoluble, even as the ideal community in nineteenth-century literature is frequently involved with some common assumption quite unsupported by fact. George and Lennie's unreal hope for a farm is what binds them to each other, based as it is on the unique contribution each makes to it: George provides an articulateness impossible to Lennie's slow mind; Lennie, the faith itself, the deep conviction which the more rational George cannot sustain alone. A more complicated version of a similar theme exists in Faulkner's *Light in August,* in the contrast between the improbable and comic union of Byron Bunch with Lena Grove and the Jefferson society of fierce black-white division which has presided over the murder and castration of Joe Christmas.

The invasion of the pastoral by an agent of technology occurs in several twentieth-century works, one example of which—Norris' *The Octopus*—Marx singles out in his "Two Kingdoms of Force." Such an invasion also pervades Sherwood Anderson's *Poor White,* a novel describing the sudden industrialization of a small Ohio town. At the novel's conclusion Anderson brings together the images of a farm at night, the child Clara McVey is now carrying within her, and the sounds of the factories:

As they went past the barns and the bunkhouses where several men now slept they heard . . . above the sound of the animals stirring in the barns . . . another sound, a sound shrill and intense, greetings perhaps to an unborn Hugh McVey. For some reason, perhaps to announce a shift in crews, the factories of Bidwell that were engaged in night work set up a great whistling and screaming.

Finally, the resistance of an unyielding environment to a persistent, expansive consciousness is apparent particularly in the work of Faulkner. In *The Sound and the Fury* Quentin Compson attempts to convert what he considers his sister Caddy's sordid promiscuity into an *imagined* incest with himself, a "world elsewhere" of outrage which frees him from the banality of merely ordinary sexual transgression. In a later novel, *Absalom, Absalom!,* Faulkner provides this same Quentin with a still broader consciousness, allowing him to imagine a coherent and convincing narrative out of the confusing materials of Thomas Sutpen's life.

It is debatable whether any of these radical oppositions are ever reconciled, but occasionally in our modern literature they come close to joining. The hero of Hemingway's *The Old Man and the Sea,* for instance, is able to rescue from his defeat by the sharks a triumph that transforms him into an image of Christ, and Bellow's Moses Herzog is able to declare out of his chaotic mental journey through past and present some sense of identity: *"I am pretty well satisfied to be, to be just as it is willed. . . ."*

Reconciled or not, the oppositions, the tensions have remained for our age as they were for our American past—the substructure of all our writers' quest to *be* writers. And these tensions are there basically out of what may well be a genuine rupture of purpose, of conviction, present from the beginning, that has forced our writers continually to confront the problem of bringing these forces together. Or, to put it another way, they are there out of some need, indigenous to our identity as Americans, to assert the supremacy of ourselves and our imaginations to whatever experience can offer. And for this it has been necessary to keep those tensions alive—to insist on their survival in order to continue to test our efforts to resolve them. In a curious way we have courted the frustration inherent to any commitment to the existence of tension; but we have courted it only because it has guaranteed the privilege of imagining, to one degree or another, reconciliation.

The Broken Circuit

RICHARD CHASE

A CULTURE OF CONTRADICTIONS

The imagination that has produced much of the best and most characteristic American fiction has been shaped by the contradictions and not by the unities and harmonies of our culture. In a sense this may be true of all literatures of whatever time and place. Nevertheless there are some literatures which take their form and tone from polarities, opposites, and irreconcilables, but are content to rest in and sustain them, or to resolve them into unities, if at all, only by special and limited means. The American novel tends to rest in contradictions and among extreme ranges of experience. When it attempts to resolve contradictions, it does so in oblique, morally equivocal ways. As a general rule it does so either in melodramatic actions or in pastoral idyls, although intermixed with both one may find the stirring instabilities of "American humor." These qualities constitute the uniqueness of that branch of the novelistic tradition which has flourished in this country. They help to account for the strong element of "romance" in the American "novel."

By contrast, the English novel has followed a middle way. It is notable for its great practical sanity, its powerful, engrossing composition of wide ranges of experience into a moral centrality and equability of judgment. Oddity, distortion of personality, dislocations of normal life, recklessness of behavior, malignancy of motive—these the English novel has included. Yet the profound poetry of disorder we find in the American novel is missing, with rare exceptions, from the English. Radical maladjustments and contradictions are reported but are seldom of the essence of form in the English novel, and although it is no stranger to suffering and defeat or to triumphant joy either, it gives the impression of absorbing all extremes, all maladjustments and contradictions

41

into a normative view of life. In doing so, it shows itself to derive from the two great influences that stand behind it—classic tragedy and Christianity. The English novel has not, of course, always been strictly speaking tragic or Christian. Often it has been comic, but often, too, in that superior form of comedy which approaches tragedy. Usually it has been realistic or, in the philosophical sense of the word, "naturalistic." Yet even its peculiar kind of gross poetic naturalism has preserved something of the two great traditions that formed English literature. The English novel, that is, follows the tendency of tragic art and Christian art, which characteristically move through contradictions to forms of harmony, reconciliation, catharsis, and transfiguration.

Judging by our greatest novels, the American imagination, even when it wishes to assuage and reconcile the contradictions of life, has not been stirred by the possibility of catharsis or incarnation, by the tragic or Christian possibility. It has been stirred, rather, by the aesthetic possibilities of radical forms of alienation, contradiction, and disorder.

The essential difference between the American novel and the English will be strongly pointed up to any reader of F. R. Leavis's *The Great Tradition*. Mr. Leavis's "great tradition" of the novel is really Anglo-American, and it includes not only Jane Austen, George Eliot, Conrad, and Henry James but, apparently, in one of its branches Hawthorne and Melville. My assumption in this book is that the American novel is obviously a development from the English tradition. At least it was, down to 1880 or 1890. For at that time our novelists began to turn to French and Russian models and the English influence has decreased steadily ever since. The more extreme imagination of the French and Russian novelists has clearly been more in accord with the purposes of modern American writers than has the English imagination. True, an American reader of Mr. Leavis's book will have little trouble in giving a very general assent to his very general proposition about the Anglo-American tradition. Nevertheless, he will also be forced constantly to protest that there is another tradition of which Mr. Leavis does not seem to be aware, a tradition which includes most of the best American novels.

Ultimately, it does not matter much whether one insists that there are really *two* traditions, the English and the American (leaving aside the question of what writers each might be said to comprise) or whether one insists merely that there is a radical divergence within one tradition. All I hold out for is a provisional recognition of the divergence as a necessary step towards understanding and appreciation of both the English and the American novel. The divergence is brought home to an American reader of Leavis's book when, for example, he comes across the brief note allotted to the Brontës. Here is Leavis's comment on Emily Brontë:

I have said nothing about *Wuthering Heights* because that astonishing work seems to me a kind of sport . . . she broke completely, and in the most astonishing way, both with the Scott tradition that imposed on the novelist a romantic resolution of his themes, and with the tradition coming down from the eighteenth century that demanded a plane-mirror reflection of the surface of "real" life. Out of her a minor tradition comes, to which belongs, most notably, *The House with the Green Shutters.*

Of course Mr. Leavis is right; in relation to the great tradition of the English novel, *Wuthering Heights* is indeed a sport. But suppose it were discovered that *Wuthering Heights* was written by an American of New England Calvinist or Southern Presbyterian background. The novel would be astonishing and unique no matter who wrote it or where. But if it were an American novel it would not be a sport; it has too close an affinity with too many American novels, and among them some of the best. Like many of the fictions discussed in this book *Wuthering Heights* proceeds from an imagination that is essentially melodramatic, that operates among radical contradictions and renders reality indirectly or poetically, thus breaking, as Mr. Leavis observes, with the traditions that require a surface rendering of real life and a resolution of themes, "romantic" or otherwise.

Those readers who make a dogma out of Leavis's views are thus proprietors of an Anglo-American tradition in which many of the most interesting and original and several of the greatest American novels are sports. *Wieland* is a sport, and so are *The Scarlet Letter* and *The Blithedale Romance, Moby-Dick, Pierre,* and *The Confidence Man, Huckleberry Finn, The Red Badge of Courage, McTeague, As I Lay Dying, The Sun Also Rises*—all are eccentric, in their differing ways, to a tradition of which, let us say, *Middlemarch* is a standard representative. Not one of them has any close kinship with the massive, temperate, moralistic rendering of life and thought we associate with Mr. Leavis's "great tradition."

The English novel, one might say, has been a kind of imperial enterprise, an appropriation of reality with the high purpose of bringing order to disorder. By contrast, as Lawrence observed in his *Studies in Classic American Literature,* the American novel has usually seemed content to explore, rather than to appropriate and civilize, the remarkable and in some ways unexampled territories of life in the New World and to reflect its anomalies and dilemmas. It has not wanted to build an imperium but merely to discover a new place and a new state of mind. Explorers see more deeply, darkly, privately and disinterestedly than imperialists, who must perforce be circumspect and prudential. The American novel is more profound and clairvoyant than the English novel, but by the same token it is narrower and more arbitrary, and it tends to carve out of experience brilliant, highly wrought fragments rather than massive unities.

For whatever reason—perhaps the nagging scrupulosity of the Puritan mind has something to do with it—the American novel has sometimes approached a perfection or art unknown to the English tradition, in which we discover no such highly skilled practitioners as Hawthorne, Stephen Crane, Henry James, or Hemingway. These writers, often overestimated as moralists, seem content to oppose the disorder and rawness of their culture with a scrupulous art-consciousness, with aesthetic forms—which do, of course, often broaden out into moral significance.

In a well known passage Allen Tate refers to the "complexity of feeling" that everyone senses in the American novel and that, as Mr. Tate says, "from Hawthorne down to our own time has baffled our best understanding." The complexity of the American novel has been much exaggerated. With the exception of one or two of James's novels no American fiction has anything like the complexity of character and event of *Our Mutual Friend,* for example. In *The Scarlet Letter* or *Moby-Dick* the characters and events have actually a kind of abstracted simplicity about them. In these books character may be deep but it is narrow and predictable. Events take place with a formalized clarity. And certainly it cannot be argued that society and the social life of man are shown to be complex in these fictions.

But of course Tate says "complexity of feeling," and he is right about that. The states of feeling, and the language in which they are caught, are sometimes very intricate in American novels. Yet these musing tides of feeling and language that make such a rich poetry in our fiction often seem to be at variance with the simplified actions and conceptions of life our novels present. The origins of this apparent anomaly must be sought in the contradictions of our culture.

Marius Bewley takes up Tate's remark in an essay called "Fenimore Cooper and the Economic Age" and traces this "complexity of feeling" to a "tension" which he finds not only in Cooper but in Hawthorne and James. It is, he thinks, a political tension in its origins, although as embodied in the works of these authors, it assumes many forms. This tension, he says, "was the result of a struggle to close the split in American experience, to discover a unity that—for the artist especially—almost sensibly *was not there.* What was the nature of the division that supported this conflict? It took on many forms concurrently; it was an opposition between tradition and progress or between the past and the future; between Europe and America, liberalism and reaction, aggressive acquisitive economics and benevolent wealth. These same divisions existed in Europe also, but there they were more ballasted by a denser social medium, a richer sense of the past, a more inhibited sense of material possibilities."

Mr. Bewley's apt discussion of the matter needs to be amended in one fundamental way. The kind of art that stems from a mind primarily moved by the impulse toward aesthetic and cultural unities and thus "struggles to close the split in American experience" as an artist might wish to close it—this kind of art is practiced often, though not always, by Henry James, but less often by Hawthorne and Cooper, and much less often by Faulkner, Melville, and Mark Twain. The fact is that many of the best American novels achieve their very being, their energy and their form, from the perception and acceptance not of unities but of radical disunities.

Like many readers of American literature, Bewley makes the mistake of assuming both that our writers have wanted to reconcile disunities by their art and their intelligence and that this is what they *should* have wanted to do. Behind this assumption is a faulty historical view, as well as a certain overplus of moralism, which neglects to observe that there have been notable bodies of literature, as well as of painting and sculpture, that have proposed and accepted an imaginative world of radical, even irreconcilable contradictions, and that with some important exceptions, the American novel (by which I mean its most original and characteristic examples) has been one of these bodies of literature.

Surely Cooper (as will be noted later) is not at his best in a novel like *Satanstoe*, which is a "culture-making" novel and in which his mind is moved by an image of aesthetic and political harmony. On the contrary he is at his best in a book like *The Prairie*, where the search for unity is not at the center of the stage and he can accept without anxiety or thought the vivid contradictions of Natty Bumppo and his way of life— those contradictions which, as Balzac saw, made him so original a conception. In this book Cooper is not inspired by an impulse to resolve cultural contradictions half so much as by the sheer romantic exhilaration of escape from culture itself, into a world where nature is dire, terrible, and beautiful, where human virtues are personal, alien, and renunciatory, where contradictions are to be resolved only by death, the ceaseless brooding presence of which endows with an unspeakable beauty every irreconcilable of experience and all the irrationalities of life.

Mr. Bewley is not alone in assuming it to be the destiny of American literature to reconcile disunities rather than to pursue the possibility it has actually pursued—that is, to discover a putative unity *in* disunity or to rest at last among irreconcilables. In *Democracy in America* Tocqueville tried to account for a number of related contradictions in American life. He noted a disparity between ideals and practice, a lack of connection between thought and experience, a tendency of the American mind to oscillate rather wildly between ideas that "are all either extremely minute and clear or extremely general and vague."

Tocqueville sought a genetic explanation for these disparities. He pointed out that in aristocratic societies there was a shared body of inherited habits, attitudes and institutions that stood in a mediating position between the individual and the state. This, he observed, was not true in a democracy, where "each citizen is habitually engaged in the contemplation of a very puny object: namely, himself. If he ever looks higher, he perceives only the immense form of society at large or the still more imposing aspect of mankind. . . . What lies between is a void." Tocqueville believed that this either/or habit of mind also owed much to the sharp distinctions made by Calvinism and its habit of opposing the individual to his God, with a minimum of mythic or ecclesiastical mediation. He found certain advantages in this "democratic" quality of mind, but he warned Americans that it might produce great confusion in philosophy, morals, and politics and a basic instability in literary and cultural values, and that consequently Americans should try to discover democratic equivalents for those traditional habits of mind which in aristocracies had moderated and reconciled extremes in thought and experience.

Tocqueville knew that the dualistic kind of thought of which he spoke was specifically American only in the peculiar quality of its origin and expression. He saw that with the probable exception of England, Europe would characteristically concern itself during the nineteenth century with grand intellectual oppositions, usually more or less of a Hegelian order. But even though the tendency of thought Tocqueville predicated belonged to Western culture generally, one is nevertheless struck by how often American writers conceive of human dilemmas according to his scheme, and how many make aesthetic capital out of what seemed to him a moral and intellectual shortcoming.

In his studies of the classic American writers, D. H. Lawrence presented his version of the contrariety, or, as he said, "duplicity" of the American literary mind by saying that he found in writers like Cooper, Melville, and Hawthorne "a tight mental allegiance to a morality which all their passion goes to destroy," a formulation which describes perfectly the inner contradiction of such products of the American imagination as the story of Natty Bumppo. In general Lawrence was thinking of an inherent conflict between "genteel" spirituality and a pragmatic experientalism which in its lower depths was sheer Dionysian or "Indian" energy and violence. Acute enough to see that the best American artistic achievements had depended in one way or another on this dualism, he seemed ready nevertheless to advocate, on moral grounds, a reconciliation of opposites, such as he thought he discerned in the poems of Whitman.

In short, like all the observers of American literature we are citing in these pages, Lawrence was trying to find out what was wrong with it. He is a sympathetic and resourceful reader—one of the best, surely, ever to turn his attention to the American novel. But he thinks that the American novel is sick, and he wants to cure it. Perhaps there is something wrong with it, perhaps it is sick—but a too exclusive preoccupation with the wrongness of the American novel has in some ways disqualified him for seeing what, right or wrong, it *is*.

Finally, there is the division of American culture into "highbrow" and "lowbrow" made by Van Wyck Brooks in 1915 in his *America's Coming-of-Age*. Brooks's essay is a great piece of writing; it is eloquent, incisive, and witty. But we have lived through enough history now to see its fundamental error—namely, the idea that it is the duty of our writers to heal the split and reconcile the contradictions in our culture by pursuing a middlebrow course. All the evidence shows that wherever American literature has pursued the middle way it has tended by a kind of native fatality not to reconcile but merely to deny or ignore the polarities of our culture. Our middlebrow literature—for example, the novels of Howells —has generally been dull and mediocre. In the face of Brooks's desire to unite the highbrow and the lowbrow on a middle ground, there remains the fact that our best novelists have been, not middlebrows, but either highbrows like James, lowbrows like Mark Twain, Frank Norris, Dreiser, and Sherwood Anderson, or combination highbrow-lowbrows like Melville, Faulkner, and Hemingway. Here again American fiction contrasts strongly with English. The English novel at its best is staunchly middlebrow. The cultural conditions within which English literature has evolved have allowed it to become a great middlebrow literature—the only one, it may be, in history.

Let us in all candor admit the limited, the merely instrumental value of the terms used in the last paragraph. They work very well, and are in fact indispensable, in making large cultural formulations. But in applying them to individual authors the terms must be constantly re-examined. We might ask, for example, whether from one point of view both Hawthorne and James performed the unlikely feat of becoming great middlebrow writers. Both of them, at any rate, achieve a kind of contemplative centrality of vision within the confines of which their minds work with great delicacy and equanimity. In so far as they do this, one certainly cannot chide them for shying away from some of the more extreme contradictions, the more drastic forms of alienation, the more violent, earthy, or sordid ranges of experience which engage the minds of Melville and Faulkner, and in fact most of our best writers. Yet to achieve a "contemplative centrality of vision" certainly requires an action of the mind; whereas the word "middlebrow," although suggesting centrality of vision, inevitably suggests, judging by our American literature, a view gained by no other means than passivity and the refusal of experience.

To conclude this brief account of the contradictions which have vivified and excited the American imagination, these contradictions seem traceable to certain historical facts. First, there is the solitary position man has been placed in in this country, a position very early enforced by the doctrines of Puritanism and later by frontier conditions and, as

Tocqueville skillfully pointed out, by the very institutions of democracy as these evolved in the eighteenth and nineteenth centuries.

Second, the Manichaean quality of New England Puritanism, which, as Yvor Winters and others have shown, had so strong an effect on writers like Hawthorne and Melville and entered deeply into the national consciousness. From the historical point of view, this Puritanism was a backsliding in religion as momentous in shaping the imagination as the cultural reversion Cooper studied on the frontier. For, at least as apprehended by the literary imagination, New England Puritanism—with its grand metaphors of election and damnation, its opposition of the kingdom of light and the kingdom of darkness, its eternal and autonomous contraries of good and evil—seems to have recaptured the Manichaean sensibility. The American imagination, like the New England Puritan mind itself, seems less interested in redemption than in the melodrama of the eternal struggle of good and evil, less interested in incarnation and reconciliation than in alienation and disorder. If we may suppose ourselves correct in tracing to this origin the prevalence in American literature of the symbols of light and dark, we may doubtless suppose also that this sensibility has been enhanced by the racial composition of our people and by the Civil War that was fought, if more in legend than in fact, over the Negro.

More obviously, a third source of contradiction lies in the dual allegiance of the American, who in his intellectual culture belongs both to the Old World and the New. These are speculative ideas which I can only hope to make concrete and relevant in the suceeding pages. I would hope to avoid, at the same time, the rather arid procedure that would result from trying to find a "contradiction" behind every character and episode.

NOVEL VS. ROMANCE

Nothing will be gained by trying to define "novel" and "romance" too closely. One of their chief advantages is that, as literary forms go, they are relatively loose and flexible. But especially in discussing American literature, these terms have to be defined closely enough to distinguish between them, even though the distinction itself may sometimes be meaningless as applied to a given book and even though, following usage, one ordinarily uses the word "novel" to describe a book like Cooper's *The Prairie* which might more accurately be called a "romance" or a "romance-novel."

Doubtless the main difference between the novel and the romance is in the way in which they view reality. The novel renders reality closely and in comprehensive detail. It takes a group of people and sets them going about the business of life. We come to see these people in their real complexity of temperament and motive. They are in explicable relation to nature, to each other, to their social class, to their own past. Character is more important than action and plot, and probably the tragic or comic actions of the narrative will have the primary purpose of enhancing our knowledge of and feeling for an important character, a group of characters, or a way of life. The events that occur will usually be plausible, given the circumstances, and if the novelist includes a violent or sensational occurrence in his plot, he will introduce it only into such scenes as have been (in the words of Percy Lubbock) "already prepared to vouch for it." Historically, as it has often been said, the novel has served the interests and aspirations of an insurgent middle class.

By contrast the romance, following distantly the medieval example, feels free to render reality in less volume and detail. It tends to prefer action to character, and action will be freer in a romance than in a novel, encountering, as it were, less resistance from reality. (This is not always true, as we see in what might be called the static romances of Hawthorne, in which the author uses the allegorical and moral, rather than the dramatic, possibilities of the form.) The romance can flourish without providing much intricacy of relation. The characters, probably rather two-dimensional types, will not be completely related to each other or to society or to the past. Human beings will on the whole be shown in ideal relation—that is, they will share emotions only after these have become abstract or symbolic. To be sure, characters may become profoundly involved in some way, as in Hawthorne or Melville, but it will be a deep and narrow, an obsessive, involvement. In American romances it will not matter much what class people come from, and where the novelist would arouse our interest in a character by exploring his origin, the romancer will probably do so by enveloping it in mystery. Character itself becomes, then, somewhat abstract and ideal, so much so in some romances that it seems to be merely a function of plot. The plot we may expect to be highly colored. Astonishing events may occur, and these are likely to have a symbolic or ideological, rather than a realistic, plausibility. Being less committed to the immediate rendition of reality than the novel, the romance will more freely veer toward mythic, allegorical, and symbolistic forms.

THE HISTORICAL VIEW

Although some of the best works of American fiction have to be called, for purposes of criticism, romances rather than novels, we would be pursuing a chimera if we tried, except provisionally, to isolate a literary form known as the American prose romance, as distinguished from the European or the American novel. In actuality the romances of our literature, like European prose romances, are literary hybrids, unique only in their peculiar but widely differing amalgamation of novelistic and romance elements. The greatest American fiction has tended toward the romance more often than the greatest European fiction. Still, our fiction is historically a branch of the European tradition of the novel. And it is the better part of valor in the critic to understand our American romances as adaptations of traditional novelistic procedures to new cultural conditions and new aesthetic aspirations. It will not change our appreciation of the originality and value of *Moby-Dick* or *The Blithedale Romance* to say that they both seem to begin as novels but then veer off into the province of romance, in the one case making a supreme triumph, in the other, a somewhat dubious but interesting medley of genres and intentions.

Inevitably we look to the writings of James Fenimore Cooper, for it was he who first fully exemplified and formulated the situation of the novelist in the New World. His first book, *Precaution*, was a novel of manners, somewhat in the style of Jane Austen. Considering this a failure, he wrote *The Spy*, a story of the Revolution, in which, following Scott, he put his characters in a borderland (in this case between the American and British armies) where the institutions and manners of society did not obtain. He sketched out in Harvey Birch the semilegendary hero who would find his full development in Natty Bumppo. As for characterization and realism of presentation, he contented himself with what he called in *Notions of the Americans* "the general picture" and "the delineation of principles"— this being, as he said, all that could be expected of the American writer, given the "poverty of materials" and the uniformity of behavior and public opinion. He introduced an element of melodrama, believing that this might be suitable to scenes set in the American forest, even though we had no mysterious castles, dungeons, or monasteries. He introduced also a certain "elevation" of style and a freedom in arranging events and attributing moral qualities to his characters. It is thus apparent that if American conditions had forced Cooper to be content with "the general picture" and "the delineation of principles" this was, if a step away from the novel form proper, a step *toward* the successful mythic qualities of the Leather-Stocking tales. Here was proof of Tocqueville's ideas that although the abstractness and generality of the democratic imagination would make unavailable some of the traditional sources of fiction, this abstractness would in itself be a new source of mythic ideality.

In Cooper's books we see what was to be the main drift of American fiction. Responding to various pressures, it would depart markedly from the novelistic tradition. When it did so, it would—with variations that may be observed in such writers as Hawthorne, Melville, Mark Twain, Faulkner, and Hemingway—become either melodrama or pastoral idyl, often both.

Although Cooper gave an indubitably American tone to romance he did so without ceasing to be, in many ways, a disciple of Scott. Another disciple of Scott, and to a lesser extent of Godwin, was Cooper's near contemporary, the South Carolina journalist and romancer William Gilmore Simms. This author is no less convinced than Cooper that romance is the form of fiction called for by American conditions. Historical romance was his particular *forte,* and his *Views and Reviews* (1845) contains an interesting investigation of the materials available to the American romancer. In his prefatory letter to *The Yemassee,* his most popular tale of Indian warfare (first published in 1835), Simms defines the romance as the modern version of epic:

You will note that I call *The Yemassee* a romance, and not a novel. You will permit me to insist on the distinction . . . What are the standards of the modern Romance? What is the modern Romance itself? The reply is immediate. The modern Romance is the substitute which the people of the present day offer for the ancient epic. The form is changed; the matter is very much the same; at all events, it differs much more seriously from the English novel than it does from the epic and the drama, because the difference is one of material, even more than of fabrication. The reader who, reading *Ivanhoe,* keeps Richardson and Fielding beside him, will be at fault in every step of his progress. The domestic novel of those writers, confined to the felicitous narration of common and daily occurring events, and the grouping and delineation of characters in the ordinary conditions of society, is altogether a different sort of composition; and if, in a strange doggedness or simplicity of spirit, such a reader happens to pin his faith to such writers alone, circumscribing the boundless horizon of art to the domestic circle, the Romances of Maturin, Scott, Bulwer, and others of the present day, will be little better than rhapsodical and intolerable nonsense.

When I say that our Romance is the substitute of modern times for the epic or the drama, I do not mean to say that they are exactly the same things, and yet, examined thoroughly . . . the differences between them are very slight. These differences depend upon the material employed, rather than upon the particular mode in which it is used. The Romance is of loftier origin than the Novel. It approximates the poem. It may be described as an amalgam of the two. It is only with those who are apt to insist upon poetry, that the resemblance is unapparent. The standards of the Romance . . . are very much those of the epic. It invests individuals with an absorbing interest—it hurries them rapidly through crowding and exacting events, in a narrow space of time—it requires the same unities of plan, of purpose, and harmony of parts, and it seeks for its adventures among the wild and wonderful. It does not confine itself to what is known, or even what is probable. It grasps at the possible; and, placing a human agent in hitherto untried situations, it exercises its ingenuity in extricating him from them, while describing his feelings and his fortunes in the process.

Loosely written as it is, this statement, with its echoes of Aristotle's *Poetics,* remains something of a classic in the history of American criticism, its general purport being one which so many of our prose fictionists have accepted. American fiction has been notable for its poetic quality, which is not the poetry of verse nor yet the domestic or naturalistic poetry of the novel but the poetry of romance. In allying romance to epic Simms was reflecting his own preoccupation with panoramic settings, battles, and heroic deeds; doubtless he had also in mind, vociferous nationalist that he was, the power of epic to mirror the soul of a people. There are many American fictions besides *The Yemassee* which remind us of epics, large and small: Cooper's *Prairie, Moby-Dick, The Adventures of Huckleberry Finn*, Faulkner's *As I Lay Dying*, for example. Yet on the whole, American fiction has approximated the poetry of idyl and of melodrama more often than of epic.

Not all of Simms's own romances have the epic quality. *Confession: or the Blind Heart* (1841), *Beauchampe* (1842), and *Charlemont* (1856) are "tales of passion" and have to do with seduction, murder, revenge, and domestic cruelty. They are dark studies in psychology that reflect Godwin and the Gothic tradition at the same time that in their pictures of town life, lawyers, court trials, and local customs they forecast later Southern writers, such as Faulkner and Robert Penn Warren. Simms's tales of passion, however, are fatally marred by the carelessness and crudity with which they are thrown toegther, and it was in the work of Hawthorne that for the first time the psychological possibilities of romance were realized.

As we see from the prefaces to his longer fictions, particularly *The Marble Faun*, Hawthorne was no less convinced than Cooper and Simms that romance, rather than the novel, was the predestined form of American narrative. In distinguishing between forms, his Preface to *The House of the Seven Gables* makes some of the same points Simms had made:

When a writer calls his work a romance, it need hardly be observed that he wishes to claim a certain latitude, both as to its fashion and material, which he would not have felt himself entitled to assume, had he professed to be writing a novel. The latter form of composition is presumed to aim at a very minute fidelity, not merely to the possible, but to the probable and ordinary course of man's experience. The former—while, as a work of art, it must rigidly subject itself to laws, and while it sins unpardonably so far as it may swerve aside from the truth of the human heart—has fairly a right to present that truth under circumstances, to a great extent, of the writer's own choosing or creation. If he think fit, also, he may so manage his atmospherical medium as to bring out or mellow the lights, and deepen and enrich the shadows, of the picture. He will be wise, no doubt, to make a very moderate use of the privileges here stated, and especially, to mingle the marvellous rather as a slight, delicate, and evanescent flavor, than as any portion of the actual substance of the dish offered to the public. He can hardly be said, however, to commit a literary crime, even if he disregard this caution.

As Hawthorne sees the problem confronting the American author, it consists in the necessity of finding (in the words of the Introduction to *The Scarlet Letter*) "a neutral territory, somewhere between the real world and fairy-land, where the Actual and the Imaginary may meet, and each imbue itself with the nature of the other." Romance is, as we see, a kind of "border" fiction, whether the field of action is in the neutral territory between civilization and the wilderness, as in the adventure tales of Cooper and Simms, or whether, as in Hawthorne and later romancers, the field of action is conceived not so much as a place as a state of mind —the borderland of the human mind where the actual and the imaginary intermingle. Romance does not plant itself, like the novel, solidly in the midst of the actual. Nor when it is memorable, does it escape into the purely imaginary.

In saying that no matter what its extravagances romance must not "swerve aside from the truth of the human heart," Hawthorne was in effect announcing the definitive adaptation of romance to America. To keep fiction in touch with the human heart is to give it a universal human significance. But this cannot be done memorably in prose fiction, even in the relatively loose form of the romance, without giving it a local significance. The truth of the heart as pictured in romance may be more generic or archetypal than in the novel; it may be rendered less concretely; but it must still be made to belong to a time and a place. Surely Hawthorne's romances do. In his writings romance was made for the first time to respond to the particular demands of an American imagination and to mirror, in certain limited ways, the American mind. In order to accomplish this Hawthorne had to bring into play his considerable talent for psychology. Cooper was not a psychologist of any subtlety and outside of the striking conception of the stoic inner life of Natty Bumppo, he gave to romance no psychological quality that might not find its close analogue in Scott. Although no one would mistake a fiction of Simms for one of Scott, Simm's originality was circumscribed by his apparent belief, as stated in the quotation above, that American romance would differ from earlier forms only because it had different material rather than a "particular mode" of rendering this material. His claim to originality was severely limited by the crudity and indecision of his literary form and of his psychological insights.

In the writings of Brockden Brown, Cooper, and Simms we have the first difficult steps in the adaptation of English romance to American conditions and needs. Following these pioneers we have had, ever since, two streams of romance in our literary history. The first is the stream that makes the main subject of this book and includes Hawthorne, Melville, James, Mark Twain, Frank Norris, Faulkner, Hemingway, and others who have found that romance offers certain qualities of thought and imagination which the American fiction writer needs but which are outside the province of the novel proper. These are writers who each in his own way have followed Hawthorne both in thinking the imagination of romance necessary and in knowing that it must not "swerve aside from the truth of the human heart."

The other stream of romance, justly contemned by Mark Twain and James, is one which also descends from Scott, and includes John Esten Cooke's *Surry of Eagle's Nest* (1866), Lew Wallace's *Ben Hur* (1880), Charles Major's *When Knighthood Was In Flower* (1899), and later books like *Gone with the Wind* and the historical tales of Kenneth Roberts. Although these works may have their points, according to the taste of the reader, they are, historically considered, the tag-end of a European tradition that begins in the Middle Ages and has come down into our own literature without responding to the forms of imagination which the actualities of American life have inspired. Romances of this sort are sometimes defended because "they tell a good story"—as opposed to the fictions of, say, Faulkner and Melville, which allegedly don't. People who make this complaint have a real point; yet they put themselves in the position of defending books which have a fatal inner falsity.

The fact is that the word "romance" begins to take on its inevitable meaning, for the historically minded American reader, in the writing of Hawthorne. Ever since his use of the word to describe his own fiction, it has appropriately signified the peculiar narrow profundity and rich interplay of lights and darks which one associates with the best American writing. It has also signified, to be sure, that common trait shared by the American romances which are discussed in this book and all other romances whatsoever—namely, the penchant for the marvelous, the sensational, the legendary, and in general the heightened effect. But the critical question is always: To what purpose have these amiable tricks of romance been used? To falsify reality and the human heart or to bring us round to a new, significant and perhaps startling relation to them?

James on the Novel vs. the Romance

In the two preceding sections of this chapter, I have tried to formulate preliminary definitions of "romance" and the "novel" and then to look at the matter in a historical perspective. In order to amplify the discussion, in both the abstract and the concrete, it will be of value at this point to return, with the aid of Henry James's prefaces, to the question of definition. In doing so, I shall risk repeating one or two observations which have already been made.

The first four prefaces James wrote for the New York edition of his works set forth, or at least allude to, the main items of his credo as a novelist, and although they are perhaps well known, there may be some advantage in looking them over again before noticing what James had to say directly about the relation of the romance to the novel. The four prefaces are those to *Roderick Hudson, The American, The Portrait of a Lady,* and *The Princess Casamassima.*

We might take as a motto this sentence, from the Preface to *The*

Princess: "Experience, as I see it, is our apprehension and our measure of what happens to us as social creatures." Although James himself does not overtly contrast his procedure with that of romance until he comes to the Preface to *The American,* we shall be justified in ourselves making the contrast, since James is obviously seeking to show, among other things, how the imperfections of romance may be avoided. And thus we reflect that, in a romance, "experience" has less to do with human beings as "social creatures" than as individuals. Heroes, villains, victims, legendary types, confronting other individuals or confronting mysterious or otherwise dire forces—this is what we meet in romances.

When James tells us that the art of the novel is the "art of representation," the practice of which spreads "round us in a widening, not in a narrow circle," we reflect on the relative paucity of "representation" in the older American romances and their tendency towards a concentrated and narrow profundity. Again we hear that "development" is "of the very essence of the novelist's process," and we recall how in romances characters appear really to be given quantities rather than emerging and changing organisms responding to their circumstances as these themselves develop one out of another. For if characters change in a romance, let's say as Captain Ahab in *Moby-Dick* or the Reverend Dimmesdale in *The Scarlet Letter* change, we are not shown a "development"; we are left rather with an element of mystery, as with Ahab, or a simplified and conventionalized alteration of character, as with Dimmesdale. Similarly, the episodes of romance tend to follow each other without ostensible causation; here too there is likely to be an element either of mystery or convention. To "treat" a subject, James says, is to "exhibit . . . relations"; and the novelist "is in the perpetual predicament that the continuity of things is the whole matter, for him, of comedy and tragedy." But in a romance much may be made of unrelatedness, of alienation and discontinuity, for the romancer operates in a universe that is less coherent than that of the novelist.

As for the setting, James says that it is not enough merely to report what it seems to the author to be, in however minute detail. The great thing is to get into the novel not only the setting but somebody's *sense* of the setting. We recall that in *The Scarlet Letter* the setting, although sketchy, is pictorially very beautiful and symbolically *à propos.* But none of the characters has a *sense* of the setting; that is all in the author's mind and hence the setting is never dramatized but remains instead a handsomely tapestried backdrop. In *Moby-Dick* the setting is less inert; it becomes, in fact, a kind of "enveloping action." Still, only in some of the scenes do we have Ishmael's sense of the setting; during most of the book Ishmael himself is all but banished as a dramatic presence.

The whole question of the "point of command" or "point of view" or "center of intelligence" is too complicated to go into here. Suffice it to say that the allotment of intelligence, the question of what character shall be specially conscious of the meaning of what happens to and around him so that we see events and people more or less through his eyes, thus gaining a sense of dramatic coherence—these questions are less and less pertinent as fiction approaches pure romance. Natty Bumppo need be conscious only of what the Indians are going to do next. Hawthorne's Chillingworth and Melville's Ahab are clairvoyantly conscious, but with a profoundly obsessive distortion of the truth. They are not placed in context in order to give concrete dramatic form to a large part of what the author sees, as is the "point of command" in a James novel; all we learn from them is how *they* see. And as I shall suggest in speaking of *The Blithedale Romance,* the dyed-in-the-wool romancer like Hawthorne merely proves that you mustn't have a central observer in your story, because if you do you simply point up the faults of romance and admit your incapacity to follow out a fully developed novelistic procedure. In the romance too much depends on mystery and bewilderment to risk a generally receptive intelligence in the midst of things. Too often the effect you are after depends on a universe that is felt to be irrational, contradictory, and melodramatic—whereas the effect of a central intelligence is to produce a sense of verisimilitude and dramatic coherence.

One or two further items from the prefaces may point up the contrast. A character, especially "the fictive hero," as James says, "successfully appeals to us only as an eminent instance, as eminent as we like, of our own conscious kind." He must not be "a morbidly special case"—but in romance he may well be. Again, says James, when economy demands the suppression of parts of the possible story they must not be merely "eliminated"; they must be foreshortened, summarized, compressed but nevertheless brought to bear on the whole. But in the looser universe of the romance, we may think "elimination" will be less criminal and unexplained hiatuses and discontinuities may positively contribute to the effect. To take an obvious case, in *Moby-Dick* we are content to think the sudden elimination of Bulkington an interesting oddity rather than a novelistic blunder and we gladly draw on the poetic capital Melville makes of it.

As for the moral significance of the novel, James sees a "perfect dependence of the 'moral' sense of a work of art on the amount of felt life concerned in producing it." We must ask, he says, "is it valid, in a word, is it genuine, is it sincere, the result of some direct impression or perception of life." These questions bear less on the romance, one of the assumptions of which is that it need not contain a full amount of felt life, that life may be felt indirectly, through legend, symbol, or allegory. Nor does the romance need the sincerity of the novel; indeed, as Lawrence points out, American romances, especially, tend to make their effect by a deep "duplicity" or ironic indirection.

To come finally to James's specific comments on the question we are considering. In the prefaces he follows his own advice as that had been expressed twenty-odd years earlier in "The Art of Fiction"—he sees no reason, that is, why the practicing writer should distinguish between novel and romance. There are good novels and bad ones, novels that have life and those that haven't—and this, for the novelist, is the only relevant question. The implication is that the novelist will be also the romancer if the "life" he is rendering extends into the realm of the "romantic." But if we are not, except as critics and readers, to distinguish between novel and romance, we still have to distinguish, within the novel that may be also a romance, the "romantic" from the "real." And this James essays in his Preface to *The American.*

In rereading this early novel James found a large element of romance in the free and easy way in which he had made his semilegendary hero Christopher Newman behave on his European travels. Particularly, James thought, the picture of the Bellegard family was "romantic." James had made them reject Newman as a vulgar manufacturer when actually common sense tells us that "they would positively have jumped at him." And James comments that "the experience here represented is the disconnected and uncontrolled experience—uncontrolled by our general sense of 'the way things happen'—which romance alone more or less successfully palms off on us." At the same time James finds an unexpected pleasure in rereading *The American,* which somewhat compensates for the lapses of verisimilitude. And his description of this pleasure makes a fair definition of the pleasure of romance—"the free play of so much unchallenged instinct . . . the happiest season of surrender to the invoked muse and the projected fable."[1]

"The disconnected and uncontrolled experience," then, is of the essence of romance, and any adequate definition must proceed from this postulate. First, however, one may clear out of the way certain conventional but inadequate descriptions of romance. It is not "a matter indispensably of boats, or of caravans, or of tigers, or of 'historical characters,' or of ghosts, or of forgers, or of detectives, or of beautiful wicked women, or of pistols and knives"—although one might perhaps be a little readier than James to think that these things might be of service. Yet one follows him assentingly when he decides that the common element in sensational tales is "the facing of danger" and then goes on to say that for most of us the danger represented by caravans and forgers is certainly benign or impotent compared with the "common and covert" dangers we face in our everyday existence, which may "involve the sharpest hazards to life and honor and the highest instant decisions and intrepidities of action."

The "romantic" cannot be defined, either, as "the far and the strange,"

---

[1] Cf. Melville's plea to his reality-minded readers for latitude in the depiction of character and incident. The ideal reader, he says, will "want nature . . . ; but nature unfettered, exhilarated, in effect transformed. . . . It is with fiction as with religion: it should present another world, and yet one to which we feel the tie." (*The Confidence Man,* Chapter 33.)

since, as such, these things are merely unknown, whereas the "romantic" is something we know, although we know it indirectly. Nor is a novel romantic because its hero or heroine is. "It would be impossible to have a more romantic temper than Flaubert's Madame Bovary, yet nothing less resembles a romance than the record of her adventures." Nor can we say the presence or absence of "costume" is a crucial difference, for "where . . . does costume begin or end."

James then arrives at the following formulation:

The only *general* attribute of projected romance that I can see, the only one that fits all its cases, is the fact of the kind of experience with which it deals— experience liberated, so to speak; experience disengaged, disembroiled, disen- cumbered, exempt from the conditions that we usually know to attach to it and, if we wish so to put the matter, drag upon it, and operating in a medium which relieves it, in a particular interest, of the inconvenience of a *related,* a measur- able state, a state subject to all our vulgar communities.

And James goes on in words that are particularly illustrative of his own art:

The greatest intensity may so be arrived at evidently—when the sacrifice of community, of the "related" sides of situations, has not been too rash. It must to this end not flagrantly betray itself; we must even be kept if possible, for our illusion, from suspecting any sacrifice at all.

In a fully developed art of the novel there is, as James says, a "latent extravagance." In novelists of "largest responding imagination before the human scene," we do not find only the romantic or only reality but a "current . . . extraordinarily rich and mixed." The great novelist responds to the "need of performing his whole possible revolution, by the law of some rich passion in him for extremes."

To have a rich passion for extremes is to grasp both the real and the romantic. By the "real," James explains, he means "the things we cannot possibly *not* know, sooner or later, in one way or another." By the "ro- mantic" he means "the things that, with all the facilities in the world, all the wealth and all the courage and all the wit and all the adventure, we never *can* directly know; the things that can reach us only through the beautiful circuit and subterfuge of our thought and our desire."

We hear much in these prefaces of the novelist's rich and mixed "cur- rent," of the possible "revolution" of his mind among extremes, of the "circuit" of thought and desire. James speaks, too, of the "conversion" that goes on in the mind of the novelist's characters between what happens to them and their *sense* of what happens to them, and of "the link of connection" between a character's "doing" and his "feeling." In other words James thinks that the novel does not find its essential being until it discovers what we may call the circuit of life among extremes or opposites, the circuit of life that passes through the real and the ideal, through the directly known and the mysterious or the indirectly known, through doing and feeling. Much of the best American fiction does not meet James's specifications. It has not made the circuit James requires of the "largest responding imagination." And the closer it has stuck to the assumptions of romance the more capital it has made, when any capital has been made, exactly by leaving the Jamesian circuits broken. That very great capital can be made in this way James does not acknowledge or know, and hence his own hostility, and that of many of his followers, to the more extreme forms of American fiction—those we associate, for example, with Brockden Brown, Poe, Melville, and Faulkner.

Nevertheless James's theory of the novel, his idea of the circuit of life which allows him to incorporate in his novels so many of the attributes of romance, is the most complete and admirable theory, as at their best James's are the most complete and admirable novels yet produced by an American. And it is against James's theory and often, though certainly not always, his practice that we have to test the achievements of his compatriots. But the danger is that in doing so we should lapse into an easy disapproval of that "rich passion . . . for extremes" which James praised on his own grounds but which may be seen operating to advantage on other grounds too.

Cultural and Literary Background:

The Type of American Experience

A. N. KAUL

To derive a culture from a certain mythic ancestry, or ideal mythic type, is a way of stating that culture's essence in narrative terms.

— KENNETH BURKE
"Ideology and Myth"

The American novelists of the nineteenth century were concerned with many sides of human experience. As happens in the case of other significant novelists of the world, the objects of their concern included the society in which they lived. Fenimore Cooper, Hawthorne, Melville, and Mark Twain were all in their different ways preoccupied with certain aspects of social life as it was shaping itself in the America of their times. Of these four, Cooper and Twain were, in some of their works, most directly concerned with the contemporary scene. Though Hawthorne's and Melville's work is seldom characterized by such directness of intention, it presents, perhaps for that very reason, a subtler and more abiding exploration of the very basis of social life and values.

It has always been difficult, however, to define the exact nature of the relation between these novelists' greatest work and the facts of American sociology as we know them. Nor is the difficulty surmounted entirely by reminding ourselves that their most significant themes were transcendent, engaging in but also going beyond the social aspect of life. The works of many of their European contemporaries (Dostoevsky and Balzac for example) also achieve a wider, if not similar, concern for the more ultimate problems of human destiny, and yet it has been comparatively easy to make this correlation in the case of European fiction. If one defines the novel as an art form entirely in terms of English and continental fiction, works like *The Deerslayer, The Scarlet Letter, Moby-Dick,* and *Huckleberry Finn* would represent an achievement which easily measures up to the requirements of great art but at the same time somehow falls below the level of the good novel. This seeming paradox has a great deal to do with the question of the relation between American society and the American novel. Lionel Trilling sees it when he observes in his essay on "Manners, Morals, and the Novel":

Now the novel as I have described it has never really established itself in America. Not that we have not had very great novels but that the novel in America diverges from its classic intention, which, as I have said, is the investigation of the problem of reality beginning in the social field. The fact is that American writers of genius have not turned their minds to society. . . . the reality they sought was only tangential to society.[1]

This perceptive formulation has a suggestiveness which goes beyond the requirements of the context in which it appears. Trilling has raised some important questions, and he briefly touches upon at least one of them when he says in a later essay that in America "the real basis of the novel has never existed—that is, the tension between a middle class and an aristocracy which brings manners into observable relief as the living representation of ideals and the living comment on ideas."[2]

To say that these observations are accurate but only negative is not to disparage Trilling, because his purpose is to provide certain fruitful comparisons rather than to argue why the American novel should not exist. It is true that some of the early American novelists themselves repeatedly evaluated their work in terms of the practice of their English contemporaries. Cooper started frankly as an imitator and perhaps never quite shook off the bad influence of Sir Walter Scott. Hawthorne admired Anthony Trollope and deprecated his own inability to write in the popular manner of the English novelists. Nevertheless, in their best work, the American novelists went their own way, and, if they felt uneasy about it, we must remember that they were creating a different kind of novel and did not enjoy our advantage of seeing it established in its own right as a vital and significant body of literature. Hence, whatever excursions we make into the realm of sociology must, in the last analysis, help our understanding of the primary fact of its enduring effectiveness. In the same way, a comparative study of the English and American novel of the nineteenth century can be useful only as a step toward a more positive account of the American novelists' concern with society and social values, even if such a comparison leads us finally to a revision of the accepted assumptions about social reality, the nature of the novelist's intention, and the relation between society and the novel.

One can thus proceed from Trilling's observations and ask: if the novel in America diverges from its "classic intention," what alternative inten-

[1] Lionel Trilling, *The Liberal Imagination* (New York, Viking Press, 1950), p. 212.
[2] Ibid., p. 260.

tion do we find informing its best examples? If the American writers of genius did not turn their minds to social description, is it not necessary to examine their attitude to the whole question of "society"? In order to understand their genius, do we not need to look more closely at what constituted the social reality of nineteenth-century America? If "the reality they sought was only tangential to society," how far did this pursuit mirror the actual conditions of the time and how far did it lead them to imaginative constructs of a life and values which can be called "social" in the best sense of the term?

The problem of realism underlies most of these questions. It can be admitted readily that in comparison with the social solidity observable in the novels of Dickens and Balzac, Hawthorne's and Melville's approach to society would indeed seem attenuated and tangential. They, as well as Cooper and Twain, would face the charge of being escapists, allegorists, day-dreamers, wishful thinkers, fantasy-mongers, romancers—they would in fact be called anything but novelists. The matter of nomenclature is relatively unimportant. What we must consider, however, is that their best works do not strike us as fairy tales or transcendental tracts which have no relevance to human problems and values, including the problems and values of man as a social being. On the contrary, they seem to us less dated and more compelling than most English fiction of about the same time. In this connection it would be well to ask ourselves why, for example, a work like *The Gilded Age*, which achieves considerable density of social description, is not for that reason a greater novel than *Huckleberry Finn,* which is also concerned, though in a different way, with society and its problems.

The main object of this book is to show how these novelists were deeply concerned with both the society of their times and an ideal conception of social relationships, and how the consequent interplay between actual and ideal social values constitutes at least a partial source of their continuing vitality. The task of relating their work with the American social reality will involve a historical essay in the nature of that reality. At this stage I will only argue that the sort of social realism which we associate with European fiction constitutes one way of approaching reality but that there is no reason to assume that it is the only way. Realism, as Karl Mannheim has pointed out, "means different things in different contexts. In Europe it meant that sociology had to focus its attention on the very severe tension between the classes, whereas in America, where there was more free play in the economic realm, it was not so much the class problems which was considered as the 'real' centre of society but the problems of social technique and organization."[3] What is said here of American sociology may be applied, *mutatis mutandis,* to American fiction. The most significant American novelists of the first sixty years of the nine-

[3] Karl Mannheim, *Ideology and Utopia,* tr. Louis Wirth and Edward Shils (London, Kegan Paul, Trench, Trübner, 1936), p. 228.

teenth century did not confine themselves wholly to the description or criticism of existing social conditions. They shared the general feeling that America was the land of social experimentation, and, while practical men battled over new political and economic institutions, they sought in their work the moral values necessary for the regeneration of human society. Exploration of existing society led them repeatedly to the theme of ideal community life.

It is against this background that we can approach those elements in the work of Cooper, Hawthorne, Melville, and Mark Twain which do not seem to fit our ordinary assumptions about the social realism of the novel. There is a way of regarding social reality which takes into account not only observable social facts but also various aspects of imaginative response to these facts; which considers such things as ideals, or mythic archetypes of thought, to be important if not readily visible components of that reality. Such an approach is especially helpful when we are dealing with a complex body of imaginative literature. To quote Karl Mannheim again:

Wishful thinking has always figured in human affairs. When the imagination finds no satisfaction in existing reality, it seeks refuge in wishfully constructed places and periods. Myths, fairy tales, other-worldly promises of religion, humanistic fantasies, travel romances, have been continually changing expressions of that which was lacking in actual life. They were more nearly complementary colours in the picture of the reality existing at the time than utopias working in opposition to the *status quo* and disintegrating it.[4]

If one accepts this statement, and if one remembers further that, according to Mannheim's unusual definition of terms, a "utopia" is an idea which is "situationally transcendant" but also realizable in actuality, one would conclude that Cooper's Leatherstocking Tales and Melville's *Typee* bear a closer relation to the social reality of nineteenth-century America than, let us say, the utopia of Jacksonian democracy which was materially working against and disintegrating the status quo of the time.

In reality, however, dissatisfaction with existing society did not make Cooper, Hawthorne, Melville, and even the Mark Twain of *Huckleberry Finn* wildly fanciful. They did not employ their imaginations in the construction of fairy tales or fantasies. As for other-worldly promises of religion, strictly speaking, these can be found only outside the work of the great novelists, in such fictions as Sylvester Judd's *Margaret: A Tale of the Real and Ideal, Blight and Bloom.* The four important novelists mentioned here derived their ideals from another source. In many different ways, they all leaned over backward and at some points achieved a sustaining contact with the great myth of America—the complex of ideas and ideals which had animated the beginnings of the experiment that had now grown into

[4] Ibid., p. 184.

the social and moral world around them. Since it recognized the limitations as well as the promises of human existence, it was not altogether an expansive myth. Nor did its promise represent even to the most sanguine mind anything more than a possibility, a suggestion of potential reality.

I am aware that one of the many dangers implicit in this kind of discussion is that it is always possible to trace many myths in the past of a country, or, rather, a myth by its very nature permits a diversity of implications to be read into it. I might therefore say at once that I am concerned with those components of the American myth which have a bearing primarily on the social concerns of the classic American novel and which, it seems to me, will help to illuminate some of its problems. My contention is that, though this myth grew out of a definite sociohistorical moment and was eventually defeated by the historical development of its own paradoxical nature, some of its essential features remained for a long time operative in the American creative sensibility. Accordingly, the best account of the particular set of implications I see in it will be a historical one.

What imaginative men will say in critical times is often revelatory of certain aspects of the national sensibility which in more normal times remain hidden from common view. A good example of this fact is provided by *I'll Take My Stand*, the documentary response of twelve famous Southerners to the great economic crisis in America. Although the whole enterprise was conducted with the air of a political gesture, the document is interesting precisely because its contributors were not politicians but primarily writers, and it is interesting to speculate whether, during the depression years, it would have been possible in any other country of the Western world to collect under a similar banner an equally intelligent set of critics, poets, novelists, sociologists, and historians. To say the least, anywhere else the program and values they advocated would have been considered too impractical to deserve serious or systematic exposition, much less to receive any attention at all. And yet some of their values —such as the desire for an unencumbered existence, for an intimate contact with the earth, for direct personal relationships rather than elaborate social arrangements—have always figured somewhere in the substratum of the American mind. To take a concrete example, "A Statement of Principles" written most probably by John Crowe Ransom and appended to the volume as an introductory essay, has the sentence: "The responsibility of men is for their own welfare and that of their neighbors; not for the hypothetical welfare of some fabulous creature called society."[5]

5 *I'll Take My Stand*, by Twelve Southerners (New York, Peter Smith, 1951), p. xviii.

Here we have in relatively simple form two important characteristics of the American sensibility: the insistence on the individual as the only proper unit of social calculus; and a definite feeling that what people generally call "society" is no more than an evil and chimerical invention that one can destroy by simply wishing it away. But this is not all. The statement contains a vague and barely perceptible reference to a third social category, for it makes one ask the simple question: Where exactly does neighborliness end and society begin? To ask such a question is to force into explicit statement an assumption concerning social values and organization that constitutes the third characteristic of the deeper American sensibility, but which has seldom, outside of certain reform movements in the nineteenth century, received rational or systematic formulation. This may be described as the concept of community life. It has figured primarily as an unstated ideal, a measuring rod rather than a blueprint for actuality. It qualifies the concept of individual freedom and prevents it from degenerating into an attitude of selfishness and irresponsibility. It postulates a set of values for relationship between individuals which, in their turn, provide a basis for the criticism of actual society when it seems to become cold and impersonal, or when its very foundations seem to rest on cruelty, greed, and acquisitiveness, to the total disregard of the claims of fellow human beings.

The career of this concept in America begins with the first settlements of New England. John Winthrop had written in "A Model of Christian Charity" which he composed during his voyage on board the *Arbella* and delivered to his fellow immigrants as an admonitory sermon on the life that lay before them:

. . . we must be knit together in this work as one man. We must entertain each other in brotherly affection; we must be willing to abridge ourselves of our superfluities, for the supply of others' necessities; we must uphold a familiar commerce together in all meekness, gentleness, patience and liberality. We must delight in each other, make others' conditions our own, rejoice together, mourn together, labor and suffer together: always having before our eyes our commission and community in the work, our community as members of the same body.[6]

The sentiment expressed here had received a practical trial almost a decade earlier in the short-lived cooperative land-farming experiment of the *Mayflower* pilgrims. Although, strictly speaking, Plymouth colony was never a communitarian settlement, it set an example for the long line of such settlements which followed it in America, and it is interesting to note the reasons for its failure as William Bradford gives them in his *History:*

[6] *The American Puritans,* ed. Perry Miller (New York, Doubleday, Anchor Books, 1956), p. 83.

For this community (so far as it was) was found to breed much confusion and discontent and retard much employment that would have been to their benefit and comfort. For the young men, that were most able and fit for labour and service, did repine that they should spend their time and strength to work for other men's wives and children without any recompense. The strong, or man of parts, had no more in division of victuals and clothes than he that was weak and not able to do a quarter the other could; this was thought injustice. The aged and graver men to be ranked and equalized in labours and victuals, clothes, etc., with the meaner and younger sort, thought it some indignity and disrespect unto them. And for men's wives to be commanded to do service for other men, as dressing their meat, washing their clothes, etc., they deemed it a kind of slavery, neither could many husbands well brook it.[7]

If we compare this passage with the one quoted from Winthrop, we notice that the cause of the failure was precisely the nonobservance of the conduct Winthrop had enjoined: the abridgment of superfluities for the supply of others' necessities; upholding a familiar commerce together in all meekness, gentleness, patience, and liberality; and remembering always the commission and community in the work as members of the same body. The surprising thing then is not that the communitarian experiment at Plymouth failed but that there should ever have been a hope of its success. Indeed, on their departure from Leyden, John Robinson, their minister, had warned the band of Puritans of this danger. "And, lastly," he wrote in a letter to "the whole company" which Bradford quotes in full, "your intended course of civil community will minister continual occasion of offence, and will be as fuel for that fire, except you diligently quench it with brotherly forbearance."[8] Winthrop and Robinson were speaking in terms of Christian social ideals, whereas Bradford, in his practical experiment, had to encounter the hard economic reality of the individual's self-interest.

These were indeed the two main drives behind the social movement which led to the settlement of America. It was a continuation of that historical moment in which religious fervor, as Mannheim says, "joined forces with the active demands of the oppressed strata of society."[9] Its animating energy had a dual purpose and a millennial character: "The impossible gives birth to the possible, and the absolute interferes with the world and conditions actual events. This fundamental and most radical form of the modern utopia was fashioned out of a singular material. It corresponded to the spiritual fermentation and physical excitement of the peasants, of a stratum living closest to the earth. It was at the same time robustly material and highly spiritual."[10]

[7] William Bradford, *Of Plymouth Plantation 1620–1647*, ed. Samuel Eliot Morison (New York, Knopf, 1959), p. 121. All references to Bradford are to this edition.

[8] Ibid., pp. 51, 369.

[9] Mannheim, p. 190.

[10] Ibid., p. 192.

The economic motivation, however, formed no part of the grand design as the Puritan leaders conceived it. It was there from the outset, but it was not acknowledged on the same terms as the religious aspect of the enterprise. Indeed, in the long line of communitarian colonies in America it was not until the nineteenth century that a colony was frankly organized as an economic experiment. Even Cotton Mather, by whose time the original energy of religious dedication was already waning, believed firmly that the earlier colonizing attempts of the English in New England had failed because "the designs of those attempts being aimed no higher than the advancement of some *worldly interests*, a constant series of disasters has confounded them." It is after this observation that Mather relates the well-known story of a preacher of his who urged his congregation in the northeastern regions "to approve themselves a *religious people*" since otherwise "they would contradict the main end of planting this wilderness." Hereupon a well-known person stood up in the assembly and cried out: "Sir, you are mistaken: you think you are preaching to the people at the Bay; our *main end* was to *catch fish*." After suitably deprecating this attitude, Cotton Mather goes on to say how his own colony was "formed upon more glorious *aims*."[11]

In 1623 Bradford does not seem to have even noticed this Cod-God paradox, this discrepancy between Winthrop's high Christian ideals, which he shared, and the conduct of his fellow colonists. The economic side of the enterprise was important to him (indeed it takes up a great part of his narrative) but it was not allowed to figure in the providential design which had sent the pilgrims across the ocean. He was content to leave the economic predilections of man alone. His final comment on the breakdown of the communitarian experiment is perhaps significant in its farsightedness and definitely more shrewd than Cotton Mather's observations quoted above: "Let none object this is men's corruption," he says, "and nothing to the course itself. I answer, seeing all men have this corruption in them, God in His wisdom saw another course fitter for them."[12]

The important thing to Bradford was the religious community, the "enjoying much sweet and delightful society and spiritual comfort together in the ways of God"[13] as he puts it in describing the Puritans' first settlement in Holland. Here also of course the individual was important; indeed he was the all-important moral integer. But he was bound by covenant both to God and to his fellow Christians in the Church. And on occasions the governor of Plymouth Colony was prepared, like the other Puritan governors of the later colonies, to enforce the requirements of the covenant by forceful exercise of civil authority and to preserve the community thus in a life of unalloyed moral purity.

[11] Cotton Mather, *Magnalia Christi Americana* (2 vols. Hartford, Silas Andrus, 1855), *I*, 65–66.
[12] Bradford, p. 121.
[13] Ibid., p. 17.

The American settlement was only partially important to the Puritans as a way of improving their material fortunes. Its main importance was that here the covenanted church could be established and maintained without challenge, interference, or persecution by any outside authority. It has been argued often and for too long that frontier conditions lead to individualism. As recently as 1961 we find Edwin T. Bowden connecting the theme of "human isolation" in the American novel with "the frontier isolation," and vaguely confusing both with the historical force of individualism.[14] As a matter of fact, as we shall see, the theme of the nineteenth-century novelists was not physical isolation but moral alienation, or, as Emerson saw it, solitude in the midst of society. The movement toward individual freedom, as it is scarcely necessary to insist at this late day, was older and more extensive in origin. Like many other ideas which later blossomed in America, like Puritanism itself, its roots were in Europe. The difference lay in the fact that on this continent there was no older order, no constituted order at all, to hinder its growth. The only countervailing force was provided by ideals; like this first Puritan ideal of a commonwealth, a close-knit community of like-minded believers and worshipers.

By itself the frontier leads neither to an unfettered individualism nor to a restrictive society. The wilderness is by its very nature as much a temptation to capriciousness and irresponsibility as it is a force for social cohesion, for bringing people together in the face of a vast and unknown or hostile environment. If it provides an opportunity for the assertion of romantic individual freedom, it also inevitably brings about the less romantic but more necessary mutual self-help associations such as existed in all frontier stations. On the same scene the Indian way of life had for centuries enforced successfully a very severe tribal discipline without mass defection or desertion by individual members of the tribe. Thus the importance of the virgin continent lay precisely in the fact that, as far as society and civilization are concerned, it was a *tabula rasa,* an invitation to create and construct, a visible proof that ideals need not always end in starry-eyed idealism. It gave rise to Daniel Boone and the Western myth. But it also provided the theater for the practical enactment of hundreds of variously motivated experiments in communitarian living which began in the seventeenth century and continued well into the nineteenth. For their bearing on the American sensibility, both these facts are important. A common theme of the American imagination has been the problem of reconciling individual freedom with a mode of social life to which the individual can give his allegiance without danger of impairing his moral, spiritual, or psychological integrity. It is a theme of the utmost importance in our own day, and this may well be among the

---

[14] Edwin T. Bowden, *The Dungeon of the Heart: Human Isolation and the American Novel* (New York, Macmillan, 1961).

reasons why the nineteenth-century novelists' exploration of the values involved in the problem seems so vitally significant to the readers of the twentieth century.

To return to William Bradford, the most fascinating thing about his history is the bold outline of its narrative. It stands as a sort of imaginative archetype of American experience even as it may be taken for the first statement of the American myth. Divested of its endless details about shipping costs, adventurers, beaver-skins, and such other things, the frame of the story presents an epic reference: the solemn exodus of a band of people from a corrupt world and their journey across the ocean to build a New Jerusalem upon a virgin land. The Christ and Virgil whom Cotton Mather later called upon to inspire his own history, combine with effortless ease in the narrative of this literal-minded Puritan to whom the past was represented mainly by the Bible and the future by a great hope. Like the ancient bards, he himself remains anonymous, while the hero of his tale is not man but men, the constant and strangely moving "They" of the narrative.

At the same time, the story is also the unfolding of a phase in the endless drama between God and Satan—the two invisible but primary actors. With this extension we have that supramundane reference, that metaphysical dimension, which, in one form or another, is always present in the great American novels of the nineteenth century but which rarely emerges from the more purely social preoccupation of European fiction. Bradford's history is set in motion by those "wars and oppositions [which] . . . Satan hath raised, maintained and continued against the Saints, from time to time, in one sort or other."[15] Oppressed in this manner, rather than submit to the machinations of Satan acting through his surrogates in a depraved society, the saints decide to separate themselves from such a society altogether and remove themselves to "some of those vast and unpeopled countries of America" which are "devoid of all civil inhabitants."[16] Once there, with "the mighty ocean which they had passed" separating them "from all the civil parts of the world," they can hope to find no "friends to welcome them nor inns to entertain or refresh their weatherbeaten bodies; no houses or much less towns to repair to, to seek for succour."[17] All that can sustain the small community is the spirit of God and the inward conviction of the righteousness of their course.

Here we have, in terms of the language and outlook of the early seventeenth century, the basic pattern of the drama which, in other and varying terms, was to find recurrent expression in subsequent American imaginative literature. Put in a simplified form, it may be described as the theme of separation from an established society in search of a more

[15] Bradford, p. 3.
[16] Ibid., p. 25.
[17] Ibid., pp. 61–62.

satisfying community life. Society, the individual, and community—the main points of this triadic theme—were variously termed and defined by the various persons with whom I am chiefly concerned. Nevertheless, they figured in the imaginations of all of them. And together with this pre-occupation went a brooding sense of forces beyond man's reach and of a reality which is not man-made but which man must take into account: what I have called the metaphysical dimension of their vision.

The first separation from Europe was not the end but only the be-ginning of a process which was to repeat itself endlessly in America. It is fitting therefore that Bradford, whose narrative began with the first Puritan community's removal to Holland, should describe toward the end of the book, in what is one of its most moving passages, the separation of the younger members from the parent church, not as individuals assert-ing their freedom but only "like children translated into other families"[18] —the old narrator preserving bravely the intimate imagery of communal feeling while the elegiac note of the passage indicates that its lack of basis in actual social relationships was already becoming apparent.

"God in His wisdom," as Bradford says, had seen "another course fitter" for the Americans. This was the course of individualism, and it was not long before the covenanted community began to feel the strain of the paradox which lay at the center of its life, and the severe unity of the Puritan church itself was disturbed by dissension. By the time we come to Cotton Mather's history, after the turn of the century, the narrator has emerged from communal anonymity and assumed the first-person singular, and Bradford's collective biography has given place to a collec-tion of individual biographies. The fragmentation is accompanied by an increasing relaxation of religious discipline, a process of secularization which leads us gradually from the world of the Puritans to the age of Enlightenment in the eighteenth century. Cotton Mather may be said to reflect the stage of transition. A Janus-like figure, he is inspired by the ideals of the past and disturbed by what he can see of the future. The voice that speaks to us in the *Magnalia* is unable either to recapture the simple serenity of Bradford or to achieve the self-possession and shrewd dignity of Franklin's *Autobiography*.

Benjamin Franklin himself represents the consummation of the shift to economic and political individualism in America. There is something almost symbolic in his departure from Boston to begin his career in Philadelphia, the capital of the frontier state which was also to provide the scene for the next important literary performance in America. Frank-lin marks a nearly complete disseverance from the past. He lives entirely in the present and looks only toward the future. In him God seems indeed to have rivaled Defoe's creative power and produced an individual who can be called the single-handed author of his own world. No mists of

18 Ibid., p. 334.

metaphysical doubt cloud his vision. The science of electricity and mechanics has banished the theology of sin and damnation. The doctrine of salvation has yielded to the principle of self-help, and in place of spiritual communion we now have philanthropic association.

Much of this would apply also to Crèvecoeur who, as a literary figure, is more interesting for my purpose. A friend of Benjamin Franklin and a true Franklinian character, this "American Farmer" seems to have played more adroitly than the sage Doctor himself the role that Europe expected of a backwoods settler. *Letters from an American Farmer* is, as the title makes clear, aimed directly at Europe. Especially intended for European consumption are, apart from the bold touches of incipient literary romanticism, such tales (related with a seemingly meticulous concern for literal truth) as the one about the American owl whose wings measured 5′ 3″ or the 171 bees which Crèvecoeur exhumed from the "craw" of a kingbird and laid out "on a blanket in the sun" only to witness that "54 returned to life, licked themselves clean, and joyfully went back to the hive; where they probably informed their companions of such an adventure and escape, as I believe had never happened before to American bees!"[19] However, if we remember Crèvecoeur today as more than a pleasant *raconteur* it is because, under all the romantic nonsense of his work, we discover a serious attempt at exploring the meaning of America in terms of the assumptions prevalent in his time. This attempt is not altogether a matter of rational social analysis. *Letters from an American Farmer* has another serious aspect, a more imaginative dimension which goes beyond the world of Benjamin Franklin and points toward Fenimore Cooper and the other novelists of the nineteenth century.

Of course, the Franklinian side of the work is more readily noticeable. The values which dominate the book are the same that Franklin preached and practiced: individualism, industry, sobriety, and honesty. The individual is seen essentially in economic terms, and Crèvecoeur shares the enlightened view that human character is environmentally determined. Linked with this are his freedom from religious orthodoxy and the insistence on manners as the representative identity of man. If he is not entirely optimistic, he shows a consistent belief in the virtues of expanding civilization. Whether or not Crèvecoeur is to be regarded as an early Romantic, his book certainly does not celebrate the myth of the noble savage. He is far too decidedly a child of the eighteenth century to hold such a view. He firmly believes in the moral superiority of a settled agrarian life over that of wandering hunters, and he sees the lone pioneers of the forest as the most depraved class of American citizens. As an agrarian, though he values his closeness to nature immensely, the fact of

[19] The edition used for quotations from Crèvecoeur is Hector St. John de Crèvecoeur, *Letters from an American Farmer*, New York, Dutton, Everyman's Library, 1951.

decisive importance to him is his being a freeholder. Unlike Wordsworth, he has nothing but pity for the European farmers who live close to the earth but do not own it. And as for the primitive African, he is neither a noble nor an ignoble savage. In the South, where he is kept in bondage and ignorance, the slave is rude and depraved, while in the North, where he is trained in the ways of civilization, he is as decent a human being as his master. In the last letter, Crèvecoeur does not expound his scheme of going to live in an Indian tribe without expressing a hope that he may be able to civilize the savages, especially through the art of inoculation in which his wife possesses much skill.

The first eight of Crèvecoeur's twelve letters thus provide a discursive answer to his celebrated question ("What then is the American, this new man?") mainly in terms of the economic and political differences between Europe and America. The American, Crèvecoeur says, is a European or the descendant of a European "who, leaving behind him all his ancient prejudices and manners, receives new ones from the new mode of life he has embraced, the new government he obeys, and the new rank he holds." In the "great American asylum" the poor immigrant is freed from the oppression of a feudal society, from the taxation of landlord, church, and monarch, from "involuntary idleness, servile dependence, penury, and useless labour." "Here religion demands but little of him; a small voluntary salary to the minister, and gratitude to God; can he refuse these?" Be he a trader, farmer, craftsman, or a common laborer, he will be rewarded amply for his labor, so that in time he will cast off his servile timidity and acquire the dignity and self-confidence of a true human being. No wonder Crèvecoeur should exclaim: "We have no princes, for whom we toil, starve, and bleed: we are the most perfect society now existing in the world."

Here we have struck perhaps for the first time that note of conscious superiority of American over European social institutions, of pride in democratic equality and abundance of opportunity, which we hear again and again in the subsequent literature of the country, though with increasingly critical qualifications. Crèvecoeur's own book is far from lacking in critical reference. However, before considering this aspect of it, it would be well to remind ourselves of its contextual breadth by turning a century and a half backward to the pilgrims or about the same number of years forward to modern times. William Bradford had also spoken of Americans as Europeans escaping oppression, when, after describing their landing, he asked whether future generations ought not to remember that their "fathers were Englishmen which came over this great ocean, and were ready to perish in this wilderness" but the Lord "heard their voices" and "delivered them from the hand of the oppressor."[20] The sense of mission, however, the urgency of high idealism, which he intended to

20 Bradford, p. 63.

transmit with this appeal did not endure for long in the face of the ascendant power of economic individualism. It was an inevitable development, but also one with which the American imagination could never wholly reconcile itself. The tensions created by this uneasy sense of disequilibrium have tended to produce a variety of attitudes, ranging from an unreasoned but acute sense of betrayal to more thoughtful criticism. For example, to take a recent formulation, this is how Richard Hofstadter sums up the chief characteristics of American politics in the "Introduction" to his book *The American Political Tradition:*

> However much at odds on specific issues, the major political traditions have shared a belief in the rights of property, the philosophy of economic individualism, the value of competition; they have accepted the economic virtues of capitalist culture as necessary qualities of man. Even when some property right has been challenged—as it was by followers of Jefferson and Jackson—in the name of the rights of man or the rights of the community, the challenge, when translated into practical policy, has actually been urged on behalf of some other kind of property. . . . American traditions also show a strong bias in favor of equalitarian democracy, but it has been a democracy in cupidity rather than a democracy of fraternity.

Crèvecoeur's account of the advantages of democracy is in keeping with this tradition, especially when he is describing the economic benefits that the country offers to the prospective "new man": "Here the rewards of his industry follow with equal steps the progress of his labour; his labour is founded on the basis of nature, *self-interest;* can it want a stronger allurement?" In moral terms, this is a far cry from Winthrop's social ideal, which would require men to labor to supply other people's necessities.

Crèvecoeur, however, experiences no misgivings as he continues his undaunted exposition of this theme in the next five letters. Having described the new man as an agrarian, he shifts the scene to the islands of Nantucket and Martha's Vineyard. The sea suggests to him no "romantic" or "metaphysical" associations; it is only a setting for the fishing industry and for trade. If the continental American labors on the land, the democratic man on these islands plows the sea. In either case the world presents an uncomplicated and hopeful prospect. Indeed it is not until the ninth letter that we find Crèvecoeur striking the first disturbed notes of a contrary and larger theme. The occasion is provided by his visit to Charleston and his witnessing of the "facts" of Negro slavery as it is practiced in the South. The question that he now asks is not "What then is the American, this new man?" but "What then is man; this being who boasts so much of the excellence and dignity of his nature, among that variety of unscrutable mysteries, of unsolvable problems, with which he is surrounded?" To this somewhat Melvillian question Crèvecoeur proceeds to give an answer with which Melville could easily sympathize. Though even Negroes have hearts in which "noble dispositions can grow," by and large, everywhere, and at all times, men have proved themselves to be little better than predatory animals. What does the history of the earth show us "but crimes of the most heinous nature, committed from one end of the world to the other? We observe avarice, rapine, and murder, equally prevailing in all parts." Perhaps we can flatter ourselves with the thought that a kindly nature has implanted in us a spirit of stoical endurance which enables us to reconcile ourselves to the severities of her dispensation. "Yet if we attentively view this globe, will it not appear rather a place of punishment, than of delight? . . . Famine, diseases, elementary convulsions, human feuds, dissensions, etc., are the produce of every climate; each climate produces besides, vices, and miseries peculiar to its latitude." The evil in human nature rivals the perversity of physical nature to such an extent that

one would almost believe the principles of action in man, considered as the first agent of this planet, to be poisoned in their most essential parts. We certainly are not that class of beings which we vainly think ourselves to be; man an animal of prey, seems to have rapine and the love of bloodshed implanted in his heart . . . If Nature has given us a fruitful soil to inhabit, she has refused us such inclinations and propensities as would afford us the full enjoyment of it. Extensive as the surface of this planet is, not one half of it is yet cultivated, not half replenished; she created man, and placed him either in the woods or plains, and provided him with passions which must for ever oppose his happiness; everything is submitted to the power of the strongest; men, like the elements, are always at war; the weakest yield to the most potent; force, subtlety, and malice, always triumph over unguarded honesty and simplicity.

"Such," the passage concludes, "is the perverseness of human nature; who can describe it in all its latitude?"

This is a Crèvecoeur who is not often recognized and who seems to subscribe neither to the rational optimism of the eighteenth century nor to the "romantic" ideas of the essential goodness of man and nature. The imagination that lies behind this letter (as well as the last one) would reveal him rather as possessing a closer kinship with the novelists of the nineteenth century. The American farmer is no longer the unreserved celebrator of democratic man and economic competitiveness, for he sees that human beings share the predatory characteristics as well as the passions of cruelty and violence which, in previous letters, he had discovered everywhere in the animal kingdom. The law of mutual destructiveness, which governs the world of nature, provides also the key to the history of human society. Accordingly, where he had expressed a firm belief in the virtues of civilization, he now regards both society and the wilderness as morally equivocal:

If from this general review of human nature, we descend to the examination of what is called civilised society; there the combination of every natural and artificial want, makes us pay very dear for what little share of political felicity we enjoy. It is a strange heterogeneous assemblage of vices and virtues, and of a variety of other principles, for ever at war, for ever jarring, for ever producing some dangerous, some distressing extreme. Where do you conceive then that nature intended we should be happy? Would you prefer the state of men in the woods, to that of men in a more improved situation? Evil preponderates in both; in the first they often eat each other for want of food, and in the other they often starve each other for want of room.

This passage, apart from its own significance, provides also the proper background for an understanding of the strange last letter, entitled "Distresses of a Frontier Man," which is in some ways the most interesting of the whole set, and which develops further the theme of "civilized society." In letter 9 immediately after the lines quoted above, Crèvecoeur had concluded that for his own part he thought that the vices and miseries to be found in civilization exceed those of the wilderness "in which real evil is more scarce, more supportable, and less enormous." Now, as the attributes of "society"—war, destruction, and pillage—invade his backwoods sanctuary, the paradox acquires the immediacy and urgency of a personal problem, so that he forms and expounds at length the scheme of abandoning his house and farm and seeking refuge in the less complicated life of an Indian tribe. "Yes," he declares, "I will cheerfully embrace that resource, it is an holy inspiration."

It would be easy to form out of this letter a neat little bridge for crossing over to Cooper's Leatherstocking Tales in the next century. It would be equally easy to dismiss it as a vulgar contraption of the romantic writer at his worst. Nevertheless, as I have tried to point out earlier, it is a mistake to regard Crèvecoeur as being altogether a literary showman of current attitudes. Not even the most liberal discounting of his obvious posturing for effect can wholly eliminate the imaginative core of his meaning, for, like Cooper after him, he shows a serious if unsophisticated concern for the values implicit in the drama of rival civilizations. Even in this letter he does not at any place suggest an unqualified approval of the primitive tribal life. On the contrary, he consistently maintains his earlier critical ambiguity. He is repeatedly worried by the fear that his young son may slip permanently from the higher agrarian life of his father into the savage hunting state. He insists that the family will maintain their own separate forms of worship under the wigwams. He even hopes that his influence may help the Indians to acquire certain aspects of civilization. And finally he presents his decision as an inevitable but perhaps only a temporary choice.

It is not important to inquire into the actual facts which lay behind the dramatization of this choice. To argue whether these reflections had their origin in the Indian raid on his house or in the conflict of loyalties he experienced during the Revolutionary War would be about as meaningful as to speculate whether Crèvecoeur could actually have encountered the caged Negro whose plight he describes with incredible flourishes of melodrama at the end of Letter 9. It is much more important to note that the sense of pervasive uneasiness that he had communicated in that letter, is now imaginatively recreated as a feeling of total betrayal. The society he had described as the most perfect "now existing in the world" and as being free of any laws except those of a lenient and protective nature has now become encumbered "either with voluminous laws, or contradictory codes, often galling the very necks of those whom they protect." And gone too is the early assurance in the value of absolute individualism: "Whichever way I look, nothing but the most frightful precipices present themselves to my view . . . what is man when no longer connected with society . . . He cannot live in solitude, he must belong to some community bound by some ties, however imperfect."

Here again is the enactment of the American drama of organized society and the individual who says: *Non serviam!* Speaking in a different context, Crèvecoeur had said of Europe in Letter 3: "There the plenitude of society confines many useful ideas, and often extinguishes the most laudable schemes which here ripen into maturity." The new world has freed the American from social enslavement, and yet, as we have seen here, his sense of individual freedom leads inevitably in the end to an equally strong desire to belong to a group larger than himself, an irresistible urge toward social community. "I resemble, methinks," Crèvecoeur goes on to say in memorable language, "one of the stones of a ruined arch, still retaining that pristine form that anciently fitted the place I occupied, but the centre is tumbled down; I can be nothing until I am replaced, either in the former circle, or in some stronger one."

If the new social circle of Crèvecoeur's choice turns out to be the Indian tribe, it is not altogether for the romantic reason that the primitive savages are "much more closely connected with nature than we are; they are her immediate children, the inhabitants of the woods are her undefiled offspring: those of the plains are her degenerated breed, far, very far removed from her primitive laws, from her original design." Undoubtedly, there is a good deal of such reasoning, but Crèvecoeur also goes behind it to make more valid discriminations. The two main aspects of the Indian communal life which he considers especially valuable, and which he sees also as providing a commentary on the practices of the society he has decided to abandon, are its social cohesiveness and its freedom from avarice. In a passage that recalls with fine irony the dominant theme of the early letters—America as the promise of material prosperity—he says:

Thus shall we metamorphose ourselves, from neat, decent, opulent planters . . . into a still simpler people divested of every thing beside hope, food, and the raiment of the woods: abandoning the large framed house, to dwell under the wigwam; and the featherbed, to lie on the mat, or bear's skin. There shall we sleep undisturbed by fruitful dreams and apprehensions.

But what Crèvecoeur admires more is the tribal social system which is "sufficiently complete to answer all the primary wants of man, and to constitute him a social being." There must be "in their social bond something singularly captivating, and far superior to anything to be boasted of among us," because, as Crèvecoeur maintains, drawing an unusually long bow, thousands of Europeans have become Indians whereas not a single Indian has adopted the white man's civilization. Discord and strife between members of the same community are unknown to them; although the white people have selfishly drawn them into their quarrels, "a civil division of a village or tribe, are events which have never been recorded in their traditions." Religion, which provides the cause for a hundred disputes in civilized society, is, among the Indians, only an agency of harmony and universal brotherhood. "Each worship with us, hath, you know, its peculiar political tendency," Crèvecoeur writes, explaining the salutary influence that he expects the simple Indian faith to exercise on his children; "there it has none but to inspire gratitude and truth: their tender minds shall receive no other idea of the Supreme Being, than that of the father of all men, who requires nothing more of us than what tends to make each other happy."

To ask whether such Indians existed anywhere outside of Crèvecoeur's imagination would be as irrelevant as to remember that he never went to live among their tribes. As an imaginative writer, and not unlike some novelists of the next century, his purpose in introducing this example of ideal community life is not to describe an actual people in a factual place but rather to create a set of values by means of which he can evaluate the society of his time.

The thousands of frontier men who succeeded Crèvecoeur on the American scene did not share his misgivings about the course America was taking. Individualism, as Ralph Gabriel has pointed out, was the most dominant force behind the developments of the nineteenth century. Its pressure was not only advancing men over the continent along an ever-extending frontier but also breaking down social institutions in the older settled areas. "Aristocracy," Tocqueville observed, "had made a chain of all the members of the community, from the peasant to the king; democracy breaks that chain and severs every link of it."[21] Even in religion there was a shift, as Gabriel points out, from Calvin's monarch-God to Horace Bushnell's conception of Jesus as the divine man, "Ameri-

---

[21] Alexis de Tocqueville, *Democracy in America*, ed. Phillips Bradley (2 vols. New York, Knopf, 1956), 2, 99. All references to Tocqueville are to this edition.

can Christianity" emphasizing the individual and his emotions rather than institutional observances.[22]

Insofar as individualism represented an advance in human values, its virtues were recognized implicitly or overtly by all thoughtful Americans of the nineteenth century. But it was also creating an atomistic society of isolated human beings which lacked moral and social purpose as much as it did any principle of cohesiveness. Writing in the last decades of the century, Henry Adams reviewed the situation of 1800 in the following words:

In the early days of colonization, every new settlement represented an idea and proclaimed a mission. . . . No such character belonged to the colonization of 1800. From Lake Erie to Florida, in long, unbroken line, pioneers were at work, cutting into the forests with the energy of so many beavers, and with no more express moral purpose than the beavers they drove away. The civilization they carried with them was rarely illumined by an idea; they sought room for no new truth, and aimed neither at creating, like the Puritans, a government of saints, nor, like the Quakers, one of love and peace; they left such experiments behind them, and wrestled only with the hardest problems of frontier life.

It is not surprising, Adams goes on to say, that foreign observers as well as the Americans of the sea coast did not admire this development, asserting that

virtue and wisdom no longer guided the United States! What they saw was not encouraging. . . . Greed for wealth, lust for power, yearning for the blank void of savage freedom such as Indians and wolves delighted in,—these were the fires that flamed under the caldron of American society, in which, as conservatives believed, the old, well-proven, conservative crust of religion, government, family, and even common respect for age, education, and experience was rapidly melting away, and was indeed already broken into fragments, swept about by the seething mass of scum ever rising in greater quantities to the surface.[23]

Not all Americans, certainly not the great novelists of the nineteenth century, who were acutely aware of the situation described by Adams, were by any means conservatives. They did not wish to see Tocqueville's hierarchic chain of aristocratic institutions reimposed upon their society. On the contrary, they wanted to preserve the gains of democracy and looked forward to the realization of social possibilities which they believed to be inherent in the democratic principle itself. Nor were many foreign observers necessarily antagonistic to American democracy just

[22] Ralph Henry Gabriel, *The Course of American Democratic Thought* (New York, Ronald Press, 1956), p. 33.

[23] Henry Adams, *History of the United States* (9 vols. New York, Scribner's, 1890–91), *1,* 177–78.

because they found themselves among its critics. If Dickens considered the Eastern Penitentiary in Philadelphia an inhuman institution, it was only after he had discovered that the inmates of the many asylums, poorhouses, hospitals, and prisons at South Boston "are surrounded by all reasonable means of comfort and happiness that their condition will admit of; are appealed to, as members of the great human family, however afflicted, indigent, or fallen; are ruled by the strong Heart, and not by the strong . . . Hand."[24] In "Concluding Remarks"—the last chapter of *American Notes*, in which he presents his view of "the general character of the American people, and the general character of their social system"—he begins by observing that Americans are "by nature, frank, brave, cordial, hospitable, and affectionate. Cultivation and refinement seem but to enhance their warmth of heart and ardent enthusiasm." He goes on to add, however, that these qualities are "sadly sapped and blighted in their growth among the mass" by that "great blemish in the popular mind of America . . . Universal Distrust." Linking this distrust itself with the American's "love of 'smart' dealing," he locates the ultimate root of the evil in "the national love of trade."[25] This diagnosis is paralleled by Emerson's criticism in "New England Reformers": "This whole business of Trade gives me to pause and think, as it constitutes false relations between men"[26] or again in "Man the Reformer":

The ways of trade are grown selfish to the borders of theft, and supple to the borders (if not beyond the borders) of fraud. . . . I leave for those who have the knowledge the part of sifting the oaths of our customhouses; I will not inquire into the oppression of the sailors; I will not pry into the usages of our retail trade. I content myself with the fact that the general system of our trade (apart from the blacker trades, which, I hope, are exceptions denounced and unshared by all reputable men), is a system of selfishness; is not dictated by the high sentiments of human nature; is not measured by the exact law of reciprocity, much less by the sentiments of love and heroism, but is a system of distrust, of concealment, of superior keenness, not of giving but of taking advantage.

We can notice here how the principle of self-interest, which Crèvecoeur had recognized as the strongest allurement that America offers to the "new man," has degenerated into selfishness and mutual distrust. We must notice, too, that for Dickens, as well as for Emerson, these characteristics of a commercial culture are evil primarily because they warp natural feelings and destroy human relations, for this was also the main point of the nineteenth-century novelists' criticism of their society.

[24] Charles Dickens, *American Notes and Pictures from Italy* (London, Oxford University Press, 1957), p. 53.

[25] Ibid., pp. 244–46.

[26] The edition used for quotations from Emerson is *Emerson's Complete Works*, 12 vols. Boston, Houghton, Mifflin, Riverside Edition, 1888–93.

And if Dickens' survey led him to conclude that the American people would be well advised to love "the Real less, and the Ideal somewhat more" and to encourage "a wider cultivation of what is beautiful without being eminently and directly useful,"[27] we must not forget that a few years later, in his story "The Artist of the Beautiful," Hawthorne attempted to give imaginative embodiment to precisely the same idea.

These men of imagination thus recognized the relation between economic forces and moral values. But, insofar as the emphasis falls on the moral consequences rather than the economic machinery of the system, they viewed the freedom of the individual as something real and meaningful. In the lecture on "New England Reformers," Emerson, by way of illustrating his concept of the sufficiency of the private man, relates the story of the individual who was excommunicated by his church on account of his connection with the antislavery movement and who thereupon promptly and boldly "excommunicated the church, in a public and formal process." Society thus presented the image of a body of men unfettered by any restrictive pressures, liberated from the restraints of religious, social, and economic institutions, enjoying a freedom of thought and action such as individuals had not known in any other place and time, and yet the world these men were creating was coming to rest increasingly on the foundations of selfishness, distrust, and crass materialism.

These products of individualism were not only falsifying social relations but abstracting from them all human content, so that the most alarming feature of this society was the isolation of its members. Tocqueville observed that democratic equality "places men side by side, unconnected by any common tie,"[28] and Emerson exclaimed in "Society and Solitude": "But how insular and pathetically solitary are all the people we know!" Emerson's position on this question of insularity and social relatedness, as on so many other questions, is interesting partly because of his dialectical manner of arguing both sides of a case. On the one hand, he seems undoubtedly to approve this tendency and to approximate closely his popular image as the champion of the self-reliant individual, of "the great Transcendental fallacy" as Daniel Aaron calls it. Nevertheless, as Aaron points out: "He was both the critic and the celebrator of his and subsequent generations, the Yea-sayer and the Nay-sayer."[29] Many positive elements of his attitude were shared by his contemporaries, not excluding the novelists, because, if their awareness of the limitations of individualism went beyond his, they, as much as he, took individual freedom as their starting point. If he seems to insist more on the individual's standing alone, a part at least of his reason is

[27] Dickens, p. 248.
[28] Tocqueville, 2, 102.
[29] Daniel Aaron, *Men of Good Hope* (New York, Oxford University Press, 1951), p. 7.

the same as theirs, for, as he says in his essay on "Friendship": "To stand in true relations with men in a false age is worth a fit of insanity, is it not?" And finally, if in "Society and Solitude" he talks of the "necessity of isolation which genius feels," it is, as he goes on to say, a "tragic necessity . . . irresistibly driving each adult soul as with whips into the desert, and making our warm covenants sentimental and momentary." A little later he adds, as though by way of a conscious comment on the other and better-known side of his own attitude: "But this banishment to the rocks and echoes no metaphysics can make right or tolerable. . . . A man must be clothed with society, or we shall feel a certain bareness and poverty, as of a displaced and unfurnished member."

Thus, while the practical-minded citizens of America were pushing forward to reap the benefits of unrestrained freedom, its philosophers, poets, and novelists were pondering the loss of moral and social values that went with the development. If the former lacked, as Adams said, all sense of moral purpose, the latter were deeply aware of the missionary tradition which had accompanied the settlement of America. No one doubted the necessity of destroying older social institutions. But what had happened to the expectations of a new society, the hope of a regenerated humanity, the vision of New Jerusalem? The American philosophers and poets felt that the process of democracy had defeated its promise.

A visionary conception of society provided more than the measuring rod of their criticism; from it came also their positive social values. In this sense the myth of America was still operative in the nineteenth century. An ideal society could be created as soon as the individuals concerned subscribed to the ideal principle which was to inform it. Since Americans were no longer the victims of old institutions but the prospective creators of new ones, the decisive factor was the moral regeneration of the individual. Emerson's answer to "this whole business of Trade" in "New England Reformers" was simple: "Let into it the new and renewing principle of love." For, as he had said in "Man the Reformer": "We must be lovers, and at once the impossible becomes possible." This was also Whitman's answer in 1864 when, after his disillusionment with the workings of practical democracy, he wrote in a characteristic vein: "The final meaning of Democracy through many transmigrations is to press on through all ridicules, arguments, and ostensible failures to put in practice the idea of the sovereignty, license, sacredness of the individual. This idea isolates, for reasons, each separate man and woman in the world;— while the idea of Love fuses and combines the whole. Out of the fusing of these twain, opposite as they are, I seek to make a homogeneous Song."[30]

The visionary aspect of the American tradition was not, however,

[30] *Walt Whitman's Workshop,* ed. C. J. Furness (Cambridge, Harvard University Press, 1928), pp. 127–28.

monopolized by literary artists. The great type of American social experience—separation from a corrupt society to form an ideal community—was receiving practical enactment in the numerous experiments of the contemporary communitarians. The first colonies were settled in the second half of the seventeenth century by foreign sectarians such as the Dutch Mennonites and Labadists. During the eighteenth century the Moravians and the Shakers had great success with their Utopian settlements, illustrating, as Arthur Bestor has said, "the process that was repeated time after time in America in the seventeenth, eighteenth, and nineteenth centuries."[31] In the nineteenth century the movement was considerably accelerated and the number of utopian colonies increased to well beyond 200, the experiments exciting widespread interest, both critical and enthusiastic.

Though the seminal idea of these colonies was in all cases brought over from Europe, the schemes came to full flower only in the new world, showing how persistently America figured in people's imagination as the bright hope of Europe. If Europe represented the hard facts of social reality, America was seen as approximating the possibility of ideal community life. In the nineteenth century, however, the communitarian tradition registered certain developments which were more significant than the quantitative increase in the number of experiments. In the first place, it was no longer restricted to foreign immigrants or to groups which continued to regard themselves as alien. As general social conditions in America itself grew unsatisfactory, American intellectuals, artists, and reformers started experimenting with utopian colonies of their own. A more important development lay in the fact that, in keeping with the general tendency of the nineteenth century, the economic and social implications of the communitarian way of life began to supersede its earlier religious and theological inspiration. Even the older utopian groups regarded themselves increasingly as communitarians first and sectarians second. When the followers of Father Rapp established the third of their villages in 1825, they called it not Harmony, as on both previous occasions, but Economy. The apostles of this new phase of communitarianism were Fourier and Owen.

Nevertheless, in America, unlike Europe, there was a continuity of tradition between the secular communities of the nineteenth century and the religious fervor of the seventeenth. "In America, and America alone, the religious socialism of the seventeenth century evolved without a break into the secular socialism of the nineteenth."[32] This transmission of communitarian tradition is illustrated by Brook Farm. Two years and a half before its establishment, its founder, George Ripley, visited the German sectarian community at Zoar, and his wife wrote enthusiastically about its

[31] Arthur Eugene Bestor, Jr., *Backwoods Utopias* (Philadelphia, University of Pennsylvania Press, 1950), p. 26.

[32] Ibid., p. 38.

way of life. The first prospectus of Brook Farm made allusion to the Moravians, the Shakers, and the Rappites, while Hawthorne, who joined the community early in its career, had already shown interest in the Shakers by publishing two tales about them in the 1830s. "The communitarian tradition influenced Brook Farm," Mr. Bestor concludes, "and Brook Farm, in turn, passed the influence along. The Fruitlands experiment of Bronson Alcott . . . was in some measure its offshoot, for Alcott had participated in the original plans for Brook Farm, and inaugurated his own experiment only when convinced that the older community was 'not sufficiently ideal.' "[33]

Hawthorne, of course, had the strongest critical reservations about the whole communitarian enterprise, and their nature was such that they would be shared by many of his contemporaries who never made the experiment of actually living in a utopian community, or even paid much attention to the movement. But before taking this up, it would be well to note two aspects of communitarian thought which represent the nineteenth-century residuum of the American myth and which bear a certain resemblance to the pattern of social experience as revealed in American imaginative literature. The first of these is the idea of the complete regeneration of society that we find in the American Fourierites and Owenites as much as in Emerson, who says in "New England Reformers": "It is handsomer to remain in the establishment . . . than to make a sally against evil by some single improvement, without supporting it by a total regeneration." Closely linked with this are the communitarians' refusal to work within the established society and their habit of viewing the two principles, the social and the communitarian, as mutually exclusive. These two concepts were termed differently by different persons but always with this suggestion of mutual incompatibility: Fourier called them "society" and "association," the American Fourierist Albert Brisbane, "civilization" and "association," and the elder Henry James, "civilization" and "society." As is obvious, "civilization" had thus a special connotation. Albert Brisbane prefaced his very popular book *Social Destiny of Man*, published in 1840, with a chapter entitled "Explanation of Terms," where he defined civilization as "the social system in which we live, *as it now is*, with all its defects and the little good it may possess."[34] It is useful to remember this while approaching the long line of American fictional heroes who abandon "civilization" in one form or another, for their decision represents the rejection of a particular social order and not of the social principle itself. It does not lead them ultimately to absolute individual freedom; more often it marks the beginning of a search for true community life.

[33] Ibid., p. 51.
[34] Albert Brisbane, *Social Destiny of Man* (Philadelphia, C. F. Stollmeyer, 1840), p. xi.

Two Kingdoms of Force

LEO MARX

A continent ages quickly once we come. The natives live in harmony with it. But the foreigner destroys, cuts down the trees, drains the water, so that the water supply is altered and in a short time the soil, once the sod is turned under, is cropped out. . . . The earth gets tired of being exploited. A country wears out quickly unless man puts back in it all his residue and that of all his beasts. When he quits using beasts and uses machines, the earth defeats him quickly. The machine can't reproduce, nor does it fertilize the soil, and it eats what he cannot raise. A country was made to be as we found it. We are the intruders. . . . Our people went to America because that was the place to go then. It had been a good country, and we had made a bloody mess of it. . . .

ERNEST HEMINGWAY
The Green Hills of Africa

I

On the morning of July 27, 1844, Nathaniel Hawthorne sat down in the woods near Concord, Massachusetts, to await (as he put it) "such little events as may happen." His purpose, so far as we can tell, was purely literary. He had no reason to believe that anything memorable would happen and, except in a literary sense, nothing did. He sat there in solitude and silence and tried to record his every impression as precisely as possible. The whole enterprise is reminiscent of the painstaking literary exercises of his neighbor, Henry Thoreau. Before Hawthorne was done, in any case, he had filled eight pages of his notebook. What he wrote is of course not a finished piece of work, yet the surprising fact is that neither is it a haphazard series of jottings. If it has a kind of unity it is because one incident, an unexpected encounter with a machine, dominates the rest of his impressions. Around this "little event" a certain formal—one

84

might almost say dramatic—pattern takes shape. It is to this pattern that I want to call attention. Looking at it closely—at the way ideas, emotions and other images group themselves about the image of the machine—we can observe the formation (on a microscopic scale to be sure) of a seminal theme in our literature.

To begin with, Hawthorne describes the setting, known in the neighborhood as "Sleepy Hollow":

. . . a shallow space scooped out among the woods, which surrounded it on all sides, it being pretty nearly circular, or oval, and two or three hundred yards—perhaps four or five hundred—in diameter. The present season, a thriving field of Indian corn, now in its most perfect growth, and tasselled out, occupies nearly half of the hollow; and it is like the lap of bounteous Nature, filled with bread stuff.

Then, in minute detail, he records what he sees and hears close by. "Observe the pathway," he writes, "it is strewn with little bits of dry twigs and decayed branches, and the sere and brown-oak leaves of last year that have been moistened by snow and rain, whirled about by harsh and gentle winds, since their departed verdure. . . . " And so on. What counts here, needless to say, is not the matter so much as the feeling behind it. From several pages in this vein we get an impression of a man in almost perfect repose, idly brooding upon the minutiae of nature, and now and then permitting his imagination a brief flight. Along the path, for example, he notices that "sunshine glimmers through shadow, and shadow effaces sunshine, imaging that pleasant mood where gaiety and pensiveness intermingle." For the most part, however, Hawthorne is satisfied to set down unadorned sense impressions, and especially sounds —sounds made by birds, squirrels, insects and moving leaves.

But then, after a time, the scope of his observations widens. Soon another kind of sound comes through. He hears the village clock strike, a cowbell tinkle, and mowers whetting their scythes.

He shifts from images of nature to images of man and society without any perceptible change of mood or tone. Indeed he makes a point of the fact that "these sounds of labor" do not "disturb the repose of the scene" or "break our sabbath, for like a sabbath seems this place, and the more so on account of the cornfield rustling at our feet." The passage is an elaborate evocation of a state of being in which there is no anxiety or tension or conflict. Hawthorne achieves the effect by describing the sequence of delicate sounds that interlace mind, nature and society. But in the end what imparts most force to the sense of all-encompassing harmony and unity is a vivid contrast:

But, hark! there is the whistle of the locomotive—the long shriek, harsh, above all other harshness, for the space of a mile cannot mollify it into harmony. It tells a story of busy men, citizens, from the hot street, who have come to spend a day in a country village, men of business; in short, of all unquietness; and no wonder that it gives such a startling shriek, since it brings the noisy world into the midst of our slumbrous peace. As our thoughts repose again, after this interruption, we find ourselves gazing up at the leaves, and comparing their different aspects, the beautiful diversity of green. . . .

These casual notes, I repeat, make an excellent starting point for a study of the image of the machine and its remarkable career in American writing. But this is not to imply that there was anything remarkable about Hawthorne's response to mechanization. Quite the contrary. Two years earlier, for example, Ralph Waldo Emerson had made a similar, if more whimsical, entry in his journal:

I hear the whistle of the locomotive in the woods. Wherever that music comes it has its sequel. It is the voice of the civility of the Nineteenth Century saying, "Here I am." It is interrogative: it is prophetic: and this Cassandra is believed: "Whew! Whew! Whew! How is the real estate here in the swamp and wilderness? Ho for Boston! Whew! Whew! . . . "

So far from being original, in fact, Hawthorne's image of the machine was closer to being a literary commonplace. Nor was it particularly American, as anyone familiar with the literature of the age will recognize. For example, the same year as the "little event" at Sleepy Hollow, Wordsworth wrote a sonnet for a campaign of protest against a projected railroad through the lake country. It began: "Is then no nook of English ground secure/From rash assault?" And it ended with a plea to the "beautiful romance/Of nature" to "protest against the wrong." By setting the machine in opposition to the tranquillity and order located in the landscape, Hawthorne, like Wordsworth, makes it an emblem of the artificial, of the unfeeling utilitarian spirit, and of that fragmented, modern style of life that allegedly follows upon the assumptions of scientific rationalism. Both writers treat the new technology as another cause of what Wordsworth likes to call the "fever of the world."

But surely this is a familiar pattern. We all know that in England during the "industrial revolution" writers, along with most other sensitive men, were repelled by the ugliness, squalor and suffering associated with the machine power, and that their revulsion sharpened the taste, already strong, for images of rural felicity. For at least half a century before now, at least as far back as the work of William Blake, feelings of this kind had been hastening the massive shift in point of view we call the romantic movement. If Hawthorne's reaction is at all typical, and I submit that it is, then the image of the new technology held by American writers is of the very essence of the romantic; it expresses that total romantic "protest," to use Whitehead's wonderfully acute phrase, "in behalf of the organic." At first glance, then, the most striking thing about Hawthorne's image of the machine is its unmitigated conventionality.

What makes this fact even more striking, of course, is our knowledge of American differences. We know that in America the new technological order *was* different. By the time of Hawthorne's visit to Sleepy Hollow many if not most Americans, like most visitors from abroad, recognized that in this country mechanization did not mean what it had meant in England.[1] At this time, moreover, when steamboats and factories and railroads were beginning to transform the native landscape, the idea of a unique affinity between America and the machine became popular. That idea, needless to say, is still very much with us. Even today, when the great scientific-technological revolution of our time is about to reach the most "backward" nations—when it so patently has become an international phenomenon—this notion of a special affinity between America and technology persists. We see it everywhere. It is reflected, for instance, in the universal habit of representing America with symbols drawn from the iconography of industrialism. The slogan at this moment in the Soviet Union is "Overtake America!" All the world, in short, acknowledges that America's experience of technology has been exceptional. Where else has there been anything to compare with the speed, intensity and, in a manner of speaking, success, with which young America embarked upon mechanization? To ask the question is to indicate why we might have expected to find a less conventional image of the machine in our literature. Why is it, under the circumstances, that our most perceptive writers seem merely to repeat a stock response of the European romantics?

The answer, let me say in advance, is that they only *seem* to do so, and that their reaction eventually does take on the color of native experience. But to say this is not to deny either the presence or the power of the convention at the outset. Right here we are at the point where "sociological" critics of literature often leave the track of plausibility. They forget that we have no business looking to art for direct, which is to say extraconventional, ties with events—with history. They forget, in other words, that lines leading from social fact to literary artifact invariably pass through the realm of inherited form and convention. In this instance, to

[1] A new exploration of the early phase of American industrialism seems to be under way. Consider, for example, the unpublished study by Marvin M. Fisher, "From Wilderness to Workshop: The Response of Foreign Observers to American Industrialization, 1830–1860," University of Minnesota, 1958; Hugo A. Meier, "American Technology and the Nineteenth-Century World," *American Quarterly*, X (1958), 116–130; "Technology and Democracy, 1800–1860," *Mississippi Valley Historical Review*, XLIII (1957), 618–640; Charles L. Sanford, "The Intellectual Origins and New-Worldliness of American Industry," *Journal of Economic History*, XVIII (1958), 1–16; John E. Sawyer, "The Social Basis of the American System of Manufacturing," *Journal of Economic History*, XIV (1954), 361–379. All of this research would seem to support the theory that industrialism under American conditions was significantly different from the British and in general the European equivalent.

be specific, our writers first saw the new machine power largely as they had been prepared to see it by other writers. Hence their use of a literary and transparently derivative image of the menacing machine. But today, looking back over American writing during the past century, we can see that they invested the device with a singular intensity of thought and feeling. For reasons I mean to discuss, our writers have responded to the onset of industrialism with a heightened sensitivity to its implications. To get at their response, let us turn to a few of the classics of American literature which contain variants of the Sleepy Hollow motif.

II

A perfect illustration may be found in the chapter on "Sounds" in *Walden*.[2] Thoreau, incidentally, began his stay at the pond during the summer of 1845, just a year after Hawthorne's encounter with the train. Of course Thoreau, who is in a sense testing the transcendental mode of perception, makes a far more calculated effort than Hawthorne to endow sensory impressions with symbolic overtones. The previous chapter is about "Reading," or what Thoreau would call the language of metaphor. What now concerns him most is the way sounds, and particularly sounds of nature, typify the language, as he puts it, that "all things speak without metaphor." If described with sufficient precision the naked fact of sensation may also be made to unfold its meaning—or so he would like to think. Hence he begins with an account of magnificent summer days when, like Hawthorne at the Hollow, he does nothing but sit "rapt in a revery, amidst the pines and sumachs, in undisturbed solitude and stillness." We get another celebration of idleness and of that sense of solidarity with the universe that presumably comes with close attention to the language of nature. But here, as he does throughout *Walden*, Thoreau reinforces this affirmation by juxtaposing another, a social reality. The tracks of the Fitchburg Railroad touch the pond not far from his hut, and so form the "link," as he says, by which he is "related to society." Once again, an auditory image conveys the essential quality of this relation:

The whistle of the locomotive penetrates my woods summer and winter, sounding like the scream of a hawk sailing over some farmer's yard, informing me that many restless city merchants are arriving within the circle of the town. . . .

This is not the place for detailed analysis of the elaborate figurative passage that follows. To do it justice it would be necessary to describe

2 The self-contained character of the railroad episode in *Walden* is suggested by the fact that it is one of the passages Thoreau had published separately in *Sartain's Magazine* in July 1852. The passage was revised before the final version. See J. Lyndon Shanley, *The Making of Walden* (Chicago, 1957), 31.

the intricate contrast between the image of the pond and that of the railroad, and indeed the relations between these controlling figures and the thematic structure of *Walden* as a whole. Only by way of its central images can we arrive at a full appreciation of the book's meaning. But for the moment we need only note the over-all design of the passage, and its striking similarity to the Sleepy Hollow episode. Like Hawthorne, Thoreau uses the image of the machine to convey certain decisive tensions of the age—and at least one of its certainties. The certainty is change itself—the kind of change associated with the railroad. For Thoreau, as for Melville's Ahab, the machine is the type and agent of an irreversible process—not alone technological change, but the implacable advance of history. "We have constructed a fate," he writes, "an *Atropos,* that never turns aside." In concluding the episode, he describes a cattle train going by, and that provides another vivid auditory image. As the train moves off into the distance, the air is filled with the bleating of calves and sheep. And so, Thoreau remarks in his driest tone, is our "pastoral life whirled past and away."

So far my examples may give the impression that this complex of images appealed only to writers somehow within the transcendental or Concord sphere of influence. But that is not true. Turning now to a later work that belongs to quite another strain in our literature—or so we have assumed—let us consider an episode in *The Adventures of Huckleberry Finn.* Although Samuel Clemens did not publish his masterpiece until 1885, he set the action in the same critical period (1835–1845) we have been discussing. We recall that after Huck escapes from his father and organized society in general, he lives for a time on Jackson's Island. Here everything is "dead quiet" and life is easy. Nature supplies fruit and berries and fish. The island, needless to say, is another of those idyllic retreats so endlessly fascinating to the American imagination.

But the life that Huck and Jim lead on Jackson's Island should not be confused with the ideal style of primitivism. When Huck first comes upon Jim and learns that he has been living on "strawberries and such truck" Huck is incredulous. " 'Is that what you live on?' " he asks, " '. . . ain't you had nothing but that kind of rubbage to eat?' " Huck has no illusions about noble savagery. In order to get from discomfort or constraint or cruelty he repeatedly moves in the direction of—but by no means all the way to—the freedom of nature. He is untouched by piety about the superiority of the natural to the artificial. When he escapes from Pap's cabin he shrewdly "borrows" some meal and bacon and sugar to supplement the bounty of the countryside. In addition, he takes along a frying-pan, a coffee-pot, some tin cups, a knife, a gun, and some fishhooks. What I am saying is that Jackson's Island is the scene of a pastoral, not a primitive, retreat. The traditional landscape of pastoral occupies a middle-ground somewhere between raw nature and urban civilization. Even the raft is made of cut lumber, not logs.

After a rise in the river, Huck and Jim penetrate the innermost recesses of the island. Clemens describes what they do in a passage suggestive of our vernacular landscape tradition in painting, and especially of Edward Hicks and his celebrated work, "The Peaceable Kingdom":

Daytimes we paddled all over the island in the canoe. It was mighty cool and shady in the deep woods even if the sun was blazing outside. We went winding in and out amongst the trees; and sometimes the vines hung so thick we had to back away and go some other way. Well, on every old broken-down tree you could see the rabbits and snakes and such things; and when the island had been overflowed a day or two they got so tame, on account of being hungry, that you could paddle right up and put your hand on them if you wanted to; but not the snakes and turtles—they would slide off in the water.

The idyll ends abruptly when Huck discovers that the villagers are about to search the island. That is when he and Jim begin their down-stream journey by raft. But in fact the idyll is not over. The raft now becomes a mobile extension of the island, a floating platform of freedom. On the raft the fugitives continue to enjoy many of the delights they had known on the island, and above all the sense of the bounty, beauty and serenity of life in accommodation to the rhythms of nature. The river helps to insulate them from the hostile, slave society. It helps, that is, until a machine intrudes upon the scene:

. . . all of a sudden she bulged out, big and scary, with a long row of wide-open furnace doors shining like red-hot teeth, and her monstrous bows and guards hanging right over us. There was a yell at us, and a jingling of bells to stop the engines, a pow-wow of cussing and whistling of steam—and as Jim went overboard on one side and I on the other, she came smashing straight through the raft.

Now here is another variation upon the Sleepy Hollow pattern. Clemens provides his hero with an Arcadian landscape, a profound sense of harmony with nature, and then he causes the sudden, menacing obtrusion of the machine. And these, as we shall see, are merely the more obvious and superficial parallels.

At this point, however, some objections surely will be raised. It will be said that Samuel Clemens held quite another view of industrial progress than the one implied here; that he admired steamboats; that he did not necessarily think of them as tokens of mechanization, and so on; that, in short, we have no right to attach any special significance to this passage. At first sight these arguments are compelling. It is of course true that we cannot take this episode as a considered statement about industrialization. No one can deny that Clemens often expressed approval of the changes associated with technological progress. In rebuttal perhaps we could show, as I do elsewhere,[3] that he felt more than a little uncertainty upon this score by the time he wrote *Huckleberry Finn*. But for the moment, let us put that consideration aside and, to make the point as emphatic as possible, we will assume that except for the book itself all the evidence does indeed support the still popular notion of Clemens as an unwavering celebrant of industrial progress. Even if this were true we would, in my opinion, still be justified in taking this episode very seriously indeed. Here the lesson of criticism is clear. In the face of a discrepancy between what a writer tells us directly, in his own words so to speak, and what is implied by his work, it is to his work that we owe the more serious attention. As between mere opinion and the indirection of art, we assume that art springs from the more profound and inclusive experience.

But this is not to say that we may interpret the episode in *Huckleberry Finn* just as we would the one in *Walden*. To do so would be to ignore a vital difference between them. The image of the machine in *Walden* is manifestly symbolic; in *Huckleberry Finn* it is not. Clemens surely did not want us to extend the meaning of his words so far as Thoreau did. Indeed, it is more than likely that he did not *intend* any heightened or symbolic significance whatever. If we could ask him he would no doubt say that he was using a commonplace event of steamboat days merely to get Huck and Jim ashore. Yet on reflection it is impossible to drop the matter there. The symbolism may not be fully under control, and for all we know it may have got there inadvertently, but it is there nonetheless.

We cannot forget that in this book the raft is more than a raft; it is the location of freedom and love and pleasure. Huck tells us that much again and again. Furthermore, steamboats *in this book* (waiving the question of what they may have meant to Samuel Clemens) are associated with conspiracy, crime, violence and the spurious romanticizing of Sir Walter Scott. Steamboats intrude the culture of the shore into life on the river. In truth, all of the controlling themes of *Huckleberry Finn* are implicated in this brief passage. But then another question arises. If Clemens does not consciously impart significance to the image of the steamboat smashing the raft, how does it get there? Part of the answer lies in the fact that here Clemens, whether he knows it or not, is working with a pattern of image and idea by no means of his own invention. The Sleepy Hollow pattern has a conventional character, and like all literary conventions, it must be regarded as a creation of culture. By using the pattern, then, a writer inescapably brings to his work some of the thought and feeling that the culture has invested in it. And it is perfectly conceivable for him to be unaware of this transfer of meaning. How this happens becomes more apparent when we recognize the symbolic sig-

---

[3] "The Pilot and the Passenger: Landscape Conventions and the Style of *Huckleberry Finn*," *American Literature*, XXVIII (1956), 129–146.

nificance of these images outside of "high" culture, that is, in the quasi-popular expression of the age.

But to return to the image of the interrupted idyll. The ominous sound of the steamboat bearing down upon the raft, like the train breaking in upon the revery of Hawthorne or Thoreau, is without question a refracted image of industrialization. It is a sound that first broke upon the American consciousness about 1840, and since then it has reverberated endlessly in our literature. More often than not the machine is made to appear with startling suddenness. Sometimes, as in the episodes we have considered, it abruptly enters the Happy Valley; in other cases an observer suddenly comes upon it. We recall, for example, that arresting moment when the narrator of Herman Melville's tale, "The Tartarus of Maids," is trying to find a paper mill in the mountains; he drives his sleigh into a deep hollow between hills that rise like steep "walls," and still he can't see the place when, as he says, "Suddenly a whirring, humming sound broke upon my ear. I looked, and there, like an arrested avalanche, lay the large white-washed factory."

Again and again our writers have made some such encounter the occasion for a dramatic moment of revelation. We think, for example, of the opening chapter of *The Octopus,* where Frank Norris describes Presley's walk at sunset through the lush San Joaquin Valley. It is a lovely, mild evening. The poet is in a revery. "All about, the feeling of absolute peace and quiet and security and untroubled happiness and content seemed descending from the stars like a benediction. . . . But suddenly there was an interruption." By now it is dark and the train, "its enormous eye, Cyclopean, red, throwing a glare far in advance," comes thundering down the track and smashes its way through a herd of sheep, flinging their bodies into the air, snapping their spines against fence posts, and knocking out their brains. When the "iron monster" has passed, Norris tell us, all sense of peace has been "stricken from the landscape"; Presley listens to the agonized cries of the wounded animals and the blood seeping down into the cinders, and thus the theme of the novel is set.

Years later John Steinbeck was to employ much the same device to set the Joads on their epic westward journey. In *The Grapes of Wrath* it is the arrival of the tractors that announces the separation of the Joads from their farm:

The tractors came over the roads and into the fields, great crawlers moving like insects, having the incredible strength of insects. They crawled over the ground, laying the track and rolling on it and picking it up. Diesel tractors, puttering while they stood idle; they thundered when they moved, and then settled down to a droning roar. Snubnosed monsters, raising the dust and sticking their snouts into it, straight down the country, across the country, through fences, through dooryards, in and out of gullies in straight lines. They did not run on the ground, but on their own roadbeds. They ignored hills and gulches, water courses, fences, houses.

To prefigure his major theme Steinbeck contrasts two attitudes toward the land. First, he describes the state of mind of the man who drives one of the tractors. "The driver sat in his iron seat and he was proud of the straight lines he did not will, proud of the tractor he did not own or love, proud of the power he could not control." Here Steinbeck is working in a convention that includes, for example, *The Octopus*, Eugene O'Neill's *The Hairy Ape*, Sherwood Anderson's *Poor White* and John Dos Passos's *U.S.A.* In all of these works the controlling idea of a modern America is a metaphoric extension of the machine image. The machine is both physical object and token of a set of economic and social relations. That is obvious enough. What is less obvious, however, is that the machine has penetrated and conquered the mind. By this I mean that the attributes of the actual machine, especially its iron impersonality and irresistible power, represent what is most compelling to the man who operates it. And invariably his state of mind is compared, as in *The Grapes of Wrath*, to another:

And when that crop grew, and was harvested, no man had crumbled a hot clod in his fingers and let the earth sift past his fingertips. No man had touched the seed, or lusted for the growth. Men ate what they had not raised, had no connection with the bread. The land bore under iron, and under iron gradually died; for it was not loved or hated, it had no prayers or curses.

This recurrent theme is often mistaken for simple nostalgia—a lament for a doomed agrarian society. Of course the agrarian ideal did embrace many of the values that Steinbeck and others regard as threatened by mechanization. Yet something much more fundamental is involved. To appreciate this fact one has only to notice how often American writers set the machine in opposition to a landscape that is neither idyllic nor bucolic. We think of the grave opening lines of T. S. Eliot's "The Dry Salvages," so reminiscent, as Lionel Trilling has observed, of the river passages in *Huckleberry Finn*. Thus Eliot invokes the "strong brown god" of the Mississippi as:

>   . . . almost forgotten
> By the dwellers in cities—ever, however, implacable,
> Keeping his seasons and rages, destroyer, reminder
> Of what men choose to forget. Unhonoured, unpropitiated
> By worshippers of the machine, but waiting, watching and waiting.

Again, at the end of "The Bear," William Faulkner uses much the same motif to extend the meaning of the final revelation. Only on his last trip into the wood does young Ike McCaslin grasp the true significance of his experience with the bear and the wild. Now he sees that all along his own destiny has been joined with that of the land itself. With the image of the train in mind he now recognizes what the machine had portended from the beginning, and that "running . . . between the twin walls of impenetrable and impervious woods" it had brought "with it into the doomed wilderness, even before the actual axe, the shadow and the portent of the new mill. . . ." It is true that the machine stands for industrialization in this American fable. But for Faulkner, as for Eliot, what the machine threatens cannot be adequately represented by any benign, tidy, sunlit landscape of the agrarian celebration.

It would be simple but tedious to extend this canvass indefinitely. Anyone who knows American writing will think of countless other examples, passages from the work, let us say, of Sarah Orne Jewett, Walt Whitman, Willa Cather, Robert Frost, Hart Crane—as a matter of fact, it is more difficult to think of a major writer upon whom this pattern has failed to exercise its fascination. But my point is not simply that the pattern recurs endlessly in our lierature; that is only one measure of its significance. What is more important, as Henry James tells us, is its inexhaustible power to evoke the distinctive qualities of American experience.

Early in *The American Scene* where James, after a long absence, records his renewed impressions of his native land, he dwells upon a scene in Farmington, Connecticut. James had traveled to New England almost immediately after landing in New York, and the region impresses him, for reasons that he admits may be shamelessly subjective, as a veritable "Arcadia." The autumn countryside gives James a sense of "some bedimmed summer of the distant prime flushing back into life." The landscape around Farmington, in particular, renews for him that older vision of "the social idyll, of the workable, the expensively workable, American form of country life; and, in especial, of a perfect consistency of surrender to the argument of a verdurous vista." Here, says James, is the American village at its best, where a "great elm-gallery happens to be garnished with old houses, and the old houses happen to show style and form and proportion. . . ." What finally is most striking, however, about the picture of the white village, with its high thin church steeple, so archaic in modern America as to seem almost a heraldic emblem, is another object in close juxtaposition, representing the present, the positive. It is the railway crossing. Out of the contrast James gains a new perception. While the church now seems a mere monument embellished upon some large white card, the railroad becomes for him the localization of "possible death and destruction," and the total impression is one of a "kind of monotony of acquiescence." But James' particular rendering of the scene, so reminiscent of a similar moment of acquiescence in Hawthorne's *Seven Gables,* is less important here than his conclusion. After some reflection upon Farmington, he concludes that this complex of images "contains . . . the germ of the most final of all .. . generalizations."

What he sees in Farmington, James is saying, is not one among many American scenes, but a thematic or, if you will, a symbolic tableau. It figures forth a controlling idea, the very marrow of his subject, which happens to be America. Mindful of the omnipresence of the Sleepy

Hollow pattern in our literature, we are in a position to be even more emphatic than James. True, the scene he describes differs from Hawthorne's "original" in many important ways, and so do all the variations on the pattern that we have adduced. Yet perhaps by now the common denominator has become evident. In each case the significance of the pattern arises from the opposition between two cardinal images of value. One usually is an image of landscape, either wild or, if cultivated, rural; the other is an image of industrial technology. Sometimes, of course, the cardinal image is not actually present but is represented by lesser or associated images. In any event, the common and distinguishing feature of the motif is the sharp conflict of meaning and value evoked by the clash of images. The contrast between them arouses a sense of dislocation, conflict and anxiety. All established ideas are called into question. Of course I do not mean that the pattern is the key to every work in which it appears. Considered individually, as a matter of fact, many of its appearances may be of no great significance. But considered in their totality they constitute a supreme metaphor of contradiction in our culture.

III

Of late much has been written, notably by Lionel Trilling, R. W. B. Lewis and Richard Chase, about the contradictions said to embody what is most distinctive in our culture.[4] Mr. Chase, with brilliant results, has applied this dialectical concept of culture to the tradition of the American novel. He shows that on the whole what distinguishes the American from the British strain in fiction is precisely what Hawthorne meant when he distinguished between a "romance" and a "novel." Like most ideas that characterize American culture, this distinction did not originate here. But Mr. Chase argues persuasively that it did have a special appeal to the native imagination—a state of mind formed, even more than that of England, by the contradictions rather than the unities and harmonies of culture. Hence the tendency in our fiction towards abstraction, away from the specification of social actualities, and away, above all, from the preoccupation with those subtle relations of property, class and status that form the substance of the great Victorian novel. Instead of writing the novel of social verisimilitude, our writers have fashioned their own kind of melodramatic, Manichean, all-questioning fable (or romance) in which they carry us, in a bold leap, beyond ordinary social experience and into the realm of abstract morality and metaphysics. Mr. Chase's theory works best for writers like Hawthorne and Melville, but it illuminates the broad tendency of our literature as well. No one, in my opinion, has come

[4] I am thinking of Trilling's essay, "Reality in America," in *The Liberal Imagination;* Lewis's *The American Adam* . . . (Chicago, 1955); and Chase's *The American Novel and Its Tradition* (New York, 1957).

closer than Mr. Chase to defining that elusive quality of Americanness in our classic American literature.

But if we ask *why* these qualities are peculiar to our literature, Mr. Chase gives us only a cursory answer. The question, to be sure, does not really engage him. He is interested in literary consequences, not historic causes. Though he admits that the peculiar traits of American writing must be traceable to historic fact, he does not fully recognize the relevance to his thought of certain supreme facts of life in nineteenth century America. Above all, I am thinking of the unbelievably rapid mechanization of an under-developed society. Within the lifetime of a single generation a rustic and in large part wild or prehistoric landscape was transformed into the site for the world's most productive industrial machine. It would be difficult to imagine more profound contradictions of value or meaning than those made palpable by this fact. Henry Nash Smith has shown the remarkable extent to which images of landscape, and particularly the image of America as a new garden of the world, served to define the promise of our national existence. Yet just at the moment when society overcame the wilderness, the industrial technology called into question the assumptions underlying the idea of America as agrarian paradise. A contradictory view of man's relation to nature, though it had been present from the beginning of our history, now was made visible. It was represented by the machine. All of this was happening between 1830 and 1850, when our first significant literary generation was coming to maturity. Hence if we are concerned to know *why* our literature rests, as Mr. Chase says it does, "in contradictions and among extreme ranges of experience," then we had best look closely at the image of the machine, and its relation to the dominant themes in American writing.

To return again to the notes Hawthorne made in 1844, we can be sure that he was fully aware of the machine as a symbol of certain contradictory tendencies in his society. Only the year before he had published "The Celestial Railroad," a wonderfully compact satire upon the American faith in progress. In this sketch the new railroad is the vehicle for an illusory voyage of salvation. The American "Christian," unlike Bunyan's original, actually turns out to be on the road to hell. But there is no need to go beyond the Sleepy Hollow notes to demonstrate Hawthorne's awareness of the machine as a sign of an historic and social contradiction. He depicts the Hollow as a miniature of the American landscape, half wilderness, half corn-field—emblem of Nature's bounty. Here is an idealized pastoral world, and it encompasses not only wilderness and farm, but village and church as well. Auditory images carry a large burden of Hawthorne's meaning, as they do in Thoreau's and Clemens' versions of pastoral. The ties that bind society and nature are represented by a harmonious blend of sounds. We hear the mowers whetting their scythes, the church bells ringing, and the unending hum and stir of nature. There is no discord. What we have, in short, is an auditory evocation of an organic community, a style of life very much like life in the hut at Walden or on Huckleberry Finn's raft.

But the onrush of the machine, also evoked by a sound, shatters the images of wholeness. The remorseless shriek of the locomotive banishes all harmony. As Frank Norris says in describing the bloody aftermath of the machine's passage, "The sense of peace . . . security . . . and . . . contentment was stricken from the landscape." In Hawthorne's notes, too, the machine is an agent of contradiction. It introduces the thought of citizens from the hot street, "men of business; in short of all unquietness. . . ." Throughout our literature the machine is to the ideal society what a hideous noise is to a delicate sonata. If the new technology does not literally smash into the symbol of utopian aspiration, as the steamboat smashes into Huck's raft, it invariably threatens it. Auditory imagery is particularly effective in suggesting the extension of a mechanized society's power into the realm of mind itself. Just as the harsh noise penetrates and fills the inner recesses of consciousness, so the external arrangements of life threaten, much more than before, to dominate the inner being. Noise here is an agent of alienation. In Sleepy Hollow, it cuts off the flow of sensation from the world of natural fecundity, thus separating man from a prime source of meaning and value. The community evoked by the machine is a drab, commercial city—a center of restless and, indeed, meaningless activity. It anticipates that dark vision of modern society that T. S. Eliot has made famous: a wasteland inhabited by "worshippers of the machine."

And yet, for all these unmistakable overtones of social or historic significance, it must not be thought that our writers necessarily use the image of the machine to direct attention to the historic fact of industrialization. To imply that would be to misconstrue their aims—to take the literary means for an end. As Emerson remarked, the artist "must" employ symbols in use in his day and nation, not in order to point in the direction of society, but rather to establish that interplay between art and experience that enables the great writer to "convey his enlarged sense to his fellow-men." In the case of Hawthorne at Sleepy Hollow, it is obvious that what chiefly interests him is not the contradiction between agrarian and industrial social orders. Here the contrast between the machine and the garden chiefly represents a conflict between two *psychic* states. Until he hears the train's whistle Hawthorne knows a serenity that approaches euphoria. The very lay of the land bespeaks a singular insulation from disturbance, and so enhances the feeling of perfect repose. It is in fact a cocoon of freedom from anxiety, guilt and conflict of all kinds—a veritable shrine of the pleasure principle. If this reading of a "Freudian" connotation seems to be pressing matters too far, consider how often our writers describe the machine as an invader of an enclosed space, a world set apart or somehow identified with an image of encircled

felicity. In addition to the Hollow itself, we think of Clemens' island and
the raft, Thoreau's hut beside a pond, Norris' valley, Faulkner's space
between impenetrable walls of forest and, as we shall see in a moment,
Melville's whale skeleton. In Sleepy Hollow the machine is menacing
reality. Its noise is unsettling, piercing, implacable; it is a token of harsh,
masculine aggressiveness, in sharp contrast to the feminine, submissive
overtones of the pastoral image. When the noise fills the air the soothing
sense of invulnerability is lost.

Right here we see, on a microscopic scale to be sure, how historic fact
is attuned to literary theme. The appearance of that machine is associated, in Hawthorne's imagination, with that conflict between the natural
and the artificial, between heart and head, love and power that we find
everywhere in his work. And it arouses a mood of alienation and loss that
pervades our literature. Hence the contrast between images of landscape
and of technology evokes endlessly suggestive metaphors of contradiction.
They have been used to express the opposition between ideas in every
important field of social value: social, psychological and even metaphysical. The relevance of the historic fact of sudden mechanization to the
marked metaphysical quality of our literature is not far to seek. After all,
a technological revolution, far more than any political change, calls into
question man's underlying relation to nature and, indeed, the very nature
of nature. It is not surprising, therefore, that the abstract significance of
the pattern should be apparent in that most metaphysical of American
novels—*Moby Dick.*

In Chaper 102 ("A Bower in the Arsacides"), after Melville has described virtually every feature of the whale, he comes to the question of
its innermost structure. "It behoves me," he has Ishmael remark, "to get
him before you in his ultimatum; that is to say, in his unconditional
skeleton." Whereupon Ishmael tells of an adventure he had had many
years before the fated voyage of the *Pequod*. Having been invited by
Tranquo, king of Tranque (an imaginary land of Melville's invention), to
spend a holiday in a seaside glen, he sees among the treasures of this
primitive people a skeleton of a great sperm whale. It has been moved
from the beach where it was found to a lush green glen, where the priests
had converted it into a temple.

It was a wondrous sight. The wood was green as mosses of the Icy Glen; the
trees stood high and haughty, feeling their living sap; the industrious earth
beneath was a weaver's loom, with a gorgeous carpet on it, whereof the ground-
vine tendrils formed the warp and woof, and the living flowers the figures.

Given the terms of Melville's fable, here inside the whale we are as close
to the center of things as we are likely to get. The skeleton is a primitive
temple of nature. The priests keep a holy flame burning within, and the
"artificial smoke" pours out of the hole where the real watery jet once had
come forth.

But as Ishmael moves further into the whale, the image shifts. The bones of the skeleton are criss-crossed with vines and through them the sunlight seems "a flying shuttle weaving the unwearied verdure." All at once the intricate structure of bones, the smoke pouring out, the light working through the lacing of leaves—all these combine to give him the impression that he is inside a textile factory. Melville uses the device for a characteristic metaphoric flight. Wherefore, asks Ishmael, "these ceaseless toilings? Speak, weaver!—stay thy hand!—but one single word with thee!" He pursues the analogy between human and natural productivity. What is the ceaseless striving for? Why is whale oil produced? What, in short, is the purpose of the *Pequod's* quest? Needless to say, the skeleton does not yield a direct answer, but it leaves him with a conviction of the irrational compulsion back of both "natural" and human productivity.

Nay—the shuttle flies—the figures float from forth the loom; the freshet-rushing carpet for ever slides away. The weaver-god, he weaves; and by that weaving is he deafened, that he hears no mortal voice; and by that humming, we, too, who look on the loom are deafened; and only when we escape it shall we hear the thousand voices that speak through it. For even so it is in all material factories.

Once again technology as noise comes between man and meaning, and so the episode contributes to Ishmael's growing skepticism. It is a bold conceit, this factory inside the whale—another vivid allegory of American experience: the hero deliberately making his way to the heart of primal nature only to find, when he arrives, a token of advancing industrial power. While the over-arching contradictions of *Moby Dick* are moral and metaphysical, not topical or historical, the fact remains that Melville's great theme of the ambiguity of nature—the whiteness of the whale—coincides with the paradox at the core of the Sleepy Hollow motif.

The essence of the matter, in metaphysical terms, is the conflict between polar conceptions of man's relations to nature. Much more is involved than the contrast between agrarian and industrial technologies, yet that contrast is a perfect metaphor of the more enduring difference. One technology is typified by the relatively direct extraction of value from nature as in farming, fishing, trapping and hunting. Here man accommodates himself to the uncontrolled rhythms of organic process. The machine technology, on the other hand, cuts man loose from such intimate relatedness to nature; it involves an assertion of his dominion over the merely organic. The difference, to be sure, is relative, and it shifts from one epoch to another. It is interesting, for example, that in earlier versions of literary pastoral the farmer often was cast in the anti-pastoral role as compared to the traditional hero, the shepherd. In modern times the farmer takes on an aura of pastoral piety, while the man at the

machine is the antagonist. In any event, the contrast between the landscape and technology expresses a contradiction that has profoundly engaged the American imagination: the simultaneous pull of the opposed
ideals of primitivism and progress, hence the need for reconciliation—
that is, for the discovery of a symbolic terrain neither wild nor urban.

What I am saying is that the dialectical tendency of mind—the habit
of seeing life as a collision of radically opposed forces and values—has
been accentuated by certain special conditions of experience in America.
Above all, it is connected with the sudden emergence of industrial power
in a nation that had identified itself with a virgin landscape. No single
work exhibits this connection so dramatically as *The Education of Henry
Adams.* The theme of the book is the pulling apart, in Adams' experience
as in the culture generally, of feeling and intellect, love and power.
Adams adroitly builds the story up to 1900 and his discovery, as in a
moment of religious exaltation, of the relation between his two master
symbols—the Virgin and the Dynamo. But it is curious that in order to
set his theme, right at the beginning of the book, Adams turns back to
the year of Hawthorne's visit to Sleepy Hollow. In 1884, as he sees it in
retrospect, the forces of history bore down upon him and fixed his fate.
That was the year, he says, when

> . . . the old universe was *thrown into the ash-heap* and a new one created. He
> and his eighteenth century, troglodytic Boston *were suddenly cut apart—
> separated forever*—in act if not in sentiment, by the opening of the Boston and
> Albany Railroad; the appearance of the first Cunard steamers in the bay; and
> the telegraphic messages which carried from Baltimore to Washington the news
> that Henry Clay and James K. Polk were nominated for the Presidency. This
> was in May, 1844; he was six years old; his new world was ready for use, and
> only fragments of the old met his eyes.[5]

A sense of the transformation of life by technology dominates *The Education* as it does no other book. This is partly because Adams comes at
the theme with the combined techniques of the cool historian and the
impassioned poet.

In the passage just quoted, for example, we can distinguish two voices.
The voice of the historian tells us the news. He regards industrial power
as an objective "cause" of change in American society. And he is able to
draw a direct line of connection from these changes to his own life. It is
technology (the new railroads, steamboats and telegraph) that has
separated Adams from his family's eighteenth century tradition. Writing
in this vein Adams virtually endorses a theory of technological determinism. "As I understand it," he wrote to his brother while at work on the
book, "the whole social, political and economical problem is the resultant
of the mechanical development of power." All through *The Education* we

[5] My emphasis.

hear the voice of the historian directing our attention to technology as an impersonal and largely uncontrolled force acting upon human events. The historian provides us with statistics on accelerating coal and steel production; he makes us aware of the impact of the new power upon society quite apart from the way it strikes him. But the voice of the poet continually chimes in. He charges historical fact with emotion by using images such as (in the passage above) "thrown into the ash-heap," and submerged metaphors: "suddenly cut apart—separated forever." The poet invests the whole statement with traumatic overtones that give the sudden appearance of the machine the effect of an irrevocable fatality, like the cutting of an umbilical cord. The historian tells us what happened to America and to Adams, but the poet tells us how we should feel about what happened.

Moving back and forth between conceptual statements about the growth of power and sensory impressions of the same process, Adams raises his theme to a melodramatic pitch. The machine image serves to convey both an inward and an historical contradiction. Early in the book, for instance, he describes a journey he took in 1858 through the English Black District. It was, he writes, a "plunge into darkness lurid with flames." There, in the center of industrial England, Adams suddenly had a "sense of unknown horror in . . . [the] weird gloom which then existed nowhere else, and never had existed before, except in volcanic craters." Here he is working in the tradition of Sleepy Hollow; what he stresses above all else in his acute sense of the *"violent contrast* between this dense, smoky impenetrable darkness, and the soft green charm that one glided into as one emerged. . . ."[6] The scene is England, but the sensibility is American. What strikes the American with particular force is the violent contrast between the industrial and the natural landscapes. If we turn to Carlyle or Ruskin or Morris we may find similar passages, but in general the English writer is more likely to regard the new power as a threat to some cherished ideal of high civilization or art or craftsmanship.

Adams' evocation of horror in the presence of the machine reaches its climax in the account of the Paris Exposition of 1900 where, in a celebrated passage, "he found himself lying in the Gallery of Machines . . . his historical neck broken by the sudden irruption of forces totally new." Confronting the new dynamos he felt an impulse to pray, much as Christians prayed to the cross—or to the Virgin. And here all the polarities of the book, not least among them the sharp contrast between the weird smoky gloom and the soft green charm of the landscape, culminate in his celebrated symbolic tableau: the conflict between "two kingdoms of force which had nothing in common but attraction": one represented by the Dynamo, the other by the Virgin. If the tendency towards an ab-

[6] My emphasis.

stract or dialectical view of life is a distinctive characteristic of American culture, then *The Education of Henry Adams* is one of the most American of books. Indeed, Adams uses the opposition between the Virgin and the Dynamo to figure forth an all-embracing conflict: a clash between past and present, unity and diversity, love and power. In his Manichean fashion he marshals all conceivable values. On one side he lines up heaven, beauty, religion and reproduction; on the other: hell, utility, science and production.

The Education of Henry Adams embodies a view of life that had been implicit in the Sleepy Hollow convention from the beginning. Of course there is a world of difference between the complex and highly wrought pattern contrived by Adams and the off-hand, Wordsworthian impression of the machine that Hawthorne had set down in 1844. What had begun as a casual notation now appears as an elaborate, tragic and all-inclusive thematic figure. And yet it is impossible to miss the continuity, or at least the similarity, between the two. Every version of the Sleepy Hollow motif depicts some aspect of the clash between the two sovereign kingdoms of force. I do not mean that the device is everywhere as important as it is in *The Education,* or that all writers who use it have in mind precisely the same antinomies. But the over-all pattern, and particularly the emotional pattern, is in essence the same wherever we find this root metaphor of contradiction.

If Adams exaggerates, he does not significantly change the underlying feeling. The encounter with the machine had always been something of a shock. Now, in *The Education of Henry Adams,* we find that it not only fills the writer with awe and terror; it arouses nightmarish visions of race suicide. The book may be read as the connecting link between the age of Hawthorne and the age of Eliot. To Adams the Dynamo is the force in the twentieth century most nearly equivalent, in its command over human behavior, to the sublimated sexual vitality that built Chartres. But in all other respects the two forces are in violent opposition. One exalts, the other denies, the beauty of eros. In earlier versions of the Sleepy Hollow pattern we may find insinuations of the idea that technology threatens sexual fulfillment. (Even Hawthorne, in his insistence upon the Hollow as an emblem of natural fecundity, had implied as much.) But Adams, in using the figure of the Virgin, makes this meaning absolutely plain. "In any previous age," he remarks, "sex was strength." Now the Dynamo foreshadows an industrial society that will deny, as no other society ever had done, the creative power of eros. On one of his scales the historian places the drab, utilitarian culture of industrial America; on the other, he places Chartres and the Louvre. The choice for Adams, needless to say, is clear. All of this no doubt is obvious, but I would stress the fact that it is precisely his awareness of mechanization and its consequences that leads Adams to reaffirm the symbol of the Virgin. She represents "the highest energy ever known to man, the creator of four-fifths of his noblest art, exercising vastly more attraction over the human mind than all the steam-engines and dynamos ever dreamed of. . ."

What Hawthorne heard in the Concord woods, to use the idiom of Henry Adams, was a new outbreak of the ancient warfare between the kingdom of love and the kingdom of power. It is the same war that Mark Twain dramatizes when he describes the steamboat interrupting the idyll on the raft. It is a dominant, probably *the* dominant theme in our literature. To think of so universal a theme as "romantic" is misleading, especially if by that we mean to identify it with a particular movement in modern European literature. How much more elemental and, curiously enough, more traditional, it really is may be seen in an early statement of the theme of *The Education of Henry Adams:*

Winter and summer, then, were two hostile lives, and bred two separate natures. Winter was always the effort to live; summer was tropical license. Whether the children rolled in the grass, or waded in the brook, or swam in the salt ocean, or sailed in the bay, or fished for smelts in the creeks, or netted minnows in the salt-marshes, or took to the pine-woods and the granite quarries, or chased muskrats and hunted snapping-turtles in the swamps, or mushrooms or nuts on the autumn hills, summer and country were always sensual living, while winter was always compulsory learning.

Again there is a danger, as in the case of *Huckleberry Finn,* of confusing the dominant feeling back of the Sleepy Hollow tradition with primitivism—the impulse to reject civilization *in toto.* Certainly it is true that Adams, in the figure of the Virgin, means to celebrate an idea of freedom rooted in the memory of summer pleasures: the sensual living, the immersion in the sensations of nature, and above all, the sense of oneness with the external universe. The force of *The Education,* and of American literature generally, comes out on the side of hostility toward a society under the growing dominion of science, technology, industry, in short, the Dynamo. And yet the point is not that the Dynamo is intrinsically evil, but rather that it arrives in this country as a threat to an ideal of balance, or rhythmic harmony of existence, that Adams recalls of his childhood and that had long been associated, in the native imagination, with the virgin landscape itself. The feeling of American writers toward the machine can only be understood in relation to their feelings about the setting in which it appears. That is why the imagery of technology so often is yoked to imagery of landscape. The Sleepy Hollow pattern is the germ-cell, so to speak, of the ruling theme in our literature. The ideal vision of life that it reveals has less in common with primitivism than with the ancient tradition of pastoral.

IV

The idea of pastoral is by its very nature difficult and elusive. But the difficulty is compounded when we use the term as we do, in two quite distinct ways. Some scholars and critics use it as a name for a specific mode, or in any case a particular set of literary conventions.[7] By pastoral they mean poems that take the form of a dialogue or singing match between shepherds, or of a dirge or elegy sung by a rustic as in the work of Theocritus. This strictly formal meaning of the term, obviously enough, has little or no bearing upon American writing. No significant pastorals, in that strict sense, have been written by Americans, and as a matter of fact the pastoral mode in the English language seems to be just about dead. But pastoral is also used to refer to the motive that lies behind the form, and to the images and themes and even the conception of life associated with it. It is this second, wider sense of the term that is relevant here. To indicate just how relevant it is I want briefly to turn back to Virgil's *Eclogues,* a fountainhead of the pastoral strain in western thought and expression. Although Theocritus preceded him, it was Virgil who first created the symbolic landscape, a blend of myth and reality, that is particularly relevant to the American imagination. As Bruno Snell remarks, Virgil "discovered" Arcadia.[8] Here are the opening lines of the first eclogue as translated recently by E. V. Rieu.[9] A shepherd, Meliboeus, is speaking to another shepherd:

Tityrus, while you lie there at ease under the awning of a spreading beech and practice country songs on a light shepherd's pipe, I have to bid good-bye to the home fields and the ploughlands that I love. Exile for me, Tityrus—and you lie sprawling in the shade, teaching the woods to echo back the charms of Amaryllis.

Tityrus answers with praise of a patron who lives in Rome, and to whom he owes his liberty and his "happy leisure." He calls the man a god, and promises to honor him with sacrifices. "He gave the word," Tityrus says, "and my cattle browse at large, while I myself can play the tunes I fancy on my rustic flute." And then Meliboeus speaks again:

Don't think that I am jealous. *My* only feeling is amazement—with every farm in the whole countryside in such a state of chaos. Look at myself, unfit for the road, yet forced to drive my goats on this unending trek. See, Tityrus, I can

---

[7] A notable example is Walter W. Greg, *Pastoral Poetry & Pastoral Drama* (London, 1906).

[8] Bruno Snell, "Arcadia: The Discovery of A Spiritual Landscape," in *The Discovery of the Mind, The Greek Origins of European Thought,* tr. T. G. Rosenmeyer (Oxford, 1953).

[9] Virgil, *The Pastoral Poems* (Penguin Classics, 1956).

hardly drag this one along. Just now, in the hazel thicket here, she bore two kids—I had been counting on them—and had to leave the poor things on the naked flints. Ah, if I had not been so blind, I might have known that we are in for this disaster. Often enough I had been warned by Heaven, when lightning struck the oats.

Now what is most striking, when we read these lines with the Sleepy Hollow motif in mind, is the similarity of the root conflict, and of the over-all pattern of images and ideas.

At the outset we are introduced to an idealized landscape. Tityrus, lying at ease in the shade of the beech, enjoys all the satisfactions of the pastoral utopia: peace, plenty, leisure—his condition is joy itself—and it all arises from his harmonious relation to the natural environment. The harmony may be described in any of several vocabularies, ranging from those associated with the more material to the more abstract forms of experience. It is, for example, economic. Nature apparently supplies all of the contented shepherd's needs, and what is more, nature does virtually all of the work. A similar interchange between man and nature accounts for the fulfillment of his less tangible needs. For instance the poet, by using an auditory image, makes palpable the power of the landscape to inspire an esthetic delight: the woods "echo back" the notes of the pipe. The esthetic pleasure, moreover, is not easily distinguished from what can only be called a religious or metaphysical relation. Nature here is not merely a passive object of perception; it is responsive to man. By insisting that the woods "echo back" the countryman's music—a recurrent device in pastoral—Virgil evokes that sense of relatedness between man and not-man that is akin, in feeling if not in concept, to prayer or revelation. In classical Greek thought this feeling *was* in fact regarded as religious. In Virgil the point of the transcendent experience is that the consciousness of the shepherd shares a principle of order with the non-conscious. We delight in echoes because the sounds we make are answered, as it were, by the inanimate universe. From the beginning, in other words, pastoral contains the promise of the spiritual serenity that religion also would provide.

What makes the promise all the more precious, of course, is the contrast between the joy of one shepherd and the plight of the other. No sooner does Virgil sketch in the Arcadian landscape than he reveals quite another kind of world pressing in from without. It is the menacing world of the great city, of organized power, of all collective discipline and constraint. It is, in a word, Rome. Like many of Virgil's countrymen at the time the eclogues were written, Meliboeus has been evicted. (The evictions actually were effected in order to provide land for veterans of the imperial army.) We are made to feel that the immediate setting, a place of tender feeling and contentment, is an oasis in a land of tragic disorder. Every farm in the countryside, according to the dispossessed shepherd, is in a state of chaos. The encroaching power threatens the very principle of natural fertility. (Meliboeus has been forced to abandon the newborn kids). What we feel about his situation is at every point the opposite of what we feel about Tityrus'. Having been divested of his land, Meliboeus faces a prospect of unending anxiety, deprivation and work. Nowadays we should call his state of mind one of alienation. While Tityrus continues to sing the praises of his patron, Meliboeus describes his own fate:

. . . the rest of us are off; some to foregather with the Africans and share their thirst; others to Scythia, and out to where the Oxus rolls the chalk along; others to join the Britons cut off as they are by the whole width of the world. Ah, will the day come, after many years, when I shall see a place that I can call home . . . ?

What chiefly concerns him is his enforced separation (being "cut off") from the landscape of his desire, a lovely "green hollow":

Forward, my goats; forward, the flock that used to be my pride. Never again, stretched out in some green hollow, shall I spy you far away, dangling on the rocky hillside where the brambles grow. There will be no songs from me, my goats, and I shall lead you no more to crop the flowering clover and the bitter willow shoots.

The contrast between the situation of the shepherds, and between the two kingdoms of force, Arcady and Rome, could not be more complete. For that reason the pastoral conception of life has been mistaken for an outright repudiation of organized society. But the theme of pastoral is not the same as the simplistic, black and white theme of romantic primitivism. Even in the few lines quoted from Virgil we get some notion of the complexity of insight that is generated by the initial conflict. It is important to notice, for example, which of the shepherds the poet endows with the more profound sense of lyrical identification with nature.

Happy old man! You will stay here, between the rivers that you know so well, by springs that have their Nymphs, and find some cool spot underneath the trees. Time and again, as it has always done, the hedge there, leading from your neighbour's land, will have its willow-blossom rifled by Hyblaean bees and coax you with a gentle humming through the gates of sleep. On the other side, at the foot of the high rock, you will have the vine-dresser singing to the breezes, while all the time your dear full-throated pigeons will be heard, and the turtle-dove high in the elm will never bring her cooing to an end.

The dispossessed shepherd speaks these lines. There can be no doubt that the intensity of his praise for the bucolic style of life stems from what he suffers of civilization. The pastoral impulse, in other words, is formed under pressure from hostile forces. Virgil underscores this point by having the fortunate shepherd, who is in a position to enjoy the felicity of life in Arcadia, pay his respects to Rome. Instead of lapsing into mindless country pleasures, he insists upon his debt to a patron at the center of power. Without such support, he says, he would have neither freedom nor leisure to enjoy. The irony is one that writers with a strong bent toward primitivism are likely to miss. In Virgil's poem the joys of Arcady exist only by virtue of the power of Rome.

The pastoral impulse, then, is an impulse toward reconciliation.[10] In the face of civilization's encroaching power, the pastoral poet reaffirms the need for a balance of human experience. Nothing makes the mediating character of the impulse so clear as the spatial symbolism in which it is expressed. The poet invests his affirmation in the image of a lovely green hollow. To arrive at this haven it is necessary to move away from Rome in the direction of nature, away from the repressions of the city toward the license of the wilderness. But the movement stops far short of unimproved, raw nature. "Happy old man!" the unfortunate shepherd says to his friend in the first eclogue. "So your land will still be yours. And it's enough for you, even though the bare rock and the marshland with its mud and reeds encroach on all your pastures. Your pregnant ewes will never be upset by unaccustomed fodder; no harm will come to them . . . " In Virgil's poem the ideal pasture has two vulnerable frontiers. One faces toward Rome, the other toward intractable nature. The ruling impulse here is to discover that middle ground where the opposing forces of love and power, nature and civilization, may be reconciled.

With Virgil's poem in view it is easier to see the special relevance of the pastoral motive to the interpretation of American experience. From the beginning the conditions of life in the new world invested the ancient theme with a singular intensity of meaning—with fresh and vivid symbols. Here, after all, is a society that came into being when advanced parties of western civilization invaded a prehistoric landscape. They moved from east to west, away from Rome toward the wilderness. The movement may be understood as an effort to create what one classical scholar, describing Virgil's Arcadia, calls a "half-way land" where the "curents of myth and empirical reality flow into one another."[11] In place of Sicily, the setting Theocritus had used, Virgil set his shepherds down in Arcadia, a land that was real yet remote enough to be

---

[10] My own thinking about the nature of pastoral has been stimulated by William Empson, *Some Versions of Pastoral* (London, 1950); Erwin Panofsky, "Et in Arcadia Ego," first printed in Raymond Klibansky and H. Paton, eds., *Philosophy & History* (Oxford, 1936), 223–254, and later revised in Erwin Panofsky, *Meaning in the Visual Arts* (New York, 1957), 295–320; Renato Poggioli, "The Oaten Flute," *Harvard Library Bulletin*, XI (Spring, 1957), 147–184; and Hallett Smith, "Pastoral Poetry," in *Elizabethan Poetry, A Study in Conventions, Meaning and Expression* (Cambridge, Mass., 1952), 1–63.

[11] Snell, 283.

endowed with the legendary glow of the golden age. And that, as everyone knows, is how the new world first struck the imagination of Europe.

But I do not mean to suggest that the pastoral image of America was meaningful only in the initial phase of our history. The dramatic "invasion" of the unspoiled country did not occur only once, when colonists first set foot on the eastern shore. It was reenacted again and again from the time of Jamestown, in 1607, until the nineteenth century when, with the onset of industrialism and the closing of the frontier, the drama of the new beginning reached something like a climax. At that time the image of the machine took hold of the native imagination. These historical circumstances help to account for the striking resemblance between the Sleepy Hollow pattern and the thematic design of Virgil's poem, first published in 39 B.C.

But of course there are vital differences between American and traditional versions of pastoral. In the typical American fable, such as *Walden* or *Huckleberry Finn* or "The Bear," the recoil from civilization is much more powerful than in Virgil's poem. Back of this radical thrust toward nature we can discern the combined force of nineteenth century ideas and of the unique American situation. It carries the hero to the very edge of anarchic primitivism. Can he make his way back to a landscape of reconciliation? What direction does he take? For that matter, can there be such a landscape in the presence of the Dynamo? It is not surprising that our writers have no answers to these questions, or that a strong tragic undertone may be felt in American pastoral. For the contrast between the two cardinal images of value, the machine and the native landscape, dramatizes the great issue of our culture. It is the germ, as Henry James put it, of the most final of all questions about America.

Self and Environment

RICHARD POIRIER

The most interesting American books are an image of the creation of America itself, of the effort, in the words of Emerson's Orphic poet, to "Build therefore your own world." American writers who make this effort are, in one sense, only doing what writers, especially in the romantic tradition, have always done. To "enclose" the world, as Emerson puts it, so that "Time and space, liberty and necessity, are left at large no longer," is to do no more in Concord than had already been done in Coleridge's lime tree bower. But such images have a recognizable uniqueness when they occur in American books. They are bathed in the myths of American history; they carry the metaphoric burden of a great dream of freedom—of the expansion of national consciousness into the vast spaces of a continent and the absorption of those spaces into ourselves. Expansive characters in Cooper or Emerson, Melville, James, or Fitzgerald are thus convinced as if by history of the practical possibility of enclosing the world in their imaginations. It is as if the conventions of English romantic poetry could in America take on the life of prose, assume a reality that even history might recognize and that novels could report as news. Let us for the moment assume with Hegel that "freedom" is a creation not of political institutions but of consciousness, that freedom is that reality which the consciousness creates for itself. The assumption makes it more understandable that the creation of America out of a continental vastness is to some degree synonymous in the imagination with the creation of freedom, of an open space made free, once savagery has been dislodged, for some unexampled expansion of human consciousness.

I shall accordingly treat books and paragraphs of books as scale models of America. For if in American history some ideal national self has had to contend from the outset with realities of time, biology, economics, and social custom, so in American literature the individual self has had to struggle into life through media of expression shaped by these realities. My demonstrations involve none of the usual connections between historical events and literary events, since I question the possibility of knowing what these are in relation to one another. Instead, I propose to measure this struggle for consciousness, personal and national, within the language of particular works. Sometimes, as in Cooper, the existence of the struggle is evident mostly in absurdities of style; at other times, as in Emerson, the struggle is merely evoked rather than made, as in Thoreau, the very substance of metaphor. Mark Twain tries to avoid the struggle, Huck Finn gets him into it, but he then drops Huck as a subject of interest in the very book named for him and turns his attention to a survey of the environmental forces within which not even a confused consciousness of freedom, like Huck's, can possibly come to full life. Later, Dreiser will derive energy from a kind of fascinated surrender to the mysterious forces that in the City destroy freedom and even any consciousness of its loss.

The books which in my view constitute a distinctive American tradition within English literature are early, very often clumsy examples of a modernist impulse in fiction: they resist within their pages the forces of environment that otherwise dominate the world. Their styles have an eccentricity of defiance, even if the defiance shows sometimes as carelessness. Cooper, Emerson, Thoreau, Melville, Hawthorne, Mark Twain, James—they both resemble and serve their heroes by trying to create an environment of "freedom," though as writers their efforts must be wholly in language. American books are often written as if historical forces cannot possibly provide such an environment, as if history can give no life to "freedom," and as if only language can create the liberated place. The classic American writers try through style temporarily to free the hero (and the reader) from systems, to free them from the pressures of time, biology, economics, and from the social forces which are ultimately the undoing of American heroes and quite often of their creators. What distinguishes American heroes of this kind from those in the fiction of Mrs. Wharton, Dreiser, or Howells is that there is nothing within the real world, or in the systems which dominate it, that can possibly satisfy their aspirations. Their imagination of the self—and I speak now especially of heroes in Cooper, Melville, James—has no economic or social or sexual objectification; they tend to substitute themselves for the world. Initially and finally at odds with "system," perhaps their best definition is Henry James Sr.'s description of the artist as hero. In a passage, later given at some length, where he affirms a parallel between the writer, struggling to express himself in language, and the defiant hero, contending with the recalcitrant materials of reality, the artist is described as "the man of whatsoever function, who in fulfilling it obeys his own inspiration and taste, uncontrolled either by his physical necessities or his social obligations." The artist-hero may be, as he often is in American literature, an athlete, a detective, or a cowboy, his technical skills being as disciplined as the skills of art.

James's description might as easily come from Emerson, specifically from his essay "The Poet." It reflects a transcendentalist idea of style— not that style should mediate between the self and society but that it should emanate from the self as a leaf from a tree, expanding itself naturally to nourish, color, and become the world. Emerson himself, as "transparent eyeball," is only the first of the many similar figures in American literature who thus "swell" into shapes or defy the realities of space and time.

In works where this expansion of self occurs there is less a tendency to criticize existing environments—for that one would read Howells or Sinclair Lewis—than an effort to displace them. So that even at the moment of worldly defeat the hero has managed to create, like the exiled Coriolanus, at least the illusion of "a world elsewhere." Works like *Moby-Dick* or *The Ambassadors*, for example, are *designed* to make the reader feel that his ordinary world has been acknowledged, even exhaustively, only to be dispensed with as a source of moral or psychological standards. They are written so as finally not to be translatable into those standards, and their extravagances of language are an exultation in the exercise of consciousness momentarily set free. We can say of two American writers as different as Melville and James that both are quite willing, for themselves and for their heroes, to accept the appearance of failure in the interests of this free exercise of consciousness.

To make an environment in language that thwarts any attempts to translate that language into the terms of conventional environments is to write with a complexity that few even now are willing to allow to the novel or to any kind of prose. Indeed it is significant that most adverse criticism of, say, Melville or James, displays a marked failure to give requisite attention to the demanding styles by which these writers create an imaginary environment that excludes the standards of that "real" one to which most critics subscribe.

I am making a distinction between works that create through language an essentially imaginative environment for the hero and works that mirror an environment already accredited by history and society. This distinction is usually explained, more often than not explained away, by saying that the first kind of environment belongs to the romance and that the second belongs to the novel. Hawthorne provides, in his Preface to *The House of the Seven Gables*, the *locus classicus*:

When a writer calls his work a Romance, it need hardly be observed that he wishes to claim a certain latitude, both as to its fashion and material, which he would not have felt himself entitled to assume had he professed to be writing a Novel. The latter form of composition is presumed to aim at a very minute fidelity, not merely to the possible, but to the probable and ordinary course of man's experience. The former—while, as a work of art, it must rigidly subject itself to laws, and while it sins unpardonably so far as it may swerve aside from the truth of the human heart—has fairly a right to present that truth under circumstances, to a great extent, of the writer's own choosing or creation. If he thinks fit, also, he may so manage his atmospherical medium as to bring out or mellow the lights and deepen and enrich the shadows of the picture. He will be wise, no doubt, to make a very moderate use of the privileges here stated, and, especially, to mingle the Marvellous rather as a slight, delicate, and evanescent flavor, than as any portion of the actual substance of the dish offered to the public. He can hardly be said, however, to commit a literary crime even if he disregard this caution.

Sorted out for us here are two kinds of fictional environment I have been trying to describe: one might be called the provided environment, the other an invented environment. But it is regrettable that Hawthorne chose to elevate distinctions about environment, which is after all only one aspect of fiction, into distinctions between genres. Use of the terms "romance" and "novel" have in fact prevented rather than encouraged serious consideration of the American obsession with inventing environments that permit unhampered freedom of consciousness. Obsession is not too strong a word if English fiction is brought in for contrast. One of the first English novels comparable to the American fiction of civilization and the frontier is *Robinson Crusoe,* but it is indicative of the American emphases of Cooper, of Mark Twain, of Thoreau, though Thoreau gives a whole chapter of *Walden* to bourgeois considerations of economy, that Defoe's novel is a sort of idyllic parable of man's gaining merely economic control over an environment out of which he could try to make anything he chose. A true born Englishman, he has no interest whatever in the merely visionary possession of landscape, which a later chapter of this book traces throughout American literature. This comparison suggests what is, for other reasons, too, an inescapable conclusion: the strangeness of American fiction has less to do with the environment in which a novelist finds himself than with the environment he tries to create for his hero, usually his surrogate.

There is an evident reluctance on the part of American writers to admit that they intend to promote eccentricity both in the heroes of their works and in the environments provided for them. It is as if our writers wanted, in commenting on their own work and on the works of one another, to hide what they most wanted to do, and to hide their true intentions under disingenuous complaints that they are victims of historical necessity. They ask us to believe that the strange environments they create are a consequence not of their distaste for social, economic, and biological realities but of the fact that these aren't abundant enough in American life. Cooper, Hawthorne, James, and commentators who follow them, all suggest that they would be happier if the social "texture" of

American life were "thicker" even while they make every sort of literary effort to escape even the supposedly thin "texture" which American society does not provide. In the passage from Hawthorne, in similar passages from Cooper and James, the talk about "romance" is always connected with the supposition that America could not provide an environment which sustained American novelists. "This country," Cooper writes in his *Preface to Home as Found*, "in its ordinary aspects, probably presents as barren a field to the writer of fiction, and to the dramatist, as any other on earth; we are not certain we might not say the most barren. . . . It would be indeed a desperate undertaking, to think of making anything interesting in the way of a *Roman de Société* in this country." And it is from such arguments that American writers and critics have made the by no means necessary extrapolation that Americans of genius were forced to write romances rather than novels.

The categorization of American fiction into novels, and, more numerously, into romances, even when the categories are made subtle by Richard Chase in *The American Novel and Its Tradition* has tended to obscure the more challenging questions: Are not certain kinds of experience much harder to put into language than other kinds? Are there not some states of consciousness that resist dramatic formulation, regardless of the genre in which the effort is made, because in dialogue or in actions they automatically become "like" some conventional states of consciousness that are less transcendental than perverse? When scenes occur in American literature that by standards of ordinary life are foolish, preposterous, or sexually irregular they are usually interpreted in one of three, all relatively unsatisfactory, ways: they are translated into psychosexual terms with the implication that because we have thereby discovered something covert we have therefore revealed "more" than the obvious, idealistic, or ideological reading. Or they are discussed merely as metaphoric expressions of one or another recurrent myth in romantic or American literature, with little, usually no attention to the fact that the expression of this myth often does unwittingly raise questions about sex and psychology. Or they are much more simply disposed of with the observation that after all they belong to a romance, since of course they could not have occurred in a novel.

All three procedures, but noticeably the last, have the same basic deficiency: a tendency to treat experiences in fiction as if somehow they existed independently of the style which creates them and which creates, too, the environment in which these experiences make or do not make sense. It is as though we apprehended these experiences not through the media of language at this particular point or at that one, but within the baggy categories of "romance," or "myth," "realism," or "naturalism." The crucial problem for the best American writers is to evade all such categorizations and to find a language that will at once express and protect states of consciousness that cannot adequately be defined by conventional formulations even of more sophisticated derivation from Marx, Freud, or Norman O. Brown. The problem is stylistic. Quite locally so in the sounds and shapes of words. Genres have no instrumentality for expression, especially those of "novel" and "romance." These so-called genres have none of the ascertainable conventions of style that can legitimately be associated with such genres as the pastoral or the epic. One can see and hear language, see and hear the struggle in a voice to find a language appropriate to some mysterious state of consciousness; but no one has ever seen or heard language that necessarily belongs to a novel rather than a romance.

Once beyond the superficiality of genre criticism and the limitations of other more sophisticated categorizations, what is most interesting in American literature is the attempt in the writing to "build a world" wherein, say, even drunkenness might be the rule of the day. I mention drunkenness not only because it is a fairly common way of at least temporarily modifying one's relationship to customary environment. It is also William James's example when he is discussing in *Varieties of Religious Experience* a problem in life much the same as the problem I am considering in literature:

Inner happiness and serviceability do not always agree. What immediately feels most 'good' is not always most 'true,' when measured by the verdict of the rest of experience. The difference between Philip drunk and Philip sober is the classic instance in corroboration. If merely 'feeling good' could decide, drunkenness would be the supremely valid human experience. But its revelations, however acutely satisfying at the moment, are inserted into an environment which refuses to bear them out for any length of time. The consequence of this discrepancy of the two criteria is the uncertainty which still prevails over so many of our spiritual judgments. There are moments of sentimental and mystical experience . . . that carry an enormous sense of inner authority and illumination with them when they come. But they come seldom, and they do not come to every one; and the rest of life makes either no connection with them, or tends to contradict them more than it confirms them. Some persons follow more the voice of the moment in these cases, some prefer to be guided by the average results. Hence the sad discordancy of so many of the spiritual judgments of human beings. . . .

According to William James there is a necessary discontinuity between revelatory moments, always sporadic and infrequent, and the "environment" in which people ordinarily pass their time. In discovering the nature of environment, in life or in a book, we must, taking a hint from this passage, look not only at the way space is filled but also at the way time is customarily measured. The proportions of time authorized for any given activity, like getting drunk, are as important as "place" to our understanding of environment.

Though James is talking about careers in life, of Philip drunk and

Philip sober, what he implies is still more decisively true of books. In literature environment is usually discussed in terms of place, or a social class, or a historical situation. This is only a convenience and it necessarily confuses what the books truly offer. As I use the word "environment," it means not the places named in a novel, like Chicago, let us say. Environment refers instead to the places filled in a book, filled with words that might indeed pretend to describe Chicago, but which in fact set a boundary on a wholly imaginary city in which the community of language shared by reader, characters, and author necessarily limits the possible shapes that action, persons, and language itself can assume. Nor does environment in a book mean, except in a most superficial sense, a time when events occur, be it 1966 or 1914. As I use the word "environment" with respect to a particular work, I mean the *proportions* of time that a writer feels he can give to some as against other kinds of events. In this sense, environment is really a derivative of such technical accomplishments as pacing and intensity, the weight of language at some points rather than at others. Why is it that often we remember vividly a particular scene that upon inspection turns out to have lasted only a few pages in a book of several hundred? From the answer to such a question we can discover that a writer could only give to moments of greatest illumination in his book, moments at which he seems to expend his genius most authentically, a small proportion of time and space as against what he felt required to give to "the rest of life."

Thinking of environment in American books as comparative units of space and time, a reader makes an obvious and very poignant discovery. What we remember about a book or a writer—and this is notably true in American literature—is often the smallest, momentary revelations that nonetheless carry, like the mystical experience to which William James alludes, an "enormous sense of inner authority." Much of this book is given over to a close look at such "passages" (the term "passages" could not be more apt) and to examining why they sometimes exist, with relation to the rest of the books in which they occur, much as do James's drunken or mystical experiences when these are "inserted into an environment which refuses to bear them out for any length of time." The rest of life, like the rest of a book, "tends to contradict them more than it confirms them."

The greatest American authors really do try, against the perpetually greater power of reality, to create an environment that might allow some longer existence to the hero's momentary expansions of consciousness. They try even when they are sure of failing, as Hawthorne was; they struggle for years in the face of failure, as Mark Twain did with his finest book, and as Melville did with most of his; and when they succeed, as James sometimes does, it is only that they may then be accused of neglecting the "realities" of sex, economics, or social history.

A novel as familiar as *Huckleberry Finn* is perhaps illustration enough

of the problem of environment. Briefly, the book creates two environments for the hero, the raft and the shore. The environment of the shore
is an investment in history and locale; Jim and Huck's few moments on
the river, before they are joined by the King and the Duke, are a retreat
from history; they are quite literally out of place and beyond economics.
To remember the novel is spontaneously to remember the raft scenes,
and yet looking back at the text we discover that the space and time
given the scenes on the raft constitute less than a tenth of the whole, and
that even on the raft Huck's mind is contaminated by the values of the
shore. What Mark Twain discovered at the point of his famous and pro-
longed difficulties after Chapter xv was that even his limited effort to
create an environment alternative to the shore had made his task impossible. He must, finally, "insert" Huck back into his customary environment. He must, in effect, destroy him. Huck as a character, created mostly
in his soliloquies up through Chapter xv, is replaced by another figure,
using the same nature, but able to exist within the verbal world of the last
two thirds of the novel, a world demonstrably less free than the verbal
world or environment of the first third. *Huckleberry Finn* is a kind of
history of American literature and it is altogether superior to most of what
passes for histories of American literature. It is superior because it brings
within its covers a conflict too often discussed as if it merely split American fiction, or the works of American writers, down the middle. On the
one side we have the "romantic," and on the other we have the "realistic"
or "naturalistic" schools. None of the interesting American novelists can
be placed on either side of this dichotomy. Nearly all of them are writing
in protest against the environment of the "rest of life" which contradicts the
dreams of their heroes and heroines. The distinction to be made is between those whose protests sometimes take the form of creating in their
works an alternative environment, as James and sometimes Faulkner have
tried to do, as Mark Twain for a while did do, and those for whom the
environment of the real world simply overpowers, as it does in *Huckleberry Finn,* any effort of the imagination to transcend it. In this case the
imagination, as in the novels of Dreiser and Edith Wharton, can only
reproduce the effect of environment as force.

II

The idea that through language it is possible to create environments
radically different from those supported by economic, political, and social
systems is one of the sustaining myths of any literature. It is a myth in one
sense because it is historically invalid: the enormous contrivances of style
called forth by this effort are themselves an admission that the environment thus created has an existence only in style. Not God, not religion,

not reality, history, or nature, but style is its only authority. It is a myth in another sense because writers do not want to believe, repetitively, despite history and their own experience, in the transcendent power of their own stylistic enterprise. The repetition and persistence of this myth has been especially evident in American literature for the obvious reason that for the only time in history men could, with the prospects of a new continent, actually believe in their power at last to create an environment congenial to an ideal self. American literature is thus full of images equivalent to the frontier. As Edwin Fussell shows, Walden is the West for Thoreau. On the pond he can build an environment for himself in which not only wilderness but also the civilizing technologies are made subservient to him. *Walden* is only one of the examples of something like an obsession in American literature with plans and efforts to build houses, to appropriate space to one's desires, perhaps to inaugurate therein a dynasty that shapes time to the dimensions of personal and familial history. Most of the houses in Cooper answer these ambitions, as does the Grangerford house in *Huckleberry Finn,* the House of the Seven Gables, Fawns in James's *Golden Bowl,* Sutpen's Hundred in Faulkner's *Absalom, Absalom!,* Silas Lapham's house, Gatsby's estate, and even the remade country house of Bellow's *Herzog.* Coincident with some of these are the American theorists of housing and of space, Horatio Greenough, Louis Sullivan, Frank Lloyd Wright, and that great historian of space, power, and architecture Henry Adams.

The building of a house is an extension and an expansion of the self, an act by which the self possesses environment otherwise possessed by nature. By an act of building, so the theorists I've mentioned would have it, it is possible to join forces with the powers of nature itself, to make its style your style. But this conjunction is possible only if the imagination and space are freed from the possessive power of all that is not nature: from systems of any kind that derive from society and history, from, often as not, "Europe."

From the outset American writers (or architects) who wanted in America to create environments in concert with the formative powers of nature found that they had first to rid themselves and America of styles imposed upon them by history. Even the men who dispossessed the Indian could only possess, could only *see* America through the styles and instrumentalities of the old world. According to Faulkner's Isaac McCaslin, the land was

"already tainted even before any white man owned it by what Grandfather and his kind, his fathers, had brought into the new land which He had vouchsafed them out of pity and sufferance, on condition of pity and humility and sufferance and endurance, from that old world's corrupt and worthless twilight as though in the sailfuls of the old world's tainted wind which drove the ships—"

The theme of "possession" and of "dispossession," one of the subjects of Chapter II of this book, finds its greatest contemporary expression in *The Bear,* where the hero rejects both his historical and his economic inheritance so that he might live in an environment where time (his relation to family and family past) and space (the wilderness, and the plantation he is to inherit) are redeemed by his sacrifice of profit from either, his relinquishment both of a sexual and of an economic identity. In all respects he gives up the house of his ancestors.

The images of housing, of possession, and of achieving by relinquishment of one's inheritance some original relation to time and space—all these are parts of what we recognize in the characteristic career of American heroes and heroines. But all these images serve equally well to describe the activites of American writers and their relation to literary styles and conventions. Thus at the point in *Democratic Vistas* just before he claims that he "can conceive a community, today and here" where "perfect personalities without noise meet," Whitman complains, in a way almost tiredly conventional by 1871, that "Of course, in these States, for both man and woman, we must entirely recast the types of highest personality from what the oriental, feudal, ecclesiastical worlds bequeath us, and which yet possess the imaginative and aesthetic fields of the United States."

Whitman's critical utterances are an example of how aesthetic theories of literary independence and originality, the preoccupation of American writers from nearly the beginnings of our literature, are an analogue to the effort by American fictional heroes to free themselves from the conventions of historically rooted environments. Whitman in his poetry fashions a poetic style wherein as both writer and hero of the poems he can be the gregarious flirt and voyeur that he was. His is a style in which the "I" escapes the limited relations permitted in environments fostered by society and expands to include anything, which in his case means everything. In quite other ways, the same omniverousness is evident in the later James. There, the environment which is James's style—an extraordinary invention in the history of language—makes it natural for the author to have total entry into the consciousness of all of his characters. James's later novels have the quality of vast interior monologues with James playing all the parts at will. Thoreau's *Walden* is perhaps more explicit than any other American book about the connections between a defiant hero literally building a world of his own—this is also, of course, the subject of *The Golden Bowl*—and the writer who looks upon writing as analogous to building. Like Whitman, and like the later James, Thoreau *is* his style. His style is itself the hero of the book: it is in substance the writer's self, the various selves that he absorbs, and it is a mirror of the creative originality of the hero-poet.

Significantly, in none of these books, not even when they permit a dialogue, is there allowance made for a style that is not the characteristic style of the author. And I have purposely selected very familiar examples in fiction, prose, and poetry. Necessarily, "perfect personalities without noise meet" in Whitman's charming picture: the only noise is the writer's own, speaking for everyone. The artist becoming "God" through his creative activity is an ambition implicit in the whole idea of creating environments where worldly distinctions among persons are of no consequence. "Spring," in *Walden* is a grotesque image of this process. It is an account of Thoreau's vision of the "excrementitious" flow of sand and vegetation in the season of rebirth and a vision of himself within this flow as "but a mass of thawing clay." Continually fluid, leading on to shapes not yet apprehended and never to be fixed, "nature" is "the laboratory of the Artist who made the world and me." To nature as an artist Thoreau joins his own plastic powers, his own activities as a poet-maker. That is what he means by a "living" artist: "the earth is not a mere fragment of dead history," he writes, "stratum upon stratum like the leaves of a book,[1] to be studied by geologists and antiquarians chiefly, but living poetry like the leaves of a tree, which precede the flowers and fruit."

Here, as in Emerson's essay on "The Poet" and in his admiration for the author of *Leaves of Grass,* is an early form of an aesthetic which is sometimes thought to be contemporary. It is an aesthetic so devoted to the *activity* of creation that it denies finality to the results of that activity, its objects or formulations. Art is an action not a product of action. To be creative is to discover one's affinity with "God" and thereby one's superiority to the works of men. Emerson's "Poet," like that version of him who is Thoreau, therefore rejects even the solidity of his own constructions, of his own created environments. No wonder American writers have always been outspoken in praise of self-contradiction, of "whim," and repetition. Self-contradiction suggests the unfinished life within the always expanding frontiers of the self—"do I contradict myself?/very well then I contradict myself,/(I am large, I contain multitudes)"—while repetition allows for endless variations within single things. There are at least thirteen of Wallace Stevens's blackbirds as well as thirteen ways of looking at one of them, and the third of Miss Stein's roses is, by the very act of naming it, not the second and not the first. Even any so-called "American" style would be a prison, if we accept the dictate of Emerson that "every thought is also a prison; every heaven is also a prison."

Something that in historically credited environments has a place and function is not even recognizable in that other environment of the artist which exists in a continually fluid state, continually transforming itself into new and mysterious forms. The notion has informed the most popular

[1] This expression, or naming, Emerson writes, "is not art but a second nature grown out of the first as a leaf out of a tree," a figure that in our own century has found its way not only into the architectural theories of Louis Sullivan but also into his drawings of compound leaf forms to illustrate the organic and functional principles of *A System of Architectural Ornament.*

idioms about America. The metaphor of America as a melting pot, for example, implies that the final product will, like Emerson's Poet, be a composite figure who "stands among partial men for the complete man." Emerson's Poet can have no established nationality; he is not imagined as having even a particular occupation, including the occupation of poet as we normally think of it. He is supposed to be simply and magnificently himself in whatever he chooses to do. The role of the artist is clarified a good deal by Emerson's friend and contemporary Henry James, Sr. in an almost unknown short lecture, already mentioned, in *Moralism and Christianity:*

Who, then, is the perfect or divine man, the man who actually reconciles in himself all the conflicting elements of humanity? Is any such man actually extant? If so, where shall we find him?

We find him in the aesthetic man, or Artist. But now observe that when I speak of the aesthetic man or Artist, I do not mean the man of any specific function, as the poet, painter, or musician. I mean the man of whatsoever function, who in fulfilling it obeys his own inspiration or taste, uncontrolled either by his physical necessities or his social obligations. He alone is the Artist, whatever be his manifest vocation, whose action obeys his own internal taste or attraction, uncontrolled either by necessity or duty. The action may perfectly consist both with necessity and duty; that is to say, it may practically promote both his physical and social welfare; but these must not be its animating principles, or he sinks at once from the Artist into the artisan. The artisan seeks to gain a livelihood or secure an honorable name. He works for bread, or for fame, or for both together. The Artist abhors these ends, and works only to show forth that immortal beauty whose presence constitutes his inmost soul. He is vowed to Beauty as the bride is vowed to the husband, and Beauty reveals herself to him only as he obeys his spontaneous taste or attraction.

The reason accordingly why the painter, the poet, the musician, and so forth, have so long monopolized the name of Artist, is, not because Art is identical with these forms of action, for it is identical with no specific forms, but simply because the poet, painter, and so forth, more than any other men, have thrown off the tyranny of nature and custom, and followed the inspirations of genius, the inspirations of beauty, in their own souls. These men to some extent have sunk the service of nature and society in the obedience of their own private attractions. They have merged the search of the good and the true in that of the beautiful, and have consequently announced a divinity as yet unannounced either in nature or society. To the extent of their consecration, they are priests after the order of Melchisedec, that is to say, a priesthood which, not being made after the law of a carnal commandment, shall never pass away. And they are kings, who reign by a *direct* unction from the Highest. But the priest is not the altar, but the servant of the altar; and the king is not the Highest, but a servant of the Highest. So painting, poetry, is not Art, but the servant and representative of Art. Art is divine, universal, infinite. It therefore exacts to itself infinite forms or manifestations, here in the painter, there in the actor; here in the musician, there in the machinist; here in the architect, there in the dancer; here in the poet, there in the costumer. We do not therefore call the painter or poet, Artist, because painting or poetry is a whit more essential to Art than ditching is, but simply because the painter and poet have more frequently exhibited the life of Art by means of a hearty insubjection to nature and convention.

When, therefore, I call the Divine Man, or God's image in creation, by the name of Artist, the reader will not suppose me to mean the poet, painter, or any other special form of man. On the contrary, he will suppose me to mean that infinite and spiritual man whom all these finite functionaries represent indeed, but whom none of them constitutes, namely, the man who in every visible form of action acts always from his inmost self, or from attraction, and not from necessity or duty. I mean the man who is a law unto himself, and ignores all outward allegiance, whether to nature or society. This man may indeed have no technical vocation whatever, such as poet, painter, and the like, and yet he will be none the less sure to announce himself. The humblest theatre of action furnishes him a platform. I pay my waiter so much a day for putting my dinner on the table. But he performs his function in a way so entirely *sui generis,* with so exquisite an attention to beauty in all the details of the service, with so symmetrical an arrangement of the dishes, and so even an adjustment of everything to its own place, and to the hand that needs it, as to shed an almost epic dignity upon the repast, and convert one's habitual "grace before meat" into a spontaneous tribute, instinct with a divine recognition.

The charm in this case is not that the dinner is all before me, where the man is bound by his wages to place it. This every waiter I have had has done just as punctually as this man, which attests that in doing it, he is not thinking either of earning his wages, or doing his duty toward me, but only of satisfying his own conception of beauty with the resources before him. The consequence is that the pecuniary relation between us emerges in a higher one. He is no longer the menial, but my equal or superior, so that I have felt, when entertaining doctors of divinity and law, and discoursing about divine mysteries, that a living epistle was circulating behind our backs, and quietly ministering to our wants, far more apocalyptic to an enlightened eye than any yet contained in books.

The ease with which the elder James finds the artist in occupations as mundane as waiting on table is one indication that an essentially Emersonian concept of style involves much more than a standard merely of literary performance. Emerson himself remarks that "poets are thus liberating gods." Believing with James that poets "more than any other men, have thrown off the tyranny of nature," Emerson also used the title Poet to designate anyone of any occupation who in the exercise of it fully realizes the self or the selves that are in him. Emerson and Henry James Sr. affirm what could in any case be inferred from the great American books: an identification of the writer, idealized as a liberator of consciousness, with the heroes of a more practical, worldly, and physical achievement. These heroes may be men of "whatsoever function," but in a significant number of cases they too are "liberators." Deerslayer shows his daring mostly in freeing his friends and himself from captivity, so does Huck Finn, and so, too does Faulkner's Charles Mallison of *Intruder in the Dust*. The stories of Poe and of Melville are full of imprisonments and efforts at liberation, while James, like Hawthorne, evolved a style meant to liberate his heroes from those, like the governess in *The Turn of the Screw*, who would "fix," imprison, or "know" others.

The situation can be described in terms of rather crude historical progression. It could be said that the theories of literary and stylistic independence, articulated if not originated by Emerson, were gradually transmuted into an ideal of heroic character asserting its independence of oppressive environments and of prefabricated social styles. So, too, the difficulties of Cooper and Emerson in achieving stylistic independence are translated, as it were, by Hawthorne, and increasingly by American novelists after him, into the central dramatic situation of their works. In this, as in many other ways, Salinger's Holden Caulfield is a merely stock character enacting the American hero's effort, more significantly illustrated by Isabel Archer, to express the natural self rather than merely to represent, in speech and manner, some preordained social type.

Defiance of convention by a writer in his style or by a character in his actions is necessarily part of the effort to create a new environment or to escape the confinements of an old one. Again, we can think of the sequence of American literature almost novelistically, each chapter modifying the concerns tentatively revealed in a previous one. Thus, when Cooper in 1828 remarks in *Notions of a Travelling Bachelor* that "it is quite obvious that, so far as taste and forms alone are concerned, the literature of England and that of America must be fashioned after the same models," he is rather passively describing a cultural situation that was later to be the provocation for Emerson's "The American Scholar" and for Whitman's *Democratic Vistas*, where, forty-three years after Cooper, Whitman would still be complaining that "as yet America has artistically originated nothing." Cultural dependence in Mark Twain became the object of satire, though he was himself its victim, and it was fable-ized in Henry James's international novels, both early, in *The Europeans*, and late, in *The Ambassadors*. In summary, Cooper describes conditions which in Emerson fostered a myth of newness, a myth that gets enacted humanly by Huck Finn, a character whose consciousness exceeds the "style" to which the book as well as Huck are ultimately forced to surrender.

Recognizing the chasm between a fully developed consciousness of self and the socially accepted styles by which that self can get expressed, Henry James developed a style which pays almost no deference to what we recognize as the language of ordinary social intercourse. It is a style that instead gives credence and support to extraordinary, almost grotesque expansions of consciousness, grotesque in the sense that the consciousness thus rendered is very often a mixture of James's own intrusive sensibility and the generally more limited ones of the characters of his later books. But even James was not able wholly to protect such heroes from questions prompted by the reader's commitment to a society and a language existent outside of James's books. There have, as a result, been endless debates about the significance in psychological and social terms of the renunciations of any customary forms of happiness at the end of nearly all his novels, noticeably at the end of *The Portrait of a Lady, The Spoils of Poynton, The Wings of the Dove,* and *The Ambassadors.* The problem is evidence of the distinctive American quality of James. The crisis in the most interesting American works often occurs at those moments when the author tries to externalize the inner consciousness of his hero, tries to insert it, to borrow William James's metaphor, into social and verbal environments that won't sustain it. And the crisis is confronted not only by the heroes but also by their creators when it comes to conceiving of some possible resolution to the conflict of inner consciousness or some suitable external reward for it.

Describing the situation in images which most often embody it in American literature, we can say that American writers are at some point always forced to return their characters to prison. They return them to "reality" from environments where they have been allowed most "nakedly" to exist, environments created by various kinds of stylistic ingenuity. They "clothe" them and subject them to questions of a social and sexual nature which it has been their and their creator's intention to avoid. When Isaac, in Faulkner's *The Bear,* enters the woods as a boy of ten, for example, it is, we are told, as if he is going back in time, leaving any historically formed environment. He feels that he is witnessing his own birth, "the wagon progressing not by its own volition but by attrition of their intact yet fluid circumambience, drowsing, earless, almost lightless." This image is contrived to imitate the movement of a baby out of the womb and into the world, the hero's imagined denudation being a prelude not only to his eloquent later choice of what he calls "dispossession," but to the necessities which accompany that choice: of a lonely, sexless, childless life.

In a companion story to *The Bear, Delta Autumn,* Faulkner gives a savage rightness to the the question asked of Isaac, now an old man, by the mulatto mistress of his nephew: what, she asks, can he know about love. The issue Faulkner recognizes here, and has the genius to exploit, is nearly everywhere a tension in American literature: the tension of bringing into conjunction the environment of nakedness, where there is no encumbrance to the expression of the true inner self, and the environment of costume, of outer space occupied by society and its fabrications. The utter simplicity of Gatsby's room is another example of what one might call the environment of inner space, intended to show the meaninglessness of the festooned life that Gatsby presents to the world. The configuration in Fitzgerald has already been anticipated, of course, in the nakedness enjoyed by Huck and Jim, when Huck does not have to go out in the disguises by which he "fits into" society. Similarly, a return to "nakedness" is also for Emerson the virtue of the woods: where "a man casts off his years as a snake his slough, and at what period soever of life is always a child," even while his own style has often a contrasting, sometimes debilitating "dress" and elegance.[2] And while Thoreau is not generally credited with having had an influence on Henry James, it seems likely that in *The Portrait of a Lady*, Thoreau's disquisition on "Clothing" was on the periphery of James's satiric intention when, to Madame Merle's belief that "we are each of us made up of a cluster of appurtenances," he lets Isabel respond that

"I don't know whether I succeed in expressing myself, but I know that nothing else expresses me. Nothing that belongs to me is any measure of me; on the contrary it's a limit, a barrier, and a perfectly arbitrary one. Certainly the clothes which, as you say, I choose to wear, don't express me; and heaven forbid they should!"

"You dress very well," interposed Madame Merle, skillfully.

"Possibly; but I don't care to be judged by that. My clothes may express the dressmaker, but they don't express me. To begin with, it's not my own choice that I wear them; they are imposed upon me by society."

Madame Merle's answer—"Should you prefer to go without them?"—terminates the discussion. But meanwhile James shows his willingness consciously to expose his heroine to standards which usually embarrass those earlier American writers who share many of Isabel's ideas and indulge themselves in many of the images she also uses. Of course the Emersonianism here is Isabel's not James's, whose allegiances were, in any case, as much to the social as to the transcendental expressions of the self. But the passage nonetheless illustrates James's tenderness for ideals of *self*-expression as against expression by which the self is filtered through representative or acquired styles. This concern passes to him from Emerson (and James's father) through the whole body of American literature.

To a degree that forces on us a critically retrospective look at American

2 The romantic tradition by which the virtues of nakedness get connected with the virtues of childhood is understandably translated into distinctly American educational theories designed to preserve the style of youth and childhood. Among the relevant texts would be Louis Sullivan's *Kindergarten Chats*, John Dewey, *In the School and Society*, and A. F. Chamberlain who in *The Child: A Study in the Evolution of Man* makes an explicit connection between childhood, as one of the best "furnishings" of man, and the creation of art. "Youth was furnished in the order of natural development to the animal as a means of utilizing and controlling the wealth of innate instincts and impulses in a new and higher fashion . . . man especially possess(es) youth because it was necessary to create art (and civilization) from instincts through the transforming power of play." See Sherman Paul, *Louis Sullivan: An Architect in American Thought*, Prentice-Hall, 1962, Chapter IV.

literature, James recognizes the impossibility of "naked" self-expression, the illusion that, like Emerson's "Poet," one can "turn the world to glass." In one sense his novels are about the disaster of assuming that within the environments provided by society there can be any allowance of space for the free expansion of the inner self. Opposed to any such translations and metamorphoses of the self are realities represented not only by the fashion of wearing clothing. Standing in opposition also, are the fashions of language, the elemental social necessities of life implicit even in the agreement to use language in its inherited and publicly accepted forms.

There are two characteristics of language and of literature that are at odds with the Emersonian ideal of building a world of one's own. First of all, there is the acceptance by any writer, and conspicuously by Emerson himself, of certain decorums in his address to an imagined audience, of certain shared suppositions—"this is how an essay sounds" or "this is an acceptable voice for a novel." The "I" that is heard in the voice is therefore unlikely to be the same "I" that is projected by images of the liberated self or the Artist. Second, there is the convention in nineteenth-century fiction of dialogue, even if the dialogue is sometimes wholly recollected or imagined in a single mind. Subscription to the convention of dialogue means that in American fiction certain ideas that sound absurd in anything but monologue or soliloquy become the subject of conversation. Such dialogue, notably in Cooper, Hawthorne, and Melville, is quite often pointlessly stilted and literary. It is as if these writers felt that dialogue was forced upon them. In some measure it was, since dialogue presupposes an accommodation to aspects of reality for which these writers have an evident distaste: the necessity of social intercourse, the acceptance of literary and social conventions in the definition of the Self, the acceptance of other selves *as* other. Cooper and Melville, for instance, want to believe in the possibility that the self can expand not merely in the presence of natural force but also in the company of other people, that the same self can carry on polite conversations and be, in one form or other, something as non-human as a "transparent eyeball."

Stressing these essential facts about American literature, one has to confront some of the issues raised by Leslie Fiedler. I want to say at the outset that *Love and Death in the American Novel* is to my mind probably the best single book on American fiction ever written, and it is surely unsurpassed in its definition of Gothicism as a characteristic of that fiction. The book has been most resented for its purported emphasis on sexual perversity in American literature and in its use of this as an index to certain historical and cultural tensions. Actually Fiedler is altogether less daring and less insistent on this aspect of our literature than was Lawrence in his much earlier study, and he is in no sense as moralistic about sex as a literary component. If Huckleberry Finn were the boy next door, it would probably hurt him more to call him homo-erotic than to call him Faustian, but Fiedler knows that as applied to fictional characters either designation is mythic, not accusatory. What he forgets is that either designation is also destructive of what Huck more *particularly* offers us in his style or in his contribution to a novel so full of the struggle for verbal consciousness. One of the troubles with Fiedler's argument is that it is often initiated by an emphasis on "character," as if "character" existed in nineteenth-century American fiction in the unfractured form it usually takes in English fiction of the same period. He can therefore insist on the significance of certain acts or words as if they refer to "character" and its psychological structure when more often these acts and words belong instead to some larger metaphorical significance in a work to which sexual psychology is merely incidental or irrelevant. Huck and Jim lying naked together on the raft are in fact looking less at each other than at the stars or the river; their nakedness expresses less about their feelings for each other than about their assertion of freedom, as necessary for the white boy as for the Negro slave, from the world of costume, of Style.

Fiedler's work is a brilliant example of mythopoeic criticism given its fullest exposition three years before *Love and Death in the American Novel* by Northrop Frye in *Anatomy of Criticism.* In Fiedler as in Frye is the assumption that mythopoeic and archetypal constructs have some existence more historically and scientifically demonstrable than the existence of a so-called text. The "text" thus becomes, as Fiedler is happy to assert, "merely one of the contexts of a piece of literature," though this creates a problem in semantics which it is not my responsibility here to unravel.[3] Fiedler's methods are not essentially different from those of other commentators who are concerned with recurrences of literary motifs and with the elaboration of these into archetypes or myths. It may be more provocative but it is not more or less valid to reduce American literature to certain versions of sexual dislocation than to reduce it to versions of Eden, Christ, or the Frontier. Because even granting the rewards of mythopoeic readings, one then wants to go on to something more important: an investigation of the career of *topoi* in their passage through inhospitable verbal contexts, through conventions of expression and through literary structures that distort them, giving even to a commonplace romantic image of "nakedness" some peripheral suggestions of "innocent homosexuality." The suggestions *are* peripheral, however—a consequence of literary rather than psychological conditions. What is centrally important is the evidence almost everywhere in American literature of an idealistic effort to free the heroes' and the readers' consciousness from categories not only of conventional moralities but also of mythopoeic interpretation.

[3] See my review of *Love and Death in the American Novel* in *Daedalus,* Winter 1961, pp. 167–72.

The result is a struggle to create through language an environment in which the inner consciousness of the hero-poet can freely express itself, an environment in which he can sound publicly what he privately is. Emphasis on the element of struggle in giving even a temporary existence to this environment means that the archetypes, images, themes, or ideas that have been the main concern of most recent studies of American literature are in this study only of incidental or procedural use. In treating such items as the "eye," "nakedness," "infancy," "new-ness," my concern is with the shapes given such images and ideas when they are under the pressures of various stylistic contexts. What immediately strikes a reader of almost any American classic, of which *Moby-Dick* might be an example, is that his attention is grasped less by images or the significances attached to them, both being usually obvious and often banal, than by the peculiar archness with which they get expressed. *Moby-Dick* is not written as cryptography but as mystery. The agitations of voice, the playfulness through which symbols emerge and then dissolve, the mixtures of incantatory, Biblical, polite, and vernacular language in this and other American books—these are what demand our attention altogether more than do ideas or themes extracted by critics in the interest of tidying up what is mysterious or confused. Marius Bewley's title for a book on American literature, *The Eccentric Design*, therefore promises that he will come much nearer the central problems of that literature than does the title of a more recent book by Tony Tanner, *The Reign of Wonder*, with its implied emphasis on intentions, on ways of perceiving in American literature rather than on ways of expressing what is perceived. However, Mr. Tanner's book turns out to be full of very rewarding speculations; it traces important continuities among American books with tact and unusual discrimination. What is more, he is alert to the problem of stylization, notably in vernacular literature and in the prose-poetry of Gertrude Stein and Henry James. But while showing us how "nearly all American writers have found it difficult to move beyond the first step [of seeing like children] to find satisfactory forms," he then admits that "This phenomenon poses a problem which is obviously beyond the scope of this book."

Trying myself to meet this problem, to make it, in fact, the subject of this book, I share Mr. Tanner's nervousness. The critic who offers the most help is D. H. Lawrence in *Studies in Classic American Literature*, probably the crucial study of American literature. Such a claim can be justified even though the book manages to ignore Emerson, Mark Twain, and Henry James. It illustrates how a work of critical genius can cover a subject even while neglecting large areas of it. The explanation, in this instance, is that Lawrence was himself by temperament an "American" writer working within the conventions of English literature. He was not only responsive to the main lines of force in

American literature; he himself accelerated them. In Lawrence, with a degree of consciousness never attained by any American writer, are the struggles, difficulties, and tensions that went into the writing of the best American books. So much did he feel these tensions that perhaps his clearest expression of them comes when he is talking not about American writing at all, but about his own. Thus in describing what he is trying to do in *Women in Love,* he speaks of that novel as an effort to find a mode of expression for ideas that are struggling into a life which language, and only language, can give them:

> Man struggles with his unborn needs and fulfilment. New unfoldings struggle up in torment in him, as buds struggle forth from the midst of a plant. Any man of real individuality tries to know and to understand what is happening, even in himself, as he goes along. This struggle for verbal consciousness should not be left out in art. It is a very great part of life. It is not superimposition of a theory. It is the passionate struggle into conscious being.
>
> We are now in a period of crisis. Every man who is acutely alive is acutely wrestling with his own soul. The people that can bring forth the new passion, the new idea, this people will endure. Those others, that fix themselves in the old idea, will perish with the new life strangled unborn within them. Men must speak out to one another.
>
> In point of style, fault is often found with the continual, slightly modified repetition. The only answer is that it is natural to the author; and that every natural crisis in emotion or passion or understanding comes from this pulsing, frictional to-and-fro which works up to culmination.

The notion that to bring forth a new passion or a new idea involves verbal struggle against established forms is given a somewhat ironic confirmation by the fact that the notion is itself one of the most persistent conventions of literature. Stylistic revolution is not the exclusive product of any particular historical situation, or the exclusive property of any national literature. If it seems to belong to American writing at the time of Cooper and Emerson, it also belongs to the America of Hamlin Garland and later of Hemingway. If it belonged to English and American poetry when Pound wrote "Make It New," to English poetry when Wordsworth and Coleridge wrote the Preface to the second edition of the *Lyrical Ballads,* it also belonged to Samuel Daniel, some two hundred years earlier, when he announced the fitness of English for rhymed verse. When Gertrude Stein laid down the law that "A rose is a rose is a rose" she was being repetitious with an intention already described. She probably did not intend also to be almost directly repetitious of Emerson in "Self Reliance":

> Man is timid and apologetic; he is no longer upright; he dares not say "I think," "I am," but quotes some saint or sage. He is ashamed before the blade of grass or the blowing rose. Those roses under my window make no reference to

former roses or to better ones; they are for what they are; they exist with God to-day. There is no time to them. There is simply the rose. . . .

In declaring the freedom of words from the significances which history has imposed on them even a writer as notoriously original as Miss Stein finds herself as imitator.

One struggle in American literature is to assert against conventional styles another kind of style that has been defined, out of Emerson and Whitman, by Louis Sullivan when he referred to style as "a consistent and definite expansion of pronounced personality." This struggle cannot wholly be explained simply by reference to some particular historical phenomenon, even one as staggering as the offering to men's imagination of a new world. All we can say is that American literature does offer the most persistent, the most poignantly heroic example of a recurrent literary compulsion, not at all confined to our literature, to believe in the possibilities of a new style.

The American Adam and the Fortunate Fall

R. W. B. LEWIS

[THE AMERICAN ADAM: WHITMAN]

I

The fullest portrayal of the new world's representative man as a
new, American Adam was given by Walt Whitman in *Leaves of Grass*
—in the liberated, innocent, solitary, forward-thrusting personality
that animates the whole of that long poem. *Leaves of Grass* tells us
what life was made of, what it felt like, what it included, and what it
lacked for the individual who began at that moment, so to speak, where
the rebirth ritual of *Walden* leaves off. With the past discarded and
largely forgotten, with conventions shed and the molting season concluded, what kind of personality would thereupon emerge? What would
be the quality of the experience which lay in store for it?

Leaves of Grass was not only an exemplary celebration of novelty in
America: it also, and perhaps more importantly, brought to its climax
the many-sided discussion by which—over a generation—innocence replaced sinfulness as the first attribute of the American character. Such a
replacement was indispensable to Whitman's vision of innocence, though,
of course, it did not account for his poetic genius. But the fact was that,
of all the inherited notions and practices which the party of Hope studied
to reject, by far the most offensive was the Calvinist doctrine of inherited
guilt: the imputation to the living individual of the disempowering effects
of a sin "originally" committed by the first man in the first hours of the
race's history. In New England, where the argument was most intense,
the traditional view of human character was that of Orthodox Calvinism.
And Calvinism, according to the hopeful, not only maintained doctrines
of ancient and obscure origin; it even argued in one of them that an

130

ancient and obscure misdemeanor could have a positive effect upon the living man. Traditionally, an inherited taint was postulated coldly in an inherited dogma. It was time to renounce both the taint and the dogma.

The Unitarians—and among them, especially, the Unitarian wit and healer, Dr. Oliver Wendell Holmes—mounted the strongest attack against the doctrine of inherited guilt; and their efforts are to be noted before coming to Whitman. But the Unitarian attitude is not easily disentangled from the general epidemic of confidence in human nature which seemed to be spreading everywhere and which even infected the party of Memory. Indeed, the nostalgic had been watching the new cheerfulness with increasing agitation for a number of years, and thought they could spot it within their own citadels. One of them put the case as follows: "For a considerable time past, it has been unhesitatingly maintained that all mankind . . . are born free from sin and have no moral corruption of nature or propensity of evil—that they are perfectly innocent—that they . . . come into existence in the same state in which Adam was before the fall." One might think that this polemic was directed against Emerson, who was known to believe that "the entertainment of the proposition of depravity is the last profligacy and profanation," and who smiled his acknowledgment of "each man's innocence"; or perhaps against Thoreau, who found that "the impression made on a wise man is that of universal innocence"; or else against Walt Whitman, the self-styled "chanter of Adamic songs." In fact, its target lay inside its own party; it was a reaction as early as 1828 to the whispers of extremely modified hope which could be heard at Calvinist Yale in the gentle voices of men like Nathaniel Taylor.

It is not easy to imagine that anyone who held, as Taylor did, that "the entire moral depravity of mankind is by nature," that sin is a real and universal thing to be "truly and properly ascribed to *nature* and *not* to circumstances," and that men sin "as soon as they become moral agents . . . *as soon as they can*," was considered a dangerous radical. But Taylor was regarded as such, and so even was Moses Stuart, professor of theology at relentlessly orthodox Andover. For these men seemed to be retreating some small distance at least from the sound principles of Jonathan Edwards. They seemed to be saying and teaching that, although human beings did observably disobey the commandments of God, they did so on their own, by assertion of their own nature, and not because of a total corruption transmitted at the instant of their conception from a diseased ancestry originally and fatally infected by Adam. They seemed to be embracing the false doctrine which had given rise to all the grievous dissensions of New England Protestantism; they seemed, almost, as bad as the Unitarians.[1]

[1] Cf. Sidney Earl Mead, *Nathaniel William Taylor* (Chicago, 1942), p. 215; the orthodox attitude suggested that "the Unitarians will just send out a boat and tow [Taylor] in." In his *Autobiography* (New York, 1869), p. 157, Lyman Beecher re-

But there was no stopping the force of the new optimism. Everybody professed a little of it, and everybody complained that his neighbor was professing too much. The march of heresy was punctuated by the blows visited by one combatant upon the head of him next on the left. While Moses Stuart was being chided for yielding an inch on total depravity, he himself was busy replying to the larger yieldings indicated by the sermons and essays of Unitarians Channing and Andrews Norton; and the dismay of Norton at being, as said, so badly misconstrued by Moses Stuart exploded in the rage and fear aroused by Emerson's sublimely confident address to the Harvard Divinity School in 1836. Theodore Parker, in turn, after valiantly reinforcing Channing's hopeful Unitarian gospel, was almost hustled out of the American Unitarian Association, since, as Lowell put it, "from their orthodox kind of dissent, he dissented." The human stock, one might say, tracing the development chronologically, was rising steadily, until it achieved its highest value in the figure of Adam. The status of Jesus declined proportionately, or, at least, it continued to until Emerson, who deified everybody, also deified Jesus once more—thereby, in a characteristic Emersonian paradox, demonstrating the fulness of Jesus' humanity.

The Unitarians, consequently, stood at approximately the middle point in the controversy—between someone like Moses Stuart, on the one hand, and Emerson, on the other. They took their name from their rejection of the Trinity in favor of Unity; but if they could get along without two of three persons of the Trinity, it was because of a prior conviction about the nature of man.

As the Unitarian minister and historian of the movement, George A. Ellis, wrote in 1857, looking back on *A Half-Century of the Unitarian Controversy*, "The doctrine, that God visited the guilt of Adam's personal sin upon the unborn millions of his posterity . . . was infinitely more objectionable to some liberal Christians than the Trinitarian theory." To the Unitarians, the Calvinist picture of man sounded like this:

A corrupted nature is conveyed by ordinary generation, to all of Adam's posterity, in consequence of his personal sin. . . . If this Orthodox doctrine is not a most shameful trifling with solemnities, as well as with language, it asserts that, by the constitution and appointment of God, the one man Adam had like power to communicate a vitiated nature, like a hereditary disease, not merely to the bodies, but to the souls of all human beings. . . . This doctrine either contradicts truth and reason, in affirming that any one can be partaker in sin committed before his birth, or it contradicts justice and righteousness, by subjecting us to punishment for the offence of another.

---

called the utter dismay with which he heard a colleague express doubt about the depravity of infants: "The moment I heard that, I saw the end. I never felt so bad." Cf. also "Backgrounds of Unitarian Opposition to Transcendentalism," by Clarence A. Faust, *Modern Philology*, February, 1938; and Joseph Haroutinian, *Piety versus Moralism* (New York, 1932).

That was the issue, as the Unitarians read it, on the whole correctly, in the contemporary discussion. If all the force and meaning of the old idea of original sin had disappeared from the religious consciousness of the day, it was largely the fault of orthodoxy, the religious element in the party of Memory. For that party, too, argued the case in almost exclusively historical terms, affirming the enslavement of the present by the past as heatedly as the hopeful insisted on its freedom. But the orthodox showed little awareness of the organic vitality of history, of the way in which the past can enliven the present: the past was simply the place where the issues had been decided, and the decision was all that mattered. The orthodox habit of presenting the end-product of religious belief drained of the spiritual impulses which had gone into the historical shaping of it led to a frozen but fragile structure, and one not likely to hold very long against the assaults of the opposition. The energetic hostility of the hopeful to the influence of the past, to the transmission of anything—be it laws, property, or ideas—gathered against the doctrine of transmitted guilt—and overwhelmed it.

The stand on the Trinity followed. For if the individual started on his spiritual career with an unsullied conscience, there was no need for expiation; there was no need, as the Unitarians were willing to say quite explicitly, of a propitiation for our sins. The sacrifice of the god satisfied a human yearning for a redemption possible only by a divine action; but the yearning vanished along with the sense of sin. The reason for the divinity of Jesus evaporated; and he became, like Paul, one of the most admirable of the characters in ancient history. The third member of the Trinity was no less rapidly defunctionalized by the hopeful attitude; for in a view which rested upon a freedom from history, upon a lack of communion between one generation and the next, there was no function for a continuing presence in time and history, for a guaranty of the unity of all ages.

The Unitarian *controversy* can be dated, as George Ellis dated it, from about 1805, when the Unitarian theories about man and God were introduced at Harvard by Henry Ware and given some sanction by his position as Hollis Professor of Divinity. Unitarianism itself, of course, went back much farther. Most of its doctrine had been preached by such disciples of Enlightenment and such anti-Edwardseans as Charles Chauncy and Jonathan Mayhew (who died in 1766). The natural goodness of man, the unlikelihood of hell, the benevolence and probable singularity of God were none of them novel propositions. They had made their appearance with the birth of Christianity; and the various heresies about the nature of Jesus, with their shifting corollaries about the nature of man, had been meticulously outlawed one by one in the great church councils of the first Christian centuries. They have recurred since at such regular intervals that their appearance can never be adequately explained in terms of immediate intellectual "background." Perhaps social psychology would be more helpful: what governs the rise and fall of man's evaluation of himself?

. . . .

. . . The excitement of life, for the hopeful, lay exactly in its present uniqueness; the burden of doubt and guilt had been disposed of when the whole range of European experience had been repudiated, for the burden was the chief product of that experience. The individual moral course was thus to be plotted—not in terms of readjustment or of identification with any portion of the past, and much less in terms of redemption—but simply in terms of the healthy cultivation of natural, unimpaired faculties.

The American was to be acknowledged in his complete emancipation from the history of mankind. He was to be recognized now for what he was—a new Adam, miraculously free of family and race, untouched by those dismal conditions which prior tragedies and entanglements monotonously prepared for the newborn European. Nathaniel Hawthorne, in his sympathetic and ironic way, had already furnished the working metaphor for this phase in the career of the New World's representative man: in a companion piece to "Earth's Holocaust," a fantasy called "The New Adam and Eve." It was the story of a second pair created after "the Day of Doom has burst upon the globe and swept away the whole race of man"—two pure people "with no knowledge of their predecessors nor of the diseased circumstances that had become encrusted around them." Innocent, cheerful, curious, they start forth on their way to discover, as Adam is made to observe, "what sort of world this is, and why we have been sent hither." Holmes, still insisting on the enabling portion of the past, could not have told them much about their fresh and purified world. But Walt Whitman, in *Leaves of Grass,* was ready to tell them everything.

II

Whitman appears as the Adamic man reborn here in the 19th century [JOHN BURROUGHS (1896)].

In his old age, Dr. Holmes derived a certain amount of polite amusement from the poetry of Walt Whitman. Whitman, Holmes remarked, "carried the principle of republicanism through the whole world of created objects"; he smuggled into his "hospitable vocabulary words which no English dictionary recognizes as belonging to the language—words which will be looked for in vain outside of his own pages." Holmes found it hard to be sympathetic toward *Leaves of Grass;* it seemed to him windy, diffuse, and humorless; but his perceptions were as lively as ever. In these two observations he points to the important elements in Whitman which are central here: the spirit of equality which animated the surging catalogues of persons and things (on its more earthly level, not unlike Emerson's lists of poets and philosophers, with their equalizing and almost leveling tendency); the groping after novel words to identify novel experiences; the lust for inventiveness which motivated what was for Whitman the great act, the creative act.

Holmes's tone of voice, of course, added that for him Whitman had gone too far; Whitman was too original, too republican, too entire an Adam. Whitman had indeed gone further than Holmes: a crucial and dimensional step further, as Holmes had gone further than Channing or Norton. In an age when the phrase "forward-looking" was a commonplace, individuals rarely nerved themselves to withstand the shock of others looking and moving even further forward than they. Emerson himself, who had gone so far that the liberal Harvard Divinity School forbade his presence there for more than thirty years, shared some of Holmes's feeling about Whitman. When his cordial letter welcoming *Leaves of Grass* in 1855 was published in the *New York Tribune*, Emerson muttered in some dismay that had he intended it for publication, he "should have enlarged the *but* very much—enlarged the *but*." *Leaves of Grass* "was pitched in the very highest key of self-reliance," as a friend of its author maintained; but Emerson, who had given that phrase its contemporary resonance, believed that any attitude raised to its highest pitch tended to encroach dangerously on the truth of its opposite.

It would be no less accurate to say that Walt Whitman, instead of going too far forward, had gone too far backward: for he did go back, all the way back, to a primitive Adamic condition, to the beginning of time.

In the poetry of Walt Whitman, the hopes which had until now expressed themselves in terms of progress crystallized all at once in a complete recovery of the primal perfection. In the early poems Whitman accomplished the epochal return by huge and almost unconscious leaps. In later poems he worked his way more painstakingly up the river of history to its source: as, for example, in "Passage to India," where the poet moves back from the recently constructed Suez Canal, back past Christopher Columbus, past Alexander the Great and the most ancient of heroes and peoples, to the very "secret of the earth and sky." In the "beginning," John Locke once wrote, "all the world was America." Whitman manages to make us feel what it might have been like; and he succeeds at last in presenting the dream of the new Adam—along with his sorrows.

A measure of Whitman's achievement is the special difficulty which that dream had provided for others who tried to recount it. Its character was such that it was more readily described by those who did not wholly share in it. How can absolute novelty be communicated? All the history of the philosophy of language is involved with that question, from *The Cratylus* of Plato to the latest essay on semantics; and one could bring to bear on it the variety of anecdotes about Adam's naming the animals by the disturbingly simple device of calling a toad a toad.

Hawthorne conveyed the idea of novelty by setting it in an ancient pattern: allowing it thereby exactly to be *recognized;* and reaching a sharpness of meaning also to be found in Tocqueville's running dialectic of democracies and aristocracies. Whitman employed the same tactic when he said of Coleridge that he was "like Adam in Paradise, and just as free from artificiality." This was a more apt description of himself, as he knew:

> I, chanter of Adamic songs,
> Through the new garden the West,
>   the great cities calling.

It is, in fact, in the poems gathered under the title *Children of Adam* (1860) that we have the most explicit evidence of his ambition to reach behind tradition to find and assert nature untroubled by art, to re-establish the natural unfallen man in the living hour. Unfallen man is, properly enough, unclothed as well; the convention of cover came in with the Fall; and Whitman adds his own unnostalgic sincerity to the Romantic affection for nakedness:

> As Adam, early in the morning,
> Walking forth from the bower refresh'd with sleep,
> Behold me where I pass, hear my voice, approach,
> Touch me, touch the palm of your hand to my body
>   as I pass,
> Be not afraid of my body.

For Whitman, as for Holmes and Thoreau, the quickest way of framing his novel outlook was by lowering, and secularizing, the familiar spiritual phrases: less impudently than Thoreau but more earnestly, and indeed more monotonously, but with the same intention of salvaging the human from the religious vocabulary to which (he felt) it had given rise. Many of Whitman's poetic statements are conversions of religious allusion: the new miracles were acts of the senses (an odd foreshortening, incidentally, of Edwards' Calvinist elaboration of the Lockian psychology); the aroma of the body was "finer than prayer"; his head was "more than churches, bibles and all creeds." "If I worship one thing more than another," Whitman declaimed, in a moment of Adamic narcissism, "it shall be the spread of my own body." These assertions gave a peculiar stress to Whitman's seconding of the hopeful belief in men like gods: "Divine am I, inside and out, and I make holy whatever I touch." Whitman's poetry is at every moment an act of turbulent incarnation.

But although there is, as there was meant to be, a kind of shock-value in such lines, they are not the most authentic index to his pervasive Adamism, because in them the symbols have become too explicit and so fail to work symbolically. Whitman in these instances is stating his position and contemplating it; he is betraying his own principle of indirect statement; he is telling us too much, and the more he tells us, the more we seem to detect the anxious, inflated utterance of a charlatan. We cling to our own integrity and will not be thundered at. We respond far less willingly to Whitman's frontal assaults than we do to his dramatizations; when he is enacting his role rather than insisting on it, we are open to persuasion. And he had been enacting it from the outset of *Leaves of Grass*.

This is the true nature of his achievement and the source of his claim to be the representative poet of the party of Hope. For the "self" in the very earliest of Whitman's poems is an individual who is always moving forward. To say so is not merely to repeat that Whitman believed in progress; indeed, it is in some sense to deny it. The young Whitman, at least, was not an apostle of progress in its customary meaning of a motion from worse to better to best, an improvement over a previous historic condition, a "rise of man." For Whitman, there was no past or "worse" to progress from; he moved forward because it was the only direction (he makes us think) in which he could move; because there was nothing behind him—or if there were, he had not yet noticed it. There is scarcely a poem of Whitman's before, say, 1867, which does not have the air of being the first poem ever written, the first formulation in language of the nature of persons and of things and of the relations between them; and the urgency of the language suggests that it was formulated in the very nick of time, to give the objects described their first substantial existence.

Nor is there, in *Leaves of Grass*, any complaint about the weight or intrusion of the past; in Whitman's view the past had been so effectively burned away that it had, for every practical purpose, been forgotten altogether. In his own recurring figure, the past was already a corpse; it was on its way out the door to the cemetery; Whitman watched it absent-mindedly, and turned at once to the living reality. He did enjoy, as he reminds us, reciting Homer while walking beside the ocean; but this was just because Homer was exempt from tradition and talking at and about the dawn of time. Homer was the poet you found if you went back far enough; and as for the sea, it had (unlike Melville's) no sharks in it— no ancient, lurking, destructible evil powers. Whitman's hope was unspoiled by memory. When he became angry, as he did in *Democratic Vistas* (1871), he was not attacking his generation in the Holgrave manner for continuing to accept the old and the foreign, but for fumbling its extraordinary opportunity, for taking a wrong turn on the bright new highway he had mapped for it. Most of the time he was more interested in the map, and we are more interested in him when he was.

It was then that he caught up and set to music the large contemporary conviction that man had been born anew in the new society, that the race was off to a fresh start in America. It was in *Leaves of Grass* that the optative mood, which had endured for over a quarter of a century and had expressed itself so variously and so frequently, seemed to have been transformed at last into the indicative. It was there that the hope that had enlivened spokesmen from Noah Webster in 1825 ("American glory begins at the dawn") to the well-named periodical, *Spirit of the Age* in 1849 ("The accumulated atmosphere of ages, containing stale ideas and opinions . . . will soon be among the things that were")—that all that stored-up abundance of hope found its full poetic realization. *Leaves of Grass* was a climax as well as a beginning, or rather, it was the climax of a long effort to begin.

This was why Emerson, with whatever enlarged "buts" in his mind, made a point of visiting Whitman in New York and Boston; why Thoreau, refusing to be put off "by any brag or egoism in his book," preferred Whitman to Bronson Alcott; and why Whitman, to the steady surprise of his countrymen, has been regarded in Europe for almost a century as unquestionably the greatest poet the New World has produced: an estimate which even Henry James would come round to. European readers were not slow to recognize in Whitman an authentic rendering of their own fondest hopes; for if much of his vision had been originally imported from Germany and France, it had plainly lost its portion of nostalgia en route. While European romanticism continued to resent the effect of time, Whitman was announcing that time had only just begun. He was able to think so because of the facts of immediate history in America during the years when he was maturing: when a world was, in some literal way, being created before his eyes. It was this that Whitman had the opportunity to dramatize; and it was this that gave *Leaves of Grass* its special quality of a Yankee Genesis: a new account of the creation of the world—the creation, that is, of a new world; an account this time with a happy ending for Adam its hero; or better yet, with no ending at all; and with this important emendation, that now the creature has taken on the role of creator.

It was a twofold achievement, and the second half of it was demanded by the first. We see the sequence, for example, in the development from section 4 to section 5 of "Song of Myself." The first phase was the identification of self, an act which proceeded by distinction and differentiation, separating the self from every element that in a traditional view might be supposed to be part of it: Whitman's identity card had no space on it for the names of his ancestry. The exalted mind which carried with it a conviction of absolute novelty has been described by Whitman's friend, the Canadian psychologist, Dr. R. M. Bucke, who relates it to what he calls Whitman's "cosmic consciousness." "Along with the consciousness of the cosmos [Dr. Bucke wrote], there occurs an intellectual enlightenment which alone would place the individual on a new plane of existence— would make him almost a member of a new species." *Almost a member of a new species:* that could pass as the slogan of each individual in the

party of Hope. It was a robust American effort to make real and operative the condition which John Donne once had merely feared:

> Prince, Subject, Father, Son are things forgot,
> For every man alone thinks he has got
> To be a Phoenix and that then can he
> None of that kind, of which he is, but he.

Whitman achieves the freedom of the new condition by scrupulously
peeling off every possible source of, or influence upon, the "Me myself,"
the "what I am." As in section 4 of "Song of Myself":

> Trippers and askers surround me
> People I meet, the effect upon me of my early life, or the
>   ward and the city I live in or the nation. . . .
> The sickness of one of my folks, or of myself, or the ill-
>   doing or loss or lack of money, or depressions or exaltations,
> Battles, the horror of fratricidal wars, the fever of doubtful
>   news, the fitful events,
> These come to me days and nights and go from me again,
> But they are not the Me myself.
> Apart from the pulling and hauling stands what I am;
> Stands amused, complacent, compassionating, idle, unitary;
> Looks down, is erect, or bends an arm on an impalpable
>   certain rest,
> Looking with side-curved head curious what will come next,
> Both in and out of the game, and watching and wondering
>   at it.

There is Emerson's individual, the "infinitely repellent orb." There is also
the heroic product of romanticism, exposing behind the mass of what
were regarded as inherited or external or imposed and hence superficial
and accidental qualities the true indestructible secret core of personality.
There is the man who contends that "nothing, not God, is greater to one
than one's self."

There, in fact, is the new Adam. If we want a profile of him, we could
start with the adjectives Whitman supplies: amused, complacent, com-
passionating, idle, unitary; especially unitary, and certainly very easily
amused; too complacent, we frequently feel, but always compassionate—
expressing the old divine compassion for every sparrow that falls, every
criminal and prostitute and hopeless invalid, every victim of violence or
misfortune. With Whitman's help we could pile up further attributes, and
the exhaustive portrait of Adam would be composed of a careful gloss on
each one of them: hankering, gross, mystical, nude; turbulent, fleshy,
sensual, eating, drinking, and breeding; no sentimentalist, no stander
above men and women; no more modest than immodest; wearing his hat

as he pleases indoors and out; never skulking or ducking or deprecating; adoring himself and adoring his comrades; afoot with his vision.

> Moving forward then and now and forever,
> Gathering and showing more always and with velocity,
> Infinite and omnigenous.

And announcing himself in language like that. For an actual illustration, we could not find anything better than the stylized daguerreotype of himself which Whitman placed as the Frontispiece of the first edition. We recognize him at once: looking with side-curved head, bending an arm on the certain rest of his hip, evidently amused, complacent, and curious; bearded, rough, probably sensual; with his hat on.

Whitman did resemble this Adamic archetype, according to his friend John Burroughs. "There was a look about him," Burroughs remembered, "hard to describe, and which I have seen in no other face,—a gray, brooding, elemental look, like the granite rock, something primitive and Adamic that might have belonged to the first man." The two new adjectives there are "gray" and "brooding"; and they belong to the profile, too, both of Whitman and of the character he dramatized. There was bound to be some measure of speculative sadness inherent in the situation. Not all the leaves Whitman uttered were joyous ones, though he wanted them all to be and was never clear why they were not. His ideal image of himself—and it is his best single trope for the new Adam—was that of a live oak he saw growing in Louisiana:

> All alone stood it and the mosses hung down from the
>   branches,
> Without any companion it grew there uttering joyous
>   leaves of dark green,
> And its look, rude, unbending, lusty, made me think of
>   myself.

But at his most honest, he admitted, as he does here, that the condition was somehow unbearable:

> I wondered how it could utter joyous leaves standing alone
>   there without a friend near, for I knew I could not. . . .
> And though the live-oak glistens there in Louisiana solitary
>   in a wide flat space,
> Uttering joyous leaves all its life without a friend a lover
>   near,
> I knew very well I could not.

Adam had his moments of sorrow also. But the emotion had nothing to do with the tragic insight; it did not spring from any perception of a genuine hostility in nature or lead to the drama of colliding forces. Whitman was wistful, not tragic. We might almost say that he was wistful because he was not tragic. He was innocence personified. It is not difficult to marshal a vast array of references to the ugly, the gory, and the sordid in his verses; brought together in one horrid lump, they appear as the expression of one who was well informed about the shabby side of the world; but though he offered himself as "the poet of wickedness" and claimed to be "he who knew what it was to be evil," every item he introduced as vile turns out, after all, to be merely a particular beauty of a different original coloration. "Evil propels me and reform of evil propels me, I stand indifferent." A sentiment like that can make sense only if the term "evil" has been filtered through a transfiguring moral imagination, changing in essence as it passes.

That sentiment, of course, is not less an expression of poetic than of moral motivation. As a statement of the poetic sensibility, it could have been uttered as easily by Shakespeare or Dante as by Whitman. Many of the very greatest writers suggest, as Whitman does, a peculiar artistic innocence, a preadolescent wonder which permits such a poet to take in and reproject whatever there is, shrinking from none of it. But in Whitman, artistic innocence merged with moral innocence: a preadolescent ignorance of the convulsive undertow of human behavior—something not at all shared by Dante or Shakespeare. Both modes of innocence are present in the poetry of Walt Whitman, and they are not at any time to be really distinguished. One can talk about this image of moral innocence only in terms of his poetic creation.

"I reject none, accept all, then reproduce all in my own forms." The whole spirit of Whitman is in the line: there is his strategy for overcoming his sadness, and the second large phase of his achievement, following the act of differentiation and self-identification. It is the creative phase, in that sense of creativity which beguiles the artist most perilously into stretching his analogy with God—when he brings a world into being. Every great poet composes a world for us, and what James called the "figure in the carpet" is the poet's private chart of that world; but when we speak of the poet's world—of Dostoevski's or Balzac's—we knowingly skip a phrase, since what we mean is Dostoevski's (or Balzac's) selective embodiment of an already existing world. In the case of Whitman, the type of extreme Adamic romantic, the metaphor gains its power from a proximity to the literal, as though Whitman really were engaged in the stupendous task of building a world that had not been there before the first words of his poem.

The task was self-imposed, for Whitman's dominant emotion, when it was not unmodified joy, was simple, elemental loneliness; it was a testimony to his success and contributed to his peculiar glow. For if the hero of *Leaves of Grass* radiates a kind of primal innocence in an innocent world, it was not only because he had made that world, it was also because he had begun by making himself. Whitman is an early example, and perhaps the most striking one we have, of the self-made man, with an undeniable grandeur which is the product of his manifest sense of having been responsible for his own being—something far more compelling than the more vulgar version of the rugged individual who claims responsibility only for his own bank account.

And of course he was lonely, incomparably lonely; no anchorite was ever so lonely, since no anchorite was ever so alone. Whitman's image of the evergreen, "solitary in a wide, flat space . . . without a friend a lover near," introduced what more and more appears to be the central theme of American literature, in so far as a unique theme may be claimed for it: the theme of loneliness, dramatized in what I shall later describe as the story of *the hero in space*. The only recourse for a poet like Whitman was to fill the space by erecting a home and populating it with companions and lovers.

Whitman began in an Adamic condition which was only too effectively realized: the isolated individual, standing flush with the empty universe, a primitive moral and intellectual entity. In the behavior of a "noiseless, patient spider," Whitman found a revealing analogy:

> A noiseless, patient spider
> I mark'd, where, on a little promontory, it stood out,
>   isolated,
> Mark'd how, to explore the vacant, vast surrounding,
> It launched forth filament, filament, filament, out of itself,
> Ever unreeling them—ever tirelessly speeding them.

"Out of itself." This is the reverse of the traditionalist attitude that, in Eliot's phrase, "home is where one starts from." Whitman acted on the hopeful conviction that the new Adam started from himself; having created himself, he must next create a home. The given in individual experience was no longer a complex of human, racial, and familial relationships; it was a self in a vacant, vast surrounding. Each simple separate person must forge his own framework anew. This was the bold, enormous venture inevitably confronted by the Adamic personality. He had to become the maker of his own conditions—if he were to have any conditions or any achieved personality at all.

There were, in any case, no conditions to *go back to*—to take upon one's self or to embody. There is in fact almost no indication at all in *Leaves of Grass* of a return or reversion, even of that recovery of childhood detected in *Walden*. Whitman begins after that recovery, as a child, seemingly self-propagated, and he is always going *forth;* one of his pleasantest poems was constructed around that figure. There is only the open road, and Whitman moves forward from the start of it. Homecoming is for the exile, the prodigal son, Adam after the expulsion, not for the new unfallen Adam in the western garden. Not even in "Passage to India" is there a note of exile, because there is no sense of sin ("Let others weep for sin"). Whitman was entirely remote from the view of man as an orphan which motivated many of the stories of Hawthorne and Melville and which underlay the characteristic adventure they narrated of the search for a father. Hawthorne, an orphan himself and the author of a book about England called *Our Old Home,* sometimes sent his heroes to Europe to look for their families; Melville dispatched his heroes to the bottom of the sea on the same mission. This was the old way of posing the problem: the way of mastering life by the recovery of home, though it might require descent to the land of the dead; but Whitman knew the secret of his paternity.

Whitman was creating a world, even though he often sounds as though he were saluting a world that had been lying in wait for him: "Salut au monde." In one sense, he is doing just that, welcoming it, acknowledging it, reveling in its splendor and variety. His typical condition is one of acceptance and absorption; the word which almost everyone who knew him applied to his distinguishing capacity was "absorptive." He absorbed life for years; and when he contained enough, he let it go out from him again. "I . . . accept all, then reproduce all in my own forms." He takes unflagging delight in the reproductions: "Me pleased," he says in "Our Old Feuillage"; it is the "what I am." But the pleasure of seeing becomes actual only in the process of naming. It is hard to recall any particular of life and work, of men and women and animals and plants and things, of body and mind, that Whitman has not somewhere named in caressing detail. And the process of naming is for Whitman nothing less than the process of creation. This new Adam is both maker and namer; his innocent pleasure, untouched by humility, is colored by the pride of one who looks on his work and finds it good. The things that are named seem to spring into being at the sound of the word. It was through the poetic act that Whitman articulated the dominant metaphysical illusion of his day and became the creator of his own world.

We have become familiar, a century after the first edition of *Leaves of Grass,* with the notion of the poet as the magician who "orders reality" by his use of language. That notion derived originally from the epochal change—wrought chiefly by Kant and Hegel—in the relation between the human mind and the external world; a change whereby the mind "thought order into" the sensuous mass outside it instead of detecting an order externally existing. Whitman (who read Hegel and who wrote a singularly flatulent poetic reflection after doing so) adapted that principle to artistic creativity with a vigor and enthusiasm unknown before James Joyce and his associates in the twentieth century. What is implicit in every line of Whitman is the belief that the poet *projects* a world of order and meaning and identity into either a chaos or a sheer vacuum; he does not *discover* it. The poet may salute the chaos; but he creates the world.

Such a conviction contributed greatly to Whitman's ever enlarging idea of the poet as the vicar of God, as the son of God—as God himself. Those were not new labels for the artist, but they had been given fresh currency in Whitman's generation; and Whitman held to all of them more ingenuously than any other poet who ever lived. He supervised the departure of "the priests" and the arrival of the new vicar, "the divine litteratus"; he erected what he called his novel "trinitas" on the base of "the true son of God, the poet"; he offered himself as a cheerful, divine scapegoat and stage-managed "my own crucifixion." And to the extent that he fulfilled his own demands for *the* poet—as laid down in the Preface to *Leaves of Grass* and in *Democratic Vistas*—Whitman became God the Creator.

This was the mystical side of him, the side which announced itself in the fifth section of "Song of Myself," and which led to the mystical vision of a newly created totality. The vision emerges from those lyrical sweeps through the universe in the later sections of the poem: the sections in which Whitman populated and gave richness and shape to the universe by the gift of a million names. We can round out our picture of Whitman as Adam—both Adam as innocent and Adam as namer—if we distinguish his own brand of mysticism from the traditional variety. Traditional mysticism proceeds by denial and negation and culminates in the imagery of deserts and silence, where the voice and the being of God are the whole of reality. Whitman's mysticism proceeds by expansive affirmation and culminates in plenitude and huge volumes of noise. Traditional mysticism is the surrender of the ego to its creator, in an eventual escape from the limits of names; Whitman's is the expansion of the ego in the act of creation itself, naming every conceivable object as it comes from the womb.

.   .   .   .

[THE FORTUNATE FALL: HENRY JAMES, SR.]

James was perhaps the most energetically hopeful man of his generation, with a hope, so to speak, exploding out of the tensions lying behind it. He was possessed of a transcendent cheerfulness derived from the experience and the full knowledge of tragedy. His cheerfulness was consequently less fragile and more solid than the buoyant innocence of the party of Hope. Along with a very few others, James suggested how the drama of Adam should proceed, or how, to put it differently, the young culture should finally achieve its maturity. James was convinced that the story was not yet finished.

This is to say—and it was the elder James's conscious intention—that he began his account of the representative American spiritual adventure where the professedly hopeful left off. His observations about some of them indicate as much: he referred to Emerson as his fair unfallen friend, and he decided later about Thoreau that he was "literally the most child-like, unconscious and unblushing egotist it has ever been my fortune to encounter in the ranks of manhood." The phrases build into a partial statement of James's program for Adam: for in order to enter the ranks of manhood, the individual (however fair) had to *fall*, had to pass beyond childhood in an encounter with "Evil," had to mature by virtue of the destruction of his own egotism. James's entire intellectual effort—the whole burden of what his wife and his children affectionately and vaguely called "father's ideas"—may be described as an immense salvaging of the American Adam. For unless he were salvaged, James felt, he would never be saved; and, unlike Whitman or Thoreau, James did believe that the moral problem was salvation rather than self-development.

. . . .

James looked forward with no less assurance than Emerson and Whitman to a human achievement of perfection; but the signal difference between James and his unfallen friends is indicated by his statement (in the letter about Whitman) that the perfection he had in mind was one "to which manifestly no one is born, but only *re*-born." His italics emphasized the same conviction in the sentence which followed: "We come to such states not by learning, only by *unlearning*." What had to die, what had to be unlearned, was the proposition, writ so extensively in *Leaves of Grass*, that the individual was the source of his own being. "He lived and breathed," William was to say about his father, "as one who knew he had not made himself." This was the knowledge which led him to his major principles: principles which, like the impulse behind them, were less intellectual concepts than (in William's words) "instinct and attitude, something realised at a stroke and felt like a fire in the breast." Such knowledge, moreover, was an accomplishment, gained through a kind of suffering so comprehensive that it might accurately be called a kind of death. Of his many narrations of this liberating tragedy, perhaps the most succinct occurs in *Society the Redeemed Form of Man* (1879):

The only hindrance to men's believing in God as a creator is their inability to believe in *themselves* as created. Self-consciousness, the sentiment of personality, the feeling I have of life in myself, absolute and underived from any other save in a natural way, is so subtly and powerfully atheistic, that, no matter how loyally I may be taught to insist upon creation as a mere traditional or legendary fact, I never feel inclined personally to believe in it, save as the fruit of some profound intellectual humiliation or hopeless inward vexation of spirit. My inward afflatus from this cause is so great, I am conscious of such superabounding personal life, that I am satisfied, for my own part at least, that my sense of self-hood must in some subtle exquisite way find itself wounded to death—find itself *become death*, in fact, *the only death I am capable of believing in*—before any genuine resuscitation is at all practicable for me.

This was the view of human development that motivated James's repeated observation that "the first and highest service which Eve renders
Adam is to throw him out of Paradise." James regarded the contemporary
ideal of man as Adam in Paradise as adolescent rubbish; "every man who
has reached even his intellectual teens," he wrote, "begins to suspect that
life is no farce . . . that it flowers and fructifies on the contrary out of the
profoundest tragic depths"; and he trained his most trenchant rhetoric
on the Adamic figure. The heroic and winsome hero of the idealists appeared, under the eye of the elder James, as "a dull, somnolent, unconscious clod," as an "innocent earthling," as "imbecile, prosaic, unad-
venturous." James clung to the older ending of the story of creation, just
as he continued to prefer the old "virile" pessimistic spirit of religion to
the "cuddling-up-to-God" of the "feeble Unitarian sentimentality." In the
Book of Genesis he found an allegory of every individual's spiritual adventure, of everyone, that is, who had the energy to grow up. Growing up
required the individuating crisis which in Genesis is dramatized as the
fall of Adam: the fatal, necessary quickening within the unconscious
chunk of innocence of the awareness of self.

The capital sin in the Jamesian universe was just this exclusive *self-
consciousness*, egotism, "proprium," or "selfhood," as he variously labeled
it. This was about as far as many personalities had the power to travel;
this was, for example, the limit of Thoreau's accomplishment; it was
about as far as the American culture had come: but James watched ex-
pectantly for that "transformation-scene in human affairs" (in his son
Henry's phrase) which would affect the drama of the culture and which
might be observed in the private history of certain individuals. That
transformation-scene, the second and greater crisis in experience, led
from total self-distrust to a rebirth of the personality as a *social* being:
one might say, to rebirth as a citizen of the holy and glorious city of
James. The new form of man, "the redeemed form of man," was society;
only the sin made possible the rebirth; and, for all its tragedy, it was a
necessary sin, and a subject for rejoicing.

James himself had undergone the entire complex experience, from an
early self-assertiveness, through the fearful evening in England in the
spring of 1844 when he was smitten by "a perfectly insane and abject
fear" which reduced him "from a state of firm, vigorous, joyful manhood
to one of almost helpless infancy," to a far more vigorous new life dedicated to preaching his own brand of socialism. It was in the light of his
own recollections that James could announce the ineluctable requirement
of a tragic *fall* in such robustly hopeful accents.

He examined the alternative hypothesis, which seemed to motivate the
expressions and the conduct of the Adamists. Supposing, James asked,
that their dream was a true dream and that men, in America or anywhere else, were truly sinless, truly exempt from the temptation and the
fall. The condition they would enjoy would in that case, however pleas-

ant, be aimless and "horticultural"; there would be no rise and no ambition to rise to the nobler condition of genuine manhood. The inadequacy of Adamism was eloquently set forth:

In Adam, then, formed from the dust and placed in Eden, we find man's natural evolution distinctly symbolized—his purely instinctual and passional condition—as winning and innocent as infancy no doubt, but also, happily, quite as evanescent. It is his purely genetic and *premoral* state, a state of blissful infantile delight unperturbed as yet by those fierce storms of the intellect which are soon to envelope and sweep it away, but also unvisited by a single glimpse of that Divine and halcyon calm of the heart in which these hideous storms will finally rock themselves to sleep. Nothing can indeed be more remote (except in pure imagery) from distinctively *human* attributes, or from the spontaneous life of man, than this sleek and comely Adamic condition, provided it should turn out an abiding one: because man in that case would prove a mere dimpled nursling of the skies, without ever rising into the slightest Divine communion or fellowship, without ever realising a truly Divine manhood and dignity.

That paragraph (it is from *Christianity the Logic of Creation* [1857]) condenses one of the most telling critiques ever formulated of an enduring phase of the American cultural temperament. And its tone is no less revealing than its content. There was nothing in James of that inverted pride in evil that has become almost the national counterpart of the continuing claim of innocence. Someone remarked to a friend of his that James puzzled him because "if he has a preference it is for evil"; but James's response to the conventional embrace of despair was summed up in a comment on Carlyle (Carlyle who, according to James's correspondent, pronounced "his usual putrid theory of the universe" in a series of remarks "interpolated with convulsive laughter"): "Never was anything more false than this worship of sorrow by Carlyle; he has picked it up out of past history and spouts it for mere display . . . it is the merest babble." James escaped the sterilities of both sides—the arrested development of infantile innocence and the premature old age of a paralyzing absorption with sin—by seeing the moral problem in unvarying dramatic terms: as a process, a story, with several grand climacterics.

It was this sense of a plot in experience that gave manifest sincerity to his account of the Fall—of Adam's fall and the fall of "every son of Adam"—as essentially fortunate. "Any one with half an eye," he wrote, "can see . . . that 'Adam's fall,' as it is called, was not that stupid lapse from the divine favor which it has vulgarly been reputed to have been, but an actual rise to the normal human level." He went on: "We certainly may, if we like, continue to vote this manly act of Adam disastrous . . . but to the deathless immortal part of man . . . it is anything but disastrous. It is an every way upward step indeed, pregnant with beatific consequences. . . . And accordingly every son of Adam . . . welcomes this puny, silly death, which inwardly *is* his proper consciousness, as his inevitable and unconscious resurrection to life." James's picture of the falling and the fallen was lit up at each instant by the radiance of the *vita nuova* which the "silly death" alone made possible.

But as we read these passages, we recover some of our original regret over the perverseness of his language. It was an extraordinarily private language; in his manipulation of it, James shows us the Emersonian man, spontaneously marking great truths with no regard whatever for their diversified historical formulations. His friend Garth Wilkinson indicated an important difference between himself and James when he acknowledged his own insistent attention to history. And we are not helped by James's habit of assaulting past doctrines in terms that suggest he must be thinking about their opposites. Even his son William, not the most dependable guide to intellectual history, had to comment upon his father's remarkable ignorance of the past: an ignorance which partly prevented him from communicating his analysis of the present.

For what James had hit on by the sheer force of his speculation was a variation on a very ancient theme: the theme of the "fortunate fall." In the history of Christian theology, the theme can be traced back almost to the fourth century A.D., and its most enduring formulation came in the medieval hymn which is sung during the Holy Saturday Mass.[2] The hymn is exultant; it is known, indeed, as the "Exultet"; it is the most poetic and the most transcendently hopeful answer that Christianity ever contrived to the old puzzle about the existence of evil in a world created by a benevolent God. "O felix culpa!" the hymn exclaims: "quae talem et tantum meruit habere redemptorem." ("O happy sin! to deserve so great a redeemer"). The theological implication is: that happiness may be predicated of the sin because, as a consequence of it, the world was enlarged and enlightened through the figure of the Redeemer and the joy of the Atonement. It is the imputation to the human event of the quality of the divine action. And the hymn thus paradoxically rejoices in the enforced departure of Adam from Eden: "O certe necessarium Adae peccatum"—certainly Adam's sin was necessary.

The Christian suggestion teeters on the verge of heresy, and, for all its cheerfulness, it has always made its proponents uneasy. But as a metaphor in the area of human psychology, the notion of the fortunate fall has an immense potential. It points to the necessary transforming shocks and

---

[2] See the essay, "Milton and the Paradox of the Fortunate Fall," in Arthur O. Lovejoy, *Essays in the History of Ideas* (Baltimore, 1948). Professor Lovejoy begins by quoting some lines from *Paradise Lost* (Book XII, ll. 462 ff.), beginning with Adam's response to the Archangel Michael: "O Goodness infinite, Goodness immense! /That all this good of evil shall produce,/And evil turn to good. . . . Full of doubt I stand,/Whether I should repent me now of sin/By me done or occasioned, or rejoice/ Much more that much more good thereof shall spring." Professor Lovejoy then traces the history of this paradox from the early centuries up to the writing of Milton.

sufferings, the experiments and errors—in short, the experience—through which maturity and identity may be arrived at. This was just the perception needed in a generation that projected as one of its major ideals the image of man as a fair unfallen Adam. The claims of newborn innocence for the individual in America inevitably elicited the response that innocence is inadequate for the full reach of human personality; that life, in James's words, "flowers and fructifies . . . out of the profoundest tragic depths." The ancient theme of the fortunate fall might have conveyed James's meaning with weight and authority.

How it might do so has been demonstrated in a later day by the extraordinarily dense little statement of dreaming Earwicker in Joyce's *Finnegans Wake:* "O foenix culprit! ex nickylow malo comes micklemassed bonum." Some of the nearly endless suggestions and combinations there are the following: that out of evil (malo), though it is related to the devil (nick) and is itself a nothingness (nickylow—*nihilo*), comes a vastness (mickle, mass) of good; a good symbolized by Michaelmas. Through the experience of evil, the perpetrator of the *culpa,* the culprit, is reborn like the phoenix; and thus the culprit is happy after all (*felix*).

Joyce was the very type of imagination in total communion with the whole of a many-stranded past. Henry James the elder, sharing his age's enthusiastic rejection of the past, was quite the opposite type. He had vaulted to the insight; but he lacked the language to articulate it. James had none of the dour nostalgic belief in inherited depravity; he accepted the principle that men began like Adam. But he went on to ask whether men must remain in the state of Adam—whether life had not more to offer than "this sleek and comely Adamic condition." He could not clearly and finally answer his own question: perhaps just because the insight he had seized upon was essentially dramatic and could therefore be better described in action than argued in syllogisms. The vocabulary he really needed was, one may hazard, the language of narrative literature. But James apparently never realized that something like a "fortunate fall"— explained and justified in terms much like his own—was central to the fiction of his friend Hawthorne and of Hawthorne's friend Melville. And he did not live long enough to read in his son Henry's novels a very comparable principle spelled out in extraordinary dramatic detail.

· · · · · · ·

THE RETURN INTO TIME: HAWTHORNE

. . . The essential continuity of American fiction explains itself through this historic transformation whereby the Adamic fable yielded to what I take to be the authentic American narrative. For much of that fable remained in the later narrative: the individual going forth toward experience, the inventor of his own character and creator of his personal history; the self-moving individual who is made to confront that "other"— the world or society, the element which provides experience. But as we move from Cooper to Hawthorne, the situation very notably darkens; qualities of evil and fear and destructiveness have entered; self-sufficiency is questioned through terrible trials; and the stage is set for tragedy. The solitary hero and the alien tribe; "the simple genuine self against the whole world"—this is still the given, for the American novelist. The variable is this: the novelist's sense of the initial tension—whether it is comforting, or whether it is potentially tragic; whether the tribe promises love, or whether it promises death.

Hawthorne was perhaps the first American writer to detect the inevitable doubleness in the tribal promise. For he was able by temperament to give full and fair play to both parties in the *agon:* to the hero and to the tribe as well. And, having done so, he penetrated to the pattern of action—a pattern of escape and return, at once tragic and hopeful—which was likely to flow from the situation as given. In addition, Hawthorne felt very deeply the intimacy between experience and art, and he enacted a change as well in the resources and methods of the narrative art: something which mirrored, even while it articulated, his heroes' and heroines' adventures. Finally, it was Hawthorne who saw in American experience the re-creation of the story of Adam and who, more than any other contemporary, exploited the active metaphor of the American as Adam—before and during and after the Fall. These are the three aspects of Hawthorne that I shall consider.

The opening scene of *The Scarlet Letter* is the paradigm dramatic image in American literature. With that scene and that novel, New World fiction arrived at its first fulfilment, and Hawthorne at his. And with that scene, all that was dark and treacherous in the American situation became exposed. Hawthorne said later that the writing of *The Scarlet Letter* had been oddly simple, since all he had to do was to get his "pitch" and then to let it carry him along. He found his pitch in an opening tableau fairly humming with tension—with coiled and covert relationships that contained a force perfectly calculated to propel the action thereafter in a direct line to its tragic climax.

It was the tableau of the solitary figure set over against the inimical society, in a village which hovers on the edge of the inviting and perilous wilderness; a handsome young woman standing on a raised platform, confronting in silence and pride a hostile crowd whose menace is deepened by its order and dignity; a young woman who has come alone to the New World, where circumstances have divided her from the community now gathered to oppose her; standing alone, but vitally aware of the private enemy and the private lover—one on the far verges of the crowd, one at the place of honor within it, and neither conscious of the other—who must affect her destiny and who will assist at each other's destruction. Here the situation inherent in the American scene was seized entire and without damage to it by an imagination both moral and visual of the highest quality: seized and located, not any longer on the margins of the plot, but at its very center.

The conflict is central because it is total; because Hawthorne makes us respect each element in it. Hawthorne felt, as Brown and Cooper and Bird had felt, that the stuff of narrative (in so far as it was drawn from local experience) consisted in the imaginable brushes between the deracinated and solitary individual and the society or world awaiting him. But Hawthorne had learned the lesson only fitfully apprehended by Cooper. In *The Scarlet Letter* not only do the individual and the world, the conduct and the institutions, measure each other: the measurement and its consequences are precisely and centrally what the novel is about. Hester Prynne has been wounded by an unfriendly world; but the society facing her is invested by Hawthorne with assurance and authority, its opposition is defensible and even valid. Hester's misdeed appears as a disturbance of the moral structure of the universe; and the society continues to insist in its joyless way that certain acts deserve the honor of punishment. But if Hester has sinned, she has done so as an affirmation of life, and her sin is the source of life; she incarnates those rights of personality that society is inclined to trample upon. The action of the novel springs from the enormous but improbable suggestion that the society's estimate of the moral structure of the universe may be tested and found inaccurate.

The Scarlet Letter, like all very great fiction, is the product of a controlled division of sympathies; and we must avoid the temptation to read it heretically. It has always been possible to remark, about Hawthorne, his fondness for the dusky places, his images of the slow movement of sad, shut-in souls in the half-light. But it has also been possible to read *The Scarlet Letter* (not to mention "The New Adam and Eve" and "Earth's Holocaust") as an indorsement of hopefulness: to read it as a hopeful critic named Loring read it (writing for Theodore Parker's forward-looking *Massachusetts Quarterly Review*) as a party plea for self-reliance and an attack upon the sterile conventions of institutionalized society. One version of him would align Hawthorne with the secular residue of Jonathan Edwards; the other would bring him closer to Emerson. But Hawthorne was neither Emersonian nor Edwardsean; or rather he was both. The characteristic situation in his fiction is that of the Emersonian figure, the man of hope, who by some frightful mischance has stumbled into the time-burdened world of Jonathan Edwards. And this grim picture is given us by a writer who was skeptically cordial toward Emerson, but for whom the vision of Edwards, filtered through a haze of hope, remained a wonderfully useful metaphor.[3] The situation, in the form which Hawthorne's ambivalence gave it, regularly led in his fiction to a moment of crucial choice: an invitation to the lost Emersonian, the thunder-struck Adam, to make up his mind—whether to accept the world he had fallen into, or whether to flee it, taking his chances in the allegedly free wilderness to the west. It is a decision about ethical reality, and most of Hawthorne's heroes and heroines eventually have to confront it.

That is why we have the frantic shuttling, in novel after novel, between the village and the forest, the city and the country; for these are the symbols between which the choice must be made and the means by which moral inference is converted into dramatic action. Unlike Thoreau or Cooper, Hawthorne never suggested that the choice was an easy one. Even Arthur Mervyn had been made to reflect on "the contrariety that exists between the city and the country"; in the age of hope the contrariety was taken more or less simply to lie between the restraints of custom and the fresh expansiveness of freedom. Hawthorne perceived greater complexities. He acknowledged the dependence of the individual, for nourishment, upon organized society (the city), and he believed that it was imperative "to open an intercourse with the world." But he knew that the city could destroy as well as nourish and was apt to destroy the person most in need of nourishment. And while he was responsive to the attractions of the open air and to the appeal of the forest, he also understood the grounds for the Puritan distrust of the forest. He retained that distrust as a part of the symbol. In the forest, possibility was unbounded; but just because of that, evil inclination was unchecked, and witches could flourish there.

For Hawthorne, the forest was neither the proper home of the admirable Adam, as with Cooper; nor was it the hideout of the malevolent adversary, as with Bird. It was the ambiguous setting of moral choice, the scene of reversal and discovery in his characteristic tragic drama. The forest was the pivot in Hawthorne's grand recurring pattern of escape and return.

It is in the forest, for example, that *The Scarlet Letter* version of the pattern begins to disclose itself: in the forest meeting between Hester and Dimmesdale, their first private meeting in seven years. During those years, Hester has been living "on the outskirts of the town," attempting to cling to the community by performing small services for it, though there had been nothing "in all her intercourse with society . . . that made her feel as if she belonged to it." And the minister has been contemplating the death of his innocence in a house fronting the village graveyard. The two meet now to join in an exertion of the will and the passion for free-

---

[3] Cf. the fine observation and the accompanying discussion of Mark Van Doren, in *Nathaniel Hawthorne* (1949), p. 162: "Hawthorne did not need to believe in Puritanism in order to write a great novel about it. He had only to understand it, which for a man of his time was harder."

'es that they can escape along
ection it goes "backward to the
deeper it goes, and deeper into
.ves will show no vestiges of the
roused by their encounter drives
heart of the society, to the peni-
: of the book's structure.

harp, the agony so intense. But the
: *Faun,* as Miriam and Donatello flee
oded Apennines to waste their illicit
ley must return to Rome and the re-
true that Zenobia, in *The Blithedale*
. her flight: because her escape consum-
drowns in the river running through the
. Zenobia, who is often associated in the
narrator s ⌐   of Eve, is too much of an Eve to survive
her private calamity.   e usual outcome—more usual, that is, with
Hawthorne—is realized in a sort of tremulous parody by the abortive
train ride of Hepzibah and Clifford Pyncheon in *The House of the Seven
Gables*—"the flight of the two owls," who get only a station or so along
the line into the country before limping back to town to confess to a
crime which has not after all been committed.

It is poor Clifford who most blatantly gives voice to the contemporary
aspirations imitated in these journeys, as he babbles on in an echo of the
hopeful language he must have heard from Holgrave, the daguerreotypist.
Homelessness, he explains to an embarrassed fellow-passenger, is the
best of conditions; "the soul needs air: a wide sweep and a frequent
change of it." He sees "the world and my best days before me" and is
sure the flight has restored him to "the very heydey of my youth." These
exclamations comprise the first principles of Adamism; Clifford trembles
in the untenable belief that he has fulfilled the action attributed (by
Lawrence) to Cooper's Hawkeye—the motion "backwards from old age
to golden youth." The ironic context for his babbling and the total collapse that it rapidly leads to reveal that here, for the first time in
American fiction, the story of Adam has become an element of the story
actually being narrated—and so begins to suffer serious modifications.
Clifford, too, wants to make that leap from memory to hope; his Adamic
ambition is an ingredient in the novel; but his leap is Icarian.

Many things are being *tested* as well as exemplified in these circular
journeys, in the pattern of escape and return. Among them, the doctrine
inherited from Edwards that "an evil taint, in consequence of a crime
committed twenty or forty years ago, remain[s] still, and even to the end
of the world and forever." Among them, too, the proposition, implicit in
much American writing from Poe and Cooper to Anderson and Hemingway, that the valid rite of initiation for the individual in the new world

is not an initiation *into* society, but, given the character of society, an initiation *away from it:* something I wish it were legitimate to call "*de*initiation." The true nature of human wickedness is also in question. Hawthorne's heroes and heroines are almost always criminals, according to the positive laws of the land, but Hawthorne presumed all men and women to be somehow criminals, and himself not the least so. The elder James reported to Emerson how Hawthorne had looked to him at a Saturday Club meeting in Boston: "like a rogue who finds himself in the company of detectives"; we can imagine him there: furtive, uneasy, out of place, half-guilty and half-defiant, poised for instant flight. No doubt it was because he appraised his personal condition this way that Hawthorne so frequently put his characters in the same dilemma: James's comment is a droll version of the opening glimpse of Hester Prynne. And no doubt also this was why Hawthorne so obviously sympathized with what he nevertheless regarded as an impossible enterprise—the effort to escape.

But if he customarily brought his sufferers back *into* the community; if he submitted most of his rogues to ultimate arrest; if the "evil taint" does turn out to be ineradicable, it was not because Hawthorne yielded in the end to the gloomy doctrine of Edwards. It was much rather because, for all his ambivalence, Hawthorne had made a daring guess about the entire rhythm of experience and so was willing to risk the whole of it. His qualifications as a novelist were at stake; for if the guess had been less comprehensive, he would have been a novelist of a very different kind: an inferior Melville, perhaps, exhausting himself in an excess of response to every tragic, new, unguessed-at collision. But if the guess had been any more certain, he might scarcely have been a novelist at all, but some sort of imperturbable tractarian. As it was, he could share some part of the hope of motivating the flight; he could always see beyond the hope to the inevitable return; and he could even see a little distance beyond the outcome of surrender to the light and strength it perhaps assured.

Beneath the sunshine that illuminates the soul's surface, he once wrote, there is a region of horror that seems, to the inward traveler, "like hell itself," and through which the self wanders without hope; but deeper still there is a place of perfect beauty. He was not often so certain, but that was the substance of his guess about experience. And this is why there is always more to the world in which Hawthorne's characters move than any one of them can see at a glance. There is more than the surface sunshine covering the whole horizon of the hopeful of his day or his fiction—his "new Adam and Eve," the comfortable customers of his "Celestial Railroad," in their untested faith in human purity and in a new world all the braver because it had stamped out the past. But there is more too, much more, than the darkness, the monsters, and the divers shapes which tormented the souls of the lost and the guilty—Mr. Hooper behind his black veil, Reuben Bourne of "Roger Melvin's Burial," young

Goodman Brown. There was still some fulfilment of the spirit, some realization of the entire self which it was worth losing one's self to find; only the lost, indeed, were likely to find it on their return journey, though a soul might shrivel, like young Brown's, in the process.

The Continuity of American Poetry

ROY HARVEY PEARCE

[Antinomianism]

. . . [T]he achievement of American poetry is a good measure of the achievement of American culture as a whole. The poet's particular relation to his culture—his self-imposed obligation to make the best possible use of the language he is given—is such as to put him at the center of the web of communications which gives his culture its characteristic style and spirit. The poet continually inquires into the genuineness and comprehensiveness of that style and spirit. He asks—above all, in the United States he has asked—how much it has cost to achieve them. And he measures the cost in terms of something as simple, and as difficult, as his sense of the dignity of man.

As the idea of the dignity of man has been threatened in American culture, and as it has survived, so has the idea of poetry itself. American poets have always been conservatives—often so radical in their conservatism as to seem to be revolutionaries, when all they are trying to do is to work such transformations on language as would enable their readers to understand the nature of the threat, the means whereby it might be resisted, and the conditions of survival. The net result is that poets have as often as not been put on the defensive by those whom they would defend. The history of their writing, the history their writing makes, manifests their continuing heroic role, on the margin of the American sensibility, yet plunging directly to its vital center.

The history—as we can construct it after the fact, knowing in the beginning how it will end—has a simple plot. I have come to think it is perhaps too simple. The simplicity derives from the American poet's compulsion (or obligation) again and again to justify his existence as poet. American poetry is characteristically tendentious, over-committed, programmatic, self-conscious, often—even in its moments of grandeur—provincial and jejune. It begins with the efforts of seventeenth-century Puritans to make poems in a world dedicated to the proposition that man could really "make" nothing. Thus, whatever else they may have intended, there is a curious antinomianism—to use a good Puritan word—in their poetry; and it is this antinomianism—*in extremis,* as it were—which increasingly characterizes the work of later poets, who of necessity write in what is essentially a Puritan tradition. American poets, however much they have wanted to say yes, have never been able to conceive of doing so until they have said no. The classic statement surely is Melville's, in his letter to Hawthorne, 16 April (?) 1851: "There is the grand truth about Nathaniel Hawthorne. He says NO! in thunder; but the Devil himself cannot make him say *yes.* For all men who say *yes,* lie; and all men who say *no,*—why, they are in the happy conditions of judicious, unincumbered travellers in Europe; they cross the frontiers into Eternity with nothing but a carpet-bag,—that is to say, the Ego. Whereas those *yes*-gentry, they travel with heaps of baggage, and damn them! they will never get through the Custom House. . . ." The question has always been: What is the necessary relationship of the poet's inevitable yes to his compulsive no. How say no with Ahab, so to say yes with Ishmael?

In short, the power of American poetry from the beginning has derived from the poet's inability, or refusal, at some depth of consciousness wholly to accept his culture's system of values. By the nineteenth century that refusal, freed from its matrix in Puritan dogma, had been in effect transformed into its opposite, a mode of assent; and the American poet again and again imaged himself—in Emerson's and Whitman's word—as an Adam who, since he might well be one with God, was certainly one with all men. The continuity of this narrative is that of the antinominian, Adamic impulse, as it thrusts against a culture made by Americans who come more and more to be frightened by it, even as they realize it is basic to the very idea of their society: one (in Whitman's words) of simple, separate persons, yet democratic, en-masse.

In Whitman, brought to a boil as he was by Emerson, the impulse led to a discovery of the American version of "modern" poetry, in which the poet quite self-consciously takes over as trustee of language and the ways of language with the sensibility. In the 1850's Whitman jotted down in his notebook: "A perfect user of words uses things—they exude in power and beauty from him—miracles in his hands—miracles from his mouth. . . ." And also: "Likely there are other words wanted.—Of words wanted, the matter is summed up in this: When the time comes for them to represent any thing or state of things, the words will surely follow. . . ."[1] The task set for modern man, would he preserve, or recover, his dignity, is not only to mean what he is saying, but know it.

[1] *An American Primer,* ed. H. Traubel (Boston, 1904), pp. 14, 21.

What the American poet does with his "modernism," how he contains it—this is the central subject of this book. The "Americanness" of American poetry is, quite simply, its compulsive "modernism"—or, with some poets in the twentieth century, its compulsive "traditionalism," which is, ironically enough, a form of "modernism." The conditions of modern life, of nineteenth- and twentieth-century life, have in the United States as elsewhere brought the poet to discover in the antinomian impulse a necessary means to the freedom without which there could not be a full sense of that sort of community in which men may realize the dignity which makes them human. The American poet, in his dedication to the idea of the dignity of man, has had as his abiding task the reconciliation of the impulse to freedom with the impulse to community, as the use of language in poetry may help bring it about.

I shall deal in turn with expressions (and with repressions too) of that twin impulse up to our own times, when it has been followed out to its bitterest and fullest implications (by Wallace Stevens) and when it has been subjected to a "mythic," orthodox religious transformation, whereby, as it is shown to be "merely" human, it becomes the means of demonstrating its own inadequacy (by T. S. Eliot.) The narrative, as I shall indicate in the Afterword, properly closes with Stevens and Eliot. The one stakes all on the radical sufficiency of humanism; the other, on its radical insufficiency. For the one, freedom, as it is manifested in poetry, guarantees us all the community we can desire; for the other, community, likewise as it is manifested in poetry, guarantees us all the freedom we can bear. In the later work of Stevens and Eliot, the impulse, no longer taken for granted, is conceived of as fixing a set of either/or alternatives: at the extreme, man as against God. It might well be that the alternatives are false. But, in any case, the impulse—which is the impulse to find a place for poetry in the life of modern man—persists. And now, in our own time, there is set for poets the task of finding new modes of reconciliation.

·   ·   ·   ·   ·   ·   ·

[THE ADAMIC VS. THE MYTHIC]

In one sense, then, the history of American poetry is the history of an impulse toward antinomianism: an antinomianism which in the nineteenth century and after seemed to be the last refuge of man in a world he was by then willing, or daring, to admit he himself had made and was therefore obliged to make over. Or, from a related point of view: That history is the record of a gradual but nonetheless revolutionary shift in the meaning of "invention": from "coming upon" something made and ordered by God, to "making" and "ordering"—transforming—something, anything, into that which manifests above all man's power to make and to order. By the end of the revolution, the thing made came to be an occasion only for the making—with the poet instructing his reader, not in what it means to contemplate creations, but rather to participate in the creating. The antinomian drive to accept only one's own testimony as to the worth and authority of the powers-that-be became the "Romantic" drive to testify that one can really know only one's own power, and yet that an element of such knowledge is the realization that all other men have this power too. Whereas the Puritan community was made up of individuals whose sense of their individuality told them only that they were nothing except as God made them so, the "Romantic" community was made up of individuals who could acknowledge God only to the degree that their idea of the godhead demonstrated that they were nothing except as their individuality made them so. In seventeenth-century New England, antinomianism was taken to threaten the existence of the community. In the nineteenth century, antinomianism was taken to make the community possible. We are so familiar with the latter formulation (contained, most notoriously, in Whitman's hymning at once the simple, separate person, yet democratic, en-masse) that we do not associate it with the first, which it inverts and so transforms. The transformative continuity of the first formulation into the second is, in fact, the great leap of the human spirit (*genus Americanus*) with which our poetry came into being: the paradox of a Puritan faith at once reborn and transformed, its principle of negation transmuted into a principle of affirmation.

. . . .

The Adamic poem—to define it as a basic style, a kind of ideal type— is one which portrays the simple, separating inwardness of man as that which at once forms and is formed by the vision of the world in which it has its being. Expressively, this poem is one which makes us aware of the operation of the creative imagination as an act of self-definition— thus, whether the poet wills it or not, of self-limitation. The poem may nominally argue for many things, may have many subjects, may be descriptive of the world at large; but always it will implicitly argue for one thing—the vital necessity of its own existence and of the ego which creates and informs it. Its essential argument, its basic subject, is the life of poetry itself, as this life makes viable a conception of man as in the end, whatever commitments he has had to make on the way, radically free to know, be, and make himself.

. . . .

Pound's hope for [a] fit audience though few rose out of his belief not only that a new kind of poetry was needed but that the older kind was no longer viable. (The older kind was, to be sure, the nineteenth-century Whitmanian kind; and the new kind was in the end simply a revival of one of the oldest kinds.) By the 1920's, with the *Cantos,* he came to believe he had established that new kind: a new mode of the imagination, whereby he might literally create that audience (in his highest hopes, it was to be a new "popular" audience). He would literally create (where Whitman would have released) its essential humanity: to have great audiences there must be great poets. This mode was that of what I shall call the *mythic* poem, because it would depend for its authority on a power which is by definition beyond man and his works. Moreover, as we shall see in the next chapter, it was for such a poem, so named, that poets in this vein most often called when they came to justify their way with language. With Pound's pronouncements, with his rising fame as critic, editor, and literary advisor in general, the mythic poem began to achieve status as a literary form—for a time seemingly the chief literary form of the twentieth-century. Robinson—not to say the multitude of poetasters— had driven the poem conceived in the image of an American Adam as far as it could go, and had turned in his later work to something approximating the mythic poem. Frost, in all his power and magnificence, could only make this traditional American mode a means to wise caution and skepticism. After Pound there was Eliot, and then the Fugitives—chiefly Ransom and Tate. With them, the mythic poem took its appropriate shape, as it leaned toward regionalism, tradition, orthodox religion, and an overpowering sense of the past—all principles of continuity derived from those large, extra-human, form-giving patterns of belief and commitment called myths. As some poets became clearer and clearer as to the stake they had in the principle of myths, others as a consequence became clearer and clearer as to the need not only for a genuine revival of the Adamic poem but for a reconception of its form-giving principle. The continuity of the Adamic poem called forth its apparent opposite, the mythic poem; and this in turn called forth a revival of the Adamic poem. Pound claimed to have set in motion a "counter-current." But the current of the continuity of American poetry from the seventeenth century to the twentieth still ran strong, stronger indeed because of the counter-current which it ran against. An issue, the central issue of twentieth-century American poetry, was joined.

·   ·   ·   ·   ·   ·   ·

[Eliot and the Mythic Poem]

In 1932 Pound, as was his habit, set his readers straight about the meaning of his own work and Eliot's:

"[Mr Eliot] displayed great tact, or enjoyed good fortune, in arriving in London at a particular date with a formed style of his own. He also participated in a movement to which no name has ever been given.

"That is to say, at a particular date in a particular room, two authors, neither engaged in picking the other's pocket, decided that dilutation of *vers libre,* Amygism, Lee Masterism, general floppiness had gone too far and that some counter-current must be set going."[2]

In Eliot's work the counter-current, as Pound testified later in the same essay, did not really begin to move until that (apocryphal?) particular date in a particular room. Still, there were sufficient anticipatory and pre-figurative signs of the movement.

The protagonists of the poems collected in *Prufrock and Other Observations* (1917) are such as to manifest the very exhaustion of the ego which set Pound and Eliot to searching for a new (or, as they came to insist, renewed) poetic mode. The "Lady" whose "Portrait" Eliot draws is like someone out of E. A. Robinson; but there is in this poem none of the precision and self-defeating honesty of Robinson's best portraits. Observing his Lady, listening to her, meditating her fate, the poet concludes:

> Well! and what if she should die some afternoon,
> Afternoon grey and smoky, evening yellow and rose;
> Should die and leave me sitting pen in hand
> With the smoke coming down above the housetops;
> Doubtful, for a while
> Not knowing what to feel or if I understand.

This is honest enough, but really not very clear. Indeed, such clarity as the poem has resides in its epigraph, from *The Jew of Malta:*

> *Thou has committed—*
> *Fornication; but that was in another country,*
> *And besides, the wench is dead.*

We gather that it is that other country which the poet cannot understand. Obviously lacking in "Portrait of a Lady" is the motivating force, the sense of the human situation, which will make for continuity and integral, not to say organic, form. Eliot could not (would not?) endow the speaker with such insight into motivation as would make of the poem that sort of whole composition in which one part leads to and demands the next. In short, from the very beginning the autobiographical mode, much less the narrative, has simply not been Eliot's *métier.*

If it be objected that the whole of Eliot's work is the record of a spiritual autobiography, I would grant the objection and then point out that spiritual autobiographies derive their motivating force not from the lesser spirits whose autobiographies they are but from a greater spirit

---

[2] Quoted from *The Criterion,* July 1932, in Espey, *Ezra Pound's Mauberly,* p. 25. The actual meeting seems to have taken place late in 1914, when Conrad Aiken, who had succeeded in getting Miss Monroe to publish "Prufrock" in *Poetry,* either took Eliot to Pound or gave him a letter of introduction. (See Aiken's and Eliot's recollections as quoted in Charles Moorman, *Ezra Pound* [New York, 1960], pp. 165–168.)

which informs the lesser—from history, or myth, or God. As a matter of fact, in the long run Eliot's sense of that greater spirit, being increasingly motivated thus, is much surer than Pound's; for in Pound that greater spirit tends, in spite of his efforts in the *Rock-Drill Cantos* and later, increasingly to reflect merely "the cultural" and can be formulated and objectified in terms whose adequacy no one but Pound can judge.

As "The Love Song of J. Alfred Prufrock" is in every way the other side of the coin from "Portrait of a Lady," it manifests the fact that the counter-current was moving even before Pound began to have his influence on Eliot. The epigraph from Dante defines the limiting situation of the poem. From the beginning we are given the self-portrait of a man who knows his own inadequacy to draw it and suffers accordingly. The "metaphysical" conceits in the poem are appropriate to this man for whom formal ratiocination must take the place of simple, spontaneous thought, analysis the place of the exercise of the sensibility. Prufrock's is yet another exhausted ego, able to celebrate, in pathetic irony, only its own exhaustion. Choosing such a one for his protagonist, Eliot can in bitter pity reveal to us Prufrock's abject inferiority to even "the women [who] come and go / Talking of Michelangelo," not to say the Hamlet who, in so far as he can bring himself to have one, is his ego ideal. The poet surely is not Prufrock; yet Prufrock is surely an aspect of the poet's sensibility, one which must carry its self-exhaustion to the end, so that there will be achieved that spiritual vacuum which only a greater spirit can fill. The formal achievement of this poem, since it has come to be archetypal for the formal achievement of so many other poems, is one which we too easily fail to see: In "Prufrock" Eliot measures the failure of a modern sensibility in the very terms which, so he believes, will, after the failure has been measured and faced up to, constitute its means to success. One's residual impression is neither of a protagonist, a poem, nor a poet, but of a force which teaches the last to care enough for the first so that he can destroy him in the second. As early as "Prufrock," then, Eliot knew how to care and not to care.

For the poet writing in this mode, the formal problem is one of sustaining the nice tension between caring and not caring—looking to that restoration of modern man from the ruins of nineteenth-century egocentrism, while yet not strengthening his ego so much as to set him once more on his way to his own ruination. Eliot's search for the means to this end is well known, as are the means themselves. The search and the means discovered are recorded in a vast literature of exegesis and redaction. Techniques, models, sources, parallels, and the like—Eliot had recourse to them, because only they could furnish him the means of defining, as opposed to creating or re-creating, the modern ego. Indeed, he has gone so far as to minimize his own ultimate role as the maker of his poems, as though this might smack of that fatal egocentrism. The emphasis in his criticism, and that which his has so greatly influenced, has been on the poet as "craftsman," not "maker."

The history of Eliot's poetry before his major achievement, "The Waste Land" (1922) is the history of a technique, a technique which would make possible the restoration of the idea of man as the creature, not the creator, of his world. In the course of events, that world would turn out not to be his after all. Most important here are the Sweeney poems and the kind they exemplify: hyperallusive, written in a quatrain imitated from Gautier, with a diction modeled after Laforgue's; in a tone recalling Donne's; and intended to carry over some of the disciplined rigor and inclusiveness of sensibility of all the poets whose work they echo. The Eliot of the Sweeney poems, as we have been often told, is the poet of the unification (following upon the dissociation) of the modern sensibility. But he would show that the means whereby to strive for that unification have been given to him and are by no means his alone. At one extreme is "Burbank with a Baedeker: Bleistein with a Cigar." Here, beginning with his inordinately complex epigraph (drawing from at least five writers), Eliot views with rather heavy-handed irony the descent into meaninglessness of one European tradition. At the other extreme, is "Sweeney among the Nightingales," in which the American, savage and vulgar in his blind egocentrism, is defined in relation to a larger, alien kind of order in which he cannot participate. Such poems are dazzling, to be sure; but they suffer from their own sort of over-insistence and do not quite avoid the ambiguous dangers of their kind. For their protagonists are so exhausted of their egos as not to be persons at all, just functions of their creator's understandable anxiety about the state of the world and those who inhabit it.

"Gerontion" (1920), which seems originally to have been intended to be part of "The Waste Land,"[3] is the first of Eliot's great poems in the mode he has made both his own and his culture's. Here Eliot begins to move from denial for the sake of denial to denial for the sake of affirmation. The mode is one in which the effect is not of creating but of being created. This is the basic style of the poem of the counter-current and compares with that of, say, Emerson's poems as do the *Cantos* with *Song of Myself*. In "Gerontion," as in "Prufrock," there is a delicately balanced portrayal of a protagonist against the backdrop of his world; still, he exists only in so far as he can "use" the elements of that backdrop in composing his so wearily pathetic song of himself. As the poem develops, the backdrop comes to have much more substantiality than does he who places himself (or should one say: is placed?) against it. The form of the poem is set initially by the tension of protagonist against background and finally by the collapse of that tension, as the protagonist loses himself in

[3] See Grover Smith, T. S. *Eliot's Poetry and Plays* (Chicago, 1956), pp. 65–66.

the background. The title indicates that the modern ego is characteristically that of an old man (like Tiresias in "The Waste Land"), living out his dry days, bravely allowing his sense of the past to tell him what he is and, in the telling, to overwhelm him. He dreams of the juvenescence of the year in which "Came Christ the tiger." This Christ is not yet God; he is rather the Christ-figure of "The Waste Land": one among several who manifest that gift of grace and order for which modern man yearns and which he yet fears. In this poem Eliot comes to see that his problem, modern man's problem, is one of a history, his own, which man cannot forget. The cluttered memories which fill the old man's mind are fused into a single pattern because, adding up to his history, they define the single pattern of his life. We do not look for him to initiate his thoughts and work them through; he is his thoughts; he is, in the end, *only* his thoughts, his memory, his history.

Here, most clearly, the Adamic principle of nineteenth-century American poetry is foresworn; or rather, here Adam is taken to be modern man's ancestor in historical fact, not an ever-contemporary, ever-possible image after which he must model himself:

> After such knowledge, what forgiveness? Think now
> History has many cunning passages, contrived corridors
> And issues, deceives with whispering ambitions,
> Guides us by vanities. Think now
> She gives when our attention is distracted
> And what she gives, gives with such supple confusions
> That the giving famishes the craving.

This, as it has often been observed, was the lesson into which Henry Adams (whose work is alluded to in "Gerontion") educated himself. He too came to believe that the American ego, like that of all modern men, was about to exhaust itself and its potential for creativity. With Eliot, he too could say, "We would see a sign!" The sign would not only signify the destiny of man, now ready to face fully up to his fate; it would *be* that destiny and that fate. In "Gerontion" the ego learns to submit itself to history, so to achieve a modicum of definition and understanding. But beyond "Gerontion" there are "The Waste Land," "Ash Wednesday," and *Four Quartets.* Beyond history, there is myth, and then—but only then—God's Word. Part of Eliot's greatness as a poet is the result of his extraordinary honesty with himself and his language. Having always been superbly conscious of what he has been about, Eliot early furnished the appropriate glosses. The first is from "Tradition and the Individual Talent" (1919): "What happens [to the poet] is a continual surrender of himself as he is at the moment to something which is more valuable. The progress of an artist is a continual self-sacrifice, a continual extinction of personality."

The second is from his essay on William Blake (1920): "Had [Blake's gifts] been controlled by a respect for impersonal reason, for common sense, for the objectivity of science, it would have been better for him. What his genius required, and what it sadly lacked, was a framework of accepted and traditional ideas which would have prevented him from indulging in a philosophy of his own, and concentrated his attention upon the problems of the poet. . . . The concentration resulting from a framework of mythology and theology and philosophy is one of the reasons why Dante is a classic, and Blake only a poet of genius. The fault is perhaps not with Blake himself, but with the environment which failed to provide what such a poet needed; perhaps the circumstances compelled him to fabricate, perhaps the poet required the philosopher and mythologist. . . . "

The third is from his essay on *Ulysses* (1923): "In using the myth in manipulating a continuous parallel between contemporaneity and antiquity, Mr. Joyce is pursuing a method which others must pursue after him. They will not be imitators, any more than the scientist who uses the discoveries of an Einstein in pursuing his own, independent, further investigations. It is simply a way of controlling, of ordering, of giving a shape and a significance to the immense panorama of futility and anarchy which is contemporary history. . . . Instead of narrative method, we may now use the mythical method. It is, I seriously believe, a step toward making the modern world possible for art. . . . "[4] With such glosses Eliot projects the technique of his poetry into poetics.

The idea of a poetry grounded in myth entailed the idea of a poetry ordered and controlled by protagonists who were no more than, or as much as, *personae*—the alternative depending upon the reader's prior commitments. The *personae* of poems in the Adamic mode are in conception diametrically opposed to those in poems in the mythic mode. Whereas in the former, a *persona* is simply one of the shape-shifting forms the poet can assume, in the latter, a *persona* is a role—its design grounded in an order of being beyond any poet's shape-shifting powers—which the poet must discipline himself into playing. In the former, the protagonist must learn to take off his mask; in the latter, he must learn to put it on. Pound's *personae* (he gave this name, of course, to an early collection of his poems) are different from Browning's, who is said in this to be his great master, primarily as they are to be distinguished one from another. They are different too from Whitman's, since they derive from the poet's need to discover himself as possibly someone else, not from his need to discover everyone else as ultimately projections of himself, or of an in-

---

[4] The first of these essays, printed originally in *The Egoist,* has been widely reprinted, of course. The second, called originally "The Naked Man" for its publication in the *Athenaeum,* is reprinted in the *Selected Essays.* The third, printed originally in *The Dial* as "Ulysses, Order, and Myth" has been reprinted, so far as I know, only in M. Schorer, J. Miles, and G. Mackenzie, eds., *Criticism: The Foundations of Modern Literary Judgement* (New York, 1948), pp. 269–271.

exhaustible communal self. Thus with Eliot's *personae* too—but in a more extreme sense than with Pound's. For Eliot—and surely this is an aspect of his final superiority to Pound—has been able to look outward, not inward, behind the *personae* which he believes it is man's inevitable obligation to assume. He has discovered for us again and again that he can make sense out of the obligation only if he can know truly who has put it upon man. Such knowledge is mythic knowledge; for the obligation, as Eliot's late poems understand it, comes from God; and the record of man's bearing up under it is part of that matrix of transhistorical narrative which is myth.

Thus Eliot's is *the* poetics of the counter-current. It constitutes a theory of the mythic poem; and a considerable portion of its force as theory is the product of a certain over-determination in the sensibility of its originator and those for whom he speaks. For the mythic poem—like its counterpart, the Adamic poem—is an over-determined poem. It asks too much of both its protagonists and its readers; for it asks them that they reject utterly the principle of personality (to recall the social scientist's terms) and as utterly opt for the principle of culture. It boldly faces the possibility (for by the time of the First World War it surely was at least a possibility) that the life-style projected by the Adamic poem might not be capable of coming to grips with the problems set for it by history, tradition, and orthodoxy. Rather, that style made for the shaping of personalities whose sense of the power of their own egos dulled, even obliterated, their sense of the power of the culture—the history, tradition, and orthodoxy—which in such great part had made them what they were. They had thus broken off the continuity between their past and their present; and so, strictly speaking, the narrative whereby they might grasp that continuity was by now impossible. The extremity of the situation into which they had got themselves called for extreme measures. Now, in all his agony, modern man might see how the very loss of that continuity argued all the more for the need for its recovery. The only means, a means which Eliot quite frankly realized was extreme, was that surrender of the self whereby the hope for an immanent narrative was resigned in favor of a hope for a transcendent myth. Thus over-determination was quite consciously acknowledged to be the price for making the modern world possible for art.

In the light of such concerns, Eliot's relation to Whitman, like Pound's, marks an impasse, or crossroads, in the continuity of American poetry.[5] Eliot's pronouncements on Whitman indicate that the latter was the demon whose achievement it was to torment any American who would dare write poetry in any mode but his. Whitman wanted, so it seemed in retrospect, to transmute the forms of ordinary discourse into verse; his

[5] See S. Musgrove, *T. S. Eliot and Walt Whitman* (Wellington, New Zealand, 1952). The example I give below is from this book, pp. 54–55.

chief means of doing so was to emphasize and reinforce their rhythms by an extraordinarily varied and subtle use of parallelism and repetition. Eliot could not avoid being "influenced" by Whitman in this matter—either directly or indirectly (indirectly as Whitman, like Poe, in effect tutored the French symbolist and post-symbolist poets who, as is well known, so much influenced Eliot). Moreover, as we shall see, when Eliot thought of Pound's achievement, he perforce thought of Whitman's. He would seem to have been aware of Pound's concern to do right what Whitman, for all his noble intentions, had done wrong.

Consider this single pair of examples. First, from Whitman's "Song of the Open Road":

> Allons! to that which is endless as it was beginningless,
> To undergo much, tramps of days, rests of nights,
> To merge all in the travel they tend to, and the days and
>   nights they tend to,
> Again to merge them in the start of superior journeys,
> To see nothing anywhere but what you may reach it and
>   pass it,
> To conceive no time, however distant, but what you
>   may reach it and pass it,
> To look up or down no road but it stretches and waits for
>   you, however long but it stretches and waits for you,
> To see no being, not God's or any, but you also go thither,
> To see no possession but you may possess it, enjoying all
>   without labor or purchase, abstracting the
>   feast yet not abstracting one particle of it . . .
>
> (Section 13)

Compare:

> To arrive where you are, to get from where you are not
>   You must go by a way wherein there is no ecstasy.
> In order to arrive at what you do not know
>   You must go by a way which is the way of ignorance.
> In order to possess what you do not possess
>   You must go by a way of dispossession
> In order to arrive at what you are not
>   You must go through the way in which you are not.
> And what you do not know is the only thing you know
> And what you own is what you do not own
> And where you are is where you are not.
>
> ("East Coker," III)

There is in the passage from Eliot not only an echo of Whitman's phrasing but, more important, an echo of the metering of syntax—this last an aspect of Eliot's notion of the "music of poetry." ("My words echo / Thus, in your mind," he wrote in "Burnt Norton.") However it got to Eliot, the influence is obvious enough. The very obviousness lends all the more significance to the fact that Eliot "uses" the Whitmanian style to deny the cogency and truth of what Whitman would say. Unlike Whitman's vocabulary even in this, for him, relatively "contemplative" passage, Eliot's is here stripped bare, so that the repetitions are all the more insistent and the insistence all the more powerful. The Whitmanian mode is made to negate itself and generate its opposite; a wholly personal style takes on a grand impersonality. Where Whitman, as always, would "merge all" in the image of himself, Eliot would order all so that, as the poem develops, he might catch a glimpse of the image of the Other. By the time of the *Quartets,* Eliot's mythic poetry had achieved the status of ritual, thus projecting in all its purity and inclusiveness the one myth which was, in its oneness, by definition not a myth. He had managed to use the Whitmanian sensibility, among many others, as a means of discovering that the Whitmanian "content" involved an egocentric predicament so terrible that it could be resolved only by beginning all over again, at the beginning, with the Whitmanian ego and its basic style, and reaching out toward that Other to whose existence its predicament had blinded it. Thus in 1928, commending Pound's verse as genuinely "original," Eliot found it necessary to claim that Whitman, another originator, was only a great writer of prose and that the content of his work was in "large part . . . claptrap."[6] This is but a way of saying that Whitman's poetics was deficient because it kept him from achieving that orthodox, classical, even royalist view of life—deriving from what I have, following Eliot, called the mythic—which, as it should have made for the continuity of American life, so should have made for the continuity of American poetry. Eliot has been happier with Poe, whose torment he can interpret as a product of his being alienated by the sort of life in which Whitman seemed so much at home.

For Eliot the deficiency of American life—a deficiency characteristic of all mass-democratic life—was directly responsible for the deficiency of American poetry. The difference between him and his forebears in the continuity, however, lies not in the fact that he has discovered such a deficiency, for certainly they did too. Rather, it lies in the fact that he cannot, as they could, conceive of anything immanent in that life which might   remedy the deficiency. He would attune himself to its rhythms, but he would then change them so that they would be in concord with something outside of American life—indeed, outside of all

[6] *Selected Poems of Ezra Pound* [1928], "Introduction," p. 10. Cf. his earlier claim that Whitman was outdated, that his undoubted skill in versification was unrelated to his political, social, religious, and moral ideas, which were "negligible." (*Nation and Athenaeum,* xv [1926], p. 426 and xli [1927], p. 302.)

"merely" human life. Pound has gone to history for his source of mythic renewal. Eliot has gone through history, so to go beyond myth.

The mythic poem, reflecting the grave lucubrations of its author, has deliberately asked too much of its readers. But, as Eliot's public career shows, it has also asked too much of itself: that it establish the trans-historical scaffolding upon which a strictly historical narrative of the origin and destiny of modern man might be erected; that, through it, tradition and a sense of the past might be recovered; that, in opposition to the Adamic poem and its rejection of the past for the present, it might show how the past and the present are inextricably involved in a single continuum. The mythic poem can indeed do all these things, but its maker cannot stop there. Being what he is, having to reject even the minimal claims of the Adamic poem, he too has created his own extreme situation, wherein he has had finally to reject the very history toward the reestablishing of whose force and meaning he originally directed his poetry. Rejecting history means to a degree rejecting also the very men whose history it is. If "Gerontion" demanded "The Waste Land," then surely "The Waste Land" demanded "Ash Wednesday" and the *Four Quartets*.

.   .   .   .

[STEVENS AND THE ADAMIC POEM]

Among twentieth-century American poets, the profoundest yes was Wallace Stevens', and it was hard-earned, as the lines quoted above indicate. His is a central achievement in twentieth-century American poetry. Acknowledging this fact, one of his younger peers, Theodore Roethke, has written a "Rouse" for Stevens, at the end of which he explodes, "Brother, he's our father!"

Yet Stevens has most often been described as at worst a dandy and a connoisseur of chaos (this last is the ironic title of one of his poems) and at best a poet so "pure" as to be bereft of any significant affiliation with the tradition of American poetry. The tendency, on the whole, has been to interpret him as a kind of post-post-*symboliste*, dwelling by choice in the universal intense inane. Whereas it has been not too difficult to accommodate a Williams on the one hand and an Eliot on the other to our conception of the evolution of poetry and poetics in the United States, only now are we beginning to realize that Stevens has an important place in that conception too—along with Eliot's, perhaps the most important of all. For in his work—if only we will at last give it the devoted study we have given to Eliot's—the continuity of the most deeply rooted tradition of American poetry, what I have called its Adamic phase, reaches the point of no return. "I'm ploughing on Sunday, / Ploughing North America," he wrote in an early poem

"Ploughing on Sunday" and so defined his major concern—to deal with Sunday, not workaday, matters: aspiration, understanding, belief, commitment in the North American portion of the modern world. In this penultimate chapter, then, I shall consider Stevens' work as it brings my narrative to an end, or a stasis.

What we have seen in the last chapter is the emergence, achieved by a breaking-through, of new modes of creativity, centering on new modes of egocentrism, deriving from renewed affirmations. The affirmations are renewed because they result from a reexamination of the poetics of the Emersonian tradition as it was called into question by Pound, Eliot, and the others. The implicit Adamic protagonist in poetry of this mode is no longer much concerned about who made him and to what end. His abiding concern is with what *he* can make, his own creations— as at once objects and acts: in epistemological language, as subjects. No longer, as with the major poets of the American Renaissance, does he work with an assurance that there is ultimately some transcendental rationale for his compulsion to egocentrism; if there is a transcendent reality, he can conceive of it only in his own image and know it only as his own creation. His poetry is formally freer, more contingent, more given over to sheer invention (and sometimes to mere *expertise*) than that of his nineteenth-century forebears. For the nineteenth-century celebration of the communal experience of the individual, it substitutes invention of the individual experience of the communal: *The Bridge* for "Crossing Brooklyn Ferry"; "all ignorance toboggans into know" for "Bacchus"; *The Divine Pilgrim* for "Israfel"; "Poetry / I too dislike it" for "This is my letter to the World"; "By the road to the contagious hospital" for "There's a certain slant of light." These poems evidence a discovery, made as the result of a desperate need to save himself alive, that the poet's sole ground of being is himself, that his spirit is his sensibility, that his worship is his poetry. But what precisely does he worship, and why? This was the grand question to which Stevens finally addressed himself, but only after he had exercised to the fullest his ability to demonstrate that the world as man could know it made asking this question imperative.

More clearly than any of his contemporaries, Stevens realized the characteristic difficulties and complexities faced by the American poet in the modern world, and he was determined from the outset to resolve them. He discovered that the sort of poetry he wanted was nothing if not egocentric; that it had to make do without the authorization of form and motivation to be got from myths or gods; that it was quite literally humanistic.[7] He dared carry to a conclusion the American poet's search

[7] The evidence is in the poems, of course. But it is also in the prose meditations with which late in his career Stevens justified his way with poetry. On the "romantic," see, e.g., "Two or Three Ideas" [1951], in *Opus Posthumous*, ed. S. F. Morse (New York,

for the poem so pure that, in being created, it could be said to create and thus to initiate that infinite series of transformations whereby man could learn to live with his own need to be sufficient unto himself: whereby man could be said to invent himself, or the possibility of himself. Stevens sought not to transcend his sense of human limitations but to find and contain the center from which the limiting force radiated. The poem he sought—and, especially toward the end of his life, with superbly lucid awareness of what he was seeking—was one of a creative process purified in such a way that all men could share in it. It was to be a poem in which all men could come to behold, stripped of its antecedents and consequences, that which made them human.

The logic of Stevens' quest led him to conclude that this poem, and its maker too, could exist only as a "supreme fiction," a postulate—an "abstract" idea to be discovered in the process of evoking in poems the qualities and conditions of the fully imaginative life of the mind. In 1954 he wrote that he still wanted "to find out whether it is possible to formulate a theory of poetry that would make poetry a significant humanity of such a nature and scope that it could be established as a normal, vital field of study for all comers."[8] In a way, certainly, the statement is outlandishly naïve—as though poetry has not always been a "significant humanity." The evidence of Stevens' work and its culminating place in the continuity of American poetry, however, may direct that we see him as quite willing to be naïve if he needed to be —just so that, in the face of all the obstacles set up by modern life, he might work toward making a significant poetry of humanity. Yet again we have the problem of that transformative relation between poetry and anti-poetry whereby man may once more discover his truest and highest self in his world.

As he insisted again and again, Stevens' essential subject was the life of the imagination (sometimes he said "mind")—thus for him, the life of man. His version of that subject was essentially an indigenous one, an American version of the compulsive modern question: Who am I? Indeed: What am I? True, much of the language and the formal qualities of his poetry reflect his extraordinary, if eccentric, sense of the relevance of European (especially French) poetry and poetics for his own work. Yet like Emerson, Poe, and many Americans before him, he sought in other writers and in other cultures the means not to have ideas but to express them. He sought the means of validating his own

1957), pp. 214–215. On myths and gods, see the remarks scattered among the "Adagia," *ibid.*, pp. 157–180.

[8] This is in a letter to Archibald MacLeish, in which Stevens declined to accept the Norton Professorship at Harvard for 1955–1956 on the grounds that he needed the time to devote himself to writing and thinking—not to say, to taking care of his business affairs. See *Opus Posthumous*, p. xvi. A more succinct version of this is "The Theory of Poetry is the Theory of Life" ("Adagia," *ibid.*, p. 178).

insights and doing his own work. The process is an interesting one and deserves to be studied further. But such study, I suspect, will only serve (as it has already served) to bring us back to the authentic Stevens—the poet who with great and painful deliberation took upon himself the burden of giving back to the world (in the words of "To the One of Fictive Music") the use of that imagination which it had spurned and now craved.

He too associated his role with Whitman's:

> In the far South the sun of autumn is passing
> Like Walt Whitman walking along a ruddy shore.
> He is singing and chanting the things that are
>   part of him,
> The words that were and will be, death and day.
> Nothing is final, he chants. No man shall see the
>   end.
> His beard is of fire and his staff is a leaping flame.
> ("Like Decorations in a Nigger Cemetery," 1935)[9]

Stevens is another sun ("son?") of autumn. (Generally in the poems "sun" = "reality," and "autumn"—like "spring"— = the poet's season, since it is one in which he is protected from the sun, yet is not, as in winter, denied it.) His chant is Whitman's, as is his subject.[10]

There are, to be sure, great differences between the two poets, as there always must be in the growth and development characteristic of genuine continuity. (Likewise, Stevens' identification of himself with Whitman is in the long run a matter incidental to the range and import

[9] I give the dates of the poems, as is my general practice, according to their first publication in book form, although, whenever possible, I follow the text of the *Collected Poems* (New York, 1954). Stevens' revisions are not such as to alter the original meaning of his poems, only to refine it.

[10] Stevens would seem to have been quite clear as to the "American" quality of his poems. In 1950 he was asked: "Is it nonsense to talk of a typical American poem? If not, what, in your opinion are the qualities which tend to distinguish a poem as 'American'?" He wrote in answer: "At bottom this question is whether there is such a thing as an American. If there is, the poems that he writes are American poems. And a typical American poem is merely a matter of choice as between one of his poems and another. It must be as easy to distinguish an American poem from a Maori poem as it is to distinguish an American from a Maori. While it is not always so easy to distinguish an American poem from an English poem, after all would *Snow-Bound* sound quite like an English poem to you? Would you be likely to mistake *Leaves of Grass* for something English? *Snow-Bound* is a typical American poem. The poems in *Leaves of Grass* are typical American poems. Even if a difference was not to be found in anything else, it could be found in what we write about. We live in two different physical worlds and it is not nonsense to think that that matters." (*Focus Five: Modern American Poetry*, ed. B. Rajan [London, 1950], pp. 183–184.) Cf. a note in *Opus Posthumous*, p. 176: "Nothing could be more inappropriate to American literature than its English source since the Americans are not British in sensibility." This theme is developed at length in a 1953 letter quoted by Samuel French Morse in his Introduction to his selection of Stevens' *Poems* (New York, 1959), pp. vi–vii.

of his poetry; here—like his looking to   recent European writers and painters—it is yet another means of consolidating gains and formulating insights.) Stevens' worldliness and sophistication, his consternation in the face of his "innocence," leads him in the end to write with a curious kind of "philosophical" impersonality. We seek for a maker, but in vain; for we find only the making. Whitman's poems are too often dominated by their maker and not released to have their own life; they are so often compulsively personal. Stevens' devotion to the intrinsic perfection of the poem is of a kind which was apparently beyond Whitman's desire. In Stevens there is always in view, perhaps too much so, an end to which Whitman's overwhelming sense of his own power blinded him: that the poem, the creative act, must be made continually to point beyond itself to the problems of belief which its existence raises. If Whitman could not achieve the requisite self-abnegation, Stevens is perhaps only too willing to strive for it. His poems, particularly the later ones, record the striving: "If the mind is the most terrible force in the world, it is also the only force that defends us against terror. Or, the mind is the most terrible force in the world principally in this, that it is the only force that can defend us against itself. The modern world is based on this pensée." The reader of these words from Stevens' commonplace book will recognize in them the leading motives of much of his poetry and poetics. So with these: "The transition from make believe for one's self to make believe for others is the beginning, or the end, of poetry in the individual." And these: "The final belief is to believe in a fiction, which you know to be a fiction, there being nothing else."[11] Nothing else, that is, except him who made the fiction. The history of Stevens' poetry is the history of making and meditating upon that fiction and upon the nature and end of its maker.

Thus the world in which Stevens' history unfolds is one characterized above all by an extreme version (I should guess that it is the extremest and that Stevens meant it to be so) of that radical opposition which has obsessed so many major American poets. It is the opposition between the poetic and anti-poetic—between the self (or, in Stevens' more usual terms, the imagination, or the mind) and a reality which is not part of that self but must be brought into its purview, composed, and so (as it were) re-created. The "jar" which Stevens placed "upon a hill in Tennessee" did give order to the "wilderness" around it; but

> It did not give of bird or bush,
> Like nothing else in Tennessee.
> ("Anecdote of the Jar," 1923)

Logically: the man-made object (one cannot but think of a mason jar and recall that in the 1920's, especially in the South, mason jars were

[11] "Adagia," *Opus Posthumous*, pp. 173–174, 169, 163.

often filled with corn whiskey—i.e. moonshine) creates by composing, not by bringing into being, as does everything—i.e., not nothing—else in Tennessee. Thus the self does not create the world, the "reality" ("the veritable *ding an sich*," as Stevens is willing to call it in "The Comedian as the Letter C") on which it is operative. Rather it creates its versions of the world, which come to be versions of itself in the act of exercising its primary function: at the least, to realize its humanity; at the most, to make men human.

The poetry which Stevens wanted was to be grounded in a human-ism so powerful that even God would be under its sway. (One of Stevens' commonplaces reads: "This happy creature—It is he that in-vented the Gods. It is he that put into their mouths the only words they have ever spoken." Another reads: "After one has abandoned a belief in god, poetry is that essence which takes its place as life's re-demption."[12] God, then, has not given reality to man; nor has man given reality to God; he has given God to reality. Man, indeed, would finally give himself to reality, only to discover himself there already. Stevens' ultimate vision, he was sure, did not contradict his initial and initiating sense of the radical opposition of self and reality. Rather the one was entailed by the other. The technique of poetry and its theory, as he developed them, described—or better, *was*—the process of entailment.

From the very beginning, Stevens was working toward the end which is manifest in such a poem as "The Rock" of 1954. Substantively, he worked toward that end as, first only in poems but later also in writings on poetics, he moved from envisioning reality, then to dramatizing the predicament of him who had the vision, then meditating the meaning of the predicament, and then once more to the envisioning. The late vision differs from the early in this: that at the end Stevens wants to conceive of confronting and knowing reality directly, not as it might be meditated by the formal elegancies of an ultimate composer of words. Poetic form is made to negate itself and to point to an ultimate vision beyond poems, to poetry as an ultimate and inclusive poem. The radical opposition of self and reality is by no means done away with. Rather, it is defined so sharply and evoked so clearly as itself to con-stitute a means toward realization of the ultimate poem. Such realization is possible only for that self which, in its direct transactions with reality, has learned to acknowledge its own limitations and now aspires not to transcend but to contain them. The means to such containment is the ultimate poem, which is the locus of the ultimate poet and thus of the creative principle itself. We must call to mind the Supreme Fiction toward the definition and realization of which all of Stevens' poems seem, in retrospect, to have tended. In Stevens' attempts to

[12] *Ibid.*, pp. 167, 158.

evoke the Supreme Fiction, with the desire for transcendence supplanted by the more appropriate desire for containment, the continuity of American poetry reached its apogee.

·   ·   ·   ·   ·   ·   ·

[THE FUTURE OF AMERICAN POETRY]

Certainly the situation of American poetry has been the sort which we now know always and everywhere to have been characteristic of American life: a situation of extreme alternatives, each seemingly ruling out the possibility of the other. The basic styles of the poetry which was meant to comprehend this situation came to be as extreme. They manifested, as only poetic styles can, the two radically opposed ways of life open to modern man in the world he had made for himself. The poet, searching among the actualities of his culture for a means to authorize his very existence as poet, could not compromise. Either the world was his, or he was the world's.

But the Common Reader says: both alternatives are true, and at once; so that they are not really alternative but complementary. The poet agrees with us when he puts himself in the position of the Common Reader—which is to say, critic and theorist. But as poet he is maker, expresser, culture hero. He wills himself to be possessed by our language, so that he may learn how much of it he can possess and still be himself. He imagines what it would be like to act upon not what we hope for, but what we have. He tells us what our lifestyle really is, what it really entails, even as we hope to make it something better, something more adequate to our vision (or should it be memories?) of *communitas*. He hopes to make it something better and more adequate too, but he works toward this by discovering for us that which is good in what we actually have.

He is trustworthy, worthy of himself and the rest of us, only when he does so. Like us, when he theorizes and rationalizes, when he makes big plans, sets out on large projects, and issues lengthy manifestoes, he is utopian and so no necessary part of the sort of inside narrative which this study aspires to be. Take the imagist movement, for example. Its early promulgators wanted a hard, dry, individualistic poetry which would argue against the dangers of romanticism and its egocentrism. (T. E. Hulme called romanticism "spilt religion.") That is, they wanted to have both a poetic style which would make for a poetry of particularist, ego-centered insight and also a system of belief, a dogma, which, in its concern for order and reason, would deny the validity of such insight. No wonder, then, that recent critics have been able to make out a "romantic" quality in poets like Eliot who, for all their declared "anti-romanticism," derive to a significant degree from the imagist movement! No wonder that imagism could, as it developed from a doctrine to a poetic mode, produce a pair of poets as antipathetic as William Carlos Williams and Ezra Pound: the one devoted to the "measure" (the style of the poet as he makes the image); the other devoted to the "ideogram" (the style of the image as it makes the poet).[13] Such are the vagaries of proper literary history; and this is only one example of the many that could be given. An inside narrative like this one, however, is something else. For its subjèct is the life of poems, not of poets and the movements in which they have participated.

Its denouement, then, is bound up in the fact of that insistent opposition: the egocentric as against the theocentric, man without history as against history without man, the antinomian as against the orthodox, personality as against culture, the Adamic as against the mythic. These are theoretical limits. In practice the opposition is perhaps a simpler affair: man against himself.

In modern times the great figures in the opposition have been Stevens and Eliot. Stevens, however, was the aggressor in way that Eliot did not have to be. Stevens had continually to justify poetry; Eliot, more and more assured that such justification was beyond the power of man, had only to write it. It might well be that Stevens' later poems are not really poems; that looking so compulsively toward the decreative, they fail to be creative, fail to sustain themselves as self-contained works of art. We can read Eliot without believing in his ideas, because we can believe in his poems and so entertain the troubling notion that the ideas just *may* be true. This is not so with the Stevens of the poems ranging from "Notes toward a Supreme Fiction" to "The Rock." For these poems are not such as to bid us only to entertain their ideas seriously; they demand of us rather that we absolutely believe or disbelieve in them. One thinks of the Emerson of the great essays and of the Emersonian hope for a writer of the future who would take upon himself the duties of poet, philosopher, and priest. The terrible predicament of the writer in the egocentric tradition is that he must, by his own definition of his task, take all forms of knowledge as his province and is therefore driven to set himself in opposition to those who say, by a definition they derive from their sense of tradition, that this is impossible. Even if Stevens' later writing is not quite poetry, we must attend closely to it. Perhaps it is something beyond poetry. In any case, it is, for good and for bad, one of the most elaborate

[13] See Stanley Coffman, *Imagism: A Chapter for the History of Modern Poetry* (Norman, 1951); Murray Krieger, *The New Apologists for Poetry* (Minneapolis, 1956); and Frank Kermode, *Romantic Image* (London, 1957).

apologies for poetry conceived of in modern times. More important, it is as a consequence one of the most elaborate apologies for man.

. . . .

The history of American poetry is the history of a search for the discipline authorized by one's sense of oneself as a person, living fully in the world and yet capable of imagining what it would be like to live apart from it. The abiding questions that American poets have had to ask are: Whence the authority? What is left, ineradicable, when one imagines oneself living apart from the world? How does what is left serve to give structure and meaning to poems, and thus to the lives of those who may read them? We may recall the epigraph of this book: "It is very unhappy, but too late to be helped, the discovery we have made that we exist. That discovery is called the Fall of Man." We should note well that Emerson continues, with his usual discomforting honesty: "Ever afterwards, we suspect our instruments." So that we may say further that the history of American poetry is the history of the search, originating in doubt, for an instrument which is beyond doubting. But it is an instrument which, for all its power, cannot deal with its own history, which is the history not just of the poet, but of all those whose instrument it should be. More than this: the instrument is such that he who uses it can treat of the lives and deeds of others only on his own terms. With such an instrument, he can do no more than postulate the character and quality of the other, hoping desperately that his postulation will be in accord with the facts of the matter. Certitude, not understanding, has been the American poet's boon.

"Our relations to each other," Emerson wrote in "Experience," "are oblique and casual." The antinomian strain in American poetry, once having achieved its mastery, has made for only iterated and reiterated songs of oneself. The power and authority is there; and we are grateful. We are led, at the very least, to our own songs of ourselves. But we ask again and again: what next? The answer, not an inconsiderable one to be sure, is: listen to your neighbor sing the song of himself. Listen to him as he is himself as surely as you are yourself. We seek in Whitman, for example, evidence of an understanding of the intrinsic nature of the multitudes of persons, places, and things he hymned; and we hear only Whitman; and we are, if we have the courage, driven to listen to ourselves, then perhaps to others. We seek in Stevens evidence of the riches of the world as it was before he put it into poems, what he so bluntly called "reality"; and we find only evidence of Stevens' power to confront the world on his own terms and to teach us that it may be possible for us to do likewise. At the very least, we may find ourselves, or even our Supreme Fiction. In the world which we have made, this is no small reward. Still, Stevens' own words are a sharp indication of the limits of his achievement: "Life is an affair of people not of places. But for me life is an affair of places [is there a pun on *topoi*?] and that is the trouble."[14]

We want more; we have to want more. We want to reveal to our-selves the possibility of a better world. We turn to Eliot and the poets in the mythic line, who also wanted more. But we find that for them too people must finally become places, occasions—worthwhile not in-trinsically but only as they can be made out to share some universal, depersonalizing vitality, some myth beyond myth. Theirs is a better world, to be sure, but it is not grounded in ours—or at least, it does not give ours the respect that some of us feel is due to it. Such poets are well figured by the "wounded surgeon" of "East Coker" (in the *Quartets*) who must perforce be healed before he can heal. In these poets, we find not Emerson's and Stevens' optative mood but an im-perative mood which directs that we look at others like us only that we may turn our eyes from them to something grander. The mythic poets can know no history either; for although they look to history, it is only so they can look beyond it. They might well be figured as so many unparadised Adams, refusing to look at anything but Him who has unparadised them. Whereas Stevens as poet knows only man, Eliot as poet knows only God: Be used, lest you be tempted to use. Now, sensing the curious lack of a dramatic sense among our poets—Eliot's rituals turned melodramas to the contrary notwithstanding—we ask: But what has happened to *men*? What has happened to the indicative mood?

I suggest that our poets have perforce sacrificed men for the sake of man; further, that they have done so because they could do nothing else; that the task our culture in its history has thus far set for them is precisely this—to defend man. In the long run, the grounds for the defense—radically humanistic as in the Adamic tradition, ultimately Christian as in the mythic tradition—really do not matter. For, de-fending man, they have defended the idea of poetry. That is to say, they have defended the idea of man as maker—this against all those forces of modern rationalized, technified, bureaucratized society which would have man made (or processed), not making.

Further, they have defended man by showing that he at his best can make sense out of his world, no matter what its inherent confu-sions; that he can make, or discover, or make-and-discover, meaning. Thus, in recent times particularly, the basic style of both the Adamic and the mythic poem has derived from the poet's concern to declare that language, in spite of all that we may do to it, is inherently mean-ingful—no matter what the ultimate source of meaning—because poems made out of it can manifest its capacity to mean. Stevens writes that

[14] *Ibid.*, p. 158.

"The poem is the cry of its occasion." Eliot searches for the relation of the word to the Word. They see that if meaningfulness disappears as a meaningful category, then surely we will be lost. If man is indeed against himself, then he must defend himself against himself. With poems, surely, he may even mount a counter-offensive. This is the great triumph of American poetry from the Puritans to Stevens and Eliot.

The triumph was gained, however, at a great sacrifice. For *men,* the whole texture of relationships which ineluctably goes with the idea of *men,* have had in the course of that triumph no major defender— at least among poets. *Men* cannot be defended until the sense of the Adamic and the mythic have been restored to their proper balance, until the ground of poetry is taken to be not only the poet but the very history which, with his poems, he helps make and the community which he helps build. Herein the poet is no worse off than those of his contemporaries who think hard about related problems in politics, education, social theory, and religion. He is perhaps better off than they. For he has worked with what he has, not with what he might have or would like to have.

All this we now know well. We are tempted, in our disappointment over what we do not have, to forget what we do have. It has been the burden of this book to indicate in some detail what we do have. Moreover, if we are dissatisfied, it is in significant measure because poets writing now—poets of the generations after Eliot's and Stevens'—are dissatisfied. As poets must be, they are ahead of us. The older poets among them turn to forms which allow them a moderate and moderating humanism, a humanism of a kind which was impossible for their forebears. They look outward and see a world which wondrously could very well, and probably will, exist without them. The tension slackens; the mood grows warmly humble; love is received as well as given. As for the younger poets: We note the confusions and ineffectualities in so much of their work; but we should note also its aspirations. They snipe savagely at each other and, happily, catch us in their cross-fire. They now play it too safe, now take suicidal risks, now are timidly domestic, now yawpishly barbarous. But they do try unashamedly to comprehend love, family, and community, do try to proclaim the brotherhood of man. Above all, rising to the threats and opportunities which the new modes of mass communication offer them, they want to make poetry once more something that is spoken and heard, not just read and meditated. They want to make of it a means to, not just an index of, *communitas.* If they fail to see that it has been so all along, that is because, like the rest of us, they find it terribly difficult to learn that even as they make history, history makes them.

We say that they have no proper sense of direction. But that is, I think, because it is precisely they who are trying to find a sense of direction for us—knowing full well that, moving in the direction set by Stevens, Eliot, and their peers, we have come to the end of a line. Some of them cannot bring themselves to admit that it was a line whose full length we had to travel in order to get where we are. But no matter. We have only to watch and wait, satisfied in the knowledge that we can at least be pretty sure how far we have come and how it was to get here.

The continuity of one phase of American poetry ends with Stevens' last poems and their complement in Eliot's. For, if nothing else, the effort of Stevens and Eliot in pushing the implications of the Adamic and mythic modes to their farthest limits (who could conceive of going farther than "The Rock" or the *Four Quartets?*) has shown us and the poets who speak on our behalf that we have reached a point of no return. Whatever American poetry looks to be in the future, it will be something essentially different from what it has been in the past. I should guess that Stevens, like Eliot, has more in common with Poe and Emerson than he will have with whoever writes major poetry in the next half-century. It might well be that there will be no American poetry in the next half-century, that it will be a new international poetry, deriving from a sense of the do-or-die universal community of men. Whatever else, it must surely be a poetry of *men:* men conceived as in their history representing the infinite range of possibilities of being and acting open to them when they realize that as man they are nothing if not men.

II

Representative Men

Among a democratic people poetry will not be fed with legends or the memorials of old traditions. The poet will not attempt to people the universe with supernatural beings, in whom his readers and his own fancy have ceased to believe; nor will he coldly personify virtues and vices, which are better received under their own features. All these resources fail him; but Man remains, and the poet needs no more. The destinies of mankind, man himself taken aloof from his country and his age and standing in the presence of Nature and of God, with his passions, his doubts, his rare prosperities and inconceivable wretchedness, will become the chief, if not the sole, theme of poetry among these nations.

ALEXIS DE TOCQUEVILLE
Democracy in America

*L*IKE all the heroes of legend and literature, the American hero must cope with his solitude, the loneliness in which he moves for much of his fabled journey. But unlike other heroes, and this of course has been a defining quality of our central literary characters, he frequently sustains that solitude—he calls it independence—even in his inevitable return to the society he has originally fled. His re-entry is often less than wholehearted, a grudging surrender to pressures too powerful to withstand or a faintly deceptive truce in which he tries to retain his radical isolation even in the midst of society—and it is often difficult to tell whether a particular character (Hester Prynne, for example) is of the first party or the second. Or it may be that return is only a pause before moving again into a larger arena, an existential spaciousness of mind or wilderness where the individual is freer to discover the shape and limits of his being.

As American writers have constantly searched for a literary form adequate to the distinctive American experience, so the American hero (in this sense the surrogate of his creator) has sought an action adequate to himself. And he is convinced from the very beginning that his solitariness—which is to say his freedom from all encumbrance—is necessary to his quest. Thus his characteristic gesture is always to begin by achieving independence, to rebel against the given contexts. He does this sometimes by a literal departure from society, as D. H. Lawrence and Leslie Fiedler make clear in two of the following essays; and sometimes by abandonment of, not society, but the conventions and assumptions which support it.

In either case the hero moves into a new physical or psychic sphere, which both attracts and repels by its enormous openness. Emerson, alone in the woods, believing that in the distant horizon "man beholds somewhat as beautiful as his own nature"; and Melville's Pip, momentarily isolated in the Pacific, "in the middle of such a heartless immensity, my God! who can tell it?"—both of these are testing the ambivalence of solitude and space, testing whether finally it be possibility or vacancy.

Daniel Hoffman, concerned here with the social complexities of this rebellion-creation theme, writes near the end of his *Form and Fable in American Fiction:*

The free man in the free society would have to create his own order anew from the chaos out of which he had emerged; and that chaos seemed all the more threatening because it was largely by his own will that the established order of the social and the supernatural world had been destroyed. Yet the inherited order was itself an intolerable threat to the existence and self-knowledge of the individual, representing stasis, rigidity, the defeat of every force save inertia.

Of course the opportunity "to create his own order anew" always contains the possibility that none will satisfy, thus dooming the hero to a chaos of incessant metamorphosis. "Step outside the narrow borders of what men call reality," Ralph Ellison writes in *Invisible Man*, seeing the possibilities and the requirements, "and you step into chaos . . . or imagination."

Perhaps the quest is lonely because, as Fiedler points out, the most obvious relationship—marriage—is precisely the symbol of what the hero most wishes to escape: "a compromise with society, an acceptance of responsibility and drudgery and dullness." Or perhaps, as the Puritan believed, because the most serious affair of life is the relationship between self and God, in which both society and church are somewhat negligible before the status, elect or damned, of the private soul. Whatever the motivating force—and in each work the metaphors shift—the hero's solitude has been as important as his quest, sufficiently so to confuse us at times as to whether he is in flight or in pursuit, whether he merely escapes or seeks as well, whether the beast whose image haunts him is behind, beyond, or within.

Paradoxically, coexistent with this prevailing solitariness has been a series of significant relationships, frequently of an unconventional kind. Yet we find these, in general, to be highly symbolical in nature rather than literal. Leatherstocking-Chingachgook, Ishmael-Queequeg, Huck-Jim, Quentin-Shreve, Ike McCaslin-Sam Fathers, the heroes of Saul Bellow and their various dark doubles, or those of Bernard Malamud and their angels, refugees, and beggars come to advise and instruct, perhaps liberate if understood—in all these cases the hero's momentary companion is an alter ego, some version of himself, or a type of that "protective figure" we are accustomed to find in myth and dream. They exist—only superficially characterized—like patrons or even God-given aids, to educate the hero, to make available to him some priceless wisdom of tolerance or dignity. They are not so much human beings as agents to provide comfort or aid in the midst of difficulty, or, if the hero is weak, to reveal to him his failure. Sometimes, as in the case of Leatherstocking, hero and agent participate in a love and brotherhood which only confirms the former in the loneliness he has chosen. In Norman Mailer's essay, "The White Negro," the companion is the black man, yet still a kind of agent, in this case the authentic existentialist who provides the white man with a mode and movement that give his need for rebellion a suitable language.

To quote Daniel Hoffman again:

. . . in these romances the individual is defined not, as in the novels of Dickens, Flaubert, or Tolstoy, by his complex interrelationships with others who represent various social classes and their values. Instead he is defined by his relations to characters representing the contending forces in his own psyche or the alternative commitments of belief, value, and action available to him.

The hero's companions, in other words, are not so much human beings as the keys to his own identity. Insofar as his quest remains the probing of that identity, and the "other" remains a subordinate figure, he retains his inviolate privacy.

This question of relationship is tied in three of the following essays to the question of race; and that discussion of the one leads to discussion of the other would seem to be a suitable reflection of the literature itself. It remains a significant fact that our greatest writers, particularly in the nineteenth century, have revealed on occasion a profound awareness which our nation at large seems only to have come upon in recent times: namely, the conviction that the destiny of the white man is deeply involved with that of the dark man. Certainly in Cooper, Poe, Melville, Twain, and Faulkner there is a sense of an inexpressible tie—at times a bondage—of white to dark, as if the definition of the American hero's quest waits, more than anything else, on the full recognition of the darkness which is, in part, himself, and without which his quest is doomed to indecisiveness.

In each of our critics the function of the dark man is generally similar to that of the "companion" in the hero's characteristic relationship mentioned above. D. H. Lawrence, in the earliest of these essays, sees the Indian as similar to the landscape itself, which "has never been at one with the white man." Thus the coming together of the white European and "the aboriginal demon hovering over the core of the continent" is linked with the hero's capacity—still limited —to "open out a new great area of consciousness, in which there is room for the red spirit too." In Fiedler, the relationship between the white and dark becomes a "metaphor of holy marriage": the most striking image the American writer can create of the hero's need to "project an engagement with life which [does] not betray the self." And in Mailer's "The White Negro," the white man—if he is brave enough—moves from society to the existential region of the black, where he can learn the possibilities of living "in the enormous present."

The development of the interracial theme in the nineteenth century is clear enough, since it stands at the center of some of our most important books. In Cooper the relationship between white and Indian may seem almost gratuitous, since Leatherstocking is whole unto himself, dependent on no one but nature; yet obviously the relationship is necessary to Cooper as artist, the image of "a new human relationship" which he conceives largely as a symbolic gesture, not quite completed even as a fictional representation. With *Moby Dick* the South-Sea islander is the soother of the white man's soul (as the black cabin boy is able to calm, temporarily, even the wilder soul of Ahab), and ultimately the savior of his body, as Queequeg's coffin—the sign of his capacity to come to terms with death—becomes the life raft of Ishmael. By the time of *Huckleberry Finn* Jim would seem to have become the *only* means by which the white hero may achieve a complete sense of human decency and dignity—genuine moral insight as the black man's gift to the white master. Ironically enough, Huck's new moral status renders him totally unfit for white society.

Such awareness of race on the part of our writers has been, however, an extremely complex one, and by no means free of racism and condescension. Leatherstocking tries us all with his endless harangue on the "natur'" and "gifts" of red man and white, the treachery which is somehow natural to the Indian but which the white acquires only through training; we must cope in Melville with the racial nightmare of *Benito Cereno* as well as the egalitarianism of *Moby Dick;* and, for all his grace, suggests Daniel Hoffman, Twain's "Nigger Jim" sometimes resembles painfully none other than a Minstrel Mr. Bones. More recently we have seen similar ambivalences in Faulkner, in the psychological disturbance which he often attributes to his mulattoes—as if projecting a fear of miscegenation—or the ease with which, through the voice of Ike McCaslin, he consigns black people to further oppression: "Binding them for a while yet, a little while yet. Through and beyond that life and maybe through and beyond the life of that life's sons. . . ." It is a punishment he tries to modify through praise: "But not always, because they will endure. They will outlast us. . . . They are better than we are. Stronger than we are." Yet there seems a quality of relief in the praise, as if in uttering it the speaker has bought himself some time, additional generations before he will have to face that full meeting which he still dreads.

To look at the problem in another way, one might say that our writers have frequently chosen the dark man as a companion for the white precisely because of those racist assumptions which insist that the relationship *remain* limited, thus allowing the hero that essential isolation he values more than brotherhood or equality. And of course in all these characterizations of nonwhites we still find the situation pointed to earlier: the companion as mere agent rather than as a fully developed being in his own right. He has remained, in other words, strictly a symbolic projection of the white hero, a metaphor of some buried psychic force or the large unknown itself—elsewhere imaged as the sea or forest—the new "context" in which the isolated white man defines only himself.

W. H. Auden, making reference to Twain, Melville, and Whitman, sums up our literature's notion of relationship in this way:

Jim, who has been [Huck's] "buddy" . . . is left behind like an old shoe, just as in *Moby Dick* Ishmael becomes a blood-brother of Queequeg and then forgets all about him. Naturally the daydream of the lifelong comrade in adventure often appears in American literature:

> Comerado, I give you my hand!
> I give you my love more precious than money,
> I give you myself before preaching or law;
> Will you give me yourself? will you come travel with me?
> Shall we stick by each other as long as we live?
> WHITMAN, "*Song of the Open Road.*"

but no American seriously expects such a dream to come true.

In his *Waiting for the End,* Fiedler sees signs of a shift from this type of characterization, and perhaps by extension an abandonment of the whole practice of the companion, white or black, as instrument. He singles out Norman Mailer's essay "The White Negro" as an instance of more promising attitudes: ". . . the new dream begins with the old, in fact presupposes it; but goes further, for it not only imagines joining with Indian or Negro in pseudo-matrimony, or being adopted by some colored foster-father, but being reborn as Indian or Negro, *becoming the other.*"

II

The question remains of course: what exactly are these heroes after? We are hindered here by the hero's peculiar negativism, for his chief characteristic, aside from his incessant movement, is his large capacity to say explicitly what he will *not* be. The terms of his own self-accounting are usually the terms of the condition he has just fled. It is civilization, convention, and "Pap" which precipitate Huck's flight; an inner despair, a "damp, drizzly November in my soul" which sends Ishmael on his ocean voyage; and in the opening chapter of *Walden,* an account of an increasingly wayward civilization that justifies the journey Thoreau is about to take. That a more positive articulateness about this matter should be difficult is also part of the very nature of the quest itself: for to define its aim is what the quest is really all about. The purpose of going to Walden Pond, Thoreau tells us, is "to live life deliberately, to front only the essential facts of life"—a vague enough statement, but only if one persists in asking the wrong question. One goes to Walden to learn the distinctive character of one's journey, to discover the extent to which that journey may fill out the unknown corners of oneself, may become, in other words, an adequate metaphor of the hero. As the poet Theodore Roethke put it: "I learn by going where I have to go."

The quest is to discover the unique shape of life itself. In "Self-Reliance" Emerson writes: "Life only avails, not the having lived. Power ceases in the instant of repose; it resides in the moment of transition from a past to a new state, in the shooting of the gulf, in the darting to an aim." Power is neither in the past nor in the new state; it is in the *moment of transition.*

Over a century after "Self-Reliance" Norman Mailer describes the October 1967 march on the Pentagon in *Armies of the Night:*

you created the revolution first and learned from it, learned of what your revolution might consist and where it might go out of the intimate truth of the way it presented itself to your experience. Just as the truth of his material was revealed to a good writer by the cutting edge of his style . . . so a revolutionary began to uncover the nature of his true situation by trying to ride the beast of his revolution.

And he is at the Pentagon because, like Thoreau's Walden Pond, it is at that moment the place where experience is best confronted, the apt corner into which life can be driven to see if it be mean or sublime; and to see the darkening outlines of one's own being, as well as *its* meanness or sublimity.

To push off, in other words, is to face the possibility not merely of having to slay whatever dragon a hero may encounter; it is to have to create the quest as one goes along, by way of instruments necessarily unpredictable because they have never been used. The ones whose identity and use he already knows, like Ahab's quadrant and Ike McCaslin's gun, like the orthodox Puritan attitude toward adultery, or an *antebellum* Missouri morality regarding theft and slavery—these are the structures of order the hero has chosen to leave behind.

III

Daniel Hoffman's "The American Hero: His Masquerade" is a study of those characters of the American folk imagination who have most influenced American writers of fiction. Beginning with "literary" characters—the hero of Ben Franklin's *Autobiography* and the figure of Andrew the Hebridean from Crèvecoeur's *Letters from an American Farmer*—Hoffman discovers a central core of "metamorphosis, adaptability, and indomitable self-mastery," characteristics he considers basic to popular conceptions of "the American, this new man." This character divides into two broad types of folk hero, the Yankee and the frontiersman, each of whom evolves through a complex range of categories. The Yankee moves from his original role as the country bumpkin in the city to his more comfortable one as plain-speaking and perceptive Yankee villager, and finally to the Yankee peddlar, the "myth of innocence" transformed to a "myth of competence." The frontiersman, while retaining the basic optimism and resiliency of the Yankee, adds a blend of ruthlessness and sentimentality, brutality combined with a deep nostalgia over the passing of his wilderness surroundings.

The American writer, however, by no means uses these folk heroes uncritically in his fictions; in fact, much of the drama of our books lies in the authors' willingness to "project elements of the American folk hero into situations with which his spiritual immaturity and his lack of human depth make him inadequate to deal." His penchant for metamorphosis becomes in fiction the crucial problem of identity itself; and the conviction of mastery of self and nature becomes the great delusion, at times the eventual despair, of many of our fictional heroes.

An additional tension emerges from the conflict of these indigenous American folk heroes with older, world mythologies. Even at the level of the folk imagination, and certainly in the actual literature, the hero continues to be defined by his rebelliousness: "Far from reenacting the death and resurrection of the Corn Spirit, or the psychic childhood of the race, the hero of the American romance cuts himself off from the history of the world which bears these traditions. His dilemma is to discover the new myths which viably take the place of those he has discarded."

Later in his *Form and Fable,* Hoffman discovers an unusually fine example of this rebellion—and its consequences—in Hawthorne's "My Kinsman Major Molineux," in which the American folk image of the young Yankee, Robin, is played off against the ancient image of the scapegoat king, in this case Robin's own kinsman. The outwardly simple tale becomes, in Hoffman's discussion, a complex treatment of freedom and responsibility, rebellion and guilt, vividly revealed by attention to the conflict of two strains of folklore.

With D. H. Lawrence's "Fenimore Cooper's Leatherstocking Novels" we move from the discussion of the folk hero to the full-fledged literary creation: Cooper's frontiersman, who in many ways remains our culture's dominant image of itself. Lawrence traces Leatherstocking through the odd sequence of metamorphoses in which Cooper imagined his hero, from the old Natty Bumppo of *Pioneers* (1823) to the young Deerslayer (1841), a progression consistent with Hoffman's notion of outwardly shifting identity as a characteristic of the American hero. Ultimately for Lawrence, Leatherstocking is "the essential American soul . . . hard, isolate, stoic, and a killer": possessed of the American hero's basic inviolateness, penetrated neither by Indian nor landscape, and perfectly prepared to kill without guilt or apology. He is conceived—somewhat miraculously, given Lawrence's account—out of the divided imagination of Cooper, torn between Europe and America, civilization and savagery, the "genteel continent" and the "tomahawking continent"; and with him Cooper also creates "the nucleus of a new society, . . . a new human relationship" between the white man and the Indian. This is the relationship which is finally not completed by Cooper, and Lawrence sees this as an indication of the direction in which American literature must move in order to fulfill itself.

Lawrence's *Studies in Classic American Literature* is ultimately an insistence that rebellion is not enough, that a perennial shattering

of the given contexts is useless unless succeeded by the establishment of new contexts. In his opening essay he writes, "Men are free
when they are in a living homeland, not when they are straying and
breaking away. . . . Men are free when they belong to a living,
organic, *believing* community. . . . Not when they are escaping to
some wild west." On the one hand he recognizes Cooper's achievement—the creation of an authentic American hero; but now that
hero must move into some kind of new community. In this respect
Lawrence speaks from the center of his own English background,
and to some extent in the language of the traditional English novel.
He cannot conceive of a truly significant literature defined more by
escape than return, by rebellion more than a constructive building
of new alternatives. His book, consequently, articulates the most
serious challenge our writers have had to face: what, in fact, to *do*
with this hero once he is fully imagined.

Leslie Fiedler's *Love and Death in the American Novel* is one of
the most original treatments of American literature ever attempted.
In its emphasis on the terror and "innocent homosexuality" in our
literature it has disturbed many readers, yet there is no gainsaying
the literary facts upon which he bases his argument: the prevalence
of violence; the frequent desertion of society, of wife and family;
and, at the center of many of our books, those significant relationships between male characters, frequently of different races, which
replace the heterosexual relationships that usually occupy the European novelist. In the essay reprinted here, Fiedler works not only
with fiction by various hands (Irving, Melville, Twain, Faulkner,
Hemingway, Bellow), but also with examples of popular culture,
such as movies, detective fiction, and the comic strips. From "Rip
Van Winkle" on up, from this first example of a "fundamental
American archetype," Fiedler develops intricate variations on a
major fictional narrative: the man who departs from society and all
its paraphernalia of job, responsibility, wife and children, for a
wilderness of good liquor and jovial male companions, an "eternal
playtime in the hills."

Cognizant of those basic tensions discussed in Part I of the present
collection, Fiedler adds the startling discovery that "there is finally
no heterosexual solution which the American psyche finds completely satisfactory, no imagined or real consummation between
man and woman found worthy of standing in our fiction for the
healing of the breach between consciousness and unconsciousness,
reason and impulse, society and nature." Instead of the "hetero-

sexual solution" the American writer has preferred "a sentimental relationship at once erotic and immaculate, a union which commits its participants neither to society nor sin"—and this can be only the innocent "homoerotic" love of boys.

Fiedler elaborately fills in the requirements of such encounters: the natural Eden, the white questing lover, and the dark "anti-bride." When completed, these relationships become images standing "for the healing of the social conflicts which most irk us, and before which we feel most powerless and baffled."

Norman Mailer's "The White Negro" is not intended as a piece of literary criticism; it is a discussion not so much of the characters who make up our contemporary fiction as a description of a particular kind of man currently emerging on the social scene, and, perhaps by way of implication, a projection of the kind of hero Mailer believes the American writer must begin to comprehend and, hopefully, re-create in fiction. Mailer's psychopathic hipster—the American existentialist—who emerges when "the bohemian and the juvenile delinquent came face-to-face with the Negro," is clearly distinguished from those "absurd" heroes—the picaros, the schlemiels, and holy fools—who have become the most popular image of the American hero in current fiction. David D. Galloway has concisely defined the type: "Both clown and saint find themselves in conflict with a world that seems infinitely resourceful in its devices for crippling or murdering the self; as a minimal requirement the clown withstands this reality, the saint transcends it, and in the most optimistic embodiments, they transform reality."

It is perhaps not too much of an oversimplification to say that such a hero, clown *or* saint, is precisely what Mailer is trying to get away from. The hipster is clearly in the same "infinitely resourceful" world as they are, but he refuses either to "withstand" or "transcend" the real; rather, in Mailer's terms, he chooses to "accept the terms of death." He insists that life is a purposeful drama of choice and risk and responsibility—that man acts and receives immediate return, reward or punishment, for his actions, and that his courage and skill, or lack of these, are the sole components of his own destiny.

Mailer's objections to much of the most important fiction being written today is apparent in his comments, in various places, on Saul Bellow; and it is also apparent that the nature of the created hero is central to his objections: "[Bellow] must give evidence, as must Styron, that he can write about men who have the lust to struggle with the history about them." And elsewhere: ". . . the hero of moral earnestness, the hero Herzog .and the hero Levin in Malamud's *A New Life,* are . . . passive, timid, other-directed, pathetic, up to the nostrils in anguish: the world is stronger than they are; suicide calls."

In a curious sense "The White Negro" looks both to the future and the past. Suggesting that the hipster may be "a new kind of personality which could become the central expression of human nature before the twentieth century is over," Mailer clearly implies the kind of hero with whom an ambitious novelist must deal; yet, at the same time his essay is filled with the echoes of nineteenth-century American romantics, as if he were seeking to re-create that theater of openness and possibility which exists at the center of our classic American books. Faced with the possibilities of instant atomic death or the death of conformity to a prodigious State, Mailer writes:

the only life-giving answer is to accept the terms of death . . . to divorce oneself from society, to exist without roots, to set out on that uncharted journey with the rebellious imperatives of the self. In short, whether the life is criminal or not, the decision is to encourage the psychopath in oneself, to explore that domain of experience where security is boredom and therefore sickness, and one exists in the present, in that enormous present which is without past or future, memory or planned intention. . . .

One turns immediately to Emerson, who spoke of "the moment of transition" rather than the "uncharted journey," nonconformity rather than rebelliousness, the God within rather than the psychopath. The similarities in kind, if not degree, are clear enough.

Even in his awareness of possibilities far grimmer than anything Emerson could have imagined, Mailer retains also that curious blend of the "pragmatic" with the "mystic," the earthly and every day with the cosmic, that characterizes not only the thought of Emerson but of many of his contemporaries, as well as the Puritans. As D. H. Lawrence once observed of *Moby Dick:* "And all this practicality in the service of a mad, mad chase." Mailer's hipster has as his immediate object the "apocalyptic orgasm," and while Emerson would doubtless have seen the goal as incredibly base, he would most certainly have understood Mailer's language in describing it: ". . . the apocalyptic orgasm often remains as remote as the Holy Grail." Later Mailer writes, to be with it is to have grace, is to be closer to the secrets of that inner unconscious life which will nourish you if you can hear it, for you are then nearer to that God which every hipster believes is located in the senses of his body. . . . not the God of the churches but the unachievable whisper of mystery within the sex, the paradise of limitless energy and perception just beyond the next wave of the next orgasm.

Mailer's language here, obviously chosen with deliberateness, of grace, God, mystery, paradise, and perception is the language in which the American writer has always expressed even his less lofty pursuits.

In attempting to see a line of development between Mailer's conception of the American hero and that of the other critics, we must take note also of the question of solitude. It might appear that Mailer, in proposing an ecstatic sexual commitment as the sign of his hero's success, is breaking with that theme of inviolate privacy that seems central in earlier American literature. Yet one wonders whether the true goal is the shared orgasm or the grace—which the Puritan knew to be an eminently private matter. Certainly the "Hip morality," as Mailer describes it, is private indeed: "to be engaged in one primal battle: to open the limits of the possible for oneself, for oneself alone, because that is one's need."

Mailer goes on to say that "in widening the arena of the possible, one widens it reciprocally for others as well, so that the nihilistic fulfillment of each man's desire contains its antithesis of human cooperation." This sounds much like Whitman's "And what I assume you shall assume,/ For every atom belonging to me as good belongs to you"; and in neither case does one have the impression that the individual's primary obligation is to the larger community of men.

IV

Earlier in this essay we cited D. H. Lawrence's considerable reservations about a literature preoccupied with rebellion rather than with the culmination of rebellion in the creation of a "living, organic, *believing* community." He also strongly implies the inadequacy of a solitary hero whose lack of concrete direction is matched by his inability to enter into genuine relationship—society—with another human being, preferably his racial opposite. At the conclusion of his essay on Cooper's Leatherstocking tales, Lawrence makes both a criticism and a prediction: "This is the very intrinsic-most American. He is at the core of all the other flux and fluff. And when *this* man breaks from his static isolation, and makes a new move, then look out, something will be happening." The question to be raised is whether, even now, the American hero has made his "move," at least in Lawrence's terms. Even in Mailer's essay we read of "a life committed to the notion that the substratum of existence is the search, the end meaningful but mysterious." Where in this kind of thinking can Lawrence's new contexts, the new masters, come from? How can the American writer, in other words, "free" his hero from his isolation; how can he discover that social situation in which the hero can move without sacrificing too much of what has gone into his making?

An essential problem of many of our twentieth-century writers has been exactly this: how to bring their distinctive hero into some kind of meaningful social context; how to convert that curious need for solitude and space, for freedom and breadth, into effective social action. How, indeed, can they rescue the hero from "static isolation," create out of his character—rather than in violation of it— some capacity for "movement," for viable activity in the context of recognizable society.

The hero of Ellison's *Invisible Man* is a prototype of the difficulty. We find him, at the end of the novel, in the isolated cellar to which all his efforts to participate effectively in the community have led him; it is this cellar from which the novel is "spoken." In no social role—intellectual, kowtowing administrator, Communist, revolutionary, nihilist—has he been able to discover an adequate context to what he vaguely senses is his essential being. Yet, for all his failures, he says: "The hibernation is over. I must shake off the old skin and come up for breath. . . . I'm coming out, no less invisible without it, but coming out nevertheless. And I suppose it's damn well time."

Whatever the courage and optimism of that cry, however, the most intolerable privacy which is prison remains the fate, not only of "invisible man," but of many of those literary characters who have tried to "move" into some version of the social arena. In *Native Son, The Catcher in the Rye, The Fixer, Herzog, The Confessions of Nat Turner, Armies of the Night,* or even Nabokov's *Lolita,* are just a few of those heroes who have attempted to convert vision into action, to have something "happen" in a book about America, but who are finally confined—or flee—to the static isolation of the jail or some equivalent of it. There, of course, in characteristic American style, they can dare to imagine what in the community would be intolerable; they can enjoy a freedom of being because there is no doing, no action by which to diminish it. Within the very pit of society's impoverishment an enormous psychic sea of possibility opens again. But it opens at a considerable cost—which our writers seem now to understand perfectly.

The American Hero:
His Masquerade

DANIEL G. HOFFMAN

'Something further may follow of this Masquerade.'
—MELVILLE, *The Confidence-Man*

ONE

'What then is the American, this new man?' asked Crèvecoeur in 1782,[1] posing at the birth of the Republic the question of national identity which our writers have never since ceased trying to answer. Even from the earliest settlement the conviction loomed large that human nature itself was changed by being transplanted to new circumstances. The Puritans had felt as a divine visitation the call to leave the Old World for the New and found under God's will a new Zion in the wilderness. By the middle of the eighteenth century the thoughts of emigration and the untamed land continued to sway men's minds. We have noted in the paradisal symbolism of the frontier that the wilderness becomes the fecund Garden of tall-tale fame. Melville would envisage the West as inhabited by 'the White Steed of the Prairies. . . . A most imperial and archangelical apparition of that unfallen western world, which to the eyes of the old trappers and hunters revived the glories of those primeval times when Adam walked majestic as a god, bluff-browed and fearless.' Characteristically, Melville mythicized into more heroic dimensions a conviction of popular culture. The Enlightenment version of the 'bluff-browed and fearless' American settler was indeed unfallen and Adamic, but not quite as majestic or godlike as Melville proposes. This we can see in Crève-

---

[1] Hector St. Jean de Crèvecoeur, *Letters from an American Farmer* (New York, 1957.)

196

coeur's answer to his own question, 'What then is the American, this new man?'

He is an American, who, leaving behind him all his ancient prejudices and manners, receives new ones from the new mode of life he has embraced, the new government he obeys, and the new rank he holds. . . . The American is a new man, who acts on new principles; he must therefore entertain new ideas, and form new opinions. From involuntary idleness, servile dependence, penury, and useless labour, he has passed to toils of a very different nature, rewarded by ample subsistence.—This is an American.

The character of this new man soon clearly revealed itself. At first there was the miraculous rebirth of the British serf as a freeholder in the New World; the career of one such serf, Andrew the Hebridean, was appended to the third of Crèvecoeur's *Letters from an American Farmer*. But one need not be born a serf on the isle of Barra to be reborn in the American colonies. That rebirth and metamorphosis are the bywords of American life is among the lessons in Benjamin Franklin's *Autobiography*. That work and Crèvecoeur's are the earliest and most influential examples of the new American character in literature. As yet the lineaments of that character are 'colonial,' the products rather of general political and social institutions than of the special culture of a particular region. Such localization was the next step in the development of popular concepts of character. Along the northeastern seaboard a well-defined type, the Yankee, developed early in folklore and, by the 1830's, appears in popular culture to have displaced the undifferentiated American of the Franklin and Crèvecoeur variety. A parallel development along the frontier brought the character of the Backwoodsman into folktales, almanacs, popular fiction, theatricals, and, in the person of Davy Crockett, into national political prominence. Metamorphosis, adaptability, and indomitable self-mastery are the qualities these three types of the hero share. Whether actual men or fictitious characters, these heroes insist upon the constancy of the self behind their changing masks. Yet, as the more reflective minds of Hawthorne, Melville, and Twain used these popular stereotypes in their fiction, the question of identity could not so casually be laid to rest. Crèvecoeur's question, What is the American, becomes for their characters, Who am I? Which of my masks is Me?

Andrew the Hebridean, however, felt no such ambiguity about *his* identity.

All I wish to delineate [Crèvecoeur writes] is, the progressive steps of a poor man, advancing from indigence to ease; from oppression to freedom; from obscurity and contumely to some degree of consequence—not by virtue of any freaks of fortune, but by the gradual operation of sobriety, honesty, and emigration.

To succeed, Andrew must cast off his ancient heritage as though it were a chrysalis. Only then can the real man within come forth in all his human power, sustained by the laws; for 'we are the most perfect society now existing in the world.' Arriving in Philadelphia, Andrew is befriended by the benevolent American Farmer who assures him that 'Your future success will depend entirely upon your own conduct; if you are a sober man . . . laborious, and honest, there is no fear that you will do well.' No less than twelve times do these adjectives, the apices of bourgeois virtue, come together in Crèvecoeur's discourse on Andrew. It is true that the Hebridean does not know how to handle a hoe or an axe, and that his wife must be apprenticed in a friendly kitchen to learn the rudiments of pioneer housekeeping. These skills being soon acquired, Crèvecoeur and a friend stake Andrew to a hundred acres of land. The ever benevolent farmer invites the neighborhood to a frolic; amid the convivial folk festival of house-raising a new American is born:

When the work was finished the company made the woods resound with the noise of their three cheers, and the honest wishes they formed for Andrew's prosperity. . . . Thus from the first day he had landed, Andrew marched towards this important event: this memorable day made the sun shine on that land on which he was to sow wheat and other grain. . . . Soon after, further settlements were made on that road, and Andrew, instead of being the last man towards the wilderness, found himself in a few years in the middle of a numerous society. He helped others as generously as others had helped him. . . . he was made overseer of the road, and served on two petty juries, performing as a citizen all the duties required of him.

The combination of his own sobriety, industry, and honesty with 'our customs, which indeed are those of nature' and our laws, which derive 'from the original genius and strong desire of the people,' leads ineluctably toward the triumphant transformation of Andrew. By Crèvecoeur's time, deistic optimism had for many colonists quite replaced the earlier Puritan emphasis on original sin. Man, in accordance with the new philosophy of the age, is inherently good, and America, being free from the inherited evils and injustices of Europe, offers him the unprecedented opportunity to be reborn to a brighter destiny. Although neither Crèvecoeur nor his age held credence in such superstitions as witchcraft or wonders, surely this transformation of a peasant into a free American is as miraculous an instance of shape-shifting as anything reported at Salem. The power of transformation, of self-transformation, is no longer seen as malevolent. It partakes of the same beneficent energy that populates the forests and the farmyards with prodigious plenitude of game and fecundity of crops. Already the American character is defined as the exercise of metamorphic power.

Crèvecoeur's ingenuous account of Andrew is the prototype of the

Horatio Alger story. It is the new fairy tale of the new man on the new continent. He begins life in Europe, in the state of subjection to which history has condemned him. But by emigrating to the New World,

He begins to feel the effects of a sort of resurrection; hitherto he had not lived but simply vegetated; he now feels himself a man, because he is treated as such.

His symbolic gesture is to discover his own humanity in a land where all men hold the highest and equal rank of citizens.

In time the American hero developed a more sophisticated character. The next representative hero adapted himself to almost all of the human possibilities of thought and action in his time. Benjamin Franklin begins his dizzying progress in much the same vein that Crèvecoeur had begun Andrew's adventures:

Having emerged from the poverty and obscurity in which I was born and bred, to a state of affluence and some degree of reputation in the world, and having gone so far through life with a considerable share of felicity, the conducting means I made use of, which with the blessing of God so well succeeded, my posterity may like to know, as they may find some of them suitable to their own suitations, and therefore fit to be imitated.

It is worth reading that Franklin formed the plan of his life upon his reading of Cotton Mather's *Essays To Do Good*. Although the didacticism of his purpose perpetuates the Puritan emphasis on studying the example of a holy life, his goal is not holiness. It is success. The simple bourgeois formula of honesty, sobriety, and industry which brought about Andrew's resurrection is elaborated in Franklin's famous table of virtues, as well as in a hundred examples drawn from his own life. One cannot gainsay D. H. Lawrence's mockery of Benjamin for his denial that 'The soul of man is a dark vast forest, with wild life in it. Think of Benjamin fencing it off! . . . He made himself a list of virtues, which he trotted inside like a gray nag in a paddock.' This charge, or at least its spirit, was anticipated by Melville. As one who dived deep into the recesses of the self, he could not help but find Franklin's character a shallow show of outward versatility lacking inner conviction. Thoreau was more in tune with the popular culture of the time when he wrote, 'Franklin—there may be a line for him in the future classical dictionary, recording what that demigod did, and referring him to some new genealogy. "Son of _____ and _____. He aided the Americans to gain their independence, instructed mankind in economy, and drew down lightning from the clouds." ' [2] It was his role as rebel rather than as conciliator, and his hardheaded virtues and practical approach to the mastery of life which made the hero of the *Auto-*

[2] Quoted by F. O. Matthiessen, *American Renaissance* (New York, 1941). p. 636.

biography seem a prototypical figure among his countrymen. Quite consistent with these qualities was his rationalistic derision of the superstitions of Puritan times in his bagatelle, 'A Witch Trial at Mount Holly.'

In the midst of so much that is admirable in Franklin's career, what seems to have most appealed to the popular mind were the ingredients of a stock figure, half wily savant, half homely philosopher. The emergent Yankee trickster was already limned in Ben's burning his light later than his rival's, pushing a wheelbarrow down Main Street to promote his own reputation for industry, rising in the world by the heft of his own cunning till at last he dines with kings. Allied with this emphasis on the too-clever side of Ben is the popular confusion of Franklin himself with Poor Richard, his fictitious gaffer who paved *The Way to Wealth* with proverbs. 'Love your neighbor; yet don't pull down your hedge'; 'Write with the learned, pronounce with the vulgar'; 'Fish and visitors stink after three days'; 'If you would be wealthy, think of saving as well as getting.' These apothegms of bourgeois caution could, like his tricksy maneuvers to get ahead, be regarded as somewhat incompatible with the other Franklin of popular tradition—the wise statesman, the original scientist, the patriarchal patriot. Mark Twain, in a sketch at Franklin's expense, complained that 'His maxims were full of animosity toward boys. Nowadays a boy cannot follow out a single natural instinct without tumbling over some of those everlasting aphorisms and hearing from Franklin on the spot.' Franklin, pretending industriousness, might say 'Procrastination is the thief of time,' but Mark Twain knows better: 'In order to get a chance to fly his kite on Sunday he used to hang a key on the string and let on to be fishing for lightning.'

> He was always proud of telling how he entered Philadelphia for the first time, with nothing in the world but two shillings in his pockets and four rolls of bread under his arm. But really, when you come to examine it critically, it was nothing. Anybody could have done it.[3]

In a trenchant satirical sketch of Franklin, Melville presents the sententious, calculating sage at Passy, in whom 'The diplomatist and the shepherd are blended; a union not without warrant; the apostolic serpent and dove.' This portrait, in *Israel Potter,* is perhaps as shrewd an assessment of Franklin's virtues and as striking an indictment of his faults as the narrator of the *Autobiography* has ever received. Melville ranks him with Jacob in the Bible, and Hobbes, as 'labyrinth-minded, but plainspoken Broad-brims . . . keen observers of the main chance; prudent courtiers; practical Magians in linsey-woolsey.' The dualism of his personality, the contrast between his humble beginnings and the worldly, so-

---

[3] 'The Late Benjamin Franklin,' in *Sketches New and Old, Writings of Mark Twain* (New York, 1917), XXIII, 188–92.

phisticated, and cunning old soothsayer Israel Potter meets in Paris, makes Franklin suspect:

Having carefully weighed the world, Franklin could act any part in it. By nature turned to knowledge, his mind was often grave, but never serious. At times he had seriousness—extreme seriousness—for others, but never for himself. . . . This philosophical levity of tranquility, so to speak, is shown in his easy variety of pursuits. Printer, postmaster, almanac maker, essayist, chemist, orator, tinker, statesman, humorist, philosopher, parlour man, political economist professor of housewifery, ambassador, projector, maxim-monger, herbdoctor, wit: Jack of all trades, master of each and mastered by none—the type and genius of his land. Franklin was everything but a poet.

In his protean and hydra-headed versatility the metamorphic Franklin seemed a moral chameleon. Who and what is he, ultimately, underneath all these rebirths and resurrections? Franklin's own character exhibited in its most highly developed form that versatility which frontier conditions and a limited population made necessary in a new country. De Tocqueville had noticed the premium placed in America on the Jack-of-all-trades, at the expense of the master-craftsman who was useless beyond his one specialty. If this prized versatility did not long outlast the division of labor brought about by post-bellum industrialization, it was characteristic of American life in the early nineteenth century. This was true on every level of society, from the farmer-mechanic-peddler to the likes of George Washington and Thomas Jefferson, both of whom were quondam philosophers, scientists, architects, statesmen, politicians, and farmers. That the plebeian Franklin should have been the most successful citizen of this universe suggests the remarkable degree of social and intellectual mobility possible even before the establishment of the Republic.

Franklin's philosophy was too self-confident for us to view his life as a search for values, although he so viewed his early years. He soon enough found the set of values—respectability and probity in business, an accommodating deism in religion, a faith of serving God through service to man in public life—which he followed throughout the rest of his long career. His intellectual energy was equalled only by his curiosity, and his theoretical interests never far outran his pragmatism in applying new concepts. No sooner had he discovered the electric nature of lightning than he patented a lightning-rod! Here was Yankee science at its birth, in which intuitive hunches lead to the discovery of great principles, and those discoveries to immediate applications.

But if Franklin had no doubt about his own identity, we cannot say the same for every young man who emulated him by trying half a dozen careers. Washington Irving and Walt Whitman taught school and edited newspapers and entered politics before discovering their essential selves. Melville of course was teacher, clerk, sailor, whaler, captive of cannibals, and Polynesian beachcomber until he found by the accident of writing his adventures that literature was his true career. Mark Twain started out as cub pilot, miner, and itinerant journalist, before making the literary strike that uncovered his richest ore. What a man does determines in the long run what he is. These writers did not know who they were until they found their right vocations. Yet their writings are populated with American characters who, true to the expansive spirit of the age, move from one identity to another with neither effort, preparation, nor reflection. At the same time, however, the problem of identity, of discovering the essential self, has been a particularly acute one in American literature. With so many selves to choose from, anyone who does have deeper commitments to the life of the spirit than Melville detected in Ben Franklin must discover which of his own masks is made of the flesh and skin of the face that wears it.

The metamorphic variety of American life and the impetus it gave toward self-determined transformation is thus made spectacularly apparent in Ben Franklin's career. Franklin, with his universality, fairly represents the nascent American character. In popular culture and our early literature, however, native characters did not have Franklin's easy movement through all the conditions of life. They began as local characters whose idiosyncrasies were typical of their regions. From the first the colonies had been differentiated by their several creeds, methods of settlement, and systems of government. These differences, to which was added the greatest difference of all—that between the life of the settled seaboard and the harsh existence of the frontier—are already visible in the earliest depictions of indigenous character. As befits a national literature in its primitive beginnings, these earliest depictions often appear in theatricals. They were, in fact, ritualistic portraits in which the several identities of the American were enacted and revealed. Whether as Yankee peddler or Kentucky boatman, metamorphosis, on a humbler level than Franklin's yet just as self-determined and as optimistic, was at the core of their nature.

Two

One evening in Boston, in 1838, a crowd in a theatre gasped with awe and terror as Dan Marble, the famous Yankee actor, deliberately leaped over Niagara Falls—from the very roof of the theatre, seventy feet above the stage—to reappear, ebulliently, in a pool of foam. The piece of which this leap was the climax was *Sam Patch: or, The Daring Yankee*. Many in the audience had already seen, or would soon see, the renowned James Hackett, another actor, in his famous impersonation of Nimrod Wildfire, 'The Lion of the West.' This remarkable hero of *The Kentuckian; or, A Trip to New York*, in his buckskin and powder-horn, characteristically admonished an English fop.

If you think to get rid of me without exchanging a shot, you might as well try to scull a potash kettle up the falls of Niagara with a crowbar for an oar.

Defying the falls of Niagara, as Carlyle observed at about this time, was a proverbial expression of the American Spirit. And so were the two rodomontade braggarts on the stage. The Yankee and the Frontiersman had come out of the country village and the virgin timber, shouting their boasts, revelling in their own rusticity. These two plays were but selected instances in a flood of stage pieces, journalistic sketches, almanac characters, humorous collections, folk-told yarns, ballads, doggerel verses, and songs which limned their collective portraits in the early nineteenth century. Not only did they body forth the types already long familiar to the popular mind; their adventures, as sung, written, read, and enacted in crude though symbolic gestures, exemplified the attitudes toward character and destiny of the popular culture whose creatures they became.

The impulse which launched these rustic heroes on their impudent careers reverberated too in the aphoristic profundity of a voice much more couth than theirs. While Nimrod Wildfire and Sam Patch cavorted on their respective stages, in a nearby lecture hall another crowd leaned forward in hushed attention to a seer's admonishment:

There is a time in every man's education when he arrives at the conviction that envy is ignorance; that imitation is suicide; that he must take himself for better or for worse as his portion . . . The power which resides in him is new in nature, and none but he knows what that is which he can do, nor does he know until he has tried. . . .

Whoso would be a man must be a nonconformist. . . . No law can be sacred to me but that of my own nature. Good and bad are but names very readily transferable to that or this; the only right is what is after my constitution, the only wrong what is against it.

The evening's lecture was 'Self-Reliance'; the lecturer, an accomplished impersonator who, on other nights, would be billed as 'The Hero,' 'The Poet,' 'The Philosopher,' 'The American Scholar,' 'The Man of the World,' 'The Reformer,' 'The Transcendentalist.' A decade later he would be characterized in Lowell's 'A Fable for Critics' as

> A Greek head on right Yankee shoulders, whose range
> Has Olympus for one pole, for t'other, the Exchange.

These lines on Emerson, from the pen which in that same year (1848) immortalized the Yankee type in the homely guise of Hosea Biglow, suggest the kinship of the Sage of Concord with the rude and rustic stereotype of regional popular character. The same contradictions that Lowell finds in Emerson he sees in the Yankee at large—'A strange hybrid, indeed, did circumstance beget, here in the New World, upon the old Puritan stock, and the earth never before saw such mystic-practicalism, such niggard geniality, such calculating-fanaticism, such cast-iron enthusiasm, such sour-faced humor, such close-fisted generosity.'[4]

Emerson's transcendental counsel has its affinities with the self-assertive folk spirit of both the Yankee and the Kentuckian. Half mystical though his vision of the world might be, in his attempts to ground the perception of the spirit in the experience of the senses he even leaned toward the folk vocabulary of the time.[5] Yet these affinities with popular culture in Emerson's essays were but fragmentary, compared with the effect the popular stereotypes of character would have on the fiction of his contemporaries, Hawthorne and Melville, and after them, Mark Twain.

What were these images? How did they evolve?

The origin of the very name *Yankee* is a mystery, a secular mystery. *The Dictionary of American English* discovers the term to be no older than the French and Indian War, when it was apparently the cognomen of certain regiments from Connecticut. In any case, we owe to the British redcoats of the Revolution the distinctive sobriquet, for it was they who used it to deride their homespun foes. If we knew who first coined the term we might also be able to know the original author of the song, 'Yankee Doodle.' This catchy fife tune soon enough passed into folk provenience. Its verses recapitulated the adventures of a nascent folk hero—the young man from the provinces who comes to town to enlist in the Continentals and make his way in the world. In the decades after the Revolution this high-stepping, wide-eyed naïf underwent some interesting transmogrifications and enjoyed some adventures as yet unsuspected by the Down East seamen, merchants, and farmers who rallied to Paul Revere's harried cry. 'Yankee Doodle' became a stock property of the Yankee drama which emerged just after the Revolution—the rustic Jonathans, Jedediahs, and Ichabods of a score of plays announced their independence as they whistled, sang or recited the famous song. Even before the song got into plays—the Yankee first walks onstage as the rustic servant Jonathan in Royall Tyler's famous comedy, *The Contrast* (1787)—it had inspired many a stanza depicting rustic life in original poems which took their rhythm and refrain from its well-nigh universal popularity. Among the most popular of these was a broadside written in 1795 by Thomas Green Fessenden, 'Jonathan's Courtship,' known also as 'The Country Lovers':

---

[4] 'Introduction' to *The Biglow Papers*, first series; *Works* (Boston and New York, 1890), VIII, 35.

[5] See John Q. Anderson, 'Emerson and the Language of the Folk,' in Mody C. Boatright, et al., ed., *Folk Travelers* (Dallas, 1953), pp. 152–9; and C. Grant Loomis, 'Emerson's Proverbs,' *Western Folklore*, XVII (Oct. 1958), 257–62.

A merry tale will I rehearse,
    As ever you did hear, sir,
How Jonathan set out so fierce
    To see his dearest dear, sir.

Yankee Doodle, keep it up,
    Yankee doodle dandy,
Mind the musick—mind the step,
    And with the girls be handy. . . .

'Miss Sal, I's going to say, as how
    'We'll spark it here tonight,
'I kind of love you, Sal, I vow,
    'And Mother said I might.' . . .
        Yankee doodle &c. . . .

'Are you the lad who went to town,
    'Put on your streaked *trowses,*
'Then vow'd you could not see the town,
    'There were so many houses?'
        Yankee doodle, &c. . . .

Here was Jonathan Jolthead, rustic swain: circumlocutious, head abulge with gossip and afire with witchcraft superstition, bashful, tongue-tied, and afraid for his life of sparking. A more amusing picture of a farm boy's discomfiture in romance was not rhymed again for half a century, until Lowell wrote 'The Courtin'.' Fessenden's broadside was at once reprinted, anthologized, and republished in his *Original Poems* (London, 1805; Philadelphia, 1806). Its comic portrayal of the New England rustic represents the first stage in the emergence of the Yankee as a character type.[6]

The second stage is his appearance in plays. The earliest stage Yankees, like Jonathan in *The Contrast,* were usually bumpkin servants on their first trip to town; but soon the Yankee end-man became the center of the show. By the 1820's such character actors as Dan Marble and Yankee Hill were commissioning plays in which to exhibit their mastery of the stereotyped comic character. To the original qualities of rusticity, boastfulness, inquisitiveness, and independence, played off against the mores of a more highly polished urban society, the Yankee as hero added a bracing bravery, downright honesty, and upstanding moral certitude. These sterling qualities were often exhibited in plots of treacle which in-

[6] In the preface to his London edition Fessenden wrote, 'My allusions and metaphors are mostly taken from objects which I saw in America around me. My nymphs and swains are not of Arcadian breed. My Jonathans and my Tabithas are more like the Cloddipoles and Blouzelindas of Gay than the Damons and Daphnes of Pope; and I will not assert, that I have not, in some instances, *caricatured* the manners of the New England rusticks. Still, however, the peasantry of New England, as described in my poems, will be found to bear some semblance to what they are in real life.' (p. xi.)

volved the attempt of a villain to seduce or abduct the heroine—dastardly knavery foiled by the indomitable Jonathan. In Richard M. Dorson's detailed study of these early plays, at least eleven examples of stock Yankee characters appear before 1819. Since these all conform to a single type rather than exhibit individual characteristics, Dorson concludes that 'it is more probable that a permanent Yankee folk type existed apart from [Tyler's] dramatic imagination and was adopted, and not created, by the playwrights.' The facts that the playwrights sometimes used the Yankee traits as a disguise for other characters and that these plays have repeated references to the Yankee as 'an original,' 'a perfect natural,' 'a real live Yankee,' indicate the 'existence of a mythical Yankee who was properly the property of the folk.' Further evidence is the 'tendency to give individual examples of the genus a common name, Jonathan.'[7] Tyler's play stated the theme which most of the later stage Yankees repeated: the contrast between the polished manners of the English dandy (aped by his obsequious butler), who proves to be both a villain and a fraud, and the dashing honesty and manliness of the American swain, aided by his oafish, naïve, and bungling Yankee servant, Jonathan, who has a heart of gold beneath a comically unsophisticated exterior.

On stage the Yankee had been the country clown in the city. A smart Down East editor, Seba Smith of Portland, hit upon the notion of rusticating the now-familiar Yankee character, and exhibiting him against the background of his native village. Happily, Smith was able to elaborate this conception, having an unusual ear for the cadences and vocabulary of actual New England country speech and a sense of humor which delighted in comic portraiture as well as in political satire. Once Jonathan is recast as Major Jack Downing of Downingville, Away Down East in the State of Maine, he suddenly ceases to be the oafish victim of his own unfamiliarity with the decorum of the city. The Yankee as countryman reverses the role. He now plays a version of Pastoral, in which he possesses the limitless wisdom of his motherwit. It is the complexities of an overweening sophistication, both social and political, which get the short end of the axe handle when measured against his horse sense, honesty, and shrewdness in appraising human motives. Smith could take advantage, in the Major Jack Downing papers, of the satirical possibilities offered him by a character both naïve and clairvoyant. Thus Major Downing, as a political commentator, acts on the presumption that in a democracy the common citizen can address the head of the State (he writes directly to General Jackson), since the Government cares as much about each of the people as the people care about the Government. His

---

[7] 'The Yankee on the Stage—A Folk Hero of American Drama,' *New England Quarterly*, XII (Sept. 1940), 467–93, esp. pp. 468, 472, 480–82.

native village is named for his grandfather, a doddering gaffer who de-
tains every passerby with his endless account of the 'fatigue of Burgwine.'
The old soldier's discursive garrulity, first published in 1833, would not
be matched in print until Mark Twain wrote down 'His Grandfather's Old
Ram' in *Roughing It* (1871). The Major's grandfather was not only a
Revolutionary soldier, but also a pioneer. It is curious how his settling as
far Down East as he could go prefigures the western treks of so many
later veterans and folk heroes. When Major Downing first appears, then,
he is seen in the settlement his own family had founded and lived in for
three generations. This roots him to a place in a way that most Yankee
characters are not rooted in popular lore; at the same time Downingville
prefigures the Jalaam of Lowell's *Biglow Papers,* the Poganuc and Oldtown of Mrs. Stowe's novels, the Deep Haven of Miss Jewett's stories,
the Tilbury Town of Robinson's poems, and so represents a large forward
step in the development of New England's regional literature.

On the 18th of January, 1830, readers of the Portland, Maine, *Daily
Courier* first made the acquaintance of Jack Downing. In a letter to his
cousin Ephraim Downing, 'up in Downingville,' Jack declared as how he
had come to Portland to 'sell my load of axe handles, and mother's
cheese, and cousin Nabby's bundle of footings.' While in town he has
'been to meeting, and to the museum, and to both Legislaters, the one
they call the House, and the one they call the Sinnet.' Of course this village boy is the yokel of Yankee jokelore, who doesn't get the point at all
of the political wrangling he sees. But as a matter of fact the parlia-
mentary wranglers look pretty venal and stupid when measured against
his clear notions of how a democratic legislature ought to conduct itself.
This simple pattern of using the good life of the bumpkin village to
measure the devious city takes full advantage of the nostalgia for a
golden age of simplicity. The rural village appears constantly in American
literature, oratory, and thought as an almost-contemporary symbol of the
Golden Age. Associated with this concept are several other equally
seminal notions: Rousseau's ideal of the Noble Natural Man, Crèvecoeur's
idealization of the farmer, Jefferson's of the artisan and farmer class; and
the opposite but complementary conceptions about the city as the place
of evil. The usual pattern of one numerous genre of the American novel is
to move an innocent character from his country home into the temptations and evils of city life. This pattern conforms not only to that found
in the 'young man from the province' class of novels, but also to the
movement of populations in the American nineteenth and twentieth centuries.

With the Rural Village as the locus of a paradisal symbolism in folklore and popular culture, we may well expect to find secular analogues
to the Fall. Seba Smith achieved a delicate balance in Jack Downing
between innocence and knowledge; his Major—his whole village of

Downingville—has a knowledge which does not cost them their Down East paradise because it is instinctual knowledge, not the hard, mean knowledge gained by experience. Their innate good natures and their birthright of Yankee wisdom make such characters as Major Downing inviolable against chicanery. (The stage Yankee, too, had been a towering pine tree of natural goodness and virtue.) But when the Yankee character is uprooted from the stabilizing influences of village life, and, in accordance with the mercantile temper of the times, takes to the roads with a pack of notions, clocks, and nutmegs, the moral quality of our delight in the folk character is perceptibly altered. President Timothy Dwight of Yale College, 'whose experience with the peddlers of Connecticut must have been extensive,' inveighed against their effect upon mercantile morality in New England:

Men, who begin life with bargaining for small wares, will almost invariably become sharpers. The commanding aim of every such man will soon be to make a good bargain: and he will speedily consider every gainful bargain as a good one. The tricks of fraud will assume, in his mind, the same place, which commercial skill and an honourable system of dealing hold in the mind of a merchant. Often employed in disputes, he becomes noisy, pertinacious, and impudent. . . . I believe this unfortunate employment to have had an unhappy influence on both the morals and manners, of the people.[8]

Doubtless there were honest peddlers, but nobody told stories about *them*. In folk anecdote and jokelore the itinerant Yankee peddler came into focus. The sketches featured his pack of notions and his sharp bargaining ways. They told of the Connecticut peddler who tried to sell brooms to the merchants of Providence. (This one was recorded in 1852, three decades after President Dwight's jeremiad.) Having no luck, at last he found a dealer who 'would put his goods at cost price, for the sake of trading.' After long negotiations they agreed to terms: payment for the brooms to be half in cash and half in goods. The brooms unloaded and cash payment made, the merchant asked, 'Now, what will you have for the remainder of your bill?'

The peddler scratched his head . . . walked the floor, whistled, drummed with his fingers on the head of a barrel. By and by, his reply came—slowly and deliberately.

'You Providence fellers are cute, you sell at cost . . . and make money. I don't see how 'tis done. Now I don't know about your goods, barrin' one article, and, ef I take anything else, I may be cheated. So, seein' as t'won't make any odds with you, I guess I'll take brooms. I know them like a book, and can swear to what you paid for 'em.'

[8] *Travels in New-England and New-York* (1821), quoted by G. L. Kittredge, *The Old Farmer and His Almanack* (Cambridge, 1904), p. 145.

Note that this sharp deal was driven because both merchant and peddler pitted wits for the sake of trading. There were countless stories of similar shrewdness.[9]

The heroes of folklore and of popular culture inevitably display those qualities of character which their celebrants admire. Since the recorded anecdotes of the nineteenth century contain so many yarns of this type, we may well ask ourselves what indeed is the significance of the popularity of the Yankee peddler as a roguish picaro. In an interesting discussion of the relation between mythical concepts and personal identity, Jerome S. Bruner remarks on two basic mythic plots:

the plot of innocence and the plot of cleverness—the former being a kind of Arcadian ideal, requiring the eschewal of complexity and awareness, the latter requiring the cultivation of competence almost to the point of guile. The happy childhood, the good man as the child of God, the simple plowman, the Rousseauian ideal of natural nobility—these are the creatures of the plot of innocence. At the other extreme there are Penelope, the suitors, and Odysseus. . . . New versions arise to reflect the ritual and practice of each era—the modifications of the happiness of innocence and the satisfaction of competence.[10]

For early nineteenth-century America, the Yankee villager is one expression of the myth of innocence, the Yankee peddler of the myth of competence. But our native trickster hero has of course sold his soul for knowledge—not that he ever thinks about his soul in the crafty jokelore that preserves the shards from which his *Odyssey* might have been written. Even in the most ambitious attempts to give the peddler a name, a face, a personality, he remains rather the shifty, sparring, crafty side of a man than does he become a personality nearly as well-rounded as Major Downing.

It was a Nova Scotian judge named Thomas Chandler Haliburton who took up Seba Smith's idea of a series of satirical newspaper sketches about a single regional character, and substituted for the village yokel of Downingville a master of shifts and disguises in the itinerant profession. By 1837 Haliburton had published in book form his first collection, *The Clockmaker, or the Sayings and Doings of Samuel Slick*. His Sam Slick is admirable, as tricksters are, without being exactly *likeable*. He

---

[9] On the development of the Yankee peddler see Rourke, *American Humor*, pp. 3–32; Walter Blair, *Native American Humor* (New York, 1937), pp. 17–62; Richardson Wright, *Hawkers & Walkers in Early America* (Philadelphia, 1927). The broom story is from the *Yankee Blade* (Boston, 24 Jan. 1852), reprinted in R. M. Dorson, *Jonathan Draws the Long Bow* (Cambridge, 1946), pp. 81–2. P. T. Barnum told the same yarn a different way, with the merchant outwitting the peddler, in *Struggles and Triumphs*, ed. G. S. Bryan (New York, 1927), pp. 48–50; reprinted in Botkin, *A Treasury of American Folklore*, pp. 394–5. For other yarns see Dorson, *Jonathan*, pp. 78–94; Botkin, *A Treasury of New England Folklore* (New York, 1947), pp. 2–63.

[10] 'Myth and Identity,' *Daedalus* (Spring 1959), pp. 353–4.

peddles his clocks and opinions up and down New England, Canada, the West, and even visits England and the Continent in a series of books that spanned the next twenty years. Fencing wits with whoever crosses his path, he assumes changes of costume (Easterner's broadcloth or Westerner's leggings), temperament, or opinion as the occasion warranted. Like the Connecticut broom peddler, he trades just for the sake of trading; he goes the broom peddler one better, trading not for profit but for pure pride:

> I met a man this morning, said the clockmaker, from Halifax, a real conceited lookin' critter as you een a most ever seed, all shines and didos. He looked as if he had picked up his airs arter some officer of the regulars had worn 'em and cast 'em off. . . .
> Well, says he to me, with the air of a man that chucks a cent into a beggar's hat, a fine day this sir. Do you actily think so said I? and I gave it the real Connecticut drawl. Why, said he, quite short, if I didn't think so, I wouldn't say so. Well says I, I don't know, but if I did think so, I guess I wouldn't say so. Why not? says he— Because, I expect, says I, any fool could see that as well as me; and then I stared at him, as much as to say, now if you like that are swap, I am ready to trade with you agin as soon as you like.[11]

Now the yokel comes out on top against the city slicker, a further reversal of the earlier Yankee role.

By the Civil War the Yankee stereotype had divided in the popular mind, as journalists and dramatists spawned two varieties of Yankee creatures to catch the public fancy. His shrewd, narrow-nosed commercialism and self-seeking aspects, joined to his impervious egotism and colossal self-satisfaction, made for a caricature of the already proverbial type. Sam Slick was the most popular expression of this side of the Yankee—albeit Lowell accused him of being a slander against the regional character. To the South, in Alabama, another rogue's adventures were laughingly devoured in the newspapers where Johnson J. Hooper first published his *Adventures of Simon Suggs* (reprinted in book form, 1845). Hooper's hero, whose motto proclaimed 'IT IS GOOD TO BE SHIFTY IN A NEW COUNTRY,' is the most fully developed American picaro before Melville's *The Confidence-Man*. In this introductory passage his creator allows us a glimpse behind the comic mask Simon usually wore:

> The shifty Captain Suggs is a miracle of shrewdness. He possesses in an eminent degree, that tact which enables man to detect *the soft spots* in his fellow, and to assimilate himself to whatever company he may fall in with. Besides, he has a quick, ready wit, which has extricated him from many an unpleasant predicament, and which makes him whenever he chooses to be so— and that is always—very companionable. In short, nature gave the Captain the

---

11 T. C. Haliburton, 'A Yankee Handle for a Halifax Blade,' *The Clockmaker* (Philadelphia, 1837), pp. 101–2.

precise intellectual outfit most to be desired by a man of his propensities. She sent him into the world a sort of he-Pallas, ready to cope with his kind from infancy, in all the art by which men 'get along' in the world; if she made him in respect to his moral conformation, a beast of prey, she did not refine the cruelty by denying him the fangs and the claws.[12]

One instance of his avarice and shifty deception is already familiar in Mark Twain's borrowing from 'Simon Suggs Attends a Camp Meeting' for his description of the spiritual and literal piracy of the King in *Huckleberry Finn* (chap. 20).

Yet the native picaro had admirable qualities too—his enterprise, his adaptability, and his peddler's mission (whatever the motive) of bringing the comforts of civilization to every cabin on the farthest frontier. In the 1840's a folk hero embodying these qualities appeared. First in cabins and farms along the Muskingum valley, then in the pages of Henry Howe's *Historical Collections of Ohio,* and eventually in the folklore and fiction of the entire country, the adventures of Johnny Appleseed grew even more miraculously than did the orchards he had planted. Paddling down the Ohio to Marietta at the mouth of the Muskingum, then up that stream to its tributaries' tributaries, John Chapman set out apple seeds to make ready the earth for populations yet unborn. He also left behind him books, which he split into sections and passed out to lonely settlers on one trip, circulating the fragments from cabin to cabin on his return. Beloved by the Indians, he was immune to their ferocities during the War of 1812; in fact he saved many settlers from their vengeance. He befriended the animals; if he saw one abused by its master he would buy it and give it away to a more humane pioneer. Johnny Appleseed spoke frequently with angels.

It does not matter that a painstaking biography of John Chapman shows him to have been a Yankee trader after all. Born in Leominster, Massachusetts, in 1774, he appeared, during his travels in Ohio, to be as representative a Yankee type in his "mystic-practicalism' as any friend of Hosea Biglow in Jalaam. First, his mysticism. Robert Price has shown how theologically sophisticated was this early disciple of Swedenborg and how important his role in spreading the doctrine of the New Jerusalem on the unpromisingly hard terrain of the Ohio frontier. He even offered to trade some of his land to the New Church in return for shipments of Swedenborg's tracts, which he would disseminate on his journeys. This offer points to the conclusion that Johnny Appleseed was no 'pauper philanthropist'—actually he owned hundreds of acres of choice Ohio land and based his seemingly eccentric life on a sound principle of economics. 'The one unique thing about John's seedling tree business . . . was his scheme for moving it with the frontier.'[13] These facts,

[12] *Adventures of Captain Simon Suggs* (Philadelphia, 1845), pp. 12–13.
[13] Robert Price, *Johnny Appleseed: Man and Myth* (Bloomington, Ind., 1954), p. 38. A popular romanticized account, from which the foregoing details are drawn,

which Price spent years tracking down, were obliterated by the popular image of Johnny Appleseed, as it was embellished and romanticized in succeeding decades. To become this humble image of the Hero as Civilizer, Sam Slick had to cast off all his characteristics but his garments and his peripatetic ways. Gone are the shiftiness, the cunning, the insidious sophistry, the trade for the sake of trading. To bring religion and reading to the trappers and woodsmen in their lonely cabins, to enrich the hillsides with orchards for the sake of mankind yet to come, this peddler all but denies his Yankee lineage.

Yankee self-assertion—the impulse of self-definition through symbolic action—appears most dramatically in the figure of Sam Patch. Like Johnny Appleseed, Patch was an actual person, a textile worker in Pawtucket, Rhode Island, who attracted local attention by plunging, feet first, from the roof of a shed into the river beneath. Spurred on to seek fortune and national fame by spectacular leaps, Sam Patch abandoned his loom for a grand tour of waterfalls. Heralded by handbills proclaiming his motto, 'Some things may be done as well as others,' he climbed to flimsy platforms and plunged into the swirling froth. Sam conquered the great Niagara, but the Falls of Genesee at last proved his undoing. Attempting his feat after one too many drinks of whiskey, he lost his poise about twenty feet from the water and landed sideways. As often happens, a mysterious death may catapult a poseur into legendary fame. Sam's body didn't come to the surface for six months. By then it was far too late to prove that he was dead. He had jumped through the bowels of the world and turned up alive in the South Seas.[14] He was also knocking about the American West, as alleged by many travellers. While some might scoff, none could deny that he had been on the stage of many a theatre. As Nature imitates Art, so men are tempted to assume the role of the heroes in their myths: Dan Marble leaped from the height of the theatre into a trap in the floor, behind the pool of water, where a bedspring padded with shavings cushioned his fall. Even more significant than professional theatricals, however, 'the jumping mania affected audiences. Clerks jumped counters, farmers jumped fences, boys and old folks vied in "doing" Sam Patch.'[15]

---

is W. D. Haley, 'Johnny Appleseed: A Pioneer Hero,' *Harper's New Monthly Magazine*, XLIII (Nov. 1871), 830–36; reprinted in Botkin, *A Treasury of American Folklore*, pp. 261–70.

[14] In an amusing sidelight by one folk hero on another, Sam Slick tells Edward Everett of Congress about Patch: 'The last dive he took was off the falls of Niagara [sic] and he was never heered of again till tother day, when Captain Enoch Wentworth, of the Susy Ann Whaler, saw him in the South Sea. Why, says Captain Enoch to him, why Sam, says he, how on airth did you get here? I thought you was drowned at the Canadian line. Why, says he, I didn't get *on* airth here at all, but I came right slap *through* it. . . . If I don't take the shine off the Sea Serpent, when I get back to Boston, then my name's not Sam Patch.' Haliburton, *The Clockmaker*, p. 46.

[15] The fragments of this curious saga are assembled in R. M. Dorson, 'Sam Patch, Jumping Hero,' *New York Folklore Quarterly*, I (Aug. 1945), pp. 132–51. The latest

Here was a natural subject for celebration by these very clerks and farmers. Sam's common origin, his braggadocio, and senseless defiance of danger—not to mention his showmanship—objectified in one symbolic act the qualities of self-assertive independence, rebellion against convention and authority, and, above all, self-reliance no matter what the stakes or the odds. These attributes had long been rooted in the American grain, in the Yankee character, and the boys and oldsters jumping fences to 'do' Sam Patch were in a sense performing a ritual by which they asserted that for them, too, 'Some things may be done as well as others.' Those things included plunging from the security of seaboard cities into the unfathomed perils of the wilderness.

THREE

The settlers of the West developed images of their indigenous traits too. In the period before the Civil War the prototypical frontiersman, like his Yankee counterpart, provided a multiple image. At first, as Backwoodsman, he is a type of the Natural Man, inherently superior to civilized decadence, his egalitarian goodfellowship not quite disguised by his shaggy exterior and helliferocious manner of speech. Backwoods brawlers must have formed an unofficial fraternity throughout the sparsely settled districts of the young Republic, for early travellers' journals report countless instances of their ear-chewing, cheek-ripping, eye-gouging battles. Augustus Baldwin Longstreet gives vivid descriptions of such fights, and of a lone plowboy's rehearsal of one, in his *Georgia Scenes, Characters, Incidents, &c. in the First Half Century of the Republic,* a work which in 1835 marks the inception of a Frontier literature comparable to the Yankee regional writings discussed above. But Longstreet's 'The Fight' and 'Georgia Theatrics' were no exaggerations of the real thing; if elaborated with tall talk and touched with fantasy, they were yet based on life.

The frontiersman, it is well to remember, was not always a Westerner, but he was usually farther west than the seaboard Yankee. In the early days of the republic the frontier was often just a few miles inshore or a few hundred yards from the inland village or town. In her study, 'The Rise of Theatricals,' Constance Rourke identifies the first frontiersman intended for the American stage as 'A minor character called Raccoon or Coony in the early comic opera *The Disappointment* [who] seems to have been a frontiersman, but the piece was never performed . . . though it was twice printed, in 1787 and 1796, and so must have had some sort of circulation.' By a curious coincidence Royall Tyler's Jonathan emerged

---

literary recrudescence of Sam Patch is to appear as one of the aspects of the hero of William Carlos Williams's epic poem *Paterson* (New York, 1948), pp. 24-7, 48f.

on the stage at the same time (1787), and our two principal character types have been in tandem almost ever since. In her tantalizingly unspecific way Miss Rourke adds that 'With his braggadocio and half-Indian way he was pictured in a few stories of the War of 1812.' Just which stories, whether drama or fiction, she does not say, but she does remark that 'Cockalorum . . . the lively typical figure with his . . . gaudy hunting costume was not to emerge noticeably in the theater until 1822, when he appeared with a rush—to music, gusty music, a song, "The Hunters of Kentucky," which celebrated those backwoods Kentuckians, "half horse, half alligator," who had helped Jackson win the Battle of New Orleans.'[16]

The frontiersman's earliest full-dress appearance in fiction is, surprisingly, in a famous sketch by our first gentleman of polished letters. Brom Bones, in Washington Irving's 'The Legend of Sleepy Hollow,' demonstrates already in 1819 that the Dutch rowdies of the upper Hudson Valley were frontiersmen of the same stamp as the Ohio riverboatmen and Missouri trappers. Lacking the stories of the War of 1812 mentioned by Rourke, however, it would seem that the first frontiersman actually to appear in a stage play is the character Opossum in Alphonso Wetmore's three-act farce, *The Pedlar,* 'Written for the St. Louis Thespians, By Whom It Was Performed with Great Applause' in early 1821. In the final curtain speech Opossum reveals the original on whom his character was doubtless based: 'If you'll let me live single, till after the dog days, Mike Fink and I will go and catch a barr, and we'll have a barbecue, for wedding supper, any how.'[17] In earlier speeches Opossum reproduces the boisterous brag of the backwoods bully:

I'm half sea horse & half sea serpent. Did you ever see my coon dog, stranger? (*Whistles.*) Which eye shall I take out, Mary? . . . I'll tell you, stranger, my name is Opossum—I'm a 'wild-cat'—I've got the swiftest horse, the sharpest shooting rifle, and the prettiest sister—so if you offer to wrestle with her again, you must run faster than the yankee pedlar did, or my coon dog will tree you.

There is, inevitably, a 'yankee pedlar' in the piece:

Nutmeg: Halloo the house! I suppose the old cogger is not up yet. He little thinks the greatest genius in the universe, now stands before his door, ready to cheat him out of half he is worth. (*Window opens, old Prairie puts his head and the muzzle of a rifle out.*)
    Old Prairie. Who the devil are you, Mr. Impudence?
    Nutmeg. A travelling merchant, sir—all the way over the mountains, from

---

[16] Rourke, *The Roots of American Culture* (New York, 1942), pp. 125–6. The song is reprinted from Samuel Woodward's *Melodies, Duets, Trios . . .* (1826) in Botkin, *A Treasury of American Folklore*, pp. 9–10.
    [17] Alphonso Wetmore, *The Pedlar* (St. Louis, 1821), facsimile reprint edited by Scott C. Osborn (Lexington, Ky., 1955), p. 34.

the town of New Haven, with a cart load of very useful, very desirable and very pretty notions: such as, tin cups and nutmegs, candlesticks and onion seeds, wooden clocks, flax seed and lanterns, Japanned coffee pots, and tea *sarvers,* together with a variety of cordage and other dry goods.

By the end of Act I, Nutmeg has sold a lantern to every member of Old Prairie's household and has cheated the sailor Harry Emigrant in a horse-swap.

Contrasted to his shrewdness with its smack of the countinghouse is the energetic activism of the frontiersman. A drunken boatman enters, singing:

> *Boatman.* Quarter less twain. (*Opossum rises, and advances.*)
> *Opossum.* Who are you, stranger?
> *Boatman.* A steam boat, damn your eyes.
> *Opossum.* Then I'm a Missouri snag—I'm into you.
> *Boatman.* I'm full of chain pumps—come on—I'm a five horse team.
> *Opossum.* Then I'll blaze your leader. (*Strikes him in the face . . .*)
> *Boatman.* No gouging?
> *Opossum.* And no ear biting . . .

It is obvious that these three characters, who so closely resemble the Yankee peddlers and ring-tailed roarers of the Jacksonian newspaper sketches a decade later, are based on the already widely known stock figures of oral tradition. Yet *The Pedlar* is not lacking in literary derivations. As Scott C. Osborn's preface to the recent reprint observes, Wetmore's piece is 'A crude mixture of melodrama, farce, low comedy, Restoration comedy, and intrigue play . . .' *The Pedlar* is 'derivative almost throughout,' based entirely on stock devices—'disguises, mistaken identities, assignations, the fortuitous discovery of a long-lost son and a will, the eloping couples.' The characters too are dramatic conventions: the female wit, the clever servant, the discomfited father, the old man in love with a young girl; 'Pecanne is a Lydia Languish, Opossum a Tony Lumpkin, Harry Emigrant an imitation of salty-spoken sailors from Wycherly on.' Two scenes are adapted from *She Stoops To Conquer,* while 'Nutmeg's lament for the loss of his wares is a burlesque of Wolsey's farewell to his greatness.' The playwright who combined dependence upon all of these eighteenth-century staples with realistic observations of frontier life and the adaptation of native stereotypes from oral tradition was a Connecticut-born soldier, merchant, lawyer, publisher, and sometime author. Osborn concludes that '*The Pedlar* has no literary value,' and that its only merit 'lies in its Western characters and local color.' Part of its historical value, however, is to remind us of the complexity of the literary matrix into which characters, themes, and settings from folklore were introduced. Even so crude a production as *The Pedlar* (the only play by a man who was after all a literary amateur) demonstrates the cultural background—richly cosmopolitan, by folk standards—of the earliest drama on the American frontier.

The Pedlar illustrates one of the knottiest problems involved in understanding the absorption of folk materials into literature. The transformation to which folklore is necessarily subjected by the literary imagination complicates its identification. Even when the author retells verbatim stories from oral tradition, he is never a folk redactor. The literary context in which he places such tales is itself a change worked upon them. He may enclose the folk motifs in a more elaborate literary structure or contrast them to a different frame of reference than would a folk raconteur telling the same story. Further, he may extend and develop germinal plots or characters. One of the most important functions of folk materials in literature is to offer contrasts to the materials drawn from traditions other than the folk. The interplay of native folklore and European literary traditions is one of the important sources of tension in much American writing. Mark Twain, for instance, made Tom Sawyer a repository of chivalric notions from *Don Quixote* and Sir Walter Scott, while Huck Finn, with his protean disguises, superstitions, innocence, and closeness to nature, is a figure embodying many themes, traits, and motifs of American folklore.

Wetmore's frontiersman had alluded to Mike Fink, the original on whom his own braggart prowess was modelled, almost a decade before Fink himself became the hero of a cult of popular literature which lasted into the 1880's. Walter Blair and Franklin Meine, who reconstructed Fink's biography and reprinted the literature about him, find considerable evidence that in the decade of the 1820's Mike Fink had already become a hero of oral folklore.[18] Like Sam Patch and Johnny Appleseed, Mike was at first just a real man, born in Fort Pitt (Pittsburgh) around 1770 when that rowdy and endangered settlement comprised twenty cabins. Life there hardened the men and boys who lived it, and Mike, as a settler who knew him records, became a prodigy of physical strength, appetites, and endurance. He was soon a supermarksman and a famous hunter.

Mike was bred as an Indian fighter. He had an appetite for that business, which was his first career. Later, when Pittsburgh had grown and the Indians retreated, he became a keelboatman. When the steamboats encroached on the keel- and flat-boats he went west of the rivers and began his third career as a trapper. In each of his manifestations he retreated from society to preserve his own savage nature from change.

[18] *Half Horse Half Alligator: The Growth of the Mike Fink Legend* (Chicago, 1956), pp. 43–55, 260. All of the ensuing accounts of Fink are taken from this collection with the exception of Mike's setting a woman's hair afire, from Henry Howe, *The Great West* (New York, 1857), pp. 277–8, reprinted in Botkin, *A Treasury of American Folklore,* pp. 34–5.

During his lifetime Fink was the hero and scourge of towns along the Ohio and the Mississippi. In time he became the archetype of his breed. 'He was in fact a Mississippi river-god, one of those minor deities whom men create in their own image and magnify to magnify themselves,' Miss Rourke claims for him.[19] Whether fact or legend, the stories told about him typified popular attitudes toward the men who first rid the wilderness of Indians and split the silence of the waters with their boat-horns and ballads of Shawneetown.

Who could have foretold that the first scribe to record the tough saga of this shaggy boatman would be a contributor to a satin-bound ladies' annual? True, *The Western Souvenir, A Christmas and New Year's Gift for 1829,* was published in Cincinnati, and its editor, James Hall, declared independence from Eastern originals, saying, 'It is written and published in the Western country . . . and is chiefly confined to subjects connected with the history and character of the country which gives it birth.' Although Hall, a leading early writer of the Ohio Valley, wrote much of the contents, his work was overshadowed by 'The Last of the Boatmen,' contributed by Morgan Neville. This author had actually known Mike Fink during his own Pittsburgh boyhood. Just as Longstreet in *Georgia Scenes* and Hooper in *Adventures of Simon Suggs* would describe the outrageous barbarity and guile of frontiersmen from the viewpoint of an observer from a higher culture, so did Neville present his uncouth Achilles as a picturesque specimen of an already vanishing phase of Western life. Unlike the later writers from the South, Neville does not abandon his own hifalutin' style to reproduce the barbaric yawp of his subject. He tells of meeting Mike, while on a riverboat, and witnessing Mike's feat of shooting a tin cup from his brother's head —the William Tell motif in buckskins; recounts Mike's prowess at killing an Indian; alludes to 'a thousand legends [that] illustrate the fearlessness of his character'; and reports that his hero died when, performing his tin cup shoot, he aimed too low, and a friend of the victim, 'suspecting foul play, shot Mike through the heart before he had time to re-load his rifle.'

In addition to these simple motifs Neville contributes a picturesque description of his hero and a set of ennobling comparisons:

With a figure cast in a mold that added much of the symmetry of an Apollo to the limbs of a Hercules, he possessed gigantic strength. . . . At the court of Charlemagne he might have been a Roland; with the Crusaders he would have been the favorite of the Knight of the Lion-heart; and in our revolution, he would have ranked with the Morgans and Putnams of the day. He was the hero of a hundred fights, and the leader in a thousand daring adventures. . . . Wherever he was an enemy, like his great prototype, Rob Roy, he levied the

[19] *American Humor,* p. 54.

contribution of Black Mail for the use of his boat. . . . On the Ohio, he was known among his companions by the appellation of the 'Snapping Turtle'; and on the Mississippi, he was called 'The Snag.'

Within the next two decades Fink's adventures were retold and elaborated in such repositories of Western local color as the Cincinnati *Western Monthly Review,* the St. Louis *Reveille,* and the nationally admired *Spirit of the Times;* the authors were such then-prominent litterateurs of the West as Timothy Flint, Thomas Bangs Thorpe, John S. Robb, and Emerson Bennett. Briefer, more vigorous sketches than theirs appeared in the Davy Crockett Almanacks for 1837, 1839, and 1850–53. None of these writings is in itself of first quality, but taken together they form a strong subliterary tradition which defines the anarchic frontiersman's character with a clarity that helps us understand the significance of the type in the writings of Melville and Twain.

The Mike Fink sketches present an unwitting mixture of sentimentality and barbarism. When looking for a fight, Mike Fink announces himself in Emerson Bennett's version of the ringtailed roarer's brag:

Hurray for me, you scapegoats! I'm a land-screamer—I'm a watchdog—I'm a snapping turckle—I can lick five times my own weight in wildcats. I can use up Injuns by the cord. I can swallow niggers whole, raw, or cooked. I can out-lick, out-dance, out-jump, out-dive, out-drink, out-holler, and out-lick any white thing in the shape o' human that's put foot within two thousand miles o' the big Massassip . . .

John S. Robb improved upon the original tale of Mike's marksmanship. He has Mike take up the taunt, 'Why, you couldn't hit the hinder part of that nigger's heel up thar on the bluff, 'thout damagin' the bone.' Dead-eye Fink fired in jest; when the local magistrate tried to arrest him for the prank, Mike quipped, 'I want you to pay me for trimmin' the heel of one of your town niggers! I've just altered his breed, and arter this his posterity kin warr the neatest kind of a boot!' To cure 'a woman who passed for his wife' of winking at another man, Mike made her lie down in a bed of leaves which he then set afire. He kept her there till her hair blazed; this was quite a joke.

Thomas Bangs Thorpe, the author of 'The Big Bear of Arkansas,' wrote of Mike in 'The Disgraced Scalp Lock' (1842). His Fink gives a brave Indian the mortal insult of plucking a feather from his headdress; he pursues Mike a thousand miles down the river but Fink's rifle cheats the Indian of a deserved revenge. Mike's philosophy is dualistic in this sophisticated adventure story: on the one hand he gives us the ruthless wilderness code which Uncle Ben, in Arthur Miller's *Death of a Salesman,* will preach in mid-twentieth-century: 'I was never particular about what's called a fair fight. . . . It's natur that the big fish should eat the little ones.' But speaking in a different voice, Thorpe's Mike transcends his time in this lament:

What's the use of improvements? When did cutting down trees make deer more plenty? Who ever found wild buffalo or a brave Indian in a city? Where's the fun, the frolicking, the fighting? Gone! Gone! The rifle won't make a man a living now—he must turn nigger and work.

The woodsman who makes possible the coming of civilization cries out in nostalgia and bitterness against the things he has wrought. Mike Fink, the retrograde bully and roustabout, is here made to mouth the ambivalent feelings of a more polite public regarding the destruction of the wilderness Eden—in which his cruelties were never called to account—by the oncome of civilization, law, and restraint.

However savage such men as Mike Fink were in fact, their unknowing roles as harbingers of civilization justified an idealization of the frontiersman's character:

Though held in sort a barbarian, the backwoodsman would seem to America what Alexander was to Asia—captain in the vanguard of conquering civilization. Whatever the nation's growing opulence or power, does it not lackey his heels? Pathfinder, provider of security to those who come after him, for himself he asks nothing but hardship. Worthy to be compared with Moses in Exodus, or the Emperor Julian in Gaul, who on foot, and bare-browed, at the head of covered or mounted legions, marched so through the elements, day after day. The tide of emigration, let it roll as it will, never overwhelms the backwoodsman into itself; he rides upon advance, as the Polynesian upon the comb of the spray.

This is Melville, eulogizing the frontiersman in *The Confidence-Man* (1857). Melville's woodsman is not Mike Fink but another Ohio Valley character first drawn by James Hall, who had published Neville's sketch of Fink in 1829. Three years later Hall, in his *Legends of the West*, outlined the career of one Colonel Moredock, a monomaniacal Indian-hater. Although Moredock's passion invests his character with a tragic dignity lacking in Fink, it is noteworthy that Melville's treatment of the woodsman, whom he presents ideally and then in the grimness of his barbarous fixation, parallels the dualistic popular conceptions of frontier character.

A decade after *The Pedlar* appeared, the poets William Cullen Bryant and Fitz-Greene Halleck served, with Prosper Wetmore, as judges of a contest offering a three hundred dollar prize for 'an original comedy whereof an American should be the leading character.' The winner was James Kirke Paulding with his farce, *The Lion of the West*. The play was produced the following year (1831), but in the course of its theatrical history it was twice rewritten—the second time, for its London run in 1833, by William Bayle Bernard who retitled it *The Kentuckian, or A Trip to New York*. Bernard's, presumably, is the version in which James H. Hackett, the actor-producer who offered the original prize, continued to appear in America as Nimrod Wildfire for over two decades. Yet with the exception of a single speech of backwoods braggadocio quoted in the *Daily Louisville Public Advertiser* for October 17, 1831, the text of Paulding's play disappeared and *The Lion of the West* has been known only by reputation for 125 years. Now, thanks to the resourceful literary detection of James N. Tidwell, the text of Bernard's adaptation has been recovered from the British Museum.[20] There is some doubt as to how closely the Bernard text resembles Paulding's original, yet a comparison of the condensed newspaper extract, the backwoodsman's brag, with the corresponding passage in Tidwell's edition shows only minor discrepancies. I quote the entire speech to show, among other things, the development of rhetorical bragging over the rough-and-ready brawling of Wetmore's Opossum. Nimrod Wildfire tells the following yarn to illustrate to an English merchant the fighting customs of his native region:

Well, I'll tell you how it was. I was riding along the Mississippi one day when I came across a fellow floating down the stream sitting cock'd up in the starn of his boat fast asleep. Well, I hadn't had a fight for as much as ten days—felt as though I must kiver myself up in a salt bin to keep—'so wolfy' about the head and shoulders. So, says I, hullo, stranger, if you don't take keer your boat will run away wi'you. So he looked up at me 'slantindicular,' and I looked down on him 'slanchwise.' He took out a chaw of tobacco from his mouth and, says he, I don't value you tantamount to that, and then he flopp'd his wings and crowed like a cock. I ris up, shook my mane, crooked my neck, and neighed like a horse. Well, he runs his boat foremost ashore. I stopped my waggon and set me triggers. Mister, says he, I'm the best man—if I ain't, I wish I may be tetotaciously exflunctified! I can whip my weight in wild cats and ride strait through a crab apple orchard on a flash of lightning—clear meat axe disposition! And what's more, I once back'd a bull off a bridge. Poh, says I, what do I keer for that? I can tote a steam boat up the Mississippi and over the Alleghany mountains. My father can whip the best man in old Kaintuck, and I can whip my father. When I'm good natured I weigh about a hundred and seventy, but when I'm mad, I weigh a *ton*. With that I fetched him the regular Ingen warwhoop. Out he jumped from his boat, and down I tumbled from my waggon—and, I say, we came together like two steam boats going sixty mile an hour. He was a pretty severe colt, but no part of a priming to such a feller as me. I put

---

[20] By a coincidence the Bernard text was discovered at the same time by Nils Erik Enkvist, *American Humour in England before Mark Twain* (Abo, Finland, 1953), p. 22. The condensation of Nimrod's brag appears in M. M. Mathews, *The Beginnings of American English* (Chicago, 1931), pp. 116–17; and in Botkin, *A Treasury of American Folklore*, pp. 13–14. The full text appears in *The Lion of the West*, ed. James N. Tidwell (Stanford, 1954), pp. 54–5.

it to him mighty droll—tickled the varmint till he squealed like a young colt, bellowed 'enough' and swore I was a 'rip staver.' Says I, *ain't* I a horse? Says he, stranger, you're a *beauty* anyhow, and if you'd stand for Congress I'd vote for you next *lection*. Says I, would you? My name's Nimrod Wildfire. Why, I'm the yaller flower of the forest. I'm all *brimstone but* the *head,* and that's *aky fortis.*

In the literary development of cockalorum bragging, Paulding's version stands midway between Wetmore's crude reduction of the real thing and Mark Twain's still more rhetorical grandiloquence in the raftsmen's fight in the third chapter of *Life on the Mississippi.* The voyage of *The Lion of the West,* and its influence upon later characterizations of the frontiersman, may be inferred from the popularity of this one speech. We can assume that the Louisville paper was, like most other journals of the time, widely exchanged, and that Nimrod Wildfire's boast was widely read by editors and journalists elsewhere on the frontier. It was also much copied and plagiarized. A Paulding scholar has made two interesting discoveries about this fight anecdote: first, Paulding himself had written a similar sketch fourteen years earlier in *Letters from the South* about a battle between a bateaux-man and a wagoner; and second, the much superior version from his play was lifted by the author of *The Sketches and Eccentricities of Col. David Crockett of West Tennessee* (1833), who changed little beside the name of the candidate in the next election.[21] This, however, was fair enough, since Paulding had modelled Nimrod Wildfire on Davy Crockett in the first place. When, according to one observer, 'at Crockett's request Hackett gave the play in Washington,' and came on stage in the character of Wildfire, he 'bowed first to the audience and then to Crockett. The redoubtable Davy returned the compliment to the amusement and gratification of the spectators.'[22]

The pattern of humor in *The Lion of the West* devolves upon the contrast between Nimrod Wildfire and one Mrs. Wollope, an English lady bearing an unmistakable resemblance to the author of the recently published *Domestic Manners of the Americans.* Arriving in America, she remarks:

At length I've reached the scene of my experiment. To ameliorate the barbarism of manners in America has been the ruling wish of my life . . . the plan I have concerted is founded, I conceive, on a true knowledge of the national character. The root of all the evils of this country is familiarity—where every one is equal, every one is familiar; and this is linked with another barbarism—the women here like those of Turkey are treated as domestic slaves. Now my system is to raise my own sex to its proper dignity, to give them the command and so refine the men.

[21] Floyd C. Watkins, 'James Kirke Paulding's Early Ring-Tailed Roarer,' *Southern Folklore Quarterly,* XV (Sept. 1951), 183–7.

[22] Tidwell, 'Introduction' to *The Lion of the West,* p. 8.

It is curious to see how this sententious and self-righteous English-woman (as Paulding depicts her) offers, as the butt of the satire, two opinions which other American authors would find in the native grain. James Fenimore Cooper and Herman Melville (in *The Confidence-Man*) would have no quarrel with her suspicion of the evils of egalitarian dogma; while Hawthorne, in *The Blithedale Romance* and Henry James in *The Bostonians* would show the passion for feminist agitation to be, as James observes in his notebook, 'the most salient and peculiar point in our social life.' As a dramatic work *The Lion of the West* is slapdash; its humor is rudimentary, its situations stock, and Paulding's opinions pretty chauvinistic. The comedy runs along these lines:

Caesar. Gemman at de bar send you his card.
Mrs. Wollope. His card—the king of clubs? (*Turns it over and reads*) Colonel
   Wildfire. Is he a gentleman?
Caesar. Don't know, marm—said he was a horse. (*Exit*)
Mrs. Wollope. A horse! Oh, of the horse—a cavalry officer—the very thing I
   wished to see. Now for a specimen of an American gentleman.

Wildfire enters, brings forward two chairs, sits in one and puts his feet on the other. Mrs. Wollope inquires where he is from:

Wildfire. Old Kaintuck's the spot. There the world's made upon a large scale.
Mrs. Wollope. A region of superior cultivation—in what branch of science do
   its gentlemen excel?
Wildfire. Why, madam, of all the fellers either side of the Alleghany hills, I
   myself can jump higher—squat lower—dive deeper—stay longer under and
   come out drier.

A moment later he tells her the yarn of the hat floating in the swamp —when he lifted it with his whip, 'a feller sung out from under it, Hallo stranger, who told you to knock my hat off? . . . I'm doing beautifully—got one of the best horses under me that ever burrowed—claws like a mole.' 'This,' says Mrs. Wollope, 'shall be the first well authenticated anecdote in my perusal.'[23] If the Englishwoman is an overbearing snob, the backwoodsman is likewise a caricature, although of course a kindly one. His integrity as one of Nature's noblemen makes a manly contrast to the cowardice of another character, a fraudulent English lord. The Flower of the Forest always shows his virtues best when played off against the decadence and the moral decay which our popular

---

[23] This yarn became, or had already become, one of the most popular tall tales on the frontier. Paulding's is the earliest version I have found, but others appear in Thoreau's *Walden* (1854); in *The Spirit of the Times* (1856); in Rourke, *American Humor*, pp. 37–8 (printed without attribution); in Vance Randolph, *We Always Lie to Strangers* (New York, 1951), pp. 253–4.

mythology viewed as the inevitable burdens of complex social organization and of the aristocratic past.

The figure of Nimrod Wildfire in Paulding's play lends support to Mody Boatright's contention that 'tall talk . . . is a notification of the repudiation of the values of the outsiders, that is, of gentility. . . . The frontier braggart assumed the role expected of him; but in exaggerating it to comic epic proportions, he satirized it.'[24] The difficulty with this argument is that on occasion the satire becomes the thing itself. This we may observe in the case of Davy Crockett, the real-life original of Paulding's Nimrod Wildfire.

FOUR

Colonel Crockett has but lately died another death. For almost a century, only folklorists studying the heroes of nineteenth-century tall tales or historians interpreting the Age of Jackson concerned themselves with the life and supposed writings of David Crockett or with the fragmentary yarns and apocryphal legends which became attached to his name. The resurrection of Davy Crockett as a temporary hero of contemporary culture is a sociological phenomenon of great interest. Why should this all-but-forgotten congressman from the canebrakes, this picturesque bear-killing, yarn-spinning, hard-drinking Indian fighter with no qualification for public life other than his gregarious manner and ready tongue, suddenly become a national infatuation whose fame was celebrated in every medium of mass communication, whose name endorsed a hundred and one products in the market place?

In considering Crockett's recent resurrection it is well to remember that he had had two earlier careers as a figure in the popular imagination. The first corresponds more or less to the events of his own lifetime, as they are recounted in his 'autobiography.' This is the Crockett whom V. L. Parrington attacks in *Main Currents of American Thought* —the ignoramus who buys his constituents drinks to win their votes, the wise-cracking hick whose folksy jokes distract the crowd from the serious speeches of his better-qualified opponents. This is the Crockett who boasts that 'at the age of fifteen, I did not know the first letter in the book,' and then when appointed a magistrate he could scarcely sign his name but "relied on natural born sense, and not on law to guide me; for I had never read a page of law book in all my life.'[25] The popular appeal of this Crockett is easy to assess, even though the book

[24] *Folk Laughter on the American Frontier*, p. 22.
[25] *The Autobiography of David Crockett*, ed. Hamlin Garland (New York, 1923), pp. 36, 90.

to which a friend more literate than he signed his name (*A Narrative of the Life of David Crockett . . .* [1834]) is one of the most pedestrian and circumstantial of American biographies. Crockett's amanuensis (the evidence compiled by James A. Shackford[26] indicates that he was Thomas Chilton) was not an able writer. Only in the accounts of the Colonel's electioneering does his style approach the vividness of a well-told yarn; this, despite the opportunities many Indian fights and bear hunts afforded him to draw the long bow. Despite its flatness, however, this life of Crockett had popular appeal because his career confirmed a stereotyped pattern of American life. It tells 'how I worked along to rise from a canebrake to my present station in life,'[27] and gives jocular intimations that a seat in Congress is only a way-station on the road to the White House. This is not merely a success story, a rags-to-riches fable; it is an incarnation of the democratic dogma at its lowest level. The Crockett of *A Narrative* professes to love his parents, to share his meat with the hungry, to be a brave fighter and a skilled hunter, to stand on his principles against even President Jackson; but what makes him a success is none of these virtues. It is his ability to feel out the meanest level of approach in dealing with his constituents, to conceal from them his ignorance of the matters on which he will have to deliberate, and to undercut his opponents in stumping the district. The appeal of Crockett as politician is dangerous and demagogic. As Randall Jarrell has remarked in quite another connection, 'When you defeat me in an election simply because you were, as I was not, born and bred in a log cabin, it is only a question of time until you are beaten by someone whom the pigs brought up out in the yard.'

But Crockett as politician fades from the popular memory even during his own lifetime, and the outlines of the second phase of his renown begin to emerge. Now, in *Colonel Crockett's Exploits and Adventures in Texas* (1836) the magnetism of Crockett the frontiersman already attracts incident and anecdote from free-floating comic tradition, both oral and journalistic, and his adventures verge on the fabulous. The climax of course is the apocryphal account of his heroic death at the Alamo. Thereafter, as Constance Rourke observes in her biography of Crockett, the popular imagination took license to make of Crockett what it would. The best indication of what his second image became is found in the anecdotes from the Crockett almanacs collected in Richard M. Dorson's *Davy Crockett: American Comic Legend*. Here is a genre of popular literature—the yarn—scarcely removed from oral tradition; the best of these almanac stories derive their rhetorical structure, their vividly animistic imagery, and their compelling combination of the humorous, the grotesque, the heroic, and the horrible from the art

---

[26] *David Crockett, The Man and the Legend* (Chapel Hill, 1956), pp. 89–90.
[27] *Autobiography,* ed. Garland, p. 111.

of the folk raconteur.[28] Here we find Crockett supernaturally hideous, Crockett entering the animal world, Crockett displaying Jovian and Promethean prowess, Crockett screaming his brag, Crockett snapping fire and lightning from his knuckles, Crockett climbing Niagara, Crockett saving the earth from extinction with a kick and a daub of bear-oil when the sun freezes fast on its axis.

The diction of these fantasies is as remarkable as their situations; the yarns abound in such prodigies of the language as 'tetotatious,' 'exfluncate,' 'absquatulate,' 'slantindicular.' Where the Crockett of the autobiographies congratulated himself on his own illiteracy, these etymological sideshows are obviously parodies of the Latinate vocabulary and rhetorical fustian of the high oratorical style of the time. To have invented or understood the point of such words as these, one would have to be capable of comprehending Mr. Henry Clay, and perhaps of declining Latin nouns oneself.

'Popular declamation of the '30's and '40's has often been considered as bombast when it should be taken as comic mythology,' Miss Rourke observes.[29] This mythology, like every other, must embody widely shared convictions about man's place in the universe. When Crockett appears as a virtual demigod he does indeed represent communal values colored by folk fantasy. He symbolizes man's uneasy relation to nature on the frontier. His aggressions against bears and his command of lightning and waterspouts are surely imaginative reactions to peril. If this second Crockett is mythological, the myth is that man can easily conquer nature and control it. In the most Promethean of his exploits—his rescuing the world from icy darkness by freeing the earth and sun from the frozen machinery of the universe—his reward is not the vulture and the rock, but this:

The sun walked up beautiful, salutin' me with sich a wind o' gratitude that it made me sneeze. I lit my pipe by the light o' his topknot, shouldered my bear, an' walked home, introducin' people to the fresh daylight with a piece of sunrise in my pocket.

There is not even the recognition of tragic possibility, much less of tragic fate, in these ebullient assertions of man's superhuman powers. The frontiersman knew tragedy enough in the life he lived and the deaths he died, but his folktales and popular writings transformed the materials of tragic life into either melodrama or farce. The folk imagination dealt with such realities as death and decomposition by affirming

---

[28] I have analyzed the narrative craft of some of these stories in *Paul Bunyan, Last of the Frontier Demigods* (Philadelphia, 1952), pp. 41–3. See Howard Mumford Jones's introduction to Dorson's collection; and, for bibliographical references, Dorson's article, 'The Sources of *Davy Crockett: American Comic Legend,' Midwest Folklore*, VIII (1958), 143–9.

[29] *American Humor*, p. 64.

their existence in terms so outrageously revolting as to deny the mere realities themselves their due in human feeling.

It is apparent that this phase of Crockett's fame corresponds to a passing phase of American history. With the settlement of the frontier, the supplanting of the clearing by the village, the dominance of industry over a handcraft and agrarian economy, and especially the accelerating effects of the Civil War upon social change, the fantasies of Crockett from the ante-bellum frontier faded from the popular mind. Except in Texas, where the Alamo and its traditions have always been revered, Crockett was all but forgotten.

Why, then, was Davy Crockett revived on a nation-wide scale in the 1950's? Did his most recent image draw on either the demagogy of his first popular appearance or the folk fantasy of the second? It is obvious that the third Crockett is an artifact not of folklore but of contemporary popular culture. There was no current oral tradition of folktales to be tapped by the authors of television and radio scripts, comic strips, juvenile storybooks, songs, and jingles. Both the historical Crockett and the almanac folk hero had been so long dead that the new Crockett could be made—would have to be made, to fit contemporary needs and to dramatize contemporary concepts of character.

We can relate the Crockett fad to the increasing antiquarian interest in certain folkloristic materials from the American past. Stanley Hyman, among others, has commented on the growing vogue for 'the folksy' in the theatre, the dance, painting, and other arts.[30] The art forms of popular culture are among the most potent of 'technicways' (to use Howard Odum's term), ready at a moment's notice to create new images to satiate the hungers of the popular imagination. The manufactured heroes of mass media thus fulfill an important function in maintaining the stability of certain values in contemporary society. One such value is the illusion of continuity with the historical past. As many observers have remarked, the need for cultural roots seems to be proportionately greater as the rate of social change increases. The disruptive effects on the sense of personal identity of rapid technological change, the high rate of social and spatial mobility, and the insecurities inevitable in a culture where status is (or is thought to be) achieved rather than ascribed—all these factors make attractive the common sharing of references to the national past. This complex of factors applies to the appeal of Davy Crockett even though the majority of the American population is descended from forebears who came to this country after Crockett had died. But since the vision of the national past shared in popular culture is created and presented by the technicways, what is

[30] Stanley Edgar Hyman, 'The American Folksy,' *Theatre Arts*, XXXIII (April 1949), 42–5.

shared is the past that the present desires, not the actual traditions (folkways) of the past as it really was.

Again, if we consider Crockett with the other heroes of juvenile popular culture, we observe that the fantasies they offer of escape from the present are conceived in terms of two contrary simplifications of life. One—the category to which Crockett belongs—presents an idealized past in which technology and science are absent; the other looks forward to a future still more technological and scientific than the present. The alternation between these two juvenile utopias has, I suspect, been going on for quite a time. One would need precise information on the respective reigns of such figures as Tom Swift, Tom Mix, Buck Rogers, the Lone Ranger, and Superman, as well as Davy Crockett. Underlying the variations of these heroes' fantasy-worlds there is of course a basic pattern of similarity. They all not only invite their audiences to escape into the remoteness of the Vanished American West or of the Supercity of the Future; they also reinforce certain values in the world from which they offer escape. The morality of their fantasy-worlds is absolute—no gradations of innocence or guilt. Consequently their decisiveness is never hedged about by such deterrents to immediate action as the complex circumstances of actual life usually and painfully provide. The security they offer is that of absolute rightness combined with force. This is obviously a dangerous simplification, but an attractive one. Crockett, whose motto, as everyone knows, was *'Be sure you're right, then Go Ahead!'* fits well into this pattern of super-confident, self-righteous individualism.

While alternation between the Western Folk Hero and the Future Spaceman (or perhaps their simultaneous appeal) seems to characterize popular culture, we may wonder why the recent version of the Westerner was not the usual cowboy but a long-forgotten backwoods politician. Surely the identity of the heroes of juvenile popular culture bears some relation to the preoccupations of the adult world. Is there some possible connection between the rise of the resurrected Crockett and the going-ahead of Senator McCarthy? Although some observers felt that the Crockett boom ended because the hero had been 'oversold' and his youthful public simply tired of him, it may not be irrelevant to note that Crockett faded from the airwaves a little after McCarthyism ceased to be the most sensational feature of the political scene.

Among the literary manifestations of the recent Crockett fad were two reprintings of his supposed autobiographies.[31] Both run together the three narratives of 1834, 1835, and 1836 without indicating where one ends and the other begins, and they make many unacknowledged

[31] *The Life of Davy Crockett* (New York, Citadel Press and Signet Books, 1955).

deletions from Hamlin Garland's already condensed text. For instance in the new editions we find the following passage:

I let the people know as early as then, that I wouldn't take a collar around my neck.

(Citadel edition, p. 130; Signet edition, p. 87)

In the Garland edition this passage occurs on page 111, Chapter XIII of *A Narrative of the Life of David Crockett* . . . (1834), and reads:

I let people know as early as then, that I wouldn't take a collar around my neck with the letters engraved on it,

> MY DOG.
> ANDREW JACKSON

Why is the legend on Davy's collar inadmissible now? Because Andy Jackson too is a hero of consequences who stands in the popular mind for the same values imputed to Crockett: coonskin democracy, the triumph of the common man. Crockett's opposition to Jackson's western land policy no longer interests us. In the pantheon of our popular culture we cannot have such a repudiation of one hero by another who represents the same values, for how then could we affirm those values? Accordingly, the new editions of Crockett's life do not make much sense, for the embarrassing fact of his opposition to Jackson is so intrinsic to the political part of the text that it cannot be eliminated by an editor's shears.

Half a century ago Frank Norris in an eloquent polemic declaimed:

The plain truth of the matter is that we have neglected our epic . . . no contemporaneous poet or chronicler thought it worth his while to sing the song or tell the tale of the West because literature in the day when the West was being won was a cult indulged in by certain well-bred gentlemen in New England who looked eastward to the Old World, to the legends of England and Norway and Germany and Italy for their inspiration, and left the great, strong, honest, fearless, resolute deeds of their own contemporaries to be defamed and defaced by the nameless hacks of the 'yellow back' libraries. . . .

And the Alamo! . . . the very histories slight the deed . . . Yet Thermopylae was less glorious, and in comparison with that siege the investment of Troy was mere wanton riot. . . . Young men are taught to consider the 'Iliad,' with its butcheries, its glorification of inordinate selfishness and vanity, as a classic. Achilles, murderer, egoist, ruffian, and liar, is a hero. But the name of Bowie, the name of the man who gave his life to his flag at the Alamo, is perpetuated only in the designation of a knife. Crockett is the hero only of a 'funny story' about a sagacious coon.[32]

[32] Frank Norris, 'Essays on Authorship,' in *Complete Works* (New York, 1903), IV, 280–81.

We can no longer blame the gentility of Eastern writers for our failure to have created an epic of the Alamo or to have supplanted Achilles with Colonel Crockett. Although the age of epic literature would seem to be long since over, such a literature may yet come from the winning of the West. It will first require our recognition as a national culture that Prometheus chained to the rock is not only myth but reality, while the image of Davy Crockett striding over the hills, exempt from sacrifice for the piece of sunlight in his pocket, is our nation's self-defeating dream.

FIVE

The American folk hero is startlingly different from most of the great heroes of myths or of Märchen. Unlike them, the American has no parents. He has no past, no patrimony, no siblings, no family, and no life cycle, because he never marries or has children. He seldom dies. If death does overtake him, it proves to be merely a stage in his transformation to still another identity. No one has cursed his birth or set him afloat on the sea; neither was he suckled by a beast nor rescued by a cowherd from the fierce elements to which a tyrannous father had condemned him. Although he may wear many disguises, it cannot be usually said that he returns incognito to his homeland, rids his country of scourges, and is recognized as the throne's true heir. The pattern of action of the hero tale, as outlined by Lord Raglan in *The Hero*, does not fit very well the adventures of our plebeian peddlers, brawlers, and emergent capitalists. Nor can we apply to them with much confidence Otto Rank's view that myths of the hero are created 'by means of retrograde childhood fantasies' in which the Oedipal 'family romance of neurotics' become universalized as the life histories of mythical heroes.[33] Our folk heroes have no family romances. Among our group of heroes only the careers of Franklin and Crockett begin to approach the fullness of the human life cycle in their respective autobiographies. In popular culture we have seen how Franklin is reduced to the get-ahead Poor Richard while Crockett becomes the go-ahead woodsman whose varied exploits in guile, hunting, and conquest of nature are entirely discontinuous, a collection of motifs rather than a coherent story. Other men who became folk heroes—Fink, Patch, Johnny Appleseed—left behind a still more fragmentary basis for their reputations. Each lived in the minds of his celebrants and emulators as an instance of metamorphosis culminating in a single dramatic gesture. From Andrew the Hebridean onward, that gesture was the annunciation of their own destinies as self-made men, their abandoning

[33] *The Myth of the Birth of the Hero* (New York, 1959), pp. 69, 84.

an old self for rebirth in a new. But after Andrew the old self that was let die was not that of a European peasant; it was simply an earlier incarnation of a character whose essence was not radically altered by his assumption of successive roles.

The American folk hero appears as a generic expression of the youthful culture which produced him. His characteristic virtues are the qualities of youth: indomitable self-confidence, and a courage in his adaptation to the world which proves almost an heroic denial that tragedy can be possible for *him*. But from another perspective the virtues of youth are the defects of immaturity. In his easy progress from one role to another without ever being compelled to accept the full commitment of spirit to any, the ever-popular image of the American folk hero exists on a psychological plane comparable to that of adolescent or pre-adolescent fantasy. In every culture the concept of maturity implies a full commitment to fixed values; until modern times these values were sacred. Their fixity had been established by supernatural powers, and the passage from childhood to maturity was marked by initiatory rites in which the sacred knowledge that came to the present from the beginning of time was passed on to the initiate. To be worthy of this knowledge the child in him had to die; his soul had to seek its sources in the power that created the world; and he had then to be reborn into his responsibilities and his grace. Before the submission to this immutable pattern, however, the child-spirit can envisage any or all fulfillments of the potentialities of its psychic energies. In the American folk hero the transformations are metamorphoses without being rebirths. The concentration of psychic energy necessary for spiritual commitment and spiritual change is not apparent in either the bourgeois get-ahead values of Ben Franklin–Poor Richard or in the sly or boisterous go-ahead values of Sam Slick–Davy Crockett. Only in the person of the American Literatus Walt Whitman does the power of self-determined metamorphosis approach the transcendent heroism of those myths of the Old World from which all our folk images attempted to liberate us. For only in Whitman is the assertion of selfhood made with such all-encompassing passion as to become in itself an escape from selfhood. The 'self' Walt sings is, as Richard Chase observes,[34] a metaphor with the power of myth, linking the ego to the entire world of apprehended sense and transforming all that it encompasses into 'a knit of identity.'

Identity, as de Tocqueville foresaw, would prove an elusive and prepossessive concern for an egalitarian society. The American temperament has always favored activism over meditation; the typical self-discovery of the American character has been conceived as an immersion in experience, rather than as contemplative withdrawal. It is as though the more reality one's experiences could encompass or be touched by, the nearer

[34] In *Walt Whitman Reconsidered* (New York, 1955).

one could come to self-definition. Consequently, the metamorphic pattern of American life and of the American folk hero's career sets its exemplars in linear motion through as many conditions of 'reality' as possible. These metamorphoses, as we have seen, are only outwardly comparable to the rebirths achieved by initiatory rites in cultures or institutions of sacred orientation. Their function, nonetheless, is a ritualistic one: not a *rite de passage* but a ritual of intensification, in which the powers of the self are affirmed, reinforced, and glorified by each demonstration of their success-ful use. These powers prove the self spiritually indomitable and adaptable to the wildest vicissitudes of fortune or nature. The historical and folk examples we have traced prove not only these considerable positive powers, but also the limitations of the American notion of selfhood. The self-determinative hero turns out to have as his goals a set of concepts more characteristic of the culture of the early American republic than of human history at large. His character is aggressive, competitive, shrewd. He seeks mastery over nature. With respect to society, he seeks to demon-strate superiority over other individuals but not ordinarily does he recog-nize society as an organic structure, in which power can be exercised for extra-personal ends.

Since the exposition of character is both an aim and method of fiction, what could American authors make of the fragmentary folk sagas which outlined the folk concepts of heroic personality? These sketches could be taken uncritically, accepted in the same spirit of resilience in which they were offered by the popular mind. Hawthorne's peddler Dominicus Pike, his Holgrave in *The House of the Seven Gables*, Melville's Ishmael, Twain's Huck Finn, all reflect both the metamorphoses and the self-reliance of the folk models we have examined. But these authors could use the same folk concepts to create characters whose qualities they viewed with the greatest reservations. Often these characters, critically examined by their authors, are presented in situations which define their fates as representative of the national destiny. Hawthorne's Robin in 'My Kinsman, Major Molineux,' Melville's Captain Delano in 'Benito Cereno,' his Ahab and the whole cast of *The Confidence-Man,* Twain's Duke and Dauphin, all project elements of the American folk hero into situations with which his spiritual immaturity and his lack of human depth make him inadequate to deal. Further, the literary enlargement of the native folk heroes is often drawn against a contrasting set of heroic values, those of the world-mythical heroes whose fates and powers are so different from their own. Thus Hawthorne contrasts his Yankee Robin against the ancient ritualistic figure of the Dying King; Ishmael presents himself as a Yankee, both bumpkin dupe and trickster; while Ahab, though in part a frontiersman—an 'Arkansas duellist'—also subsumes the attributes of a Slayer of the Beast (Perseus, St. George), a shaman, and a Christ. Huck Finn, as I have mentioned, represents the triumphantly moral American imagination in contrast to the decadent European chivalric romanticism of Tom Sawyer. The patterns seem as capable of variation as the imaginations of their authors could make them. The depictions of native character, whether sympathetic or critical, and tensions between them and representatives of the older heroic traditions in world mythology, contribute much to the sense of largeness, of archetypal representativeness, which we find in the American prose romance. This representativeness is certainly not the function of surface realism. It inheres in the romance because the characters themselves are so often modelled on half-legendary archetypes projected fragmentarily by the folk imagination.

Fenimore Cooper's
Leatherstocking Novels

D. H. LAWRENCE

In his Leatherstocking books, Fenimore is off on another track. He is no longer concerned with social white Americans that buzz with pins through them, buzz loudly against every mortal thing except the pin itself. The pin of the Great Ideal.

One gets irritated with Cooper because he never for once snarls at the Great Ideal Pin which transfixes him. No, indeed. Rather he tries to push it through the very heart of the Continent.

But I have loved the Leatherstocking books so dearly. Wish-fulfilment!

Anyhow one is not supposed to take LOVE seriously, in these books. Eve Effingham, impaled on the social pin, conscious all the time of her own ego and of nothing else, suddenly fluttering in throes of love: no, it makes me sick. Love is never LOVE until it has a pin pushed through it and becomes an IDEAL. The ego turning on a pin is wildly IN LOVE, always. Because that's the thing to be.

Cooper was a GENTLEMAN, in the worst sense of the word. In the Nineteenth Century sense of the word. A correct, clock-work man.

Not altogether, of course.

The great National Grouch was grinding inside him. Probably he called it COSMIC URGE. Americans usually do: in capital letters.

Best stick to National Grouch. The great American grouch.

Cooper had it, gentleman as he was. That is why he flitted round Europe so uneasily. Of course in Europe he could be, and was, a gentleman to his heart's content.

"In short," he says in one of his letters, "we were at table two counts, one monsignore, an English Lord, an Ambassador, and my humble self."

Were we really!

How nice it must have been to know that one self, at least, was humble.

233

And he felt the democratic American tomahawk wheeling over his uncomfortable scalp all the time.

The great American grouch.

Two monsters loomed on Cooper's horizon.

MRS. COOPER	MY WORK
MY WORK	MY WIFE
MY WIFE	MY WORK

THE DEAR CHILDREN
MY WORK! ! !

There you have the essential keyboard of Cooper's soul.

If there is one thing that annoys me more than a business man and his BUSINESS, it is an artist, a writer, painter, musician, and MY WORK. When an artist says MY WORK, the flesh goes tired on my bones. When he says MY WIFE, I want to hit him.

Cooper grizzled about his work. Oh, heaven, he cared so much whether it was good or bad, and what the French thought, and what Mr. Snippy Knowall said, and how Mrs. Cooper took it. The pin, the pin!

But he was truly an artist: then an American: then a gentleman.

And the grouch grouched inside him, through all.

They seemed to have been specially fertile in imagining themselves "under the wigwam," do these Americans, just when their knees were comfortably under the mahogany, in Paris, along with the knees of

4 Counts
2 Cardinals
1 Milord
5 Cocottes
1 Humble self.

You bet, though, that when the cocottes were being raffled off, Fenimore went home to his WIFE.

Wish Fulfilment		Actuality
THE WIGWAM	*vs.*	MY HOTEL
CHINGACHGOOK	*vs.*	MY WIFE
NATTY BUMPPO	*vs.*	MY HUMBLE SELF

Fenimore lying in his Louis Quatorze hôtel in Paris, passionately musing about Natty Bumppo and the pathless forest, and mixing his imagination with the Cupids and Butterflies on the painted ceiling, while Mrs. Cooper was struggling with her latest gown in the next room, and déjeuner was with the Countess at eleven. . . .

Men live by lies.

In actuality, Fenimore loved the genteel continent of Europe, and waited gasping for the newspapers to praise his WORK.

In another actuality, he loved the tomahawking continent of America, and imagined himself Natty Bumppo.

His actual desire was to be: *Monsieur Fenimore Cooper, le grand écrivain américain.*

His innermost wish was to be: Natty Bumppo.

Now Natty and Fenimore arm-in-arm are an odd couple.

You can see Fenimore: blue coat, silver buttons, silver-and-diamond buckle shoes, ruffles.

You see Natty Bumppo: a grizzled, uncouth old renegade, with gaps in his old teeth and a drop on the end of his nose.

But Natty was Fenimore's great Wish: his wish-fulfilment.

"It was a matter of course," says Mrs. Cooper, "that he should dwell on the better traits of the picture rather than on the coarser and more revolting, though more common points. Like West, he could see Apollo in the young Mohawk."

The coarser and more revolting, though more common points.

You see now why he depended so absolutely on MY WIFE. She had to look things in the face for him. The coarser and more revolting, and certainly more common points, she had to see.

He himself did so love seeing pretty-pretty, with the thrill of a red scalp now and then.

Fenimore, in his imagination, wanted to be Natty Bumppo, who, I am sure, belched after he had eaten his dinner. At the same time Mr. Cooper was nothing if not a gentleman. So he decided to stay in France and have it all his own way.

In France, Natty would not belch after eating, and Chingachgook could be all the Apollo he liked.

As if ever any Indian was like Apollo. The Indians, with their curious female quality, their archaic figures, with high shoulders and deep, archaic waists, like a sort of woman! And their natural devilishness, their natural insidiousness.

But men see what they want to see: especially if they look from a long distance, across the ocean, for example.

Yet the Leatherstocking books are lovely. Lovely half-lies.

They form a sort of American Odyssey, with Natty Bumppo for Odysseus.

Only, in the original Odyssey, there is plenty of devil, Circes and swine and all. And Ithacus is devil enough to outwit the devils. But Natty is a saint with a gun, and the Indians are gentlemen through and through, though they may take an occasional scalp.

There are five Leatherstocking novels: a *decrescendo* of reality, and a crescendo of beauty.

1. *Pioneers:* A raw frontier-village on Lake Champlain, at the end of the eighteenth century. Must be a picture of Cooper's home, as he

knew it when a boy. A very lovely book. Natty Bumppo an old man, an old hunter half civilized.

2. *The Last of the Mohicans:* A historical fight between the British and the French, with Indians on both sides, at a Fort by Lake Champlain. Romantic flight of the British general's two daughters, conducted by the scout, Natty, who is in the prime of life; romantic death of the last of the Delawares.

3. *The Prairie:* A wagon of some huge, sinister Kentuckians trekking west into the unbroken prairie. Prairie Indians, and Natty, an old, old man; he dies seated on a chair on the Rocky Mountains, looking east.

4. *The Pathfinder:* The Great Lakes. Natty, a man of about thirty-five, makes an abortive proposal to a bouncing damsel, daughter of the Sergeant of the Fort.

5. *Deerslayer:* Natty and Hurry Harry, both quite young, are hunting in the virgin wild. They meet two white women. Lake Champlain again.

These are the five Leatherstocking books: Natty Bumppo being Leatherstocking, Pathfinder, Deerslayer, according to his ages.

Now let me put aside my impatience at the unreality of this vision, and accept it as a wish-fulfilment vision, a kind of yearning myth. Because it seems to me that the things in Cooper that make one so savage, when one compares them with actuality, are perhaps, when one considers them as presentations of a deep subjective desire, real in their way, and almost prophetic.

The passionate love for America, for the soil of America, for example. As I say, it is perhaps easier to love America passionately, when you look at it through the wrong end of the telescope, across all the Atlantic water, as Cooper did so often, than when you are right there. When you are actually *in* America, America hurts, because it has a powerful disintegrative influence upon the white psyche. It is full of grinning, unappeased aboriginal demons, too, ghosts, and it persecutes the white men like some Eumenides, until the white men give up their absolute whiteness. America is tense with latent violence and resistance. The very common sense of white Americans has a tinge of helplessness in it, and deep fear of what might be if they were not common-sensical.

Yet one day the demons of America must be placated, the ghosts must be appeased, the Spirit of Place atoned for. Then the true passionate love for American Soil will appear. As yet, there is too much menace in the landscape.

But probably, one day America will be as beautiful in actuality as it is in Cooper. Not yet, however. When the factories have fallen down again.

And again, this perpetual blood-brother theme of the Leatherstocking novels, Natty and Chingachgook, the Great Serpent. At present it is a sheer myth. The Red Man and the White Man are not blood-brothers: even when they are most friendly. When they are most friendly, it is as a rule the one betraying his race-spirit to the other. In the white man—rather highbrow—who "loves" the Indian, one feels the white man betraying his own race. There is something unproud, underhand in it. Renegade. The same with the Americanized Indian who believes absolutely in the white model. It is a betrayal. Renegade again.

In the actual flesh, it seems to me the white man and the red man cause a feeling of oppression, the one to the other, no matter what the good will. The red life flows in a different direction from the white life. You can't make two streams that flow in opposite directions meet and mingle soothingly.

Certainly, if Cooper had had to spend his whole life in the backwoods, side by side with a Noble Red Brother, he would have screamed with the oppression of suffocation. He had to have Mrs. Cooper, a straight strong pillar of society, to hang on to. And he had to have the culture of France to turn back to, or he would just have been stifled. The Noble Red Brother would have smothered him and driven him mad.

So that the Natty and Chingachgook myth must remain a myth. It is a wish-fulfilment, an evasion of actuality. As we have said before, the folds of the Great Serpent would have been heavy, very heavy, too heavy, on any white man. Unless the white man were a true renegade, hating himself and his own race-spirit, as sometimes happens.

It seems there can be no fusion in the flesh. But the spirit can change. The white man's spirit can never become as the red man's spirit. It doesn't want to. But it can cease to be the opposite and the negative of the red man's spirit. It can open out a new great area of consciousness, in which there is room for the red spirit too.

To open out a new wide area of consciousness means to slough the old consciousness. The old consciousness has become a tight-fitting prison to us, in which we are going rotten.

You can't have a new, easy skin before you have sloughed the old, tight skin.

You can't.

And you just can't, so you may as well leave off pretending.

Now the essential history of the people of the United States seems to me just this: At the Renaissance the old consciousness was becoming a little tight. Europe sloughed her last skin, and started a new, final phase.

But some Europeans recoiled from the last final phase. They wouldn't enter the *cul de sac* of post-Renaissance, "liberal" Europe. They came to America.

They came to America for two reasons:

1. To slough the old European consciousness completely.
2. To grow a new skin underneath, a new form. This second is a hidden process.

The two processes go on, of course, simultaneously. The slow forming of the new skin underneath is the slow sloughing of the old skin. And sometimes this immortal serpent feels very happy, feeling a new golden glow of a strangely-patterned skin envelop him: and sometimes he feels very sick, as if his very entrails were being torn out of him, as he wrenches once more at his old skin, to get out of it.

Out! Out! he cries, in all kinds of euphemisms.

He's got to have his new skin on him before ever he can get out.

And he's got to get out before his new skin can ever be his own skin.

So there he is, a torn, divided monster.

The true American, who writhes and writhes like a snake that is long in sloughing.

Sometimes snakes can't slough. They can't burst their old skin. Then they go sick and die inside the old skin, and nobody ever sees the new pattern.

It needs a real desperate recklessness to burst your old skin at last. You simply don't care what happens to you, if you rip yourself in two, so long as you do get out.

It also needs a real belief in the new skin. Otherwise you are likely never to make the effort. Then you gradually sicken and go rotten and die in the old skin.

Now Fenimore stayed very safe inside the old skin: a gentleman, almost a European, as proper as proper can be. And, safe inside the old skin, he *imagined* the gorgeous American pattern of a new skin.

He hated democracy. So he evaded it, and had a nice dream of something beyond democracy. But he belonged to democracy all the while.

Evasion!—Yet even that doesn't make the dream worthless.

Democracy in America was never the same as Liberty in Europe. In Europe Liberty was a great life-throb. But in America Democracy was always something anti-life. The greatest democrats, like Abraham Lincoln, had always a sacrificial, self-murdering note in their voices. American Democracy was a form of self-murder, always. Or of murdering somebody else.

Necessarily. It was a *pis aller*. It was the *pis aller* to European Liberty. It was a cruel form of sloughing. Men murdered themselves into this democracy. Democracy is the utter hardening of the old skin, the old form, the old psyche. It hardens till it is tight and fixed and inorganic. Then it *must* burst, like a chrysalis shell. And out must come the soft grub, or the soft damp butterfly of the American-at-last.

America has gone the *pis aller* of her democracy. Now she must slough even that, chiefly that, indeed.

What did Cooper dream beyond democracy? Why, in his immortal friendship of Chingachgook and Natty Bumppo he dreamed the nucleus of a new society. That is, he dreamed a new human relationship. A stark, stripped human relationship of two men, deeper than the deeps of sex. Deeper than property, deeper than fatherhood, deeper than marriage, deeper than love. So deep that it is loveless. The stark, loveless, wordless unison of two men who have come to the bottom of themselves. This is the new nucleus of a new society, the clue to a new world-epoch. It asks for a great and cruel sloughing first of all. Then it finds a great release into a new world, a new moral, a new landscape.

Natty and the Great Serpent are neither equals nor unequals. Each obeys the other when the moment arrives. And each is stark and dumb in the other's presence, starkly himself, without illusion created. Each is just the crude pillar of a man, the crude living column of his own manhood. And each knows the godhead of this crude column of manhood. A new relationship.

The Leatherstocking novels create the myth of this new relation. And they go backwards, from old age to golden youth. That is the true myth of America. She starts old, old, wrinkled and writhing in an old skin. And there is a gradual sloughing of the old skin, towards a new youth. It is the myth of America.

You start with actuality. *Pioneers* is no doubt Cooperstown, when Cooperstown was in the stage of inception: a village of one wild street of log cabins under the forest hills by Lake Champlain: a village of crude, wild frontiersmen, reacting against civilization.

Towards this frontier-village, in the winter time, a negro slave drives a sledge through the mountains, over deep snow. In the sledge sits a fair damsel, Miss Temple, with her handsome pioneer father, Judge Temple. They hear a shot in the trees. It is the old hunter and backwoodsman, Natty Bumppo, long and lean and uncouth, with a long rifle and gaps in his teeth.

Judge Temple is "squire" of the village, and he has a ridiculous, commodious "hall" for his residence. It is still the old English form. Miss Temple is a pattern young lady, like Eve Effingham: in fact she gets a young and very genteel but impoverished Effingham for a husband. The old world holding its own on the edge of the wild. A bit tiresomely too, with rather more prunes and prisms than one can digest. Too romantic.

Against the "hall" and the gentry, the real frontiers-folk, the rebels. The two groups meet at the village inn, and at the frozen church, and at the Christmas sports, and on the ice of the lake, and at the great pigeon shoot. It is a beautiful, resplendent picture of life. Fenimore puts in only the glamour.

Perhaps my taste is childish, but these scenes in *Pioneers* seem to me marvellously beautiful. The raw village street, with woodfires blinking through the unglazed window-chinks, on a winter's night. The inn, with the rough woodsmen and the drunken Indian John; the church, with the snowy congregation crowding to the fire. Then the lavish abundance of Christmas cheer, and turkey-shooting in the snow. Spring coming, forests all green, maple-sugar taken from the trees: and clouds of pigeons flying from the south, myriads of pigeons, shot in heaps; and night-fishing on the teeming, virgin lake; and deer-hunting.

Pictures! Some of the loveliest, most glamorous pictures in all literature.

Alas, without the cruel iron of reality. It is all real enough. Except that one realizes that Fenimore was writing from a safe distance, where he would idealize and have his wish-fulfilment.

Because, when one comes to America, one finds that there is always a certain slightly devilish resistance in the American landscape, and a certain slightly bitter resistance in the white man's heart. Hawthorne gives this. But Cooper glosses it over.

The American landscape has never been at one with the white man. Never. And white men have probably never felt so bitter anyhwere, as here in America, where the very landscape, in its very beauty, seems a bit devilish and grinning, opposed to us.

Cooper, however, glosses over this resistance, which in actuality can never quite be glossed over. He *wants* the landscape to be at one with him. So he goes away to Europe and sees it as such. It is a sort of vision.

And, nevertheless, the oneing will surely take place—some day.

The myth is the story of Natty. The old, lean hunter and backwoodsman lives with his friend, the grey-haired Indian John, an old Delaware chief, in a hut within reach of the village. The Delaware is christianised and bears the Christian name of John. He is tribeless and lost. He humiliates his grey hairs in drunkenness, and dies, thankful to be dead, in a forest fire, passing back to the fire whence he derived.

And this is Chingachgook, the splendid Great Serpent of the later novels.

No doubt Cooper, as a boy, knew both Natty and the Indian John. No doubt they fired his imagination even then. When he is a man, crystallized in society and sheltering behind the safe pillar of Mrs. Cooper, these two old fellows become a myth to his soul. He traces himself to a new youth in them.

As for the story: Judge Temple has just been instrumental in passing the wise game laws. But Natty has lived by his gun all his life in the wild woods, and simply childishly cannot understand how he can be poaching on the Judge's land among the pine trees. He shoots a deer in the close season. The Judge is all sympathy, but the law *must* be enforced. Bewildered Natty, an old man of seventy, is put in stocks and in prison. They release him as soon as possible. But the thing was done.

The letter killeth.

Natty's last connection with his own race is broken. John, the Indian, is dead. The old hunter disappears, lonely and severed, into the forest, away, away from his race.

In the new epoch that is coming, there will be no Letter of the Law.

Chronologically, *The Last of the Mohicans* follows *Pioneers*. But in the myth, *The Prairie* comes next.

Cooper of course knew his own America. He travelled west and saw the prairies, and camped with the Indians of the prairie.

The Prairie, like *Pioneers*, bears a good deal the stamp of actuality. It is a strange, splendid book, full of sense of doom. The figures of the great Kentuckian men, with their wolf-women, loom colossal on the vast prairie, as they camp with their wagons. These are different pioneers from Judge Temple. Lurid, brutal, tinged with the sinisterness of crime; these are the gaunt white men who push west, push on and on against the natural opposition of the continent. On towards a doom. Great wings of vengeful doom seem spread over the west, grim against the intruder. You feel them again in Frank Norris' novel, *The Octopus*. While in the West of Bret Harte there is a very devil in the air, and beneath him are sentimental self-conscious people being wicked and goody by evasion.

In *The Prairie* there is a shadow of violence and dark cruelty flickering in the air. It is the aboriginal demon hovering over the core of the continent. It hovers still, and the dread is still there.

Into such a prairie enters the huge figure of Ishmael, ponderous, pariah-like Ishmael and his huge sons and his were-wolf wife. With their wagons they roll on from the frontiers of Kentucky, like Cyclops into the savage wilderness. Day after day they seem to force their way into oblivion. But their force of penetration ebbs. They are brought to a stop. They recoil in the throes of murder and entrench themselves in isolation on a hillock in the midst of the prairie. There they hold out like demi-gods against the elements and the subtle Indian.

The pioneering brute invasion of the West, crime-tinged!

And into this setting, as a sort of minister of peace, enters the old, old hunter Natty, and his suave, horse-riding Sioux Indians. But he seems like a shadow,

The hills rise softly west, to the Rockies. There seems a new peace: or is it only suspense, abstraction, waiting? Is it only a sort of beyond?

Natty lives in these hills, in a village of the suave, horse-riding Sioux. They revere him as an old wise father.

In these hills he dies, sitting in his chair and looking far east, to the forest and great sweet waters, whence he came. He dies gently, in physical peace with the land and the Indians. He is an old, old man.

Cooper could see no further than the foothills where Natty died, beyond the prairie.

The other novels bring us back east.

The Last of the Mohicans is divided between real historical narrative and true "romance." For myself, I prefer the romance. It has a myth-meaning, whereas the narrative is chiefly record.

For the first time, we get actual women: the dark, handsome Cora and her frail sister, the White Lily. The good old division, the dark sensual woman and the clinging, submissive little blonde, who is so "pure."

These sisters are fugitives through the forest, under the protection of a Major Heyward, a young American officer and Englishman. He is just a "white" man, very good and brave and generous, etc., but limited, most definitely *borné*. He would probably love Cora, if he dared, but he finds it safer to adore the clinging White Lily of a younger sister.

This trio is escorted by Natty, now Leatherstocking, a hunter and scout in the prime of life, accompanied by his inseparable friend Chingachgook, and the Delaware's beautiful son—Adonis rather than Apollo—Uncas, the Last of the Mohicans.

There is also a "wicked" Indian, Magua, handsome and injured incarnation of evil.

Cora is the scarlet flower of womanhood, fierce, passionate offspring of some mysterious union between the British officer and a Creole woman in the West Indies. Cora loves Uncas, Uncas loves Cora. But Magua also desires Cora, violently desires her. A lurid little circle of sensual fire. So Fenimore kills them all off, Cora, Uncas, and Magua, and leaves the White Lily to carry on the race. She will breed plenty of white children to Major Heyward. These tiresome "lilies that fester," of our day.

Evidently Cooper—or the artist in him—has decided that there can be no blood-mixing of the two races, white and red. He kills 'em off.

Beyond all this heart-beating stand the figures of Natty and Chingachgook: the two childless womanless men of opposite races. They are the abiding thing. Each of them is alone, and final in his race. And they stand side by side, stark, abstract, beyond emotion, yet eternally together. All the other loves seem frivolous. This is the new great thing, the clue, the inception of a new humanity.

And Natty, what sort of a white man is he? Why, he is a man with a gun. He is a killer, a slayer. Patient and gentle as he is, he is a slayer. Self-effacing, self-forgetting, still he is a killer.

Twice, in the book, he brings an enemy down hurling in death through the air, downwards. Once it is the beautiful, wicked Magua—shot from a height, and hurtling down ghastly through space, into death.

This is Natty, the white forerunner. A killer. As in *Deerslayer*, he shoots the bird that flies in the high, high sky, so that the bird falls out of the invisible into the visible, dead, he symbolizes himself. He will bring the bird of the spirit out of the high air. He is the stoic American killer of the old great life. But he kills, as he says, only to live.

Pathfinder takes us to the Great Lakes, and the glamour and beauty of sailing the great sweet waters. Natty is now called Pathfinder. He is about thirty-five years old, and he falls in love. The damsel is Mabel Dunham, daughter of Sergeant Dunham of the Fort garrison. She is blonde and in all things admirable. No doubt Mrs. Cooper was very much like Mabel.

And Pathfinder doesn't marry her. She won't have him. She wisely prefers a more comfortable Jasper. So Natty goes off to grouch, and to end by thanking his stars. When he had got right clear, and sat by the campfire with Chingachgook, in the forest, didn't he just thank his stars! A lucky escape!

Men of an uncertain age are liable to these infatuations. They aren't always lucky enough to be rejected.

Whatever would poor Mabel have done, had she been Mrs. Bumppo? Natty had no business marrying. His mission was elsewhere.

The most fascinating Leatherstocking book is the last, *Deerslayer*. Natty is now a fresh youth, called Deerslayer. But the kind of silent prim youth who is never quite young, but reserves himself for different things.

It is a gem of a book. Or a bit of perfect paste. And myself, I like a bit of perfect paste in a perfect setting, so long as I am not fooled by pretense of reality. And the setting of Deerslayer *could* not be more exquisite. Lake Champlain again.

Of course it never rains: it is never cold and muddy and dreary: no one ever has wet feet or toothache: no one ever feels filthy, when they can't wash for a week. God knows what the women would really have looked like, for they fled through the wilds without soap, comb, or towel. They breakfasted off a chunk of meat, or nothing, lunched the same, and supped the same.

Yet at every moment they are elegant, perfect ladies, in correct toilet.

Which isn't quite fair. You need only go camping for a week, and you'll see.

But it is a myth, not a realistic tale. Read it as a lovely myth. Lake Glimmerglass.

Deerslayer, the youth with the long rifle, is found in the woods with a big, handsome, blond-bearded backwoodsman called Hurry Harry. Deerslayer seems to have been born under a hemlock tree out of a pinecone: a young man of the woods. He is silent, simple, philosophic, moralistic, and an unerring shot. His simplicity is the simplicity of age rather than of youth. He is race-old. All his reactions and impulses are fixed, static. Almost he is sexless, so race-old. Yet intelligent, hardy, dauntless.

Hurry Harry is a big blusterer, just the opposite of Deerslayer. Deerslayer keeps the centre of his own consciousness steady and unperturbed. Hurry Harry is one of those floundering people who bluster from one emotion to another, very self-conscious, without any centre to them.

These two young men are making their way to a lovely, smallish lake,

Lake Glimmerglass. On this water the Hutter family has established itself. Old Hutter, it is suggested, has a criminal, coarse, buccaneering past, and is a sort of fugitive from justice. But he is a good enough father to his two grown-up girls. The family lives in a log hut "castle," built on piles in the water, and the old man has also constructed an "ark," a sort of house-boat, in which he can take his daughters when he goes on his rounds to trap the beaver.

The two girls are the inevitable dark and light. Judith, dark, fearless, passionate, a little lurid with sin, is the scarlet-and-black blossom. Hetty, the younger, blond, frail and innocent, is the white lily again. But alas, the lily has begun to fester. She is slightly imbecile.

The two hunters arrive at the lake among the woods just as war has been declared. The Hutters are unaware of the fact. And hostile Indians are on the lake already. So, the story of thrills and perils.

Thomas Hardy's inevitable division of women into dark and fair, sinful and innocent, sensual and pure, is Cooper's division too. It is indicative of the desire in the man. He wants sensuality and sin, and he wants purity and "innocence." If the innocence goes a little rotten, slightly imbecile, bad luck!

Hurry Harry, of course, like a handsome impetuous meat-fly, at once wants Judith, the lurid poppy-blossom. Judith rejects him with scorn.

Judith, the sensual woman, at once wants the quiet, reserved, unmastered Deerslayer. She wants to master him. And Deerslayer is half tempted, but never more than half. He is not going to be mastered. A philosophic old soul, he does not give much for the temptations of sex. Probably he dies virgin.

And he is right of it. Rather than be dragged into a false heat of deliberate sensuality, he will remain alone. His soul is alone, for ever alone. So he will preserve his integrity, and remain alone in the flesh. It is a stoicism which is honest and fearless, and from which Deerslayer never lapses, except when, approaching middle age, he proposes to the buxom Mabel.

He lets his consciousness penetrate in loneliness into the new continent. His contacts are not human. He wrestles with the spirits of the forest and the American wild, as a hermit wrestles with God and Satan. His one meeting is with Chingachgook, and this meeting is silent, reserved, across an unpassable distance.

Hetty, the White Lily, being imbecile, although full of vaporous religion and the dear, good God, "who governs all things by his providence," is hopelessly infatuated with Hurry Harry. Being innocence gone imbecile, like Dostoevsky's Idiot, she longs to give herself to the handsome meat-fly. Of course he doesn't want her.

And so nothing happens: in that direction. Deerslayer goes off to meet Chingachgook, and help him woo an Indian maid. Vicarious.

It is the miserable story of the collapse of the white psyche. The white man's mind and soul are divided between these two things: innocence and lust, the Spirit and Sensuality. Sensuality always carries a stigma, and is therefore more deeply desired, or lusted after. But spirituality alone gives the sense of uplift, exaltation, and "winged life," with the inevitable reaction into sin and spite. So the white man is divided against himself. He plays off one side of himself against the other side, till it is really a tale told by an idiot, and nauseating.

Against this, one is forced to admire the stark, enduring figure of Deerslayer. He is neither spiritual nor sensual. He is a moralizer, but he always tries to moralize from actual experience, not from theory. He says: "Hurt nothing unless you're forced to." Yet he gets his deepest thrill of gratification, perhaps, when he puts a bullet through the heart of a beautiful buck, as it stoops to drink at the lake. Or when he brings the invisible bird fluttering down in death, out of the high blue. "Hurt nothing unless you're forced to."And yet he lives by death, by killing the wild things of the air and earth.

It's not good enough.

But you have there the myth of the essential white America. All the other stuff, the love, the democracy, the floundering into lust, is a sort of by-play. The essential American soul is hard, isolate, stoic, and a killer. It has never yet melted.

Of course the soul often breaks down into disintegration, and you have lurid sin and Judith, imbecile innocence lusting, in Hetty, and bluster, bragging, and self-conscious strength, in Harry. But there are the disintegration products.

What true myth concerns itself with is not the disintegration product. True myth concerns itself centrally with the onward adventure of the integral soul. And this, for America, is Deerslayer. A man who turns his back on white society. A man who keeps his moral integrity hard and intact. An isolate, almost selfless, stoic, enduring man, who lives by death, by killing, but who is pure white.

This is the very intrinsic-most American. He is at the core of all the other flux and fluff. And when *this* man breaks from his stoic isolation, and makes a new move, then look out, something will be happening.

The American Hero and the Evasion of Love

LESLIE FIEDLER

The failure of the Sentimental Love Religion and the rejection of the Protestant Virgin are the two most critical and baffling facts of the history of the novel in America. But that failure and that rejection are inevitable, granted the profound division in the American awareness of women, arising from an impossible demand that they represent at once the ruined and redeeming virgin-bride dreamed by Sentimentalism, and the forgiving mother, necessary to sustain an imaginary American commonwealth of boy-children, camerados at work and play.

Perhaps the clue to an essential difficulty is here. If marriage dismays the American writer, though his earlier European prototypes assured him it was salvation itself; and if lawless passion unnerves him, though his later European colleagues assure him that it "justifies all"—this is because both marriage and passion impugn the image of woman as mother, mean the abandonment of childhood. The keynote of our special sentimentality had been set even before the mid-nineteenth-century American renaissance by Nathaniel Parker Willis. Writing of that soon-forgotten figure some fifty years after his debut, Oliver Wendell Holmes remembered that in 1830 "Willis was by far the most prominent young American author"! He recalled his epicene grace, "something between a remembrance of the Count D'Orsay and an anticipation of Oscar Wilde," and compared him to a portrait of Hippolytus: "the beautiful young man who had kindled a passion in the heart of his wicked step-mother."

There could be no apter image to preside over the birth of our literature: the evocation of a delicate homosexuality, fleeing from gross female assault and haunted by the incest taboo. And even more to the point are the verses which Holmes quotes from Willis, written when he had already won the fame he desired, but was appalled to realize that he had swapped time for success, was over the sill of manhood:

> I'm twenty-two, I'm twenty-two,—
> > They idly give me joy,
> As if I should be glad to know
> > That I was less a boy.

It is maturity above all things that the American writer fears, and marriage seems to him its essential sign. For marriage stands traditionally not only for a reconciliation with the divided self, a truce between head and heart, but also for a compromise with society, an acceptance of responsibility and drudgery and dullness. To this ultimate surrender, the Young Werther had preferred death; and Werther, as we have noticed earlier, was the moral guide of the first hero of American fiction.

It is more complicated even than this, however; for marriage also means an acceptance of the status of a father: an abandonment of the quest to deliver the captive mother and an assumption of the role of the ogre who holds her in captivity. There is no authentic American who would not rather be Jack than the Giant, which is to say, who would not choose to be "one of the boys" to the very end. The ideal American postulates himself as the fatherless man, the eternal son of the mother.

He does not, of course, see himself as the swaggering son of the continental imagination, the adulterer who in every cuckolded husband humiliates his father and revenges his mother. Romantic adultery is regarded with horror by the American bourgeois and the classic American novelist alike, for it is hopelessly involved with a European class society abandoned forever; by most of our writers it is not really regarded at all, only ignored at the prompting of a largely unconscious self-censorship. To our writers, for whom courtly love is something learned about in school, extramarital passion seems not only an offense against the mother, but also, like marriage itself, a disclaimer of childhood: a way of smuggling adult responsibility and guilt in through the back door. Only a temporary alliance with a savage maiden whose language one cannot understand: a mindless, speechless, brief encounter in some tropical Happy Valley appears to our traditional writers a possible image for a love which does not compromise freedom. But in the end, even this seems to them not quite safe.

There is finally no heterosexual solution which the American psyche finds completely satisfactory, no imagined or real consummation between man and woman found worthy of standing in our fiction for the healing of the breach between consciousness and unconsciousness, reason and impulse, society and nature. Yet in no nation in the world are those cleavages more deeply felt, declared, indeed, in the very pattern of historical life, visibly represented by the frontier. And in no nation is the need to heal such divisions more passionately recognized. The quest which has distinguished our fiction from Brockden Brown and Cooper, through Poe and Melville and Twain, to Faulkner and Hemingway is the search for an innocent substitute for adulterous passion and marriage alike. Is there not, our writers ask over and over, a sentimental relationship at once erotic and immaculate, a union which commits its participants neither to society nor sin—and yet one which is able to symbolize the union of the ego with the id, the thinking self with its rejected impulses?

We have already noticed that the first legend to seize the American imagination is the story of Rip Van Winkle, which has outlived the general reputation of its author, and which for years continued, as a popular drama, to reach the kind of audience to whom books remain forever a mystery. It is all a joke, of course, the jocular tale of a man who wakes up to find, when he has slept off his superhuman drunk, that he has also slept away the life of the shrew who bullied him, as well as that of George III, who had oppressed his country. Even as such a jest, however, the Rip archetype possesses surprising vitality, surviving to this day in the comic strip "Bringing Up Father," whose very title refers ironically to American woman's image of herself as a culture bearer, the civilizer of her spouse.

Though the Catskills for which Jiggs lights out is Dinty Moore's saloon, the alcoholic aroma of his escape remains the same as Rip's; and though Maggie takes opera lessons and aspires to "high society," she is still Mrs. Rip, a status-striving shrew. There is something already a little old-fashioned about "Bringing Up Father," both in its up-from-the-working-class background and in the frankness with which it reveals the power struggle between husband and wife. The true Rip type—whether embodied in Jiggs or Major Hoople or the Uncle Willie of "Moon Mullins"—seems faintly archaic, a hangover from a more brutal age, before one spouse had agreed to put down the rolling pin or the other to bend the elbow no longer. The successor of Rip-Jiggs is Dagwood Bumstead, who goes to work every day and welcomes the tyranny of Blondie as quite what his own inadequacy demands and merits. On the most popular level, the image of the wife as shrew seems to be dying, abandoned to middlebrow novelists like Philip Wylie or quite serious calumniators of the female like Faulkner or Hemingway or Wright Morris. The disreputable figure of Rip himself dies harder, appearing with all his old scapegrace charm in, for instance, Faulkner's "Uncle Willy," where he is portrayed as the small boys' ally in their war against the mothers. "He wasn't anybody's uncle, but all of us, and grown people, too, called him . . . Uncle Willy." It is a hopeless war these days, the war against good women; and Uncle Willy, who cannot sleep away the lifetime of his opponents, is driven out of town.

Sometimes, in more serious books, Rip doffs his comic role and appears in new guises, less the clown but still essentially the man on the run from his wife. In the unwritten story of "Agatha," he teased the imaginations of Hawthorne and Melville in the form of the sailor, Robertson: that anti-Enoch Arden who returns from a long absence to find his former wife, not married again but still waiting—and flees again westward to a new escape. In *The Wonder Book,* Hawthorne through his alter ego Eustace Bright had already gone on record as refusing to re-tell the tale of Rip in its original version, though begged to by eager children. "Among those misty hills, he said, was a spot where some old Dutchmen were playing an everlasting game of nine-pins and where an idle fellow whose name was Rip Van Winkle had fallen asleep and slept away twenty years at a stretch." It is interesting to note how gun, dog and wife disappear from this discreet summary, to which Eustace Bright will add no more. "But the student replied that the story had been told once already, and better than it ever could be told again, and that no-body would have a right to alter a word of it until it should have grown as old as 'The Gorgon's Head.' . . ." "The Gorgon's Head"—it is an odd association, which evokes the missing wife at a symbolic remove, as the female face which turns the beholder to stone!

Despite his disclaimer, however, Hawthorne actually did rewrite Irving's tale, or at least embodied certain of its elements in the shadowy sketch which he called "Wakefield." It is not quite a story, this ironic little portrait of a man endowed with "a quiet selfishness . . . a peculiar sort of vanity . . . a disposition to craft," who one day steps out of his door and, for the legendary twenty years, remains away, merely as "a little joke . . . at his wife's expense," "a long whimwham." But the joke is finally at Wakefield's expense, since outside the purlieus of his own home, he becomes for Hawthorne a hopelessly alienated man: "the Outcast of the Universe." Hawthorne's story is racked, that is to say, by a guilt entirely absent in Irving's tale, in which there is no note of equivocation about the joyousness of Rip's deliverance: "there was one species of despotism under which he had long groaned and that was petticoat government. Happily that was at an end; he had got his neck out of the yoke of matrimony, and could go in and out whenever he pleased. . . ."

What is posed originally as an innocent lark soon becomes problematic; for the myth of Rip is more than just another example among the jollier fables of masculine protest; it is the definition, made once and for all—as Eustace Bright justly observes—of a fundamental American archetype. In some ways, it seems astonishingly prophetic: a forecast of today's fishing trip with the boys, tomorrow's escape to the ball park or the poker game. Henpecked and misunderstood at home, the natural man whistles for his dog, Wolf, picks up his gun and leaves the village for Nature—seeking in a day's outing what a long life at home has failed to provide him. It is hard to tell whether he is taking a vacation or making a revolution, whether his gesture is one of evasion or of subversion; but in any case, he seeks some ultimate Good symbolized by the keg of excellent Hollands and the male companions, who do not even talk (that is the province of his wife), merely indicate the liquor and continue with their game—their eternal playtime in the hills.

It is scarcely surprising that such a legend would have a special appeal for Melville, whose whole writing career represents, as it were, an escape to an inner Catskills, a Happy Valley of natural ease and male camaraderie, into which his imagination had translated the experience of his early manhood. To no one did marriage seem so utterly Paradise lost (as we have observed in looking at *Mardi*); to no one did bachelorhood appear so enviable a state. In "Benito Cereno," the innocent ship which Captain Delano leaves to plunge into a web of horror and intrigue is called *The Bachelor's Delight;* in *Moby Dick,* the last glimpse of joy and peace enjoyed by the crew of the *Pequod* comes in their encounter with another whaler named the *Bachelor;* while one of Melville's most intriguing short stories contrasts "The Tartarus of Maids" with "The Paradise of Bachelors." No wonder, then, that Melville turns at the end of his life to the most traditional of all American fables of anti-marriage. His idyllic tale, a composite of verse and prose, was intended as part of a volume he was preparing in his last years to dedicate to his wife. Like that other ambiguous tribute, *Mardi*, "Rip Van Winkle's Lilac" demands some knowledge of the language of flowers for a full understanding; but even to a cursory reader its essential meaning is clear. Melville's tale is an apology for the original Rip, put in the mouth of a bohemian painter, who prefers the shadow of the lilac tree reputed to have been planted by Rip's own hand to the shelter of the whitewashed church. The implication is that art is nurtured not by institutionalized religion but by the impulse which leads man to overthrow petticoat tyranny and head for the hills.

But why has Melville symbolized Rip's heritage by a lilac? For what precisely does it stand, this casual gift of the lazy reprobate to the American artist? We are told two things about it: first, that its blossoms have replaced Dame Van Winkle's pot of pinks and hollyhocks; and second, that its trunk stands in the place of a willow which endured as long as the house lasted and could not be cut down by Dame Van Winkle's ax. But pinks represent both boldness and woman's love, while hollyhocks stand for ambition and fecundity. Opposed to these symbols of aggressive, fertile femaleness, the lilac bloom betokens humility and the joy of youth—appropriate to the modest companionship of boys. The willow, of course, figures forth mourning, the blight that cannot be removed as long as hearth and home continue; while the lilac bush means joy, the rapture which arises when both have become dust. The gift book for Mrs. Melville, who in its code is called "Winnifred" (which means, appropriately enough "White Phantom"!), is entitled *Weeds and Wildings, with a Rose or Two.* What tender meanings roses had for Melville, we know from his portrait of that rosy and beloved boy Billy Budd; but Mrs. Melville, it is interesting to note, suffered from rose fever!

II

Though the myth of Rip Van Winkle embodies the sketch of an alternative to married life, in Irving's version, the mountain spree is tucked away in a few lines, Rip plunged unceremoniously into his Big Sleep—as if to suggest that the escape from the shrew can only be dreamed, not lived. Even on a more serious level, some American writers follow his lead, making not the search for an erotic substitute but the simple failure of married love their essential theme. Hawthorne, for instance, peoples his tales, as we have already seen, with a succession of Wakefieldian "outcasts," capable only of beholding love but not of sharing it. Disconcertingly, he offers such impotent Peeping Toms as prototypes of the American artist.

The metaphor of the trapped spectator is a kindlier one than that of the Peeping Tom, but it describes the same kind of peripheral observer, who is reborn in the form of James's Lambert Strether in *The Ambassadors*. Though the remote original of his character was William Dean Howells, James refused in the end to make him an artist, even a *poète manqué* like Coverdale. "I can't make him a novelist—too like W.D.H.," he wrote to himself. ". . . But I want him 'intellectual' . . . fine, clever, literary almost: it deepens the irony, the tragedy. The Editor of a Magazine—that would come nearest. . . ." A good deal of Howells remains, nonetheless, and even a judgment on Howells; for the "happy ending" of *The Ambassadors* is one of the saddest in all our literature, leaving us with the heartbreaking image of Strether as the man who *sees* everything but can do nothing, understands everything but can possess nothing.

James is not quite candid, however, insisting that Strether's choice of impotence is a willed, a moral act, and that his very voyeurism is insight and "vision." Miss Gostrey, however, is not deceived. When she asks Strether quite directly whether he will not remain in Europe, not take his reward, not, in effect, take her—Strether answers that to be right he must "not, not out of the whole affair . . . have got anything" for himself except "wonderful impressions," which is to say, thrilling peeps into reality. "It's you who would make me wrong," he tells Maria Gostrey; but she protests, "It isn't so much your *being* 'right'—it's your horrible sharp eye for what makes you so." But Strether is really nothing but that "horrible sharp eye," which is his sole organ of morality; and, in this sense at least, he is his own author: less Howells than Henry James who began with "pedestrian gaping" along Broadway, and remained always the big-eyed child, imagining "the probable taste of the bright compound wistfully watched in the confectioner's window, unattainable, impossible. . . ." It is this James who invents the technique of the "center of consciousness," i.e., a device for making the peeper the focus of a work of art, and who insists that "art deals with what we see." It is only in the work of art that

James, like Coverdale before him, can possess symbolically what in reality he cannot touch; and of his very limitations he makes the form and substance of his fiction, which is not, as he liked to boast, "felt life" so much as "*seen* life."

For all his subtlety and tact, James is basically, hopelessly innocent, an innocent voyeur, which is to say, a child! And he is, indeed, the first novelist to do in full consciousness what Twain in *Huckleberry Finn* did just once unawares: present the complexities of adult experience as perceived by a pre-adolescent mind. The child character, made compulsory in our books by the restrictions of gentility and the fear of sex, is first used in *What Maisie Knew* to confront rather than evade experience. James's novel, like the later books which follow its pattern, is a kind of initiation story, though it deals not with a full-scale initiation from innocence to maturity but with a quasi initiation that ends in a withdrawal. In the Jamesian version of the Fall of Man, at any rate, there are four actors, not three: the man, the woman, the serpent, and the child, presumably watching from behind the tree.

The Peeping Child is only a junior version of the Peeping Tom as pallid poet or aging editor of a magazine; but it has had a special appeal to the American imagination. In *What Maisie Knew*, James not only invents the fable, but sets the technique for presenting it; and, indeed, the vicarious ocular initiation presupposes the convention of controlled point of view. Once James has shown how to do it, novelist after novelist sets himself to portraying the corrupt world as reflected in the innocent eye. Eye to the crack in the door, ear attuned from the bed where he presumably sleeps —curious or at idle play, the innocent observer stumbles upon the murderer bent over the corpse, the guilty lovers in each other's arms, the idolized jockey in a whorehouse, a slattern on his knee, and, like the boy in Sherwood Anderson's story, is left, crying, "What did he do it for? I want to know why."

The end of innocence via the ocular initiation is bafflement and nausea; beyond the cry of the kid at the window, it is hard to imagine a real acceptance of adult life and sexuality, hard to conceive of anything but continuing flight or self-destruction. This many American writers besides Anderson see quite clearly; Faulkner, for instance, presents a similar insight, though with a brutality and terror beside which Anderson's sentimentality is revealed in all its inadequacy. Quentin Compson, who has watched as a child an adult drama of passion and death in "That Evening Sun Go Down," relives it as an adolescent witness and peripheral actor in *The Sound and the Fury* and *Absalom, Absalom!;* then dies by his own hand on the verge of manhood, refusing to step over the mystic barrier of twenty-one. Joe Christmas, in *Light in August,* on the other hand, manages to reach the age of Christ at the crucifixion, even after his induction into nausea at the age of five. But at fourteen, he cruelly kicks the naked black girl upon whom he might have lost his virginity; and at thirty-three, decapitates the aging woman who has made him her lover, thus assuring his own eventual lynching. Impotence and sadist aggression, suicide direct or indirect; it is not only to Faulkner that these seem the choices for an American whose imagination is fixed forever on one of the two major crises of pre-adolescent emotional life. Yet it is around these crises that our literature compulsively circles: the stumbling on the primal scene, mother and father caught in the sexual act (or less dramatically, the inference of that scene from creaking springs and ambiguous cries); or the discovery of heterosexual "treachery" on the part of some crush, idolized in innocent homosexual adoration.

In our time, the subterfuges which have traditionally concealed from author and audience alike the true nature of the castrated peeper are no longer necessary. By 1926, it was possible for Hemingway in *The Sun Also Rises* (and thirty years later, even a movie version could make the point unequivocally—though not without some show of daring) to portray an emasculated Jake Barnes, all of whose desperate clutching of Brett creates between them a friction which only erodes, never sparks to life. To be sure, Hemingway tells us that it is "the War" which has afflicted Jake with the absurd wound which he examines in the mirror of his lonely room; but "the War" is merely a convenient tag for the failure of values and faith which converted a generation of young American writers to self-hatred, bravado, and expatriation. The same forces, at any rate, which have "emancipated" Brett have unmanned Jake; forced him into the role not only of witness to Brett's love affairs, but of pimp as well—setter-up of scenes which, beheld or imagined, can only drive him to queasy despair. From the time of Hemingway, impotence has been a central symbol in our fiction, a felt clue to the quality of American life, erotic and spiritual.

Faulkner, who is Hemingway's contemporary and admirer, has exploited the same theme, conceiving as eunuchs both Flem Snopes, symbol of the new bourgeoisie, the sterile lover of money, and Popeye, the spawn of urban alleys, Prohibition, and the hysteria of the Great Depression. The self-pity, which in Hawthorne, James, and even Hemingway has softened the horror of the portrait of the American as impotent voyeur, the insistence that, for better or worse, he is an intellectual, "one of us"— disappears in *Sanctuary*. The dreadfully intelligent eye of Strether has become the absurd and moronic stare which the name Popeye implies; and it looks not out of the face of a gentleman, but from the rat's face (when he watches her in the barn, Popeye seems to Temple one of the smaller rodents) of a killer. He is the ultimate, as he is the most revolting, avatar of the desexed seducer, but he is also a terrible caricature of the child witness, not like Peter Pan one who chooses not to grow up, but one who cannot. "And he will never be a man properly speaking," a doctor says of Popeye when he is five, ". . . he will never be any older than he is now."

When Popeye leans over the bed in Madame Reba's whorehouse, watching Temple Drake perform the act of darkness of which he is incapable ("the two of them would be nekkid as two snakes, and Popeye hanging over the foot of the bed without even his hat off, making a kind of whinnying sound"), he is projecting a brutal travesty of the American artist, helpless and fascinated before the fact of genital love. Similarly, in that other central "love" scene, in which Popeye rapes Temple with the corncob, Faulkner is parodying his own blasphemy of the Pale Protestant Virgin—portraying the hysterical masculine protest of his time in the image of the maimed male, revenging himself on woman who has maimed him with the first instrument that comes to hand, a weapon in place of the phallus.

But he is revealing, too, the secret of the descendants of Natty Bumppo in popular literature: those cowboys, for instance, who ride off into the sunset leaving the girls they have rescued behind; and they have been postulated as virile without sexuality, their only weapons (like Popeye's) in their hands, for only thus can they be imagined as representing the innocence of the West. The taboo that separates them from the women they preserve is so unself-consciously accepted, so widely known, that a television comedian can set the nation to laughing with a quip about the unconventional cowboy who insisted on kissing the girl in the last scene and was trampled to death by his jealous horse.

But just as Natty became with the westward expansion a cowpuncher, with the retreat from the frontier, he was urbanized into the image of the private detective, called—in the language of that literature itself—the "private eye," the peeper institutionalized at last. Through the corrupt city, the innocent tough guy who finally sees all, though he is slugged, doped, sapped, shot at, and bribed on the way to his vision, moves on an immaculate journey. The undraped daughters of the rich, tight-breasted virgins and nymphomaniac night-club entertainers, tempt him with their proffered bodies; but he is faithful only to his buddies, and like Lambert Strether, to "what is right."

In a typical gesture, the shamus of *The Maltese Falcon* (1930) sends the sexually attractive woman who loves him off to jail; but even this rejection is finally not decisive enough. From Dashiell Hammett, the private eye is passed on to Raymond Chandler and from him to Mickey Spillane, who recreates him at last for the ultimate audience—the readers of pocket-books, who put down their quarters in millions in search of myths more appropriate to their lives than those of high literature. In Spillane's Mike Hammer, Faulkner's Popeye is reborn as a culture hero, a chevalier of the city streets, blasting down the female he never manages quite to possess, and who, dead in one book, rises up in the next, phallic and aggressive, deadly whether clothed or nude. "She was a beautiful evil goddess with a gun in her hand," he writes in *The Big Kill* of Marsha, who lies dead a moment later, shot by the kid she has spurned and wounded: "the tongue of flame that blasted from the muzzle seemed to lick out across the room with a horrible vengeance that ripped all evil from her face, turning it into a ghastly wet red mask that was really no face at all." The climax of *Vengeance Is Mine,* however, is really more satisfactory, since it is Mike Hammer himself who does the shooting, and he blasts not the face of the goddess but the naked body of a luscious blonde, making the only penetration possible to the cripple of love with the slug of a .45.

III

When the Hawthorne-James-Faulkner gambit is refused and the American writer does not make impotence itself his subject, he is left to choose between the two archetypes of innocent homosexuality and unconsummated incest: the love of comrades and that of brother and sister. From his trip to Europe, undertaken just after he had finished *Moby Dick,* Melville brought back with him not only the oleograph reproduction of Guido Reni's "Beatrice Cenci" mentioned earlier but also a life-long memory of the relief sculpture of Antinoüs, favorite boy of the Emperor Hadrian, a work of art ("head like moss-rose with curls and buds—rest all simplicity") then on display in the Villa Albani. He returned, that is to say, from his cultural pilgrimage with an icon of incest justified and of homosexuality glorified, in memory of which it is perhaps fair to call the themes we have been describing the Antinoüs archetype and the Cenci archetype.

Both themes are juvenile and regressive, that is, narcissistic; for where woman is felt to be a feared and forbidden other, the only legitimate beloved is the self. Pure narcissism cannot, however, provide the dream and tension proper to a novel; the mirror-image of the self is translated in the American novel either into the flesh of one's flesh, the sister as *anima;* or into the comrade of one's own sex, the buddy as *anima.* Certainly, Melville's greatest work is essentially an account, as he himself hints, of "Narcissus, who because he could not grasp the tormenting, mild image he saw in the fountain, plunged into it and was drowned": but the alter ego of Narcissus-Ishmael is projected as the Polynesian cannibal, Queequeg, in whom the seeker in quest of his own "tormenting, mild image" finds a genuine other. Marriage to a woman would have seemed to Melville's hero intolerable; only through a pure wedding of male to male could he project an engagement with life which did not betray the self.

This is an alternative deeply appealing to the American mind and essentially congenial to the American experience. If one considers the series of distinguished fictions which begins with Cooper's Leatherstocking Tales and passes through Poe's *Narrative of A. Gordon Pym* (as well as his abortive *Journal of Julius Rodman*), Dana's *Two Years Before the Mast,* Melville's whole body of work culminating in *Moby Dick,* Twain's *Huckleberry Finn* and Henry James's "The Great Good Place," and is refurbished in our own time in such works as Faulkner's "The Bear" as well as Hemingway's *The Sun Also Rises* and *The Old Man and the Sea,* it is evident that there is an archetype at work, a model story, appearing and reappearing in a score of guises, haunting almost all our major writers of fiction.

What is hard to understand at first is why middle-class readers were not appalled at the implications of the homoerotic[1] fable, opposed as it is to almost everything in which middle-class society pretends to believe. Only by assuming an unconscious marginal rejection of the values of that society on the part of all or most of its members can we come to terms with its glorification of a long line of heroes in flight from woman and home. Cooper's Natty flees the settlements and the prospect of marriage with squaw or pale-face maiden; Melville's Ishmael rejects his cruel stepmother and the whole world of security she represents; Poe's Gordon Pym deceives and defies his family to go to sea; Twain's Huck evades all the women who try, with rigor or gentleness, to redeem his orphaned state; James's Dane flees from his social commitments to ladies and ladies' luncheons. None of these protagonists, moreover, manages to disown all female ties without seeming to reject life itself. "Whenever it is a damp, drizzly November in my soul," Ishmael remarks, "then, I account it high time to get to sea as soon as I can. This is my substitute for pistol and ball. With a philosophical flourish Cato throws himself upon his sword; I quietly take to ship."

Yet for a man to love death is not nearly so suspect in bourgeois America as for him to love another man; and in all the classic American books we have been examining, there are hints of such a love: in some, buried deep beneath the ken of the authors themselves, in others moving just beneath a transparent surface. How could Antinoüs come to preside over the literature of the nineteenth-century United States, which is to say, at a time and in a place where homosexuality was regarded with a horror perhaps unmatched elsewhere and ever? Certainly, in the popular literature of the period, the "sissy," the effeminate boy, nearest thing to a fairy mentionable in polite books, was a target upon which the fury of a

---

[1] "Homoerotic" is a word of which I was never very fond, and which I like even less now. But I wanted it to be quite clear that I was not attributing sodomy to certain literary characters or their authors, and so I avoided when I could the more disturbing word "homosexual." All my care has done little good, however, since what I have to say on this score has been at once the best remembered and most grossly misunderstood section of my book. *Ubi morbus, ibi digitus.*

self-conscious masculinity vented itself with especial venom. In the long run, however, so violent a disavowal of male inversion fostered an ignorance of its true nature; the "sin" or "crime" of homosexuality was conceived only in the grossest physical terms, so that a love as abstract and unconsummated as Dante's for Beatrice (or Shakespeare's for his aristocratic boy!) seemed unexceptionable to the most genteel. Mothers, indeed, rejoiced at "harmless" romantic attachments between their sons, conceiving of them as protecting against the lure of the flesh, which might lead to venereal diseases or the impregnation of quite undesirable lower-class girls. Even in the minds of women, that is to say, "evil love" could only be conceived of in connection with "evil women," and the relations of males seemed therefore healthy by definition. Indeed, to this very day, anyone who suggests that such relations are occasionally at least ambiguous is regarded as a disturber of the peace, a public enemy.

In our native mythology, the tie between male and male is not only considered innocent, it is taken for the very symbol of innocence itself;[2] for it is imagined as the only institutional bond in a paradisal world in which there are no (heterosexual) marriages or giving in marriage. Paradisal, however, means for hardheaded Americans not quite real; and there is, in fact, a certain sense of make-believe in almost all portrayals of the holy marriage of males, set as they typically are in the past, the wilderness, or at sea—that is to say, in worlds familiar to most readers in dreams. After Mark Twain, one of the partners to such a union is typically conceived of as a child, thus inviting the reader to identify the Great Good Place where the union is consummated with his own childhood, a region more remote and less real to the grown man than the dimmest reaches of pre-history. It is Stephen Crane who finds the proper name for that Neverland, calling it "Whilomville," which is to say a town which never had an "is" but only a half-recalled, half-invented "was." Everywhere in our classic fiction—in Cooper's use of the historical past, in Melville's evocation of his own receding youth, in Twain's or Faulkner's reversion to a rural boyhood, there is implicit a suggestion that the Edenic affair is lived out in a Garden in the process of being destroyed. The sound of axes is heard; the trees fall; the ground is broken for factories and stores; and the reader feels that he is being asked to recreate in fantasy a place to which neither he nor the author can ever return— the "home" to which the American writer complains he cannot go back again.

---

[2] Things have changed radically in this regard, however. When the traditional sentimental relationship of white man and colored is evoked these days, it is likely to be quite the opposite of innocent, as the following passage from James Purdy's *Cabot Wright Begins* spectacularly indicates: "Taking Winters Hart's left hand in his, Bernie held his friend's dark finger on which he wore a wedding-ring, and pressed the finger and the hand. Far from being annoyed at this liberty, Winters Hart was, to tell the truth, relieved and pleased. Isolation in a racial democracy, as he was to tell Bernie later that night, as they lay in Bernie's bed together, isolation, no thank you."

In our classic fiction, the heroes of such attempts at evasion are shown, at their stories' close, remanded to the world of reality. Ishmael, "alone escaped alive," comes back to tell his tale, Gordon Pym to write down his authentic account of adventure, Huck Finn to take another whirl at being civilized. Though he is already speaking of his next escape, even the motherless boy is last presented at the moment of his restitution to the society of women. Henry James, too sophisticated to equivocate about the reality of the Great Good Place, portrays his hero as awaking from a simple dream, from a twelve-hour sleep. Natty alone is never portrayed outside the universe of fantasy; pursuing the elusive West to the very end, he makes of his death the ultimate escape, for which his later avatars yearn but which they can never seem quite to attain. Those others act out not a permanent removal from the society which irks them, but an outing, a long excursion. Tom Sawyer's career as a pirate parodies the dream to which his author subscribed, gives the whole game away: the vows of eternal alienation and the message to Aunt Polly concealed in a pocket all the time: "We ain't dead—we are only off being pirates."

Perhaps it is this sense of make-believe which redeems so subversive a theme for the most genteel and diffident reader. It represents a projection, entertained *without final faith*, of a way of life hostile to the accepted standards of the American community: a counter-family that can only flourish in a world without women or churches or decency or hard work, living what one is tempted to call "life with father," or, more precisely, "life with foster-father." Such terms seem to hold up well enough, superficially at least, in describing the erotic tie at the heart of *Huckleberry Finn*, for instance, or those in fictions like Faulkner's "The Bear" and *Intruder in the Dust,* as well as in certain stories by Stephen Crane and Sherwood Anderson. In these fictions, a small boy is represented as turning to a colored foster-father in revulsion from a real father, felt as brutal or ineffectual or effete; or he is portrayed as seeking out the dark-skinned, outcast male in an attempt to escape the mothers of his world, who are wholly committed to respectable codes of piety and success.

Such a reading, however, only seems satisfactory if we set a book like Mark Twain's in the context of a popular tradition which falsifies him even as it derives from him: the vulgarized juvenile, which descends by way of Stephen Crane's *Whilomville Stories* to the heavy-handed cuteness of Booth Tarkington's *Penrod.* In that middlebrow line of descent, the filial relationship of Negro and child is transformed into the stereotype which William Lyon Phelps describes condescendingly in a foreword to Crane's tales of childhood: "Little children and big Africans make ideal companions, for the latter have the patience, inner sympathy, forbearance, and unfailing good humor necessary to such an association. Both Stephen Crane and Booth Tarkington have given us permanent drawings in black and white." Twain's treatment of Jim in *Huckleberry*

Finn is, however, complex enough to preserve him from becoming a merely stereotypical darkie; and that very complexity makes it impossible to describe him as just a substitute father. Sometimes he seems more servant than father, sometimes more lover than servant, sometimes more mother than either! His relationship with Huck must be seen not against the later sentimental tradition of "little children and big Africans," but against an earlier tradition of more nearly coeval loving pairs like Natty and Chingachgook, Gordon Pym and Dirk Peters, Ishmael and Queequeg. In Jim, Huck finds the pure affection offered by Mary Jane without the threat of marriage; the escape from social obligations offered by Pap without the threat of beatings; the protection and petting offered by his volunteer foster-mothers without the threat of pious conformity; the male companionship offered by the Grangerfords without the threat of the combat of honor; the friendship offered by Tom without the everlasting rhetoric and make-believe. Jim is all things to him: father and mother and playmate and beloved, appearing naked and begowned and be-whiskered and painted blue, and calling Huck by the names appropriate to their multiform relationship: "Huck" or "honey" or "chile" or "boss," and just once "white genlman."

It is an impossible society which they constitute, the outcast boy and the Negro, who, even for Huck, does not really exist as a person: a society in which, momentarily, the irreparable breach between black and white seems healed by love. Huck, who offends no one else, begins by playing in Tom's company a stupid joke on the sleeping Jim; then almost kills him as the result of another heartless stunt; teases him to the point of tears about the reality of their perils on the river; and finally joins with Tom once more to inflict on Jim a hundred pointless torments, even putting his life in unnecessary danger. And through it all, Jim plays the role of Uncle Tom, enduring everything, suffering everything, forgiving everything—finally risking a lynching to save "Marse Tom's" life. It is the Southerner's dream, the American dream of guilt remitted by the abused Negro, who, like the abused mother, opens his arms crying, "Lawsy, I's mighty glad to git you back agin, honey."

Only on the unstable surface of the river and in the dark of night, can such a relationship exist, and its proper home is the raft, which floats on the surge of flood-time into the story, a gift from the non-Christian powers of Nature. "There warn't no home like a raft, after all . . . ," Huck reflects. "You feel mighty free and easy and comfortable on a raft." But the very essence of life on a raft is unreality. "The motion of the raft is gentle, and gliding, and smooth, and noiseless . . . ," Twain writes in *A Tramp Abroad;* "under its restful influence . . . existence becomes a dream . . . a deep and tranquil ecstasy." Yet the dream of life on the river always threatens to turn for Twain into a nightmare. In 1906, he comments on a recurring dream in which he was once more piloting a boat down the Mississippi:

It is never a pleasant dream, either. I love to think about those days, but there's always something sickening about the thought . . . and usually in my dream I am just about to start into a black shadow without being able to tell whether it is Selma Bluff, or Hat Island, or just a black wall of night.

The idyll of Huck and Jim is a dream at whose heart lurks a nightmare. All about them on the lawless river, crime is plotted and violence done, while the river itself is ever ready to mislead and destroy with fog or storm or snag. Thieves and murderers seek the same avenue of escape which Huck and Jim follow in domestic peace. And at last, in the persons of the Duke and Dauphin, the evil of river life invades the raft itself. The floating island paradise becomes an occupied country, a place where absurd and sodden scoundrels hatch deceit and seek to avoid retribution. There is no way to escape evil forever, no absolute raft; and once the home of Huck and Jim has been invaded, they cannot manage to establish their little Eden again. For a moment after the fiasco at the Wilks', it seems as if Huck and Jim are about to recapture their first freedom: "it *did* seem so good to be free again and all by ourselves on the big river, and nobody to bother us." But the King and Duke appear at the last minute, and Huck collapses into despair: "it was all I could do to keep from crying."

If one moves from a literal to a symbolic level, the difficulties involved in reading Jim and Huck as father and son become even greater. It is hard to think of a figure, union with whom signifies a coming to terms with the natural and impulsive, as finally paternal; much more suitable is the metaphor of the spouse. Only marriage is a relationship complicated enough to stand for so complicated and ambiguous a cluster of meanings; the search for a parent, a master, a slave, an equal, a companion, a soul— a union with one's deepest self which is simultaneously a rejection of the community to which one was born. This Melville, at least, most canny and conscious of all exploiters of this common theme, realized with great clarity, working out the metaphor of the holy marriage in great detail in the pages of *Moby Dick*, to which we must turn for clues to what elsewhere remains confusing and confused.

Three elements are necessary for the *hierogamos:* the longed-for spouse, the questing lover, and the sacred setting. The setting, though it is, of course, only another projection of the world of instinct represented by the desired spouse, is of great symbolic importance. It is an Eden, to be sure, which is to say, a place out of time and history, as well as beyond the bounds of society; but it is a natural Eden, nature as Eden. Only in the mind of Henry James is that Great Good Place portrayed as an ordered and cultivated garden, though even for him it provides a vantage point from which one can look out "over a long valley to a far horizon," like some "old Italian picture." More typically, it is portrayed as a campsite in the wilderness, a raft floating down the river, an isolated valley on a South Sea island, a lonely wood sought as a refuge from combat, a ship on the open sea. What it cannot be is city or village, hearth or home; for isolation is the key, the non-presence of the customary—in the words of Henry James, "the absence of what he didn't want." And what "he" especially does not want is *women!*

In America, the earthly paradise for men only is associated, for obvious historical reasons, with the "West"; and it is possible to regard the classic works which we have been discussing, in this sense, as "Westerns." Despite certain superficial differences, they are, indeed, all closely related to the pulp stories, the comic-books, movies, and TV shows, in which the cowhand and his side-kick ride in silent communion through a wilderness of sagebrush, rocks, and tumbleweed. The Western, understood in this way, does not even require an American setting, being reborn, for instance, in Hemingway's *The Sun Also Rises* in the improbable environs of Paris and Burguete. One must not be confused by the exotica of expatriation: bullfights, French whores, and *thés dansants.* Like the American East, Paris in Hemingway's book stands for the world of women and work, for "civilization" with all its moral complexity, and it is presided over quite properly by the bitch-goddess Brett Ashley. The mountains of Spain, on the other hand, represent the West: a world of male companions and sport, an anti-civilization, simple and joyous, whose presiding genius is that scarcely articulate arch-buddy, "good, old Bill."

For Hemingway there are many Wests, from Switzerland to Africa; but the mountains of Spain are inextricably associated in his mind with the authentic American West, with Montana whose very name is the Spanish word for the mountains that make of both isolated fastnesses holy places. It is in the Hotel Montana that Lady Ashley ends up after her abortive romance with the bullfighter Romero; and it is from the University of Montana that Robert Jordan, hero of *For Whom the Bell Tolls,* takes off to the Spanish Civil War. But it is not only a pun that binds together for Hemingway his two paradisal retreats; it is also the sacred sport of fishing. Though the monastery of Roncesvalles stands on a peak high above Jake's place of refuge, it serves only to remind Hemingway's characters of a religion now lapsed for them. "It's a remarkable place," one of them says of the monastery; but Bill, the good companion, observes mournfully, "It isn't the same as fishing, is it?"

It is in the trout stream of Burguete that Jake and Bill immerse themselves and are made whole again and clean; for that stream links back to the rivers of Hemingway's youth, the rivers of upper Michigan, whose mythical source is the Mississippi of Tom Sawyer and Huck Finn. "We stayed five days at Burguete and had good fishing. The nights were cold and the days were hot. . . . It was hot enough so that it felt good to wade in the cold stream, and the sun dried you when you came out. . . ." They are boys again, back on Jackson's Island, which is to say, safe in the

Neverland of men without women. Jake is, in his quest for the Great Good Place, at one with almost all the other heroes of Hemingway; though somehow it is he who has managed to find again the magical stream of which the wounded, half-mad *tenente* in "Now I Lay Me" can only dream: "I would think of a trout stream I had fished along when I was a boy and fish its whole length carefully in my mind. . . . But some nights I could not fish, and on those nights I was cold-awake and said my prayers over and over. . . ."

In the double-barreled story, "Big Two-Hearted River," it is impossible to tell whether the hero (called Nick this time) is moving through reality or fantasy. We can know only that he has returned, or dreams he has returned, once more to the River that is always different and always the same; and that this time he fishes it inch by inch to the edge of the tragic swamp which he will not enter. This time there is no question of choosing between fishing and praying; fishing has become clearly a prayer, or at least a ritual, in the midst of which a disguised prayer is uttered in the guise of a childish epithet. "Chrise," Nick says at one point, when he knows he is at last really *there*, "Geezus Chrise," and Hemingway tells us he says it "happily." In the dreams of the River both in "Now I Lay Me" and "Big Two-Hearted River," however, the Hemingway hero imagines himself alone; in *The Sun Also Rises*, a second self is with him, a companion to share the inarticulate sentimentality that becomes finally too embarrassing to bear, bursting with pure masculine love. "'Old Bill' I said. 'You bum!'" And when the time for parting comes, when the bluff, immaculate honeymoon is over, when the telegram arrives to announce that the outsiders are coming, Brett and Cohen, woman and Jew, it is a third fisherman, an Englishman called Harris, who blurts out in his drunkenness what neither Jake nor Bill can quite confess: "I've not had so much fun since the war. . . . We *have* had a good time."

What Hemingway's emphasis on the ritual murder of fish conceals is that it is not so much the sport as the occasion for immersion which is essential to the holy marriage of males. Water is the symbol of the barrier between the Great Good Place and the busy world of women; and everywhere in our fiction, the masculine paradise is laved by great rivers or the vast ocean, washed by the ripples of Lake Glimmerglass or the spume of Glens Falls, even—in Poe—drowned, swallowed up in a liquid white avalanche: "and now we rushed into the embraces of the cataract, where a chasm threw itself open to receive us." Not only in chronicles of shipwreck like *Gordon Pym* or *Moby Dick*, but even in so mild an account of masculine evasion as James's "The Great Good Place," the metaphor of a descent into the waters prevails; though to be sure, in the case of James we are reminded of the bathtub or hydrotherapy rather than a plunge into the maelstrom: "He didn't want, for a time, anything but just to *be* there, to steep in the bath. He was in the bath yet, the broad deep bath of stillness. They sat in it together now with the water up to their chins. . . . He had been sunk that way before, sunk . . . in another flood. . . . *This* was a curtain so slow and tepid that one floated practically without motion and without chill."

To descend into the charmed waters where one can float "practically without motion" is, in effect, to die; and the flight to the watery world is a kind of suicide, a quietus self-imposed. Melville, in whom much that is elsewhere implicit is made explicit, makes it clear that the land is the realm of the super-ego, the water that of the id; and he at least does not hesitate long between them. Like Bulkington, the supernumerary hero of *Moby Dick,* he turns his own back on the "leeward land": "The port would fain give succor; the port is pitiful; in the port is safety, comfort, hearthstone, supper, warm blankets, friends, all that's kind to our mortalities. . . . But in landlessness alone resides the highest truth, shoreless, indefinite as God—so better is it to perish in that howling infinite, than to be ingloriously dashed upon the lee, even if it were safety."

Better death than castration, articulate Melville cries; but he does not foresee death as inevitable for the man who plunges into the "all-subduing" element, the shoreless wastes of his own unconsciousness. What seems a suicide may be in the end a baptism and a transfiguration, an immersion and a resurrection. "Take heart, take heart, O Bulkington . . . ," Melville writes at the close of the "six-inch chapter" which he calls Bulkington's "stoneless grave"; "Up from the spray of thy ocean-perishing—straight up, leaps thy apotheosis!" So (in gentle parody) Tom Sawyer is resurrected after "drowning," while Huck, presumably slaughtered like a pig, takes the plunge and lives again; so Ishmael, drawn into the ocean whirlpool, or Gordon Pym, sucked into the chasm beneath the cataract, emerge unscathed to write gospel accounts of their survival. The picnic, the day's outing from which the male fugitive returns, is also a watery grave; and though, like the Ancient Mariner, the survivor lives on chiefly to tell his tale, he returns purged and guiltless.

In fact, only he is guiltless in our world; for—our classical novelists believe with Shakespeare—no man born of woman is innocent enough to combat evil without being converted into its image. Each must be born again, the second time not of the murky flood of blood, amniotic fluid, and milk which characterizes female gestation, but out of the immaculate flux of waters which characterizes a birth into the world of men without women. A new birth implies a new family, a wifeless and motherless one, in which the good companion is the spouse and nurse, the redeemed male the lover and child, each his own progenitor and offspring. The disgust of the American male at our original birth is most clearly and passionately expressed in Melville's sketch called "The Tartarus of Maids." In this extraordinary piece, Melville describes the processes of natural gestation (to him a mechanical and brutal function) from inside, as it were—in terms of a guided tour through a paper mill. Proceeding from a "large bespattered place, with two great round vats in it, full of a wet, weedy-looking stuff, not unlike the albuminous part of an egg" into a "room, stifling with a strange, blood-like, abdominal heat," he beholds at last the end product of a process which takes "nine minutes to the second": "suddenly, I saw a sort of paper-fall, not wholly unlike a water-fall; a scissory sound smote my ears, as of some cord being snapped; and down dropped an unfolded sheet of perfect foolscap, with my 'Cupid' half faded out of it, and still moist and warm . . . here was the end of the machine." To convert into "royal sheets" the "imperfect foolscap" produced by a female machine, which is powered by the fall of "Blood River" through what Melville calls the "Black Notch," is no easy task. They must either be re-immersed, as we have seen, in the waters of life which seem those of death, or else be dipped into an altogether alien bloodstream.

The alternative to immersion and rebirth is the baptism in the blood of a beast. Quite often, indeed, the holy marriage is sanctified by the ritual killing of a totem, the ram offered in the place of Isaac; though in the American version of the fable of sacrifice it is Isaac who kills the beast, becomes his own father at the moment of killing him, while the colored mother-midwife-beloved stands by as witness. From Natty Bumppo's first deer to the buck whose shooting by young Ike McCaslin is described in Faulkner's "Delta Autumn," such doomed animals play a leading role in American fiction. When Ike is smeared with the blood of his victim by Sam Fathers, half-Indian, half-Negro ("and Sam dipped his hands into the hot blood and marked his face forever while he stood trying not to tremble"), even the scarcely literate can understand the ritual that is being performed. Indeed, with the expulsion of sex from polite novels and the consequent demotion of the hero to childhood, such outdoor stories became a staple of middlebrow literature. In the forest rather than brothel or bedroom, through murder rather than sex, the child enters manhood, trembles with nausea over the broken bird or lifeless rabbit rather than the spread-eagled whore.

In our more serious fictions, from *Moby Dick* to Faulkner's "The Bear" or Hemingway's *The Old Man and the Sea*, such tales are redeemed from sentimentality by making of the animals involved not mere occasions for the loss of virginity but monstrous embodiments of the natural world in all its ambiguous and indestructible essence. Either, like Moby Dick, such totemic beasts are ubiquitous and immortal; or, like Big Ben, the bear of Faulkner's story, they cannot be destroyed until "the last day"; or, like the giant swordfish of *The Old Man and the Sea*, they cannot be brought back as trophies. They are sacred embodiments of power, taboo objects whose death is a blasphemy if it is not a rite. Behind all such tales echoes the reproach of God to Job: "Canst thou catch Leviathan with a hook!" and their guilt-ridden protagonists regret the violence they enact even as they enact it. It is the boast of the young Isaac McCaslin and his hunting companions that they go to the woods once a year "not to hunt bear and deer but to keep yearly rendezvous with the bear which

they did not even intend to kill." Yet *finally* the bear dies as lesser bears
have died before him, the whale is harpooned and stripped, the swordfish mounted above the fireplace, and (as was foretold) the innocent
world ends; for Ishmael and Ike McCaslin live, after all, in America,
where the way is opened for the rape of nature by the pioneers who come
to it in love and in search of communion. At any moment, the pure
huntsman may find himself transformed into his anti-image, the Faustian
man—Captain Ahab, who thrusts at the unfallen world not in reverence
but in rage.

But worse is yet to come—for after the tragic betrayal, the comic anticlimax follows fast. Natty Bumppo gives way to the bounty-hunter, to
Buffalo Bill; and Buffalo Bill is followed by the dude with pack animal
and guide and whisky bottle, playing Indian and fleeing his wife! The
real end of the flight to the forest never changes, only the equipment and
the ideological justification. Like the dude who emulates him, the hero
did not go out alone to encounter the spirit of the wilderness—but
traveled always with a companion and guide; and like the hero, the dude
still hunts some excuse to justify the ideal community of buddies isolated
from the world, pursues the "primitive area," in which alone such a community can survive.

IV

But who are these good companions in their archetypal reality, as
dreamed by our greatest writers rather than travestied by our poor selves?

The questing lover is, in general, a surrogate for the artist, the articulate
man (Natty, grandfather of them all, is garrulous to a fault), whose tale
is presented typically in the form of a first-person narrative, journal, diary,
or running reminiscence: "And I only am escaped alone to tell thee." He
is the artist projected as a pariah, an Ishmael—not *le grand écrivain
américain*, which was, on occasion at least, as we have noticed, Cooper's
conscious self-image. In Poe, for instance, Julius Rodman, the hero of his
incomplete Western, is obviously intended to suggest the author; dwarfed,
hypochondriac, oddly Semitic in appearance ("He was . . . not more than
five feet three or four inches high . . . with legs somewhat bowed. . . .
His physiognomy was of a Jewish cast . . ."), Rodman anticipates the
westward trek of Lewis and Clark "urged solely by a desire to seek in the
bosom of the wilderness, that peace which his peculiar disposition would
not suffer him to enjoy among men."

It is Melville, however, who most consciously works out the figure of
the fugitive-lover artist and gives him his generic name. In his series of
portraits of the artist as outcast, he blends the Old Testament archetype
of Hagar's unwanted son (Redburn is already called a "sort of Ishmael")
with the figure of the taboo wanderer, about whom he had learned some-

thing during his sojourn in the islands of the South Pacific. Sometimes the rejected son is a merely comic character in Melville, a *schlemiel* with an absurd name, a ridiculous jacket, an outlandish vocabulary, and pretensions to gentility; but he is always threatening to take on tragic overtones. And often, indeed, he is mythicized into an almost divine presence, at once accursed and a source of blessing, Prometheus himself. The "I" of *Typee* is incapable of taking seriously his own godhead, but he has been renamed Tommo and started on the long road toward apotheosis; while the very title of Melville's next book, *Omoo*, is a Polynesian word for the untouchable Wanderer. In *Mardi*, the protagonist is not merely called Taji, another name for the taboo man, but is transformed into that semi-mythical figure. *Redburn* and *White Jacket*, intended potboilers, return to the comic version of the theme, qualifying its serious implications with a playful irony; but in *Moby Dick*, Ishmael takes on once again the full stature of the alienated man, though he enters the novel as a rather absurd greenhorn, apparently fitter for gags and pratfalls than the tragic illumination toward which he really moves.

Everywhere the figure of the Stranger moves through Melville's work: as the rich boy turned writer in *Pierre*, as the early avatars of the Confidence Man, as the exiled Israel Potter, as the ultimately alienated protagonist of "Bartleby the Scrivener," condemned to prison and madness and death. Snob, greenhorn, madman, *schlemiel*, god and exile: the Outsider has a score of forms in Melville's fiction, but he remains, in his various masquerades, always the artist, society's rejected son with his "splintered heart and maddened hand . . . turned against the wolfish world." Though Outsider, he is not alien; invariably a native white American in Melville, he remains so as Twain's Huck and Faulkner's Ike McCaslin and Hemingway's Nick Adams or Jake Barnes: lonelier and lonelier in a country overrun by other stocks; "Chinese and African and Aryan and Jew, all breed and spawn together until no man has time to say which one is which nor cares. . . ."

Typically white and Anglo-Saxon (even Poe's Rodman turns out really to have been "a native of England where his relatives were of excellent standing"), the artist surrogate in the homoerotic Western is a disaffected child of the reigning race and class. He is no late arrival, no member of a dusky or non-Aryan race (when Saul Bellow re-imagined Huck Finn as a young Chicago Jew in *The Adventures of Augie March*, scarcely any of his readers recognized the affiliation), but a renegade from respectability and belongingness. He has cut himself out of the community that bred him in a desire to embrace some alien shadow-figure symbolizing the instinctive life despised by his white, Anglo-Saxon parents and his fated white, Anglo-Saxon wife.

But who is the alien helpmeet for him? There are various versions of the shadow-spouse in our literature, fumblings in various directions toward the definition of a type symbolically appropriate; but they finally cohere in a single image.

In the remote prototype of Irving, there is no single good companion but an indefinite group of European ghosts out of which a single voice speaks the only word Rip Van Winkle hears—his own name! In Melville, there are several attempts at portraying the appropriate mate, from Toby, who is the narrator's companion in the valley of the Typees, to the various avatars of Jack Chase, the Handsome Sailor who appears in person in *White Jacket* and who haunted Melville until the end of his life. The Sailor is represented by Bulkington in *Moby Dick* ("full six feet in height, with noble shoulders, and a chest like a cofferdam . . ."), and finally by Billy himself in *Billy Budd*, whose dedication recalls in Melville's last days his first love: "To Jack Chase . . . Wherever that great heart may now be . . ." But Billy is Jack Chase recast in the image of Antinoüs ("head like moss-rose with curls and buds"), so "welkin-eyed," angelic and beautiful that he threatens to quite give away the homosexual secret he embodies. The first Jack Chase is the idol of White Jacket, but more usually the love which the Handsome Sailor stirs is more ambiguous, verges on hatred and destruction. It is as if something in Melville himself, aware of what is from the conventional point of view dangerous in his yearning for his six-foot, Anglo-Saxon beauties, drove him to portray that yearning chiefly in dark parody; the relationship of Billy Budd and Claggart, who could have loved Billy "but for fate and ban."

Even outside his treatment of the Handsome Sailor theme, Melville turned on occasion to descriptions of such murderous and passionate relations between males. Steeling himself to kill his cousin and boyhood friend, thus insuring his own eventual death, Pierre cries out, "Oh Glen! Oh Fred! most fraternally do I leap to your rib-crushing hugs! Oh, how I love ye two, that yet can make me lively hate. . . ." And even the utterly hostile cohabitation of Benito Cereno and the slave Babo is an obscene parody of the intimate bond of lovers.

Melville is, of course, not alone among American writers in portraying such sinister relationships; and one of the most notable examples is to be found in the work of Hawthorne, whose own relation to Melville turned from an initial deep affection to coldness and distrust. Surely no loving tie is closer than the one established between Chillingworth and Dimmesdale in *The Scarlet Letter*, as the cuckold penetrates in icy intimacy his cuckolder's psyche. Hester, Chillingworth, and Dimmesdale stand to each other in that odd relationship which European critics call the unnatural triangle, in which two men are bound to each other through the woman they jointly possess, as they cannot "for fate and ban" possess each other.

In our own time, the unnatural triangle recurs in Saul Bellow's *The Victim* (1947), where it assumes a peculiarly American mutilated form, being, in effect, a triangle without an apex or with only a hypothetical

one, which is to say, a triangle without a woman! Indeed, the whole of
Bellow's work is singularly lacking in real or vivid female characters;
where women are introduced, they appear as nympholeptic fantasies,
peculiarly unconvincing. His true world is a world of men in boarding
houses, men whose wives are ill, or have left them, or have gone off on
vacation; and the deepest emotions he evokes are those which simultaneously join together and separate father and son, brother and sister,
con-man and victim. This holds true throughout the body of his work,
from *Dangling Man* to *Seize the Day*, and is even seen, in a bizarre context, in *Henderson the Rain King*, in which Bellow actually returns (three
times over) to the convention of the dark companion.[3] But in no book
does the involvement of mates quivering between poles of attraction and
repulsion take on a more crucial importance than it has in *The Victim*.
Asa Leventhal, the hero of that novel, finds his lover-enemy Kirby Allbee
in his very bed, but finds him there not with his wife but a casual whore.
What binds the two men together is not the ambivalent tie of the cuckold
and the cuckolder but of the Jew and anti-Semite. Bourgeois and bohemian, secure citizen and self-torturing bum, Semite and Anglo-Saxon,
recent immigrant and old American—they are bound together by their
manifold contrasts. Nothing renders them more "dependent for the food
of spiritual life" upon each other than Allbee's indecent need for Jews
to define his existence by defining a difference, or Leventhal's secret
hunger for a hatred that can mark off the boundaries of his identity.

It is this realization on Bellow's part which differentiates his book from
the host of righteous, liberal tract-novels about the problem of anti-
Semitism, makes it a complex study of the deeper levels of life, on which
the erotic and political fuse into a single passion, baffling but human. That
passion is founded in a terrible physical intimacy which Bellow renders
in terms of sheer nausea. "Leventhal . . . was so conscious of Allbee, so
certain he was being scrutinized, that he was able to see himself as if
through a strange pair of eyes: the side of his face, the palpitation of his
throat, the seams of his skin. . . . Changed in this way into his own observer, he was able to see Allbee, too . . . the weave of his coat, his rag-
gedly overgrown neck . . . the color of the blood on his ear; he could even
evoke the odor of his hair and skin. The acuteness and intimacy of it
astounded him, oppressed and intoxicated him." And when Allbee begs
to touch Leventhal's hair—that alien, wiry, Jewish hair—actually reaches
out and takes it in hand, the gesture is like a sexual assault; "He fingered

[3] With the publication of *Herzog*, Bellow has simultaneously entered the lists of
best-sellers and embraced the subject matter of popular ladies' fiction (my best friend
betrayed me with my wife); but Madeleine, the wife, seems a nightmare projection
bred by baffled malice rather than a realized woman; and Herzog's passionate involvement with her remains, therefore, unconvincing. The most moving and credible relationship in the book is that between Herzog and his faithless friend, Valentine Gersh-
bach, who turns out to be the most vital and believable human being created in the
book. Bellow remains the laureate of such disturbing and ambiguous encounters.

Leventhal's hair, and Leventhal found himself under his touch and felt incapable of doing anything. But then he pushed his hand away, crying 'Lay off!' " After this, there is no climax possible except the "rib-crushing hug." Leventhal, the physical spell broken, drives the shoddy parasite out of his apartment by brute force. "Allbee fell back a few steps and, seizing a heavy glass ashtray, he aimed it menacingly. . . . Leventhal made a rush at him. . . . Pinning his arms, he wheeled him around and ran him into the vestibule. . . . The door, as Leventhal jerked it open, hit Allbee in the face. He did not resist. . . ." It is the consummation: an orgasm of violence, entailing a separation.

It is a long way from *Billy Budd* to *The Victim;* and by Bellow's time the Anglo-Saxon beauty, seedy and corrupt, has become the tormentor, while his swarthy opponent has taken on the sympathetic role. Melville is not yet ready to dissolve in irony the contrast of good blonde and evil brunette; as a matter of fact, his Billy is simply the Fair Maiden translated in sex—too much the Anglo-Saxon Virgin still to represent the dangerous and forbidden Eros which the good companion must embody. A *white* anti-bride will not in the long run really do: not the Good Bad Boys who accompany Tom Sawyer to Jackson's Island or their grown-up equivalent, the "old Bill" of *The Sun Also Rises,* not certainly the "Brother" of Henry James's "The Great Good Place," "a man of his own age, tired distinguished modest kind. . . ." In *Gordon Pym,* one can watch Poe learning as he goes that the Anglo-Saxon alter ego is no fit partner in the holy marriage of males, see how he abandons Pym's white shipmate, Augustus Bernard, to clear the way for the half-breed Dirk Peters. But the prototype had already been established by Cooper in the dusky figures of the Last Mohicans, father and son.

In dreams of white men, psychologists tell us, the forbidden erotic object tends to be represented by a colored man, such a figure as the "black pagod of a fellow," the "grand sculptured bull," "so intensely black that he must needs have been . . . of the unadulterable blood of Ham" whom Melville evokes for a moment at the beginning of *Billy Budd.* So in the communal American dream of love (beneath which lurks, for all the idyllic surface, a sense of trifling with taboos), the spouse of the pariah is properly of another race, a race suppressed and denied, even as the promptings of the libido are suppressed and denied. In the Leatherstocking Tales, the anti-wife is the dispossessed Indian; in *Gordon Pym,* the half-mad breed; in *Huckleberry Finn,* the Negro slave; in *Moby Dick,* the uprooted Polynesian (even as in *Two Years Before the Mast,* which may have given Melville his cue); in Faulkner's "The Bear," the old man, half-Chickasaw and half Negro. In Sam Fathers, "son of a Negro slave and a Chickasaw chief," one meaning of the dark skin is made clear; for his coloredness is taken as an ensign of kinship with the wilderness and the beasts who inhabit it. "Because there was," Faulkner writes, "something running in Sam Fathers' veins which ran in the veins of the buck too. . . ."

Edenic nature, the totem, and the dark spouse: these are three symbols for the same thing—for the primitive world which lies beyond the margins of cities and beneath the lintel of consciousness.

V

Whatever the symbolic necessities which demand that the male *hierogamos* be inter-racial as well as homoerotic, that marriage takes on, by virtue of crossing conventional color lines, a sociological significance as well as a psychological and metaphysical one.[4] The elopement of the good companians comes, therefore, to stand for the healing of the social conflicts which most irk us, and before which we feel most powerless and baffled. Such a sociological extension of meaning by no means cancels out but rather enriches other, more profound significances and gives to them their peculiarly American form.

There is, of course, in the European novel—and even the drama, epic, and romance which precede the emergence of that genre—a tradition of the pseudo-marriage of males, stretching from, say, Don Quixote and Sancho Panza through Leporello and Don Juan, Robinson Crusoe and Friday to Pickwick and Sam Weller. *Robinson Crusoe,* in particular, seems to embody an archetype much like that which haunts our classic fiction; and this is proper enough for a novel so bourgeois and Protestant that one is tempted to think of it as an American novel before the fact. The protagonists are not only black and white, but they exist on the archetypal island, cut off from the home community by the estranging sea. Cannibal and castaway, man-eater and journal-keeper, they learn to adjust to each other and to domesticity, on what is surely the most meager and puritanic Eden in all literature.

In *Robinson Crusoe,* however, the male relationship, even after shipwreck and abandonment, is kept rigidly within the European class-patterns of master and man. Within this convention (the Shakespearean convention, one wants to call it, for it is part of the basic symbolic structure of Shakespeare's work) the advocacy of the "natural" way of life is entrusted to the servant, and by virtue of that fact, clearly identified as inferior. The servant is, by definition, a comic character, who can never be taken quite seriously, never really understood as an ideological rival to his master. He can be cowardly, greedy, and carnal without stirring anything in us but smug condescension (cf. the role of the lazy, fearful tom-catting darkie in the popular arts up to the very present); he can eat

---

[4] Recently, we have grown more and more aware of how in the Civil Rights Movement the aspirations of Negroes for full freedom and the struggle of homosexuals to be accepted are oddly intermingled. And it is no use protesting (as Ralph Ellison has done, for instance) that they should be kept separate and pure. For better or for worse, they are mythically one in our deepest imaginations, as, indeed, James Baldwin has tried to make manifest—however shrilly and ineptly—in *Another Country.*

flesh on Friday or loose his bowels over his horse in a moment of terror like Sancho Panza, for *nothing is at stake.* The servant may represent the protest of the unconscious against the ego ideals for which his master stands, but there is no equivocation about their relative rank or importance. To side with Leporello against Don Juan, Caliban against Prospero is unthinkable; and even Robinson Crusoe, good bourgeois that he is, teaches Friday "master" as his first word!

In America, however, we are a nation of Calibans and Leporellos and Sancho Panzas—of "fugitive slaves." Europe is the master from which we have all fled. It is hard therefore for even the most class-conscious writer to keep his characters in their traditional places; Cooper himself, Tory-democrat that he is, proves incapable of defining Natty and Chingachgook in terms of a strict hierarchical relationship either to each other or to the "ladies and gentlemen," those supernumeraries in the plot who are presumably their betters. Melville, Twain, Faulkner, even a homemade dandy like Poe, quite frankly abandon the attempt. Who is the better man, Gordon Pym or Dirk Peters, Isaac McCaslin or Sam Fathers, Huck or Nigger Jim, Ishmael or Queequeg? Though Jim is presumably a slave and calls even Huck a "young gentleman," the whole point of the work is that Jim is "free as any cretur." The rapid mobility of American social life, as well as its establishment by masterless men, makes it only too easy to conceive the relationship of instinct and ego, white and black, not as a tie between servant and master but as a marriage of equals.

Yet there are forces in our life, almost as profound and aboriginal, which work against such a concept. The Northern European white, blue-eyed stock which originally settled the United States, shabby as it was in its origins, soon set itself up as a ruling class eager to protect its hegemony and its purity, a purity especially identified with its pale, genteel women busy in schools and churches. The drama of an equal meeting and mating of Caucasian and colored men was remanded quite early to a mythical *state of nature,* or at least to the nearest equivalent of that state, the frontier, where trapper and Indian guide bedded down together. In the settlements, such equality could scarcely survive beside the facts of social organization: the Negro confined to his ghettos, the Indian harried and driven continually westward, the Polynesian sailor restricted to the waterfront city of cheap saloons and brothels.

There is an almost hysterical note to our insistence that the love of male and male does not compete with heterosexual passion but complements it; that it is not homosexuality in any crude meaning of the word, but a passionless passion, simple, utterly satisfying, yet immune to lust—physical only as a handshake is physical, this side of copulation. And yet we can never shake off the nagging awareness that there is at the sentimental center of our novels, where we are accustomed to find in their European counterparts "platonic" love or adultery, seduction, rape, or long-drawn-out flirtation, nothing but the love of males! What awaits us are the fugitive slave and the no-account boy side by side on a raft borne by the endless river toward an impossible escape; or the pariah sailor waking in the tattooed arms of the brown harpooner on the verge of some impossible quest. To emphasize the purity of such unions, the fact that they join soul to soul rather than body to body, they are typically contrasted with mere heterosexual passion, the dubious desire which threatens always to end in miscegenation. Yet, though such confrontations seem only to contrast the homoerotic and heterosexual ways of joining white and black, they suggest disconcertingly a general superiority of the love of man for man over the ignoble lust of man for woman.

It is for this reason, perhaps, that the colored rival of the wife is presented typically with the stigmata of something dangerous and disgusting as well as forbidden. Chingachgook wears a death's-head on his chest and a scalp at his belt, while Queequeg is horridly tattooed and bears with him a phallic god and shrunken head; even Jim, who possesses no particularly repulsive characteristics, makes his first appearance with his head muffled in a blanket—scaring Huck half to death—and is dyed, before the voyage is over, a sickening blue. The most monstrous of all the dark companions is Poe's hybrid Dirk Peters, who assumes in the course of Poe's description of him not only a bestial aspect but something of the appearance of a gnome or kobold, which is to say, the surviving image in the mind of *homo sapiens* of the stunted proto-men that they destroyed, the first dispossessed people, whose memory survives to haunt our fairy tales and nightmares. But the Neanderthal gnome is also the model for popular notions of "devils" or "demons," quite properly assimilated to the primordial figure that symbolizes our broken link with the animal world. For better or worse, the love-affair with the "Black Man" carries with it diabolic implications, hints of a union with infernal forces, as well as salvational overtones, promises of psychic redemption. And in *Moby Dick* Melville attempts to embody both in the two dark-skinned characters, supernumeraries in the action, who represent the polar aspects of the id, beneficent and destructive. The first is the Polynesian harpooner, Queequeg, whose relationship to Ishmael threatens to take over the entire book in its first portion; and the second is the Parsee, Fedallah, who is yoked to Ahab by a link as passionate, though quite different from that which joins the first two. The Parsee and the Polynesian are associated with two other representatives of the primitive, also harpooners, the Indian, Tashtego, and the African, Dagoo. Yellow, brown, red, and black, they seem, considered together, rather emblems than characters, signifying the four quarters of the globe and the four elements as well, for Dagoo is carefully identified with the earth, Tashtego with the air, the Parsee with fire, and Queequeg with water. Only Queequeg and Fedallah *thematically* matter, however, since they alone are used to represent the basic conflict which lies at the heart of the book, the struggle between love and death. Queequeg stands for the redemptive baptism of water (or sperm), and around him the "Western" or sentimental story which is one half of *Moby Dick* develops; while Fedallah stands for the destructive baptism of fire (or blood), and around him the gothic or Faustian romance which is its other half unfolds. But it is Queequeg who wins, though the two never meet face to face, Eros which triumphs over Thanatos.

The White Negro

Superficial Reflections on the Hipster

NORMAN MAILER

Our search for the rebels of the generation led us to the hipster. The hipster is an enfant terrible *turned inside out. In character with his time, he is trying to get back at the conformists by lying low . . . You can't interview a hipster because his main goal is to keep out of a society which, he thinks, is trying to make everyone over in its own image. He takes marijuana because it supplies him with experiences that can't be shared with "squares." He may affect a broad-brimmed hat or a zoot suit, but usually he prefers to skulk unmarked. The hipster may be a jazz musician; he is rarely an artist, almost never a writer. He may earn his living as a petty criminal, a hobo, a carnival roustabout or a free-lance moving man in Greenwich Village, but some hipsters have found a safe refuge in the upper income brackets as television comics or movie actors. (The late James Dean, for one, was a hipster hero.) . . . It is tempting to describe the hipster in psychiatric terms as infantile, but the style of his infantilism is a sign of the times. He does not try to enforce his will on others, Napoleon-fashion, but contents himself with a magical omnipotence never disproved because never tested. . . . As the only extreme nonconformist of his generation, he exercises a powerful if underground appeal for conformists, through newspaper accounts of his delinquencies, his structureless jazz, and his emotive grunt words.*

—*"Born 1930: The Unlost Generation"*
by Caroline Bird
Harper's Bazaar, *Feb. 1957*

Probably, we will never be able to determine the psychic havoc of the concentration camps and the atom bomb upon the unconscious mind of almost everyone alive in these years. For the first time in civilized history, perhaps for the first time in all of history, we have been forced to live with the suppressed knowledge that the smallest facets of our personality or the most minor projection of our ideas, or indeed the absence of ideas and the absence of personality could mean equally well that we might still

274

be doomed to die as a cipher in some vast statistical operation in which our teeth would be counted, and our hair would be saved, but our death itself would be unknown, unhonored, and unremarked, a death which could not follow with dignity as a possible consequence to serious actions we had chosen, but rather a death by *deus ex machina* in a gas chamber or a radioactive city; and so if in the midst of civilization—that civilization founded upon the Faustian urge to dominate nature by mastering time, mastering the links of social cause and effect—in the middle of an economic civilization founded upon the confidence that time could indeed be subjected to our will, our psyche was subjected itself to the intolerable anxiety that death being causeless, life was causeless as well, and time deprived of cause and effort had come to a stop.

The Second World War presented a mirror to the human condition which blinded anyone who looked into it. For if tens of millions were killed in concentration camps out of the inexorable agonies and contractions of super-states founded upon the always insoluble contradictions of injustice, one was then obliged also to see that no matter how crippled and perverted an image of man was the society he had created, it was nonetheless his creation, his collective creation (at least his collective creation from the past) and if society was so murderous, then who could ignore the most hideous of questions about his own nature?

Worse. One could hardly maintain the courage to be individual, to speak with one's own voice, for the years in which one could complacently accept oneself as part of an elite by being a radical were forever gone. A man knew that when he dissented, he gave a note upon his life which could be called in any year of overt crisis. No wonder then that these have been the years of conformity and depression. A stench of fear has come out of every pore of American life, and we suffer from a collective failure of nerve. The only courage, with rare exceptions, that we have been witness to, has been the isolated courage of isolated people.

2

It is on this bleak scene that a phenomenon has appeared: the American existentialist—the hipster, the man who knows that if our collective condition is to live with instant death by atomic war, relatively quick death by the State as *l'univers concentrationnaire,* or with a slow death by conformity with every creative and rebellious instinct stifled (at what damage to the mind and the heart and the liver and the nerves no research foundation for cancer will discover in a hurry), if the fate of twentieth-century man is to live with death from adolescence to premature senescence, why then the only life-giving answer is to accept the terms of death, to live with death as immediate danger, to divorce oneself from society, to exist without roots, to set out on that uncharted journey into the rebellious imperatives of the self. In short, whether the life is criminal or not, the decision is to encourage the psychopath in oneself, to explore that domain of experience where security is boredom and therefore sickness, and one exists in the present, in the enormous present which is without past or future, memory or planned intention, the life where a man must go until he is beat, where he must gamble with his energies through all those small or large crises of courage and unforeseen situations which beset his day, where he must be with it or doomed not to swing. The unstated essence of Hip, its psychopathic brilliance, quivers with the knowledge that new kinds of victories increase one's power for new kinds of perception; and defeats, the wrong kind of defeats, attack the body and imprison one's energy until one is jailed in the prison air of other people's habits, other people's defeats, boredom, quiet desperation, and muted icy self-destroying rage. One is Hip or one is Square (the alternative which each new generation coming into American life is beginning to feel), one is a rebel or one conforms, one is a frontiersman in the Wild West of American night life, or else a Square cell, trapped in the totalitarian tissues of American society, doomed willy-nilly to conform if one is to suceed.

A totalitarian society makes enormous demands on the courage of men, and a partially totalitarian society makes even greater demands, for the general anxiety is greater. Indeed if one is to be a man, almost any kind of unconventional action often takes disproportionate courage. So it is no accident that the source of Hip is the Negro for he has been living on the margin between totalitarianism and democracy for two centuries. But the presence of Hip as a working philosophy in the sub-worlds of American life is probably due to jazz, and its knifelike entrance into culture, its subtle but so penetrating influence on an avant-garde generation—that postwar generation of adventurers who (some consciously, some by osmosis) had absorbed the lessons of disillusionment and disgust of the twenties, the depression, and the war. Sharing a collective disbelief in the words of men who had too much money and controlled too many things, they knew almost as powerful a disbelief in the socially monolithic ideas of the single mate, the solid family and the respectable love life. If the intellectual antecedents of this generation can be traced to such separate influences as D. H. Lawrence, Henry Miller, and Wilhelm Reich, the viable philosophy of Hemingway fit most of their facts: in a bad world, as he was to say over and over again (while taking time out from his parvenu snobbery and dedicated gourmandize), in a bad world there is no love nor mercy nor charity nor justice unless a man can keep his courage, and this indeed fitted some of the facts. What fitted the need of the adventurer even more precisely was Hemingway's categorical imperative that what made him feel good became therefore The Good.

So no wonder that in certain cities of America, in New York of course, and New Orleans, in Chicago and San Francisco and Los Angeles, in such

American cities as Paris and Mexico, D.F., this particular part of a generation was attracted to what the Negro had to offer. In such places as
Greenwich Village, a ménage-à-trois was completed—the bohemian and
the juvenile delinquent came face-to-face with the Negro, and the hipster
was a fact in American life. If marijuana was the wedding ring, the child
was the language of Hip for its argot gave expression to abstract states of
feeling which all could share, at least all who were Hip. And in this
wedding of the white and the black it was the Negro who brought the
cultural dowry. Any Negro who wishes to live must live with danger from
his first day, and no experience can ever be casual to him, no Negro can
saunter down a street with any real certainty that violence will not visit him
on his walk. The cameos of security for the average white: mother and the
home, job and the family, are not even a mockery to millions of Negroes;
they are impossible. The Negro has the simplest of alternatives: live a
life of constant humility or ever-threatening danger. In such a pass where
paranoia is as vital to survival as blood, the Negro had stayed alive and
begun to grow by following the need of his body where he could. Knowing in the cells of his existence that life was war, nothing but war, the
Negro (all exceptions admitted) could rarely afford the sophisticated
inhibitions of civilization, and so he kept for his survival the art of the
primitive, he lived in the enormous present, he subsisted for his Saturday
night kicks, relinquishing the pleasures of the mind for the more
obligatory pleasure of the body, and in his music he gave voice to the
character and quality of his existence, to his rage and the infinite variations of joy, lust, languor, growl, cramp, pinch, scream and despair of his
orgasm. For jazz is orgasm, it is the music of orgasm, good orgasm and
bad, and so it spoke across a nation, it had the communication of art even
where it was watered, perverted, corrupted, and almost killed, it spoke
in no matter what laundered popular way of instantaneous existential
states to which some whites could respond, it was indeed a communication by art because it said, "I feel this, and now you do too."

So there was a new breed of adventurers, urban adventurers who
drifted out at night looking for action with a black man's code to fit their
facts. The hipster had absorbed the existentialists synapses of the Negro,
and for practical purposes could be considered a white Negro.

To be an existentialist, one must be able to feel oneself—one must know
one's desires, one's rages, one's anguish, one must be aware of the character of one's frustration and know what would satisfy it. The overcivilized
man can be an existentialist only if it is chic, and deserts it quickly for
the next chic. To be a real existentialist (Sartre admittedly to the contrary) one must be religious, one must have one's sense of the "purpose"—
whatever the purpose may be—but a life which is directed by one's faith
in the necessity of action is a life committed to the notion that the substratum of existence is the search, the end meaningful but mysterious;
it is impossible to live such a life unless one's emotions provide their pro-

found conviction. Only the French, alienated beyond alienation from their unconscious could welcome an existential philosophy without ever feeling it at all; indeed only a Frenchman by declaring that the unconscious did not exist could then proceed to explore the delicate involutions of consciousness, the microscopically sensuous and all but ineffable *frissons* of mental becoming, in order finally to create the theology of atheism and so submit that in a world of absurdities the existential absurdity is most coherent.

In the dialogue between the atheist and the mystic, the atheist is on the side of life, rational life, undialectical life—since he conceives of death as emptiness, he can, no matter how weary or despairing, wish for nothing but more life; his pride is that he does not transpose his weakness and spiritual fatigue into a romantic longing for death, for such appreciation of death is then all too capable of being elaborated by his imagination into a universe of meaningful structure and moral orchestration.

Yet this masculine argument can mean very little for the mystic. The mystic can accept the atheist's description of his weakness, he can agree that his mysticism was a response to despair. And yet . . . and yet his argument is that he, the mystic, is the one finally who has chosen to live with death, and so death is his experience and not the atheist's, and the atheist by eschewing the limitless dimensions of profound despair has rendered himself incapable to judge the experience. The real argument which the mystic must always advance is the very intensity of his private vision—his argument depends from the vision precisely because what was felt in the vision is so extraordinary that no rational argument, no hypotheses of "oceanic feelings" and certainly no skeptical reductions can explain away what has become for him the reality more real than the reality of closely reasoned logic. His inner experience of the possibilities within death is his logic. So, too, for the existentialist. And the psychopath. And the saint and the bullfighter and the lover. The common denominator for all of them is their burning consciousness of the present, exactly that incandescent consciousness which the possibilities within death has opened for them. There is a depth of desperation to the condition which enables one to remain in life only by engaging death, but the reward is their knowledge that what is happening at each instant of the electric present is good or bad for them, good or bad for their cause, their love, their action, their need.

It is this knowledge which provides the curious community of feeling in the world of the hipster, a muted cool religious revival to be sure, but the element which is exciting, disturbing, nightmarish perhaps, is that incompatibles have come to bed, the inner life and the violent life, the orgy and the dream of love, the desire to murder and the desire to create, a dialectical conception of existence with a lust for power, a dark, romantic, and yet undeniably dynamic view of existence for it sees every man and woman as moving individually through each moment of life forward into growth or backward into death.

3

It may be fruitful to consider the hipster a philosophical psychopath, a man interested not only in the dangerous imperatives of his psychopathy but in codifying, at least for himself, the suppositions on which his inner universe is constructed. By this premise the hipster is a psychopath, and yet not a psychopath but the negation of the psychopath, for he possesses the narcissistic detachment of the philosopher, that absorption in the recessive nuances of one's own motive which is so alien to the unreasoning drive of the psychopath. In this country where new millions of psychopaths are developed each year, stamped with the mint of our contradictory popular culture (where sex is sin and yet sex is paradise), it is as if there has been room already for the development of the antithetical psychopath who extrapolates from his own condition, from the inner certainty that his rebellion is just, a radical vision of the universe which thus separates him from the general ignorance, reactionary prejudice, and self-doubt of the more conventional psychopath. Having converted his unconscious experience into much conscious knowledge, the hipster has shifted the focus of his desire from immediate gratification toward that wider passion for future power which is the mark of civilized man. Yet with an irreducible difference. For Hip is the sophistication of the wise primitive in a giant jungle, and so its appeal is still beyond the civilized man. If there are ten million Americans who are more or less psychopathic (and the figure is most modest), there are probably not more than one hundred thousand men and women who consciously see themselves as hipsters, but their importance is that they are an elite with the potential ruthlessness of an elite, and a language most adolescents can understand instinctively, for the hipster's intense view of existence matches their experience and their desire to rebel.

Before one can say more about the hipster, there is obviously much to be said about the psychic state of the psychopath—or, clinically, the psychopathic personality. Now, for reasons which may be more curious than the similarity of the words, even many people with a psychoanalytical orientation often confuse the psychopath with the psychotic. Yet the terms are polar. The psychotic is legally insane, the psychopath is not; the psychotic is almost always incapable of discharging in physical acts the rage of his frustration, while the psychopath at his extreme is virtually as incapable of restraining his violence. The psychotic lives in so misty a world that what is happening at each moment of his life is not very real to him whereas the psychopath seldom knows any reality greater than the face, the voice, the being of the particular people among whom he may find himself at any moment. Sheldon and Eleanor Glueck describe him as follows:

The psychopath . . . can be distinguished from the person sliding into or clambering out of a "true psychotic" state by the long tough persistence of his anti-social attitude and behaviour and the absence of hallucinations, delusions, manic flight of ideas, confusion, disorientation, and other dramatic signs of psychosis.

The late Robert Lindner, one of the few experts on the subject, in his book *Rebel Without a Cause—The Hypnoanalysis of a Criminal Psychopath* presented part of his definition in this way:

. . . the psychopath is a rebel without a cause, an agitator without a slogan, a revolutionary without a program: in other words, his rebelliousness is aimed to achieve goals satisfactory to himself alone; he is incapable of exertions for the sake of others. All his efforts, hidden under no matter what disguise, represent investments designed to satisfy his immediate wishes and desires. . . . The psychopath, like the child, cannot delay the pleasures of gratification; and this trait is one of his underlying, universal characteristics. He cannot wait upon erotic gratification which convention demands should be preceded by the chase before the kill: he must rape. He cannot wait upon the development of prestige in society: his egoistic ambitions lead him to leap into headlines by daring performances. Like a red thread the predominance of this mechanism for immediate satisfaction runs through the history of every psychopath. It explains not only his behaviour but also the violent nature of his acts.

Yet even Lindner who was the most imaginative and most sympathetic of the psychoanalysts who have studied the psychopathic personality was not ready to project himself into the essential sympathy—which is that the psychopath may indeed be the perverted and dangerous front-runner of a new kind of personality which could become the central expression of human nature before the twentieth century is over. For the psychopath is better adapted to dominate those mutually contradictory inhibitions upon violence and love which civilization has exacted of us, and if it be remembered that not every psychopath is an extreme case, and that the condition of psychopathy is present in a host of people including many politicians, professional soldiers, newspaper columnists, entertainers, artists, jazz musicians, call-girls, promiscuous homosexuals and half the executives of Hollywood, television, and advertising, it can be seen that there are aspects of psychopathy which already exert considerable cultural influence.

What characterizes almost every psychopath and part-psychopath is that they are trying to create a new nervous system for themselves. Generally we are obliged to act with a nervous system which has been formed

from infancy, and which carries in the style of its circuits the very contradictions of our parents and our early milieu. Therefore, we are obliged,
most of us, to meet the tempo of the present and the future with reflexes
and rhythms which come from the past. It is not only the "dead weight
of the institutions of the past" but indeed the inefficient and often anti-
quated nervous circuits of the past which strangle our potentiality for
responding to new possibilities which might be exciting for our individual
growth.

Through most of modern history, "sublimation" was possible: at the
expense of expressing only a small portion of oneself, that small portion
could be expressed intensely. But sublimation depends on a reasonable
tempo to history. If the collective life of a generation has moved too
quickly, the "past" by which particular men and women of that generation may function is not, let us say, thirty years old, but relatively a hundred or two hundred years old. And so the nervous system is overstressed
beyond the possibility of such compromises as sublimation, especially
since the stable middle-class values so prerequisite to sublimation have
been virtually destroyed in our time, at least as nourishing values free of
confusion or doubt. In such a crisis of accelerated historical tempo and
deteriorated values, neurosis tends to be replaced by psychopathy, and
the success of psychoanalysis (which even ten years ago gave promise of
becoming a direct major force) diminishes because of its inbuilt and characteristic incapacity to handle patients more complex, more experienced, or
more adventurous than the analyst himself. In practice, psychoanalysis has
by now become all too often no more than a psychic blood-letting. The
patient is not so much changed as aged, and the infantile fantasies which
he is encouraged to express are condemned to exhaust themselves against
the analyst's nonresponsive reactions. The result for all too many patients
is a diminution, a "tranquilizing" of their most interesting qualities and
vices. The patient is indeed not so much altered as worn out—less bad,
less good, less bright, less willful, less destructive, less creative. He is thus
able to conform to that contradictory and unbearable society which first
created his neurosis. He can conform to what he loathes because he no
longer has the passion to feel loathing so intensely.

The psychopath is notoriously difficult to analyze because the fundamental decision of his nature is to try to live the infantile fantasy, and in
this decision (given the dreary alternative of psychoanalysis) there may
be a certain instinctive wisdom. For there is a dialectic to changing one's
nature, the dialectic which underlies all psychoanalytic method: it is the
knowledge that if one is to change one's habits, one must go back to the
source of their creation, and so the psychopath exploring backward along
the road of the homosexual, the orgiast, the drug-addict, the rapist, the
robber and the murderer seeks to find those violent parallels to the violent
and often hopeless contradictions he knew as an infant and as a child. For
if he has the courage to meet the parallel situation at the moment when

he is ready, then he has a chance to act as he has never acted before, and in satisfying the frustration—if he can succeed—he may then pass by symbolic substitute through the locks of incest. In thus giving expression to the buried infant in himself, he can lessen the tension of those infantile desires and so free himself to remake a bit of his nervous system. Like the neurotic he is looking for the opportunity to grow up a second time, but the psychopath knows instinctively that to express a forbidden impulse actively is far more beneficial to him than merely to confess the desire in the safety of a doctor's room. The psychopath is ordinately ambitious, too ambitious ever to trade his warped brilliant conception of his possible victories in life for the grim if peaceful attrition of the analyst's couch. So his associational journey into the past is lived out in the theatre of the present, and he exists for those charged situations where his senses are so alive that he can be aware actively (as the analysand is aware passively) of what his habits are, and how he can change them. The strength of the psychopath is that he knows (where most of us can only guess) what is good for him and what is bad for him at exactly those instants when an old crippling habit has become so attacked by experience that the potentiality exists to change it, to replace a negative and empty fear with an outward action, even if—and here I obey the logic of the extreme psychopath—even if the fear is of himself, and the action is to murder. The psychopath murders—if he has the courage—out of the necessity to purge his violence, for if he cannot empty his hatred then he cannot love, his being is frozen with implacable self-hatred for his cowardice. (It can of course be suggested that it takes little courage for two strong eighteen-year-old hoodlums, let us say, to beat in the brains of a candy-store keeper, and indeed the act—even by the logic of the psychopath—is not likely to prove very therapeutic, for the victim is not an immediate equal. Still, courage of a sort is necessary, for one murders not only a weak fifty-year-old man but an institution as well, one violates private property, one enters into a new relation with the police and introduces a dangerous element into one's life. The hoodlum is therefore daring the unknown, and so no matter how brutal the act, it is not altogether cowardly.)

At bottom, the drama of the psychopath is that he seeks love. Not love as the search for a mate, but love as the search for an orgasm more apocalyptic than the one which preceded it. Orgasm is his therapy—he knows at the seed of his being that good orgasm opens his possibilities and bad orgasm imprisons him. But in this search, the psychopath becomes an embodiment of the extreme contradictions of the society which formed his character, and the apocalyptic orgasm often remains as remote as the Holy Grail, for there are clusters and nests and ambushes of violence in his own necessities and in the imperatives and retaliations of the men and women among whom he lives his life, so that even as he drains his hatred in one act or another, so the conditions of his life create it anew in him until the drama of his movements bears a sardonic resemblance to the frog who climbed a few feet in the well only to drop back again.

Yet there is this to be said for the search after the good orgasm: when one lives in a civilized world, and still can enjoy none of the cultural nectar of such a world because the paradoxes on which civilization is built demand that there remain a cultureless and alienated bottom of exploitable human material, then the logic of becoming a sexual outlaw (if one's psychological roots are bedded in the bottom) is that one has at least a running competitive chance to be physically healthy so long as one stays alive. It is therefore no accident that psychopathy is most prevalent with the Negro. Hated from outside and therefore hating himself, the Negro was forced into the position of exploring all those moral wildernesses of civilized life which the Square automatically condemns as delinquent or evil or immature or morbid or self-destructive or corrupt. (Actually the terms have equal weight. Depending on the telescope of the cultural clique from which the Square surveys the universe, "evil" or "immature" are equally strong terms of condemnation.) But the Negro, not being privileged to gratify his self-esteem with the heady satisfactions of categorical condemnation, chose to move instead in that other direction where all situations are equally valid, and in the worst of perversion, promiscuity, pimpery, drug addiction, rape, razor-slash, bottle-break, what-have-you, the Negro discovered and elaborated a morality of the bottom, an ethical differentiation between the good and the bad in every human activity from the go-getter pimp (as opposed to the lazy one) to the relatively dependable pusher or prostitute. Add to this, the cunning of their language, the abstract ambiguous alternatives in which from the danger of their oppression they learned to speak ("Well, now, man, like I'm looking for a cat to turn me on . . . "), add even more the profound sensitivity of the Negro jazzman who was the cultural mentor of a people, and it is not too difficult to believe that the language of Hip which evolved was an artful language, tested and shaped by an intense experience and therefore different in kind from white slang, as different as the special obscenity of the soldier which in its emphasis upon "ass" as the soul and "shit" as circumstance, was able to express the existential states of the enlisted man. What makes Hip a special language is that it cannot really be taught—if one shares none of the experiences of elation and exhaustion which it is equipped to describe, then it seems merely arch or vulgar or irritating. It is a pictorial language, but pictorial like nonobjective art, imbued with the dialectic of small but intense change, a language for the microcosm, in this case, man, for it takes the immediate experiences of any passing man and magnifies the dynamic of his movements, not specifically but abstractly so that he is seen more as a vector in a network of forces than as a static character in a crystallized field. (Which latter is the practical view of the snob.) For example, there is real difficulty in trying to find a Hip substitute for "stubborn." The best possibility I can come up with is: "That cat will never come off his groove, dad." But groove implies movement, narrow movement but motion nonetheless. There is really no way to describe someone who does not move at all. Even a creep does move—if at a pace exasperatingly more slow than the pace of the cool cats.

4

Like children, hipsters are fighting for the sweet, and their language is a set of subtle indications of their success or failure in the competition for pleasure. Unstated but obvious is the social sense that there is not nearly enough sweet for everyone. And so the sweet goes only to the victor, the best, the most, the man who knows the most about how to find his energy and how not to lose it. The emphasis is on energy because the psychopath and the hipster are nothing without it since they do not have the protection of a position or a class to rely on when they have overextended themselves. So the language of Hip is a language of energy, how it is found, how it is lost.

But let us see. I have jotted down perhaps a dozen words, the Hip perhaps most in use and most likely to last with the minimum of variation. The words are man, go, put down, make, beat, cool, swing, with it, crazy, dig, flip, creep, hip, square. They serve a variety of purposes and the nuance of the voice uses the nuance of the situation to convey the subtle contextual difference. If the hipster moves through his life on a constant search with glimpses of Mecca in many a turn of his experience (Mecca being the apocalyptic orgasm) and if everyone in the civilized world is at least in some small degree a sexual cripple, the hipster lives with the knowledge of how he is sexually crippled and where he is sexually alive, and the faces of experience which life presents to him each day are engaged, dismissed or avoided as his need directs and his lifemanship makes possible. For life is a contest between people in which the victor generally recuperates quickly and the loser takes long to mend, a perpetual competition of colliding explorers in which one must grow or else pay more for remaining the same (pay in sickness, or depression, or anguish for the lost opportunity), but pay or grow.

Therefore one finds words like go, and make it, and with it, and swing: "Go" with its sense that after hours or days or months or years of monotony, boredom, and depression one has finally had one's chance, one has amassed enough energy to meet an exciting opportunity with all one's present talents for the flip (up or down) and so one is ready to go, ready to gamble. Movement is always to be preferred to inaction. In motion a man has a chance, his body is warm, his instincts are quick, and when the crisis comes, whether of love or violence, he can make it, he can win, he can release a little more energy for himself since he hates himself a little less, he can make a little better nervous system, make it a little more possible to go again, to go faster next time and so make more and thus find more people with whom he can swing. For to swing is to communicate, is to convey the rhythms of one's own being to a lover, a friend, or an audience, and—equally necessary—be able to feel the rhythms of their response. To swing with the rhythms of another is to enrich oneself—the conception of the learning process as dug by Hip is that one cannot really learn until one contains within oneself the implicit rhythm of the subject or the person. As an example, I remember once hearing a Negro friend have an intellectual discussion at a party for half an hour with a white girl who was a few years out of colleage. The Negro literally could not read or write, but he had an extraordinary ear and a fine sense of mimicry. So as the girl spoke, he would detect the particular formal uncertainties in her argument, and in a pleasant (if slightly Southern) English accent, he would respond to one or another facet of her doubts. When she would finish what she felt was a particularly well-articulated idea, he would smile privately and say, "Other-direction . . . do you believe in that?"

"Well . . . No," the girl would stammer, "now that you get down to it, there is something disgusting about it to me," and she would be off again for five more minutes.

Of course the Negro was not learning anything about the merits and demerits of the argument, but he was learning a great deal about a type of girl he had never met before, and that was what he wanted. Being unable to read or write, he could hardly be interested in ideas nearly as much as in lifemanship, and so he eschewed any attempt to obey the precision or lack of precision in the girl's language, and instead sensed her character (and the values of her social type) by swinging with the nuances of her voice.

So to swing is to be able to learn, and by learning take a step toward making it, toward creating. What is to be created is not nearly so important as the hipster's belief that when he really makes it, he will be able to turn his hand to anything, even to self-discipline. What he must do before that is to find his courage at the moment of violence, or equally make it in the act of love, find a little more between his woman and himself, or indeed between his mate and himself (since many hipsters are bisexual), but paramount, imperative, is the necessity to make it because in making it, one is making the new habit, unearthing the new talent which the old frustration denied.

Whereas if you goof (the ugliest word in Hip), if you lapse back into being a frightened stupid child, or if you flip, if you lose your control, reveal the buried weaker more feminine part of your nature, then it is more difficult to swing the next time, your ear is less alive, your bad and energy-wasting habits are further confirmed, you are farther away from being with it. But to be with it is to have grace, is to be closer to the secrets of that inner unconscious life which will nourish you if you can hear it, for you are then nearer to that God which every hipster believes is located in the senses of his body, that trapped, mutilated and nonetheless megalomaniacal God who is It, who is energy, life, sex, force, the Yoga's *prana,* the Reichian's orgone, Lawrence's "blood," Hemingway's "good," the Shavian life-force; "It"; God; not the God of the churches but the unachievable whisper of mystery within the sex, the paradise of limitless energy and perception just beyond the next wave of the next orgasm.

To which a cool cat might reply, "Crazy, man!"

Because, after all, what I have offered above is an hypothesis, no more, and there is not the hipster alive who is not absorbed in his own tumultuous hypotheses. Mine is interesting, mine is way out (on the avenue of the mystery along the road to "It") but still I am just one cat in a world of cool cats, and everything interesting is crazy, or at least so the Squares who do not know how to swing would say.

(And yet crazy is also the self-protective irony of the hipster. Living with questions and not with answers, he is so different in his isolation and in the far reach of his imagination from almost everyone with whom he deals in the outer world of the Square, and meets generally so much enmity, competition, and hatred in the world of Hip, that his isolation is always in danger of turning upon itself, and leaving him indeed just that, crazy.)

If, however, you agree with my hypothesis, if you as a cat are way out too, and we are in the same groove (the universe now being glimpsed as a series of ever-extending radii from the center), why then you say simply, "I dig," because neither knowledge nor imagination comes easily, it is buried in the pain of one's forgotten experience, and so one must work to find it, one must occasionally exhaust oneself by digging into the self in order to perceive the outside. And indeed it is essential to dig the most, for if you do not dig you lose your superiority over the Square, and so you are less likely to be cool (to be in control of a situation because you have swung where the Square has not, or because you have allowed to come to consciousness a pain, a guilt, a shame or a desire which the other has not had the courage to face). To be cool is to be equipped, and if you are equipped it is more difficult for the next cat who comes along to put you down. And of course one can hardly afford to be put down too often, or one is beat, one has lost one's confidence, one has lost one's will, one is impotent in the world of action and so closer to the demeaning flip of becoming a queer, or indeed closer to dying, and therefore it is even more difficult to recover enough energy to try to make it again, because once a cat is beat he has nothing to give, and no one is interested any longer in making it with him. This is the terror of the hipster—to be beat—because once the sweet of sex has deserted him, he still cannot give up the search. It is not granted to the hipster to grow old gracefully —he has been captured too early by the older dream of power, the gold fountain of Ponce de León, the fountain of youth where the gold is in the orgasm.

To be beat is therefore a flip, it is a situation beyond one's experience, impossible to anticipate—which indeed in the circular vocabulary of Hip is still another meaning for flip, but then I have given just a few of the connotations of these words. Like most primitive vocabularies each word is a prime symbol and serves a dozen or a hundred functions of communication in the instinctive dialectic through which the hipster perceives his experience, that dialectic of the instantaneous differentials of existence in which one is forever moving forward into more or retreating into less.

5

It is impossible to conceive a new philosophy until one creates a new language, but a new popular language (while it must implicitly contain a new philosophy) does not necessarily present its philosophy overtly. It can be asked then what really is unique in the life-view of Hip which raises its argot above the passing verbal whimsies of the bohemian or the lumpenproletariat.

The answer would be in the psychopathic element of Hip which has almost no interest in viewing human nature, or better, in judging human nature, from a set of standards conceived a priori to the experience, standards inherited from the past. Since Hip sees every answer as posing immediately a new alternative, a new question, its emphasis is on complexity rather than simplicity (such complexity that its language without the illumination of the voice and the articulation of the face and body remains hopelessly incommunicative). Given its emphasis on complexity, Hip abdicates from any conventional moral responsibility because it would argue that the result of our actions are unforeseeable, and so we cannot know if we do good or bad, we cannot even know (in the Joycean sense of the good and the bad) whether we have given energy to another, and indeed if we could, there would still be no idea of what ultimately the other would do with it.

Therefore, men are not seen as good or bad (that they are good-and-bad is taken for granted) but rather each man is glimpsed as a collection of possibilities, some more possible than others (the view of character implicit in Hip) and some humans are considered more capable than others of reaching more possibilities within themselves in less time, provided, and this is the dynamic, provided the particular character can swing at the right time. And here arises the sense of context which differentiates Hip from a Square view of character. Hip sees the context as generally dominating the man, dominating him because his character is less significant than the context in which he must function. Since it is arbitrarily five times more demanding of one's energy to accomplish even an inconsequential action in an unfavorable context than a favorable one, man is then not only his character but his context, since the success or failure of an action in a given context reacts upon the character and therefore affects what the character will be in the next context. What dominates both character and context is the energy available at the moment of intense context.

Character being thus seen as perpetually ambivalent and dynamic enters then into an absolute relativity where there are no truths other than the isolated truths of what each observer feels at each instant of his existence. To take a perhaps unjustified metaphysical extrapolation, it is as if the universe which has usually existed conceptually as a Fact (even if the Fact were Berkeley's God) but a Fact which it was the aim of all science and philosophy to reveal, becomes instead a changing reality whose laws are remade at each instant by everything living, but most particularly man, man raised to a neo-medieval summit where the truth is not what one has felt yesterday or what one expects to feel tomorrow but rather truth is no more nor less than what one feels at each instant in the perpetual climax of the present.

What is conseqeunt therefore is the divorce of man from his values, the liberation of the self from the Super-Ego of society. The only Hip morality (but of course it is an ever-present morality) is to do what one feels whenever and wherever it is possible, and—this is how the war of the Hip and the Square begins—to be engaged in one primal battle: to open the limits of the possible for oneself, for oneself alone, because that is one's need. Yet in widening the arena of the possible, one widens it reciprocally for others as well, so that the nihilistic fulfillment of each man's desire contains its antithesis of human co-operation.

If the ethic reduces to Know Thyself and Be Thyself, what makes it radically different from Socratic moderation with its stern conservative respect for the experience of the past is that the Hip ethic is immoderation, childlike in its adoration of the present (and indeed to respect the past means that one must also respect such ugly consequences of the past as the collective murders of the State). It is this adoration of the present which contains the affirmation of Hip, because its ultimate logic surpasses even the unforgettable solution of the Marquis de Sade to sex, private property, and the family, that all men and women have absolute but temporary rights over the bodies of all other men and women—the nihilism of Hip proposes as its final tendency that every social restraint and category be removed, and the affirmation implicit in the proposal is that man would then prove to be more creative than murderous and so would not destroy himself. Which is exactly what separates Hip from the authoritarian philosophies which now appeal to the conservative and liberal temper—what haunts the middle of the twentieth century is that faith in man has been lost, and the appeal of authority has been that it would restrain us from ourselves. Hip, which would return us to ourselves, at no matter what price in individual violence, is the affirmation of the barbarian, for it requires a primitive passion about human nature to believe that individual acts of violence are always to be preferred to the collective violence of the State; it takes literal faith in the creative possibilities of the human being to envisage acts of violence as the catharsis which prepares growth.

Whether the hipster's desire for absolute sexual freedom contains any genuinely radical conception of a different world is of course another matter, and it is possible, since the hipster lives with his hatred, that many of them are the material for an elite of storm troopers ready to follow the first truly magnetic leader whose view of mass murder is phrased in a language which reaches their emotions. But given the desperation of his condition as a psychic outlaw, the hipster is equally a candidate for the most reactionary and most radical of movements, and so it is just as possible that many hipsters will come—if the crisis deepens—to a radical comprehension of the horror of society, for even as the radical has had his incommunicable dissent confirmed in his experience by precisely the frustration, the denied opportunities, and the bitter years which his ideas have cost him, so the sexual adventurer deflected from his goal by the implacable animosity of a society constructed to deny the sexual radicals as well, may yet come to an equally bitter comprehension of the slow relentless inhumanity of the conservative power which controls him from without and from within. And in being so controlled, denied, and starved into the attrition of conformity, indeed the hipster may come to see that his condition is no more than an exaggeration of the human condition, and if he would be free, then everyone must be free. Yes, this is possible too, for the heart of Hip is its emphasis upon courage at the moment of crisis, and it is pleasant to think that courage contains within itself (as the explanation of its existence) some glimpse of the necessity of life to become more than it has been.

It is obviously not very possible to speculate with sharp focus on the future of the hipster. Certain possibilities must be evident, however, and the most central is that the organic growth of Hip depends on whether the Negro emerges as a dominating force in American life. Since the Negro knows more about the ugliness and danger of life than the white, it is probable that if the Negro can win his equality, he will possess a potential superiority, a superiority so feared that the fear itself has become the underground drama of domestic politics. Like all conservative political fear it is the fear of unforeseeable consequences, for the Negro's equality would tear a profound shift into the psychology, the sexuality, and the moral imagination of every white alive.

With this possible emergence of the Negro, Hip may erupt as a psychically armed rebellion whose sexual impetus may rebound against the antisexual foundation of every organized power in America, and bring into the air such animosities, antipathies, and new conflicts of interest that the mean empty hypocrisies of mass conformity will no longer work. A time of violence, new hysteria, confusion and rebellion will then be likely to replace the time of conformity. At that time, if the liberal should prove realistic in his belief that there is peaceful room for every tendency in American life, then Hip would end by being absorbed as a colorful figure in the tapestry. But if this is not the reality, and the economic, the social, the psychological, and finally the moral crises accompanying the rise of the Negro should prove insupportable, then a time is coming when every political guidepost will be gone, and millions of liberals will be faced with political dilemmas they have so far succeeded in evading, and with a view of human nature they do not wish to accept. To take the desegregation of the schools in the South as an example, it is quite likely that the reactionary sees the reality more closely than the liberal when he argues that the deeper issue is not desegregation but miscegenation. (As a radical I am of course facing in the opposite direction from the White Citizen's Councils—obviously I believe it is the absolute human right of the Negro to mate with the white, and matings there will undoubtedly be, for there will be Negro high school boys brave enough to chance their lives.) But for the average liberal whose mind has been dulled by the committee-ish cant of the professional liberals, miscegenation is not an issue because he has been told that the Negro does not desire it. So, when it comes, miscegenation will be a terror, comparable perhaps to the derangement of the American Communists when the icons to Stalin came tumbling down. The average American Communist held to the myth of Stalin for reasons which had little to do with the political evidence and everything to do with their psychic necessities. In this sense it is equally a psychic necessity for the liberal to believe that the Negro and even the reactionary Southern white are eventually and fundamentally people like himself, capable of becoming good liberals too if only they can be reached by good liberal reason. What the liberal cannot bear to admit is the hatred beneath the skin of a society so unjust that the amount of collective violence buried in the people is perhaps incapable of being contained, and therefore if one wants a better world one does well to hold one's breath, for a worse world is bound to come first, and the dilemma may well be this: given such hatred, it must either vent itself nihilistically or become turned into the cold murderous liquidations of the totalitarian state.

6

No matter what its horrors the twentieth century is a vastly exciting century for its tendency to reduce all life to its ultimate alternatives. One can well wonder if the last war of them all will be between the blacks and the whites, or between the women and the men, or between the beautiful and ugly, the pillagers and managers, or the rebels and the regulators. Which of course is carrying speculation beyond the point where speculation is still serious, and yet despair at the monotony and bleakness of the future have become so engrained in the radical temper that the radical is in danger of abdicating from all imagination. What a man feels is the impulse for his creative effort, and if an alien but nonetheless passionate instinct about the meaning of life has come so unexpectedly from a virtually illiterate people, come out of the most intense conditions of exploitation, cruelty, violence, frustration, and lust, and yet has succeeded as an instinct in keeping this tortured people alive, then it is perhaps possible that the Negro holds more of the tail of the expanding elephant of truth than the radical, and if this is so, the radical humanist could do worse than to brood upon the phenomenon. For if a revolutionary time should come again, there would be a crucial difference if someone had already delineated a neo-Marxian calculus aimed at comprehending every circuit and process of society from ukase to kiss as the communications of human energy—a calculus capable of translating the economic relations of man into his psychological relations and then back again, his productive relations thereby embracing his sexual relations as well, until the crises of capitalism in the twentieth century would yet be understood as the unconscious adaptations of a society to solve its economic imbalance at the expense of a new mass psychological imbalance. It is almost beyond the imagination to conceive of a work in which the drama of human energy is engaged, and a theory of its social currents and dissipations, its imprisonments, expressions, and tragic wastes are fitted into some gigantic synthesis of human action where the body of Marxist thought, and particularly the epic grandeur of *Das Kapital* (that first of the major *psychologies* to approach the mystery of social cruelty so simply and practically as to say that we are a collective body of humans whose life-energy is wasted, displaced, and procedurally stolen as it passes from one of us to another)—where particularly the epic grandeur of *Das Kapital* would find its place in an even more God-like view of human justice and injustice, in some more excruciating vision of those intimate and institutional processes which lead to our creations and disasters, our growth, our attrition, and our rebellion.

HIPSTER AND BEATNIK: A FOOTNOTE TO "THE WHITE NEGRO"

Hipster came first as a word—it was used at least as long ago as 1951 or 1952, and it was mentioned in the New Directions blurb on Chandler

Brossard's *Who Walk In Darkness*. It came up again from time to time, notably in Ginsberg's *Howl* ("Angel-headed hipsters"), and was given its attention in *The White Negro*. Then came *On The Road*, and with Kerouac's success, The Beat Generation (a phrase first used by him many years ago, and mentioned several times in articles by Clellon Holmes) was adopted by the mass-media. Beatnik came into existence a year later, in the summer or fall of 1958, the word coined by a San Francisco columnist, Herb Caen. The addition of "nik" however—"nik" being a pejorative diminutive in Yiddish—gave a quality of condescension to the word which proved agreeable to the newspaper mentally. "Beatnik" caught on. But one no longer knew whether the Beat Generation referred to hipsters or beatniks or included both, and some people to avoid the label of beatnik began to call themselves Beats.

Since there is no authority to order this nomenclature, it is anyone's right to set up his surveyor's marks as he chooses, and I will make the attempt here, for I think there are differences, and they should be noted. The Beat Generation is probably best used to include hipsters and beatniks. Not too many seem to use the word Beats; it is uncomfortable on the tongue; those who refuse to let it die seem to use it as an omnibus for hipster and beatniks, a shorthand for saying The Beat Generation. This last term is itself an unhappy one, but since it has entered the language, one may as well live with it. Still, it must be said that the differences between hipsters and beatniks may be more important than their similarities, even if they share the following general characteristics: marijuana, jazz, not much money, and a community of feeling that society is the prison of the nervous system. The sense of place is acute—few care to stay away for long from the Village, Paris, North Beach, Mexico, New Orleans, Chicago and some other special cities. Hipster and Beatnik both talk Hip, but not in the same way—the beatnik uses the vocabulary; the hipster has that muted animal voice which shivered the national attention when first used by Marlon Brando.

Now the differences begin. The hipster comes out of a muted rebellion of the proletariat, he is, so to say, the lazy proletariat, the spiv; nothing given to manual labor unless he has no choice. The beatnik—often Jewish —comes from the middle class, and twenty-five years ago would have joined the YCL. Today, he chooses not to work as a sentence against the conformity of his parents. Therefore he can feel moral value in his good-bye to society. The hipster is more easygoing about the drag and value of a moneyless life of leisure.

Their bodies are not the same. A hipster moves like a cat, slow walk, quick reflexes; he dresses with a flick of chic; if his dungarees are old, he turns the cuffs at a good angle. The beatnik is slovenly—to strike a pose against the middle class you must roil their compulsion to be neat. Besides—the beatnik is more likely to have a good mind than a good body. While he comes along with most hipsters on the first tenet of the faith:

that one's orgasm is the clue to how well one is living—he has had less body to work with in the first place, and so his chances for lifting himself by his sexual bootstraps are commonly nil, especially since each medieval guild in the Beat Generation has invariably formed itself on a more or less common sexual vitality or lack of it. The boys and girls available to the average beatnik are as drained as himself. Natural that the sex of the beatnik circles in, and mysticism becomes the Grail—he ends by using his drug to lash his mind into a higher contemplation of the universe and its secrets, a passive act, onanistic; the trance is coveted more than any desire to trap it later in work or art. The beatnik moves therefore onto Zen, the search for a lady ends as a search for *satori*—that using a drug goes against the discipline of Zen is something he will face later.

The hipster has a passing respect for Zen, he doesn't deny the experience of the mystic, he has known it himself, but his preference is to get the experience in the body of a woman. Drugs are a gamble for him, he gambles that the sensitivity of his libido on marijuana will help him to unlock the reflexes of his orgasm. If marijuana and the act take more out of him than he gets back, he is not likely to consider himself in good shape. Whereas a beatnik might. Who cares about impotence if one finds within it the breath of a vision? The beatnik, then, is obviously more sentimental—he needs a God who will understand all and forgive all. The hard knowledge of the hipster that you pay for what you get is usually too bitter for the beatnik. But then, the hipster is still in life; strong on his will, he takes on the dissipation of the drugs in order to dig more life for himself, he is wrestling with the destiny of his nervous system, he is Faustian. The beatnik contemplates eternity, finds it beautiful, likes to believe it is waiting to receive him. He wants to get out of reality more than he wants to change it, and at the end of the alley is a mental hospital.

If a hipster has a fall, it is to death or jail. Psychosis is not for him. Like a psychopath, he is juggling the perils of getting your kicks in this world, against the hell (or prison) of paying for them in the next. The hipster looks for action, and a bar with charge is where he goes when marijuana has turned him on—the beatnik, more at home with talk, can be found in the coffeehouse. The poet is his natural consort, his intellectual whip, even as the criminal, the hip hoodlum, and the boxer is the heart of knowledge for the hipster who ducks the psychotic relations between beatniks as too depressing, a hang-up, they go nowhere which can nourish him. The beatnik is in the line of continuation from the old bohemian, and nowhere near in his tradition to the hipster whose psychic style derives from the best Negroes to come up from the bottom. Yet the beatnik is to the Left of the other, for the hipster is interested in exploring the close call of the Self, and so has to collaborate more with the rhythms and tastes of the society he quit. It is not that the hipster is reactionary, it is rather that in a time of crisis, he would look for power, and in the absence of a radical spirit in the American air, the choices of power which will present themselves are more likely to come from the Right than the moribund liberalities of the Left. The beatnik, gentle, disembodied from the race, is often a radical pacifist, he has sworn the vow of no violence— in fact, his violence is sealed within, and he has no way of using it. His act of violence is to suicide even as the hipster's is toward murder, but in his mind-lost way, the beatnik is the torch-bearer of those all-but-lost values of freedom, self-expression, and equality which first turned him against the hypocrisies and barren cultureless flats of the middle class.

For years now, they have lived side by side, hipster and beatnik, white Negro and crippled saint, their numbers increasing every month as the new ones come to town. They can be found wherever one knows to look, in all their permutations and combinations, in what is finally their un-classifiable and separate persons. I have exaggerated some tendencies, and made some divisions, but I have also blurred the spectrum of indi-viduality by creating two types who never exist so simply in the real life of any Village ferment. If there are hipsters and beatniks, there are also hipniks and beatsters like Ginsberg and Kerouac, and across the spectrum like a tide of defeat—rebellion takes its price in a dead year and a dead-ened land—there are the worn-out beats of all too many hipsters who made their move, lost, and so have ended as beatniks with burned-out brains, listening sullenly to the quick montage of words in younger beat-niks hot with the rebellion of having quit family, school, and flag, and on fire with the private ambition to be charged one day so high as to be a hipster oneself.

III

From Puritanism to the Present

The sign and credentials of the poet are that he announces that which no man foretold. He is the true and only doctor; he knows and tells; he is the only teller of news, for he was present and privy to the appearance which he describes. He is a beholder of ideas and an utterer of the necessary and casual. . . . The poet has a new thought; he has a whole new experience to unfold; he will tell us how it was with him, and all men will be the richer in his fortune. For the experience of each new age requires a confession, and the world seems always waiting for its poet.

RALPH WALDO EMERSON
"The Poet"

THE critics whose essays appear in Part I of this book all start with the same assumption: that there is a body of literature called American literature, a body composed of all the imaginative works written by Americans from the beginning of our country up to the present. Their task, then, is to make claims about that body, to search out the various themes and techniques which give it more than a chronological form. But the writers in Part III start from some different assumptions. They assume that American literature hangs together with more than just chronology, but they also make two further claims: First, that within the whole of American literature there exist parts that have an integrity of their own, and, second, that whole as the parts might be they merge quite naturally into those that surround them. The task, then, of the writers represented here is to give meaning to, to explain, to identify the various ways in which American literature breaks into parts and the various ways those parts connect, even though complete and autonomous in themselves.

Before discussing the various essays which follow, we might say a few more words about these two claims that underlie them. The first emerges from a statement by A. O. Lovejoy in *The Great Chain of Being:*

There are . . . implicit or incompletely explicit *assumptions,* or more or less *unconscious mental habits,* operating in the thought of an individual or a generation. It is the beliefs which are so much a matter of course that they are rather tacitly presupposed than formally expressed and argued for, the ways of thinking which seem so natural and inevitable that they are not scrutinized with the eye of logical self-consciousness, that often are most decisive of the character of a philosopher's doctrine, and still oftener of the dominant intellectual tendencies of an age.

What Lovejoy is arguing is that if we look hard enough at an age, a group of thinkers, a collection of literary works, we will find unity where at first glance diversity seemed to abound. As varied as a group of writers might be in subject and technique, we will discover that they all share, quite unconsciously, the same point of view, the same frame of mind.

We can understand the second claim better by beginning with Perry Miller's argument "that certain basic continuities persist in a culture . . . which underlie the successive articulation of 'ideas.'" At first glance Miller's argument might appear to be synonymous with the assumption, made by writers in Part I, that an entire body of literature has a form beyond the chronological. But the emphasis in that assumption is on sharing, on having qualities in common, while Miller's emphasis is on continuity. Another way of putting it is this: Miller is opting for a view which rejects the popular modern notion that history is discontinuous, that events and persons exist in a kind of vacuum, unrelated in any way to those events or persons that are historically on either side of them. For Miller, as well as for others in Part III, the unity of contiguous ages, groups of thinkers, collections of works is a rather paradoxical one, for it is a unity which somehow generates another unity—a succeeding age, group, collection—without destroying itself. How this can be will appear as we turn to discussing the essays that follow.

John Lynen's "The Design of Puritan Experience" is an attempt to articulate the habit of mind which lay behind all the Puritans' beliefs. In going behind those beliefs, Lynen is able to avoid the common prejudices about Puritanism and to say something fresh about a much studied subject. For Lynen the essence of Puritanism is to be found in an attitude toward time, in the belief that "eternity and the present are the only relevant points of view," in "the harsh simplification . . . which makes truth take the form of timeless generalizations and renders experience a purely present event." How it was that for the Puritans "eternity and the present [were] the only relevant points of view" is a question which Lynen answers with reference to Puritan theology. But for the student of literature what is important is the influence of such a belief about time. Lynen discusses this influence rather fully in the essay which follows, shows rather conclusively that from the Puritans' belief about time came the didactic intent of their literature, its frequent use of analogy and symbol, and the static quality of its narratives. The last point is particularly important. Lynen shows how in narrative Puritan authors arrest "time, yet [make] it seem to run on toward infinity," present the "whole story in small before working it out in detail," and find it necessary to convert "story into state of mind and vice versa." Seeing this, we see that the Puritan frame of mind has continued to influence American literature, for what Lynen says about Puritan narrative is true, in the first case, of a book like *Light in August,* in the second, of books like *Huckleberry Finn* and *The Sun Also Rises,* and in the third, of *Moby Dick* and *Absalom, Absalom!.*

Perry Miller's "From Edwards to Emerson" is also an attempt to say something about the influence on American thought and literature of Puritanism. Miller begins his essay by asking whether Transcendentalism is not a native movement rather than an import from England and Germany. He gives an affirmative answer, one which traces Transcendentalism back to Puritanism and in the process relates Jonathan Edwards to Emerson. Miller shows first how mysticism and pantheism arose out of the Puritans' premises, how, to be specific, both Jonathan Edwards and Ralph Waldo Emerson had roots in Puritanism no matter how different their specific theologies might have been. This is to say that in the emotional component of their theologies Edwards and Emerson had common ancestors, but Miller goes on to show another way in which they were related to the Puritans and thereby to each other. In his words:

What is persistent, from the covenant theology (and from the heretics against the covenant) to Edwards and Emerson is the Puritan's effort to confront, face to face, the image of a blinding divinity in the physical universe, and to look upon that universe without the intermediacy of ritual, of ceremony, of the Mass and the confessional.

The emphasis here is on the individual confronting God without the support of history, community, or doctrine. That this emphasis is one which continues, though often in secularized form, throughout American history and literature all students of literature will agree.

Lynen's essay, then, is one which defines the essence of Puritanism, and Miller's is one which extends that essence, defined in different terms, down to the time of Emerson. The third essay in this section, F. O. Matthiessen's "Man in the Open Air" (all except section three of his last chapter in *American Renaissance*), attempts to articulate what was central to the age of Emerson. Matthiessen begins by suggesting that the age of Emerson discovered the value of myth. What Matthiessen means by myth is never made explicitly clear in the pages we reprint, but in the first of those pages we find him talking of translating the then into the now, private fact into generalizations, the moment into something much larger. Myth, then, becomes a way of explaining, of relating, of giving meaning. It becomes a point of view or a frame of mind by which one gives order and intelligibility to the raw facts of experience. In Matthiessen's opinion, the dominant myth in the age of Emerson was a view of history which was anti-aristocratic, anti-great men, anti-magnificent events. It was a view of history which celebrated democracy and the common man. It was a view that history must tell us of the social state of the people, the relation of the cultivator to the soil, the relation of class to class. It is well to know what songs the peasant sung; what prayers he prayed; what food he ate; what tools he wrought with; what tax he paid; how he stood connected with the soil; how he was brought to war; and what weapons armed him for the fight.

The whole of *American Renaissance* is Matthiessen's exploration of the myth of democracy as it manifested itself in the works of Thoreau, Emerson, Hawthorne, Melville, and Whitman, but in the final pages of his essay that we print we find a brief summary of the exploration. As brief as it is, it is sufficient to show that what bound together the age of Emerson, especially the imaginative writers in that age, was a commitment to democracy.

Leslie Fiedler's "The Unbroken Tradition" argues that "the essential shape and direction of American poetry had been established by the middle of the nineteenth century." So while the age was held together by a particular view of history, it was also generating poetic trends which Fiedler believes have dominated our verse up to the present. As fathers of these trends, Fiedler names Longfellow, Poe, Whitman, and Emerson. Longfellow was the first of the best-selling poets, a model for advanced poets to define themselves against, the original poet as widow or spinster. Longfellow's influence has been on third-rate poets, but Poe's has been perhaps even less. With the exception of his influence on French symbolist poets, Poe has, in Fiedler's view, been only a model for adolescents first writing poetry. Yet his poetry haunts us, for in its anti-rationalist, anti-literary, and anti-communicative state it reminds us of so much that has happened in both modern poetry and modern life. Fiedler's third trend in American poetry is the one which most readers probably think of as characteristically American, that trend in which Whitman is the first and largest figure. It is a trend, and here Fiedler is related to Matthiessen, which in theme is democratic and nationalistic, and in technique is expansive and prophetic. The ancestors of Whitman still write today, but even poets whose work has been in another tradition have felt the need to take account of him. Thus it was that Pound had to make a pact with Whitman before he could work out his own idiom. Finally, and easy to forget, comes the line of poetry which began with Emerson. In this line, Fiedler argues, the poetry is of winter—cold and sparse—and the poet is a philosopher. It is this line which allows us to assimilate into the tradition of American literature the poetry of Emily Dickinson, E. A. Robinson, and Robert Frost.

Fiedler's essay is an effort to trace an American genre, but the one which follows it, Everett Carter's "Realism to Naturalism," is an attempt to define and trace related but different modes. He begins by defining what points of view or habits of mind the realists shared. These were essentially the beliefs that the scientist was a hero, that therefore science provided the basis for a valid system of thought, that just as science was an appropriate way of analyzing the physical world so literature was the means for studying society, that literature (especially fiction) was to tell the truth about the ordinary world of society, that in order to tell the truth the gap between fiction and reality had to be narrowed, and finally that fiction therefore had to be autobiographical. All this the realists discussed by Carter more or less believed. How their beliefs changed enough in order for naturalism to emerge is the burden of his final pages printed here. Once literature began to move away from the surface into the human mind and out into the life of the entire human race, and once some of the pessimistic possibilities inherent in Darwin's thought had taken shape, naturalism was born. The result was a literature characterized by misery, a loss of confidence, and a deterministic view of man's condition.

With Carter we come to the end of American literature in the nineteenth century. When we move to American literature of the twentieth century, we discover something new. No longer is the task of the critic to search out what is common to modern American literature (though, to be sure, many have tried to do this), but rather his goal is to relate modern American literature to modern literature. The assumption is that in the twentieth century literature goes international, and therefore what is important in modern literature is not the American component but the modern.

In "The Modern Element in Modern Literature" Lionel Trilling discusses his experiences in teaching a course in modern literature at Columbia. What he concluded as he taught the course over a period of years was that he should concentrate on those works, and thereby those subjects and forms, which have most influenced modern literature. In other words, Trilling concluded that to read modern literature we must know what it is that modern authors have unconsciously assumed and believed. In Trilling's opinion the most important of these assumptions and beliefs have to do with myth, the possibility of the Dionysian in human affairs, the substitution of art for ethics as man's primary metaphysical activity, the disbelief in the value of civilization, the rise of the anti-hero, and the rejection of commonsense and the commonplace life.

As Trilling's essay makes clear, he feels that to get at what is common to modern literature we may best read a number of influential nineteenth-century works. Trilling believes, in other words, in the continuity of the last two centuries. But J. Hillis Miller in "The Poetry of Reality" challenges this continuity, questions in particular the common assumption that modern poetry is an extension of romanticism. And in arguing for discontinuity, of course, Miller separates himself from the other critics in this section. Miller sees poetry before the twentieth century and since the rise of romanticism as featuring a radical separation of the subjective from the objective, the mind from everything which is out there. This is a poetry in which consciousness is the foundation for everything else and in which a radical nihilism comes to dominate. The nihilism, Miller holds, becomes difficult to bear, and thus many modern poets are driven to means for escaping it. The only escape is to abandon the earlier frame of mind, to give up the independence of the ego, to efface the mind before reality, to let go of power over things, and thereby to get back into the world. In other words, in modern poetry, especially in the poets discussed by Miller—Yeats, Eliot, Thomas, Stevens, Williams—we have an attempt made to heal the breach between subject and object, the mind and the world. The result is a poetry in which "the mind is dispersed everywhere in things and forms one with them," in which "elements once dispersed are gathered together in a new region of correspondence," and in which "the instant's motion is a space grown wide, and within that brief space of time all existence is named, captured, and revealed."

Miller's essay is an interesting one, especially because he reveals the modern poet at work in our behalf. The essays in this section which come before Miller's all help us to understand our past and thereby to gain some insight into who we are in the present. But Miller's piece is at least partially concerned with our future. If he is right, then modern poets are not just trying to explain us to ourselves but are also looking for ways to save us from ourselves. In doing this, the poets are proving once more that science is not enough to meet the world with, and in pointing to what modern poets have been up to Miller proves that criticism at its best is a sustaining endeavor.

The Design of Puritan Experience

JOHN F. LYNEN

Thus there may exist provisional origins, which practically and in fact form the first beginnings of the particular tradition held by a given community, folk or communion of faith; and memory, though sufficiently instructed that the depths have not actually been plumbed, yet nationally may find reassurance in some primitive point of time and, personally and historically speaking, come to rest there.

—THOMAS MANN

The Puritan quality that has persisted in American literature, even to our own time, is not a creed or set of general propositions. And it is not something "handed down" from father to son. Its mode of transmission has been subtler and less conscious. Perhaps it had best be called a habit of mind, in that habit suggests learning of the most direct kind, the way in which the child is conditioned not just by what those around him say and do but by their manner—the style of their statements and the world their most casual gestures imply. Ideas inculcated and those later acquired from books can mean, after all, only what the point of view the child learned at a much more primitive stage will allow. So conceived, the habit of mind is not the content of experience but its form and condition. It exists in the child before he has sufficiently mastered language to understand ideas, and it is doubtless intimately connected with the possibilities his language system offers. It is a set of assumptions which are for the most part tacit and unrecognized, just because they are the most fundamental ones and are accepted without reserve or the criticism which would bring them into view—accepted as the terms of experiencing, without which experience would not be possible.

If the Puritan influence is found at this most basic and intimate level of mind, one can see not only why it persists but why, with respect to American literature, it is something less, as well as more, than a cause.

The convenience of arranging our thoughts historically in a cause-and-effect sequence makes it very tempting to assume that Puritan theology came first and a certain sensibility was then created by the way dogma affected the mind. But when one asks whether the sequence couldn't be reversed—whether the habit of mind expressed itself by creating Puritan theology, rather than the theology producing the sensibility, as if from whole cloth—it becomes clear that priority in time is not so relevant as logical priority. No doubt the habit of mind and the theology grew up together, each fostering the other, but it is the habit of mind that has proved more fundamental, since it has persisted long after the doctrines of Puritanism have lost their authority. Because it is less than a religion, is merely a *form* of consciousness, it has been able to accommodate itself to altered subject matter, But while it is less than a religion, it is surely more than a theology; it is a way of thinking rather than just a particular system of thoughts.

By viewing the Puritan influence in this way, one can free oneself from the inconvenience of regarding it as strictly a matter of causation. That is, one does not have to assume that Puritan traits in later American writing are always or primarily the effect of causes originating in early New England. Of course, such causation is operative, particularly in writers as conscious of their place in the Puritan tradition as Emerson and Emily Dickinson, and thus the intricacies of Puritan theology continue to be significant even up to the close of the nineteenth century. But more often one feels that the Puritan quality of a novel or poem is a matter of relevance rather than causation—that James' *The American,* for example, illustrates the fact that James found Puritan assumptions natural rather than that he was historically conditioned to accept them. While traditions surviving from the Puritan past may indeed cause certain modes of perception to persist, such influence is dependent upon the continuing relevance of Puritan assumptions; and this relevance is exemplified by the predominant role of New England in American cultural history, when compared to other colonial subcultures which enjoyed stronger political backing and were, in the short run, more viable economically. Puritanism and its close ally, the Scottish-Irish Calvinism of the South, exerted the most lasting influence because its theology expressed the most relevant definition of the American experience. Whether the situation is that of the early settler alone in the wilderness or that of a man alone in an urbanized world, where the continuities of his culture, if not already destroyed by immigration, are in any case concealed by the shifting phantasmagoria of technological change, it is, in its essential outlines, the human situation as Puritanism pictured it—that of the individual in his isolated present moment trying to interpret the immediate by a direct reference to the eternal.

· · · · · · ·

The most profound and lasting influence of Puritanism upon the American mind has been its effect upon the sense of time. By the sharp contrast between the present and eternity which its doctrine of grace fostered, it accustomed the imagination to conceive experience in terms of the purely present in relation to a total history or conspectus of all times. In establishing this habitual view of time, Puritanism affected the very nature of the artist's medium, for since language itself is sequential, the present-eternity contrast defines experience in a manner which bears directly on the writer's problem as to how perceptions, events, and ideas are to be arranged on the page. It is this relevance of doctrine to literary form that perhaps explains why America has excelled in literature, from an earlier date and more markedly, than in any of the other arts. By shaping a particular attitude toward time, Puritanism largely determined the ways a poem or novel would be organized and so founded the drama which in one or another of certain possible ways the American author has henceforth been destined to enact.

Two aspects of New England Puritanism must be kept in mind—the relative isolation which allowed it to develop freely according to its own nature, and its special place in the evolution of Protestant theology. While, in England, Puritanism was but one among many sects and was soon forced to accommodate itself to traditions and institutions which modified it at least as much as it altered them, in New England it was the dominant sect, with the result that the challenge of alien ideologies no less than the practical problems of colonization could be dealt with within the system of strictly Puritan assumptions. That is why New England's severest problems proved to be not those created by Indian wars, British interference, or subversive foreign ideas, but the heresies and irresolvable dilemmas which the contradictions within Puritanism itself brought to light.

The sharp contrast between the present and eternity is the result of the particular phase of Protestant thought which Puritanism represents. It is the phase in which God's immanence is conceived as a presence so absolutely immediate (within the moment of regenerative experience), while God's transcendence has been given so categorical a definition (as Absolute Sovereignty), that although the two aspects of deity can still be held together in thought, the mind is forever engaged in the violent shifting of perspective between the present and eternal points of view. Looking back to the earlier phases of the Reformation, one can see that the main tendency had been toward increased abstraction: God's freedom from obligation to fallen man, and man's consequent need to rely on "justification by faith" alone, lead naturally to predestination, but in Calvin predestination is more abstractly defined to give a bolder, more severely logical statement of God's perfect foreknowledge and foreordination of all things. Thus God is defined as ever more remotely transcendent by an increased emphasis upon Absolute Sovereignty, while, conversely, God becomes more immediately present as salvation is made a question of the self's own state of mind. For to the believer the question of his election must be studied within his own experience, and since experience is always a present event, the more conscientiously he searches his experience, the more purely immediate his idea of the present becomes.

Thus, as the first and third Persons of the Trinity come to seem increasingly divergent as eternal being and immediate perception, it becomes natural to assume that the present and eternity are ultimately the only relevant points of view. But although for convenience I have spoken as if theology caused the Puritan mind to think in this way, in another sense the mentality of Protestantism caused the doctrinal development, and this is nowhere more apparent than in the way the taste for rationalistic abstractions, particularly in the use of such terms as "all," "always," and "infinite," necessitated the widening contrast between immanence and transcendence. When this contrast is pushed a little further than the Puritans or their Calvinist brethren would attempt, Trinitarian Christianity collapses into the inspirational pietism of Antinomian and Quaker, or, if the emphasis falls on clear reason rather than ardent feeling, the rationalism of the Deist and Unitarian.

In Puritanism, however, the balance is perilously maintained—a fact which I think can be recognized in the tension between its Calvinist theology and its Congregationalist polity. It is the latter which most clearly distinguishes the Puritans from the Presbyterians. In espousing a theory of church government founded upon the belief in a corporate spiritual life, the Puritans contravened the logic of predestination, for if works are of no account and salvation is through God's foreordained grace alone, church membership and obedience to the moral law can have no effect upon the life of the soul. One logical conclusion to Calvin's doctrine is thus the Antinomianism for which Anne Hutchinson was banished, and the other great controversies, those concerning "preparation," the "half-way covenant," and admission to the sacrament, also appear to have resulted from the incompatibility of predestinarian and Congregational premises. The covenant theology emphasizes a communal rather than a personal relation between man and God. It was as a people —a church and, somewhat less importantly, a nation—that the Puritans enjoyed their privileged contractual arrangements with God, while predestinarianism gives a larger emphasis to God's presence in the regenerate individual than in the community. On the surface the two views may seem to fit together, since the Church was defined as the core of believers who could attest to some personal assurance of regeneration, and there were many arguments fashioned to reconcile the two—as, for example, that good works are a sign, though not a means, of grace. But since the intricacies of such reasoning give it the air of rationalization, one should look beyond it to the basic impulse that the covenant theology manifests. This is, above all, the desire to see God as present in the everyday life of the community, a desire the more urgent in Puritanism than in the less radical forms of Protestant faith (the Lutheran and Anglican, for instance), in that Calvinist theology had more completely estranged it from the medieval Catholic view of the Church. It was, I would suggest, the remoteness which Calvinism attributed to God as transcendent ruler which explains the Puritans' desire to conceive God's presence in an area more easily perceived than the obscure interior of the individual's heart—in a community, in a church. Perhaps a Scotch Presbyterian colony in America would not have differed greatly from New England, but, even so, the Puritan allegiance to a Congregational form of church government gives added emphasis to the tension which the transcendence-immanence contrast created in the New England mind.

One clear sign of the way this duality influenced the form of Puritan literature is the didacticism so pronounced in the work of early New England authors. Not only their sermons, controversial writings, and works of mere propaganda but their lyric poems and diaries formulate meaning as a lesson and make its status as a lesson abnormally explicit. No doubt it is partly from Puritanism that later American literature derived its characteristic interest in ethical problems and the habit of formulating the answers to them in an abstract and often preachy manner; but in recognizing this connection, one is forced to ask if either a Puritan writer or an American novelist of the twentieth century is really more concerned with ethics than his European counterpart. For to say that the literary tradition which produced a *Phèdre* or a *Crime and Punishment* is less ethical would seem an absurd conclusion. My point is that Puritan literature and later American writing reflect a different, rather than a greater ethical, interest. Instead of appealing to Puritan statements about the instructive function of literature in their literary theory (the texts of which are, indeed, so scant that with respect to the purpose of art they may be thought to do no more than reflect the most commonplace of European aesthetic ideas), it would be wiser to suppose that the Puritans' didactic tendency is the result of their way of relating general ideas to the fictionally realized experience. Ethical truths become lessons delivered with didactic emphasis, not because the American writer is more earnestly concerned with morality, but because for him a generalization is an eternal truth which can only be seen by standing outside the moment of immediate experience. Moral maxims and proverbs spoken "in character" are common throughout literature; so, too, are authorial pronouncements. But what seems distinctively American is the separateness of the lesson from either the characters' world or the author's. The American writer cannot remain "in character," even in his own, if he is to deliver the truth—a fact well exemplified by Hawthorne, as compared with Dickens. The author must stand at a distance to generalize, and having left his own present, he adopts eternity as the only other possible point of view. This is not done merely to make the lesson more explicit or to show that it is universally true, but to see it at all.

There are, in the last analysis, no middle grounds between the eternity of instructive ideas and the moment of present perception. Thus fable suddenly turns into lesson, pure sensation becomes pure concept, and, conversely, the abstraction brought into experience becomes a question of conduct or technology, as one frequently observes in a Franklin, a Melville, or a Hemingway. What lies behind the Puritans' conscious belief that literature should teach lessons is the harsh simplification of time which makes truth take the form of timeless generalizations and renders experience a purely present event.

To the mind for which eternity and the present are the only relevant points of view, the most natural form of thought is analogy, and it is therefore not surprising that analogy is the dominant characteristic of Puritan literature. No other trait is so important, no other literary method so all-pervasive, for analogy is not merely a stylistic device but the very method and design of Puritan thought—a mode not only of interpretation but of having the experience to be interpreted. One can appreciate this by recollecting that New England itself was viewed as one vast analogy in which the settlers correspond to the Israelites, the wilderness to the Promised Land, and the theocratic community to the New Jerusalem.

The same thought process which created New England's essential myth and determined the broad outlines of the Puritans' image of themselves can also be seen in their abnormally great interest in providential interpretations. As the whole life of New England is viewed and, indeed, created by the analogy to ancient Israel, so every detail of public experience is to be regarded as a possible sign of God's dealings with his people. One example will suffice to illustrate this very familiar method, and I will quote from Governor Bradford as a representative of the earliest immigrants, whose mental set was established before the American land could exert the mystical influence which has so often been imputed to our geography. In recording an earthquake, Bradford writes:

It was not only on the seacoast, but the Indians felt it within land, and some ships that were upon the coast were shaken by it. So powerful is the mighty hand of the Lord, as to make both the earth and sea to shake, and the mountains to tremble before Him, when He pleases. And who can stay His hand?

It so fell out that at the same time divers of the chief of this town were met together at one house, conferring with some of their friends that were upon their removal from the place, as if the Lord would hereby show the signs of His displeasure, in their shaking a-pieces and removals from one another.[1]

Providential interpretations served as the key to personal experience as well as the concerns of the community. In fact, its public uses were

----

[1] *Of Plymouth Plantation: 1620–1647*, ed. Samuel Eliot Morison (New York, Knopf, 1952), p. 302.

probably but a consequence of the angle of vision from which the individual looked at his world. Thomas Shepard's account of a calamity
which occurred when he was on the point of setting out for America
shows how naturally the life of faith fostered the habit of analogizing.

So upon the sabbeth day morning boats came to our vessel from the town; and
so my dear wife and child went in the first boat; but here the Lord saw that
these waters were not sufficient to wash away my filth and sinfulness and therefore he cast me into the fire as soon as ever I was upon the sea in the boat, for
there my first born child very precious to my soul and dearly beloved of me was
smitten with sickness; the Lord sent a vomiting upon it whereby it grew faint,
and nothing that we could use could stop its vomiting although we had many
helps at Yarmouth and this was a very bitter affliction to me, and the Lord now
showed me my weak faith, want of fear, pride, carnal content, immoderate
love of creatures, and of my child especially, and begot in me some desires and
purposes to fear his name; but yet the Lord would not be intreated for the life
of it, and after a fortnight's sickness at last it gave up the ghost when its mother
had given it up to the Lord.[2]

That analogy could bring solace even in such heart-rending moments
shows much more effectively than its application to theological controversies and political questions how directly it manifests the essence of
the Puritan mentality.

But it may be asked whether providential interpretations are really
analogies, for Bradford's earthquake and the death of Shepard's child are
not mere parallels to God's will but enactments of it—revelations of
divine purpose within the visible event. If that is so, "Providences" are
metaphors, the two things compared becoming one in experience, whereas
analogy is the drawing of parallels between things, or contexts, which
remain distinct. And since the Puritan's whole purpose in seeking "Providences" is to see God in human events, it would therefore seem that he
aims at metaphor or symbol rather than analogy. This is true in one
sense, but false in another, for as I shall later explain, it is a matter of
point of view whether an event is an analogy or a symbol. One must
approach this difficulty by observing first that although providential
interpretation is common throughout Protestant culture, it is of exaggerated importance in Puritanism, because the more predestination is emphasized, the more every event comes to seem a sign of God's will. If all
that comes to pass is part of a fixed plan determined before the world was
created, then each happening is an indication, because a necessary element, of the total design. Thomas Shepard can make sense of his terrible
misfortune by reasoning that the child's death, like every other event in
his experience, is the inevitable means to the end which God has determined for him.

2 *The Autobiography of Thomas Shepard*, Publication of the Colonial Society of
Massachusetts, 27 (Boston, 1932), 381.

Thus, though analogy and symbol seem opposites, Puritan analogizing leads to symbolism. It is symbolism of a special and limited kind, however, a symbolism deriving from the fact that to the Puritan mind the process of drawing analogies is itself symbolic. The analogy turns into a symbol when one shifts attention from the parallel between image and meaning to the mind which discerns this relation. Conversely, because one regards the things of experience as potential analogies, they are already symbols, they already have an inherent significance rather than functioning as mere signs which point toward meanings outside themselves. To have faith is a sign of regenerative grace; to draw analogies consistent with orthodox belief is evidence that one does have faith in the perfect wisdom and power which make all things expressions of the divine will.

Charles Feidelson has demonstrated that the main literary tradition in America has been a symbolist tradition because symbolism as a way of writing grows naturally from the way the American author's mind confronts his world. Yet Feidelson's analysis tends to limit the Puritan influence upon the later development of symbolist literature and, indeed, pictures Puritanism as more nearly an obstruction than a source. While granting that "Puritan rationalism . . . predicated an indivisible unity of thought, word, and thing," a view which would seem to have fostered the symbolist method, he emphasizes the Puritan allegiance to a discursive reasoning in which words are viewed as having as their meanings discrete objects in an "atomistic" universe, and reasons that this rationalistic bent at first restrained and finally canceled the symbolist tendency.[3] Thus the emergent symbolism of the American Renaissance is primarily a reaction to rather than a development out of Puritanism. Emerson meant "to rescue the intellect by showing that the [theological] controversies grew out of the nature of logical language."[4] For present purposes a distinction must be made between two senses in which the Puritan influence is considered—the theoretical and the psychological. Feidelson's main concern is with specific theories of language, reason, and symbol, and, with respect to these, Puritanism does seem to have developed toward a rationalistic formulation which allowed no scope to the symbolic imagination. But considered within the Puritan world view and the kind of belief which the salvatory doctrines define, Puritanism seems to have favored symbolist thinking much more strongly than its conscious reasoning on this subject allowed. When one considers the self's situation as it is understood in the Puritan scheme, one can see that Puritan experience rendered the symbolist mode natural—indeed, inevitable. Granted, the Puritan writer prefers the image that is merely typical to the symbol, and his statements tend to be propositional in form: Yet the perspective from which the

[3] *Symbolism and American Literature* (Chicago, University of Chicago Press, Phoenix Books, 1953), p. 92.
[4] Ibid., p. 97.

typical image and theological idea are to be viewed has the effect of converting them into symbols. In the way they come to mind, in their happening as events in experience, they are regarded as potential symbols of the effects of grace, even though in content they remain analogues or abstract ideas. While in formal theory Puritanism developed in the manner Feidelson describes, and while it is not possible to trace a line of strictly literary influence in which Puritan poets may be seen providing an example that later poets recognized and imitated, it is safe to assume that the effects of Puritan beliefs upon the American mind habituated it to the symbolic mode of vision, with the result that eventually, in Emerson and other men of his time, the revolt against the jejune rationalism into which the formal theology had developed expressed a sensibility more fundamentally Puritan than the theoretical positions it rejects.

Admittedly, Puritan symbolism is different from that of the American Renaissance, more qualified and tentative, allowing for only momentary resolutions of the habitual analogizing. Yet American symbolism is symbolism of a particular kind, and what distinguishes it is the peculiar self-consciousness which is characteristic of Puritan experience, and which makes the symbolic process itself the center of attention. This is manifest by the very prominence—the obviousness—of the symbol in an American poem or novel. Whitman's thrush and Fitzgerald's green light, like Wallace Stevens' Susanna and Bryant's waterfowl, are more than images charged with symbolic import: their status *as* symbols is the essence of their meaning. *The Scarlet Letter* and *Moby-Dick* are two of the most characteristic as well as two of the greatest American novels because they present the most thoughtful explorations of the odd self-consciousness which makes the American abnormally aware of his symbolizing. They are also representative novels in the preference they manifest for symbols of either the most conventional or the most primitive kind. By greatly exaggerating a symbol's publicly acknowledged and traditional quality—which often produces the "gothic" effect of stylization—or by underlining the primitive aspects of symbols drawn from nature, the writer stresses the fact that his symbols are symbols indeed, and so is able to place the symbolizing process at the center of attention. A sharp contrast is usually developed between the traditional and natural symbols, so that, for example, Leatherstocking's marksmanship seems the more natural as the opposite of Judge Temple's laws and title deeds. There is often still a third sort of contrast designed for the same end: that between the dignity of conventional symbols and the humble commonplace of those derived from everyday experience. It must be stars or bowling balls, diadems or cookery, the grail or a cracked cup.

These ways of calling attention to the symbol as symbol illustrate the fact that in American literature the symbolizing can only be carried out within the larger process of studying one's own interpretation. The author's self-consciousness is but an aspect of the double view Puritanism fostered. Since he lives in a world where the level of meaning and the level of perceptions are antithetical, he is abnormally anxious to unite them in the symbol and yet painfully aware of the difficulties of doing so. Thus to symbolize and to study the symbolic process are for him the same thing. *What* the symbol means is really *how* it means, for that it has any given meaning at all is true only to the extent that the author can demonstrate how it acquires and expresses that meaning.

That a symbolism of this sort derives from the Puritan's rather simplistic contrast between the present and eternity becomes evident when one notices that, on the one hand, the meaning of such symbolism is always there—just as God's eternally preordained plan is implicit in all events—while, on the other hand, the meaning is always in the process of developing, a process which cannot end—just as for the Puritan, who could never have perfect assurance of election, each new moment initiates a fresh search for the signs of grace. The same attitude is revealed in the American writer's double view of the literary work, which he sees, on the one hand, as the touch-and-go affair of achieving "a momentary stay against confusion," and on the other, as a finite or imperfect version of the eternal poem—Poe's "plot of God." Depending on the author, the main emphasis will fall upon one or the other formula, but the two are opposite sides of the same coin. In the world of analogy the symbol's meaning is the universal order: "A leaf, a drop, a crystal, a moment of time, is related to the whole, and partakes of the perfection of the whole. Each particle is a microcosm, and faithfully renders the likeness of the world."[5] Yet because "always" and "now" are permanently separate, for there must ever be a contrast between the divine will, which is eternal, and human experience, which can only be immediately seen in a narrowly defined present, the symbol can effect but a brief and transitory reconciliation. Hence the symbolizing is an unending process. It is therefore the process of thought itself and the essential action of the poem or narrative.

. . . .

The Puritans' narrative writings reflect the dualism of the Puritan world view, for narrative action is a series of events developing sequentially through time, yet such movement cannot easily be accommodated to either the divine or human viewpoints. To God all events are simultaneously present, so that from the point of view of eternity an action is really a static pattern; and eternity is, as it were, the "whole truth"—that which the human mind approximates to the extent that it sees rightly. On the other hand, when an action is regarded from the human point of view, from the present in which a man finds himself, its narrative movement also tends to be negated. Though the present is, in one sense, the opposite of eternity—time itself, the only time which really exists—it is also a

---

[5] Emerson, *Nature,* in *The Complete Works of Ralph Waldo Emerson,* ed. Edward Waldo Emerson (12 vols. Boston, Houghton, Mifflin, 1903), I, 43.

duration within which no time passes; it exists only to the extent that time has been arrested.[6] To be sure, man sees events happen and time pass, but what is real and true in a story is to be found in the experiential now, where things simply *are*. Thus, whether consciously or not, the Puritan writer of narrative finds himself obliged to depict action through stasis. His developing story is perforce something in the past, whether or not he chooses to recount it in present-tense narration. But what is real to him is what now is or what always is. The story must therefore be brought into one or both of these areas of credible fact, and in the process it will, of course, cease to be a story—will no longer develop as a sequence of events moving forward through time.

Puritan histories are, in fact, notably static. In Bradford's *Of Plymouth Plantation,* for example, the story of cause and effect relations is much less important than the isolated episode. That it is through episodes that Bradford works is shown by the virtual disappearance of the narrative line after the arrival at Plymouth, by Bradford's admission that his data are arranged as annals, and by the difficulty the reader has in trying to place later events chronologically, with respect to each other. For example, at just which point does the story of Merrymount occur? One would have to look the matter up to answer, because, memorable and interesting as this episode is, its significance has little to do with its place in a sequence of other happenings. The causal relations are there, of course: Bradford explains how Wollaston established his trading post, how the group there fell into evil ways, how the Puritans came to take action. The meaning of the episode, however, is much less concerned with what preceded and followed it than with the reference it individually makes to transcendent truths. This is apparent in Bradford's analogy comparing the maypole to the Philistines' deity, Dagon, whose image fell to the ground in the presence of the Ark of the Covenant. Though the Puritan triumph over the revelers is a justification of the Puritan point of view and thus, it could be concluded, an explanation of what caused the successful establishment of the colony, still it should be noticed how very directly the line of causation runs back to God's will. What happened at Merrymount seems to be much less dependent upon such necessary pre-conditions as the arrival of the *Mayflower* than upon the immediate in-fluence of the divine will. Bradford implies that the nature of things in the world God has created is such that behavior so offensive to the moral law and so contrary to the interests of God's people cannot for long go unpunished. One feels that the fate of Morton and his followers would be much the same at almost any time and place. Instead of tracing out causation through a sequence of events, Bradford illustrates causation by example. This is the natural procedure for a Puritan historian, for

---

[6] What I have referred to as a present duration is sometimes termed the "specious present," presumably on the ground that it is subjective, whereas it is supposed that the time in terms of which every moment is divisible is not.

granting the assumption that to the predestinarian God all events coexist as elements of a timeless pattern, then it follows that each happening has this plan as its total meaning, and instead of sequences progressively developed in time, the historian considers each event as a unique point of view, a juncture at which the divine plan can be seen from a new angle.

It is this rationale that explains the mysterious charm and effectiveness of Bradford's history. The reader accepts it as history without quite knowing why, so much closer is it to a chronicle or memoir. Bradford seems quite innocent of the historian's usual purposes. Far from formulating any definite theory of history, he does not even seem to try very hard to prove the relevance of his theological ideas, which seem simply to be taken for granted. Having as his subject the experience of a few hundred people, he cannot focus upon events of the magnitude of those which political history has traditionally treated. On the other hand, the materials for a modern social history are too scant and incidental to place the work in that genre. Bradford's whole conception of what constitutes a historical event is, in fact, peculiar. The modern reader would agree with Bradford that the decimation of the Massachusetts Indians by plague is a historical event, but he would be inclined to laugh off the idea that the death by sickness of a cruel and profane sailor aboard the *Mayflower* was too.

One must ask, then, what point of view would allow a historian to regard both happenings as historical in the same sense. It would be one affording a perspective in which progression and development are relatively less important than the analogy between isolation occasions and eternal principles. It is with respect to causation that the sailor's death and the plague are too different to seem relevant to each other. Commines could treat such moralistic episodes historically because the persons involved are the greatest political figures, but Bradford's sailor lacks social importance and one cannot imagine how his death could possibly have much effect on other happenings. However, if the reader forgets about causation and considers instead the emblematic possibilities of our two events, he will see that they are mutually relevant. As emblems, they make reference to the same meaning.

In a very general sense all of Bradford's episodes are intended to show God's dealings with his chosen people, but this formulation is imprecise because the local significance of passages is various and usually a matter of implication. Indeed, Bradford is far less didactic than the now prevailing notions of Puritan literary theory would lead one to suppose. Rather than teaching succinct lessons, his events present different points of view, so that while all ultimately refer to God's plan, each episode reveals a unique aspect. The unity of the work is the result of Bradford's remarkable ability to make all the episodes consistent in tone and harmonious in implication. Thus, though there is a diversity of religious meanings— though, for example, the Merrymount tale focuses attention upon the ethical aspect of God's will, while such matters as the accounts of fishing and farming illustrate the chastening influences of Providence—these more particular meanings are so well integrated that the reader can infer an all-inclusive plan which is at once beyond man's understanding yet the source of reasonable explanations.

Considered by itself, the form of Bradford's history might seem fortuitous and one might be tempted to conclude that the unity of a work whose organization has so casual a look is the result, not of art, but merely of a consistent point of view. Yet such unity is a literary achievement of some importance, however unconsciously the author may have worked. The value, as art, of Bradford's literary method becomes more apparent when it is compared with that of such a contemporary historian as Edward Johnson.

Johnson has epic intentions, and his *Wonderworking Providence* begins fortissimo with an explicit account of God's purposes:

Christ Jesus intending to manifest his Kingly Office toward his Churches more fully than ever yet the Sons of men saw, even to the uniting of Jew and Gentile Churches in one Faith, begins with our English Nation (whose former reformation being vere imperfect) doth now resolve to cast down their false foundation of Prelacy, even in the hight of their domineering dignity. And therefore in the yeere 1628, he stirres up his servants as the Heralds of a King to make this proclamation for volunteers, as followeth.[7]

The Deity's instructions are then set forth in the manner of Deuteronomy. But whenever Johnson descends from the mountain of panoramic vision to the level of the modest facts he has to relate, the effect is bathetic and confusing. Not that his theme is a minor one or less than universal in meaning, but that it is of a nature unsuited to his narrative method. Portraying God acting in the manner of an epic character (consider the statement that Christ 'doth now resolve" to overthrow Prelacy) is difficult to square with predestinarian theory, but even more troublesome is the general perspective such statements assume. History is not to be seen from either of the two credible Puritan viewpoints—that of omniscience or that of the ordinary individual. Rather, it is to be witnessed in the traditional European mode of heroic narrative, where the main actors are somewhat bigger than life and their deeds are ritual enactments of communal experience rather than types of the average person's behavior. Within such a context Johnson's kind of fact is absurdly out of place, as the chapter headings frequently illustrate. Chapter 37 of Book I is entitled "Of the gratious goodness of God, in hearing his peoples' prayers in time of need, and of the Ship-loades of goods the Lord sent them in." Whether or not Johnson himself wrote the headings, the failure of tone in this one illustrates the failure of perspective throughout his history.

---

[7] *Johnson's Wonderworking Providence,* Vol. *10* of *Narratives of Early American History,* ed. J. Franklin Jameson (New York, Scribners, 1910), p. 24.

The fault is neither in the theory of providential interpretation per se nor in Johnson's quaint worldliness in using it. It is in the procedure of treating emblematic episodes as if they were events in a cause and effect sequence. Doubtless the coming of the supply ships was an important event and therefore to the Puritan mind a fitting emblem of the providential help they often received, but as an event in a narrative sequence it is inappropriate because there its cause and effect relations are too narrowly practical to tie it in on any other level than of physical causation. Providence caused the ships' arrival directly by supernatural means, not indirectly through a set of earlier events extending backward in time toward the period when the ships' keels were laid. Johnson's episodes are symbolic as individual facts rather than as parts of a larger story, with the result that his efforts to see narratively are always defeated by his unconscious preference for seeing typically.

The characteristic effect is one of petering out as the attempted narrative bogs down in random detail. For instance, when he undertakes an account "Of the laborious worke Christ's people have in planting this wilderness," he decides to proceed by using the foundation of Concord as an example, since Concord was the first inland settlement.[8] Thus, at the outset, story is replaced by emblem, since Concord's story is to stand for the whole process of colonization. Actually even Concord's story does not get told, the chapter consisting instead of an assortment of details and anecdotes, as for instance that the forest underbrush soon wears out stockings, that a maid lost her way but returned after three days, that the settlers often had no meat except such venison and "rockoons" as they could buy from the savages. Similarly, chapter 23 of Book II discusses the union of the New England colonies by giving some reasons for it and pointing out that in the resultant undertaking Massachusetts bore the greatest burden without having commensurate representation. Then the remainder and greater part of the chapter tells of Miantomeno's plot to murder Uncas and his eventual execution for the crime. The only relation of this episode to the uniting of the colonies is the incidental fact that a joint commission investigated Miantomeno's case. How the union was brought about—the events, the story—Johnson does not recount, nor does he indicate how, in terms of causation, the story about Miantomeno is related to other public events. Here, as throughout the *Wonderworking Providence,* the historian's vision is such that the customary narrative connections are out of focus .

As the most ambitious of seventeenth-century historical works, Cotton Mather's *Magnalia* provides the clearest evidence that Bradford's episodic method marks the beginning of a traditional form which becomes increasingly conscious and elaborate. The *Magnalia* begins with an account of the early years of the colony, and since this is brief, adding little to Bradford's history, from which Mather borrowed, it has the air of a

[8] Ibid., pp. 111–15.

story. But when this initial sketching out of events is completed, Mather abandons chronological narration in order to go back over the same period again and again as he recounts the lives of notable magistrates and divines. In effect, the historical period 1620–ca. 1670 is held up as a unified whole for the reader's examination, as the successive biographical chapters display it from a series of different points of view. This is not a denial of time's passing or of history as sequence so much as a reformulation of them. It is because Mather is intensely interested in history, because he regards it as the medium through which God deals with mankind, that he would break down the generalized outlines of the New England past into specific episodes. For, with respect to the nation's history, the individual "lives" are episodes, just as the remarkable Providences are. Of course there is progression of a sort in the *Magnalia:* the groups of lives tend to be arranged by generation, though not much attention is drawn to this; and while the last book and the appendix deal primarily with the Indian troubles from the seventies to the end of the century, the sketches of notable Harvard graduates mark a shift to later decades. But the chronological pattern is muted by Mather's topical and illustrative manner of dividing up his materials. It is highly significant that he prefers to treat theological matters in one book, to group all the magistrates into another, and to devote yet another to the sundry trials of New England. In a history of this scope it is something of a feat to have avoided sequential narration as effectively as Mather has. One need only compare the plan of the *Magnalia* with that of the greatest English historical work of the period, Clarendon's *True Historical Narrative of the Rebellion and Civil Wars,* to recognize how fundamental is the Puritan historian's divergence from the norm of narrative progression, which even today seems the most natural arrangement.

The objection that Mather's method may have been a merely slapdash procedure is of but slight relevance. If it were true that he simply put together a brief history, borrowing most of his materials, and then added to this a collection of "lives," sermons, and miscellaneous articles, most of which had been written at an earlier time, one would still have to conclude that the arrangement of the *Magnalia* seemed to him an entirely proper form of history. Nor does the *Magnalia's* didactic intent alter the case: that Mather thought a history so written would be effective as propaganda indicates all the more clearly that its form reflects the prevailing sense of time. Actually there is much evidence of conscious artistry in the design of the *Magnalia,* most especially in Mather's use of sermons to frame and underline his meaning.

Mather's meaning is somewhat more narrowly defined than Bradford's, since his account is specifically designed to prove that the Puritans are indeed God's chosen by recounting how in the past the Deity rewarded their righteousness and punished their backslidings. Even so, Mather's meaning is of the same sort, a meaning which is always wholly there and never changes. It is the kind of meaning which history must necessarily have to the minds of men who believe that all events issue from the will of a predestining God. It is history having a form which foreshadows many of the distinctive traits of later narrative art in America.

The first of these is the paradoxical technique of arresting time, yet making it seem to run on toward infinity. By emphasizing the isolated moment, the Puritan historian intensifies the sense of time's passing, for in stressing the sameness of all moments in their potential significance, he implies an endless succession as well as a static eternity. In American fiction this duality is manifest in the technique of containing all time within the present moment, while simultaneously extending time in such a way as to imply that what now is will always be. Thus in Faulkner's *Light in August* Lena Grove's journey traces the unending path between December and August, birth and death, while Joe Christmas' end is also a beginning—Christmas, a moment which embraces every temporal phase in a single duration.

The second of such traits—the Puritan historian's technique of presenting his whole story in small before working it out in detail—is reflected in the American novelist's tendency to begin with a symbolic episode which summarizes his action by posing the question to be explained: Isabel Archer entering the garden, Huck Finn squirming under Miss Watson's religious instruction, Jake Barnes being disconcerted by Cohn's complaint that he isn't living life to the hilt, Hester Prynne stepping onto the scaffold.

However, the most striking of the resemblances between Puritan historical writings and American novels is the convertibility of story into state of mind and vice versa. The events which occur in series as parts of a temporally unfolding action are also to be thought of as the content of an all-embracing consciousness. The journey of the *Pequod* extends temporally as a narrative what is, from another point of view, the dialectic of Ishmael's philosophizing, and the mood of Quentin Compson and his roommate, Shreve, as they converse one night in 1910 contains the whole history of the Sutpens. How a novelistic form of this kind develops from the early historians' way of treating events is most effectively suggested by a familiar poem of Emily Dickinson. When the lady in "Because I Could Not Stop for Death" discovers where her courtly escort, Death, is taking her, she sees the whole journey in an instant, and sees, too, that it is a journey without an end:

> Since then—'tis Centuries—and yet
> Feels shorter than the Day
> I first surmised the Horses Heads
> Were toward Eternity—[9]

[9] *The Poems of Emily Dickinson*, ed. Thomas H. Johnson (3 vols. Cambridge, Mass., Harvard University Press, 1958), 2, 546.

Since poetry requires a patterning which is more than merely service-able, the traits and tendencies of Puritan chronicles are even more appar-ent in efforts at verse narrative. Here the failures are instructive as demonstrations of what could not be accomplished and therefore of the limits within which a proper form would have to be found. "New Eng-land's Crisis" is an exaggerated example of the Puritan's inability to make a story "move."[10] Though Benjamin Tompson's subject is King Philip's War, which by nature would surely seem to invite a simple linear progres-sion and make any other plan seem difficult, Tompson is so fixed in his interest in the isolated episode that the task of linking the events into a sequence proves quite beyond his capabilities. Hence his work is not a narrative poem but a series of tableaux, even though they do appear in chronological order. While Tompson is no artist, his way of failing is characteristic. The static view merely arrests action rather than explain-ing it.

Wigglesworth is of course a more skillful poet—or verse-maker, at least —but *The Day of Doom* illustrates the opposite side of the Puritan's difficulties. Here sequence is all; instead of halting, the poet "runs on." Wigglesworth conceives the Last Judgment as a debate in which one by one, the classes of sinners step before God's throne to plead for salvation and Christ explains the predestinarian logic as it applies in each case. By repeating the same pattern, Wigglesworth can review the various objec-tions to his theology and through Christ's replies elucidate the Puritan system. That the monotony of this plan was not thought a fault—the poem was extremely popular—indicates that it reflects a view congenial to its audience. The preternatural smoothness of the poem as it spins on and on as equably as a cart on ball bearings must have impressed the Puritan reader with the sense of divine inevitability. Since God's will is timeless, the Last Judgment is not really an event or completed action but a con-tinuous activity—hence the oppressive monotony of Wigglesworth's repetitions: his simple linear movement is quite unsuited to his static subject, and he can only proceed by adding more and more and more.

Edward Taylor seems to have understood, as Wigglesworth did not, that the predestinarian faith bore directly upon the nature of narrative. In "God's Determinations" he provides the first example in poetry of the rather special ways of manipulating time which would become charac-teristic of American narrative literature. The beauty of this remarkable work is not at first apparent. Except for two of the poems—the "Preface" and "The Joy of Church Fellowship"—the cycle is little known, but to be appreciated it must be read as a whole, and read several times, so that the mind can learn to adjust to Taylor's particular perspective. The total design counts for a great deal, and unless one reads the poems with that whole plan in mind, most of them will seem dull or, at best, naïvely primi-

10 See *Early American Poetry* (Boston, The Club of Odd Volumes, 1896), I, 5–29.

tive. To say this is to acknowledge the poet's understanding of his theme, his sense that for him or any believing Puritan the story developing through time in a series of events must also appear, from another point of view, as a fixed pattern, God's plan. Though he clearly believes the latter to be the whole truth, his healthy respect for time gives "God's Determination," a validity lacking in *The Day of Doom*. And Taylor's purpose, unlike Wigglesworth's, is not simply that of versifying dogma; he regards doctrinal instruction as merely the means to a larger intent—to hearten and inspire the despairing soul. Thus retribution is not pictured, is scarcely mentioned in fact, and at the end he tolerantly concedes that many who never enter the chariot of the covenanted Church will get to heaven afoot. Taylor's charitable purpose commits him to viewing the things of religion from within time, as the ordinary mortal must, and here he recognizes a torturing dubiety for which faith, rather than Wigglesworth's detached logic, is the ultimate answer. Taylor was enough of a theorist to see that he could not surrender the narrow present of human understanding because he must also believe in the deity's eternal will; and he was enough of a poet to see that his dual allegiance called for narrative of a double kind.

Taylor's essential method is to construct his story in such a way that at each stage it provides both a movement and a panorama. Like the Puritan historians, he works through static episodes. The individual poem, or group of poems, constitutes an isolated moment within which nothing happens, since this moment depicts a state of mind, not an event. Seen in sequence, however, the moments represent phases in the story of the soul's development, and Taylor can therefore trace a narrative movement as he progresses through a series of contrasting states of consciousness, even though within each state time is arrested. The method would not seem very different from that which is common in the sonnet sequence were it not that Taylor has complicated it by another sort of doubleness: seen as an individual, the soul is a character developing as he moves forward through time, but since the soul is also a type—the Christian at any point in history—in the soul's story Taylor represents universal history as the static pattern of God's will.

. . . .

The mode of thought revealed in the typical features of Puritan narrative is no less apparent in the Puritan way of viewing nature. The common Christian tendency to read nature as God's second book is abnormally prominent in Puritan literature, demonstrating again the taste for analogy. But if the Puritan mind regards nature as a compendium of useful texts, it favors no less the contrary view of nature as a very direct sort of revelation. Nature is simply the creation of the transcendent deity and therefore a volume to be read as evidence of the author's intentions, but it is also a world in which God's will is continuously operative and through the presence of his will in events in nature, his immanence as the

Holy Spirit is revealed. Symbolism follows from the second view as analogy does from the first. The natural event is both God acting and yet merely a sign of his purposes. Though logic may cast doubt upon this paradox, to the Puritan mind it was valid and important.

Granted that the design of nature is not to be separated from the Creator's will—that, in as much as the order God willed at the beginning still persists, the willing also continues—Christianity nevertheless assumes that there is an absolute difference between the natural and spiritual orders. In Puritan thought this distinction receives unusual emphasis, for when the question of election becomes the self's primary concern, the means of grace acquire a corresponding interest, and when at the same time the mediation of priest, church, and sacrament is denied, God's influence upon the individual can only be considered in terms of the narrow alternatives of natural or supernatural means. In effect, no other kind of means exists. Puritanism assumed that the redeemed man is dealt with through exceptional means, while the reprobate is allowed to live out his days in the world of unredeemed nature and with the aid of his merely natural faculties, which are corrupted as a consequence of original sin. Providences are exceptional events in which God's hand interposes to alter the ordinary course of nature. The Puritan therefore always confronted the question of whether a particular event should be accounted unusual or normal. Thus Governor Bradford, after interpreting the earthquake as a sign of God's displeasure, went on to say:

It was observed that the summers for divers years together after this earthquake were not so hot and seasonable for the ripening of corn and other fruits as formerly, but more cold and moist, and subject to early and untimely frosts by which, many times, much Indian corn came not to maturity. But whether this was any cause I leave it to the naturalists to judge.[11]

The question Bradford so casually raised gives a glimpse of the problem which in Edwards was to become critical. Bradford could feel sure about the earthquake and leave the bad weather to the naturalists, but the more introspective Puritan would be forced to recognize the problem of distinguishing in his experience between those things which were in the course of nature and those which manifested the workings of grace. Even if the latter were found and the longed-for assurance obtained, nature would still remain problematical. The Puritan would still have to maintain the balance between his sense of God as transcendent ruler and as immanent Spirit, avoiding a heretical pantheism, while insisting upon God's presence in the natural phenomenon.

Taylor's "Upon a Wasp Chilled with Cold" illustrates the form of Puritan nature experience and the odd use of language it fostered. Its moralizing pattern is typical in that, like Bryant's waterfowl, the wasp is first

[11] *Of Plymouth Plantation*, p. 302.

described in a way which draws analogies to the human condition—she lies "In Sol's warm breath and shine as saving"; she rubs her head "As if her velvet helmet high/ Did turret rationality"—so that when the picture is complete, the reader has been prepared for the lesson the poet extracts:

> Lord, clear my misted sight that I
> May hence view thy Divinity,
> Some sparks whereof thou up dost hasp
> Within this little downy wasp,
> In whose small corporation we
> A school and a schoolmaster see;
> Where we may learn, and easily find
> A nimble sprit, bravely mind
> Her work in ev'ry limb: and lace
> It up neat with a vital grace,
> Acting each part though ne'er so small,
> Here of this fustian animal.[12]

"Divinity" and "grace" play the same crucial role as "Power" in Bryant's poem, striking a balance, through double-entendre, between God's immanence and transcendence. Divinity is seen as Godhead but also as mere theology; grace is meant in the spiritual sense but then as simply an outward beauty. From one point of view the wasp manifests God as present in the operations of nature; from another, it is a "school" indicating God's will through the instructive ideas it suggests. And while Taylor depends more upon such verbal wit than upon Bryant's shifting of perspective, at the end he too departs toward higher ground:

> Till I enravished climb into
> The Godhead on this ladder do:
> Where all my pipes inspired upraise
> An heavenly music, furr'd with praise.[13]

Two lines are so indicative of Puritan experience that they may fitly be quoted once again.

> Lord, clear my misted sight that I
> May hence view thy Divinity . . .

The request is a peculiar one: Taylor prays that God will empower him to find the meaning he already sees. The self-consciousness already noted —the sort of awareness which makes the American writer unusually attentive to his own symbolizing—has its source in the scruple apparent here. Knowing is not enough. The Puritan conscience demanded what

[12] *The Poems of Edward Taylor*, pp. 466–67.
[13] Ibid.

Edwards would call "a sense of the divine excellency" of religious truths rather than a merely "notional" understanding.[14] Thus the experience of nature was a crucial test; the self's spiritual condition could be seen no more clearly than in its way of responding to the physical objects immediately before it. Being able to draw appropriate lessons from nature was not a sufficient sign of grace, since the unregenerate could be as well informed in matters of doctrine and morality as the saints. One had to find evidence of something more than natural understanding, to discover the feelings of a sanctified heart. And the determining of one's true feelings was really a matter of discerning how they arose and whither they tended. The Puritan studied his symbolizing because he thought the power to interpret was in itself as auspicious a sign of grace as the interpretation. The tedious piety of Cotton Mather's journal illustrates how much assurance could be gained from the mere activity of symbolizing: a more sensitive man than Mather would have been concerned to see how well he symbolized rather than how much, would have questioned whether his feelings were behind his interpretations, whether his heart assented to the lessons he knew he ought to find, whether the motives which led to understanding were worthy, and whether the whole process of coming to know the meaning of his perceptions signified a will in harmony with God's or going its natural way.

The urgency of this self-questioning becomes understandable when one considers the terrible pressure under which the Puritan lived. Nature provided but the simplest and the clearest of the objects of his experience, in a world where all things were potential signs. Because nothing can be without significance in the creation of a predestining God, the Puritan assumed that every moment might be a revelation and that in every item he perceived there might lie a spiritual message. Fearing damnation, he sought everywhere the signs of grace; yearning for salvation, he attended upon the slightest evidence of God's regenerative spirit within his heart. Doubtless few men could sustain the requisite alertness continually, and presumably most Puritans most of the time yielded somewhat to indifference or self-deception. But the Puritan anxiety is not to be refuted by quotations from such texts as Sewall's diary, which merely reveal the evasions to be expected of an ordinary mind. To students of literature Puritanism is important mainly in its highest states of consciousness, not in phases of hebetude or collapse. And when the Puritan mind is most aware, it is a mind in doubt, a mind in that peculiar sort of doubt which makes doubting an essential function of all consciousness.

To believe that the destiny of one's soul is inalterably determined is to commit oneself to a life of continual questioning. Since it follows from

---

[14] See Edwards' sermon, "A Divine and Supernatural Light," in *Puritan Sage: Collected Writings of Jonathan Edwards,* ed. Vergilius Ferm (New York, Library Publishers, 1953), pp. 160–62, for a characteristic statement on this subject.

predestination that the man who will be consigned to flame or raised to immortal life is the very same man who is presently experiencing, the question of election is really the question of one's own state of mind.

Thus in America what Robert Langbaum has aptly termed "the poetry of experience" appears at an early date, and its Puritan origin gives it certain distinctive features which persist to our own time.[15] Such traits result from the essential purpose of the Puritan's self-examination: since his objective is to view experience as evidence of his spiritual condition, he is accustomed to studying it from the outside as a single unit or specimen; and since the truth he would find is fixed and unchanging, his attention is directed to the present as the most immediate evidence of things which always pertain as they pertain here. The person that the Puritan is in God's sight is the same person he is now. Quite naturally, then, he conceives his experience as a static present duration and isolates the moment in order to regard it as an epitome of all time.

This focusing upon the present signifies not an indifference to other times but, rather, a radically different way of getting at them. Past and future are regarded as present events of consciousness and are seen, always, in terms of how the mind is now remembering or foreseeing. It is an epitome, not a continuity, that the Puritan seeks. He is not interested in observing his present as a phase in a larger development; indeed, his religion makes such an undertaking both improper and impossible. If he writes his life story, he views the events episodically as a series of tableaux each of which contains the whole truth, rather than as happenings in a causative sequence. Because the meaning of experience is its direct reference to the eternal instead of its relation to other times, remembering, foreseeing, and generalizing are more significant in the way they happen than in what they reveal. Their content is only true and important with respect to the behavior of the mind which considers it. The past, for example, is the past as it is now known and is true only to the extent that one remembers well.

Because so definite a line is drawn about the present, the Puritan is both more aware and more interested in the way the mind transcends it. Thus, in a poetry of this kind, the shifts of perspective are just as abrupt as those that later occur in Bryant and Stevens. For the mind's positioning *is* the poetic action, and its movement from one to another point of view is the key to the meaning of its experience. Since how one perceives determines what one perceives, the poem means what the poet's mind does. If what one really is is the truth to be found, the way one thinks is the surest evidence, and if one is always the same person, one's present thinking provides the whole answer.

[15] See his *The Poetry of Experience: The Dramatic Monologue in Modern Literary Tradition* (New York, Norton, 1963).

From Edwards to Emerson

PERRY MILLER

Ralph Waldo Emerson believed that every man has an inward and immediate access to that Being for whom he found the word "God" inadequate and whom he preferred to designate as the "Over-Soul." He believed that this Over-Soul, this dread universal essence, which is beauty, love, wisdom, and power all in one, is present in Nature and throughout Nature. Consequently Emerson, and the young transcendentalists of New England with him, could look with complacence upon certain prospects which our less transcendental generation beholds with misgiving:

> If the red slayer thinks he slays,
> Or if the slain think he is slain,
> They know not well the subtle ways
> I keep, and pass, and turn again.

Life was exciting in Massachusetts of the 1830's and '40's; abolitionists were mobbed, and for a time Mr. Emerson was a dangerous radical; Dr. Webster committed an ingenious murder; but by and large, young men were not called upon to confront possible slaughter unless they elected to travel the Oregon Trail, and the only scholar who did that was definitely not a transcendentalist. Thus it seems today that Emerson ran no great risk in asserting that should he ever be bayoneted he would fall by his own hand disguised in another uniform, that because all men participate in the Over-Soul those who shoot and those who are shot prove to be identical, that in the realm of the transcendental there is nothing to choose between eating and being eaten.

It is hardly surprising that the present generation, those who are called upon to serve not merely as doubters and the doubt but also as slayers and slain, greet the serene pronouncements of Brahma with cries of dissent.

Professors somewhat nervously explain to unsympathetic undergraduates that of course these theories are not the real Emerson, much less the real Thoreau. They were importations, not native American growths. They came from Germany, through Coleridge; they were extracted from imperfect translations of the Hindu scriptures, misunderstood and extravagantly embraced by Yankees who ought to have known better—and who fortunately in some moments did know better, for whenever Emerson and Parker and Thoreau looked upon the mill towns or the conflict of classes they could perceive a few realities through the haze of their transcendentalism. They were but transcendental north-north-west; when the wind was southerly they knew the difference between Beacon Hill and South Boston. I suppose that many who now read Emerson, and surely all who endeavor to read Bronson Alcott, are put off by the "philosophy." The doctrines of the Over-Soul, correspondence and compensation seem nowadays to add up to shallow optimism and insufferable smugness. Contemporary criticism reflects this distaste, and would lead us to prize these men, if at all, for their incidental remarks, their shrewd observations upon society, art, manners, or the weather, while we put aside their premises and their conclusions, the ideas to which they devoted their principal energies, as notions too utterly fantastic to be any longer taken seriously.

Fortunately, no one is compelled to take them seriously. We are not required to persuade ourselves the next time we venture into the woods that we may become, as Emerson said we might, transparent eyeballs, and that thereupon all disagreeable appearances—"swine, spiders, snakes, pests, madhouses, prisons, enemies"—shall vanish and be no more seen. These afflictions have not proved temporary or illusory to many, or the compensations always obvious. But whether such ideas are or are not intelligible to us, there remains the question of whence they came. Where did Emerson, Alcott, Thoreau, and Margaret Fuller find this pantheism which they preached in varying degrees, which the Harvard faculty and most Boston businessmen found both disconcerting and contemptible? Was New England's transcendentalism wholly Germanic or Hindu in origin? Is there any sense, even though a loose one, in which we can say that this particular blossom in the flowering of New England had its roots in the soil? Was it foolishly transplanted from some desert where it had better been left to blush unseen? Emerson becomes most vivid to us when he is inscribing his pungent remarks upon the depression of 1837, and Thoreau in his grim comments upon the American blitzkrieg against Mexico. But our age has a tendency, when dealing with figures of the past, to amputate whatever we find irrelevant from what the past itself considered the body of its teaching. Certain fragments may be kept alive in the critical test tubes of the Great Tradition, while the rest is shoveled off to potter's field. The question of how much in the transcendental philosophy emerged out of the American background, of how much of it was not appropriated from foreign sources, is a question that concerns the entire American tradition, with which and in which we still must work. Although the metaphysic of the Over-Soul, of self-reliance, and of compensation is not one to which we can easily subscribe, yet if the particular formulations achieved by Emerson and Thoreau, Parker and Ripley, were restatements of a native disposition rather than amateur versions of *The Critique of Pure Reason*, then we who must also reformulate our traditions may find their philosophy meaningful, if not for what it held, at least for whence they got it.

Among the tenets of transcendentalism is one which today excites the minimum of our sympathy, which declared truth to be forever and everywhere one and the same, and all ideas to be one idea, all religions the same religion, all poets singers of the same music of the same spheres, chanting eternally the recurrent theme. We have become certain, on the contrary, that ideas are born in time and place, that they spring from specific environments, that they express the force of societies and classes, that they are generated by power relations. We are impatient with an undiscriminating eclecticism which merges the Bhagavad-Gita, Robert Herrick, Saadi, Swedenborg, Plotinus, and Confucius into one monotonous iteration. Emerson found a positive pleasure—which he called "the most modern joy"—in extracting all *time* from the verses of Chaucer, Marvell, and Dryden, and so concluded that one nature wrote all the good books and one nature could read them. The bad books, one infers, were written by fragmentary individuals temporarily out of touch with the Over-Soul, and are bad because they do partake of their age and nation. "There is such equality and identity both of judgment and point of view in the narrative that it is plainly the work of one all-seeing, all-hearing gentleman." We have labored to restore the historical time to Chaucer and Dryden; we do not find it at all plain that they were mouthpieces of one all-seeing agency, and we are sure that if there is any such universal agent he certainly is not a gentleman. We are exasperated with Emerson's tedious habit of seeing everything *sub specie aeternitatis*. When we find him writing in 1872, just before his mind and memory began that retreat into the Over-Soul which makes his last years so pathetic, that while in our day we have witnessed great revolutions in religion we do not therefore lose faith "in the eternal pillars which we so differently name, but cannot choose but see their identity in all healthy souls," we are ready to agree heartily with Walt Whitman, who growled that Emerson showed no signs of adapting himself to new times, but had "about the same attitude as twenty-five or thirty years ago," and that he himself was "utterly tired of these scholarly things." We may become even more tired of scholarly things when we find that from the very beginning Emerson conceived the movement which we call transcendentalism as one more expression of the benign gentleman who previously had spoken in the persons of Socrates and Zoroaster, Mohammed and Buddha, Shakespeare and St. Paul. He does not assist our quest for native origins, indeed for any origins which we are prepared to credit, when he says in 1842, in the Boston Masonic Temple, that transcendentalism is a "Saturnalia of Faith," an age-old way of thinking which, falling upon Roman times, made Stoic philosophers; falling on despotic times, made Catos and Brutuses; on Popish times, made Protestants; "on prelatical times, made Puritans and Quakers; and falling on Unitarian and commercial times, makes the peculiar shades of Idealism which we know." Were we to take him at his word, and agree that he himself was a Stoic revisiting the glimpses of the moon, and that Henry Thoreau was Cato redivivus, we might then decide that both of them could fetch the shades of their idealism from ancient Rome or, if they wished, from Timbuktu, and that they would bear at best only an incidental relation to the American scene. We might conclude with the luckless San Francisco journalist, assigned the task of reporting an Emerson lecture, who wrote, "All left the church feeling that an elegant tribute had been paid to the Creative genius of the First Cause," but we should not perceive that any compliments had been paid to the intellectual history of New England.

Still, to take Emerson literally is often hazardous. We may allow him his Stoics, his Catos and Brutuses, for rhetorical embellishment. He is coming closer home, however, when he comes to Puritans and Quakers, to Unitarian and commercial times. Whether he intended it or not, this particular sequence constitutes in little an intellectual and social history of New England: first Puritans and Quakers, then Unitarians and commercial times, and now transcendentalists! Emerson contended that when poets spoke out of the transcendental Reason, which knows the eternal correspondence of things, rather than out of the shortsighted Understanding—which dwells slavishly in the present, the expedient, and the customary, and thinks in terms of history, economics, and institutions—they builded better than they knew. When they were ravished by the imagination, which makes every dull fact an emblem of the spirit, and were not held earthbound by the fancy, which knows only the surfaces of things, they brought their creations from no vain or shallow thought. Yet he did not intend ever to dispense with the understanding and the fancy, to forget the customary and the institutional—as witness his constant concern with "manners." He would not raise the siege of his hencoop to march away to a pretended siege of Babylon; though he was not conspicuously successful with a shovel in his garden, he was never, like Elizabeth Peabody, so entirely subjective as to walk straight into a tree because "I saw it, but I did not realize it." Could it be, therefore, that while his reason was dreaming among the Upanishads, and his imagination reveling with Swedenborg, his understanding perceived that on the plain of material causation the transcendentalism of New England had some connection with New England experience, and that his fancy, which remained at home with the customary and with history, guided this choice of words? Did these lower faculties contrive, by that cunning which distinguishes them from reason and imagination in the very moment when transcendentalism was being proclaimed a saturnalia of faith, that there should appear a cryptic suggestion that it betokened less an Oriental ecstasy and more a natural reaction of some descendants of Puritans and Quakers to Unitarian and commercial times?

I have called Emerson mystical and pantheistical. These are difficult adjectives; we might conveniently begin with Webster's dictionary, which declares mysticism to be the doctrine that the ultimate nature of reality or of the divine essence may be known by an immediate insight. The connotations of pantheism are infinite, but in general a pantheist holds that the universe itself is God, or that God is the combined forces and laws manifested in the existing universe, that God is, in short, both the slayer and the slain. Emerson and the others might qualify their doctrine, but when Professor Andrews Norton read that in the woods "I become a transparent eyeball; I am nothing, I see all; the currents of the Universal Being circulate through me; I am part or particle of God," in his forthright fashion he could not help perceiving that this was both mysticism and pantheism, and so attacking it as "the latest form of infidelity."

Could we go back to the Puritans whom Emerson adduced as his predecessors, and ask the Emersons and Ripleys, not to mention the Winthrops, Cottons, and Mathers, of the seventeenth century whether the eyeball passage was infidelity, there would be no doubt about the answer. They too might call it the "latest" form of infidelity, for in the first years of New England Winthrop and Cotton had very bitter experience with a similar doctrine. Our wonder is that they did not have more. To our minds, no longer at home in the fine distinctions of theology, it might seem that from the Calvinist doctrine of regeneration, from the theory that a regenerate soul receives an influx of divine spirit, and is joined to God by a direct infusion of His grace, we might deduce the possibility of receiving all instruction immediately from the indwelling spirit, through an inward communication which is essentially mystical. Such was exactly the deduction of Mistress Anne Hutchinson, for which she was expelled into Rhode Island. It was exactly the conclusion of the Quakers, who added that every man was naturally susceptible to this inward communication, that he did not need a special and supernatural dispensation. Quakers also were cast into Rhode Island or, if they refused to stay there, hanged on Boston Common. Emerson, descendant of Puritans, found the descendants of Quakers "a sublime class of speculators," and wrote in 1835 that they had been the most explicit teachers "of the highest article to which human faith soars [,] the strict union of the willing soul to God & so the soul's access at all times to a verdict upon every question which the opinion of all mankind cannot shake & which the opinion of all mankind cannot confirm." But his ancestors had held that while the soul does indeed have an access to God, it receives from the spirit no verdict upon any question, only a dutiful disposition to accept the verdict confirmed by Scripture, by authority, and by logic. As Roger Clap remarked, both Anne Hutchinson and the Quakers "would talk of the Spirit, and of revelations by the Spirit without the Word, . . . of the Light within them, rejecting the holy Scripture"; and the Puritan minister declared that the errors of the Antinomians, "like strong wine, make men's judgments reel and stagger, who are drunken therwith." The more one studies the history of Puritan New England, the more astonished he becomes at the amount of reeling and staggering there was in it.

These seventeenth-century "infidels" were more interested in enlarging the soul's access to God from within than in exploring the possibilities of an access from without, from nature. But if we, in our interrogation of the shades of Puritans, were to ask them whether there exists a spirit that rolls through all things and propels all things, whose dwelling is the light of setting suns, and the round oceans, and the mind of man, a spirit from whom we should learn to be disturbed by the joy of elevated thoughts, the Puritans would feel at once that we needed looking after. They would concede that the visible universe is the handiwork of God, that He governs it and is present in the flight of every sparrow, the fall of every stone, the rising and setting of suns, in the tempests of the round ocean. "Who set those candles, those torches of heaven, on the table? Who hung out those lanterns in heaven to enlighten a dark world?" asked the preacher, informing his flock that although we do not see God in nature, yet in it His finger is constantly evident. The textbook of theology used at Harvard told New England students that every creature would return into nothing if God did not uphold it—"the very cessation of Divine conservation, would without any other operation presently reduce every Creature into nothing." In regard of His essence, said Thomas Hooker, God is in all places alike, He is in all creatures and beyond them, "hee is excluded *out* of no place, included *in* no place." But it did not follow that the universe, though created by God and sustained by His continuous presence, was God Himself. We were not to go to nature and, by surrendering to the stream of natural forces, derive from it our elevated thoughts. We were not to become nothing and let the currents of Universal Being circulate through us. Whatever difficulties were involved in explaining that the universe is the work of God but that we do not meet God face to face in the universe, Puritan theologians knew that the distinction must be maintained, lest excitable Yankees reel and stagger with another error which they would pretend was an elevated thought. The difficulties of explanation were so great that the preachers often avoided the issue, declaring, "this is but a curious question: therefore I will leave it," or remarking that the Lord fills both heaven and earth, yet He is not in the world as the soul is in the body, "but in an incomprehensible manner, which we cannot expresse to you." Thomas Shepard in Cambridge tried to be more explicit: the Godhead, he said, is common to everything and every man, even to the most wicked man, "nay, to the vilest creature in the world."

The same power that made a blade of grass made also the angels, but grass and angels are not the same substance, and so the spirit of God which is in the setting sun and the round ocean is not the same manifestation which He puts forth as a special and "supernatural" grace in the regenerate soul. "There comes another spirit upon us, which common men have not." This other spirit teaches us, not elevated thoughts, but how to submit our corrupt thoughts to the rule of Scripture, to the law and the gospel as expounded at Harvard College and by Harvard graduates.

The reason for Puritan opposition to these ideas is not far to seek. The Renaissance mind—which was still a medieval mind—remembered that for fifteen hundred years Christian thinkers had striven to conceive of the relation of God to the world in such a fashion that the transcendence of God should not be called in question, that while God was presented as the creator and governor of the world, He would always be something other than the world itself. Both mysticism and pantheism, in whatever form, identified Him with nature, made Him over in the image of man, interpreted Him in the terms either of human intuitions or of human perceptions, made Him one with the forces of psychology or of matter. The Renaissance produced a number of eccentrics who broached these dangerous ideas—Giordano Bruno, for instance, who was burned at the stake by a sentence which Catholics and Calvinists alike found just. The Puritans carried to New England the historic convictions of Christian orthodoxy, and in America found an added incentive for maintaining them intact. Puritanism was not merely a religious creed and a theology, it was also a program for society. We go to New England, said John Winthrop, to establish a due form of government, both civil and ecclesiastical, under the rule of law and Scripture. It was to be a medieval society of status, with every man in his place and a place for every man; it was to be no utopia of rugged individualists and transcendental freethinkers. But if Anne Hutchinson was correct, and if men could hear the voice of God within themselves, or if they could go into the woods and feel the currents of Universal Being circulate through them—in either event they would pay little heed to governors and ministers. The New England tradition commenced with a clear understanding that both mysticism and pantheism were heretical, and also with a frank admission that such ideas were dangerous to society, that men who imbibed noxious errors from an inner voice or from the presence of God in the natural landscape would reel and stagger through the streets of Boston and disturb the civil peace.

Yet from the works of the most orthodox of Calvinists we can perceive that the Puritans had good cause to be apprehensive lest mystical or pantheistical conclusions arise out of their premises. Anne Hutchinson and the Quakers commenced as Calvinists; from the idea of regeneration they drew, with what seemed to them impeccable logic, the idea that God imparted His teaching directly to the individual spirit. With equal ease others could deduce from the doctrines of divine creation and providence the idea that God was immanent in nature. The point might be put thus: there was in Puritanism a piety, a religious passion, the sense of an inward communication and of the divine symbolism of nature. One side of the Puritan nature hungered for these excitements; certain of its appetites desired these satisfactions and therefore found delight and ecstasy in the doctrines of regeneration and providence. But in Puritanism there was also another side, an ideal of social conformity, of law and order, of regulation and control. At the core of the theology there was an indestructible element which was mystical, and a feeling for the universe which was almost pantheistic; but there was also a social code demanding obedience to external law, a code to which good people voluntarily conformed and to which bad people should be made to conform. It aimed at propriety and decency, the virtues of middle-class respectability, self-control, thrift, and dignity, at a discipline of the emotions. It demanded, as Winthrop informed the citizens of Massachusetts Bay in 1645, that men forbear to exercise the liberty they had by nature, the freedom to do anything they chose, and having entered into society thereafter, devote themselves to doing only that which the authorities defined as intrinsically "good, just and honest." The New England tradition contained a dual heritage, the heritage of the troubled spirit and the heritage of worldly caution and social conservatism. It gave with one hand what it took away with the other: it taught men that God is present to their intuitions and in the beauty and terror of nature, but it disciplined them into subjecting their intuitions to the wisdom of society and their impressions of nature to the standards of decorum.

In the eighteenth century, certain sections of New England, or certain persons, grew wealthy. It can hardly be a coincidence that among those who were acquiring the rewards of industry and commerce there should be progressively developed the second part of the heritage, the tradition of reason and criticism, and that among them the tradition of emotion and ecstasy should dwindle. Even though a few of the clergy, like Jonathan Mayhew and Lemuel Briant, were moving faster than their congregations, yet in Boston and Salem, the centers of shipping and banking, ministers preached rationality rather than dogma, the Newtonian universe and the sensational psychology rather than providence and innate depravity. The back country, the Connecticut Valley, burst into flame with the Great Awakening of the 1740's; but the massive Charles Chauncy, minister at the First Church, the successor of John Cotton, declared that "the passionate discovery" of divine love is not a good evidence of election. "The surest and most substantial Proof is, *Obedience to the Commandments of God,* and the *stronger* the Love, the more uniform, steady and pleasant will be this *Obedience*." Religion is of the understanding as well as of the affections, and when the emotions are stressed at the expense of reason, "it can't be but People should run into

Disorders." In his ponderous way, Chauncy was here indulging in Yankee understatement. During the Awakening the people of the back country ran into more than disorders; they gave the most extravagant exhibition of staggering and reeling that New England had yet beheld. Chauncy was aroused, not merely because he disapproved of displays of emotion, but because the whole society seemed in danger when persons who made a high pretense to religion displayed it in their conduct "as something wild and fanciful." On the contrary, he stoutly insisted, true religion is sober and well-behaved; as it is taught in the Bible, "it approves itself to the Understanding and Conscience, . . . and is in the best Manner calculated to promote the Good of Mankind." The transformation of this segment of Puritanism from a piety to an ethic, from a religious faith to a social code, was here completed, although an explicit break with the formal theology was yet to come.

Charles Chauncy had already split the Puritan heritage. Emerson tells that Chauncy, going into his pulpit for the Thursday lecture (people at that time came all the way from Salem to hear him), was informed that a little boy had fallen into Frog Pond and drowned. Requested to improve the occasion,

the doctor was much distressed, and in his prayer he hesitated, he tried to make soft approaches, he prayed for Harvard College, he prayed for the schools, he implored the Divine Being "to—to—to bless to them all the boy that was this morning drowned in Frog Pond."

But Jonathan Edwards felt an ardency of soul which he knew not how to express, a desire "to lie in the dust, and to be full of Christ alone; to love him with a holy and pure love; to trust in him; to live upon him; to serve and follow him; and to be perfectly sanctified and made pure, with a divine and heavenly purity." To one who conceived the highest function of religion to be the promotion of the good of mankind, Jonathan Edwards stood guilty of fomenting disorders. Chauncy blamed Edwards for inciting the populace, and was pleased when the congregation at Northampton, refusing to measure up to the standards of sanctification demanded by Edwards, banished him into the wilderness of Stockbridge. Edwards, though he was distressed over the disorders of the Awakening, would never grant that a concern for the good of mankind should take precedence over the desire to be perfectly sanctified and made pure. In his exile at Stockbridge he wrote the great tracts which have secured his fame for all time, the magnificent studies of the freedom of the will, of the nature of true virtue, of the purpose of God in creating the universe, in which Chauncy and Harvard College were refuted; in which, though still in the language of logic and systematic theology, the other half of the Puritan heritage—the sense of God's overwhelming presence in the soul and in nature—once more found perfect expression.

Though the treatises on the will and on virtue are the more impressive performances, for our purposes the eloquent *Dissertation Concerning the End for which God Created the World* is the more relevant, if only because when he came to this question Edwards was forced to reply specifically to the scientific rationalism toward which Chauncy and Harvard College were tending. He had, therefore, to make even more explicit than did the earlier divines the doctrines which verged upon both mysticism and pantheism, the doctrines of inward communication and of the divine in nature. It was not enough for Edwards to say, as John Cotton had done, that God created the world out of nothing to show His glory; rationalists in Boston could reply that God's glory was manifested in the orderly machine of Newtonian physics, and that a man glorified God in such a world by going about his rational business: real estate, the triangular trade, or the manufacture of rum out of smuggled molasses. God did not create the world, said Edwards, merely to exhibit His glory; He did not create it out of nothing simply to show that He could: He who is Himself the source of all being, the substance of all life, created the world out of Himself by a diffusion of Himself into time and space. He made the world, not by sitting outside and above it, by modeling it as a child models sand, but by an extension of Himself, by taking upon Himself the forms of stones and trees and of man. He created without any ulterior object in view, neither for His glory nor for His power, but for pure joy of self-expression, as an artist creates beauty for the love of beauty. God does not need a world or the worship of man; He is perfect in Himself. If He bothers to create, it is out of the fullness of His own nature, the overflowing virtue that is in Him. Edwards did not use my simile of the artist; his way of saying it was, "The disposition to communicate himself, or diffuse his own fulness, which we must conceive of as being originally in God as a perfection of his nature, was what moved him to create the world," but we may still employ the simile because Edwards invested his God with the sublime egotism of a very great artist. God created by the laws of His own nature, with no thought of doing good for anybody or for mankind, with no didactic purpose, for no other reason but the joy of creativeness. "It is a regard to himself that disposes him to diffuse and communicate himself. It is such a delight in his own internal fulness and glory, that disposes him to an abundant effusion and emanation of that glory."

Edwards was much too skilled in the historic problems of theology to lose sight of the distinction between God and the world or to fuse them into one substance, to blur the all-important doctrine of the divine transcendence. He forced into his system every safeguard against identifying the inward experience of the saint with the Deity Himself, or of God with nature. Nevertheless, assuming, as we have some right to assume, that what subsequent generations find to be a hidden or potential implication in a thought is a part of that thought, we may venture to feel that Ed-

wards was particularly careful to hold in check the mystical and pantheistical tendencies of his teaching because he himself was so apt to
become a mystic and a pantheist. The imagery in which a great thinker
expresses his sense of things is often more revealing than his explicit
contentions, and Edwards betrays the nature of his insight when he uses
as the symbol of God's relation to the world the metaphor that has
perennially been invoked by mystics, the metaphor of light and of the
sun:

> And [it] is fitly compared to an effulgence or emanation of light from a
> luminary, by which this glory of God is abundantly represented in Scripture.
> Light is the external expression, exhibition and manifestation of the excellency
> of the luminary, of the sun for instance: it is the abundant, extensive emanation
> and communication of the fulness of the sun to innumerable beings that partake
> of it. It is by this that the sun itself is seen, and his glory beheld, and all other
> things are discovered; it is by a participation of this communication from the
> sun, that surrounding objects receive all their lustre, beauty and brightness. It
> is by this that all nature is quickened and receives life, comfort, and joy.

Here is the respect that makes Edwards great among theologians, and
here in fact he strained theology to the breaking point. Holding himself
by brute will power within the forms of ancient Calvinism, he filled those
forms with a new and throbbing spirit. Beneath the dogmas of the old
theology he discovered a different cosmos from that of the seventeenth
century, a dynamic world, filled with the presence of God, quickened
with divine life, pervaded with joy and ecstasy. With this insight he
turned to combat the rationalism of Boston, to argue that man cannot live
by Newtonian schemes and mathematical calculations, but only by surrender to the will of God, by reflecting back the beauty of God as a jewel
gives back the light of the sun. But another result of Edwards's doctrine,
one which he would denounce to the nethermost circle of Hell but which
is implicit in the texture, if not in the logic, of his thought, could very
easily be what we have called mysticism or pantheism, or both. If God is
diffused through nature, and the substance of man is the substance of
God, then it may follow that man is divine, that nature is the garment of
the Over-Soul, that man must be self-reliant, and that when he goes into
the woods the currents of Being will indeed circulate through him. All
that prevented this deduction was the orthodox theology, supposedly
derived from the Word of God, which taught that God and nature are not
one, that man is corrupt and his self-reliance is reliance on evil. But take
away the theology, remove this overlying stone of dogma from the well-
springs of Puritan conviction, and both nature and man become divine.
    We know that Edwards failed to revitalize Calvinism. He tried to fill
the old bottles with new wine, yet none but himself could savor the vin-
tage. Meanwhile, in the circles where Chauncy had begun to reëducate
the New England taste, there developed, by a very gradual process, a

rejection of the Westminster Confession, indeed of all theology, and at last emerged the Unitarian churches. Unitarianism was entirely different wine from any that had ever been pressed from the grapes of Calvinism, and in entirely new bottles, which the merchants of Boston found much to their liking. It was a pure, white, dry claret that went well with dinners served by the Harvard Corporation, but it was mild and was guaranteed not to send them home reeling and staggering. As William Ellery Channing declared, to contemplate the horrors of New England's ancestral creed is "a consideration singularly fitted to teach us tolerant views of error, and to enjoin caution and sobriety."

In Unitarianism one half of the New England tradition—that which inculcated caution and sobriety—definitely cast off all allegiance to the other. The ideal of decorum, of law and self-control, was institutionalized. Though Unitarianism was "liberal" in theology, it was generally conservative in its social thinking and in its metaphysics. Even Channing, who strove always to avoid controversy and to appear "mild and amiable," was still more of an enthusiast than those he supplied with ideas, as was proved when almost alone among Unitarian divines he spoke out against slavery. He frequently found himself thwarted by the suavity of Unitarian breeding. In his effort to establish a literary society in Boston, he repaired, as Emerson tells the story, to the home of Dr. John Collins Warren, where

he found a well-chosen assembly of gentlemen variously distinguished; there was mutual greeting and introduction, and they were chatting agreeably on indifferent matters and drawing gently towards their great expectation, when a side-door opened, the whole company streamed in to an oyster supper, crowned by excellent wines; and so ended the first attempt to establish aesthetic society in Boston.

But if the strain in the New England tradition which flowered so agreeably in the home of Dr. Warren, the quality that made for reason and breeding and good suppers, found itself happily divorced from enthusiasm and perfectly enshrined in the liberal profession of Unitarianism, what of the other strain? What of the mysticism, the hunger of the soul, the sense of divine emanation in man and in nature, which had been so important an element in the Puritan character? Had it died out of New England? Was it to live, if at all, forever caged and confined in the prison house of Calvinism? Could it be asserted only by another Edwards in another treatise on the will and a new dissertation on the end for which God created the universe? Andover Seminary was, of course, turning out treatises and dissertations, and there were many New Englanders outside of Boston who were still untouched by Unitarianism. But for those who had been "liberated" by Channing and Norton, who could no longer express their desires in the language of a creed that had been shown to be

outworn, Calvinism was dead. Unitarianism rolled away the heavy stone
of dogma that had sealed up the mystical springs in the New England
character; as far as most Unitarians were concerned, the stone could now
be lifted with safety, because to them the code of caution and sobriety,
nourished on oyster suppers, would serve quite as well as the old doctrines of original sin and divine transcendence to prevent mankind from
reeling and staggering in freedom. But for those in whom the old springs
were still living, the removal of the theological stopper might mean a
welling up and an overflowing of long suppressed desires. And if these
desires could no longer be satisfied in theology, toward what objects
would they now be turned? If they could no longer be expressed in the
language of supernatural regeneration and divine sovereignty, in what
language were they to be described?

The answer was not long forthcoming. If the inherent mysticism, the
ingrained pantheism, of certain Yankees could not be stated in the old
terms, it could be couched in the new terms of transcendental idealism, of
Platonism, of Swedenborg, of "Tintern Abbey" and the Bhagavad-Gita,
in the eclectic and polyglot speech of the Over-Soul, in "Brahma," in
"Self-Reliance," in *Nature*. The children of Puritans could no longer say
that the visible fabric of nature was quickened and made joyful by a diffusion of the fullness of God, but they could recapture the Edwardsean
vision by saying, "Nature can only be conceived as existing to a universal
and not to a particular end; to a universe of ends, and not to one,—a work
of *ecstasy*, to be represented by a circular movement, as intention might
be signified by a straight line of definite length." But in this case the circular conception enjoyed one great advantage—so it seemed at the time—
that it had not possessed for Edwards: the new generation of ecstatics had
learned from Channing and Norton, from the prophets of intention and
the straight line of definite length, that men did not need to grovel in the
dust. They did not have to throw themselves on the ground, as did Edwards, with a sense of their own unworthiness; they could say without
trepidation that no concept of the understanding, no utilitarian consideration for the good of mankind, could account for any man's existence, that
there was no further reason than "*so it was to be*." Overtones of the seventeenth century become distinctly audible when Emerson declares, "The
royal reason, the Grace of God, seems the only description of our multiform but ever identical fact," and the force of his heredity is manifest
when he must go on to say, having mentioned the grace of God, "There is
the incoming or the receding of God," and as Edwards also would have
said, "we can show neither how nor why." In the face of this awful and
arbitrary power, the Puritan had been forced to conclude that man was
empty and insignificant, and account for its recedings on the hypothesis
of innate depravity. Emerson does not deny that such reflections are in
order; when we view the fact of the inexplicable recedings "from the platform of action," when we see men left high and dry without the grace of

God, we see "Self-accusation, remorse, and the didactic morals of self-denial and strife with sin"; but our enlightenment, our liberation from the sterile dogmas of Calvinism, enables us also to view the fact from "the platform of intellection," and in this view "there is nothing for us but praise and wonder." The ecstasy and the vision which Calvinists knew only in the moment of vocation, the passing of which left them agonizingly aware of depravity and sin, could become the permanent joy of those who had put aside the conception of depravity, and the moments between could be filled no longer with self-accusation but with praise and wonder. Unitarianism had stripped off the dogmas, and Emerson was free to celebrate purely and simply the presence of God in the soul and in nature, the pure metaphysical essence of the New England tradition. If he could no longer publish it as orthodoxy, he could speak it fearlessly as the very latest form of infidelity.

At this point there might legitimately be raised a question whether my argument is anything more than obscurantism. Do words like "New England tradition" and "Puritan heritage" mean anything concrete and tangible? Do they "explain" anything? Do habits of thought persist in a society as acquired characteristics, and by what mysterious alchemy are they transmitted in the blood stream? I am as guilty as Emerson himself if I treat ideas as a self-contained rhetoric, forgetting that they are, as we are now discovering, weapons, the weapons of classes and interests, a masquerade of power relations.

Yet Emerson, transcendental though he was, could see in his own ideas a certain relation to society. In his imagination transcendentalism was a saturnalia of faith, but in his fancy it was a reaction against Unitarianism and in his understanding a revulsion against commercialism. We can improve his hint by remarking the obvious connection between the growth of rationalism in New England and the history of eighteenth-century capitalism. Once the Unitarian apologists had renounced the Westminster Confession, they attacked Calvinism not merely as irrational but as a species of pantheism, and in their eyes this charge was sufficient condemnation in itself. Calvinism, said Channing, robs the mind of self-determining force and makes men passive recipients of the universal force:

It is a striking fact that the philosophy which teaches that matter is an inert substance, and that God is the force which pervades it, has led men to question whether any such thing as matter exists. . . . Without a free power in man, he is nothing. The divine agent within him is every thing, Man acts only in show. He is a phenomenal existence, under which the One Infinite Power is manifested; and is this much better than Pantheism?

One does not have to be too prone to economic interpretation in order to perceive that there was a connection between the Unitarian insistence that matter is substance and not shadow, that men are self-determining agents and not passive recipients of Infinite Power, and the practical interests of the society in which Unitarianism flourished. Pantheism was not a marketable commodity on State Street, and merchants could most successfully conduct their business if they were not required to lie in the dust and desire to be full of the divine agent within.

Hence the words "New England tradition" and "Puritan heritage" can be shown to have some concrete meaning when applied to the gradual evolution of Unitarianism out of the seventeenth-century background; there is a continuity both social and intellectual. But what of the young men and young women, many of them born and reared in circles in which, Channing said, "Society is going forward in intelligence and charity," who in their very adolescence instinctively turned their intelligence and even their charity against this liberalism, and sought instead the strange and uncharitable gods of transcendentalism? Why should Emerson and Margaret Fuller, almost from their first reflective moments, have cried out for a philosophy which would reassure them that matter is the shadow and spirit the substance, that man acts by an influx of power—why should they deliberately return to the bondage from which Channing had delivered them? Even before he entered the divinity school Emerson was looking askance at Unitarianism, writing in his twentieth year to his southern friend, John Boynton Hill, that for all the flood of genius and knowledge being poured out from Boston pulpits, the light of Christianity was lost: "An exemplary Christian of today, and even a Minister, is content to be just such a man as was a good Roman in the days of Cicero." Andrews Norton would not have been distressed over this observation, but young Emerson was. "Presbyterianism & Calvinism at the South," he wrote, "at least make Christianity a more real & tangible system and give it some novelties which were worth unfolding to the ignorance of men." Thus much, but no more, he could say for "orthodoxy": "When I have been to Cambridge & studied Divinity, I will tell you whether I can make out for myself any better system than Luther or Calvin, or the *liberal besoms* of modern days." The "Divinity School Address" was forecast in these youthful lines, and Emerson the man declared what the boy had divined when he ridiculed the "pale negations" of Unitarianism, called it an "icehouse," and spoke of "the corpse-cold Unitarianism of Harvard College and Brattle Street." Margaret Fuller thrilled to the epistle of John read from a Unitarian pulpit: "Every one that loveth is born of God, and knoweth God," but she shuddered as the preacher straightway rose up "to deny mysteries, to deny second birth, to deny influx, and to renounce the sovereign gift of insight, for the sake of what he deemed a 'rational' exercise of will." This Unitarianism, she argued in her journal, has had its place, but the time has now come for reinterpreting old dogmas. "For one I would now preach the Holy Ghost as zealously as they have been preaching Man, and faith instead of the understanding, and mysticism instead &c—." And there, characteristically enough, she remarks, "But why go on?"

A complete answer to the question of motives is probably not possible as yet. Why Waldo and Margaret in the 1820's and '30's should instinctively have revolted against a creed that had at last been perfected as the ideology of their own group, of respectable, prosperous, middle-class Boston and Cambridge—why these youngsters, who by all the laws of economic determinism ought to have been the white-headed children of Unitarianism, elected to become transcendental black sheep, cannot be decided until we know more about the period than has been told in *The Flowering of New England* and more about the nature of social change in general. The personal matter is obviously of crucial importance. The characters of the transcendentalists account for their having become transcendental; still two facts of a more historical nature seem to me worth considering in the effort to answer our question.

The emergence of Unitarianism out of Calvinism was a very gradual, almost an imperceptible, process. One can hardly say at what point rationalists in eastern Massachusetts ceased to be Calvinists, for they were forced to organize into a separate church only after the development of their thought was completed. Consequently, although young men and women in Boston might be, like Waldo and Margaret, the children of rationalists, all about them the society still bore the impress of Calvinism: the theological break had come, but not the cultural. In a thousand ways the forms of society were still those determined by the ancient orthodoxy, piously observed by persons who no longer believed in the creed. We do not need to posit some magical transmission of Puritanism from the seventeenth to the nineteenth century in order to account for the fact that these children of Unitarians felt emotionally starved and spiritually undernourished. In 1859 James Cabot sent Emerson *The Life of Trust*, a crude narrative by one George Muller of his personal conversations with the Lord, which Cabot expected Emerson to enjoy as another instance of man's communion with the Over-Soul, which probably seemed to Cabot no more crackbrained than many of the books Emerson admired. Emerson returned the volume, accompanied by a vigorous rebuke to Cabot for occupying himself with such trash:

I sometimes think that you & your coevals missed much that I & mine found for Calvinism was still robust & effective on life & character in all the people who surrounded my childhood, & gave a deep religious tinge to manners & conversation. I doubt the race is now extinct, & certainly no sentiment has taken its place on the new generation,—none as pervasive & controlling. But they were a high tragic school, & found much of their own belief in the grander traits of the Greek mythology,—Nemesis, the Fates, & the Eumenides, and, I am sure, would have raised an eyebrow at this pistareen Providence of . . . George Muller.

At least two members of the high tragic school Emerson knew intimately and has sympathetically described for us—his stepgrandfather, the Reverend Ezra Ripley, and his aunt, Mary Moody Emerson. Miss Emerson put the essence of the Puritan aesthetic into one short sentence: "How insipid is fiction to a mind touched with immortal views!" Speaking as a Calvinist, she anticipated Max Weber's discovery that the Protestant ethic fathered the spirit of capitalism, in the pungent observation, "I respect in a rich man the order of Providence." Emerson said that her journal "marks the precise time when the power of the old creed yielded to the influence of modern science and humanity"; still in her the old creed never so far yielded its power to the influence of modern humanity but that she could declare, with a finality granted only to those who have grasped the doctrine of divine sovereignty, "I was never patient with the faults of the good." When Thomas Cholmondeley once suggested to Emerson that many of his ideas were similar to those of Calvinism, Emerson broke in with irritation, "I see you are speaking of something which had a meaning once, but is now grown obsolete. Those words formerly stood for something, and the world got good from them, but not now." The old creed would no longer serve, but there had been power in it, a power conspicuously absent from the pale negations of Unitarianism. At this distance in time, we forget that Emerson was in a position fully to appreciate what the obsolete words had formerly stood for, and we are betrayed by the novelty of his vocabulary, which seems to have no relation to the jargon of Calvinism, into overlooking a fact of which he was always aware— the great debt owed by his generation "to that old religion which, in the childhood of most of us, still dwealt like a sabbath morning in the country of New England, teaching privation, self-denial and sorrow!" The retarded tempo of the change in New England, extending through the eighteenth into the nineteenth century, makes comprehensible why young Unitarians had enough contact with the past to receive from it a religious standard by which to condemn the pallid and unexciting liberalism of Unitarianism.

Finally, we do well to remember that what we call the transcendental movement was not an isolated phenomenon in nineteenth-century New England. As Professor Whicher has remarked, "Liberal ideas came slowly to the Connecticut Valley." They came slowly also to Andover Theological Seminary. But slowly they came, and again undermined Calvinist orthodoxies as they had undermined orthodoxy in eighteenth-century Boston; and again they liberated a succession of New Englanders from the Westminster Confession, but they did not convert them into rationalists and Unitarians. Like Emerson, when other New Englanders were brought to ask themselves, "And what is to replace for us the piety of that race?" they preferred to bask "in the great morning which rises forever out of the eastern sea" rather than to rest content with mere liberation. "I stand here to say, Let us worship the mighty and transcendent Soul"—but not the good of mankind! Over and again the rational attack upon Calvinism served only to release energies which then sought for new forms of expression in directions entirely opposite to rationalism. Some, like Sylvester Judd, revolted against the Calvinism of the Connecticut Valley, went into Unitarianism, and then came under the spell of Emerson's transcendentalist tuition. Others, late in the century, sought out new heresies, not those of transcendentalism, but interesting parallels and analogues. Out of Andover came Harriet Beecher Stowe, lovingly but firmly underlining the emotional restrictions of Calvinism in *The Minister's Wooing* and *Oldtown Folks,* while she herself left the grim faith at last for the ritualism of the Church of England. Out of Andover also came Elizabeth Stuart Phelps in feverish revolt against the hard logic of her father and grandfather, preaching instead the emotionalism of *Gates Ajar.* In Connecticut, Horace Bushnell, reacting against the dry intellectualism of Nathaniel Taylor's Calvinism just as Margaret Fuller had reacted a decade earlier against the dry rationalism of Norton's Unitarianism, read Coleridge with an avidity equal to hers and Emerson's, and by 1849 found the answer to his religious quest, as he himself said, "after all his thought and study, not as something reasoned out, but as an inspiration—a revelation from the mind of God himself." He published the revelation in a book, the very title of which tells the whole story, *Nature and the Supernatural Together Constituting One System of God,* wherein was preached anew the immanence of God in nature: "God is the spiritual reality of which nature is the manifestation." With this publication the latest—and yet the oldest—form of New England infidelity stalked in the citadel of orthodoxy, and Calvinism itself was, as it were, transcendentalized. At Amherst, Emily Dickinson's mental climate, in the Gilded Age, was still Emerson's; the break-up of Calvinism came later there than in Boston, but when it had come the poems of Emily Dickinson were filled with "Emersonian echoes," echoes which Professor Whicher wisely declines to point out because, as he says, resemblances in Emerson, Thoreau, Parker, and Emily Dickinson are not evidences of borrowings one from another, but their common response to the spirit of the time, even though the spirit reached Emily Dickinson a little later in time than it did Emerson and Thoreau. "Their work," he says, "was in various ways a fulfillment of the finer energies of a Puritanism that was discarding the husks of dogma." From the time of Edwards to that of Emerson, the husks of Puritanism were being discarded, but the energies of many Puritans were not yet diverted—they could not be diverted— from a passionate search of the soul and of nature, from the quest to which Calvinism had devoted them. These New Englanders—a few here and there—turned aside from the doctrines of sin and predestination, and thereupon sought with renewed fervor for the accents of the Holy Ghost in their own hearts and in woods and mountains. But now that the restraining hand of theology was withdrawn, there was nothing to prevent them, as there had been everything to prevent Edwards, from identifying their intuitions with the voice of God, or from fusing God and nature into the one substance of the transcendental imagination. Mystics were no longer inhibited by dogma. They were free to carry on the ancient New England propensity for reeling and staggering with new opinions. They could give themselves over, unrestrainedly, to becoming transparent eye-balls and debauchees of dew.

Man in the Open Air

F. O. MATTHIESSEN

'We have had man indoors and under artificial relations—man in war, in love (both the natural, universal elements of human lives)—man in courts, bowers, castles, parlors—man in personal haughtiness and the tussle of war, as in Homer—or the passions, crimes, ambitions, murder, jealousy, love carried to extreme as in Shakespeare. We have been listening to divine, ravishing tales, plots inexpressibly valuable, hitherto (like the Christian religion) to temper and modify his prevalent perhaps natural ferocity and hoggishness—but never before have we had man in the open air, his attitude adjusted to the seasons and as one might describe it, adjusted to the sun by day and the stars by night.'

—WHITMAN

1. THE NEED FOR MYTHOLOGY

'We need a theory of interpretation or Mythology.'
—EMERSON's *Journal* (1835)

Where the age of Emerson may be most like our own is in its discovery of the value of myth. The starting point is in Emerson's 'History,' the opening essay in his first collection. He believed that history can be re-created only by a man for whom the present is alive. He had reached his initial premise of 'the identity of human character in all ages' as a schoolmaster of nineteen. But his example then was the conventional one: 'There is as much instruction in the tale of Troy as in the Annals of the French Revolution.' In his mature work the emphasis was to be reversed. He was still concerned with 'the universal nature which gives worth to particular men and things.' But his chief desire was to translate the Then into the Now. In the academic sense, his interest was unhistorical. He

343

was never satisfied with studying process. His belief that 'the use of history is to give value to the present hour' was a natural corollary to his conception of time: that when we come to the quality of the moment we drop duration altogether. The opening sentences of *Nature* were a protest against being history-ridden: 'Our age is retrospective. It builds the sepulchres of the fathers. It writes biographies, histories, and criticism. The foregoing generations beheld God and nature face to face; we, through their eyes. Why should not we also enjoy an original relation to the universe?'

His essay on 'History' was thus compelled by his deepest needs. The compensation of the isolated villager lay in Emerson's assurance that 'civil and natural history, the history of art and of literature, must be explained from individual history, or must remain words.' His idealism and his individualism, his religion and his politics joined when he said: 'I believe in Eternity. I can find Greece, Asia, Italy, Spain and the Islands, —the genius and creative principle of each and of all eras, in my own mind.' Yet he had, as always, the counterpoise to his extreme subjectivity. If all public facts were to be individualized, all private facts must be generalized. On the last page of his essay he declared that every history should be written in a wisdom that looks on facts as symbols. And though he gave only the shadowiest indication of an awareness of the intricate forces that had conditioned the activities of men in any epoch, he held fast to his conviction of the artist's responsibility to 'employ the symbols in use in his day and nation to convey his enlarged sense to his fellowmen.'

We recall that Emerson also found 'the cardinal fact' about Thoreau to be that he had learned to regard 'the material world as a means and symbol.' Thoreau's greater concentration carried him to explicit statement of the connections between symbol and myth. In his affirmation both of the moment and of all time, he often differed from Emerson only in his special philological twist: 'The life of a wise man is most of all extemporaneous, for he lives out of an eternity which includes all time.' He believed that mythology best expressed that eternal quality, and developed his meaning characteristically when reflecting on the beauty of some trout. He could hardly trust his senses as he stood over them, 'that these jewels should have swam away in that Aboljacknagesic water for so long, so many dark ages;—these bright fluviatile flowers, seen of Indians only, made beautiful, the Lord only knows why, to swim there! I could understand better for this, the truth of mythology, the fables of Proteus, and all those beautiful sea-monsters,—how all history, indeed, put to a terrestrial use, is mere history; but put to a celestial, is mythology always.'

He made the same distinctions even in less poetic moods. Delighted with the kinship between folk-tales of widely separated races, he took this for 'the most impressive proof of a common humanity.'[1] Moreover, he relived the process of myth-making for himself. He believed that 'as men lived in Thebes, so do they live in Dunstable to-day.' If mythology was more primitive than history, the nature that had inspired the myths was still flourishing. He could walk out into a world 'such as the old prophets and poets, Menu, Moses, Homer, Chaucer, walked in.' He felt certain that he could establish this identity between past and present, because he had seized upon the living principle of nature: 'If I am overflowing with life, am rich in experience for which I lack expression, then nature will be my language full of poetry,—all nature will *fable,* and every natural phenomenon be a myth.' When he looked at the result rather than the process, he said: 'A fact truly and absolutely stated . . . acquires a mythologic or universal significance.'

Those sentences bring us back to the chief propositions about the organic style. They reassert the fusion between the word and the thing. They suggest again how Grimm and others could arrive at mythology through the study of the origins of language. Emerson knew that 'language is fossil poetry.' Thoreau could back up that truth with a specific example. In studying a dictionary of the Abenaki tongue, he perceived how language provides an index to the primitive and hence real history of any race. 'Let us know what words they had and how they used them, and we can infer almost all the rest.' The Indians had left records there of what they had seen and felt and imagined, what they were.

Thoreau's major concern was with what men are. If symbols from the past could give expansion to life, his intense localism kept him aware that most people discern the heroic past only, that they read Plutarch but ignore John Brown. In the short essay on history that he wrote for *The Dial* and used again in his *Week,* the leading idea was: 'Critical acumen is exerted in vain to uncover the past; the *past* cannot be *presented;* we cannot know what we are not. But one veil hangs over past, present, and future, and it is the province of the historian to find out, not what was, but what is. Where a battle has been fought, you will find nothing but the bones of men and beasts; where a battle is being fought, there are hearts beating . . . Ancient history has an air of antiquity. It should be more modern.'

---

[1] After going by boat from Boston to Hull (1851), Thoreau remarked: 'I heard a boy telling the story of Nix's Mate to some girls, as we passed that spot, how "he said, 'If I am guilty, this island will remain; but if I am innocent, it will be washed away,' and now it is all washed away." This was a simple and strong expression of feeling suitable to the occasion, by which he committed the evidence of his innocence to the dumb isle, such as the boy could appreciate, a proper sailor's legend; and I was reminded that it is the illiterate and unimaginative class that seizes on and transmits the legends in which the more cultivated delight. No fastidious poet dwelling in Boston had tampered with it,—no narrow poet, but broad mankind, sailors from all ports sailing by.'

Thomas Mann has said almost the same things about myth. He has called it the mode of celebrating life whereby the moment becomes infinitely larger than itself, and the individual existence escapes from its narrow bounds and finds sanction and consecration. Writing about 'Freud and the Future,' he stated that 'life in the myth, life, so to speak, in quotation, is a kind of celebration, in that it is a making present of the past, it becomes a religious act, the performance by a celebrant of a prescribed procedure; it becomes a feast. For a feast is an anniversary, a renewal of the past in the present.' That is akin to Emerson's sense of what he could find in the Now, and celebrate as ecstasy. If the Now is eternal, the role of the prophet, the poet becomes the same in all incarnations and Emerson becomes Saadi, becomes a representative man.

Mann has found corroboration for his belief wherever he has turned, as did one of his 'past masters,' Nietzsche.[2] In his essay on Lessing, Mann set out to revitalize the meaning of 'classic' by giving it a mythical significance, because 'the essence of the myth is recurrence, timelessness, a perpetual present.' He has spoken in almost the same terms of why he has been drawn to re-create the legend of Joseph: ' "At any time": therein lies the mystery. For the mystery is timeless, but the form of timelessness is the now and here. . . . For the essence of life is presentness.' Freud has taught him that the infancy of a human being recapitulates the infancy of the race, and the myths are collective dreams. That Whitman arrived instinctively at the first of these truths is shown by the significance he could give to his own adolescent experience in such a poem as 'There was a child went forth.' Without ever formulating it into a theory, Melville illustrated the second truth in his chapter on 'Dreams' in *Mardi*, in his discovery of 'all the past and present pouring in me.'

The reasons why we have felt again to-day the need for the reinforcement of myth could take us too far afield into a diagnosis of modern culture. We have inevitably been even more burdened than Emerson's contemporaries by the accretions of another century of the historical method. To Lawrence the merely critical mind had become so desiccating that he could find his renewal only in the realms of the unconscious, and declared that the great myths 'now begin to hypnotize us again, our own impulse towards our own scientific way of understanding being almost spent.' Twenty years ago Eliot spoke of how *The Golden Bough* 'has influenced our generation profoundly.' What he discovered in anthropology is what Mann has also found, the reassertion—for an age almost overwhelmed by its sense of historical tendencies—of the basic dramatic patterns in the cyclic death and rebirth of nature and of man. In the

[2] An integral link between Emerson's conception of history and Mann's is provided by Nietzsche's view that 'Only the supreme power of the present can interpret the past . . . Otherwise men depress the past to their own level . . . The voices of the past speak in oracles; and only the master of the present and the architect of the future can hope to decipher their meaning.'

primitive and the remote Eliot first regained contact with sources of vitality deeper than his mind. But unlike Lawrence, he was not satisfied with the primitive for its own sake. The problem still remained to integrate its vitality with the complex life of the present. In the year after *The Waste Land,* Eliot wrote a short essay on '*Ulysses,* Order, and Myth': 'In using the myth, in manipulating a continuous parallel between contemporaneity and antiquity, Mr. Joyce is pursuing a method which others must pursue after him . . . It is simply a way of controlling, or ordering, of giving a shape and a significance to the immense panorama of futility and anarchy which is contemporary history.'

Even this glimpse of the myth-making faculty of our modern writers reveals a difference from Emerson's discovery of the paradox that 'always and never man is the same.' Emerson's innocent celebration of our common nature is radically unlike Mann's understanding of the disease latent everywhere in society, of man's corruptibility. Hawthorne is more like Eliot in his sense of the weight of the past, in his discernment of human traits which are constant beneath varying guises, and especially in his discovery of the lasting bond between the ages in man's capacity for suffering. His awareness of 'the haunted mind' also points towards our concern with the subconscious. But Hawthorne, alone of the five writers who have been the subject of this volume, did not conceive of his work in any relation to myth. He did not seek for universal analogies, but gained his moral profundity by remaining strictly a provincial and digging where he was. When he spoke of how 'all men must descend' into 'dark caverns . . . if they would know anything beneath the surface and illusive pleasures of existence,' he showed where his consciousness of suffering had brought him. He was at the threshold of the descent into myth, he was using almost Mann's words in the 'Prelude' to *Joseph and His Brothers.* By the very fact of not consciously intending it, Hawthorne thus furnishes a striking if oblique example of Emerson's and Thoreau's major reason for valuing myth: the way it reveals the inevitable recurrence of the elemental human patterns.

2. Representative Men

What Emerson conceived to be 'the symbols in use in his day and nation,' which he must use in turn if he was to express the meaning of its life, can be read most clearly in *Representative Men.*[3] Notwithstanding his satisfaction in his New England setting, he repeatedly declared that nature must be humanized, that its beauty 'must always seem unreal and mocking, until the landscape has human figures that are as good as

[3] Though not published until 1850, the substance of the book had first been delivered as lectures in the winter of 1845–6, and again in 1847–8.

itself.' His selection of such figures—Plato, Swedenborg, Montaigne, Shakespeare, Napoleon, Goethe—is by itself ample evidence of his freedom from any restrictions of nationalism. He knew that an American renaissance needed the encouragement of great writers and thinkers. His timelessness took for granted his country's immediate share in the whole cultural heritage.

One inevitable stimulus to the form of this book was Carlyle's *Heroes and Hero-Worship* (1841). But even before that appeared, Emerson had reached his own position that 'there is properly no history, only biography,' a position that Thoreau, in his confidence, carried to the point of saying, 'Biography, too, is liable to the same objection; it should be autobiography.' Carlyle's book was more than a stimulus: it provided the assumptions against which Emerson made a quiet but fundamental counterstatement. The difference between the titles is significant. 'Great men,' said Emerson, 'the word is injurious'; and his grounds for objection to Carlyle were both religious and social. The source of his own title was probably Swedenborg, whom he celebrated for daring to take the last and boldest step of genius, to provide a theory of interpretation for the meaning of existence. Emerson quoted triumphant evidence of this from *The Animal Kingdom:* 'In our doctrine of Representations and Correspondences we shall treat of both these symbolical and typical resemblances, and of the astonishing things which occur, I will not say in the living body only, but throughout nature, and which correspond so entirely to supreme and spiritual things that one would swear that the physical world was purely symbolical of the spiritual world.' Swedenborg's correspondences were in harmonious keeping with Emerson's belief that what made one man more representative than another was the degree to which he was a receptive channel for the superincumbent spirit. Emerson held Carlyle's greatest blemish to be his inadequate understanding of spirituality. As Henry James, Sr. phrased it: 'Moral force was the deity of Carlyle's unscrupulous worship,—the force of unprincipled, irresponsible will.' As a result he had glorified the strong men of history, in a sequence that devolved from Odin to Cromwell to Frederick of Prussia, and thus helped prepare the way for our contemporary fatal worship of force. Though Emerson did not phrase himself with James' terseness, he grew to realize the drastic importance of Carlyle's defect.

What Emerson wanted to say was that 'no individual was great, except through the general.' He could go so far as to speak of the 'inflamed individualism' that separated the man of power from the mass of his fellows. But he had not gone far enough to satisfy himself. As soon as he had sent *Representative Men* to press, he regretted that 'many after thoughts, as usual . . . come just a little too late; and my new book seems to lose all value from their omission. Plainly one is the justice that should have been done to the unexpressed greatness of the common farmer and laborer.' Thoreau had developed that same strain when writing his essay on Carlyle (1847). Balancing Thoreau's belief that history must be written as though it had happened to the writer was his equally strong conviction that if so written it would not be the history of reigns but of peoples. The trouble even with Carlyle's *French Revolution* was that there were no chapters called 'Work for the Month,' 'State of the Crops and Markets,' 'Day Labor'—'just to remind the reader that the French peasantry did something beside go without breeches, burn châteaus, get ready knotted cords, and embrace and throttle one another by turns.' In consequence of this lack, Carlyle did not speak to 'the Man of the Age, come to be called workingman.'

Thoreau thus phrased in its simplest form the theory of history that he believed must prevail in America. On the basis of such a theory Parker held Prescott's dramatic pageants to amount to no more than rhetorical *tours de force*, the product of a superficial aristocrat. In Parker's solid if somewhat naïve objections we come to the democratic core of New England transcendentalism. For Parker believed that an American historian must write in the interest of mankind, in the spirit of the nineteenth century. He must be occupied with the growth of institutions, not with glamorous spectacles. 'He must tell us of the social state of the people, the relation of the cultivator to the soil, the relation of class to class. It is well to know what songs the peasant sung; what prayers he prayed; what food he ate; what tools he wrought with; what tax he paid; how he stood connected with the soil; how he was brought to war; and what weapons armed him for the fight.'

Through this view of history Emerson's age found its myth. Whitman joined to the full in the objections to Carlyle. Though he valued the challenge of Carlyle's attack on democracy, and wrote his own *Democratic Vistas* (1871) partly as an answer to *Shooting Niagara* (1867), he believed the worship of heroes to be poisonous. He was sure that 'always waiting untold in the souls of the armies of common people, is stuff better than anything that can possibly appear in the leadership of the same.' Even when talking about Lincoln he said that 'man moves as man, in all the great achievements—man in the great mass.' Thoreau did not share Whitman's confidence in mass movements, and said that California was '3000 miles nearer to hell,' since its gold was a touchstone that had betrayed 'the rottenness, the baseness of mankind.' Yet even Thoreau could respond to the myth of the age when he looked (1851) at a panorama of the Mississippi. He saw in his imagination 'the steamboats wooding up, counted the rising cities, gazed on the fresh ruins of Nauvoo . . . I saw that this was a Rhine stream of a different kind; that . . . the famous bridges were yet to be thrown over the river; and I felt that *this was the heroic age itself*, though we know it not, for the hero is commonly the simplest and obscurest of men.'

Emerson penetrated to the heart of this myth in his conception (1846) of 'the central man' the creative source of all vitality. He imagined himself in talk with him, and that the voice of the central man was that of Socrates. 'Then the discourse changes, and the man, and we see the face and hear the tones of Shakespeare . . . A change again, and the countenance of our companion is youthful and beardless, he talks of form and color and the riches of design; it is the face of the painter Raffaelle.' Next it is Michel Angelo, then Dante, afterwards Jesus: 'And so it appears that these great secular personalities were only expressions of his face chasing each other like the rack of clouds.' The Orphic poet who spoke at the end of *Nature* had voiced a kindred parable of the continual renewal of man's heroic energy. Emerson felt that in *Representative Men* he had only managed to suggest this under a few shadowy guises. Looking back at this book a dozen years later, he said that he had sensed when writing it that Jesus was the 'Representative Man' whom he ought to sketch, but that he had not felt equal to the task. What he might have tried to present is suggested by a few sentences in his journal several years before (1842): 'The history of Christ is the best document of the power of Character which we have. A youth who owed nothing to fortune and who was "hanged at Tyburn,"—by the pure quality of his nature has shed this epic splendor around the facts of his death which has transfigured every particular into a grand universal symbol for the eyes of all mankind ever since.' That is similar to Melville's conception of democratic tragedy, and also to what Hawthorne had perceived in Sodoma's picture of Christ bound to a pillar—the union of suffering and majesty. But it is unlikely that Emerson would have concentrated long on the tragic aspect. Even in his journal he went on to say, 'This was a great Defeat; we demanded Victory,' and to insist on the mind's conquest of Fate.

Where he was at his best in *Representative Men* was in translating Plato into Concord, in giving a portrait of Socrates as a 'plain old uncle . . . with his great ears, an immense talker,' 'what our country-people call *an old one.*' Emerson's concern in this book with man's common nature also gave him an insight into the value of tradition that we would hardly expect from him. Elsewhere, as in 'Self-Reliance,' he often said, 'Where is the master who could have taught Shakespeare? . . . Every great man is a unique.' But here he saw that 'the rude warm blood of the living England circulated in the play, as in street-ballads.' He went even farther and declared: 'What is best written or done by genius in the world, was no man's work, but came by wide social labor, when a thousand wrought like one, sharing the same impulse.' Unhappily Emerson, as we have seen, could not make much out of that perception. The 'genius of humanity' that he announced to be his real subject could become very amorphous, most devastatingly so in his vague treatment of his modern figures, Napoleon and Goethe. It was no accident that his passage on the different incarnations of 'the central man' ended with these sentences: 'Then all will subside, and I find myself alone. I dreamed and did not know my dreams.'

. . . .

4. FULL CIRCLE

'Make-belief is an enervating exercise of fancy not to be confused with imaginative growth. The saner and greater mythologies are not fancies; they are the utterance of the whole soul of man and, as such, inexhaustible to meditation. They are no amusement or diversion to be sought as a relaxation and an escape from the hard realities of life. They are these hard realities in projection, their symbolic recognition, co-ordination and acceptance. Through such mythologies our will is collected, our powers unified, our growth controlled. Through them the infinitely divergent strayings of our being are brought into "balance or reconciliation." The "opposite and discordant qualities" of things in them acquire a form; and such integrity as we possess as "civilized" men is our inheritance through them. Without his mythologies man is only a cruel animal without a soul—for a soul is a central part of his governing mythology—he is a congeries of possibilities without order and without aim.'

—RICHARDS, *Coleridge on Imagination*

Thoreau's ability to create myth ran on a deeper level than his amused fancies about Franklin. Those fancies were the instinctive product of his sense of the age's plenitude. He would have liked Mann's description of myth as 'the holiday garment,' 'the recurrent feast which bestrides the tenses and makes the has-been and the to-be present to the popular sense.' Thoreau's own superabundant life let him find a river god in a logger on the Penobscot, it let him read in Homer about 'such a fire-eyed Agamemnon as you may see at town meetings.' He was following there one of Emerson's most fruitful leads. The birth of a first son (1836) had given Emerson's life at Concord its final consecration. He felt that he had at last reached the solidity of life's fundamental pattern: 'A wife, a babe, a brother, poverty, and a country, which the Greek had, I have.' Emerson continued these thoughts in a passage that he later incorporated into 'History': 'Our admiration of the Antique is not admiration of the old, but of the natural. We admire the Greek in an American ploughboy often.' Thoreau might have said that, but there turned out to be this crucial distinction: there was a great deal of admiration of the antique in Thoreau's practice, in the precision and toughness of language that the Greeks and Romans had taught him to be his goal. Emerson's heart, as Santayana has said, 'was fixed on eternal things,' his Now was that of the metaphysicians, and—despite his earnest desire that it should be otherwise—had very little relation to an actual present or past. Thoreau possessed more of the past, not through his mind, but as an experienced linguistic discipline. Therefore he inevitably possessed a more concrete present as well.

He re-created a basic myth because he was able to assimilate his conscious analogies into re-enacting what Emerson had perceived but could not put his muscle into, the union of work and culture. As Odell Shepard has discerned, 'This man who read his Homer in a hut by a woodland lake can show us better, perhaps, than any other teacher we have yet had how to coordinate whatever is peculiarly American with the tradition of the ages.' The day after Thoreau had settled by Walden he felt that he had found 'the very light and atmosphere in which the works of Grecian art were composed, and in which they rest.' He was glad on summer nights to sit on the shore of his Ithaca, 'a fellow-wanderer and survivor of Ulysses.' But the reason why his allusions did not become merely literary, the reason why he accomplished his rare coordination, lies in the way he reacted to his reading. Cato's *De Re Rustica* did not remain quaint for him. He described it thus (1851): 'A small treatise or Farmer's Manual of those days, fresh from the field of Roman life, all reeking with and redolent of the life of those days, containing more indirect history than any of the histories of Rome of direct,—all of that time but that time,— *here* is a simple, direct pertinent word addressed to the Romans. And where are *the Romans?*" Thoreau's answer was that the Romans are ordinarily 'an ornament of rhetoric,' but that 'we have here their *New England Farmer*, the very manual those Roman farmers read . . . as fresh as a dripping dish-cloth from a Roman kitchen.' It was as if he read the letters of Solon Robinson, and how much was paid to Joe Farrar 'for work done.'

Thoreau thus became an actor in the great cyclic drama, but did not give up his New England accent. He had not perceived more than Emerson of the New England character. For Emerson had caught its essence when observing the struggle between 'sage and savage' in Ezra Ripley (1834): 'These old semi-savages do from the solitude in which they live and their remoteness from artificial society and their inevitable daily comparing man with beast, village with wilderness, their inevitable acquaintance with the outward nature of man, and with his strict dependence on sun and rain and wind and frost, wood, worm, cow and bird, get an education to the Homeric simplicity, which all the libraries of the Reviews and the Commentators in Boston do not countervail.' Thoreau had the immeasurable benefit of such thought from the day he listened to *The American Scholar*. He could give it sturdier expression. His words ring with the authority of having experienced both halves of his comparison when he says that Minott tells his long stories with the same satisfaction in the details as Herodotus. In his sympathy with the seasons as well as with the farmers' often grim effort to wrest subsistence from them, Thoreau learned that 'the perennial mind' did not die with Cato, 'and will not die with Hosmer.' This mind was nothing rarefied; it was an integral part of the functioning of the human organism. What interested Thoreau most in literature was the expression of this mind, the insight it gave into collective existence: 'it is the spirit of humanity, that which animates both so-called savages and civilized nations, working through a man, and not the man expressing himself.' Thoreau had come to that fundamental understanding while studying the Indians, just as Mann came to it at the close of his essay on Dürer, in whose deep humanity he had found 'history as myth, history that is ever fresh and ever present. For we are much less individuals than we either hope or fear to be.'

Thoreau's accent is no less that of a New Englander for betraying an awareness of both the Romans and the Indians. Living in an age of waning Christianity, he became convinced that there was no important difference between his countrymen's religion and that of the ancient world: 'The New Englander is a pagan suckled in a creed outworn.' Thoreau's light-hearted worship of Pan set the tone for his *Week*. But much of his praise of Jupiter in place of Jehovah was designed simply to shock, and some of it is merely frivolous, gaining its license from the accepted fact of the Christian background. He struck his most autochthonous vein when he noted the difference between English and American time, how here he could penetrate almost immediately to a savage past. He was not a savage himself, more the villager than the hunter, but he felt in his world no unbridgeable gap between these roles. His sense of closeness to the Indian strengthened his hold on the primitive, and kept him from writing Victorian idylls. He was most nearly an antique Roman when he said: 'Superstition has always reigned. It is absurd to think that these farmers, dressed in their Sunday clothes, proceeding to church, differ essentially in this respect from the Roman peasantry. They have merely changed the names and number of their gods. Men were as good then as they are now, and loved one another as much—or little.'

The source of vigor in Thoreau's New England festival was his knowledge that 'the husbandman is always a better Greek than the scholar is prepared to appreciate.' The old customs still survive, even while antiquarians grow gray in commemorating their past existence. 'The farmers crowd to the fair to-day in obedience to the same ancient law, which Solon or Lycurgus did not enact, as naturally as bees swarm and follow their queen.' Thoreau's quality there, as we have found it in *Walden*, is more cultivated than wild. It is more lyric and pastoral than heroic, though this, like the question of whether he belonged to the village or to the forest or to the borderline between, is simply a matter of degree. He saw the classical present in his own surroundings just as Sarah Jewett was to do when she envisaged the Bowden family reunion in its procession across the field to the picnic grove as though it was a company of ancient Greeks going to worship the god of the harvests: 'We were no more a New England family celebrating its own existence and simple progress; we carried the tokens and inheritance of all such households from which this had descended, and were only the latest of our line.' Unlike Thoreau's, Miss Jewett's tone is generally elegiac. Robert Frost has more of Thoreau's dramatic immediacy, but since the forests have now receded and the cities have encroached on the farms, Frost's scope as a poet of nature has inevitably been contracted to the more purely personal.

The heroic quality is absent from *North of Boston,* if by that quality you mean what Thoreau could sense in Whitman, that he was 'something a little more than human.' Thoreau was not blind to the element of brag, but when he called on Whitman in Brooklyn (1856), he felt at once, 'He is apparently the greatest democrat the world has ever seen.' It is hardly necessary to dwell on Whitman's creation of myth, since it is so explicit throughout the whole breadth of his work. He looked at the past in a more reckless mood than Thoreau: 'As if the beauty and sacredness of the demonstrable must fall behind that of the mythical! As if men do not make their mark out of any times! As if the opening of the western continent by discovery and what has transpired since in North and South America were less than the small theatre of the antique or the aimless sleepwalking of the middle ages!' That was the opening blast of his 1855 preface, though he presently added:

> In the name of the States shall I scorn the antique?
> Why these are the children of the antique to justify it.

Whitman set out more deliberately than any of his contemporaries to create the kind of hero whom Emerson had foreshadowed in his varying guises of the Scholar and the Poet. Looking back over his career in his final preface, he said that *Leaves of Grass* had been impelled by his desire to realize his own personality, both physical and spiritual, in the midst of its momentous surroundings, 'to exploit that Personality, identified with place and date, in a far more candid and comprehensive sense than any hitherto poem or book.' He had said long before, 'I have but one central figure, the general human personality typified in myself.' He had felt from the time of his first *Leaves* that if his book was to be true to its American origin, it must be 'a song of "the great pride of man in himself."' What saved Whitman from the last extreme of egotism was his insistence on the typical and his boundless store of fellow-feeling. His one quarrel with Thoreau was his 'disdain for men (for Tom, Dick, and Harry): inability to appreciate the average.'[4] If the poet had discovered

---

[4] The difference between their temperaments could hardly have been revealed more characteristically than in their first meeting. Thoreau reported: 'I did not get far in conversation with him,—two more being present,—and among the few things which I chanced to say, I remember that one was, in answer to him as representing America, that I did not think much of America or of politics, and so on, which may have been somewhat of a damper to him.' Years later Whitman generalized: Thoreau 'couldn't put his life into any other life—realize why one man was so and another man not so: was impatient with other people on the street and so forth . . . We could not agree at all in our estimate of men—of the men we met here, there, everywhere—the concrete man. Thoreau had an abstraction about man—a right abstraction: there we agreed.'

himself to be at the creative center of life, with all its potential energies radiating out from him, this discovery was the property of all. Whitman wanted his book to compel 'every reader to transpose himself or herself into the central position, and become the living fountain.' He took his final pleasure in reflecting: 'I have imagined a life which should be that of the average man in average circumstances, and still grand, heroic.'

His work inevitably assumed cosmic proportions. He said that from the press of his foot to the earth sprang 'a hundred affections' that eluded his best efforts to describe them. But the language of his poems does not suggest contact with the soil so much as with the streets of Brooklyn. When he thought of the past, his instinctive analogy was:

> Lads ahold of fire-engines and hook-and-ladder ropes no less to me than the gods of the antique wars.

When he envisaged his 'stock personality' in its most godlike stature, he made it come to life by breaking into slang:

> Earth! you seem to look for something at my hands,
> Say, old top-knot, what do you want?

Otherwise his cult of himself as the bearded prophet could lead into pages of solemn straining for effect. The dichotomy that we observed in both his diction and his content expresses itself again in the contrast between Whitman's actual and ideal selves. Tocqueville foresaw his problem when he observed that the poet of democracy, having given up the past, thus ran the risk of losing part of the present in his excessive preoccupation with the future destinies of mankind. Lawrence's distinction between the poetry of the future and the poetry of the present is likewise partly relevant. Lawrence held that the first may possess the crystalized perfection of things to come, whereas the second, lacking this, seeks to catch the present in all its confusion, and is 'plasmic.' Whitman possessed none of the power of thought or form that would have been necessary to give his poems of ideal democracy any perfection, and to keep them from the barrenness of abstraction. He created his lasting image of the common man and 'the pending action of this Time and Land we swim in' when he remained the instinctual being who found no sweeter fat than stuck to his own bones.

He was never conscious of the dichotomy, but he described its consequences in his surprised and hesitant admission as an old man that Thoreau, though not 'so precious, tender, a personality' as Emerson, was 'one of the native forces' and so possibly 'bigger.' The heroic stature that Whitman recognized in Thoreau was the result of Thoreau's having lived up to his own dictum that 'it is the faculty of the poet to see present things as if . . . also past and future, as if distant or universally significant.' By so doing Thoreau made actual the classical present instead of merely perceiving it like Emerson. Whitman had neither Thoreau's lucidity nor firmness. By cutting himself loose from any past, he often went billowing away into a dream of perfectibility, which tried to make the human literally divine and was hence unreal. But because he was more porous to all kinds of experience, he gave a more comprehensive, if confused, image of his fluid age than Thoreau did.

The cult of perfection was an inevitable concomitant of the romantic cult of the future. The attitude behind both received its most searching contemporary analysis from Hawthorne. He sensed that Emerson's exaltation of the divinity in man had obliterated the distinctions between man and God, between time and eternity. Although no theologian, Hawthorne did not relax his grip on the Christian conception of time. This had been obscured by Thoreau and Whitman no less than by Emerson in their exhilaration over the fullness of the moment. Hawthorne knew that he lived both in time and out of it, that the process of man's history was a deep interaction between eternity and time, an incessant eruption of eternity into time. And he knew the tragic nature of such conflict. In spite of the capacity of man's soul to share immediately in eternal life, his finite and limited nature made it inevitable that nothing perfect could be realized in time.[5] Hawthorne's understanding of human destiny ran counter to all the doctrines of progress. It made him cling fast to the quality of actual existence even though he was aware of its impermanence; it made him insist that 'all philosophy that would abstract man from the present is no more than words.' It made him profoundly conscious that the moments of greatest human import were the moments of moral crisis, for then men and women entered most nearly into the eternal nature even as they were aware of their limitations.

Such a reading of destiny came to Hawthorne through his resistence to what he could not deem otherwise than transcendental fads. It enabled him to criticize, in *The Blithedale Romance,* one phase of the contemporary myth, the quest for Utopia. However inadequately worked out some of his social criticism may be, there is no questioning the acuity with which he saw the weaknesses of Brook Farm. He could not help feeling that its spirit was essentially that of a picnic, of an escape to a woodland paradise. As he watched the community's competition with the outside market-gardeners, he soon realized that with relation to 'society at large, we stood in a position of new hostility, rather than new brotherhood.' These views might well have seemed captious to George Ripley, who

---

[5] Our present awareness of this strain of thought has been increased by the rediscovery of Kierkegaard, and by Karl Barth's 'theology of crisis.'

gave his heart's blood to prove that such experiments could lead the way to a more just organization of society as a whole. Where Hawthorne's criticism runs no risk of being obscurantistic is in his portrait of Hollingsworth, man the reformer. There Hawthorne could make articulate his understanding of what happened when a man failed to distinguish between time and eternity, between his fallibility and his longing for the ideal. Hollingsworth was desperately earnest in his scheme for reforming criminals 'through an appeal to their higher instincts,' but he had no faint inkling of the complexity of man's nature. He was warped by his single thought, to which he would brook no opposition, and was interested in other people only to the extent that they accepted his plan. He became an incarnation of the terrible egotism that mistakes its own will for the promptings of God.

Emerson had more opportunity to study reformers than Hawthorne, since they were always swarming around him, but he never saw the problem they presented with such deadly lucidity. He found many of them bores, but he was partial to their trust in uplift, and relied on compensation to atone for their want of balance. When Thoreau and Whitman thought of a reformer, they, like Emerson, remembered the heroic affirmation of John Brown, of whom Hawthorne said: "Nobody was ever more justly hanged. He won his martyrdom fairly and took it firmly.' But both Whitman and Thoreau could have learned something from the example of Hollingsworth. Their images of the rising common man are far more compelling than anything Hawthorne conceived through Holgrave. But Whitman's belief in the poet as his own Messiah escaped Hollingsworth's tragedy only by the counterpoise of his generous warmth. And although Thoreau evaded the literal-minded apostles of improvement, his weakest element lay in the possible perfection he demanded from mankind. ('I love my friends very much, but I find that it is no use to go to see them. I hate them commonly when I am near them.') So far as there was a defect in his valiant self-reliance, it emerged when he turned his back on other men, and sought for truth not in the great and common world but exclusively within himself.

What Hawthorne found through his descent into the caverns of the heart was the general bond of suffering. His discovery gave Melville his only clue through the labyrinth of the age's confusions. He plunged deeper into the blackness than Hawthorne had, and needed more complex images to express his findings. He developed one by likening Ahab's buried life, 'his whole awful essence,' to the mystic grandeur of an ancient statue far beneath the modern surface of existence. The primitive spoke to Melville with different meanings than it did to Thoreau. He might joke about Hercules as an antique Crockett, but he did not so often think of the presentness of the past as of the pastness of the present, of its illimitable shadowy extensions backward to the roots of history, to the preconscious and the unknown. 'Ten million things were as yet uncovered to Pierre. The old mummy lies buried in cloth on cloth; it takes time to unwrap this Egyptian king. Yet now, forsooth, because Pierre began to see through the first superficiality of the world, he fondly weens he has come to the unlayered substance. But, far as any geologist has yet gone down into the world, it is found to consist of nothing but surface stratified on surface. To its axis, the world being nothing but superinduced superficies.' That is akin to Mann's reflection on the bottomless well of the past, on the incertitude of the researcher as he lets down his plummet into unfathomable depths. But the author of *Pierre* did not possess Mann's humanistic patience. He had become identified with his hero's agony: 'By vast pains we mine into the pyramid; by horrible gropings we come to the central room; with joy we espy the sarcophagus; but we lift the lid—and no body is there! appallingly vacant as vast is the soul of a man!'

Such a mood could lead only to nihilism. But the passion with which Melville made his demands upon life had given him previously an instinctive awareness of the significance of myth. He had commented in *Moby-Dick* on the loss of poetic mythology 'in the now egotistical sky.' He had sensed the primal vitality of the stories that are preserved in the popular memory, and that help keep alive the hidden strivings of the human spirit by giving them concrete shape. He had sensed too the destructive quality of the enlightened mind if by its criticism it served merely to divorce man from his past by dispelling the reality of the myths, by reducing them to a remote and naïve stage of racial development. Though Melville did not articulate his theory of history, he affirmed its values by finding figures of tragic stature on board a whaler, and in Ahab all the majesty of a Biblical king. Melville knew that beyond the bright circle of man's educated consciousness lay unsuspected energies that were both magnificent and terrifying. He wanted to rouse his country to its 'contemporary grandeur.' His detailed recording of the whaling industry sprang from his comprehension that the living facts of ordinary existence were the source of whatever heroic myths Americans could live by.

His choice of material was hardly thus deliberate, but by taking the segment of human activity that he knew best, he re-enacted through it the major significances of myth. He had been attracted to whaling as the great adventure of his day, around which had clustered such widely current legends as the one Emerson had reported in his journal (1834) after a trip from New Bedford to Boston: 'A seaman in the coach told the story of an old sperm-whale, which he called a white whale, which was known for many years by the whalemen as Old Tom, and who rushed upon the boats which attacked him, and crushed the boats to small chips in his jaws, the men generally escaping by jumping overboard and being picked up. A vessel was fitted out at New Bedford, he said, to take him. And he was finally taken somewhere off Payta Head by the *Winslow* or the *Essex*.' That was the subject for an adventure story, but the way Melville transformed his version shows the principal function of myth, its symbolizing of the fundamental truths. In his narrative of whaling Melville could see how this industry typified man's wresting a livelihood from nature and extending his power over the globe by peaceful commerce rather than by war. He could trustingly visualize the whale ship as a means of communication, battering down ancient prejudices, opening doors in the Orient, even, as we have noted, leading the way to the liberation of South America from autocratic domination and to the establishment 'of the eternal democracy' there.

But that was scarcely Melville's main theme. The dark half of his mind remembered what effect the white man had left on the South Sea islands; and as he meditated too on the brutal savagery in the conquest of the whale, his imagination stirred to the latent possibilities in the story Emerson had heard. He grasped intuitively the process that Whitehead has described: 'We inherit legends, weird, horrible, beautiful, expressing in curious, specialized ways the interweaving of law and capriciousness in the mystery of things. It is the problem of good and evil. Sometimes the law is good and the capriciousness evil; sometimes the law is iron and evil and the capriciousness is merciful and good.' Melville could not say directly whether the law was good or evil. He had been born into a world whose traditional religion was in a state of decay, and whose grim Jehovah often struck him as being only the projection of man's inexorable will to power. But as Melville responded to the Christian belief in equality and brotherhood, he poured out his praise to 'the great God absolute, the centre and circumference of all democracy.'

Melville did not achieve in *Moby-Dick* a *Paradise Lost* or a *Faust*. The search for the meaning of life that could be symbolized through the struggle between Ahab and the White Whale was neither so lucid nor so universal. But he did apprehend therein the tragedy of extreme individualism, the disasters of the selfish will, the agony of a spirit so walled within itself that it seemed cut off from any possibility of salvation. Beyond that, his theme of the White Whale was so ambivalent that as he probed into the meaning of good and evil he found their expected values shifting. His symbols were most comprehensive when they enabled him to elicit 'what remains primeval in our formalized humanity,' when they took such a basic pattern as that of his later discernment of Abraham and Isaac in Captain Vere and Billy. When the Pacific called out the response of his united body and mind, he wrote the enduring signature of his age. He gave full expression to its abundance, to its energetic desire to master history by repossessing all the resources of the hidden past in a timeless and heroic present. But he did not avoid the darkness in that past, the perpetual suffering in the heart of man, the broken arc of his career which inevitably ends in death. He thus fulfilled what Coleridge held to be the major function of the artist: he brought 'the whole soul of man into activity.'

The Unbroken Tradition

LESLIE FIEDLER

If the contemporary American poet must be understood in terms of his difficult and ambiguous relationship with the great audience, created by the dream of democracy and the fact of mass culture, he must also be understood in terms of his equally difficult and ambiguous relationship with the great tradition, impugned by the same dream of democracy and the same fact of mass culture. When Walt Whitman cries out, in his "Song of the Exposition":

> Come, Muse, migrate from Greece and Ionia,
> Cross out please those immensely overpaid accounts,
> That matter of Troy and Achilles' wrath, and Aneas',
> Odysseus' wandering,
> Place 'Removed' and 'To let' on the rocks of your snowy
> Parnassus,
> Repeat at Jerusalem . . .
> The same on the walls of your German, French and
> Spanish castles . . .

he is echoing, as befits a poet who has chosen to play the impossible role of popular spokesman, the contempt for the remote classical past and the distrust of a more recent European one that move the American mass audience in its insecurity and pride. To be sure, he is also echoing certain European aspirations, accepting the Romantic image of America and reflecting a tradition of anti-tradition already invented in the shadow of "German, French and Spanish castles." But his *posture*, at least, signifies a resolution to reject the artistocratic past in favor of a democratic future.

Here once more posture answers posture, and Poe assumes the anti-Whitmanian role: setting his poems against backgrounds vaguely Italian or German or English, anything but native American, and affecting

361

through allusion and quotation (often superficial or faked) the manner of one at home among old books and alien tongues, mouldering dungeons and mossgrown graveyards. In Poe and Whitman alike, however, in the unacknowledged borrowings of the one and the ostentatious references of the other, old-world models seem more parodied than emulated; as if in each, equal though opposite ambiguities undercut piety, turning *imitatio* to travesty. The absurdity of Whitman's attempt to dignify his diction with pseudo-borrowings from foreign tongues is well known, and there is scarcely an undergraduate in America who has not been taught to smile a little at his fondness for the non-existent word "camerados." But Poe is equally ridiculous when he affects the style of certain inferior English historical romances in "Lenore":

> And, Guy de Vere, hast *thou* no ear?—weep now or nevermore
> See! on yon drear and rigid bier low lies thy love, Lenore!

It is not entirely fortuitous, after all, that the only poet writing in English who succeeded in imitating Poe's rhythm and diction with real faithfulness is that composer of nonsense verse for children, Edward Lear. From Poe's "dank tarn of Auber" and "misty mid-region of Weir" to Lear's "Hills of Chankley Bore" is a shorter distance than any of us find it convenient or comfortable to remember.

So, too, Longfellow, when he makes his very American attempt in *Hiawatha* to adapt the meter of Finnish epic to the matter of Indian life, produces the most easily and most often parodied poem in our language. Our main poetic tradition, in all of its various lines of development, can, then, be described as essentially, if sometimes unintentionally, comic or burlesque; and it is never funnier than when it seeks to emulate European models of greater or lesser antiquity. This fact, still largely unacknowledged in classrooms, the early Eliot (before respectability overtook him) and the early Pound (before madness undid him) brought to full consciousness in a series of anti-poems which have given our age its special American savor. Mock-epic is, of course, their chosen form, and satire their mode; but the device they make most their own is the travesty-allusion: the simultaneous evocation and parody of great verses out of the past. The reader remembering at the moment he reads in Eliot's *The Waste Land:*

> When lovely woman stoops to folly and
> Paces about her room again, alone,
> She smoothes her hair with automatic hand,
> And puts a record on the gramophone.

the lovely lines of Goldsmith to which they allude (or is guided to those lines by Eliot's mock-serious footnote, "V. Goldsmith, the song in *The*

Vicar of Wakefield"), finally is unsure what is being mocked: Goldsmith, our relationship to him, us, or the poet himself? Perhaps it is really the poet, vainly attempting to hold onto a no-longer-viable tradition by means of pedantry and travesty and frustrated love. Certainly, in the great gallery of comic characters created by Eliot—Prufrock and Sweeney and Bleistein and Doris—it is the Old Possum himself who is least forgettable:

> How unpleasant to meet Mr. Eliot!
> With his features of clerical cut,
> And his brow so grim
> And his mouth so prim . . .

Yet no one has written more earnestly, and, after a while, more solemnly, about the "Tradition" and our need to attach ourselves to it than this same Mr. Eliot. Indeed, with the help of Ezra Pound, he has created a canon of works out of the past to which he has ceaselessly urged us to commit ourselves, presumably at the same moment that we embrace Anglo-Catholicism and even, perhaps, a more-or-less-synthetic British citizenship. What we are likely to overlook is the fact that his canon is home-made and—though studded with European writers—therefore peculiarly American, made in the U.S.A. at least. There is, that is to say, no desire on the part of Eliot and Pound to go back to the tradition so rousingly disavowed by Walt Whitman; for, whatever Eliot may say outside of his poetry, he knows that Americans must begin by recognizing their exclusion from the *organic* cultural community once the common heritage of all Europe. Our choice is always between living in a theoretical non-tradition made for us by Europe or in a synthetic European tradition of our own fabrication. In this sense, the effort of Pound and Eliot is a little like that of Longfellow in his raids on a score of literatures from Finland to Spain; nor is it very different from such attempts at synthesizing culture as last century's Harvard Twelve Foot Shelf of Books or this century's Hundred Great Books and Syntopicon as contrived at the University of Chicago. We may even be reminded of those contests, held annually in the provincial colleges of America, in which a prize is awarded for the best "new tradition" suggested by a student.

In any such contest, the "new tradition" of Eliot and Pound, with its demotion of Milton and Shelley, and its elevation of Donne, its snide devaluation of Goethe and its overt attack on Hugo, its apotheosis of Dante and its beatification of Guido Cavalcanti and Arnaut Daniel, would surely take the prize. In fact, it *has* been awarded the accolade of academic acceptance and is now embodied in a hundred textbooks and "taught" in ten thousand classes. Oddly enough, or perhaps not so oddly, at the moment when American literature enters the world scene, it has been accepted in some parts of Europe itself, and controls the assumptions of poets like, say, Eugenio Montale and Odysseus Elytis, and of the critics who admire them. Nonetheless, it is important to remember that the essential shape and direction of American poetry had been established by the middle of the nineteenth century, and that, far from radically altering this shape and direction, the "new canon" of Eliot and Pound is itself influenced by them.

No one writing poetry in the United States today, of course, can feel himself separate from an international movement whose boundaries cannot even be confined to what is at the moment called politically the West; nor can what has happened to American verse from, say, 1912 to the present moment, be understood unless one has taken into account the impact of French *symboliste* verse of the last century, Italian and Provençal verse of the late Middle Ages, the Japanese *Noh* play, and the short poems of Bassho, English religious poetry of the seventeenth century, and so on. Such influences have, however, been more than adequately treated in the most recent past, and offer now the rewards of scholarship rather than those of critical understanding. What needs to be emphasized is rather the sense in which American poetry has been *continuous* for the last one hundred years.

It is convenient, in attempting to make clear the nature of the continuity of American poetry, to speak of four lines of descent in our verse: the line of Longfellow, the line of Poe, the line of Whitman, and the line of Emerson. More commonly, critics speak of two only, that of Poe and that of Whitman, though sometimes they will cross generic or national boundaries and speak of Henry James or Baudelaire, rather than Poe, as the ideal anti-Whitmanian figure. Behind the twofold classification, there is always some myth of conflict, some legendary classification of the one as good, the other as evil. To V. L. Parrington, for instance, Whitman was the hero and Poe the villain; while, at a later date and under other pressures, critics like Yvor Winters or R. P. Blackmur reversed the labels, Blackmur insisting that "the influence of Whitman was an impediment to the *practice* of poetry, and that the influence of Baudelaire [he might equally as well have said Poe] is a re-animation itself." Whatever the original justification for such a twofold division, it has long worn out the pedagogical uses it may once have had, and must yield to another analysis, more firmly based in literary history and critical discrimination.

For many decades now, we have simply not spoken of Longfellow in attempting to come to terms with contemporary verse, since his influence has seemed to us neither good nor bad, just non-existent. Yet, ceasing to function as high literature, his poems have assumed another kind of life, blending into the body of sub-literature which represents the nearest thing to a common culture we possess: the culture of grade-school children. Such poems as "The Children's Hour" and "The Village Blacksmith" have a status otherwise reserved for the lyrics of long-popular songs: "Home, Sweet Home," "The Old Oaken Bucket," "Way Down upon the Swanee River," or such occasional, semi-ritual poems as "The Night Before Christmas." The authors of such songs and verses are, however, almost inevitably forgotten, though their compositions survive in the popular mind, while Longfellow is, for precisely that mind, the typical poet. Indeed, he is for many semi-literate Americans the sole poet, besides Shakespeare (whom they are likely to think of as a playwright, anyhow), whom they know by name. Puns on his eminently punnable last name can be made in jokes for third-grade children, to whom parodies of his verses are also recognizable, needing no scholarly apparatus of the kind provided by Eliot for his more recondite rewritings of Goldsmith or Baudelaire.

By the same token, however, Longfellow provides a model to advanced poets of what they must define their poetry *against*, and they are haunted by his bearded presence, the patriarchal face which once hung over their desks in classrooms where their fellows learned to hate all verse. Whenever they turn from nostalgic and evocative parody to brutal satire and burlesque, mocking popular culture at the point where it becomes bestselling poetry, they are likely to be thinking of Henry Wadsworth Longfellow. When Auden, for instance, comments ironically on overdomesticated verse ("each homely lyric thing/ On sport or spousal love or spring/ Or dogs or dusters . . . "), or E. E. Cummings travesties the cultural aspirations of Americans abroad ("O to be a metope/ now that triglyph's here"), or Robert Frost parodies didacticism with an appallingly straight face ("Better to go down dignified/ With boughten friendship at your side/ Than none at all. Provide; provide!"), each may have quite other specific anti-poets in mind; yet the total effect is of an attack on Longfellow.

Other countries have had their own best-selling poets, dispensing culture and good advice. This we know (yet we cannot help feeling that we would have been better off with Victor Hugo or Tennyson). And we know, too, that none of the other founders of the main lines of American verse managed to die without leaving behind a contribution to popular sub-poetry. With uncanny accuracy of judgment, the mass audience has found them out, and does not forget Poe's "Raven," Whitman's "O Captain, My Captain," or Emerson's "Concord Hymn." A single slip is enough; the lonely error is canonized in the collections of anti-literature which serve as children's anthologies, and the great audience is revenged on the poet who has despised it. With Longfellow, however, it is not merely a matter of a poem or two on the level of debased taste, but of many scattered through a lifetime of providing the more educated, genteel, and securely Anglo-Saxon segments of the American middle class with lucid, simple, musical, sentimental, pious, often trite reassurances that the values of their class and race were not only universal, but would survive eternally.

Life is real, life is earnest,
And the grave is not its goal.

Dust thou art, to dust returnest,
Was not spoken of the soul.

It is his good poems which are irrelevant, as we must remember at the same moment we grant that he has written them. In recent years, he has found some learned and even sensitive defenders, and it is true, as they assert, that he has written subtle and moving verse, that especially in his Dantesque moments he possesses a genuine dignity and passion. But, alas, his artistic successes somehow do not count! The Longfellow who really survives is the one who has never died, but who is re-embodied year after year in volumes of poems published at their own expense by widowed grandmothers or spinster aunts. It is not merely that he is banal or even Philistine, but that he is an "American" in a sense which had ceased, by the time he died, to move living writers: an Anglo-Saxon American comfortably at home, rather than an alienated American, a melting-pot American, a frontier American, or an expatriate American. Despite all his concern with European literature, he was for this very reason as unsympathetic to avant-garde Europeans as to the serious poets of his own land, and, unlike the other major lines of American verse, that which is derived from his example has been unable to influence or to be subsumed into the international modern style.

Certainly the line of Poe has fared much differently. He has, notoriously, influenced no adult twentieth-century American poet directly, yet his *presence* has haunted many, his ghost, for instance, inhabiting the very center of the American Hades imagined by Hart Crane in *The Bridge*. And scarcely anyone interested in verse has not, in his early adolescence, tried to write in the style of Poe; for adolescence is Poe's true homeland, the imaginary country out of space and in time of which he was, throughout his short life, a secret but loyal citizen. Grown-up Americans, however, have found it difficult to come to terms with Poe, except as re-interpreted by his great French admirers, Baudelaire and Mallarmé. He is at once too banal and too unique, too decadent and too revolutionary, too vulgar and too subtle, all of which is to say, too American, for us to bear except as reflected in the observing eye of Europe. And he is, further, the inventor of what was to become, by the twentieth century, a true international style—though it remained in his hands merely a synthetic non-rational one, learned, allusive, at ease with no mythology but acquainted with many:

Thy Naiad airs have brought me home
    To the glory that was Greece
And the grandeur that was Rome . . .

> Ah, Psyche, from the regions which
> Are Holy-Land!

The act which makes Poe a poet, which commits him to his muse is, then, an act of disengagement from the myth of America. Certainly, no poet who works in the tradition derived from his is aggressively patriotic, for the quarrel out of which he makes his poetry is inevitably the quarrel with his own country, and followers of Poe typically became expatriates —especially after World War I taught them the way to Europe. Before that time, their recourse was to total detachment from all the world they knew, and beyond which they could imagine no other, a flight to insanity based on the belief that there was no alternate way out of America. Indeed, the ultimate expatriation of madness seemed often to Poe identical with the most exquisite achievement of art, and he distinguishes scarcely at all between the poet, the aristocrat of the spirit, and the madman.

There is a politics of madness as well as an esthetics, and Poe subscribes to both. His ideal poet is an anti-democrat, too sensitive and refined to accept anything sponsored by the majority, including those norms of reality by which sanity is customarily judged. But syntax, logic, the act of predication itself, are concessions to sanity, and all these Poe, obsessively concerned with them elsewhere, would ban from the highest expression of art, from the poem.

Poe is in his verse not merely anti-rationalist, which he is willing enough to admit, he is also anti-literary, anti-communicative, which he finds it harder to confess even to himself. Yet it is for precisely this quality that the *symbolistes* hailed him, seeing in him that dissolution of statement into music which they so admired; and for this, too, Lear took him as a master, seeing in him that dissolution of sense into nonsense which so appealed to his imagination. Poe is the first modern poet, then, in the sense that he not merely registered his alienation from the larger audience, but wrote the kind of verse only the alienated poet is free to write—verse intended for fellow-poets or children, which is to say, "no one," as opposed to "everyone." Poe's awareness of his revolutionary difference from other poets of his time is, however, rather dim.

He admired extravagantly, as everyone knows, the most conventional lady poets of his own day. And his famous quarrel with Longfellow, which began with an attack on didacticism, soon settled down into a quarrel about plagiarism. The truth is that Longfellow and Poe are *both* didactic poets, though the doctrine espoused by Poe is simply that art should not subserve morality. Children of the same romantic mode, Poe and Longfellow split the famous Keatsian chestnut between them, one asserting "Beauty is truth!" while the other retorted, "Truth is beauty!" How close they could come to each other in style and theme is attested by the fact that no critic now is sure whether Longfellow's "The Beleaguered City" is an imitation of Poe's "The Haunted Palace," or vice versa, or whether both borrowed from a poem by Tennyson called "The Deserted House." There is, at any rate, more of the Philistine and commonplace, more kinship with Longfellow, in Poe than is apparent at first glance; and this is a clue, perhaps, to why the school of Poe has, in the last decades, become as genteel and respectable a part of the American establishment as that of the New England Brahmins in the nineteenth century.

Even the poems which Poe wrote *about* his own loneliness scarcely rise above banality and self-pity of the most obvious kind. When he says in "Alone," for instance:

> From childhood's hour I have not been
> As others were—I have not seen
> As others saw—I could not bring
> My passions from a common spring—

he is contributing to a body of popular jingles on the subject, usually printed only in newspapers. If this represents the "school of Poe," that school reached its end with the convict leader of the last riot in the Montana State Prison, who was found dead after the shooting had died away, these verses by his own hand in one pocket:

> Nary a word said o'er my grave,
> Not a soul to rant and rave,
> No marker of errant past,
> An individualist to the last . . .

No, it is rather as in the final lines of "Ulalume," when the poet is no longer making meaning so much as sounds, when he is reproducing in pseudo-sentences the effect of hissing or singing *la-la-la-la,* that we are at last in the presence of *poésie pure,* which is to say, ultimate or last poetry, the sort of earnest parody of serious verse appropriate to a time when the average reader no longer understands such verse:

> . . . Have drawn up the spectre of a planet
>   From the limbo of lunary souls—
> The sinfully scintillant planet
>   From the Hell of the planetary souls?

Poe tried *deliberately* to write what other difficult poetry has *accidentally* become in the ear of the sub-literate; and this is the third kind of travesty appropriate to modern verse, the other two being the mockery of middle-brow poetizing, and the parody-allusion as practiced by Pound and Eliot.

But Poe's way, too, is a way to *épater la bourgeoisie,* as certain French poets not required to read Poe in school were quick to realize; and it is their *Edgairpo,* re-imported into the United States, who became the spiritual father of all our aristocratic anti-poets, from Eliot (who began by writing as often in French as in English), through Pound and Wallace Stevens to Marianne Moore, R. P. Blackmur, and beyond. Not only in his origins but also in his pose, Poe has appealed especially to poets of the American South, to the so-called Southern agrarians, cavalier dandies all, including John Crowe Ransom, Robert Penn Warren, and Allen Tate, the last of whom has begun a long, sympathetic study of the figure he calls "Our Cousin, Mr. Poe." It is tempting, as a matter of fact, to speak of the line of Poe as a "Southern line," appropriate to a part of our country obsessed by myths of its aristocratic origins and high culture, and ridden by the fact of its impoverishment and defeat.

Utterly different in origin, tone, and appeal is the line of Whitman, whose pretensions are democratic rather than aristocratic, aggressively nationalistic rather than ostentatiously internationalist. To Whitmanians being American means despising the culture of Europe, indeed, all high culture, finally the very notion of culture itself; and, as we have already seen, their verse is dedicated not to the ironic evocation of the past in travestied quotation, nor to the creation of elegant nonsense in a simultaneous protest against and acceptance of the isolation of the poet, nor to an attack on popular vulgarization of language. The Whitmanian, indeed, has no quarrel with the esthetics of the masses, which he thinks of himself as trying to emulate; only with their politics and their morality, which he thinks of as somehow unworthy of them. His onslaught is directed against the artificial cultural heritage of the educated classes, which he regards as both pedantic and un-American, and he resists that culture in the name of the people, who for him represent the naïve, the natural, the *real.* It is raw experience for which he longs and for whose sake he disowns all literature except his own. He wants really to write the *first* poem of the world, even when he has come to his own second, or tenth, or one hundredth.

For the Whitmanian, consequently, the poet is conceived of not as the cosmopolitan dandy, but the provincial prophet, the man with a message from God, or from the people who are the voice of God. He does not, therefore, suggest or evoke, but asserts, yells, hollers, and screams, since for him poetry aspires not to the condition of music but to that of rhetoric, public speech. He has, perhaps, no assurance that he will be heard, only that he *must* be, and that is why his tone is rather the tone of one trying to shout down hecklers than of one preaching to the converted. Since he aims at convincing rather than delighting (like Poe) or instructing delightfully (like Longfellow), it is indifferent to him whether he writes in verse or prose; indeed, what he writes is likely to be deliberately ambiguous in this regard.

If there is a section of America with which poetry in the line of Whitman can be identified, it is the West, the part of our country mythically rather than historically defined. The "South" of Poe can be identified with Virginia, the "East" of Longfellow with Boston and Cambridge, but the "West" of Whitman (who, of course, did not really live in it or know it except out of books) is for one generation Kentucky, for another Ohio or Illinois, for the next Minnesota and the Dakotas, then California or Montana; and finally it ceases to exist at all except in poems like Whitman's, or in popular movies less unlike him than one thinks at first. The "West," that is to say, is not a fact of history defined once and for all and there to be accepted or rejected forever after; it is a fiction: the place to which we have not yet come or at which we have just arrived, a *theoretical* place. When Whitman talks of landscapes he knows, Brooklyn, Long Island, New York City, we believe what he writes; but when he cries, "I cross the Laramie plains, I note the rocks in grotesque shapes, the buttes. . . . I see the Monument mountain and the Eagle's nest, I pass the Promontory, I ascend the Nevadas . . ." we have the sense that he has worked it all up out of some gazetteer.

Yet actual Western poets in the generations which followed him have taken Whitman for a guide and model—Carl Sandburg, for instance, first poet of Chicago, and Edgar Lee Masters, who expressed, with political overtones, his appreciation of what is specifically new and, therefore, anti-Eastern about the author of *Leaves of Grass:* ". . . Whitman wrote for the American tribe and the American idea. . . . Whitman had the right idea, namely, that poetry, the real written word, must come out of the earth . . . It is no wonder that a man as sincere as Whitman . . . had to endure the sneers and chatter of New York critics . . . who often miss the important, the real and truly American art." To this classic populist statement, Amy Lowell gave the classic aristocratic answer, speaking from Boston and in defense of ideals more like Poe's: "Often and often I read in the press, that modern vers libre writers derive their form from Walt Whitman. As a matter of fact, most of them got it from French Symbolist poets . . ." And she adds, trying to take from Whitman his claims to Americanism as well as his prestige as a technical innovator, "It is perhaps sadly significant that the three modern poets who most loudly acknowledge his leadership are all of recent foreign extraction . . ."

Now it is, indeed, true that Whitman has appealed always to relatively *new* Americans, that is, marginal and therefore theoretical Americans, not to Anglo-Saxon Brahmins at home, like Miss Lowell, or such Brahmins exiled to the Midwest, like Eliot, nor to the offspring of upper-class Southern families, whose loyalties are sectional and whose origins tie them securely to Great Britain. It is to melting-pot Americans or to those on actual and recent frontiers, to those educated abroad, like William Carlos Williams, and whose America is therefore large and abstract, whose Americanism must be invented day by day, that he seems especially sympathetic. This is why he was at first the darling of the populist poets of the mid-West, like Sandburg and Masters, then the preferred muse of the Marxists in the United States, most of them children of recent immigrants and themselves just out of ghettos, or on the long hard way out. Americans, that is to say, who have yearned for, rather than endured, their Americanism have sought in Whitman a myth of their own lives and of their country.

Ben Maddow, a once-admired "proletarian poet" of the Thirties, will serve to represent the Marxist-Whitmanians as Edgar Lee Masters represents the populist-Whitmanians. In a poem called "Red Decision," he invokes the spirit of his master to help him prove in verse what the leaders of the American Communist Party were asserting in political manifestoes, that "Communism is the Americanism of the twentieth century":

> Broad-hearted Whitman of the healthy beard
> stiffen my infirm palate for this bread,
> whose gritty leaven shall embowel me
> to hold . . .
> in solemn hands, my tough majestic pen

This is rather Whitman parodied than Whitman emulated; for, indeed, the style of *Leaves of Grass* is, in its exaggeration, almost comic, almost caricature, a last desperate, delicate teetering on the edge of self-travesty —and pushed further it becomes a joke on those who use it. But worse was to come.

Transmitted, via the fake "native culture" (pseudo-Whitman, plus pseudo-folk-songs, plus pseudo-jazz) sponsored by the Popular Front movement, to the heart of the New Deal, this line of development from Whitman became a new official art and was exemplified, for instance, in the sound track of Pare Lorentz's *The River,* and other documentary films, as well as throwaways, campaign literature, etc. It was, at this point, that Whitmanian verse became to the living avant garde a butt and a laughing stock, not less scorned than ladylike effusions in the style of Longfellow; and W. H. Auden is able to include in a list of Philistine cultural horrors:

> . . . over-Whitmanated song
>   That does not scan,
> With adjectives laid end to end,
> Extol the doughnut and commend
>   The Common Man.

Yet just before World War I, poets in the line of Whitman and those in the line of Poe felt themselves allied in a common cause: a united front against the bourgeoisie and its dream of a poetry romantic and sentimental, Anglo-Saxon and genteel. At that point, the name of Whitman was the rallying cry of the whole literary avant garde; new sex, new society, and new poetry, these seemed the three persons of a single god (or better, devil), and Whitman was his prophet. *Poetry,* the magazine founded by Harriet Monroe, still carries a tag from Whitman, and in its pioneer days that magazine celebrated as a single syndrome, anti-conventional and anti-bourgeois, T. S. Eliot, Pound, Amy Lowell, imagism, free verse, Sandburg, Frost, and E. A. Robinson. To this blur of enthusiasm, the prophetic blur at the heart of the Whitman image corresponded exactly; he is the presiding genius of an alliance based on the single slogan: "Make it New!"

It was, however, an alliance that could not survive its first victories. Dismayed at the death of Longfellow as a living influence, the disappearance of an ideal against which to define themselves, and undone by the triumph and slow spread of the Russian revolution, its members divided against themselves. Quite soon, the socialist poets were regarding their converted Catholic confreres with hostility; the re-discoverers of metaphysical wit and classical form were watching warily the exponents of formless dithyrambics; the advocates of escape from emotion were wondering why they had ever enlisted beside the enthusiasts of phallic consciousness; the followers of *Edgairpo* separated themselves from the champions of *Leaves of Grass.* And though Ezra Pound tried to make peace ("I make a pact with you, Walt Whitman—/ I have detested you long enough), no one in Pound's own camp would believe him, Eliot insisting, for instance, "I am equally certain—it is indeed obvious—that Pound owes nothing to Whitman. This is an elementary observation . . ."

Yet one of the most admired American poets of the first half of the twentieth century attempted, in his most ambitious poem, to keep alive side by side not only the myths of Poe and Whitman but their actual influences. In *The Bridge,* Hart Crane confesses Poe as the ghost who haunts him and his country; but it is Whitman whom he honors as inspiration and guide:

> Our Meistersinger, thou set breath in steel;
> And it was thou who on the boldest heel
> Stood up and flung the span on even wing
> Of that great Bridge, our Myth, whereof I sing!

The Bridge, however, is a failure, incoherent throughout, despite occasional momentary successes; and it is never more incoherent than in the passages in which Crane attempts to evoke Whitman. Crane's whole relationship to Whitman was ambiguous in the extreme, and he had other troubles with his subject matter, each alone deep and dangerous enough to wreck a poem.

Nonetheless, the failure of *The Bridge* was interpreted not as Crane's failure but as Whitman's. The critical *locus classicus* is the review by Yvor Winters in *Poetry* for June 1930, which begins by admiring the "dignity and power" of Crane's attempt to make a Whitmanian epic, and ends by insisting that his lack of success proves "the impossibility of getting anywhere with the Whitmanian inspiration . . . it seems highly unlikely that any writer of comparable genius will struggle with it again." This contention became a basic dogma of those new critics who dominated the American scene for two decades; indeed, it is one of their few firm critical judgments about American literature, and one of the handful in any area upon which they unanimously agree. Allen Tate and R. P. Blackmur early expressed their concurrence, and by 1950 Winters' position had become orthodoxy in the academies. Here, for instance, is how the position is summed up in a handbook for college students: "But Whitman and his followers—like Robinson Jeffers, Vachel Lindsay, Edgar Lee Masters, Carl Sandburg, Stephen Vincent Benét . . . and later Paul Engle, August Derleth, Muriel Rukeyser, Ben Maddow, and Alfred Hayes . . . are not in the line of American writers who have deepened our knowledge of human motivation or action."

Not only is Whitman gone, according to this view, but two, three generations of followers with him, consigned to an outer darkness with all others who deviate "from the tradition which runs from Hawthorne and Melville through James and Eliot." Only in Europe did the wandering American, until very recently, encounter serious scholars and critics who wanted to discuss Sandburg or Edgar Lee Masters seriously, and who did not even know that Whitman's reputation had been challenged. At home only undergraduate versifiers, back-country bards, and provincial schoolmasters remained ignorant of the news that a god had died and that his prophets were unread. And these benighted few were advised, some years ago, on a black-bordered page in a little magazine called *Furioso:* WALT WHITMAN IS DEAD! As late as 1950, indeed, it would have been hard to persuade any reputable critic or respected younger poet that it would be possible ever again to write moving verse based on the examples of *Leaves of Grass.*

Easiest of the lines of American verse to forget, or remembering, to despise, is the line of Ralph Waldo Emerson. Europeans are likely to be quite unaware of its existence, and Americans to confuse it with the line of Longfellow (was not Emerson, after all, just another New England Brahmin?) or to dismiss it impatiently with a curt reference to the failure of Emerson's technique (was he not a lecturer and essayist, a master of our prose, if of anything?). Edgar Lee Masters, who at least named Emerson in order to dismiss him in favor of Whitman, was apparently thinking of *both* these objections: "It is not because Whitman is a better poet than Emerson that he may be called the father of American poetry. . . . It is because Whitman wrote for the American tribe." For a long time, indeed, it seemed as if Emerson were another once-admired poet doomed to live the sub-literary life of Longfellow: his

"Rhodora" sung in occasional school concerts chiefly for the sake of its musical setting, and his "Concord Hymn" recited in schoolrooms on patriotic occasions.

Without understanding Emerson, however, it is impossible to deal with two notable early modern American poets, Frost and E. A. Robinson, who seem otherwise unaccountable eccentrics; nor can one understand the place of Emily Dickinson between Emerson's time and our own; nor, finally, can one appreciate the true meaning of Edward Taylor, that recently rediscovered American metaphysical poet who is Emerson's ancestor, as Emerson is Emily Dickinson's. We cannot now and never really could read with pleasure Anne Bradstreet and other pre-Republican American poets celebrated in the textbooks of a generation ago, but Taylor is a seventeenth-century poet as alive for us as his English forerunner John Donne. Lines from his poems have already made their way into our new anthologies and, more significantly, into our heads, from which they will not be dislodged: the first stanzas, for instance, of "Upon a Spider Catching a Fly":

> Thou sorrow, venom Elf:
>   Is this thy play,
> To spin a web out of thyself
>   To catch a Fly?
>   For why?
>
> I saw a pettish wasp
>   Fall foul therein:
> Whom yet thy whorl pins did
>   not hasp
> Lest he should fling
>   His sting.
>
> Thus gently him didst treat
>   Lest he should pet,
> And in a froppish, aspish
>   heat
>   Should greatly fret
>   Thy net.
>
> Whereas the silly Fly,
>   Caught by its leg,
> Thou by the throat took'st
>   hastily,
> And 'hind the head
>   Bite Dead.

It is clear, as a matter of fact, that the sole line of American poetry which has an unbroken line of development as old as our country itself is the one that runs from Taylor to Emerson to Dickinson to Frost and beyond; and it is Emerson who brought it to full consciousness, at the very moment when the schools of Longfellow and Poe and Whitman were defining themselves for the first time. Yet Emerson does not exist for the imagination as do any of the other three, for he has not assumed mythic dimensions to Europeans, as have Poe and Whitman, or to the American middle classes, as has Longfellow. Emerson represents, that is to say, neither a European myth of America, nor an American myth of Europe—only a private myth of ourselves for ourselves, which somehow has appealed neither to Europeans nor to many of us. I do not mean to say that Emerson did not try to project his view of the poet in legendary guise; he was a deeply, if erratically, learned man, given to describing his ideal bard as Merlin or Uriel or Saadi; but somehow none of these tags caught on—perhaps because in his cool, almost antiseptic mind they were divested of the self-pity we seem to demand of our writers as our devil's due.

How, then, to define the Emersonian line? Perhaps the easiest way to begin is by locating it geographically in New England, in what seems at first glance the same Northeast out of which Longfellow speaks his bland and scholarly reassurance. In Longfellow, however, the emphasis is on the east of the compound sectional name; in Emerson the north. He speaks not for the self-satisfied urban center, not for the would-be cosy cosmopolitanism of Boston, but for a more provincial, a much colder Concord. He is the poet of winter, of an iciness which is not perhaps generous but is surely never sentimental. And, by the same token, he is the mouthpiece of essential Puritanism, that tough-minded view of man and God, immune alike to sentiment and gentility, which survived the collapse of the church that first nurtured it. That in our time the line of Emerson has been represented by a great poetic authority on snow and night actually called Robert *Frost* is one of those astonishingly happy accidents which almost persuade us that history is the subtlest allegorist of all. Trying to portray the typical American poet in his recent novel, *Pale Fire,* Vladimir Nabokov was unable to do better than model him on Frost and name him analogously, though not quite as satisfactorily, "Shade."

The best brief description of the Emersonian countryside is in E. A. Robinson's "New England," which in scarcely more than four verses suggests to us not only the Emersonian setting but the special quality of feeling that setting begets:

> Here where the wind is always north-north-east
> And children learn to walk on frozen toes,
> Wonder begets an envy of all those
> Who boil elsewhere with such a lyric yeast
> Of love . . .

The language, the meter reflect more than some improbably imported ideal of neo-classicism. This is cool, if not downright cold, verse: a little tight and tending to the crabbed; sometimes—less in Robinson, perhaps, than in Emerson himself—as rocky and uncomfortable as the meager landscape against which it is written. At its best, however, it is quietly tough and masculine (even in the hands of Emily Dickinson, when her female instincts do not lead her into coyness or cuteness), neither sensually self-indulgent like Poe, nor ostentatiously loose like Whitman, in whom we sense the boast of masculinity rather than the fact. This is poetry of the middle-way, neither hypnotic nor hortatory, but it is saved from the smoothness of the golden mean by a kind of blessed clumsiness.

And behind it, of course, there is a different view of the poet than those which moved Poe and Whitman and Longfellow. For Emerson, the poet is neither dandy nor agitator nor domesticated paraclete; he is, rather, a lonely philosopher or magician; a rebel, perhaps, as much as Whitman's mythical poet, but one, in Frost's phrase, "too lofty and original to rage." The voice of such a poet is neither wholly musical nor wholly rhetorical, though it partakes of both elements. When it inclines to the rhetorical, it is the speech of a man urging himself on, rather than appealing to a crowd:

> He shall not his brain encumber
> With the coil of rhythm and number,
> But leaving rule and pale forethought,
> He shall aye climb
> For his rhyme:
> Pass in, pass in, the angels say,
> In to the upper doors;
> Nor count compartments of the floors,
> But mount to Paradise
> By the stairway of surprise.

When it inclines to the musical, it is like the overheard spell some amateur magician murmurs to himself:

> Subtle rhymes with ruin rife
> Murmur in the house of life,
> Sung by the Sisters as they spin;
> In perfect time and measure, they
> Build and unbuild our echoing clay,
> As the two twilights of the day
> Fold us music-drunken in.

But at its best it is conversational, though not garrulous and effusive, rather like the cryptic interchange of two wise old friends, each of whom insists that between them the final words, the last things remain unspoken:

Askest, "How long shalt thou stay?"
Devastator of the day!
Know, each substance and relation
Through nature's operation,
Hath its unit, bound and metre . . .
But the unit of the visit,
The encounter of the wise,
Say what other metre is it
Than the meeting of the eyes?

Sometimes the Emersonian writer is content with pure musing or meditation, and stays within the confines of the lyric; but often he is moved to try his hand at myth-making or narration, and produces poems like Emerson's "Uriel," which Frost thought to be one of the greatest poems in the language. Actually "Uriel" is a retelling of the first two books of *Paradise Lost* from the point of view of the Satanic party, very terse and very American. In it the fallen angel is Prometheus rather than the Devil; and Prometheus, biographically interpreted, turns out to be the transcendentalist Emerson or, prophetically understood, the scientific relativist, Albert Einstein:

Line in nature is not found,
Unit and universe are round;
In vain produced, all rays return,
Evil will bless, and ice will burn.

Emerson himself, however, was too short-breathed and gnomic to tackle seriously the really long poem, and it remained for Frost (less happily for E. A. Robinson, too) to produce in the twentieth century, after almost everyone else had abandoned conventional drama and story-telling in verse, large poetic narratives of considerable power. Such a poem as Frost's "Witch of Coos" stands nearly alone in a time when the chief American poets had decided its mode and methods were hopelessly outdated and were searching for hints in Whitman and Pound to help them construct pseudo- or mock-epics with imagistic rather than narrative techniques. Frost and Robinson alone resisted the drift toward studied incoherence, willed dissociation, and planned irrelevance that characterized the anti-poetry of the first half of the twentieth century, just as they alone clung still to the traditional metrical forms of English poetry despite Pound's battle-cry, "Break the iambic!" Indeed, in their resolve to write poetry that scanned and told a story, Frost and Robinson came to seem allies to the Philistine opponents of the new verse, and enemies to its practitioners.

Though Frost had made an appearance or two in *Poetry*, in the exciting days just before World War I, he did not seem part of the movement that was making room for the utterly new by destroying the old: old allegiances, old esthetics, old forms. Indeed, he had to go to England before he could make a poetic reputation; there he was able to profit by the cultural lag which has kept British poetry limping along behind ours through the whole of this century, and to be accepted along with certain of the English Georgian poets, with whom he only seemed to have something essential in common. That he wrote about the countryside rather than the city appealed to a backward English audience convinced that, in their land at least (unlike France or America), poetry was going to be kept where it belonged, that is, where Wordsworth had firmly placed it at the end of the eighteenth century. But what did the landscape evoked in the title of Frost's second published book, the bleak snow-bound world of "North of Boston," have to do with the Lake Country?

Robinson had the good grace, at least, to be born in the same decade in which the Civil War ended, and to die before World War II, so that he could be comfortably placed in the past and labeled a forerunner. But Frost disturbingly survived into the present, to be honored not by a remote Theodore Roosevelt (like E. A. Robinson) but by the living and reigning exponent of the New Frontier. What to do, then, in a time like ours, with poets still available to Philistines and even Presidents, with poets who neither pretend to write first poems, in the manner of Whitman—poems before which the readers could imagine no others—nor last poems, in the manner of Poe—poems after which the reader could imagine no others? Without a sense of the Emersonian tradition and its meaning, one is tempted to class them with the poets who wrote just poems, in the manner of Longfellow, poems whose whole function is to remind the reader of all the others he has read before and shall read after. But the relevance to our present situation of what Emerson and his followers were after, and the sense in which they stand beside the Whitmanians as dissenters and disturbers of the peace (after all, it was Emerson alone, of all the poets of his day, who hailed the publication of *Leaves of Grass*), we are just now beginning to understand.

Realism to Naturalism

EVERETT CARTER

TOWARDS A PHILOSOPHY OF LITERARY REALISM

1. The Reason for Realism

> "He . . . can write solely of what his fleshly eyes have seen."
> —Henry James

But "no" is not the kind of word upon which men can build; the impulse to destroy the lie in literature was a negative impulse; and writers must not only be against something; they also have to be for something. It is not enough to be just against untruth; an artist must feel that "this world means intensely, and means good" in order to justify his absorption in its appearances. Why is it that writers over the Western world returned to the physical world for the materials of their fiction, and to an objective selection from the events of that world for their method? Part of the reason why realism came in America, of course, as it had been coming in France, and in Russia, and was to come in Spain, is that there were intellectual attitudes floating in the solution of our culture which could be precipitated by the currents of post-war developments. Some of these attitudes we have already noticed. Emersonian transcendentalism revered the smallest and most humble bits of the world of experience; it took only a change in emphasis to make over transcendental concern for the commonplace into realistic concern for the immediate, the familiar, the humble, and the low. The Scottish philosophy of common sense "dominating the intellectual atmosphere of most American colleges and universities in the decades immediately following Appomattox" filtered down into the periodicals and the newspapers to color the attitudes of the generation. The answer this philosophical school would give to the difficult problem of "how do we know things?" would be: "We know them through perceiving them"; and in reply to the skeptical doubtings of a Berkeley and a Hume about the trustworthiness of sense perceptions, they would give the "common-sense" answer: Dr. Johnson kicking the stone to prove the existence of the material. In pre-war America, too, the Brahmin civilization of Lowell and Holmes had kept very much alive the neo-classical tradition of humanism with its concern for the world of the senses, and with its fundamental distrust of the "crypts of metaphysics."

These were the native sources from which De Forest and Twain and Howells—all three of them, as well as a host of their followers later in the century—could draw when they turned naturally to a reporting of the world of their experience. In "common-sense" terms they never doubted that they need do anything else than observe carefully and honestly and report truthfully in order to arrive at truthfulness, and hence beauty, in fiction. Twain wanted above all to be authentic. No other literature is worth writing, Howells wrote to a young poet in 1867, except that which expresses the life one has lived. The only secret of art, said Howells to another friend in 1871, is to observe with the naked eye.

It is fruitless to hope to find out "why" this should be; as Howells wrote later to T. S. Perry, realism cannot be said to have been caused by anything; it just "came," and seemed "to have come everywhere at once." The generation of Howells was swinging away from the otherworldliness of Hawthorne and Poe. Almost instinctively, as we have seen, Howells read and loved those authors whose concern had been with man's social circumstance; instinctively, he turned away from Wordsworth and Coleridge, from Poe and Sir Walter Scott. He quickly abandoned his adolescent imitations of Heine, and his immature apings of the sentimentalists, and agreed with Lowell that he must write of that which he observed and knew himself. In one of his early letters to Mrs. James T. Fields after he assumed the assistant editorship of the *Atlantic*, he complained of the impossibility of finding people who could write short, lively sketches, and made it clear that he was searching for contributors who would base their work on observed material. While no discernible critical standards operated in his reviews in the first years for the *Atlantic* (he wrote in 1867 that "there is hardly any law established for criticism which has not been overthrown as often as the French government"), hints of his allegiance to fiction based upon personal experience had already begun to appear. He liked Bayard Taylor's "faithful spirit" in which he "adhered to all the facts of life he portrayed." He wrote to Don Lloyd Wyman, who wished advice, and asked if his poems expressed the life he had lived or had known, and added that only such poems are worth reading. He admired Henry Ward Beecher's "felicity in expressing the flavor and color of New England life." Mark Twain, he told readers of the *Atlantic*, had an honest and observant eye, "honest enough to let himself see the realities of human life everywhere." He cheered for T. B. Aldrich's *The Story of a Bad Boy,* which was obviously the story of the author's own life, and it was this element of autobiography which Howells seized upon as the reason for its success. Aldrich did a new thing, Howells wrote; he told "what . . . life is" instead of trying to teach "what it should be." And in this direction, Howells said, lay "the work which has long hovered in the mental atmosphere . . . pleading to be born into the world,—the American novel, namely." Soon after reading *The Story of a Bad Boy,* he started on the writing of his first novel; and it was a novel in which he simply took his experiences on his own delayed honeymoon and gave them "the form of fiction so far as the characters are concerned." He wrote his father that this was the path in literature which he believed he could make "most distinctly" his own. Henry James testified that Howells was beginning to dedicate himself to a reporting of that which his "fleshly eyes" could see.

But why should such observation be "art"? Why should people be interested in reading works based upon observation by "the naked eye"? What is the beauty and morality of a work of fiction whose base is a fidelity to actuality? Howells and Twain never considered such matters systematically. They and De Forest, and Bret Harte in the Far West, were creatures of their time. And yet their concern with the physical world had, in France, produced a social philosopher and a literary critic who gave system and justification to man's concern with the observable. And when Howells, and men who thought and wrote like him in his own age, turned their attention to a careful examination of the probable and the commonplace as the materials for their fiction, they were sometimes unconsciously, but more often consciously, basing their attitude towards fiction upon a theory of aesthetics which had been fashioned to meet the needs of a world which was being transformed by the application of the scientific method to the material and the moral universe.

2. The Scientist as the New Hero

Howells' was an age which saw about it everywhere the success of the empirical method. In the thirteen years from 1865 to 1878, applied science doubled America's capital investments; in 1864 the Bessemer process for converting iron to steel was first used commercially in America at Wyandotte, Michigan; three years later 2,600 tons of ingots were produced, a volume which increased four hundred-fold by 1879. In 1859, the first successful oil well in the United States was sunk near Titusville, Pennsylvania; by 1864 the area was producing more than 2,100,000 barrels. Railway mileage doubled in the seven years between 1865 and 1872. In this atmosphere of material expansion, the inventor became the new hero. James Parton's *Famous Americans of Recent Times* (1868) devoted a third of its space to men of science, and Howells thought that Parton wrote of them "with the most heart," that he interested the reader deeply in their lives. For the inventors, said Howells, "are the discoverers of our time, and it is they who carry forward, in their true spirit, the magnificent enterprises of other days. . . ."

While the applied sciences were transforming the face of America, the theoretical scientists were busy overhauling its mind. Darwin published his findings in 1859, two years after the first issue of the *Atlantic,* and during the next twenty years, the periodicals of the day were still busy explaining the implications of his theory to their audience. While Darwin was casting doubt on the biblical account of mankind's development, geologists like Louis Agassiz at Harvard were forcing Americans to question the literal truth of the story of the world's creation in the book of Genesis. If they were to go out to Plymouth Rock once a year, Agassiz told his listeners, and brush silk just once, and lightly, over the monolith, and keep this up until the rock was worn down to a pebble, they would have a concept of the length of time our earth was a-borning. While geologists like Agassiz were upsetting Fundamentalist religious concepts, physicians like Oliver Wendell Holmes were challenging old beliefs about the mystical origins of personality, and would have no truck with either the pessimism of the Calvinists or the optimism of Platonic concepts to which Wordsworth had given new prestige. Don't talk to me about children coming into the world trailing clouds of glory, the doctor told the minister in *Elsie Venner;* and then the man of science went on to say that children are more likely to trail clouds of hereditary mental disorders.

And with men like Agassiz and Holmes, Howells felt himself instinctively at home. We have already seen how large a part Holmes played in the early encouragement of the young poet from the West, and Howells continued to avow his indebtedness to the little doctor and his hard-headed empiricism. Like Holmes he felt "the inquiry was inquiry, to the last," and he had the "scientific conscience that refuses either to deny the substance of things unseen, or to affirm it." The "Goethean face and figure of Louis Agassiz" were also dear to Howells; he later portrayed David Sewell, the sympathetic pastor in *The Minister's Charge,* as an admirer of the geologist who could "make every inch of the earth vocal, every rock historic, and the waste places social."

The admiration for the scientist became a commonplace of realistic fiction. As the clear-eyed observer, he was portrayed as seeing through sentimentality to the truth: De Forest's Dr. Ravenel, or his young scientist in *Kate Beaumont;* Mark Twain's empiricists: the Connecticut Yankee, Tom Canty, Pudd'nhead Wilson, even Huck Finn himself. Huck was really an empiricist; his belief in magic was not unscientific; far from it; as Frazer has pointed out, the basic beliefs of magic and science are the same—each accepts as empirically true any result which consistently follows the same activities (an experiment in one case, a ritual in the other). Huck putting the legend of the genie to the test of actual performance, and rejecting the story as untrue when the stipulated action did not have the stipulated result, is a symbol of the age's trust in the scientific method: Tom Sawyer, we may remember, had insisted upon the truth of the Aladdin legend. Huck's reaction was that of the empiricist: "I got an old tin lamp and an iron ring, and went out in the woods and rubbed and rubbed till I sweat like an Injun, calculating to build a palace and sell it; but it warn't no use, none of the genies came. So I judged all that stuff was only just one of Tom Sawyer's lies." Colville in *Indian Summer* and Olney in *An Imperative Duty* are less vivid, but equally symbolic characters in their representation of the empirical attitude towards truth and morality. It is no coincidence that Olney should be portrayed as a doctor; it is equally significant that Warner and Twain made Ruth Bolton, the heroine of *The Gilded Age,* a medical scientist.

Howells' generation was one in which science, both theoretical and applied, was either capturing or oppressing the imagination of creative artists. Men of letters at this time either absorbed its truths and went on to create literature which accepted what they understood was its message about the place of observation in art, or they rejected it, and wrote sentimentally, or not at all. Thomas Bailey Aldrich mourned that

> Romance beside his unstrung lute
> > Lies stricken mute.
> The old-time fire, the antique grace,
> You will not find them anywhere.
> Today we breathe a commonplace,
> Polemic, scientific air. . . .

And Aldrich wrote novels like *Prudence Palfrey* which Howells saw were simply the sentimental stereotypes of a poet longing for what he thought was Romance. On the other hand, the Southern poet, Sidney Lanier, tried hard to make the poet at home in the new world of science; and while he failed in his own poetry, he made some remarkably acute observations about the nature of prose fiction and its relation to science, while in poetry he tried to reconcile art and empiricism:

> And Science be known as the sense making love to the All,
> And Art be known as the soul making love to the All,
> And Love be known as the marriage of man with the All—
> Till Science to knowing the Highest shall lovingly turn,
> Till Art to loving the Highest shall consciously burn,
> Till Science to Art as a man to a woman shall yearn.

The blend of the two, we see, was not signally successful. But his lectures on the novel were shrewd evaluations of the place of the scientific attitude in fiction. Like Howells and Hawthorne, he suggested that the term "Romantic" defined the literary attitude which was fundamentally poetic. The "realistic" attitude, he said, was a combination of the poetic and the scientific, while "those who entirely reject the imagination" could be termed "the Naturalistic school. We are prepared," he continued, "to study the novel as a work in which science is carried over into the region of art."

3. TAINE IN AMERICA

In France, a generation earlier, a philosopher had come forth who had made the techniques and attitudes of the new science the basis of a system of thought. August Comte had proclaimed that the scientific attitude towards society and its problems was the right one. Just as it had alone proven of use in unlocking the mysteries of the physical universe, so it would alone be of use in solving the questions of the moral universe. Comte aimed at taking human social thought out of the two childlike and adolescent stages of development—the theological, in which all phenomena are ascribed to supernatural causes, and the metaphysical, in which preformulated, *a priori* principles are considered the causes of events. The new stage, said Comte, the positive stage, is one in which the supernatural is ignored and the metaphysical is discarded, and observation, analysis, and classification take their place.

Hippolyte Taine took positivism and made it into a literary credo, and it was Taine's positivistic theory of the source and function of literary expression that became the basis of conscious American realism.

Taine was almost unknown in America before 1870. There had been a review of his work in 1861 when M. H. Harisse had summarized the latest developments in French criticism for the *North American Review*. But the attitude of this early notice was that here is a young and brilliant Frenchman with a rather difficult philosophy of aesthetics and criticism in which we are interested but with which we cannot wholly agree. Then Edward Eggleston read Taine's *Philosophy of Art in the Netherlands*, and wrote a brief review of it for the *Independent* in 1870. A few months later, he was encouraged to write a story for *Hearth and Home*. The story extended through three issues; and while he was writing it, Eggleston remembered the philosophy of art formulated by Taine—that to be a great artist, one must express one's own times, and the attitudes of one's own people; that the greatness of the art of the Netherlands was its willingness to use common materials and familiar subjects. Eggleston came to his brother, George Cary Eggleston, and announced that he was going to "write a three-number story, founded upon your experiences at Riker's Ridge." Then, George recorded, the incipient novelist went on to "set forth his theory of art—that the artist, whether with pen or brush, who would do his best work, must choose his subjects from the life that he knows." And to justify his choice of theme, Eggleston "cited the Dutch painters" as well as referring to "Lowell's success with the Biglow papers."

Out of this fortuitous combination, out of Taine, Lowell, and the desire of the *Hearth and Home* for a story from Eggleston, came *The Hoosier Schoolmaster*, an early landmark in the development of realism in America. Despite its open mawkish sentimentalism, the novel was rich with regional dialect, and remorseless in its truthful portrayal of the hard-shelled farmers of Indiana. And in 1874, Eggleston added to his picture of the Midwest in *The Circuit Rider*. In the preface to this book, he expressed with clarity and precision the aim of realism in literature, and it was an expression which clearly shows the influence of the Frenchman who pointed out that an artist must deal with his contemporaries. Eggleston asked the reader who might be offended by his treatment of the rougher side of religion to remember "the solemn obligations of a novelist to tell the truth." He insisted that the title of "novelist" could only be given to him who tries with whole soul "to produce the higher form of history, by writing truly of men as they are, and dispassionately of those forms of life that come within his scope."

Howells had hailed *The Hoosier Schoolmaster* as a contribution to the development of a native school of realism. But this review had been one of a group which Howells wrote from 1867 to 1872 which had shown a catholicity of taste confounding to any attempt to draw consistent attitudes from them. They had praised historical romances and imaginative fantasies by Edward Everett Hale, and Dion Boucicault, as well as the realism of De Forest and Eggleston. But in 1872 Howells, too, read and reviewed a work of Taine's—his *History of English Literature*.

Taine's transformation of Comte's philosophy of social positivism into the conception of literature as a product of the *"race, milieu, et moment"* of each author is well known. What has not been so well remembered was Taine's penetrating formulation of the justification for, even the necessity of, a literature which plays its part in the positivist program. Literature, Taine said in essence, must be the principal method by which society and men are observed, analyzed, and classified. Fiction should be the scientific laboratory of society—the laboratory in which the complex components of our social system are mixed with each other, so that the race may watch the experiment, see the result, and be better able to make decisions affecting its life.

· · · · · · ·

4. The Autobiographical Method: Howells

In a world where the scientific method was raising the hopes and stirring the imaginations of men, a school of letters created a literature for that world and tried to find the answers to such questions as: What is the function of literature? How do we know literature is good or bad? What kind should we write and encourage others to write? The answer Howells gave to these questions, and by giving it helped to encourage the talents of De Forest and Eggleston, Garland and Frederic, as well as the greatest of them all, Mark Twain, was simply "be true." This was to be the test of a "good" work: "Is it true?—true to the motives, the impulses, the principles that shape the life of actual men and women?" With this kind of truth, he told young writers, your books cannot be bad, morally or artistically. Without it, "all graces of style and feats of invention and cunning of construction are so many superfluities. . . ."

But then the question: How to be true in fiction?—how to say what is actual through something which is made up, invented; in short, which is a fiction? Howells knew well the depths and subtleties of the problem, knew that there were other roads to literary "truth"—the road Hawthorne took, the road Henry James was to take—roads which led through the brilliant strangeness of physical romance or the arc-lit phantasms of psychological romance. But Howells and his age felt that before writers could go *above* or *beneath*, they had to go *in*. Before they could attempt to tell the truth about the extraordinary, they had to tell the truth about the ordinary. How could they plumb the depths or reach the heights when there was so much to be learned about the levels, so much falsehood and sentiment to be dispelled before writers and readers could know the verities of their own social existence?

So this was the task the age of Howells set itself—to tell the truth, through fiction, about the ordinary world of physical experience. And the first way to do this, they felt, was to narrow the gap between fiction and nonfiction, to write fiction that was largely autobiographical, that was one's own experiences clarified by the perspective of the fictional technique. The novel, Howells felt, becomes the only true autobiography, for only by putting on the "mask" of the teller of tales can a man show his real face beneath it.

Strangely enough, as we have seen, it was Thomas Bailey Aldrich, the purveyor of sentimentalities, who brought home to Howells the lessons which the Brahmins had been trying to teach him. For with the reading of Aldrich's *The Story of a Bad Boy,* Howells became convinced that the future of his generation lay in fictionalizing its personal experience, in immersing itself in the contemporary American atmosphere and telling what it knew about life from what it had seen, heard, smelt, sensed about it.

.   .   .   .

5. The Autobiographical Method: De Forest, Harte,
Eggleston, Garland, Twain

With Howells, the group that became known as the "realists" agreed
that the way to write truthfully was to write of the life one knew, and
whenever one of their segments of clarified autobiography appeared, it
was assured of the praise of Howells and the powerful magazines for
which he wrote. De Forest's pioneer work, *Miss Ravenel's Conversion*,
gained its strength from the knowing account of the Civil War which
only someone who had campaigned in it could write. Many years after
its publication, De Forest issued the original letters which he had sent to
his family during the great cataclysm. The description of the chaotic
battle of Port Hudson, the scenes at the hospital where, for the first time,
Americans were permitted to see the realities of war, to watch the
hideous drop of amputated legs and the numb wonder of the dying, these
and scenes like them were reworked with little change from the letters
which the young captain De Forest had written when the impressions
were vivid within him. Like De Forest, his Western contemporary, Bret
Harte, thought, at least, that he was drawing his characters and actions
from the life about him, and claimed that every person in his stories had
their living counterparts. Eggleston, in the Midwest, had written his best
book, *The Hoosier Schoolmaster*, as a sentimentalized but nonetheless
fairly accurate impression of his own and his brother's experiences with
the rude farmers of Indiana and their ruder children. A generation after
he wrote it, an Indiana paper printed the death notice of one Hoosier
who had achieved his greatest fame by being the prototype of "Jeemie
Phillips," who lost the spelling bee in Eggleston's novel. Ten years after
Eggleston had met Taine through the pages of *Art of the Netherlands*,
Hamlin Garland made the impressive acquaintance of the French critic
through the pages of *The History of English Literature*, and diligently
copied word for word Taine's analysis of the duties of a writer in an age
of science. He made Taine's theory the basis of his lectures on literature
in Boston in 1884, and then, hat in hand, he waited upon the man who
was doing most to turn these theories into fruitful practice. He felt the
thrill of discipleship surging through him when the kindly Howells
smiled upon him, the day of their meeting at the "dean's" vacation home
in Auburndale, and when Howells talked to him about the simple honesty of autobiographical fiction, Garland knew he must write the story
of his own life. When *Main-Travelled Roads* appeared in 1891, tortured
triptychs of farm life on the mid-frontier as Garland and his family had
lived it, Howells could devote a large part of his "Editor's Study" to hail-
ing it as the creation out of burning dust of the truth about human
experience on the American soil.

The ultimate worth of any literary method, however, is not in the production of the good, but of the best. The works of De Forest, of Eggleston, of Garland, even of Howells are of the class of honest second-rate, occasionally pressing close to greatness, never quite pushing past to glory. But in Mark Twain, the group produced the timeless figure, one of the four or five giants of American letters. And Mark Twain, like the others, wrote according to the realists' creed and achieved his stature when transmuting the ore of his personal experience into the gold of reminiscence, autobiography, and autobiographical fiction. From the beginning Twain knew his way to lie in reporting and interpreting what he saw and heard. The Mississippi and the West provided him with all the characters he would ever encounter again: whenever he met a stranger, he knew he had met him before—on the river. And so he spun his greatness out of his experience, and when he tried to do otherwise, he wrote well, but not greatly.

Although Howells encouraged the lesser side of Twain's genius when it turned to inventions like *The Prince and the Pauper* and *A Connecticut Yankee,* his first and highest praise was reserved for works which Twain created out of his remembrance. He was first brought close to the great Westerner by the autobiographical *The Innocents Abroad,* with its large amount of "real life" in it and its fidelity to the experience of its author. Twain was raised by this criticism to the heights of exultation, and for the rest of his life he yearned to taste the rum of his friend's approval. When he had made his initial success with his travel books, he had promised to use his eyes, to see clearly with them, and report accurately. He never lost this faith in the eye as the organ of truthful perception. Truly a son of Missouri, he believed what he saw. Although he wasted very little of his energies discussing the techniques of fiction, the little criticism he did write was largely on this one theme—that the author who tells what he has seen is taking the first necessary step towards literary value, and that when he invents, he is apt to be mistaken, or sentimental, or silly. This was the sum of his attack on Fenimore Cooper, who simply had not been there and therefore simply could not know. And Twain, furthermore, was not bothered in the least, until the very end, by the possibilities of illusion, of deception by the senses. The metaphor with which he attacked Professor Edward Dowden illustrates his commonsensical attitude towards the testimony of the eyes and ears. People like Dowden, he wrote, would have us believe we are mistaken when we look at a body of water and say it is blue, since, they say, you can dip up a glassful and show it is white. But, replied Twain, the water looks blue, and it is blue.

So he wrote most of his best works about life as it looked to him, and therefore as he believed it was. After the careful reporting of *The Innocents Abroad,* he continued his recreation of personal experience with *Roughing It.* And then he made the first bridge between autobiography and autobiographical fiction in *The Gilded Age.* The amount of personal history in this book was enormous, ranging from minor detail upward through the entire story of a family and an era as Twain had seen it develop. The Hawkinses, cursed with the hopeless hope of quick, undeserved riches, and a post-war America threatened by the same corruption, were the Clemens family and the America of Twain's youth and manhood. Washington Hawkins had much of Mark himself in him, the elder Clemens were the models for the elder Hawkinses. Lafayette Hawkins, he told Howells, was his seldom-do-well brother, Orion. Colonel Sellers was copied directly from his cousin James Lampton. When the Hawkinses, on their way to a new home on the frontier, witnessed a Mississippi steamboat explosion, Mark reproduced, in the novel, the catastrophe he had personally witnessed and which he later described in *Life on the Mississippi:* even the little French Midshipman was there in the fiction, as he was in life, heroically refusing aid as he died so that others might better use it. *Life on the Mississippi,* which has come to be classed, along with *Huckleberry Finn,* as the greatest work of a great author, was a return to straight autobiography. While Joe Twichell had suggested its theme on a walk one day in Hartford, Howells gave Twain, who by then had become close to him personally as well as artistically, the impetus which set him writing one of his two masterworks. In searching for contributors who would write simply of the things they knew well, Howells turned to Twain and asked him to write of his old times on the Mississippi. Twain then sat down and did the first, and best section of the book, which appeared as a series in the *Atlantic* in 1874, and Howells told him enthusiastically that he could taste the mud in it.

Before and after *The Prince and the Pauper,* his allegory in praise of progress, Twain kept close to personal reminiscence and out of it brought *Tom Sawyer* and then *Huckleberry Finn.* In making these two stories, he selected and arranged and hence interpreted much of his rich and varied experience at Hannibal. In Tom Sawyer, he created his own image and placed it outside himself, breathed his own life into it, and with that breath, all the romantic weaknesses and sentimentalism which he knew were the qualities of every boy, but of the boy that was Sam Clemens more than most. Huckleberry Finn and his evil father were recreations of Tom Blankenship and his parents, the town drunkard of Hannibal. Nigger Jim was one of his uncle's slaves in whose memory Mark Twain fashioned the most warmly rounded Negro character in our literature. When Mark wanted to tell of river humbuggery, he did not have to go outside his own experience to make the epitomes of all duping falsity in the Duke and the Dauphin, for as a boy he had seen and reported the same swindling rascals. Their names were different, of course, and the swindles they practiced, but their spirits were the same, and undoubtedly their strangely contrasting bodies as well. They had come down the river in 1852 and had advertised the performance of a "celebrated troupe." When the suckers had paid their silver, the curtains parted to disclose the frauds posturing absurdly in a "burlesque of a farce, the dullness of which was not relieved even by the disgusting blackguardisms with which it was profusely interlarded."

As well as the squint of fraud, Twain knew well the narrowing look of pride that he drew in Colonel Sherburn's eyes as he faced the mob in *Huckleberry Finn,* and he knew the look of death in the eyes of the drunkard Boggs whom the Colonel had warned to get out of town and then had murdered when his warning went unheeded. For this drama had been enacted on the streets of Hannibal and he had watched "Uncle Sam" Smarr, the prototype of Boggs, gasping out his last breath after William Owsley had shot him down.

It was out of this kind of recreated personal experience that Mark Twain's masterworks came, the best flower of the realistic method of fiction—writing of the life one knew.

[6] THE GILDED AGE, HUCKLEBERRY FINN, AND
THE RISE OF SILAS LAPHAM

> *"Morality penetrates all things . . ."*
> —HOWELLS

The morality of the realists, then, was built upon what appears a paradox—morality with an abhorrence of moralizing. Their ethical beliefs called, first of all, for a rejection of any scheme of moral behavior imposed, from without, upon the characters of fiction and their actions. Yet Howells always claimed for his works a deep moral purpose. What was it? It was based upon three propositions: that life, social life as lived in the world Howells knew, was valuable, and was permeated with morality; that its continued health depended upon the use of human reason to overcome the anarchic selfishness of human passions; that an objective portrayal of human life, by art, will illustrate the superior value of social, civilized man, of human reason over animal passion and primitive ignorance.

The first axiom—that social life has value—was an unquestioned article of faith during this period; when it came to be seriously questioned, the age of Howells was at an end. For that age had a faith in the physical world and its meaning, a faith that, in the endless complexities, in the cracks and joints of materiality, there was a moral force which held the palpable together and gave it its meaning. Indeed, this was Howell's own metaphor: "Morality penetrates all things, it is the soul of all things." He wrote these words at the time he was reading Tolstoy, for his introduction to the great Russian in 1886 was like a religious experience to him. What had been dark and dim before—the reason for his absorption with the common, the familiar, the low—suddenly was illuminated.

And notwithstanding all his wild flings at the iniquities of man, Mark Twain, too, had this same faith in the essential morality permeating his social structure. A scene he and Warner wrote into *The Gilded Age* is almost a definition of this complex moral vision of the realist who believed he was writing a species of "objective" social history, but at the same time was writing a commentary upon that history which was based upon its essentially moral meaning. True to the realistic method as we have seen it, Twain and his collaborator took this scene from life. A woman named Laura D. Fair had, one day in 1870, bought a revolver in a shop near her home in San Francisco, had taken the ferry across the bay to Oakland, had waited until the train discharged her middle-aged lover who was returning with his recently reconciled wife and children, had stalked him until he was aboard the ferry and seated with his family about him, and then had walked up to him and put a bullet into his chest. She was tried for murder, pleaded momentary insanity, and finally was acquitted. Twain was so repelled by this example of mass unreason that he wrote the major subplot of *The Gilded Age* around Laura Hawkins, betrayed by her middle-aged lover, Colonel Phelps. Just as Laura Fair had hunted down her victim, Laura Hawkins followed Phelps to a New York hotel and shot him down under the same unambiguously premeditated circumstances. The Laura of fiction was tried and freed on the same grounds as the real Laura. There was a great scene of rejoicing in the courtroom as the women swarmed about the successful defense attorney and embraced him in a scene, the authors said, which went down in the annals of New York as "the kissing of Braham." From this point on, we must watch the fictional handling of the incident carefully. The authors described what followed: the judge rapped his gavel, and reasonably declared that the accused must be placed in an institution since it had been found, that while in a deranged condition, she had taken a life. Laura was led away to a hospital for the criminally insane, and sank back upon the cot as the door shut upon her terrible despair. But then the authors cried "wait!" And they stepped aside to tell the "dear reader" that this is what would have happened had they been writing a novel; for, they declared, the author of a novel would have had to arrange his material towards this reasonable and moral outcome; however, they were not, they said, writing a novel, but were writing history, and so they would have to reluctantly report that Laura Hawkins did not go to the insane asylum, but was driven home in a carriage amid the cheers of her admirers and left free to follow her career as a momentarily popular heroine.

Let us stop for a moment and consider the implications of this extraordinary little piece of artistic "business." The authors seem to have said, first, that fiction has an obligation to morality and to reason; that it must show the readers the way the good life should be lived. Then they declared that their work is not fiction, but history, and what they were describing was the history of their own society, a society ruled not by reason but by unreason, and therefore one in which good and evil were not followed by some kind of reward or punishment.

But we must go further before we accept this superficial analysis. For the plain fact is that Twain and Warner were not writing history, but were writing fiction. Laura Hawkins was like Laura Fair, but was not Laura Fair; her story was taken from life, but it was life selected and arranged. And to what did this arrangement eventually lead? To a scene where Laura Hawkins, reaching the depth of human misery, feeling herself worse than worthless, sells herself to be scorned and mocked by the vulgar in an almost empty auditorium, and wounded deeply with the knowledge of her own uselessness, totters off the stage to die. So in their novel which, like all realistic novels pressed close to the actual, there was still the arrangement of the "real" for moral instruction. Indeed, it was the essence of satiric realism that it should so scoff at the iniquities of society, that it should try to show Americans wherein their lives were leading to error, not because the realists hated the life they were criticizing, but because they loved it, and therefore wanted to reform it. When, at one point, Howells asked Twain for another satire on European travel, Twain replied that he could not give him one, for he hated it; and, he went on, one has to like something before one can satirize it. Believing in the essentially "moral" and "right" nature of their American society, although ready at the drop of a tort to spring to the attack of that which they loved so that it might be brought nearer to perfection, Twain and Warner could not do otherwise, in writing their "history" of the Gilded Age, than to arrange its details to show that "wrong" actions, individual and social, lead to unhappiness and ruin.

This same moral purpose, based upon a belief in an essentially moral society, operated in all of Twain's fiction, even, as we shall see, in his late and presumably "disillusioned works," and it is the force that holds together the episodic structure of *Huckleberry Finn*, the meaning that fills in and seals the joints of the rambling narrative, just as, for Twain and Howells, it held together the structure of their nineteenth-century world, making it a comedy instead of a nightmare. *Huckleberry Finn* is, on one level, a moral attack on social unreason, an indictment of social sentimentalism and a demonstration of the virtues of social empiricism. The frame of the picaresque story is the contrast between the method of reason, embodied by Huck Finn, and the method of sentimental romance, personified by Tom Sawyer, between hard-headed Huck who could be counted upon to do the right thing, and romantic Tom who could be counted on to do the wrong, and do it with a great flourish. The contrast was introduced at the beginning, when Huck described how Tom would transform the world of reality into a world of phantoms, of sheep who are maidens in distress, farmers who are knights, rusty lamps which are passports to the supernatural. And then the narrative was rounded at the end by the reintroduction of Tom who "assisted" in the ultimate freeing of Nigger Jim. This long section, covering about a third of the book, has often been called disproportionate and anticlimactic; but in one sense its very extravagance is a commentary upon Tom's "unrealism." When Jim had been betrayed by the Duke and the Dauphin, and locked up in a flimsy shack, Huck wanted to steal the key, which was hanging within easy reach, let Jim out, and then shove off down the river. But Tom Sawyer had read the *Count of Monte Cristo,* and would have none of the plan. "It's too blame simple," he said. "What's the good of a plan that ain't no more trouble than that?" He told Huck *his* scheme and Huck admitted, "I could see in a minute it was worth fifteen of mine for style, and would make Jim just as free a man as mine would, and maybe get us all killed besides." Tom nearly did get them killed, and it almost seemed as if Nigger Jim would go back to captivity when the scamp revealed the total uselessness of his dramatics, for he had known all along that Miss Watson had freed Jim in her will. This was Mark Twain's commentary upon the social inutility of sentimentalism, the wrongness of the romantic failure to face the facts of practical living.

Twain's masterwork was, then, based on a rejection of a false absolute. It also proposed as the test of a "good" action the results of that action in bettering the immediate human situation. It was, in short, a work based upon the prevailing pragmatic assumptions of the North after the Civil War. This is worth emphasizing, because *Huckleberry Finn* is, in one sense, a story of revolt against society, a tale of Huck's flight from the restrictions of civilization. It is all too easy, therefore, to read this same kind of revolt into its moral scheme as well. But in its morality, the book is not a work of revolt, but of acquiescence in the fundamental premises of the dominant American society of its time.

To see this clearly, we must become aware of the two circles of moral judgment which operate in the act of experiencing the novel. One was a morality of pragmatic humanitarianism; its premise was the right of the individual to the pursuit of happiness, regardless of the individual's color. The other was the *a priori* code of the slaveholding South which regarded the Negro not as a human being, but as a commodity; and in this frame of reference, the injunction "thou shalt not steal" became a principle which would make it a crime to aid a runaway slave. Huck feels himself completely within this Southern frame of reference, and can therefore experience only a sense of guilt when he helps Nigger Jim to escape. The reader, however, exactly reverses each one of Huck's judgments upon himself, because the book is written and must be read in the other, the general American pragmatic frame of reference.

This reversal occurs most obviously when, on the raft, Jim started daydreaming. "He was saying," Huck reported uncomfortably, "how the first thing he would do when he got to a free state he would go to saving up money and never spend a single cent, and when he got enough he would buy his wife, which was owned on a farm close to where Miss Watson lived; and then they would both work to buy the two children, and if their master wouldn't sell them, they'd get an Abolitionist to go and steal them." Huck was shocked beyond measure. "It almost froze me to hear such talk. He wouldn't ever dared to talk such talk in his life before. . . . Thinks I, this is what comes of my not thinking. Here was this nigger, which I had as good as helped run away, coming right out flat-footed and saying he would steal his own children—children that belonged to a man I didn't know, a man that hadn't ever done me no harm."

Huck thereupon decided to give Jim up to the authorities, and immediately felt "easy and happy and light as a feather right off." But when a canoe-load of white men approached, Huck put them off with a wonderfully clever ruse; and when they went and Jim was saved, Huck said: "I got aboard the raft feeling bad and low, because I knowed very well I had done wrong, and I see it warn't no use for me to try to do right; a body that don't get *started* right when he's little ain't got no show." Huck, having adopted the ethics of slavery, was convinced he was a great sinner; every time he helped Jim, he was saddened by this sense of guilt. But, of course, each time he was saddened, the reader was cheered; each time, operating under a false code, he thought he did wrong, he did right, by the true code of humanitarianism. And this irony would only be possible if Mark Twain could feel sure that the society for which he was producing *Huckleberry Finn* was a society that, by and large, accepted the code of humanitarianism. And that is why *Huckleberry Finn*, like *Miss Ravenel's Conversion*, like *A Hazard of New Fortunes*, has a happy ending. Mark Twain believed that the moral principles of his society could triumph; the slave, after all, had been freed.

NATURALISM AND INTROSPECTION

THE END OF THE COMEDY

When does an "Age" end? The very asking exposes the arbitrariness of all such divisions. We saw that the comic tone—the deep conviction of the value of the world of appearances—was the hallmark of the age of Howells. And this tone did not disappear at once, instead it trailed off like a sigh after the explosion of Haymarket. Twain was still occasionally able to crow to Howells about the immense days when it seemed, with the revolutions in South America, that republics were springing up all over the globe; Howells could agree with Norton that, after all, pleasant people were more numerous than the unpleasant; and he could say in an article bitterly critical of American life that a danger was not that Americans should praise themselves too much, but should "accuse themselves too much."

But these expressions were overwhelmed by increasing weariness and pessimism. By 1895 Twain was sixty, and Howells would become so in two more years, and they knew they were two old men whose day had passed. The death of Winifred in the first months of 1889 left Howells crushed, and the death of Susy Clemens, occurring so tragically while her parents were away on the lecture tour with which her father recouped his shattered fortunes, took the light out of Twain's world. New writers were emerging; for all the continued and unexciting faithfulness of the Garlands, the Boyesens, the Herricks, and the Fullers, there were the younger writers who took Howells as their guide up to a certain point and then, with his blessing, went on into the woods alone: there was Harold Frederic, and Stephen Crane; Theodore Dreiser and Frank Norris, all of whom published promising work in the 1890's. And while Henry James had produced good work, even great work before, his major phase lay just ahead, and his genius symptomatically came to fruition at the moment when that of Howells and Twain was dying.

After *A Hazard of New Fortunes,* Howells had little left to do. While to the outward eye he seemed to be still at the height of his fame and the fullness of his powers, there were signs of his decline. *Harper's* seemed almost eager to shake loose of some of their commitments with him, especially from his continuance of the "Editor's Study" department, about which there had been so much controversy. More important, however, was the growing evidence that he was written out, that he had said all he had to say, and only with effort could force himself to say it over again. From 1890 to 1894 his letters to Norton, along with Twain, the closest and dearest friend of his age, were full of doubts as to his ability to go on in the same line, as to his ability to continue writing fiction; even worse, doubts as to his desire to go on. At the moment of his deepest self-doubts, he was jolted by an episode involving his short-lived editorship of the *Cosmopolitan* from December, 1891, to June, 1892. He had been invited to bring all his prestige and experience to this magazine by John Brisben Walker, who, it would appear, assured him of a free hand in its conduct. Howells immediately set about soliciting material which would, it appears, have made the *Cosmopolitan* the center of the critically realistic, just as he had made the *Atlantic* the stronghold of the realistic; he wrote Garland, for example, asking him if he would do a piece on the growing Farmer's Alliance movement, or anything else on the same lines. It was quite possibly a disagreement about this kind of material that led to the breach between Walker and Howells, about which Howells was so silent, and which left him without an official editorial connection until

1900, when he relaxed into the Editor's "Easy Chair" department of *Harper's*.

In the meantime, Twain was sinking deeper into the pessimism of his later years. Whereas the early sorrows of his career—the death of his brother on the Mississippi, the death of his first son, both tragedies for which he blamed himself—had been absorbed in the general healthfulness of his optimism, the death of Susy in 1896 was the blow from which he never recovered; for the following four years, his letter paper was still edged with black in gloomy remembrance of his loss. And for the first time Howells and Twain and Aldrich began to talk about reality as if it were a dream: the present a nightmare, the past a pleasant haze of nostalgia. Do you remember, Howells wrote Aldrich, wistfully, the good times they had, the dinners at Ober's where the three of them, together with Ralph Keeler and Bret Harte and James T. Fields, would devour their flattened omelettes and beefsteak with shoe-pegs (champignons), and a blasphemous story from Fields about a can of peaches would be followed by the condescensions of Harte to Twain which must have been so severely galling to the latter. And always there would be the sigh that it all seemed like the vision in a golden haze. What a dream it has been! they would exclaim; or how like two old derelicts they were, Howells and Twain, drifting aimlessly about, their passengers gone, their compass giving no familiar readings.

In this mood Twain was oppressed by his lack of productivity and his wife would beg him to try to recapture the joy of life which had given the world Huck Finn and the Yankee. But the age whose spirit he was and whose spirit was his, was slipping away until suddenly, everyone seemed to agree at once, it was gone. And in its afterglow, the gloom of personal and financial losses deep upon him, he turned with a cry of rage upon the personal God in whom he had never really believed and the impersonal Fate in which he always had, and wrote the sombre tales of *The Man That Corrupted Hadleyburg* and *The Mysterious Stranger*.

But his pessimism never quite changed to misanthropy; he kept his belief in the goodness possible, though never prevalent, in man in his familial and social relations. We must not be misled by outcries of what seem to be man-hatred in works like *What Is Man?*; for his fiction is more revealing, showing the pervasion of his basic humanistic faith; he pictured the forces which corrupted men, or played with them as if they were meaningless toys, as a fiendish malignance, which he eventually gave the name of Satan. Should he and Howells ever see their children again? without a doubt, he said bitterly, for that would give Malignance another chance to break their hearts.

But his conception of the malice of supra-human Fate caused him to elevate Satan into supreme power in the Universe, and kept something of God among men. In the dark late years of his despair, he lost optimism, but he kept some of his faith in man. This fact has been obscured by the many evidences of the deepening pessimism of his last twenty years, with works like *The Man That Corrupted Hadleyburg* and *The Mysterious Stranger* cited to illustrate the depth of his hatred for his fellow. But when we examine works like these, what do we find?—that men in general do not come out so badly. For on the scale of increasing sympathy, we generally find that the same ordinary, common people he celebrated in *Huckleberry Finn*, like Jack Halliday who led the townspeople of Hadleyburg in their scoffing of the Incorruptibles, ranked high, while the pretentious, self-righteous "pillars of society" were very low. The commoners of Hadleyburg rose to the derision which punctured the pretensions of their respectable bankers and lawyers and civic leaders and ridiculed their own civic hypocrisy with the chorus of "You are not a baaad man." Highest in the scale of sympathies was the old couple who wrestled unsuccessfully with the superhuman temptation placed in their path by the unknown visitor, finally succumbed, and then, with their faith in themeslves shattered, were left crushed and dying. And who was lowest of all—lower even than the pompous Incorruptibles? It could not fail to be the "mysterious stranger" himself, a dehumanized figure who came into Hadleyburg, was the victim of a slight which the author did not even bother to record, and then set about coolly to destroy the village's pride with a malevolent practical "joke."

Had Mark Twain wished to change the focus of his readers' sympathies from the sinful people of Hadleyburg to their tormentor, it would have needed only the slightest of additional touches—the specifying of the man's grievance, the detailing of the injury done him, at least what he looked like, what his name was. Instead Twain kept him nameless and bodiless, an anonymous shadow who slipped into the world of men and slipped out again, and then from afar, with unfeeling malice, manipulated the strings of lustful greed and made the human puppets dance. And what must be remembered is that Mark Twain did not wholly renounce his citizenship in the commonwealth whose motto was: men are a collection of asses, and I'm the biggest ass in the collection. As a matter of fact, he had earlier told something very like the story of *The Man That Corrupted Hadleyburg*, and he had told it on himself; it was a story in *Life on the Mississippi* in which he was the one whose ethics and cupidity came into conflict, with greed the easy victor. There he had related how a dying man in Germany had entrusted him with the secret of a $10,000 cache along the Mississippi, so that the fortune might be given to the poor shoemaker to whom it rightfully belonged. It took very little effort on the part of his companions to persuade him that it would be far more charitable to keep the money themselves, for with the access of sudden fortune, the shoemaker would "shut up shop, maybe take to drinking, maltreat his motherless children. . . ." They soon had talked the poor old man down from $10,000 to a chromo sent as a sentimental remembrance. The point was that Twain immersed himself in the fallibility which he satirized, and in the later, more serious, more bitter description of human corruptibility, he did not completely lose his sense of complicity, his feeling of sympathy. And the second "mysterious stranger"—the title character of the posthumously published work which summarized his later pessimism—was Satan, and there was an undercurrent of terrible anger in the descriptions of the fiend who rules our destinies, how he creates small villages and their populations only to crush them like ants under a board. Helpless, tiny, yet compassionate, the human ants engage our whole sympathies, and our rage is not against man but against Fate.

These are the symptoms of the continuance of some elements of confidence even in Twain's later years. But these elements no longer were segments of the robust and vivifying faith which he shared with the age whose genius he was. Instead they are unintegrated parts of the darkening skepticism and doubt which gathered about his snowy eagle's head, as it was gathering about America's.

Meanwhile, new currents were beginning to flow, one of them carrying the old debris of sentiment and escapism, the other a fresh new surge towards the future. The first counter-current was the revival of historical romance, and it seemed to overwhelm the realistic movement. As early as 1893 one of Howells' fictional publishers had said that "people are getting tired of those commonplace, photographic things. They want something with a little imagination." He could not then foresee that by 1900 people would be buying *Graustarks* and *Prisoner of Zendas* by the millions. By the turn of the century, the fashion of the historical romance had not only captured the general reading public, but had reduced America's centers of culture. When early in 1900, Howells' friend W. H. Bishop invited him to speak at Yale, he warned Howells that he would be in the enemy's country, with regard to opinions about fiction, a country where the only good words were for swashbucklers and their rapiers. Howells answered that he didn't mind being in the enemy's country; he was growing used to it. The thing he complained of, he added, was that it was so poverty-stricken in ideas that a man could not live off of it. In his first essay in *Harper's* "Easy Chair" he despaired of making anyone understand "how wholly" writers of realism had been forgotten, in an age when "the cry . . . is for historical romances, which is answered with volumes in all their hundred thousands." And by 1904, *Collier's* summarized the trend of the times: "The popular novel of today is romantic—romantic in subject and effusively romantic in method. A great deal of adventure, a dash of sentiment, and a strange land for its setting make a fine recipe for a modern novel. All of this is far removed from the minute study of commonplace people which Mr. Howells has made the basis of most of his fiction."

He knew part of the reason for this; the romantic tendency was always present during the supremacy of the "natural," waiting for the time when American sensibility would once again feel the need for probing behind the world of physical appearances; but he felt, too, that there was another, baser reason for the return of interest in the "romanticistic," in the sentimentalism which took the form of the historical romance. He theorized that America's unconscious revulsion from the shameful imperialism of the Spanish-American War made it "more than ever anxious to get away from itself, and welcome the tarradiddles of the historical romancers as a relief from the facts of the odious present." In an attempt to explode these sentimentalists, Howells wrote one of his best short stories, "Editha," the tale of a girl who embodied all the nonsense about the heroic romanticism of war and whose false sense of values drove her unfortunate lover to enlist. She had visions of him returning heroically home, with some slight wound to testify his courage. Instead, he died miserably in Cuba, and his mother told Editha bluntly that her sentimentalism had killed him. "How perfectly vulgar," said one of Editha's fashionable acquaintances, when she heard of the old lady's accusation, and that helpful phrase enabled Editha to explain everything and to rest in contentment with her sentimentality.

But if the current of historical romance was broad, it was also shallow; running deeper were other currents; younger writers were gratefully accepting the encouragement Howells gave them; to the same allegiance to the truth, to the same unswerving honesty, to careful representation of the normal and the commonplace, they were adding new areas of man's knowledge of himself, going deeper into his social life, spreading wider over his political and economic life, and the unbroken line of serious writers from the 'nineties testifies to the endurance of the basic doctrines of realism. Stephen Crane in *Maggie*, Theodore Dreiser in *Sister Carrie*, Upton Sinclair, Sinclair Lewis in *Main Street, Babbitt,* and *Elmer Gantry,* James Farrell in *Studs Lonigan,* all are in a direct line of descent from Howellsian realism and critical realism. The essential similarity, yet important difference in degree, between the generations of realists was symbolized in the tone of a meeting between Howells and Theodore Dreiser in 1900. Dreiser felt that Howells "has been an influence for good in American letters" and had "used his strength and popularity in the direction of what he took to be right"; but there was scorn in Dreiser's eyes as he looked at the man whom he found to be "greater than his writings," and if that was little enough praise, "greater than his reputation." For Howells "had no direct experience" of the "great misery"; Howells had led the sheltered middle-class existence; Howells probably, as Henry James said commiseratingly of him, had known no other woman but his wife. Howells had never, like Dreiser, lived a tortured life of adolescent poverty in a house where love was a stranger; Howells had never, like Crane, slept under a Mexican sky between two bandits or lived with a "madam."

Yet when *Maggie* was refused by publisher after publisher, it was Howells who found him one, and who wrote the essay which launched the young man on his literary career. Crane was frank in his avowal of his discipleship. He was grateful in a way that was hard for him to say, he told Howells, and he always thanked God that he could have the strongest admiration for the work of a man who had been so much to him personally.

Crane believed that he was simply carrying on the work which Howells had begun: the telling of the truth about that which he knew. But there was a difference in degree, if not in kind, between his fiction and that of Howells. The younger novelists were catching and recording the first tremors of cultural change; in this instance, the tremors were of uncertainty, of loss of confidence, a loss of the buoyancy which had made possible the works of Howells, the great works of Twain, the philosophy of William James. The novels of Crane, Norris, Frederic, and Dreiser began to reflect the spread of the feeling that man is no lawgiver, but an absorber; that nature "stands firm," and man must accommodate himself to her, "must record truth, inhuman though it be, and submit to it." This was William James' statement of the "naturalistic" feeling. It also seems to be a summary of the literary position known by the same name.

It is generally agreed that naturalism, the literature of supposedly pessimistic determinism, had its major manifestation in France, especially in the works of Emile Zola. Zola was idolized by Frank Norris, who took him as master and guide, and hence, runs the argument, gave tangible proof of the emergence, in America, of a new strain of literary technique and attitude in the last decade of the nineteenth century.

What are some of the hallmarks of this supposedly new strain? We must go back to its origins to understand it. Early in his career, Zola cast about for a philosophy to inform his literature and give it meaning, and he thought he found it in Claude Bernard's description of the experimental method of science, and in his interpretations of the theories of Charles Darwin. Here Zola believed he found the rationale for a kind of literature which would report truthfully and objectively, with a passion for scientific accuracy and an overwhelming accumulation of factual detail. Since Darwin had shown that all organisms were shaped by their environment, the way to show what really happens to a person is to portray him in his social and economic surroundings, with as little selection and arrangement of the details of those surroundings as possible. And various corollaries seemed to flow from the neo-Darwinian origins of this literary theory. One of the most striking was the treatment of man as partly animal, especially with regard to his primitive drives of love, hate and hunger. The naturalistic novelist would then go further in the direction of portraying these drives than did his predecessors. A second, and more important corollary, was the assumption of a deep pessimism: for if man develops and changes solely through the buffeting of his environment, if he acts solely through the outer pressures of his heredity and environment, over neither of which he exercises any control, then there is a tendency to see him as a helpless animal without meaning and without hope, reduced to either a pawn of these two forces, or, with pessimism carried one step further (and Twain came near this position in his last years), an insect which some malignant higher force torments with titanic malice.

The first of these distinctions—the extension of truthful representation to wider areas of human experience—would not seem to warrant the division between two kinds of literary sensibility; we have seen that a man like Howells knew that realism must spread out to include these areas of experience. The realistic mode, widening in its interests from those of a Howells, to those of a Robert Herrick, and thence to the interests of a Sinclair Lewis, remained essentially the same philosophy of art, using the same techniques, but with the extension of the materials upon which these techniques were exercised. What does make a difference is the way in which the newer writers continued to shift the focus of their attention away from the individual towards the natural and social forces which seemed to be enslaving man. But even with their greater emphasis upon natural drives and environmental influence, American writers at the turn of the century did not succumb to complete pessimism. "Naturalism" in the sense of a completely pessimistic determinism never existed save in the mind of its enemies. If it is true that man is simply a helpless creature of external forces, then it follows that man can do nothing about his fate, and therefore it is useless to hope for betterment either of society or of the individual. But the original "naturalist"—the father of them all—Emile Zola, was an ardent reformer, and specifically stated that he wrote his books to show men and their conditions as they are, so that man might take heed of them and make them better. The rigid determinism that supposedly dominated naturalism and differentiated it from other types of literary sensibilities would make it quite impossible for man to affect either his own fate or the fates of others; an individual would be simply the product of external forces over which he has no control; hence there could be no question of a "right" or a "wrong" action, no question of morality, for man could only act as he must. But Zola was a self-proclaimed "experimental moralist"; the putrescent corruption of Nana's body under the ravages of smallpox gave the Rougon-Macquart cycle one of the most moral endings in all literature; the bitter indictment of the unjust social and economic scheme in *Germinal* conveyed the author's moral vision of the just society which would make such miseries impossible.

It is not strange that this should be so. Writing is painful and demands great courage, and it would be difficult to imagine anyone undergoing the strains of creation, the disillusion of watching the transcribed reality fall short of one's vision of perfection, if one believed that it all added up to nothing. Dissatisfaction with his world does one of several things to a writer; if he loses confidence in appearances, he seeks the primitive meanings which he feels are eternally there beneath the flux, or he makes a religion of art; if he remains in his world and seeks salvation in its complexities, he does what Zola did, what Howells did, what in our times a James Farrell does: he writes of things as they are so that people will understand them and try to make them better. This was the answer Danny O'Neill gave to his University of Chicago professor when asked why he wrote of the sordidness of Chicago's South Side.

And the younger American writers at the turn of the century who seem to have been dominated by the pessimistic determinism which has been called "naturalism" turn out to be either writers who wrote for reformation of man, or writers who were groping towards the meanings they felt lay under or above the ordinary world of human social relations.

Dreiser, for example, who at first glance seems so different from what went before (and was hailed by Sinclair Lewis, himself a critical realist of the twentieth century, as the pioneer of new frontiers in American literature); Dreiser's attitude seemed to be summed up in the striking symbol at the beginning of *The Financier,* when young Frank Cowperwood stood before the fishmarket's tank and watched the life-and-death struggle between a squid and a lobster, the uneven battle ending, as it must, on the side of the harder armor and sharper claws. For Cowperwood this was the sum of the world's amorality, and it has seemed the sum of Dreiser's world as well. But from the beginning, Dreiser's world of fiction was a moral one.

The fall of Hurstwood in *Sister Carrie* was as moral a tale as the career of Nana. As for the trilogy of which *The Financier* was the first part, it traced the dramatic rise of the immoralist, whose rise brought no more satisfaction than did the "rise" of Silas Lapham; and when the plan of the whole came into view, with the publication of the notes which would have formed the basis of the concluding volume, *The Stoic,* it turned out that Dreiser had designed the series to lead up to—the proof that morality has no place in the Darwinian world of tooth and claw? Hardly; Cowperwood's heirs were to be shown acknowledging that the only peace and satisfaction can come from complicity and feeling with others, and planning the return of their father's fortune to the society from which he had so unscrupulously wrested it.

In Frank Norris, the other presumed "naturalist" of the younger generation of writers, "naturalism" in the sense of pervasive pessimistic determinism is just as hard to find. In *The Octopus,* for example, Presley discovered that the master of the railroad was presumably a victim, helpless in the clutch of the supposedly inexorable laws that govern the affairs of men, just as the earth is in the grasp of natural forces. At least, that is what Shelgrim said, and presumably what Presley believed. But the total meaning of *The Octopus* added up neither to pessimism, nor even to determinism. For according to the scheme of which *The Octopus* was a part, and according to Norris' explicit statement at the end of that work, these vast cosmic forces inevitably worked for the Good. And even social determinism, as well as cosmic pessimism, was ruled out by the structure of *The Octopus,* which did nothing to show the inexorable social necessity of the railroad's actions, and everything to arouse the reader's antipathies against them. The very metaphors applied to the railroad—the title metaphor itself with its connotations of inhuman, faceless death by water —involve the reader in a fierce personal hatred for the machine which was strangling the farmers of the valley; the farmers, victims of the railroad, were warmly personalized; we sympathize with their loves, their loyalties, their griefs; and the only personalization of the cyclopian monster that came tearing through the valley, scattering the carcasses of sheep in its dumb, murderous, iron wake, was the ugly S. Behrman, a man without even a first name, a stereotypical villain if there ever was one, who met a fitting end buried under the flood of wheat pouring into the hold of the India-bound merchantman. This general tenor of criticism of things as they are was reinforced by one of the most moving juxtapositions imaginable: the scenes which alternated between the orphaned child watching her widowed mother starve to death in the bushes, and the dinner party in the sumptuous mansion on the hill just above them. Interspersed with the dying mother's words were snatches of conversation over a decadently elaborate menu, with each course specified; the alternation made an almost unbearably affecting contrast; together with the main dramatic structure of impersonal machine pitted against personal man, it made the work one which stirred the reader with a sense of the injustice and inequality of which he must take heed and change, rather than one which stunned him with a conviction of the overwhelming power of amoral forces over which man has no control, and to which he should deterministically resign himself.

"Naturalism," then, in America, seemed to be no more than a deepening and broadening of the realistic and critically realistic techniques and attitudes extended to larger areas of society. But when one reads the novels of Norris and Crane, and the later works of Harold Frederic, one becomes aware of the beginnings of a difference in kind as well as degree, a difference in treatment as well as a difference in materials. One feels that the surface that Howells revered and portrayed with such loving fidelity was beginning to break up, and through its fissures were welling strange new visions: ogres and demigods, grotesqueries, and distortions of time and space which we associated with the romantics of an earlier time. But these weird landscapes were as real as any pleasant New England countryside described so honestly by Miss Jewett, and the ogres were as genuine, if scarcely as palpable, as the hard-shelled Baptists whom Eggleston showed us. For these were the landscapes and creatures of the human mind, the richly mysterious region where the experience of the individual mind and the experience of the race seem to coalesce; where mythology appears not so much the symbolization of social pat-

terns, as of mental process; where symbols themselves take on new meanings, and become not so much discursive representations of meanings
within the story, but presentational things in themselves, the point in
palpability where the otherwise unknowable things about the human
mind are materialized.

This newer "romanticism" (as Norris termed it) was primarily interested in extending the bounds of literary investigation outward from the
normal commonplace of average civilized life in two directions: one was
downward, deeper into the inner life of the individual; the other was upward, into the life of the race. And in conducting these explorations, the
newer novelists had to abandon the objective techniques of the realists, so
well suited to truthful reporting of the average. In place of picaresque
looseness, they began to contrive carefully interlaced structures where
epical figures worked their way through patterns of symbolism; in place
of autobiographical freedom, with its apparent abstention from moralizing, they began to attempt tight contrivances which, in Norris' words,
would prove something, would "draw conclusions from a whole congeries
of forces, social tendencies, race impulses." As Howells commented, it
was the reversal of the realistic mode which in some ways resembled the
older scientific method where the documents were collected and then
the hypothesis drawn. In the newer fiction, the hypothesis, the insight,
was drawn first, and then documents collected in support of the hypothesis: "First the inference, then the fact."'

Howells had observed, and to some extent charted, the flow of these
new currents towards twentieth-century fiction, one in the direction of
the psychological, the other in the direction of the mythical, both of
which directions ultimately converged in writers like Faulkner and Steinbeck. As early as 1893 one of his fictional authors had mentioned that the
"motive" of his story might be called psychological, and his publisher had
replied: "Well, they say that the *roman psychologique* is superseding the
realistic novel in France." By 1903, Howells saw that "a whole order of
literature" had arisen to which the name "psychological" might be given,
as the term "scientific" had been applied to realism. And he saw that the
newer impulses were, in many cases, revivals of those tendencies in the
literature which dominated the age just before his own—the tendencies
best represented by Hawthorne. (He might have added, of Melville, too;
but Melville was still deep in the obscurity from which he was only
rescued in 1921.) The newer fiction, Howells said, "turning from the
superabundance of character" would "burrow far down into a soul or
two" and bend its vision inward, as did Hawthorne; or else it would take
its clue from "a poet of such epical imagination" as Emile Zola.

Howells himself made some experiments, not very successful ones, with
introspection. In several short stories and one short novel in the century's
last years he went as far as he could in the unfamiliar grounds of
psychological analysis. That this could never be very far was suggested

by one of his stories in which Wanhope, a psychologist, proposed to a group, of which the author was a member, that it conduct an investigation into dreams. "That would be rather dreadful, wouldn't it?" Howells asked. "We do dream such scandalous, such compromising things about people." One of these "compromising things" was the subject of *The Shadow of a Dream,* in which a husband's recurrent nightmare was that his best friend, who lived with him, attended his funeral and then married his widow. The husband did die, and the wife did become engaged to the friend, but broke off her impending marriage when she learned the nature of her dead husband's dream.

Although Howells tried to begin to understand this new world with its strangely different kind of reality and was sympathetic to its explorers, although he felt that the fantasy life of the mind should be respected as something "gravely significant," he could not himself develop in this line, for it was, as he confessed to Norton, a new field for his ignorance. The depths of the mind's richness or the heights of the supposed consciousness of the race were not for him, whose ground was the open, sunny meadow of normality and reason. But he could, and did, encourage the younger writers to dive and to climb.

The Modern Element in
Modern Literature

LIONEL TRILLING

. . . I approached it [a course in modern literature] with an uneasiness which has not diminished with the passage of time—it has, I think, even increased. It arises, this uneasiness, from my personal relation with the works that form the substance of the course. Almost all of them have been involved with me for a long time—I invert the natural order not out of lack of modesty but taking the cue of W. H. Auden's remark that a real book reads us. I have been read by Eliot's poems and by *Ulysses* and by *Remembrance of Things Past* and by *The Castle* for a good many years now, since early youth. Some of these books at first rejected me; I bored them. But as I grew older and they knew me better, they came to have more sympathy with me and to understand my hidden meanings. Their nature is such that our relationship has been very intimate. No literature has ever been so shockingly personal as ours—it asks every question that is forbidden in polite society. It asks us if we are content with our marriages, with our family lives, with our professional lives, with our friends. It is all very well for me to describe my course in the college catalogue as "paying particular attention to the role of the writer as a critic of his culture"—this is sheer evasion: the questions asked by our literature are not about our culture but ourselves. It asks us if we are content with ourselves, if we are saved or damned—more than with anything else, our literature is concerned with salvation. No literature has even been so intensely spiritual as ours. I do not venture to call it religious, but certainly it has the special intensity of concern with the spiritual life which Hegel noted when he spoke of the great modern phenomenon of the secularization of spirituality.

I do not know how other teachers deal with this extravagant personal force of modern literature, but for me it makes difficulty. Nowadays the teaching of literature inclines to a considerable technicality, but when the teacher has said all that can be said about formal matters, about verse-patterns, metrics, prose conventions, irony, tension, etc., he must confront the necessity of bearing personal testimony. He must use whatever authority he may possess to say whether or not a work is true; and if not, why not; and if so, why so. He can do this only at considerable cost to his privacy. How does one say that Lawrence is right in his great rage against the modern emotions, against the modern sense of life and ways of being, unless one speaks from the intimacies of one's own feelings, and one's own sense of life, and one's own wished-for way of being? How, except with the implication of personal judgment, does one say to students that Gide is perfectly accurate in his representation of the awful boredom and slow corruption of respectable life? Then probably one rushes in to say that this doesn't of itself justify homosexuality and the desertion of one's dying wife, certainly not. But then again, having paid one's *devoirs* to morality, how does one rescue from morality Gide's essential point about the supreme rights of the individual person, and without making it merely historical and totally academic?

My first response to the necessity of dealing with matters of this kind was resentment of the personal discomfort it caused me. These are subjects we usually deal with either quite unconsciously or in the privacy of our own conscious minds, and if we now and then disclose our thoughts about them, it is to friends of equal age and especial closeness. Or if we touch upon them publicly, we do so in the relative abstractness and anonymity of print. To stand up in one's own person and to speak of them in one's own voice to an audience which each year grows younger as one grows older—that is not easy, and probably it is not decent.

And then, leaving aside the personal considerations, or taking them merely as an indication of something wrong with the situation, can we not say that, when modern literature is brought into the classroom, the subject being taught is betrayed by the pedagogy of the subject? We have to ask ourselves whether in our day too much does not come within the purview of the academy. More and more, as the universities liberalize themselves, and turn their beneficent imperialistic gaze upon what is called Life Itself, the feeling grows among our educated classes that little can be experienced unless it is validated by some established intellectual discipline, with the result that experience loses much of its personal immediacy for us and becomes part of an accredited societal activity. This is not entirely true and I don't want to play the laboring academic game of pretending that it *is* entirely true, that the university mind wilts and withers whatever it touches. I must believe, and I do believe, that the university study of art is capable of confronting the power of a work of art fully and courageously. I even believe that it can discover and disclose power where it has not been felt before. But the university study of art achieves this end chiefly with works of art of an older period. Time has the effect of seeming to quiet the work of art, domesticating it and

making it into a classic, which is often another way of saying that it is
an object of merely habitual regard. University study of the right sort
can reverse this process and restore to the old work its freshness and force
—can, indeed, disclose unguessed-at power. But with the works of art of
our own present age, university study tends to accelerate the process by
which the radical and subversive work becomes the classic work, and
university study does this in the degree that it is vivacious and responsive
and what is called non-academic. In one of his poems Yeats mocks the
literary scholars, "the bald heads forgetful of their sins," "the old, learned,
respectable bald heads," who edit the poems of the fierce and passionate
young men.

> Lord, what would they say
> Did their Catullus walk this way?

Yeats, of course, is thinking of his own future fate, and no doubt there is
all the radical and comical discrepancy that he sees between the poet's
passions and the scholars' close-eyed concentration on the text. Yet for
my part, when I think of Catullus, I am moved to praise the tact of all
those old heads, from Heinsius and Bentley to Munro and Postgate, who
worked on Codex G and Codex O and drew conclusions from them about
the lost Codex V—for doing only this and for not trying to realize and
demonstrate the true intensity and the true quality and the true cultural
meaning of Catullus's passion and managing to bring it somehow into
eventual accord with their respectability and baldness. Nowadays we
who deal with books in universities live in fear that the World—which
we imagine to be a vital, palpitating, passionate, reality-loving World—
will think of us as old, respectable, and bald, and we see to it that in our
dealings with Yeats—to take him as the example—his wild cry of rage
and sexuality is heard by our students and quite thoroughly understood
by them as—what is it that we eventually call it?—a significant expression
of our culture. The exasperation of Lawrence and the subversiveness of
Gide, by the time we have dealt with them boldly and straightforwardly,
are notable instances of the *alienation of modern man as exemplified by
the artist.* "Compare Yeats, Gide, Lawrence, and Eliot in the use which
they make of the theme of sexuality to criticize the deficiencies of modern
culture. Support your statement by specific references to the work of each
author." Time: one hour. And the distressing thing about our examination
questions is that they are not ridiculous, they make perfectly good sense
—such good sense that the young person who answers them can never
again know the force, the terror, of what has been communicated to him
by the works he is being examined on.
    Very likely it was with the thought of saving myself from the necessity
of speaking personally and my students from the betrayal of the full
harsh meaning of a great literature that I first taught my course in as

literary a way as possible. A couple of decades ago the discovery was made that a literary work is a structure of words: this doesn't seem a surprising thing to have learned except in its polemical tendency which is to urge us to minimize the amount of attention we give to the poet's social and personal will, to what he wants to happen outside the poem as a result of the poem; it urges us to fix our minds on what is going on inside the poem. For me this polemical tendency has been of the greatest usefulness, for it has corrected my inclination to pay attention chiefly to what the poet *wants*. For two or three years I directed my efforts toward dealing with the matter of the course chiefly as structures of words, in a formal way with due attention paid to the literal difficulty which marked so many of the works. But it went against the grain. It went against my personal grain. It went against the grain of the classroom situation, for formal analysis is best carried on by question-and-answer, which needs small groups, and the registration for the course in modern literature in any college is sure to be large. And it went against the grain of the authors themselves—structures of words they may indeed have created, but these structures were not pyramids or triumphal arches, they were manifestly contrived not to be static and commemorative but mobile and aggressive, and one does not describe a quinquireme or a howitzer or a tank without estimating how much *damage* it can do.

Eventually I had to decide that there was only one way to give the course, which was to give it without strategies and without conscious caution. It was not honorable, neither to the students nor to the authors, to conceal or disguise my relation to the literature, my commitment to it, my fear of it, my ambivalence toward it. The literature had to be dealt with in the terms it announced for itself. As for the students, I have never given assent to the modern saw about "teaching students, not subjects"—I have always thought it right to teach subjects, believing that if one gives his first loyalty to the subject, the student is best instructed. So I resolved to give the course with no considerations in mind except my own interests. And since my own interests lead me to see literary situations as cultural situations, and cultural situations as great elaborate fights about moral issues, and moral issues as having something to do with gratuitously chosen images of personal being, and images of personal being as having something to do with literary style, I felt free to begin with what for me was a first concern, the animus of the author, the objects of his will, the things he wants or wants to have happen.

I went so far in my cultural and non-literary method as to decide that I would begin the course with a statement of certain themes or issues that might especially engage our attention. I even went so far in non-literariness as to think that my purposes would best be served if I could contrive a "background" for the works we would read—I wanted to propose a history for the themes or issues that I hoped to discover. I did not intend that this history should be either very extensive or very precise. I wanted merely a *sense* of a history, some general intuition of a past. And because there is as yet no adequate general work of history of the culture of the last two hundred years, I asked myself what books of the age just preceding ours had most influenced our literature, or, since I was far less concerned with showing influence than with discerning a tendency, what older books might seem to fall into a line the direction of which pointed to our own literature and thus might serve as a prolegomenon to the course.

It was virtually inevitable that the first work that should have sprung to mind was Sir James Frazer's *The Golden Bough,* not, of course, the whole of it, but certain chapters, those that deal with Osiris, Attis, and Adonis. Anyone who thinks about modern literature in a systematic way takes for granted the great part played in it by myth, and especially by those examples of myth which tell about gods dying and being reborn— the imagination of death and rebirth, reiterated in the ancient world in innumerable variations that are yet always the same, captivated the literary mind at the very moment when, as all accounts of the modern age agree, the most massive and compelling of all the stories of resurrection had lost much of its hold upon the world.

Perhaps no book has had so decisive an effect upon modern literature as Frazer's. It was beautifully to my purpose that it had first been published ten years before the twentieth century began. Yet forty-three years later, in 1933, Frazer delivered a lecture, very eloquent, in which he bade the world be of good hope in the face of the threat to the human mind that was being offered by the Nazi power. He was still alive in 1941. Yet he had been born in 1854, three years before Matthew Arnold gave the lecture "On the Modern Element in Literature." Here, surely, was history, here was the past I wanted, beautifully connected with our present. Frazer was wholly a man of the nineteenth century, and the more so because the eighteenth century was so congenial to him—the lecture of 1933 in which he predicted the Nazi defeat had as its subject Condorcet's *Progress of the Human Mind;* when he took time from his anthropological studies to deal with literature, he prepared editions of Addison's essays and Cowper's letters. He had the old lost belief in the virtue and power of rationality. He loved and counted on order, decorum, and good sense. This great historian of the primitive imagination was in the dominant intellectual tradition of the West that, since the days of the pre-Socratics, has condemned the ways of thought that we call primitive.

In short, Frazer—at least in his first or conscious intention—was a perfect representative of what Matthew Arnold meant by a modern age. And perhaps nothing could make clearer how the conditions of life and literature have changed in a hundred years than to note the difference between the way in which Arnold defines the modern element in literature and the way in which we must define it.

If we speak of modernity, we should have it in mind that the terms of the endowment of the Poetry Chair at Oxford required that the Professor lecture on the ancient literatures and that he speak in Latin. This will suggest that Arnold's making the idea of modernity the subject of his inaugural was not without its subversiveness. Arnold met the requirement of dealing with the classic writers—his lecture is about the modern element in the ancient literatures. But he asked for permission to lecture in English, not because he was unable to speak in Latin but because he wished to be understood by more than scholars. Permission was granted by the University, with what reluctance I do not know, or with what sad sense that another bastion of the past had fallen, and in an English which was perhaps doctoral but certainly lucid, Arnold undertook to decline what he called the modern element.

Arnold used the word modern in a wholly honorific sense. So much so, indeed, that he seems to dismiss all temporal idea from the word and makes it signify certain timeless intellectual and civil virtues. A society, he said, is a modern society when it maintains a condition of repose, confidence, free activity of the mind, and the tolerance of divergent views. A society is modern when it affords sufficient material well-being for the conveniences of life and the development of taste. And, finally, a society is modern when its members are intellectually mature, by which Arnold means that they are willing to judge by reason, to observe facts in a critical spirit, and to search for the law of things. By this definition Periclean Athens is for Arnold a modern age, Elizabethan England is not; Thucydides is a modern historian, Sir Walter Raleigh is not.

I shall not go into further details of Arnold's definition or description of the modern.[1] I have said enough, I think, to suggest what Arnold was up to, what he wanted to see realized as the desideratum of his own society, what ideal he wanted the works of intellect and imagination of his own time to advance. And at what a distance his ideal of the modern puts him from our present sense of modernity, from our modern literature! To anyone conditioned by our modern literature Arnold's ideal of order, convenience, decorum, and rationality might well seem to reduce itself to the small advantages and excessive limitations of the middle-class life of a few prosperous nations of the nineteenth century. Arnold's historic sense presented to his mind the long, bitter, bloody past of Europe, and he seized passionately upon the hope of true civilization at last achieved. But the historic sense of our literature has in mind a long excess of civilization to which it ascribes the bitterness and blood both

---

[1] I leave out of my summary account the two supreme virtues that Arnold ascribes to the most successful examples of a "modern" literature. One is the power of effecting an "intellectual deliverance," by which Arnold means leading men to comprehend the "vast multitude of facts" which make up "a copious and complex present, and behind it a copious and complex past." The other is "adequacy," the ability to represent the complex high human development of a modern age "in its completest and most harmonious" aspect, doing so with "the charm of that noble serenity which always accompanies true insight."

of the past and of the present and of which it conceives the peaceful aspects to be mainly contemptible—its order achieved at the cost of extravagant personal repression, either that of coercion or that of acquiescence; its repose otiose; its tolerance either flaccid or capricious; its material comfort corrupt and corrupting; its taste a manifestation either of timidity or of pride; its rationality attained only at the price of energy and passion.

For the understanding of this radical change of opinion nothing is more illuminating than to be aware of the doubleness of mind of the author of *The Golden Bough*. I have said that Frazer in his conscious mind and in his first intention exemplifies all that Arnold means by the modern. He often speaks quite harshly of the irrationality and the orgiastic excesses of the primitive religions he describes, and even Christianity comes under his criticism both because it stands in the way of rational thought and because it can draw men away from intelligent participation in the life of society. But Frazer had more than one intention, and he had an unconscious as well as a conscious mind. If he deplores the primitive imagination, he does not fail to show it as also wonderful and beautiful. It is the rare reader of *The Golden Bough* who finds the ancient beliefs and rituals wholly alien to him. It is to be expected that Frazer's adduction of the many pagan analogues to the Christian mythos will be thought by Christian readers to have an adverse effect on faith, it was undoubtedly Frazer's purpose that it should, yet many readers will feel that Frazer makes all faith and ritual indigenous to humanity, virtually biological; they feel, as DeQuincey put it, that not to be at least a *little* superstitious is to lack generosity of mind. Scientific though his purpose was, Frazer had the effect of validating and even of seeming to propose to modern times those old modes of experiencing the world which, beginning with the Romanticists, modern men have sought to revive in order to escape from positivism and common sense.

The direction of the imagination upon great and mysterious objects of worship is not the only means men use to liberate themselves from the bondage of quotidian fact, and although Frazer can scarcely be held accountable for the ever-growing modern attraction to the extreme mental states, to rapture, ecstasy, and transcendance, which are achieved by drugs, trance; music and dance, orgy, and derangement of personality, yet he did provide a bridge to the understanding and acceptance of these states, he proposed to us the idea that the desire for them and the use of them for heuristic purposes is a common and acceptable manifestation of human nature.

This one element of Frazer's masterpiece could scarcely fail to suggest the next of my prolegomenal works. It is worth remarking that its author is in his own way as great a classical scholar as Frazer himself—Nietzsche was the Professor of Classical Philology at the University of Basel when, at the age of 27, he published his essay, *The Birth of Tragedy*. After the appearance of this stunningly brilliant account of Greek civilization, of which Socrates is not the hero but the villain, what can possibly be left to us of that rational and ordered Greece, that modern, that eighteenth-century, Athens that Arnold so entirely relied on as the standard for judging all civilizations? Professor Kaufmann is right when he warns us against supposing that Nietzsche exalts Dionysus over Apollo and tells us that Nietzsche "emphasizes the Dionysiac only because he feels that the Apollonian genius of the Greeks cannot be fully understood apart from it." But no one reading Nietzsche's essay for the first time is likely to heed this warning. What will reach him before due caution intervenes, before he becomes aware of the portentous dialectic between Dionysus and Apollo, is the excitement of his sudden liberation from Aristotle, the joy that he takes in his willingness to believe the author's statement that, "art rather than ethics constitutes the essential metaphysical activity of man," that tragedy has its source in the Dionysiac rapture, "whose closest analogy is furnished by physical intoxication," and that this rapture, in which "the individual forgets himself completely," was in itself no metaphysical state but an orgiastic display of lust and cruelty, "of sexual promiscuity overriding every form of tribal law." This sadic and masochistic frenzy, Nietzsche is at pains to insist, needs the taming hand of Apollo before it can become tragedy, but it is the primal stuff of the great art, and to the modern experience of tragedy this explanation of it seems far more pertinent than Aristotle's, with its eagerness to forget its origin in its achievement of a noble *apatheia*.

Of supreme importance in itself, Nietzsche's essay had for me the added pedagogic advantage of allowing me to establish an historical line back to William Blake. Nothing is more characteristic of modern literature than its discovery and canonization of the primal, non-ethical energies, and the historical point could be made the better by remarking the correspondence of thought of two men of different nations and separated from each other by a good many decades, for Nietzsche's Dionysus and Blake's Hell are much the same thing.

Whether or not Joseph Conrad read either Blake or Nietzsche I do not know, but his *Heart of Darkness* follows in their line. This very great work has never lacked for the admiration it deserves, and it has been given a kid of canonical place in the legends of modern literature by Eliot's having it so clearly in mind when he wrote *The Waste Land* and his having taken from it the epigraph to "The Hollow Men." But no one, to my knowledge, has ever confronted in an explicit way its strange and terrible message of ambivalence toward the life of civilization. Consider that its protagonist Kurtz is a progressive and a liberal and that he is the highly respected representative of a society which undertakes to represent itself as benign, although in fact it is vicious. Consider too that he is a practitioner of several arts, a painter, a writer, a musician, and into the bargain a political orator. He is at once the most idealistic and the most practically successful of all the agents of the Belgian exploitation of the Congo. Everybody knows what truth about him Marlow discovers—that Kurtz's success is the result of a terrible ascendancy he has gained over the natives of his distant station, an ascendancy which is derived from his presumed magical or divine powers, that he has exercised his rule with the extreme of cruelty, that he has given himself to unnamable acts of lust. This is the world of the darker pages of *The Golden Bough.* It is one of the great points of Conrad's story that Marlow speaks of the primitive life of the jungle not as being noble or charming or even free but as being base and sordid—and for *that* reason compelling: he himself feels quite overtly its dreadful attraction. It is to this devilish baseness that Kurtz has yielded himself, and yet Marlow, although he does indeed treat him with hostile irony, does not find it possible to suppose that Kurtz is anything but a hero of the spirit. For me it is still ambiguous whether Kurtz's famous deathbed cry, "The horror! The horror!" refers to the approach of death or to his experience of savage life. Whichever it is, to Marlow the fact that Kurtz could utter this cry at the point of death, while Marlow himself, when death threatens him, can know it only as a weary greyness, marks the difference between the ordinary man and a hero of the spirit. Is this not the essence of the modern belief about the nature of the artist, the man who goes down into that hell which is the historical beginning of the human soul, a beginning not outgrown but established in humanity as we know it now, preferring the reality of this hell to the bland lies of the civilization that has overlaid it?

This idea is proposed again in the somewhat less powerful but still very moving work with which I followed *Heart of Darkness,* Thomas Mann's *Death in Venice.* I wanted this story not so much for its account of an extravagantly Apollonian personality surrendering to forces that, in his Apollonian character, he thought shameful—although this was certainly to my purpose—but rather for Aschenbach's fevered dreams of the erotic past, and in particular that dream of the goat-orgy which Mann, being the kind of writer he is, having the kind of relation to Nietzsche he had, might well have written to serve as an illustration of what *The Birth of Tragedy* means by religious frenzy, the more so, of course, because Mann chooses that particular orgiastic ritual, the killing and eating of the goat, from which tragedy is traditionally said to have been derived. A notable element of this story in which the birth of tragedy plays an important part is that the degradation and downfall of the protagonist is not represented as tragic in the usual sense of the word—that is, it is not represented as a great deplorable event. It is a commonplace of modern literary thought that the tragic mode is not available even to the gravest and noblest of our writers. I am not sure that this is the deprivation that some people think it to be and a mark of our spiritual inferiority. But if we ask why it has come about, one reason may be that we have learned to think our way back through tragedy to the primal stuff out of which tragedy arose. If we consider the primitive forbidden ways of conduct which traditionally in tragedy lead to punishment by death, we think of them as being the path to reality and truth, to an ultimate self-realization. We have always wondered if tragedy itself may not have been saying just this in a deeply hidden way, drawing us to think of the hero's sin and death as somehow conferring justification, even salvation of a sort— no doubt this is what Nietzsche had in mind when he said that "tragedy denies ethics." What tragedy once seemed to hint, our literature now is willing to say quite explicitly. If Mann's Aschenbach dies at the height of his intellectual and artistic powers, at the behest of a passion that his ethical reason condemns, we do not take this to be a defeat, rather a kind of terrible rebirth: at his latter end the artist knows a reality that he had until now refused to admit to consciousness.

This being so, how fortunate that the Anchor edition of *The Birth of Tragedy* should include Nietzsche's *The Genealogy of Morals*. For here, among many other ideas most pertinent to the *mystique* of modern literature, was the view of society which is consonant with the belief that art and not ethics constitutes the essential metaphysical activity of man and with the validation and ratification of the primitive energies. Nietzsche's theory of the social order dismisses all ethical impulse from its origins— the basis of society is to be found in the rationalization of cruelty: as simple as that. Nietzsche has no ultimate Utopian intention in saying this, no hope of revising the essence of the social order, although he does believe that its pain can be mitigated. He represents cruelty as a social necessity, for only by its exercise could men ever have been induced to develop a continuity of will: nothing else than cruelty could have created in mankind that memory of intention which makes society possible. The method of cynicism which Nietzsche pursued—let us be clear that it is a method and not an attitude—goes so far as to describe punishment in terms of the pleasure derived from the exercise of cruelty: "Compensation," he says, "consists in a legal warrant entitling one man to exercise his cruelty on another." There follows that most remarkable passage in which Nietzsche describes the process whereby the individual turns the cruelty of punishment against himself and creates the bad conscience and the consciousness of guilt which manifests itself as a pervasive anxiety. Nietzsche's complexity of mind is beyond all comparison, for in this book which is dedicated to the liberation of the conscience, Nietzsche makes his defense of the bad conscience as a decisive force in the interests of culture. It is much the same line of argument that he takes when, having attacked the Jewish morality and the priestly existence in the name of the health of the spirit, he reminds us that only by his sickness does man become interesting.

From *The Genealogy of Morals* to Freud's *Civilization and Its Discontents* is but a step, and some might think that, for pedagogic purposes, the step is so small as to make the second book supererogatory. But al-

though Freud's view of society and culture has indeed a very close affinity
to Nietzsche's, Freud does add certain considerations which are essential
to our sense of the modern disposition.

For one thing, he puts to us the question of whether or not we want to
accept civilization. It is not the first time that the paradox of civilization
has been present to the mind of civilized people, the sense that civilization makes men behave worse and suffer more than does some less
developed state of human existence. But hitherto all such ideas were
formulated in a moralizing way—civilization was represented as being
"corrupt," a divagation from a state of innocence. Freud had no illusions
about a primitive innocence, he conceived no practicable alternative to
civilization. In consequence there was a unique force to the question he
asked: whether we wished to accept civilization, with all its contradictions, with all its pains—pains, for "discontents" does not accurately describe what Freud has in mind. He had his own answer to the question—
his tragic, or stoic, sense of life dictated it: we do well to accept it, although we also do well to cast a cold eye on the fate that makes it our
better part to accept it. Like Nietzsche, Freud thought that life was justified by our heroic response to its challenge.

But the question Freud posed has not been set aside or closed up by
the answer that he himself gave to it. His answer, like Nietzsche's, is
essentially in the line of traditional humanism—we can see this in the
sternness with which he charges women not to interfere with men in the
discharge of their cultural duty, not to claim men for love and the
family to the detriment of their free activity in the world. But just here
lies the matter of Freud's question that the world more and more believes
Freud himself did not answer. The pain that civilization inflicts is that
of the instinctual renunciation that civilization demands, and it would
seem that fewer and fewer people wish to say with Freud that the loss of
instinctual gratification, emotional freedom, or love, are compensated for
either by the security of civilized life or the stern pleasures of the moral
masculine character. The possibility of options different from the one that
Freud made is proposed theoretically by two recent books, Herbert
Marcuse's *Eros and Civilization* and Norman O. Brown's *Life Against
Death*.

With Freud's essay I brought to a close my list of prolegomenal books
for the first term of the course. I shall not do much more than mention
the books with which I introduced the second term, but I should like to
do at least that. I began with *Rameau's Nephew*, thinking that the
peculiar moral authority which Diderot assigns to the envious, untalented
unregenerate protagonist was peculiarly relevant to the line taken by the
ethical explorations of modern literature. Nothing is more characteristic
of the literature of our time than the replacement of the hero by what
has come to be called the anti-hero, in whose indifference to or hatred of
ethical nobility there is presumed to lie a special authenticity. Diderot is

quite overt about this—he himself in his public character is the deuter-oganist, the "honest consciousness," as Hegel calls him, and he takes delight in the discomfiture of the decent, dull person he is by the Nephew's nihilistic mind.

It seemed to me too that there was particular usefulness in the circumstance that this anti-hero should avow so openly his *envy*, which Tocqueville has called the ruling emotion of democracy, and that, although he envied anyone at all who had access to the creature-comforts and the social status which he lacked, what chiefly animated him was envy of men of genius. Ours is the first cultural epoch in which many men aspire to high achievement in the arts and, in their frustration, form a dispossessed class which cuts across the conventional class lines, making a proletariat of the spirit.

Although *Rameau's Nephew* was not published until fairly late in the century, it was known in manuscript by Goethe and Hegel; it suited the temper and won the admiration of Marx and Freud for reasons that are obvious. And there is ground for supposing that it was known to Dostoevsky, whose *Notes from Underground* is a restatement of the essential idea of Diderot's dialogue in terms both more extreme and less genial. The Nephew is still on the defensive—he is naughtily telling secrets about the nature of man and society. But Dostoevsky's underground man shouts aloud his envy and hatred and carries the ark of his self-hatred and alienation into a remorseless battle with what he calls "the good and the beautiful," mounting an attack upon every belief not merely of bourgeois society but of the whole humanist tradition. The inclusion of *Notes from Underground* among my prolegomenal books constituted something of a pedagogic risk, for if I wished to emphasize the subversive tendency of modern literature, here was a work which made all subsequent subversion seem like affirmation, so radical and so brilliant was its negation of our pieties and assumptions.

I hesitated in compunction before following *Notes from Underground* with Tolstoy's *Death of Ivan Ilytch*, which so ruthlessly and with such dreadful force destroys the citadel of the commonplace life in which we all believe we can take refuge from ourselves and our fate. But I did assign it and then two of Pirandello's plays which, in the atmosphere of the sordidness of the commonplace life, undermines all the certitudes of the commonplace, common-sense mind.

.   .   .   .

The author of *The Magic Mountain* once said that all his work could be understood as an effort to free himself from the middle class, and this, of course, will serve to describe the chief intention of all modern literature. And the means of freedom which Mann prescribes (the characteristic irony notwithstanding) is the means of freedom which in effect all of modern literature prescribes. It is, in the words of Clavdia Chauchat, *"se perdre et même . . . se laisser dépérir,"* and thus to name the means is to make plain that the end is not merely freedom from the middle class but freedom from society itself. I venture to say that the idea of losing oneself up to the point of self-destruction, of surrendering oneself to experience without regard to self-interest or conventional morality, of escaping wholly from the societal bonds, is an "element" somewhere in the mind of every modern person who dares to think of what Arnold in his unaffected Victorian way called "the fulness of spiritual perfection." But the teacher who undertakes to present modern literature to his students may not allow that idea to remain in the *somewhere* of his mind; he must take it from the place where it exists habitual and unrealized and put it in the conscious forefront of his thoughts. And if he is committed to an admiration of modern literature, he must also be committed to this chief idea of modern literature. I press the logic of the situation not in order to question the legitimacy of the commitment, or even the propriety of expressing the commitment in the college classroom (although it does seem odd!) but to confront those of us who do teach modern literature with the striking actuality of our enterprise.

The Poetry of Reality

J. HILLIS MILLER

Reality is not that external scene but the life that is lived in it. Reality is things as they are. The general sense of the word proliferates its special senses. It is a jungle in itself.[1]

A change in literature as dramatic as the appearance of romanticism in the late eighteenth century has been taking place during the last fifty years. This book tries to explore the change through a study of six writers who have participated in it. Each of the chapters which follow attempts to show the configuration of themes which permeates one writer's work and unifies it. The chapter describes the historical milieu within which the particular worlds of the six writers may be followed in their planetary trajectories.

My interpretation of these writers questions the assumption that twentieth-century poetry is merely an extension of romanticism. A new kind of poetry has appeared in our day, a poetry which grows out of romanticism, but goes beyond it. Many twentieth-century poets begin with an experience of the nihilism which is one of the possible consequences of romanticism. My chapter on Conrad attempts to identify this nihilism by analysis of a writer who follows it into its darkness and so prepares the way beyond it. Each succeeding chapter describes one version of the journey beyond nihilism toward a poetry of reality. The new art which gradually emerges in the work of Yeats, Eliot, Thomas, and Stevens reaches full development in the poetry of William Carlos Williams.

Much romantic literature presupposes a double bifurcation. Existence is divided into two realms, heaven and earth, supernatural and natural,

---

[1] Wallace Stevens, *The Necessary Angel: Essays on Reality and the Imagination* (New York: Alfred A. Knopf, 1951), pp. 25, 26.

the "real" world and the derived world. It is also divided into subjective and objective realms. Man as subjective ego opposes himself to everything else. This "everything else" is set against the mind as object of its knowledge. Though some preromantic and romantic writers (Smart, Macpherson, Blake) speak from the perspective of a visionary or apocalyptic union of subject and object, earth and heaven, many romantic poets start with both forms of dualism. They must try through the act of poetry to reach the supersensible world by bringing together subject and object. To reach God through the object presupposes the presence of God within the object, and the romantic poets usually believe in one way or another that there is a supernatural power deeply interfused in nature.

Writers of the middle nineteenth century, as I tried to show in *The Disappearance of God*,[2] tend to accept the romantic dichotomy of subject and object, but are no longer able to experience God as both immanent and transcendent. God seems to Tennyson, to Arnold, or to the early Hopkins to have withdrawn beyond the physical world. For such poets God still exists, but he is no longer present in nature. What once was a unity, gathering all together, has exploded into fragments. The isolated ego faces the other dimensions of existence across an empty space. Subject, objects, words, other minds, the supernatural—each of these realms is divorced from the others, and man finds himself one of the "poor fragments of a broken world."[3] Accepting this situation as a necessary beginning, the Victorian poets try to reunite the fragments, to bring God back to earth as a "fusing flame" present in man's heart, in nature, in society, and in language, binding them together in "one common wave of thought and joy."[4]

Another way of thinking grows up side by side with that of the mid-nineteenth-century poets. A God who has disappeared from nature and from the human heart can come to be seen not as invisible but as nonexistent. The unseen God of Arnold or Tennyson becomes the dead God of Nietzsche. If the disappearance of God is presupposed by much Victorian poetry, the death of God is the starting point for many twentieth-century writers.

What does it mean to say that God is dead? Nietzsche's "madman" in *The Joyful Wisdom* announces the death of God, and explains it:

"Where is God gone?" he called out. "I mean to tell you! *We have killed him,* —you and I! We are all his murderers! But how have we done it? How were we able to drink up the sea? Who gave us the sponge to wipe away the whole horizon? What did we do when we loosened this earth from its sun? Whither

2 The Belknap Press of Harvard University Press, 1963.
3 Matthew Arnold's phrase, in "Obermann Once More," *Poetical Works*, ed. C. B. Tinker and H. F. Lowry (London: Oxford University Press, 1950), p. 320.
4 "Obermann Once More," pp. 320, 323.

does it now move? Whither do we move? Away from all suns? Do we not dash on unceasingly? Backwards, sideways, forewards, in all directions? Is there still an above and below? Do we not stray, as through infinite nothingness? Does not empty space breathe upon us? Has it not become colder? Does not night come on continually, darker and darker? Shall we not have to light lanterns in the morning? Do we not hear the noise of the grave-diggers who are burying God? Do we not smell the divine putrefaction?—for even Gods putrefy! God is dead! God remains dead! And we have killed him!"[5]

Man has killed God by separating his subjectivity from everything but itself. The ego has put everything in doubt, and has defined all outside itself as the object of its thinking power. Cogito ergo sum: the absolute certainty about the self reached by Descartes' hyperbolic doubt leads to the assumption that things exist, for me at least, only because I think them. When everything exists only as reflected in the ego, then man has drunk up the sea. If man is defined as subject, everything else turns into object. This includes God, who now becomes merely the highest object of man's knowledge. God, once the creative sun, the power establishing the horizon where heaven and earth come together, becomes an object of thought like any other. When man drinks up the sea he also drinks up God, the creator of the sea. In this way man is the murderer of God. Man once was a created being among other created beings, existing in an objective world sustained by its creator, and oriented by that creator as to high and low, right and wrong. Now, to borrow the passage from Bradley which Eliot quotes in the notes to "The Waste Land," "regarded as an existence which appears in a soul, the whole world for each is peculiar and private to that soul."

When God and the creation becomes objects of consciousness, man becomes a nihilist. Nihilism is the nothingness of consciousness when consciousness becomes the foundation of everything. Man the murderer of God and drinker of the sea of creation wanders through the infinite nothingness of his own ego. Nothing now has any worth except the arbitrary value he sets on things as he assimilates them into his consciousness. Nietzsche's transvaluation of values is the expunging of God as the absolute value and source of the valuation of everything else. In the emptiness left after the death of God, man becomes the sovereign valuer, the measure of all things.

Many qualities of modern culture are consonant with the definition of man as a hollow sphere within which everything must appear in order to exist. The devouring nothingness of consciousness is the will to power over things. The will wants to assimilate everything to itself, to make everything a reflection within its mirror. Seen from this perspective, romanticism and technology appear to be similar rather than antithetical.

[5] Book III, Section 125, trans. Thomas Common (New York: Frederick Ungar, 1960), pp. 167, 168.

Romanticism attempts to marry subject and object through the image. The romantic image may be the representation of object within the sphere of the subject, as in Wordsworth, or the carrying of subject into the object, as in Keats, or the wedding of subject and object, as in Coleridge, but in most of its varieties an initial dualism, apparent or real, is assumed. Romanticism develops naturally into the various forms of perspectivism, whether in the poetry of the dramatic monologue or in the novel, which, in its concern for point of view, is perfectly consonant with romanticism. The development of fiction from Jane Austen to Conrad and James is a gradual exploration of the fact that for modern man nothing exists except as it is seen by someone viewing the world from his own perspective. If romantic poetry most often shows the mind assimilating natural objects—urns, nightingales, daffodils, or windhovers—the novel turns its attention to the relations between several minds, but both poetry and fiction usually presuppose the isolation of each mind.

Science and technology, like romanticism, take all things as objects for man's representation. This may appear in a theoretical form, as in the numbers and calculations which transform into mathematical formulas everything from subatomic particles to the farthest and largest galaxies. Or it may appear in a physical form, the humanization of nature, as earths and ores are turned into automobiles, refrigerators, skyscrapers, and rockets, so that no corner of the earth or sky has not been conquered by man and made over in his image.

Romantic literature and modern technology are aspects of a world-embracing evolution of culture. As this development proceeds, man comes even to forget that he has been the murderer of God. The presence of God within the object, as it existed for the early romantics, is forgotten, and forgotten is the pathos of the Victorians' reaching out for a God disappearing over the horizon of an objectified world. The triumph of technology is the forgetting of the death of God. In the silence of this forgetting the process of universal calculation and reduction to order can go on peacefully extending its dominion. The world no longer offers any resistance to man's limitless hunger for conquest. This process has continued through the first two-thirds of the twentieth century, and is the chief determinant of man's sensibility in many parts of the world today. Many people have forgotten that they have forgotten the death of God, the living God of Abraham and Isaac, Dante and Pascal. Many who believe that they believe in God believe in him only as the highest value, that is, as a creation of man, the inventor of values.

Only if the nihilism latent in our culture would appear as nihilism would it be possible to go beyond it by understanding it. In spite of two world wars, and the shadow of world annihilation, this is a course which our civilization has not yet chosen, or had chosen for it. Nevertheless, a central tradition of modern literature has been a countercurrent moving against the direction of history. In this literature, if not in our culture as a whole, nihilism has gradually been exposed, experienced in its implications, and, in some cases, transcended.

The special place of Joseph Conrad in English literature lies in the fact that in him the nihilism covertly dominant in modern culture is brought to the surface and shown for what it is. Conrad can best be understood as the culmination of a development within the novel, a development particularly well-marked in England, though of course it also exists on the continent and in America. After the attempt to recover an absent God in nineteenth-century poetry, a subsequent stage in man's spiritual history is expressed more fully in fiction than in poetry. The novel shows man attempting to establish a human world based on interpersonal relations. In the novel man comes more and more to be defined in terms of the strength of his will, and the secret nihilism resulting from his new place as the source of all value is slowly revealed.

Conrad is part of European literature and takes his place with Dostoevsky, Mann, Gide, Proust, and Camus as an explorer of modern perspectivism and nihilism. Within the narrower limits of the English novel, however, he comes at the end of a native tradition. From Dickens and George Eliot through Trollope, Meredith, and Hardy the negative implications of subjectivism become more and more apparent. It remained for Conrad to explore nihilism to its depths, and, in doing so, to point the way toward the transcendence of nihilism by the poets of the twentieth century.

In Conrad's fiction the focus of the novel turns outward from its concentration on relations between man and man within civilized society to a concern for the world-wide expansion of Western man's will to power. Conrad is the novelist not of the city but of imperialism. Several consequences follow from this. He is able to show that society is an arbitrary set of rules and judgments, a house of cards built over an abyss. It was relatively easy for characters in Victorian fiction to be shown taking English society for granted as permanent and right. The fact that Western culture has the fragility of an edifice which might have been constructed differently is brought to light when Conrad sets the "masquerade" of imperialism against the alien jungle. With this revelation, the nature of man's will to power begins to emerge, and at the same time there is a glimpse of an escape from nihilism.

The will to power seemed a subjective thing, a private possession of each separate ego. Though the struggle for dominance of mind against mind might lead to an impasse, nonhuman nature seemed to yield passively to man's sovereign will. Everything, it seemed, could be turned into an object of man's calculation, control, or evaluation. In "Heart of Darkness" (1899) Conrad shows how imperialism becomes the expansion of the will toward unlimited dominion over existence. What begins as greed, the desire for ivory, and as altruism, the desire to carry the torch of civilization to the jungle, becomes the longing to "wring the heart" of the wilderness and "exterminate all the brutes." The benign project of civilizing the dark places of the world becomes the conscious desire to annihilate everything which opposes man's absolute will. Kurtz's megalomania finally becomes limitless. There is "nothing either above or below him." He has "kicked himself loose of the earth," and in doing so has "kicked the very earth to pieces."

It is just here, in the moment of its triumph, that nihilism reverses itself, as, in Mann's *Doktor Faustus*, Leverkühn's last and most diabolical composition leads through the abyss to the sound of children's voices singing. Conrad's work does not yet turn the malign into the benign, but it leads to a reversal which prepares for the daylight of later literature. When Kurtz's will has expanded to boundless dimensions, it reveals itself to be what it has secretly been all along: nothing. Kurtz is "hollow at the core." Into his emptiness comes the darkness. The darkness is in the heart of each man, but it is in the heart of nature too, and transcends both man and nature as their hidden substance and foundation.

When the wilderness finds Kurtz out and takes "a terrible vengeance for the fantastic invasion,"[6] then the dawn of an escape from nihilism appears, an escape through the darkness. By following the path of nihilism to the end, man confronts once again a spiritual power external to himself. Though this power appears as an inexpressibly threatening horror, still it is something beyond the self. It offers the possibility of an escape from subjectivism.

The strategy of this escape will appear from the point of view of the tradition it reverses the most dangerous of choices, a leap into the abyss. It will mean giving up the most cherished certainties. The act by which man turns the world inside-out into his mind leads to nihilism. This can be escaped only by a counterrevoluton in which man turns himself inside-out and steps, as Wallace Stevens puts it, "barefoot into reality."[7] This leap into the world characterizes the reversal enacted in one way or another by the five poets studied here.

To walk barefoot into reality means abandoning the independence of the ego. Instead of making everything an object for the self, the mind must efface itself before reality, or plunge into the density of an exterior world, dispersing itself in a milieu which exceeds it and which it has not made. The effacement of the ego before reality means abandoning the will to power over things. This is the most difficult of acts for a modern man to perform. It goes counter to all the penchants of our culture. To

[6] Quotations from "Heart of Darkness" are cited from *Youth and Two Other Stories* (Garden City, N.Y.: Doubleday, Page, 1925), pp. 118, 131, 144, 148.

[7] "Large Red Man Reading," *The Collected Poems* (New York: Alfred A. Knopf, 1954), p. 423.

abandon its project of dominion the will must will not to will. Only through an abnegation of the will can objects begin to manifest themselves as they are, in the integrity of their presence. When man is willing to let things be then they appear in a space which is no longer that of an objective world opposed to the mind. In this new space the mind is dispersed everywhere in things and forms one with them.

This new space is the realm of the twentieth-century poem. It is a space in which things, the mind, and words coincide in closest intimacy. In this space flower the chicory and Queen Anne's lace of William Carlos Williams' poems. In this space his wheelbarrow and his broken bits of green bottle glass appear. In a similar poetic space appear "the pans above the stove, the pots on the table, the tulips among them" of Stevens' "poem of life." The "ghosts" who "return to earth" in Stevens' poems are those who have been alienated in the false angelism of subjectivity. They return from the emptiness of "the wilderness of stars" to step into a tangibile reality of things as they are. There they can "run fingers over leaves/And against the moist coiled thorn."[8]

The return to earth making twentieth-century poetry possible is accompanied by the abandonment of still another quality of the old world. This is the dimension of depth. In a number of ways the world of nineteenth-century poetry is often characterized by extension and exclusion. The mind is separated from its objects, and those objects are placed in a predominantly visual space. In this space each object is detached from the others. To be in one place is to be excluded from other places, and space stretches out infinitely in all directions. Beyond those infinite distances is the God who has absented himself from his creation. The pathos of the disappearance of God is the pathos of infinite space.

Along with spatial and theological depth go other distances: the distance of mind from mind, the distance within each self separating the self from itself. If each subject is separated from all objects, it is no less divided from other subjects and can encounter them only across a gap generated by its tendency to turn everything into an image. From the assumption of the isolation of the ego develops that conflict of subjectivities which is a central theme of fiction. For Matthew Arnold and other inheritors of romanticism the self is also separated from its own depths, the gulf within the mind which hides the deep buried self. To reach that self is as difficult as to reach God beyond the silence of infinite spaces.

In the new art these depths tend to disappear. The space of separation is turned inside-out, so that elements once dispersed are gathered together in a new region of copresence. This space is often more auditory, tactile, or kinesthetic than visual. To be within it is to possess all of it,

8 "Large Red Man Reading," pp. 423, 424.

and there is no longer a sense of endless distances extending in all directions. The mind, its objects, other minds, and the ground of both mind and things are present in a single realm of proximity.

The disappearance of dimensions of depth in twentieth-century art provides special difficulties for someone trained in the habits of romanticism. An abstract expressionist painting does not "mean" anything in the sense of referring beyond itself in any version of traditional symbolism. It is what it is, paint on canvas, just as Williams' wheelbarrow is what it is. In the space of the new poetry the world is contracted to a point—the wheelbarrow, the chicory flower, the bits of green glass. The poem is "not ideas about the thing but the thing itself,"[9] part of the world and not about it. In the same way the characters of Williams' fiction, like those of the French "new novel," have little psychological depth. They exist as their thoughts, their gestures, their speech, and these have the same objective existence as the wheelbarrow or the flower. In such a world "anywhere is everywhere,"[10] and the romantic dialectic of movement through stages to attain a goal disappears. In place of advance in steps toward an end there is the continuous present of a poetry which matches in its speed the constant flight of time. Each moment appears out of nothing in the words of the poem and in that instant things emerge anew and move and are dissolved.[11]

If any spiritual power can exist for the new poetry it must be an immanent presence. There can be for many writers no return to the traditional conception of God as the highest existence, creator of all other existences, transcending his creation as well as dwelling within it. If there is to be a God in the new world it must be a presence within things and not beyond them. The new poets have at the farthest limit of their experience caught a glimpse of a fugitive presence, something shared by all things in the fact that they are. This presence flows everywhere, like the light which makes things visible, and yet can never be seen as a thing in itself. It is the presence of things present, what Stevens calls "the swarthy water/That flows round the earth and through the skies,/Twisting among the universal spaces."[12] In the same poem he gives this power its simplest name: "It is being." The most familiar object, in coming into the light, reveals being, and poetry brings being into the open by naming things as they are, in their glistening immediacy, the wheelbarrow glazed with rain water, the steeple at Farmington shining and swaying. The new poetry is therefore "the outlines of being and its expressings, the syllables of its law."[13] There outlines are glimpsed as the

[9] Stevens, *The Collected Poems,* p. 534.
[10] William Carlos Williams, *Paterson* (New York: New Directions, 1963), p. 273.
[11] See Wallace Stevens, *Opus Posthumous* (New York: Alfred A. Knopf, 1957), p. 110.
[12] "Metaphor as Degeneration," *The Collected Poems,* p. 444.
[13] "Large Red Man Reading," p. 424.

words of the poem vanish with the moment which brought them into existence. The space of such a poem is the space of the present in its evanescence. This present holds men closely with discovery as, "in the instant of speech,/The breadth of an accelerando moves,/Captives the being, widens—and was there."[14] The instant's motion is a space grown wide, and within that brief space of time all existence is named, captured, and revealed.

These are the characteristics of the domain which twentieth-century literature has come to inhabit. The entry into the new world is not easy to make and has not everywhere been made. Our culture still moves along the track laid out for it by science and dualistic thinking, and many writers remain enclosed within the old world. Moreover, every artist who crosses the frontier does so in his own way, a way to some degree unlike any other. I do not wish to minimize the differences between twentieth-century writers, but to suggest a context in which those differences may be fruitfully explored.

Examples of the new immediacy may be found in widely divergent areas of contemporary thought and art: in the flatness of the paintings of Mark Rothko and Franz Kline, as opposed to the romantic depth in the work of Paul Klee; in the "superficiality," as of a mystery which is all on the surface, of the novels of Ivy Compton-Burnett or Alain Robbe-Grillet; in the philosophy of Martin Heidegger or the German and French phenomenologists; in the descriptive linguistic analysis of Ludwig Wittgenstein and the British common language philosophers; in the poetry of Jorge Guillén, René Char, or Charles Olson; in the literary criticism of Gaston Bachelard, Jean-Pierre Richard, or Marcel Raymond. All these writers and artists have in one way or another entered a new realm, and, for all of them, if there is a fugitive spiritual power it will be within things and people, not altogether beyond them.

Yeats, Eliot, Thomas, Stevens, and Williams have played important roles in this twentieth-century revolution in man's experience of existence. Each begins with an experience of nihilism or its concomitants, and each in his own way enters the new realtiy: Yeats by his affirmation of the infinite richness of the finite moment; Eliot by his discovery that the Incarnation is here and now; Thomas by an acceptance of death which makes the poet an ark rescuing all things; Stevens by his identification of imagination and reality in the poetry of being; Williams by his plunge into the "filthy Passaic." This book traces the itineraries leading these writers to goals which are different and yet have a family resemblance. The unity of twentieth-century poetry is suggested by the fact that these authors are in the end poets not of absence but of proximity. In their work reality comes to be present to the senses, present to the mind which possesses it through the senses, and present in the words of the

[14] Wallace Stevens, "A Primitive Like an Orb," *The Collected Poems*, p. 440.

poems which ratify this possession. Such poetry is often open-ended in form. It follows in its motion the flowing of time and reveals, through this mobility, the reality of things as they are. Wallace Stevens speaks for all these poets when he affirms the union of inner and outer, natural and supernatural, in the transience and nearness of the real:

> We seek
> Nothing beyond reality. Within it,
>
> Everything, the spirit's alchemicana
> Included, the spirit that goes roundabout
> And through included, not merely the visible,
> The solid, but the movable, the moment,
> The coming on of feasts and the habits of saints,
> The pattern of the heavens and high, night air.[15]

Before following my five poets in their journeys of homecoming toward reality it will be necessary to investigate the spiritual adventure which takes Conrad to the limit of nihilism, and so opens the way beyond it.

[15] "An Ordinary Evening in New Haven," *The Collected Poems,* pp. 471, 472.

Epilogue

Form and the American Experience

RALPH ELLISON

... After the usual apprenticeship of imitation and seeking with delight to examine my experience through the discipline of the novel, I became gradually aware that the forms of so many of the works which impressed me were too restricted to contain the experience which I knew. The diversity of American life with its extreme fluidity and openness seemed too vital and alive to be caught for more than the briefest instant in the tight well-made Jamesian novel, which was, for all its artistic perfection, too concerned with "good taste" and stable areas. Nor could I safely use the forms of the "hard-boiled" novel, with its dedication to physical violence, social cynicism and understatement. Understatement depends, after all, upon commonly held assumptions and my minority status rendered all such assumptions questionable. There was also a problem of language, and even dialogue, which, with its hard-boiled stance and its monosyllabic utterance, is one of the shining achievements of twenti-eth-century American writing. For despite the notion that its rhythms were those of everyday speech, I found that when compared with the rich babel of idiomatic expression around me, a language full of imagery and gesture and rhetorical canniness, it was embarrassingly austere. Our speech I found resounding with an alive language swirling with over three hundred years of American living, a mixture of the folk, the Bibli-cal, the scientific and the political. Slangy in one stance, academic in an-other, loaded poetically with imagery at one moment, mathematically bare of imagery in the next. As for the rather rigid concepts of reality which informed a number of the works which impressed me and to which I owe a great deal, I was forced to conclude that reality was far more mysterious and uncertain, and more exciting, and still, despite its raw violence and capriciousness, more promising. To attempt to express that American experience which has carried one back and forth and up and

429

down the land and across, and across again the great river, from freight
train to Pullman car, from contact with slavery to contact with a world
of advanced scholarship, art and science, is simply to burst such neatly
understated forms of the novel asunder.

A novel whose range was both broader and deeper was needed. And
in my search I found myself turning to our classical nineteenth-century
novelists. I felt that except for the work of William Faulkner something
vital had gone out of American prose after Mark Twain. I came to believe that the writers of that period took a much greater responsibility for
the condition of democracy and, indeed, their works were imaginative
projections of the conflicts within the human heart which arose when the
sacred principles of the Constitution and the Bill of Rights clashed with
the practical exigencies of human greed and fear, hate and love. Naturally
I was attracted to these writers as a Negro. Whatever they thought of my
people per se, in their imaginative economy the Negro symbolized both
the man lowest down and the mysterious, underground aspect of human
personality. In a sense the Negro was the gauge of the human condition
as it waxed and waned in our democracy. These writers were willing to
confront the broad complexities of American life and we are the richer
for their having done so.

Thus to see America with an awareness of its rich diversity and its
almost magical fluidity and freedom, I was forced to conceive of a novel
unburdened by the narrow naturalism which has led, after so many
triumphs, to the final and unrelieved despair which marks so much of our
current fiction. I was to dream of a prose which was flexible, and swift as
American change is swift, confronting the inequalities and brutalities of
our society forthrightly, but yet thrusting forth its images of hope, human
fraternity and individual self-realization. It would use the richness of our
speech, the idiomatic expression and the rhetorical flourishes from past
periods which are still alive among us. And despite my personal failures,
there must be possible a fiction which, leaving sociology to the scientists,
can arrive at the truth about the human condition, here and now, with
all the bright magic of a fairy tale.

What has been missing from so much experimental writing has been
the passionate will to dominate reality as well as the laws of art. This
will is the true source of the experimental attitude. We who struggle
with form and with America should remember Eidothea's advice to
Menelaus when in the *Odyssey* he and his friends are seeking their way
home. She tells him to seize her father, Proteus, and to hold him fast
"however he may struggle and fight. He will turn into all sorts of shapes
to try you," she says, "into all the creatures that live and move upon the
earth, into water, into blazing fire; but you must hold him fast and press
him all the harder. When he is himself, and questions you in the same
shape that he was when you saw him in his bed, let the old man go; and

then, sir, ask which god it is who is angry, and how you shall make your way homewards over the fish-giving sea."

For the novelist, Proteus stands for both America and the inheritance of illusion through which all men must fight to achieve reality; the offended god stands for our sins against those principles we all hold sacred. The way home we seek is that condition of man's being at home in the world, which is called love, and which we term democracy. Our task then is always to challenge the apparent forms of reality—that is, the fixed manners and values of the few, and to struggle with it until it reveals its mad, vari-implicated chaos, its false faces, and on until it surrenders its insight, its truth. We are fortunate as American writers in that with our variety of racial and national traditions, idioms and manners, we are yet one. On its profoundest level American experience is of a whole. Its truth lies in its diversity and swiftness of change. . . .

Index of Authors

Index of Works